Related Titles from Morgan Kaufmann

Brave NUI World

Designing Natural User Int
for Touch and Gesture

Daniel Wigdor and Denr ...on

ISBN: 9780123822314

Guerrilla UX Research Methods

Russ Unger and Todd Zaki Warfel

ISBN: 9780123847133

Thoughts on Interaction Design, 2nd Edition

Jon Kolko

ISBN: 9780123809308

Designi... the Mind in

Jeff Johnson

ISBN: 9780123750303

Global UX

Design and Research in a Connected World

Whitney Quesenbery and Daniel Szuc

ISBN: 9780123785916

Smart Things

Ubiquitous Computing User Experience Design

Mike Kuniavsky

ISBN: 9780123756954

mkp.com

DESIGN RESEARCH THROUGH PRACTICE

From the Lab, Field, and Showroom

DESIGN RESEARCH THROUGH PRACTICE

From the Lab, Field, and Showroom

ILPO KOSKINEN
JOHN ZIMMERMAN
THOMAS BINDER
JOHAN REDSTRÖM
STEPHAN WENSVEEN

AMSTERDAM • BOSTON • HEIDELBERG • LONDON • NEW YORK • OXFORD
PARIS • SAN DIEGO • SAN FRANCISCO • SINGAPORE • SYDNEY • TOKYO
Morgan Kaufmann is an imprint of Elsevier

Acquiring Editor: Rachel Roumeliotis
Development Editor: David Bevans
Project Manager: Danielle S. Miller
Designer: Kristen Davis

Morgan Kaufmann is an imprint of Elsevier
225 Wyman Street, Waltham, MA 02451, USA

Library of Congress Cataloging-in-Publication Data
Application submitted

British Library Cataloguing-in-Publication Data
A catalogue record for this book is available from the British Library

ISBN: 978-0-12-385502-2

Printed and bound by CPI Group (UK) Ltd, Croydon, CR0 4YY

Transferred to digital print 2012

For information on all MK publications visit our website at www.mkp.com

CONTENTS

FOREWORD

Twenty-five years ago I was lucky to find a visionary designer willing to take a leap of faith in hiring me—a human scientist and researcher. That designer was the legendary Bill Moggridge, who shortly afterwards merged his company with two others to form the global design and innovation consultancy IDEO. My charge was to strengthen IDEO's human-centred approach, and to integrate research with the practice of design. Back then there were few models for me to emulate. If I'd had access to a book like this one, certainly I would have felt more confident in my early endeavours. Design researchers will find this volume an invaluable guide as they navigate the options and challenges of their practice.

But constructive design research was in its infancy then, and my activities in that moment felt more like improvisation than evolving method. For me, that's one of most exciting aspects of this book: it puts the everyday activities of designers, researchers, and design researchers in historical context and reveals their varied influences. Readers "overhear" a rich and discursive conversation among five erudite authors. Ilpo Koskinen, John Zimmerman, Thomas Binder, Johan Redstrom, and Stephan Wensveen weave together perspectives from culture, art and design, cognitive psychology, and education as they discuss the blending of design and research. It's inspiring to see, through the selected work that they share, just how far that integration has come, to see the development of distinct traditions and intent—of lab, field, and showroom—and to imagine how far these will go within another generation.

Reflecting back on my early days as a new graduate of social science, I recall being frustrated that research and design were considered separate pursuits, developing in different academic spheres. Design was largely future-oriented; research focused on the past and the present. I found myself wondering, Wouldn't it be better if we *connected* research and design? That's precisely why I joined a design consultancy: I imagined myriad opportunities to link what I'd learned about people—about their behaviour, needs, desires, habits, and perceptions—with the design of places and things.

I did find opportunities, but linking design and research wasn't as straightforward as I'd hoped. My training in academic research, which emphasised the rigorous analysis of observed conditions, undoubtedly provided me with a strong foundation. But that wasn't enough to be interesting or applicable to the work of designers. I needed to find some common ground.

What I *did* share with designers was an interest in the future, and in developing new and better products and services for people. Back then IDEO worked intensively with both emerging companies in Silicon Valley and with established manufacturers, bringing new technology to life: new input devices for computers (such as the mouse); electric charging systems for cars (anticipating the drive towards alternative fuels); digital cameras (heralding ubiquity of shared personal imagery). We sought ways to explore future possibilities, and that meant creating prototypes—tangible things we could look at, touch, share, and experience ourselves and show others. Just as the authors herein assert, we were not dealing with research that tried to describe or explain things, as "constructive research imagines new things and builds them." This was our common ground: a desire to examine and evaluate what we'd envisaged. This was crucial to learning what we needed to know to develop successful, world-changing designs.

Whether in the studio, the lab, or the field we used physical, mechanical, and interactive models—which usually represented new technology products that someday would actually get made—to help answer questions such as: How will this feel to use? Is it a good size, speed? How will it fit into daily life and support social behaviour?" By constructing prototypes, scenarios, role-playing, and body-storming we explored how to refine the design of those new things we were bringing into the world. Such design research applied whether we were developing a smart phone, reinventing a bank branch, conceiving a premium service for an airline, or creating new systems and processes for a fast-food company. It embodied the approach reflected in the current discourse about design thinking and "business in beta" which encourages companies to learn by doing—to commit resources to experimentation and prototyping as an on-going process rather than trying to pre-determine the details of a future offering through analysis.

Beyond refining the design of a future product or system, another important benefit of prototyping is in helping us explore the kinds of behaviour, attitudes and experiences that a new product, system, or technology might engender for people as individuals or communities. This is also constructive design research. It helps us answer questions like: What might it be like to design and grow artefacts from our own genetic material? How will new technology affect our experience of giving birth? Might a positive vision of the future encourage local action to minimize the effects of climate change? Here our constructions, though real, are somewhat more speculative; they are created to provide a vision for observers to explore new possibilities and how these affect their hopes, dreams, and aspirations. Such design research is close to the idea of the "showroom" explored in this book; using prototypes to provoke reaction and conversation with the ultimate goal of making a positive difference to the world we live in.

Thus, working alongside designers now for many years, I have learned that design research is about far more than creating things to be made and marketed. Design research plays an important role in illuminating and tackling many complex problems facing the world today. It encourages and enables social change and challenges assumptions and beliefs about how we live, work, and consume. It raises questions that prompt us to consider other possibilities.

As human beings we tend to shift between pondering our existence in the world—the people, places and things that comprise it—and taking action to alter it. Sometimes we're inquisitive and seek to *understand*: How do people, places, and things interact? How do they shape our experiences, habits, lifestyles, and culture? Other times we're innovative and want to effect change, to *make* new things and experiences. Human beings are both *curious* and *creative*. We are *researchers* and *designers*, in ways that are inextricably linked. At IDEO today, my colleagues and I "think to build" and "build to think" as entirely reciprocal activities.

"Design Research Through Practice" is a critical exploration of this reciprocity as it plays out in multifaceted ways in the real world. It demonstrates how different traditions of collaborative construction have bridged the gap between understanding and making, and between theoretical and actual solutions. This is not a *how-to* book (which could never feel right to design researchers anyway), but rather a thoughtful examination of exemplary practice—a *how-they-did-it* book—and an inspirational foundation for others to reflect and build upon.

Jane Fulton Suri
Managing Partner; Creative Director IDEO
May 18th 2011

PREFACE

The origins of this book are from observations we made a few years ago. It focuses on a small but growing slice of design research we call "constructive design research". There are many types of constructive design research, but only a few approaches have been successful for a decade or more. We call these approaches Lab, Field, and Showroom. They come from different places, with some having roots in universities, some in design firms, some in engineering and the social sciences, and some in contemporary art.

As we see it, design research is coming of age. Hundreds of papers have been written about design research and how it should be done. For this reason, any attempt to write about it has to be done as an informative narrative. For us, this informative narrative has been methodology — discussion of abstract principles at work behind actual research. Being abstract helps us to better understand what some of the leading design researchers are doing and why their work makes sense.

There are three main reasons for writing this book. First, design has increasingly become a growing academic field. We feel that a bird's eye perspective on it is useful for researchers, professors, and students alike. The second reason is that a PhD is fast becoming an entry criterion for teaching positions; however, this is not how design is traditionally taught: design has been like art, taught by masters to apprentices. The apprenticeship model has guaranteed that designers have sensitivities that are very difficult to put in words. To maintain these sensitivities, professors of the future need design skills, and one way to maintain these skills is to bring design into the middle of research.

The third reason for writing this book is to add tolerance. Designers are not traditionally well versed in scientific practice and tend to understand science narrowly. We still hear talks about *the* scientific method, even though there clearly are many methods. A good deal of astrophysics and geology is not experimental. In contrast, we argue that there is a need for many types of methods and methodologies in design, just as there is a need for many types of methodologies in the sciences and the social sciences.

When writing, we have kept in mind MA/MSc and doctoral students in industrial and interaction design, product design engineering, and in such emerging fields of design as services and sustainability. We also believe that what we write is useful for the increasing number of practitioners who do research for a living. By now, there is a market for design research in cities like Los Angeles, Chicago, New York, London, Copenhagen, Helsinki, Rio de Janeiro, Seoul, Hong Kong, and Milan, just to mention a few. This dual audience explains some of the features of the book. The focus on the big picture makes this book fairly abstract, but this is what universities need. Some other features help practicing designers to skim through the book quickly: it is organized in parts, we give short examples of work we find inspiring, and our writing style is deliberately non-technical.

While talking about this book, many practitioners and researchers have found it immediately useful. One word of caution is required. Many people ask how their practice fits into the Lab, Field, and Showroom framework. However, we talk about practices that are seldom pure. In fact, Chapters 7–9 look at how theory, research practice, and the social environment create commonalities between these approaches. These chapters have their origin in a "deviant case": when we realized that it is impossible to classify Ianus Keller's PhD work under Lab or Field, we took a closer look at things that bridge researchers.

Each of the writers has participated in constructive design research for the past ten years, and some considerably longer. Some of us find our academic homes outside design, some have considerable practical experience, one is an industrial designer, and one is an interaction designer. Experience in design, engineering, the social sciences, philosophy, and filmmaking are all represented here. Two authors work in art and design schools, one in a technical university, one has a double appointment between design and computer science, and one author works in a research institute focusing on interaction design. Our native languages are English, Dutch, Danish, Swedish, and Finnish and as a team, we probably understand more than 12 languages. Due to this diversity, this book covers many subjects. Hopefully this means that many kinds of designers and people interested in design can find something interesting within its covers. For us, writing this book has been a marvelous learning experience, and we hope the result is useful for our readers.

May 22, 2011
Helsinki, Finland
Ilpo Koskinen

ACKNOWLEDGMENTS

In writing this book, the authors are indebted to many people and institutions. In alphabetical order by country, our thanks go to about 15 different countries.

In Melbourne, Australia, Larissa Hjorth helped by providing a home at RMIT. Thanks also to Jesper for providing a perspective on life. There was also very useful discussion with Swinburne's Dori Tunstall in December 2009 in Aalborg, Denmark, where Nicola Morelli hosted a dinner with Dori and Pirkko Raudaskoski. In Rio de Janeiro, Andrea and Marcelo Júdice were excellent hosts during and after the carnival season in February 2010. In Denmark, we need to first thank Nicola Morelli at Aalborg University. At the Aarhus School of Architecture, Peter Krogh, Jørgen Rasmussen, Martin Ludvigsen, and Andreas Lykke-Olesen helped us, as did Sofie Beck and Maiken Hillerup Fogtmann. At the University of Aarhus we need to thank Martin Brynskov, Olav Bertelsen, Susanne Bødker, Peter Dalsgaard, Marianne Graves Petersen, Kim Halskov, Ola Iversen, and Morten Kyng. In Copenhagen, our thanks go to many people who work with Thomas Binder, but especially Eva Brandt and Joachim Halse. Thanks to Petra Ahde for providing images from her research.

When visiting Lancaster at its multifaceted Imaginations Institute, I met Tim Dant who helped me to understand sociology. People to thank in London and its vicinity include Anthony Dunne (whom I met all too briefly in Pittsburgh's Squirrel Hill), Tobie Kerridge, Bill Gaver, and David Frohlich, who organized an excellent family dinner for me and John McCarthy, who happened to be visiting London under the Icelandic ash cloud. In Sheffield, we need to say a kind word to Paul Chamberlain for telling us about Lab4Living and Jim Roddis for his broad view of PhD education in art schools in the United Kingdom. Kristina Niedderer, now in Birmingham, told us about craft research in the United Kingdom.

In Helsinki, we have to thank Tuuli Mattelmäki, Turkka Keinonen, Esko Kurvinen, and Pekka Korvenmaa. Specifically, we want to mention Jussi Mikkonen, with whom I organized two classes in 2007–2008. The basic construct of this book, Lab, Field, Showroom, first saw daylight in these classes. In Berlin, our thanks go to Martin Rinderknecht from design gallery Helmrinderknecht, which hosted the exhibition FreakShow in 2010–2011. Its curator, Sophie Lovell, also deserves credit. Another design gallery we want to thank is Z33 in Hasselt, Belgium, home to two excellent exhibitions, Designing Critical Design and Design by Performance. Kun-Pyo Lee from KAIST and now LG Electronics helped us to understand IASDR and design research in Korea and Japan, as did Jung-Joo Lee at Taik in Helsinki.

In Paris, Christian Licoppe from ParisTech was an excellent host, and thanks also go to Eric Lecolinet for organizing the opportunity to talk at SIGCHI Paris. Annie Gentes organized a pleasant dinner between myself and Armand Hatchuel and Mathias Bejean of l'Ecole des Mines. There are too many people to mention in the most amazing design culture of the world called Milan, but at the top of our list of thanks are Ezio Manzini, Francesca Rizzo, Luca Guerrini, and Anna Meroni. Other people who helped us were Alessandro Biamonti, Daria Cantu, Fabrizio Ceschin, Stefano Maffei, Francesco Trabucco, Francesco Zurlo, Roberto Verganti and, slightly later, Andrea Branzi.

At Technical University of Delft, we would like to thank Pieter Jan Stappers, Cees de Bont, Pieter Desmet, Paul Hekkert, Imre Horváth, and researchers at IO Studiolab for useful discussions and contextualizations. At Technische Universiteit Eindhoven, we are grateful for Kees Overbeeke and his research group, with special thanks to Miguel Alonso, Caroline Hummels, Pierre Levy, Oscar Tomico, and in particular, Joep Frens and Philip Ross. Kees has gathered an exceptional group of young researchers; if only all design researchers could do the same. In Eindhoven, we also benefited from discussions with Tom Djajadiningrat at Philips Design. Yolanda van Kessel and Bas Raijmakers told us about research ideas at Design Academy Eindhoven. Later, Bas also told about his work in his agency over a lunch at Spitalfields in London.

At Technical University of Porto, Carlos Aguiar was an excellent host. Latin family life is the envy of the world, and for good reason! Thanks also to Francisco Xavier De Carvalho for opening the doors to the design program of the university. When writing this book, another excellent host was Gordon Hush in Glasgow, but our thanks also extend to the very collegial staff of design programs at the renowned Glasgow School of Art. Gordon: it is my round the next time we see each other in The State. Cheers with your favorite Czech beer!

In Gothenburg, our special thanks goes to the Interactive Institute for providing excellent working conditions for me during my visit in May 2010. At Malmö's K3, we need to thank Pelle Ehn, who shared one of the last remaining copies of his PhD thesis with me, and Jonas Löwgren, who edited a special issue for the now defunct journal *Artifact*, where Binder, Redström, and I first published some of the key ideas of this book under the title Lab, Field, Gallery (Koskinen et al., 2008). Swiss Design Network sent us old proceedings from their design conferences without asking anything in return.

You must include the United States when writing about research. In Boston, thanks to the people at MIT Media Lab, and in Chicago, Kei Sato. At Savannah College of Art and Design, we need to thank Victor Ermoli for opening the doors of design to us, Jesus Rojas for showing us the industrial design department, and Joel Wittkamp and Christine Miller not only for a pleasant dinner but also for telling us about the impressive Savannah school. In Los Angeles, we learned many things from Lisa Nugent (now in New York), Yee Chan, Sean Donahue, and Serra Semi. In Pasadena, we got to know Brenda Laurel's work, which became one of the starting points for us (Laurel 2003). In Palo Alto, our thanks go to Katja Battarbee and Jane Fulton Suri at IDEO and Larry Leifer at Stanford University. In Portland, Ken Anderson and Scott Mainwaring provided us with information about ethnography at Intel and also in Silicon Valley. Jack Whalen talked about his work on PARC and helped with the manuscript when it was getting too large. Jack also wrote an inset about one particularly successful project at PART called Eureka. Last but not least, Carnegie Mellon University has an amazing group of design research scholars; we need to thank in particular Jodi Forlizzi, Dan Boyarski, Suguru Ishizaki, Eric Paulos, Haakon Faste, and Will Odom. CMU has excelled in design since Herbert Simon's heyday and continues to do so with these people.

Funding for research behind this book mostly came from the Academy of Finland and Aarhus School of Architecture, where I spent three months as visiting professor at the end of 2009. More modest help was provided by Aalto University School of Art and Design (formerly the School of Design at Taik), the Interactive Institute, and the Danish Design School.

At Elsevier and Morgan Kaufmann, we started our journey with Mary James and continued with David Bevans, Danielle Miller, and Rachel Roumeliotis.

Ilpo Koskinen, 2011

1

CONSTRUCTIVE DESIGN RESEARCH

iFloor was an interactive floor built between 2002 and 2004 in Aarhus, Denmark. It was a design research project with participants from architecture, design, and computer science. It was successful in many ways: it produced two doctoral theses and about 20 peer-reviewed papers in scientific conferences, and led to other technological studies. In 2004, the project received a national architectural prize from the Danish Design Center.

At the heart of *iFloor* was an interactive floor built into the main lobby of the city library in Aarhus. Visitors could use mobile phones and computers to send questions to a system that projected them to the floor with a data projector. The system also tracked movement on the floor with a camera. Like the data projector, the camera was mounted into the ceiling. With an algorithm, the system analyzed social action on the floor and sent back this information to the system. If you wanted to get your question brought up in the floor, you had to talk to other people to get help in finding books.

iFloor's purpose was to bring interaction back to the library. The word "back" here is very meaningful. Information technology may have dramatically improved our access to information, but it has also taken something crucial away from the library experience — social interaction. In the 1990s, a typical visit to the library involved talking to librarians and also other visitors; today a typical visit consists of barely more than ordering a book through the Web, hauling it from a shelf, and loaning it with a machine. Important experience is lost, and serendipity — the wonderful feeling of discovering books you had never heard about while browsing the shelves — has almost been lost.

A blog or a discussion forum was not the solution. After all, interaction in blogs is mediated. Something physical was needed to connect people.

A floor that would do this job was developed at the University of Aarhus through the typical design process.[1] The left row of Figure 1.1 is an image from a summer workshop in 2002, in which the concept was first developed. The second picture is from a bodystorm[2] in which the floor's behaviors were mocked up with a paper prototype to get a better grasp of the proposed idea. Site visits with librarians followed, while technical prototyping took place in a computer science laboratory at the university (left row, pictures 3–5). The system was finally installed in the library (left row, picture at the bottom). How *iFloor* was supposed to function is illustrated in the computer-generated image on the right side of the picture.

iFloor received lots of media attention; it was introduced to Danish royalty, and it was submitted to the Danish Architecture Prize competition where it was awarded the prize for visionary products (Figure 1.2). In addition, as already mentioned, it was reported to international audiences in several scientific and design conferences.

However, only half the research work was done when the system was working in the library. To see how it functioned, researchers stayed in the library for two weeks, observing and videotaping interaction with the floor (Figure 1.3). It was this meticulous attention to how people worked with the *iFloor* that pushed it beyond mere design. This study produced data that were used in many different ways, not just to make the prototype better, as would have happened in design practice.

Developing the *iFloor* also led to two doctoral theses: one focusing more on design and technology, another focusing mostly on how people interacted with the floor.[3] Andreas Lykke-Olesen focused on technology, and Martin Ludvigsen's key papers tried to understand how people noticed the floor, entered it, and how they started conversations while on it. It was this theoretical work that turned *iFloor* from a design exercise into research that produced knowledge that can be applied elsewhere. In design philosopher Richard Buchanan's terminology, it was not just a piece of clinical research; it had a hint of basic research.[4]

iFloor is a good example of research in which planning and doing, reason, and action are not separate.[5] For researchers, maybe the most important concept *iFloor* exhibits is that there is value in doing things. When researchers actually construct something, they find problems and discover things that would otherwise go unnoticed. These observations unleash wisdom, countering a typical academic tendency to value thinking and discourse over doing. A PowerPoint presentation or a CAD rendering would not have had this power.

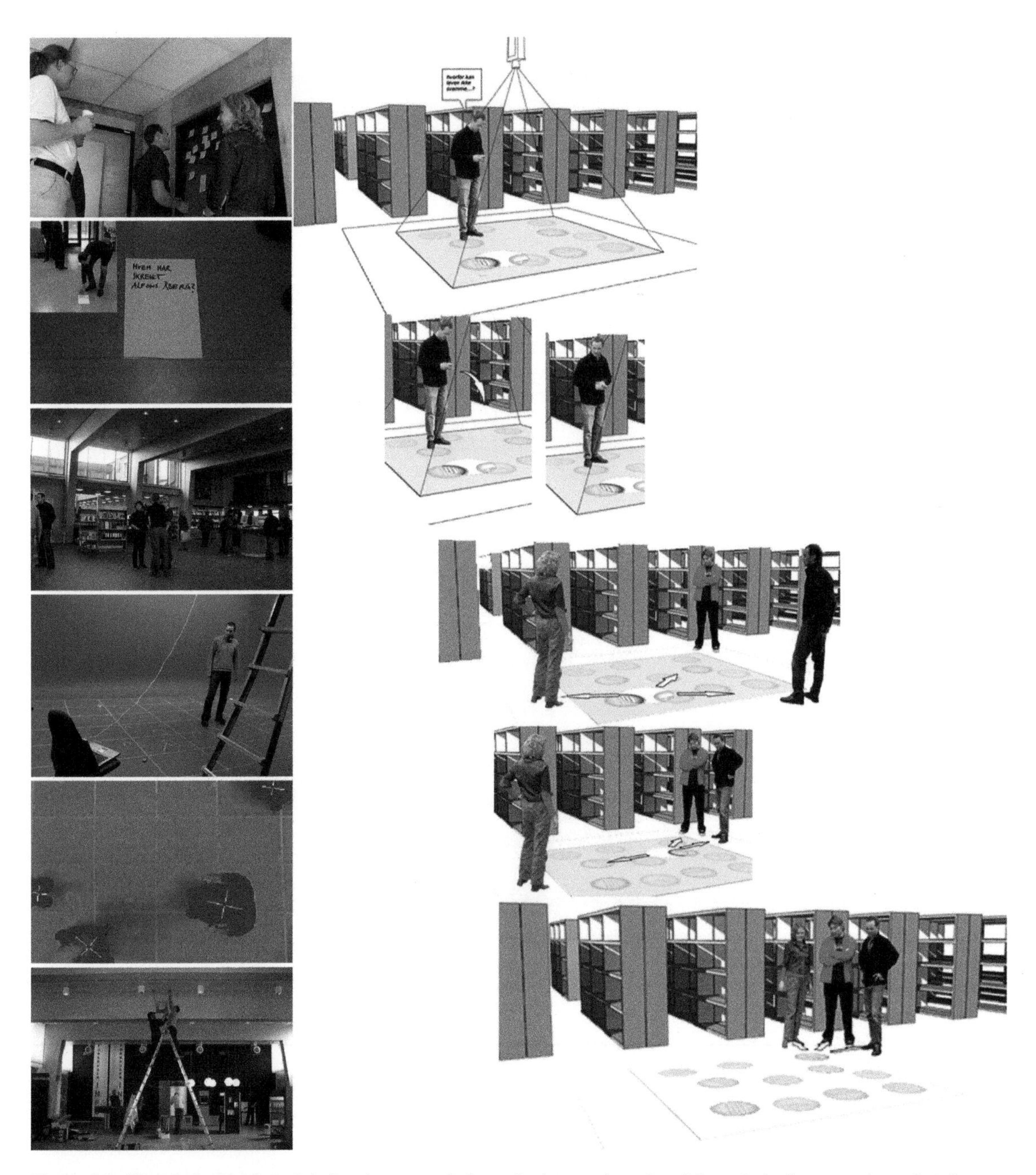

Figure 1.1 *iFloor* being designed. Left column: workshops, bodystorming, site visit, technical prototyping, what the computer saw, and building the system into Aarhus City Library. Right column: use scenario.

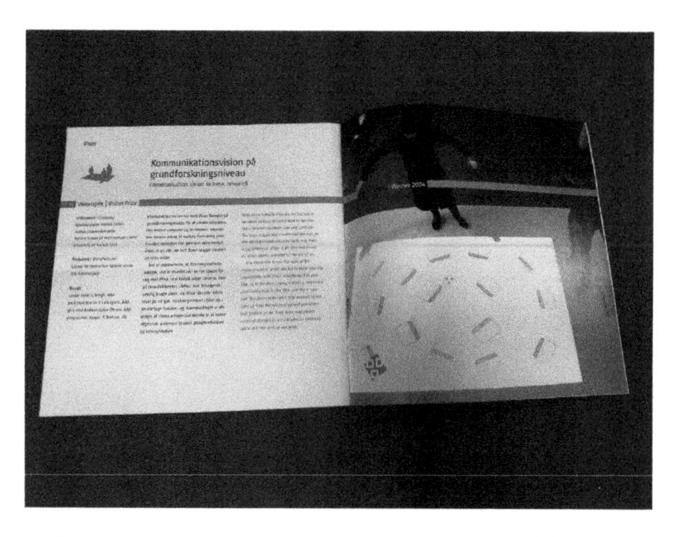

Figure 1.2 Picture of *iFloor* in Danish Design Centre's Design Prize booklet, 2004.

Figure 1.3 *iFloor* in action. Here seventh graders are exploring the floor.

1.1 Beyond Research Through Design

Usually, a research project like *iFloor* is seen as an example of "research through design." This term has its origins in a working paper by Christopher Frayling, then the rector of London's Royal College of Art (RCA)[6]. Jodi Forlizzi and John Zimmerman from Carnegie Mellon recently interviewed several experts to find definitions and exemplars of research through design. According to their survey, researchers

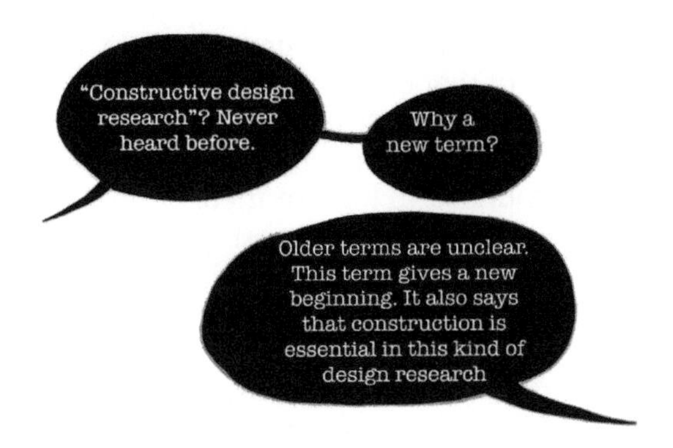

Figure 1.4 New term provides a fresh beginning.

> *make prototypes, products, and models to codify their own understanding of a particular situation and to provide a concrete framing of the problem and a description of a proposed, preferred state.... Designers focus on the creation of artifacts through a process of disciplined imagination, because artifacts they make both reveal and become embodiments of possible futures.... Design researchers can explore new materials and actively participate in intentionally constructing the future, in the form of disciplined imagination, instead of limiting their research to an analysis of the present and the past.*[7]

However, this concept has been criticized for its many problems. Alain Findeli and Wolfgang Jonas, among others, noted that any research needs strong theory to guide practice, but this is missing from Frayling's paper.[8] For Jonas, Frayling's definitions remained fuzzy. Readers get few guidelines as to how to proceed and are left to their own devices to muddle through the terrain. Jonas also says that the term provides little guidance for building up a working research practice — and he is no doubt right.

This concept fails to appreciate many things at work behind any successful piece of research. For example, the influential studies of Katja Battarbee and Pieter Desmet made important conceptual and methodological contributions in their respective programs, even though, strictly speaking, they were theoretical and methodological rather than constructive in nature. People read Kees Overbeeke's writings not because he builds things but because he has articulated many valuable ideas about interaction in his programmatic and theoretical writings. People read Bill Gaver because of his contribution to design as well as methodology, often against his wishes.[9]

For these reasons, we prefer to talk about "constructive design research," which refers to design research in which construction — be it product, system, space, or media — takes center place and becomes the key means in constructing knowledge (Figure 1.4). Typically, this "thing" in the middle is a prototype like *iFloor*. However, it can be also be a scenario, a mock-up, or just a detailed concept that could be constructed.

We focus on leading examples of constructive research but follow Frayling's empiricist and pragmatist approach rather than offer a definition grounded in logic or theory.[10] By now, we have a luxury: a body of research that does most of the things that Findeli and Jonas called forth. When looking at the 1990s, it is clear that what people like Tom Djajadiningrat in the Netherlands, Anthony Dunne in England, and Simo Säde in Finland did in their doctoral work was solid, theoretically and methodically informed research that could not have been done without a design background.[11] Ten years later, there are dozens of good examples. For this reason, we explicate practice rather than try to define a field with concepts as big as design and research.[12] Introducing a new word is an old academic trick used to avoid difficulties with existing concepts and to keep discussion open, if only for a few years.

1.2 Constructive Research in Design Research

This book looks at one type of contemporary design research. It excludes many other types, including research done in art and design history, aesthetics, and philosophy. It also skips over work done in the social sciences and design management. It leaves practice-based research integrating art and research to others. Similarly, it barely touches engineering and leaves out theory, semantics, and semiotics altogether.[13] This book will not look at research done by design researchers if there is no construction involved, unless there is a clear connection to constructive studies.[14] Finally, it will not review design research that builds on the natural sciences such as chemistry as this research is most typically done in ceramics and sometimes in glass design and conservation. We are dealing with research that imagines and builds new things and describes and explains these constructions (Figure 1.5).[15]

What constructive design research imports to this larger picture is experience in how to integrate design and research. Currently, there is a great deal of interest in what is the best way to integrate these worlds. This book shows that there are indeed many ways to achieve such integration and still be successful. We are hoping that design researchers in other fields find precedents and models in this book that help them to better plan constructive studies. For constructive design researchers, we provide ways to justify methodological choices and understand these choices.

It should be obvious that we talk about construction, not constructivism, as is done in philosophy and the social sciences.

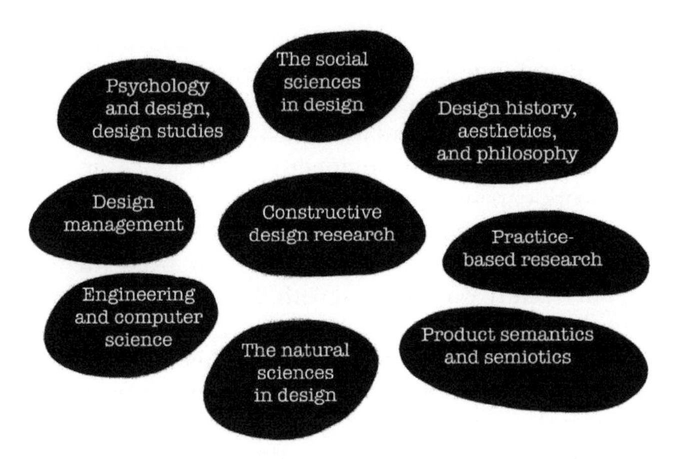

Figure 1.5 Current design research.

Constructivists are people who claim issues such as knowledge and society are constructed rather than, say, organized functionally around certain purposes, as if in a body or in a piece of machinery.[16] Many designers are certainly constructivists in a theoretical and philosophical sense, but this is not our concern. We focus on something far more concrete, that is, research like *iFloor* in which something is actually built and put to use. Not only concepts, but materials. Not just bits, but atoms.

One of the concerns many design writers have is that design does not have a theoretical tradition.[17] For us, this is a matter of time rather than definition. Theory develops when people start to treat particular writings as theories; for example, such as happened to Don Norman's interpretation of affordance. It became a theory when researchers like Gerda Smets and Kees Overbeeke in the Netherlands treated it as such.

For this reason, we focus on research programs rather than individual studies. Chapter 3 explains this concept of program in detail. Here, it is enough to say that research programs always have "a central, or core, idea that shapes and structures the research conducted."[18] Programs consist of a variety of activities ranging from individual case studies to methodology and theory building. This richness is lost in definitions of research through design that tend to place too much weight on design at the expense of other important activities that make constructive research possible.

1.3 What Is "Design"?

Any book on design has to face a difficulty that stems from the English language. The word "design" is ambiguous, as it covers both planning (of products and systems), and also what most other European languages would loosely call "formgiving."[19] The latter meaning is more restrictive than the former, which may cover anything from hair and food design to designing airplanes.

This book is not about engineering or science, it builds primarily on work carried out in art and design schools. The art and design tradition has an important message to more technically oriented designers. Above all, designers coming from the art school tradition have many ways to deal with the "halfway" between people and things.

People negotiate their way through this halfway with their eyes, ears, hands, and body, as well as their sense of space and movement and many kinds of things they are barely aware of. Although everyone lives in this halfway every second, there are few words to describe it.[20] However, it is the stuff of design education. In Sharon Poggenpohl's words, it aims at developing sensibilities of visual, material, cultural, and historical contexts.[21]

There is no reason to be romantic or cynical about these sensibilities. Designers trained in the arts are capable of capturing fleeting moments and structures that others find ephemeral, imaginative, and unstable for serious research. They are also trained in reframing ideas rather than solving known problems. Above all, they are trained to imagine problems and opportunities to see whether something is necessary or not. It is just this imaginative step that is presented in discussions on innovation in industry.[22]

1.4 Industrial Design and Interaction Design

Even in this narrow sense, design is a complex category that covers many subjects ranging from paper machines to the conceptual designs of, say, Droog Design in the Netherlands.[23] This book does not try to cover all of these topics; it mostly builds on work carried out in industrial design and interaction design — the main hubs of constructive design research (see Figure 1.6).

Industrial design and interaction design differ in many ways. The most notable differences are in tradition and technology: industrial design has roots producing material goods, and interaction design is based on computer science, film, and Web design. Industrial design is product-oriented, three-dimensional, and relies heavily on sketches, mock-ups, models, and physical prototypes. Interaction design is time-oriented and relies on personas, scenarios, narratives, and software prototypes. Also, the skills required for each type of design are different.

Figure 1.6 Industrial design and interaction design: physical things are the focus of industrial design, whereas interaction is the focus of interaction design.

Still, over the past 15 years these specialties have evolved side by side with many interaction designers with a background in industrial design and sometimes vice versa. Also, research communities overlap, sharing processes and many working practices.[24]

We believe that constructive design research continues to build on these two specialties, but with more overlap. One set of reasons lies in its technology, which is making interaction design an increasingly important design specialty. When information technology has "disappeared" from gray boxes to the environment, interaction designers increasingly deal with problems familiar to industrial designers.[25] Industrial designers, on the other hand, are increasingly using information technology (IT). Importantly, information technologies have no obvious shape. The key skills in coping with IT are not redoing and refining existing forms but imagining interesting and useful concepts that people want.[26]

1.5 Design Research in Second Modernity

Behind current research lie social forces larger than technology. After the reconstruction period after World War II, the 1960s witnessed major changes in society. Western economies became consumer driven and an ecological crisis influenced it, higher education democratized, and pop culture merged with youth culture. Media became global, taste became democratized, and there was an upheaval in politics as traditional loyalties started to crack. In the 1950s, the main arbiters of taste were the educated upper middle classes, but by the mid-1970s, up-to-date design built on sources like pop art.

However, when the 1980s arrived, society was more stable. Andrea Branzi, one of the main revolutionaries of design, wrote:

> *During the period of forced industrialization that lasted from 1920 to 1960, the hypothesis had been formed that design ought to be helpful in bringing about a standardization of consumer goods and the patterns of behavior in society. Its work lay in a quest for primary needs.... Along that fascinating road design has hunted for many years the white whale of standard products, products aimed at the neutral section of the public's taste, products intended to please everyone and therefore no one.... Then, in the mid 1960s, things began to move in exactly the opposite direction. The great, pyramid-shaped mass markets, guided by enlightened or capricious opinion leaders, gradually disintegrated into separate niches and were subsequently reformed into new and multicolored majorities. Design had to skirt its attention from mass products to those intended for limited semantic groups. From objects that set out to please everyone, to objects that picked their own consumers. From the languages of reason to those of emotion.... Then the process of transformation slowly came to an end. The mutation was complete and it is now possible to say that a new society, with its own culture and values, has taken on a fairly stable shape.*[27]

For designers, Branzi's second modernity has opened many new opportunities.[28] The first ones who seized these opportunities were graphic, industrial, and interaction designers. There are also many other characters who populate design today: service designers, design managers, community designers, and researchers. As Branzi recently noted, design has become a mass profession.[29]

There is some friction between the two modernities. Institutions like universities react to society slowly and tend to be run by those who came to the field in the first modernity. However, many designers and researchers commute across the boundary with ease. As design has become more diversified in ethnic and gender terms, such skill is in high demand; there is no way back to the first modernity dominated by white European and American men.

Research plays an increasingly important role in this transition. As Branzi's colleague Antonella Penati noted, design is coming of age. Design education was typically established in universities after World War II, making it a relative newcomer in universities. However, design is now in its third generation. As Penati explained, design is currently maturing by embracing new computer-based technologies and research.[30] Research helps designers to navigate the second modernity (Figure 1.7).

Figure 1.7 Second modernity offers many possibilities for design.

End Notes

1. See Lykke-Olesen (2006).
2. Buchenau and Fulton Suri (2000).
3. Lykke-Olesen (2006), Ludvigsen (2006).
4. See Buchanan (2001), who distinguished clinical, applied, and basic research. Clinical research consists of applying a body of (professional) knowledge to a case. Applied research applies such knowledge to a class of cases. In basic research, application is secondary: the goal is to produce knowledge that may be applied later in applied and even clinical studies.
5. As Pieter Jan Stappers (2007) from Delft University of Technology says.
6. Frayling (1993); Schneider (2008), Zimmerman et al. (2010).
7. Zimmerman and Forlizzi (2008).
8. Findeli (1998, 2006), Jonas (2007, pp. 189–192). Jonas points out some misunderstandings of Frayling as well.
9. See Gaver et al. (2004). The *Presence Project* had already been warned not to turn cultural probes into a method. Other references in this paragraph are Battarbee (2004) and Desmet (2002). Overbeeke is a professor at the Technische Universiteit Eindhoven and Gaver is a professor at Goldsmiths College in London.
10. For example, Zimmerman et al. (2007).
11. Djajadiningrat (1998), Dunne (2005), Säde (2001).
12. Andrea Branzi made a similar point regarding art and design in Burkhardt and Morotti (n.d., p. 65).
13. For history, aesthetics, and philosophy, see Dilnot (1989a,b), Julier (1991, 2008), Buchanan and Margolin (1995), Margolin and Buchanan (1995), Bürdek (2005), Fallan (2010), and Svengren (1995). For social sciences, see Molotch (2003), Brandes et al. (2009), and Shove et al. (2007). For design management, see Gorb (1990), Borja de Mozota (2003, 2006), Aspara (2009), and Verganti (2009). For artistic and so-called practice-based research, see Mäkelä and Routarinne (2007). For engineering, see Archer (1968). Product

semiotics and semiotics are explained in Krippendorff (1989, 2006), Butter (1989), and Vihma (1995). For an applied perspective, see McCoy (1996). Krippendorff's MA thesis in Ulm in 1961 was already studying semantics (see Krippendorff, 1989, p. 10, note 5). For theory, consult Branzi (1988).

14. Keinonen (1998), Desmet (2002). For user experience, see Schifferstein and Hekkert (2008).

15. See Slate (2002), Siikamäki (2006), Costa Gaspar (2003), Thampirak (2007), and Härkäsalmi (2008).

16. The classic statement is Berger and Luckmann (1967), although the history of empirical research on social construction of knowledge goes back at least to Karl Mannheim's sociology and, ultimately, German idealism in philosophy. For a philosophical critique of the notion of practice, see Turner (1994), who mostly — and in many ways, misleadingly, as Lynch (1993) pointed out — built on Ludwig Wittgenstein's discussion on rule following his criticism of practice.

17. This is the main concern for Poggenpohl and Sato (2009), perhaps partly in response to Krippendorff's (1995) fear that lacking a disciplinary basis, design always loses in collaboration with other disciplines. Krippendorff's talk is quoted in Poggenpohl (2009a, pp. 15–16).

18. Downton (2005, p. 9).

19. Germanic languages usually have separate words for planning and formgiving, including German *Gestaltung* and *Formgebung*, and also the more general *Entwurf* (verb *entwerfen*), Dutch *ontwerpen*, and Swedish *formgivning*. Latin languages build more on the idea of planning, drawing, and projecting, like the Italian *disegno* and French *conception*. Other languages, such as Finnish, build on Germanic roots; thus, *muotoilu* is a direct translation from the Swedish form, while *suunnittelu* comes from planning.

20. Merleau-Ponty 1973. As the philosopher Maurice Merleau-Ponty noted, this intertwining of the world and people had no name in philosophy. The word "experience" tries to capture it, but it is human-centric and too easy to turn into just another cognitive process. It also tends to focus on significant events rather than the prose of everyday life. The word "interaction," on the other hand, having its origins in the natural sciences, is too easy to turn into a model of a mechanism. Merleau-Ponty's term of choice was "flesh," also a less appropriate choice. Its carnal imagery downplays mindful and social aspects of human existence. This notion is from Merleau-Ponty's (1963, 1973) posthumously published essay "The Intertwining — The Chiasm." The word "prose," also from his posthumous writings, carries a heavy meaning. As Merleau-Ponty noted, our world is mostly prosaic rather than poetic. Certainly, prose dominates in design (Merleau-Ponty, 1968, 1970, pp. 65–66). Somewhat similar ideas are apparent in many other writings in design: design is about capturing something in the gray area between people and the things around them. In addition to Poggenpohl's essay quotes in this paragraph see, for example, Seago and Dunne (1999), and in particular Pallasmaa (1996, 2009), whose perceptive analysis of architecture is well in line with this understanding of design (especially Pallasmaa, 2009, pp. 11–22).

21. Poggenpohl (2009a, p. 7). She follows Polanyi's distinction between tacit and explicit knowledge, which we try to avoid in this book, as we believe it unnecessarily dramatizes the difference between design and research.

22. The second point builds on several writers. Characterizing design as an attempt to change existing situations to preferred ones comes from Herbert Simon (1996). The idea that designers reframe things through imagining several preferred situations rather than framing a problem and solving it comes from Horst Rittel and Melvin Webber (1973) and Richard Buchanan (1992). For recent discussion on design in innovation, see Verganti (2009).

23. Some caution is needed here. While it is easy to classify the work of groups like Memphis and Droog Design, and today, critical design, as conceptual work aimed at changing perceptions and ways of seeing things in design, it is equally true that these groups worked through material. Their work was certainly not designed to celebrate immaterial things like concepts. For a similar point regarding relational aesthetics, see Bourriaud (2002, pp. 46–47).

24. As with most concepts, a dose of caution helps a designer to not get distracted. If one looks at job offerings, interaction design is mostly about interfaces for the Web, computers, and machinery. In this sense, interaction design is a novelty in design, although its history goes back far longer than design folklore says. Many designers worked with interaction far before graphical user interfaces came to light in the 1980s. In a wider sense, interaction design may mean those things in which people meet their environment through some kind of computation. Here, interaction design is scarcely a novelty. For example, there are many industrial design programs that do not offer interaction design specialties. If industrial and other designers have been using interactive devices all along without specialized training, then why change? A word of warning about industrial design is also warranted, but this warning is about the relationship to product design. Usually, industrial design is an umbrella and product design a part, but the reverse holds in places like the Glasgow School of Art.

25. This sentence builds on Mark Weiser's (1991) idea of ubiquitous computing.

26. Thackara (1988), Redström (2006, pp. 123–127), Buchanan (2001). For how the object of art got dematerialized, see Lippard (1997).

27. Branzi (1988, p. 11). Castelli 1999. Contemporary design reflects change in society in that there is no common style or criteria for style today, as Catherine MCdermott 2008 and Penny Sparke 2008 have noted.

28. See Maldonado (1972, pp. 27–29). For an accessible version of Maldonado's thinking, see Gui Bonsiepe (2009, p. 125), who rightfully pays attention to a curious lack of design in a plentiful discussion of modernity in the social sciences, and compares this to Maldonado's concerns:

The debated tackling of the theme of modernity … have never taken the design dimension into consideration: design has been absent …. In [Maldonado's] essays, design is not merely understood as an incidental phenomenon or a secondary theme of modernity but, on the contrary, as a driving force of modernity itself. In the practice of design, modernity finds itself. Being radically modern means: inventing, designing, and articulating the future or modernity.

29. Branzi (2010).

30. Penati (2010).

2

THE COMING OF AGE OF CONSTRUCTIVE DESIGN RESEARCH

Most early writings on design research are built on rationalistic assumptions. Perhaps the most ambitious call for basing design on rationalistic thinking came from Herbert Simon, who proposed basing design on systems and operations analysis. For him, design became an exercise in mathematics, and the task of design research was to describe the natural and human rationalities that govern it.[1] Such rationalistic assumptions were particularly strong in the 1950s and 1960s. At that time, the studio model of the Bauhaus became too limited to respond to the demands of increasingly complex and growing industries.

However, rationalistic methods failed to get much of a following in design, probably because they barely tackled the human and artistic faces of design—for example, the "design methods movement," which bloomed for a few years in the 1960s mainly in the United States and England.[2] Writing at the end of the 1990s, Swedish designer Henrik Gedenryd noted how this movement built on operations research and systems theory, trying to lay the foundations for design on

> *logic, rationality, abstraction, and rigorous principles. It portrays, or rather prescribes, design as an orderly, stringent procedure which systematically collects information, establishes objectives, and computes the design solution, following the principles of logical deduction and mathematical optimization models.... This view is still very much alive, and there is a good reason to believe that this won't change for a long time.*
>
> *However, discontent with this approach is widespread and quite old, even though no substantive replacement has yet been proposed. Experience from design practice and from studies of authentic design processes has consistently been that not only don't designers work as design methodology says they should, it is also*

a well established fact that to do design in the prescribed manner just doesn't work.[3]

The leading rationalists like J.C. Jones and the mathematician-turned-architect Christopher Alexander quickly changed their earlier teachings about research. By the end of the 1960s, Alexander's advice was to "forget the whole thing," and Jones turned to music and poetry. In the end, they had encouraged designers to experiment with art.[4]

As Peter Downton noted, the rationalistic movement left a legacy of many useful means for improving design, but its problems went deep.[5] The rationalistic mentality faced many external problems. The 1960s saw the opening of the space era and Lyndon B. Johnson's Great Society, but is was also the high point of Branzi's first modernism. Soon after, the West was on a course to a second modernism. Along came a shift to consumer society, a general mistrust in authority, an explosive growth and diversification of higher education, and an awareness of looming ecological crises. Despite increasingly sophisticated methods aimed at handling complexity, human, social, and ecological problems proved to be "wicked" and unsolvable by rationalistic methods.[6]

In a sense, the design methods movement arrived at design when it was already too late. To claim that technical expertise somehow automatically makes the world better was hardly credible to people who had lived through Auschwitz and Vietnam.

The failure of the movement was more than a matter of changing mental landscape. The best known attempt to lay design on rational foundations was the Hochschule für Gestaltung in Ulm, Germany. Starting as New Bauhaus in 1953 with roots in art and design, by 1956 its agenda had turned to teaching teamwork, science, research, and social consciousness in a modernist spirit.[7] The Ulm school is typically seen as the first serious attempt at turning design into a science of planning.[8]

However, the Ulm experiment was short-lived. The long time head of the Ulm school, Tomás Maldonado, reflected on his experience 15 years after the school was closed.[9] For him, the main cause of failure was sticking to "the theoretical generalities of a 'problem solving' which did not go beyond a 'discourse on method' of Cartesian memory."[10] He wrote:

The driving force behind our curiosity, of our studies and of our theoretical effort consisted of our desire to furnish a solid methodological basis for design. One must admit that such a pretext was very ambitious: one attempted to force a change in the field of design which was very similar to the process which turned alchemy into chemistry. But our attempt was, as we know now, premature.[11]

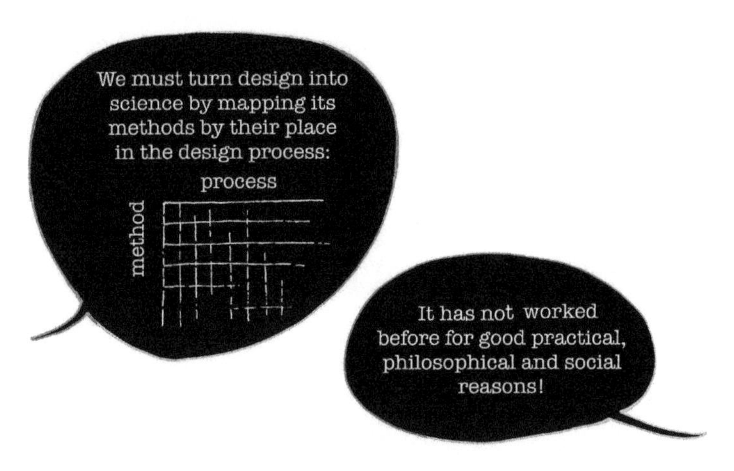

Figure 2.1 Rationalism faces post-Cartesian philosophy.

Indeed, how can anyone "solve" the problem of climate change through design? Modesty was in demand, given the scale of emerging environmental and social problems. Solving known problems rationally is a part of design, but can hardly provide anything like a solid foundation for it. Ultimately, the problem is one of creativity and critique, imagining something better than what exists, not the lack of rational justification (see Figure 2.1).

Small wonder that Gedenryd's conclusion about the usefulness of self-proclaimed rationalistic design processes was grim.[12] When he was writing his thesis, he was able to build not only on the disappointment of the rationalist program, but also on the rich debate of the limits of rationalism. For example, the Berkeley-based phenomenologist Hubert Dreyfus analyzed the assumptions at work in artificial intelligence. Despite their prowess in calculation, even the most sophisticated computers could do a few things any child could, such as speaking, understanding ambiguity, or walking. Several computer scientists followed in the footsteps of Dreyfus' critique.[13] The 1980s was a decade when most humanities and social sciences turned to French social theory and philosophy that further eroded belief in rationalism.[14] In the 1990s, Kees Dorst and Henrik Gedenryd followed Donald Schön's pragmatist perspective, arguing for seeing designers as sense-making beings rather than problem solvers.[15]

Also, there were several well-spoken critics in the field coming from the social sciences and the human-centered corner of computer science. For example, Lucy Suchman studied how people use copy machines at Palo Alto Research Center. She demonstrated how rational reasoning has little to do with how people actually use the machines, and urged designers to take social action seriously.[16] Participatory designers and critical information systems researchers borrowed from Ludwig Wittgenstein's philosophy to understand how ordinary language works at the background in any system.[17] Groups at the University of Toronto, Stanford, Carnegie Mellon, MIT, and many other American universities proved that technological research can be done without complex rationalistic methodology on pragmatic grounds.

2.1 The User-Centered Turn: Searching the Middle Way

After the demise of the design methods movement, designers turned to the behavioral and social sciences in their search to find new beginnings. In several places, user-centered design gained a foothold.[18] In terms used by Nelson and Stolterman, the rationalists were idealists in their search for truth. When this search was over, the next place to look at was the real world.[19]

This step was not radical, given designers' self-image. Designers have long seen themselves as speakers for people in the industry. The global organization for industrial designers, ICSID, defines the basic ethos of the occupation as follows:

> *Design is a creative activity whose aim is to establish the multi-faceted qualities of objects, processes, services and their systems in whole life cycles. Therefore, design is the central factor of innovative humanization of technologies and the crucial factor of cultural and economic exchange.*[20]

As this definition shows, designers see themselves as proponents of people in the industry. This self-image has more than a grain of truth, especially when designers are compared to engineers.[21] This self-image has deep historical roots. The importance of studying people was first forcefully introduced to design in post-war America, largely through practitioners like Henry Dreyfuss, one of the founding fathers of design ergonomics. In particular, Dreyfuss' books *Designing for People* and *Measures of Man* influenced generations of designers.[22]

However, it was in the 1990s that industrial design and the emerging interaction design went through the so-called user-centered turn. The key idea was that everyone has expertise of some kind and, hence, can inspire design. In retrospect, the most important ideas from this time built on usability and user-centered design.

Usability fell on the fertile ground of ergonomics and spread quickly. Its roots go back to the early 1980s, with companies such as Digital Equipment Corporation and IBM at the forefront. Early on, usability was divided into two camps: practical engineers and researchers whose backgrounds were usually in cognitive psychology.[23] Usability laboratories popped up in hi-tech companies and universities in North America, Japan, and Europe, and the academic community grew rapidly. Practitioners built on books like *Usability Engineering* by Jacob Nielsen, while the more academic field was reading books like Don Norman's *The Design of Everyday Things*.[24]

The problem with usability was that, while it did help to manage design problems with increasingly complex information technologies, it did little to inform design about the "context" — the environment in which some piece of design was meant to do its work. The image of a human being was that of an information processor, a cybernetic servomechanism.[25] Context was but a variable in these mechanisms. New, more open methods were developed, and they came from ethnography.

The design industry started to hire ethnographers in the 1970s, first in the Midwest and the Chicago area and slightly later in California.[26] The best known pioneers were Rick Robinson working for Jay Doblin and later E-Lab, and its marketing-oriented rival Cheskin. Interval Research at Stanford, funded by Microsoft's Paul Allen, hired John Hughes and Bonnie Johnson to teach fieldwork. Several anthropologists were hired by major companies in the 1990s, including Apple (1994) and Intel (1996). Another inspiration was fieldwork done in design firms like IDEO and Fitch. These were quick and rough ethnographies done very early in the design process for inspiration and provided a vision that worked as "glue" in long and arduous product development processes. Yet another American precursor was Xerox PARC, where design was infused with ethnographic techniques, ethnomethodology, and conversation analysis.[27] Through PARC, ethnomethodology influenced a field called "computer-supported collaborative work" (CSCW). The aims of much of this work were summarized by Peggy Szymanski and Jack Whalen:

> *Plainly, as social scientists these researchers were committed to understanding the fundamentally socio-cultural organization of human reasoning and action .... moreover, these researchers were equally committed to naturalistic observation of that action — to leaving the highly controlled environment of the laboratory so that what humans did and how they did it could be studied in real-world habitats and settings, under ordinary, everyday conditions.*[28]

In Europe, an important inspiration was Scandinavian participatory design, even though its radical political ideology was lost when it spread to industry. Although its direct influence was not felt much in design beyond the borders of Scandinavia, it had a degree of impact in software development and later in design in the United States.[29] It also had limited impact in art and design schools. Still, in retrospect, it managed to do two things typical to contemporary design research: working with people using mock-ups.[30]

Eureka: Fieldwork Leads to an Information System

Written by Jack Whalen

How can you design an information system that enables a firm's employees to easily share their practical knowledge, and then put this knowledge to use each and every day to solve their most vexing problems? (See Figure 2.2.)

Most companies have tackled this problem by brute force, building massive repositories of their reports, presentations, and other officially authorized documents that they hope contain enough useful knowledge to justify the effort, or by placing their faith in artificial intelligence, designing expert systems that basically try to capture that same authorized knowledge in a box. Yet everyone recognizes that much of any organization's truly valuable knowledge, its essential intellectual capital, is found in the undocumented ideas, unauthorized inventions and insights, and practicable know-how of its members. Most of this knowledge is embodied in the employee's everyday work practice, commonly shared through bits of conversations and stories among small circles of colleagues and work groups, with members filling in the blanks from their own experience.

Researchers at Xerox's renowned Palo Alto Research Center (PARC) came face to face with this reality only after they first took the artificial intelligence (AI) route, designing a sophisticated expert system for the company's field service technicians to use when solving problems with customers' copiers and printers. Its knowledge base was everything that was known about the machines — everything in "the book." But the researchers soon discovered, after going into the field and observing technicians as they went about their daily rounds, that technicians often had to devise solutions to problems for which "the book" had no answer — what you could call "the black arts of machine repair." A way to share this kind of knowledge throughout their community — an information system designed to work like those stories and conversations, and managed by the community itself — is what technicians needed most.

And so together the technicians and PARC researchers co-designed a peer-to-peer system for sharing previously undocumented solutions to machine problems that are invented by technicians around the world, and named it Eureka. From the very start, Eureka saved the company an estimated $20M annually and continues to do so, with Xerox being named "Knowledge Company of the Year" by *KMWorld Magazine* (and garnering several other IT and management awards) as a result (see Figure 2.3).

Figure 2.2 Observing technicians at work in Eureka project.

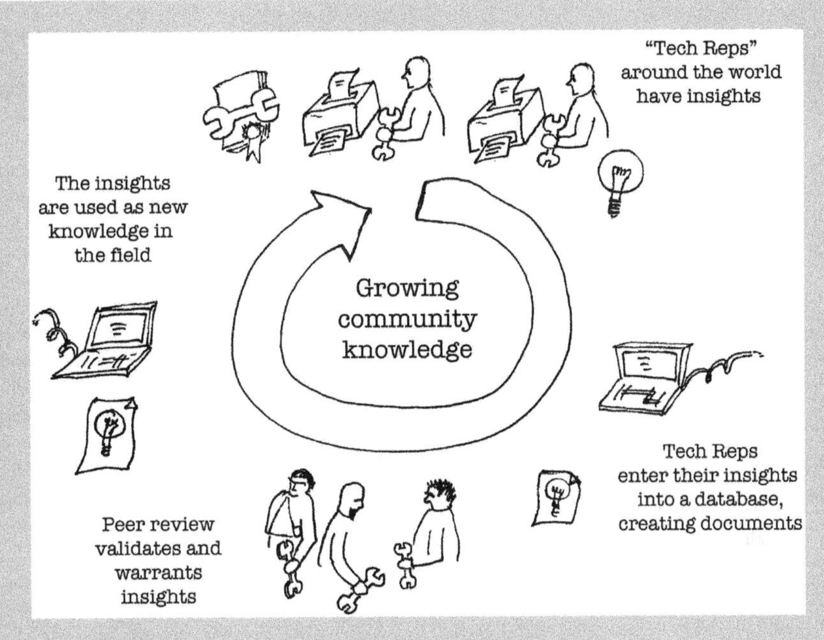

Figure 2.3 Research and design process in Eureka.

From such humble beginnings, the field has grown over the past few years into a community of industrial ethnographers sizeable enough to run an annual international conference, Ethnographic Praxis in Industry (EPIC). As its founder Ken Anderson explained, it was designed mainly to share learning between practitioners of design ethnography. Still, it also sought academic approval from the American Anthropological Association to make it more than a business conference where consultants run through their company portfolios (Figure 2.4).[31]

The outcome of this work was a series of fieldwork techniques that became popular in the second half of the 1990s. American interaction designers also created a blend of analytic

However, user-centered design had its problems too. Ethnography mainly focused on the early stages of design, and usability at its very end, which limited their usefulness. User-centered design was software-oriented in its tone, and slowly spread to other fields of design. Both were largely seen as imports from sociology, anthropology, and psychology. They were also seen as research rather than design practices. Also, if stretched to a prophecy, user-centered design fails: as Roberto Verganti argued, most products on the market are designed without much user research.[33] For reasons like these, user-centered design failed to attract a following, especially among more artistically oriented designers.

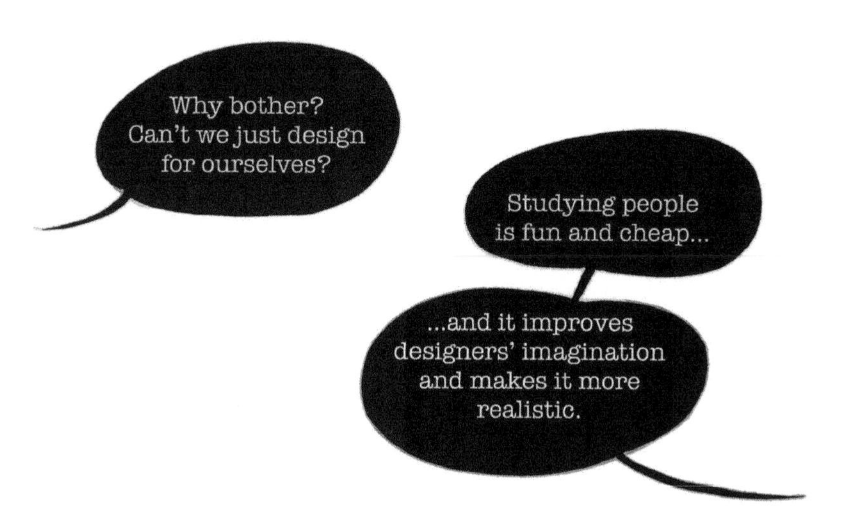

Figure 2.4 Why study people? It is not difficult and provides better results than thinking.

and communication techniques, such as "personas." These are constructed, detailed descriptions of individual characters done to both highlight research results and to encourage developers to implement the design team's design. Through scenarios, designers study the viability of these concepts in different future situations.[32]

For good reasons, both usability and user-centered design are alive and well today. In particular, they placed people into the middle of design and gave credibility to designers' claims that they are the spokespersons of people in production. It also produced many successful designs, and provided design researchers ways to publish their research.

2.2 Beyond the User

Despite these limitations, user-centered design created powerful tools for understanding people and creating designs that work. However, it was just as obvious that it was not able to respond to many interests coming from the more traditional design world. User-centered design methods may have helped to explore context for inspiration, but it left too many important sources of imagination in design unused.

Constructive design researchers have had good reasons to go back to contemporary art and design in search of more design-specific methods and ways of working (see Figure 2.5). The past 15 years have seen a proliferation of openings that not only build on user-centered design, but also go beyond it. Several research

Figure 2.5 Making people imagine is a problem in constructive design research.

groups have begun to address the problem of creativity with methodic, conceptual, technological, and artistic means.[34]

2.2.1 Design Practice Provides Methods

One push beyond the user was methodic. The 1990s and 2000s saw the growth of "generative" research methods that put design practice at the core of the research process. These design-inspired methodologies include experience prototypes, design games, and many types of traditional design tools such as collages, mood boards, storyboards, pastiche scenarios, scenarios, "personas," and various types of role-plays.[35] There is no shortage of such methods: Froukje Sleeswijk Visser listed 44 user-centered methods in her doctoral thesis at Delft, and IDEO introduced a pack of cards having 52 methods (see Figure 2.6).[36]

One striking feature of much of this work is the speed at which it has gained influence and has been adopted by its audience even beyond design. In the computer industry, scenarios and personas have become mainstream, while in industrial design, cultural probes, Make Tools, and action research have spread fast.[37] These methods have been quickly adapted to a wide variety of design work, often with a limited connection to the intentions of the original work.[38] Still, they have given designers ways to research issues like user experience. They also help to open the design process to multiple stakeholders.[39]

Figure 2.6 IDEO methods cards. These cards describe design methods in words on one page. The other side gives an illustration of the method.

2.2.2 Turn to Technology

Another important concept that has pushed design research beyond user studies can be loosely called the "sandbox culture." This is similar to engineering in Thomas Edison's Menlo Park, or in the hacker culture of Silicon Valley in the 1970s. One can, as engineers at the University of Toronto, turn a (computer) mouse into a door sensor without going into the physics of sensors. The *modus operandi* of the most successful design firm in the world over the past two decades, IDEO, has been characterized as "technology brokering": finding problems and solving them by finding answers by exploring technology creatively through engineering imagination, not scientifically.[40]

The most famous sandbox culture existed at MIT's Media Lab under the leadership of Nicholas Negroponte, where the old scientific adage "publish or perish" became "demo or die."[41] Other sandbox cultures that served as exemplars for design researchers were Toronto, Carnegie Mellon, the Interactive Television Program at Tisch School of the Arts at New York University, and Stanford's design program.[42] They showed that it is possible to do research with things at hand without complex justifications and theoretical grounds and just let imagination loose in the workshop.[43] This is typical of software design as well.[44] The prestige of these places has also given legitimacy to building new sandboxes in places like Technische Universiteit Eindhoven.

MIT Media Lab

Maybe the best known sandbox has been the Media Lab at MIT in Cambridge, Massachusetts. It was created in 1985 with a mission to explore and develop media technologies. It had precursors in New York University, where Tisch School of the Arts had run an Interactive Telecommunications Program (ITP) under Red Burns since the early 1970s.

However, while ITP focused more on media content, and gradually grew into technology, MIT focused on technology from the beginning. Its mission was to explore and develop new media technologies and to conceive and illustrate new concepts by prototyping them. This is where Media Lab started, and this is where it still stands. Its moment of glory was probably during the second half of the 1990s when the IT industry exploded with the Web and soon after with mobile technology (see Figure 2.7).

For a while, the Media Lab was one of the most closely followed research institutions in the world, as judged by the digital industries. Several other institutions were modeled after its example in Asia and Europe; the most famous of these was probably the short lived Interaction Design Institute Ivrea in Italy.

When one walks into the building in Massachusetts, there are no classrooms and corridors, only workspaces in which people sit in the middle of wires, sensors, circuits, computers, lights, and "old materials" of many sorts, most of them organized in open spaces where it is possible to walk around and try out the "old materials."

Several famous concepts have been discovered in the Media Lab. Some of the most influential in the research world have been Hiroshi Ishii's interactive ping pong table and his bottle interface for a music player.

Figure 2.7

From a constructive design research standpoint, the Media Lab well illustrates three points. First, doing is important for designers: one can create new worlds by doing. Second, design research needs design; design happens at the Media Lab, but it is not a priority. Duct tape creations are enough, because prototypes are used to illustrate technological, not design possibilities. Third, a focus on technology means that technological research comes before wrting. The Media Lab is famous for the prototypes it creaters.

The co-founder of the Media Lab, Nicholas Negroponte, is said to have replaced the old academic adage "publish or perish" with "demo or die." (See Figure 2.8.)

Figure 2.8

The main legacy of this culture is several research communities exploring new possibilities in information technology. For example, by now, there are conferences specializing in ubiquitous and pervasive computing and tangible interaction. For those constructive researchers who specialize in interactive technologies, these communities provide many types of publication possibilities. Also, by now, there are many design frameworks ranging from resonant interaction to rich and intuitive interaction. Chapter 4 presents some of these frameworks in detail.

2.2.3 Enter User Experience

In the 1990s, design researchers created many types of concepts that paved the way to constructive research. Important trailblazing work was done at IDEO and SonicRim, where Uday Dandavate, Liz Sanders, Leon Segal, Jane Fulton Suri, and Alison Black emphasized the role of emotions in experience and started to build the groundwork for empathic methodologies.[45] In Europe, the leader was probably Patrick Jordan at Philips, who claimed that design should build on pleasure rather than usability.[46] Influential studies like Maypole followed his lead, usually building on concepts like need.[47]

This hedonic and emotional movement was a useful correction to cognitive psychology, which had crept into design research through usability and design studies focusing on what designers know and how they think.[48] It remained individualistic. The key constructs of this movement were difficult to understand. It focused on measurable emotions at the expense of more finely tuned emotions like aesthetic feelings, which are crucial to design.

For reasons like this, the main conceptual innovation came to be user experience, which was open enough and avoided many of these problems.[49] It did not have unwanted connotations like the word "pleasure," and was not contested like "aesthetics," which has a history in aesthetics, art history, and philosophy. This concept has been so successful that leading universities, corporations, and design firms have built units to study user experience. Even the International Organization for Standardization (ISO) is trying to create a standard for user experience in industrial practice. Finally, pragmatist philosophy gave this concept credibility, depth, and openness.[50]

2.2.4 Design Tradition as Inspiration

Yet another push beyond user-centered design came from design. The key place was the Computer-Aided Design program in the Royal College of Art (RCA) in London. Its researchers explored new media in city space and alternative ways to design electronics. They explicitly built on art and design and had an agnostic tone when it came to science.[51]

For example, the main influence of the *Presence Project*, published in 2000, was an artistic movement called "situationism."[52] What came to be known as "critical design," on the other hand, built on designers like Daniel Weil who had questioned the design conventions of electronics.[53] Critical design was also influenced by Italian *controdesigners*, and from the Dutch design concept Droog Design, which was also inspired partly by Italian design.[54]

Today, many design researchers seek inspiration from art and design,[55] and many are also active debaters and curators.[56] The art and the design worlds are also converging commercially, with one-offs, limited editions, and prototypes becoming objects sold by major auction houses.[57] There are hundreds of books about designers' sketches in bookstores, effectively representing designers as artists. Media celebrates designers much as it has celebrated artists. Also, there have been company research centers that have had artist-in-residence programs.[58]

2.3 Between Engineering, Science, Design, and Art

This history has left a legacy to constructive design research, which lies on several foundations. A good deal of early design research was built on rationalistic models that in the beginning faced many kinds of political and scientific difficulties. Constructive design research has turned away from this foundation. Researchers seek inspiration from engineering as well as from the social sciences and design traditions. What it is doing is important: it is bringing design back to the heart of research.

By now, constructive design research has gained a degree of maturity and autonomy. There have been several milestones in this maturation. Methods like scenarios, personas, Make Tools, and the cultural probes played an important role in lowering designers' entry into research. These methods have proved that many things in design practice can be turned into research methods fairly easily. After the end of the 1990s, conferences like Design+ Emotion, Designing Pleasurable Products and Interfaces, and Nordes[59] gave designers an opportunity to explore design-related topics with little gatekeeping from other disciplines. A few influential books have served as precedents; noteworthy are Anthony Dunne and Fiona Raby's *Design Noir* and Dunne's *Hertzian Tales*. Several dozen doctoral theses build directly on design rather than borrow methodologies and concepts from other disciplines (see Figure 2.9).[60]

The development is uneven. The strongest institutions have taken leadership. Among universities, the most research-driven are well-resourced schools such as Politecnico di Milano, technical universities in Delft and Eindhoven, Carnegie Mellon University, and what was the University of Art and Design Helsinki (now a part of Aalto University). Among global companies, leaders included Intel, Microsoft, and Nokia, and some of the largest design firms like IDEO.[61] Among pioneers were Delft's IO Studiolab, which combined several studios at the end of the 1990s, Smart Products Research Group in Helsinki's UIAH, Philips' visionary programs, and Intel's anthropological fieldwork.[62]

Underneath this canopy, a good deal of the design world went on as before. However, the strongest schools and companies set examples for others to follow. Once they did the trailblazing, others found it easier to follow suit.

Although constructive design research is coming of age, this is only one part of the story. This research is typically

Figure 2.9 The two-headed design researcher (homage to Henry Dreyfuss).

multidisciplinary and takes place in institutions over which designers have little control. Constructive design researchers typically collaborate with sociologists, anthropologists, and computer scientists. In these research groups, design researchers are often junior partners who needed to follow the models of research from their more established colleagues.[63] Some consequences of this collaboration have left a mark on constructive design research. For example, experimental research became an almost unquestioned choice for constructive design researchers, especially in technical universities and the technology industry.

Design also juggles with the worlds of art and culture. Even designers who work with industry typically have one foot in art and culture, as in the famous case of Olivetti. Designers working for Olivetti in Ivrea, about 100 kilometers west of Milan, also continued living and working in Milan with company approval. This organization made it possible for designers like Ettore Sottsass and Michele de Lucchi to alternate between industrial work and Milan's artistic and intellectual milieux.[64] Today, it is easy to see a similar balancing act in some researchers' work coming from the RCA at Sheffield-Hallam University and several Scandinavian universities. These researchers sometimes work at the university and sometimes as independent designers and artists. They also mix these worlds in their work in various ways, especially in the ways in which they communicate their work through exhibitions rather than books.[65]

Constructive design research has managed to gain a degree of autonomy and recognition on its own, but it has to find its way through an environment that sets many standards for research.

In research today, coalitions are a norm, not an exception. These coalitions tend to be strategic and temporary, usually lasting for only one project, and then disappear as parties move to other projects.[66] To flourish in this environment, constructive design researchers need methodological and theoretical flexibility.

End Notes

1. Simon (1996, pp. 2–9). Perhaps characteristically, Simon's ideas remained open in *The Sciences of the Artificial.* The best way to understand this book is perhaps to see it as an opening into a new domain, a prolegomena, to borrow the words of his colleague Jim March (1978). His notes on design remained so abstract that there is simply no way to know where they would have led, should he have built a complete research program based on them. Simon's biographer, Hunter Crowther-Heyck (2005, p. 176), said that characterizing Simon's work as a collection of prolegomena is "uncharitable, but not entirely inaccurate." For more recent analyses of systems thinking in design, see Sato's notes in his 2009 paper (pp. 32–34), and Forlizzi (forthcoming).
2. Archer (1968), Jones (1992, but first edition in 1970), Alexander (1968), Simon (1996), and Lawson (1980). The most influential of these writers is probably Jones, whose text still appears, even at doctoral-level research, as the definitive document of what design research is about. His rational approach on design was based on the notion of "complexity," claiming that new problems like urban traffic systems required methods and processes that could not be found from existing design traditions. Jones' (1970) solution was a matrix in which methods were classified by their place in the design process. The process was one in which a problem was first discovered and then transformed into design ideas that were then broken into subproblems. These subproblems were to be solved one by one and then combined into alternative designs that were then evaluated to find the best solution to the problem.
3. Gedenryd (1998, p. 1).
4. The now (in)famous new introduction to Jones' (1992) *Design Methods* not only said that the rationalistic program failed but also changed its form: it referred mostly to artists like John Cage and consisted of drawings, poetry, and fictional narratives. His book *Designing Designing* (Jones, 1991) developed this radical approach further, telling designers to discard rationalism and focus on imagination instead.

   It is hard not to agree with his call, but it is also worth noting that his solution does not have to be followed, turning the very design process into a critique and even travesty of design or, by implication, design research. Here, the problem is the same as in science, but more general: scientists and social scientists sometimes turn to poetry and the performing arts in an effort to break the conventions of their craft. However, more often than not, their work is not on par with poets, performance artists, and dancers. It is far easier to behave as an artist than to be one.

   Similarly, Alexander (1971) said in an interview:

   > *There is so little in what is called "design methods" that has anything useful to say about how to design buildings that I never even read the literature any more.... I would say forget it, forget the whole thing. Period. Until those people who talk about design methods are actually engaged in the problem of creating buildings and actually trying to create buildings, I wouldn't give a penny for their efforts.*

This statement should be taken with caution. One irony here is that Alexander was talking about architecture. In this field where every building is unique, the idea of *the* method is consequently slightly offbeat. Another problem lies in the notion of method. There are methods that work perfectly well, even though their design could not be reduced to a particular method. That rationalistic methods failed does not mean that every method will fail forever. It depends on how "methods" are understood and even more on what foundations they build upon (see Chapter 7). Finally, Alexander talks about methods, not research, and these are different things.

However, Alexander points to an important issue — the connection between theory and doing. Given his background in mathematics, his interest in formalisms was understandable, but as the first ever to receive a PhD in architecture at Harvard, his theories most likely reflected his background more than his practice. Over time, the realities of practice won.

The difficulty here is that his analysis equates a person with his practice in saying that only practitioners' texts have value. This view does not take into account the social basis of architecture (or design). By his measure, a person like Kees Overbeeke has no value to design research because he is not a designer. This claim is blatantly false, and fails to take into account that Overbeeke's work is necessary in expanding design. We introduce language in detail in Chapter 3, and Overbeeke's work is essential to the welfare of one research program and contributes to design, even though his background is in psychology. Following Alexander's blindness to the social background of a discipline would be plainly destructive.

Coming from a similar background, Horst Rittel's notion of "wicked problems" is indebted to Herbert Simon's earlier work on the limits of rationality. This critique came from within the rationalist movement, and was a part of the paradigm change of the 1960s that paved the way to more philosophical criticisms of the 1980s. We will come back to these later in this chapter.

It must be noted that the design methodology movement continued to inspire design research quietly, in particular in design schools in England, with the exception of design studies, in an attempt to understand designers' thinking (Lawson, 1980, 2004; Cross, 2007; Visser, 2006). This field went into hibernation for two decades (see also Bayazit, 2004, p. 21).

5. Downton (2005, p. 35) noted how

> *Writings concerned with what design should be, have focused on attempting to improve the design process by devising a rational method.... such formulations (labeled as "Design Methods") were accompanied by virtual guarantees that their use would banish irrational design and herald the dawn of the era of rationality. Without wishing to decry such attempts, examination and attempted use over four decades have made it clear that they were ambitious and even misguided.... It is hard, perhaps impossible, to cite a single example of a building or urban design produced through the rigorous and unsullied use of one of these methods. They have left a legacy of many useful strategies and tools that can be used in research for design. The desire to promote means, if not methods, for "improving design" remains alive, although tempered with world-weary awareness, if not cynicism, of post-postmodernism. [italics removed].*

6. For wicked problems, see Rittel and Webber (1973).
7. For a recent review of teamwork and collaboration in design, see Poggenpohl (2009b, p. 139ff) who noted that collaboration has a long, though largely unwritten history in design and also reviews recent studies on managing information and communication as well as issues related to human dimensions of interdisciplinarity.

8. As Herbert Lindinger, himself trained in Ulm, noted in his introduction to a book he edited about Ulm in 1991. The school was established in 1952 as New Bauhaus. After 1956, the school first stressed teamwork, science, research, and multidisciplinary collaboration. From around 1958, scientists like Horst Rittel and Bruce Archer begun to formulate design methodology, and artistic extravagance gave way to scientific caution and value neutral design, both beliefs stemming from logical positivism. As Lindinger said, universal manifestos like "building a new culture" changed to working hypotheses, dubbing the years from 1958 to 1962 as years of "planning mania." Soon, designers became a minority in the school. There was a crisis period that led to a search for balance between theory and practice around 1962 until about 1966, with Tomás Maldonado and Bruce Archer as leading lights (Lindinger, 1991, pp. 10–12).
   As this history suggests, the school's position on theory and methodology was not consistent after 1956. As Michael Erlhoff (1991, p. 51) noted in the same collection, Ulm "took the case of modernity … back to the last phase of the Bauhaus, and carried abstraction forward into systematization. The HfG set out to be on the side of the modern age and found itself … subscribing to humanistic principles and so resisting the truth of its own modernity."
   The point, quite simply, was that the modern tendency to see the world through abstract, scientific concepts may carry the promise of a rational society, but it also leads to the horrors of the twentieth century. People at Ulm may have learned their methodology from logical positivists, but this dilemma was something they learned from the Frankfurt School of philosophers, most notably Theodor Adorno.
   Bonsiepe (1999, p. 13) listed some of the influences of the Ulm School with the demurrer "if my memory does not fail me." His list has a place for positivists, pragmatists, the Frankfurt School, and apparently the late Wittgenstein as well as systems theory, concrete art/constructivism, Abraham Moles' aesthetics of information, and as he said, to a lesser degree, surrealism.
   The case for turning design into a science was never on solid ground but was strong enough to attract people like Reyner Banham (1991, pp. 58–59), for whom Ulm was like "a breath of painfully fresh air blowing down from the snowy Kuhberg" after London, where designers still believed in old shibboleths like "form follows function." It was a place where one could take intellectual risks because every claim, no matter how outrageous, was subjected to intense research and debate.
   Andrea Branzi had the most notable alternative view of Ulm. For him, people working on the hill of Ulm were extraordinary artists who disguised themselves as ordinary artists (Branzi, 1988, p. 42). We come back to this argument in Chapter 6.
9. Here Maldonado (1972, p. 22) talked about Western rationalism in generic terms, but he captures its spirit perfectly.

   What is really happening today is that men are being transformed into things so that it will be easier to administer them. Instead of working with men, one can work with schemes, numbers, and graphs that represent men. In that context, models became more important than the objects of the persons of which they were a mere replica. For many years now, the fetishism of models, especially in the fields of economics, politics, and military strategy, has typified the attitude of the late Enlightenment of the modern technocrats.

   According to these people, perfection of the instructional and decision-making process is possible only if one succeeds in getting rid of all subjective interference with the construction and manipulation of the models used for obtaining that perfection.

By turning design into a science, one could get rid of "subjective interference" and pave the way to a world of plenty. Revolution would come by design, as Buckminster Fuller once prophesied (cf. Maldonado, 1972, pp. 27–29).

10. Maldonado (1984). This critique, somewhat paradoxically, also extends to art. In a recently republished paper *Otl Aicher*, the Bauhaus gave too much priority to art at the expense of engineering and science. It built on a Platonic idea, in which art was the means to achieve knowledge of the idea, spiritual, and abstract world that lies behind things we see.

Aicher (2009, pp. 177, 181) asked:

> *is design an applied art manifested in the elements of square, triangle, and circle, or is it a discipline that derives its criteria from the task at hand; from function, production, and technology? and noted that this conflict remained unsolved at the Bauhaus "as long as the concept of art remained taboo, as long as an uncritical Platonism of pure form remained in force as a world principle." His example of such Platonism was Rietveld's chairs that "turned out to be nothing more than Mondrians for sitting, ineffectual art objects with the pretext of wanting to be useful.*

At Ulm, the models were designers like the Eameses. As Aicher wrote, "designers like Charles Eames were the first to show what it meant to develop products on the basis of their purpose, material, and methods of manufacture — on the basis of their function," rather than on the basis of geometry. "We all had good reasons to have reservations about the Bauhaus," he concluded (Aicher, 2009, pp. 181–182). In contrast, at Ulm, "the objective was not to extend art into everyday life, to apply it. The objective was an anti-art, a work of civilization, a culture of civilization" (pp. 178, 180–181). This realization in its part paved the way for user-centered design four decades later.

11. Maldonado (1984, p. 5). In this text, Maldonado also refers to Herbert Simon's "limited rationality" thesis. We have omitted this sentence, because we see it as another attempt to salvage rationalistic thinking and its "Cartesian" view of the world as a place of individual entities that can only be known by organizing painstaking observations into more abstract, meaningful entities.

Several intellectual movements have argued that Cartesian thinking presupposes those very things that make it possible in the first place. For example, we relate to things around us not only through ideas in our minds, but also with our bodies, and more often than not with other people. If one accepts the Cartesian worldview, many things are no longer considered. Out goes working with the body and hands; out goes sketching and prototyping; out goes basing design on social meanings; and out go dreams, beliefs, and emotions. Also no longer considered are working with people, studies of non-logical things like religion, integrating non-analytic tasks done by hand, and sketchy design processes designed for flexibility. For design research, this kind of rationalism provides a particularly narrow focus. (See also Maldonado, 1991).

12. Dreyfus (1972, 1993, 2001).

13. Winograd and Flores (1987), Winograd (1996), Dourish (2002).

14. These criticisms pointed out that rationalism has limits that explained a good deal of its elegance. For example, when one does not have to deal with the body, or anything social, it is far easier to imagine people making rational decisions and, as important, obeying them. From a post-Cartesian perspective, rationalism was only possible because something in our lives made it possible: language, social action, our ability to talk and act in an orderly manner. From this perspective, rationalism is but a special case of a far more general way of thinking about humans. Rationalism works in the community when it believes in it, and has the same idea of what is relevant and what is not. This is the case in some closed, isolated communities, and certainly in some academic groups, but rarely anywhere else.

15. Schön (1983), Dorst and Dijkhuis (1995), Dorst (1997), Gedenryd (1998).
16. Suchman (1987). Another important writer who pointed out the importance of looking at social action was Edward Hutchins (1996), who introduced the notion "cognition in the wild," referring to the need to study thinking in real settings. Activity theorists added that there also was a need to look at historical background in any attempt to understand action (Kuutti, 1996).
17. In addition to Ehn (1988a), see Lyytinen (1982, 1983, 1986), Hirschheim et al. (1995), and Nurminen (1988).
18. Focusing on humans is represented in many ways. The design program's Web site at Stanford claims that the idea of human-centered design was invented at Stanford when John Arnold built the design program in the mid-1950s. This may be true, but one should also remember that in the United States, designers like Dreyfuss and Teague had already been working with the military for a long time while putting humans into the middle of design work. In Europe, the Ulm school was built on the same idea, and ISCID was already working to make humans the center point of its definition of design.

    When computers became design material in the 1990s, humans became "users," which suggests that they are seen as parts of technical systems (see Bannon, 1991). Seen against the history of design, this was an extraordinary semantic reduction. At its narrowest, people came to be seen as barely more than biological information processing units in technical systems. When reading, say, ICSID's definition of industrial design, one is struck by the discordance to its humanistic spirit.
19. Nelson and Stolterman (2003).
20. ICSID, icsid.org/about/about/articles31.htm, retrieved October 22, 2009. The definition goes back to the turn of the 1950s and 1960s and is based on Tomás Maldonado's thinking. See Anceschi and Botta (2009, p. 23), and note 5 in their text.

    Maldonado had his predecessors. Ulm's first principal, Max Bill (2009), was trained in the Bauhaus and used Bauhausian language when writing about design as a human discipline in 1954:

    > *the task of the artist is not to express himself and his feelings in a subjective way; it is to create harmonious objects that will serve people.... artists, as part of their responsibility for human culture, have to grapple with the problems of mass production.... the basis of all production should be the unity of functions, including the aesthetic functions of an object ... and the aim of all production should be to satisfy people's needs and aspirations.*

    For Maldonado and his colleagues in Ulm, the way forward was the then fashionable information theory and linguistics. Otl Aicher tells how one of the first books he acquired for the Ulm School's library was Charles Morris' *Sign Theory*. Its classification of information into semantics, syntax, and pragmatics became a theoretical foundation for him and for Maldonado. For Aicher, this classification revealed that the focus of design must be semantics, that is, communication, not the syntax of elementary geometry then prevalent in avant-garde graphic design and photography. For instance, in photography this led to a study of photojournalists like Felix H. Mann, Stephan Laurant, and Robert Capa whose job was communication, not art.

    As Aicher related (2009, pp. 183–185), studies of mathematical logic led him and Maldonado to realize that any answer they wanted to get to their questions depended on the method: "the spirit was a method, but not a substance. We experience the order of the world as the order of thought, as information."

21. For some of the paradoxes here, see Redström (2006).
22. Tilley and Dreyfuss' (2002) *The Measure of Man* in 1959 was a landmark that described the dimensions of Joe and Josephine, two average Americans. The origins of ergonomics — or human factors, as ergonomics is also called in the United States — in America are in the war. As Russell Flinchum (1997, pp. 78, 84) noted, the exact history of how ergonomics came to be established in design is probably lost in old classified materials. Ergonomics in design was largely codified by Alvin Tilley, an engineer working in Dreyfuss' design firm. Tilley used a variety of sources creatively in *The Measure of Man* (Tilley and Dreyfuss, 2002), including military sources, as well as material from Manhattan's fashion industry (Flinchum 1997, p. 87). As Flinchum also noted, the characters of Joe and Josephine were meant to be used as guidelines in preliminary investigations in design; they were never meant to be used as exact descriptions of humans (Flinchum 1997, p. 175).
23. Dumas (2007).
24. Nielsen (1993), Norman (1998), with the original in 1988.
25. For a good analysis of where this worldview came from in computer science and psychology, see Crowther-Heyck's (2005, pp. 184–274) analysis of Herbert Simon and the early stages of artificial intelligence in America.

    Few reliable sources exist about Japanese companies' user-centric practices from the 1970s and 1980s, but anecdotes reveal that they were in the frontline with the Europeans and the Americans. For instance, John Thackara (1998, p. 20) admired Sharp's "humanware design" in the 1980s, telling how the company anchored its practice in it and reversed the traditional production-led Western ways in which design attempts to fit product specifications to match factories and laboratories. Instead, "Sharp employs sociologists to study how people live and behave, and then plans products to fill the gaps they discover.... new technology is used to create when consumers are discovered to 'want,'" he wrote.
26. Wasson (2000, 2002), Cefkin (2010).
27. Szymanski and Whalen (2011), Suchman (1987), Crabtree (2003).
28. Szymanski and Whalen (2011, p. 5).
29. For a history of the early years of participatory design in the United States, see Greenbaum (2009). More history can be found in Bannon (2009). Obstacles to participatory techniques in organizations were mapped by Grudin (2009).
30. For participatory design, see Ehn (1988a), Iversen (2005), and Johansson (2005). For contextual design, see Beyer and Holtzblatt (1998). For recent work in combining anthropology and design, see Halse et al. (2010). We will come back to participatory design in Chapters 5 and 7.
31. Ken Anderson and Scott Mainwaring to Koskinen, August 19, 2010, at Hillsboro, Oregon.
32. The main statement of personas is in Cooper (1999). John Carroll has edited and written several books about scenarios (see especially Carroll, 2000).
33. Verganti (2009). One standard complaint about user-centered design is that it leads to unimaginative and conservative design. Although this is only a part of the story, there certainly is a grain of truth in this criticism. However, this criticism has its faults too: there are many examples of short-sighted, designer-driven design that has led to rubbish, and there are better ways to judge how effective a design approach is than by looking at traditional products like coffee pots and sofas. See Verganti (2009) for a defense of designer-driven design.
34. See Green and Jordan (1999) and Battarbee and Koskinen (2004, p. 5).
35. Dandavate et al. (1996), Sanders and Dandavate (1999), Brandt (2006).
36. Sleeswijk Visser (2009, p. 63).
37. Gaver et al. (1999), Mattelmäki (2006).

38. See Boehner et al. (2007).
39 For example, Sanders (2006).
40. Hargadon and Sutton (1997).
41. Our reference to "demo or die," as well as attributing it to the MIT Media Lab under Nicholas Negroponte, is from Peter Lunenfeld (2000).
42. Stanford's "d.school" is an informal name. The full correct name of the institute is Hasso Plattner Institute of Design at Stanford, after its principal source of funds.
43. For example, there exists human–computer interaction, and at least these "computings": mobile, urban, social, physical, collective, ubiquitous, embedded, proactive, and wearable. In interaction design, there are also many "interactions": tangible (Wensveen, 2004), interactive space (interactivespaces.net), aesthetic (Graves Petersen et al., 2004), rich (Frens, 2006a), intuitive (Lucero, 2009), kinesthetic, embodied (Dourish, 2002), emergent (Matthews et al., 2008), and resonant (Overbeeke et al., 2006).
44. Wroblewski (1991).
45. Dandavate et al. (1996), Segal and Fulton Suri (1997), Black (1998).
46. For a push toward hedonic psychology — psychology of pleasure — in the 1990s, see Patrick Jordan's (2000) work. For Maypole, see Mäkelä et al. (2000).
47. Maypole was a project funded by the European Union. Its aim was to study communication patterns in families to suggest new technologies. Participants were the Helsinki University of Technology (and through it, University of Art and Design Helsinki), IDEO Europe, Meru Research b.v., Netherlands Design Institute (which coordinated the project), Nokia Research Center, and the Center for Usability Research and Engineering.
Maypole did field studies of communication behavior. Based on these studies, it developed scenarios and concepts, tested methods and tools, and built prototypes that were then studied in countries like Austria and Finland. For example, one study connected a digital camera to a laptop in a back bag, which immediately allowed it to capture and send images immediately. See Mäkelä et al. (2000). For Maypole, see cordis.europa.eu/esprit/src/25425.htm, retrieved September, 12, 2010; maypole.org; and meru.nl.
48. Lawson (1980, 2004), Cross (2007).
49. For "user experience" in industry and universities, see Shedroff (2001), Forlizzi and Ford (2000), and Battarbee (2004). Theoretically, this notion is alternatively grounded in Dewey's pragmatism (1980; see McCarthy and Wright, 2004), symbolic interactionism (Battarbee, 2004), ecological psychology (Djajadiningrat, 1998, pp. 29–61), or emotional psychology (Desmet, 2002).
50. Usually the main reference is John Dewey (1980), and especially his *Art as Experience.* Over the past few years, there has been more interest in William James, but references to Dewey still dominate research.
51. See Chapter 6.
52. *Presence Project* (2001).
53. Dunne and Raby (2001), Dunne (2005).
54. For Droog, see Ramakers (2002) and Ramakers and Bakker (1998); for radical designers, see Celant in Ambasz (1972). Bosoni (2001) provides a long-term perspective on discourse in Italy.
55. There is no shortage on literature that maps the relationship of art and design. For example, for a particularly knowledgeable analysis of the relationship between pop art and design, see Bocchietto (2008). A good recent example is Stefano Giovannoni's work for Alessi (see Morozzi, 2008). A less consistent account on surrealism in design is Wood (2007).

56. For example, Alessandro Mendini works as an all-around cultural personality whose work is available in numerous designs, but is sometimes also exhibited as art (see Fiz, 2010), and Andrea Branzi continues to curate high-profile events in places such as Milan. For example, see Branzi's *Neues Europäisches Design*, which he curated with François Burkhardt in Berlin in 1991, and more recent exhibitions of *What Is Italian Design? The Seven Obsessions* in Milan's Triennale (Branzi, 2008).

57. For one-offs and prototypes, see Lovell (2009). See also Konstantin Grcic's *Design Real* (2010), which commented on this tendency by showing ordinary industrial products in a gallery. Ordinary products may lack the mystique of one-offs and prototypes, but not functionality and elegance. For how craft can be treated as art, see Ramakers and Bakker (1998) and Holt and Skov (2008).

58. For PAIR, an artist-in-residence program at Xerox's Palo Alto Research Center, see Harris (1999).

59. nordes.org.

60. Dunne and Raby (2001), Dunne (2005), Djajadiningrat (1998), Wensveen (2004), Frens (2006a), Battarbee (2004), Ludvigsen (2007).

61. See Kelley (2001) and Brown (2009).

62. For Philips, see De Ruyter and Aarts (2010) and Aarts and Marzano (2003); for Intel, see Cefkin (2010).

63. This dilemma, and a drift to the applied science model, was already discussed by Herbert Simon in *The Sciences of the Artificial*. Apparently because of prestige bestowed upon the sciences in years following World War II, leading engineering schools of that time were clearly opting for the science-based model, see Simon (1996, p. 111).

64. Ambasz (1972), Branzi (1984). The Olivetti case is from Kicherer (1990, pp. 17, 25).

65. For example, see Freak Show. Strategies for (Dis)engagement in Design, an exhibition in the HelmRinderknecht Gallery in Berlin.

66. Nowotny et al. (2008). We come back to this point at length in Chapter 3.

3

RESEARCH PROGRAMS

A philosopher of science, Imre Lakatos, once argued that progress in research ultimately lies in research programs rather than individual studies.[1] Progress happens when some piece of research adds new knowledge to or corrects a research program. A successful research program generates new content and new problems in the long run. Any successful research program also has a negative and a positive heuristic. A negative heuristic consists of a "hard core" of beliefs that is not questioned, and a protective belt of auxiliary hypotheses that can be subjected to debate and can be wrong. A positive heuristic tells which questions and objections are important and in what order they are tackled when they show up (see Figure 3.1).[2]

Lakatos' concept gives us a good understanding of how constructive design research works. For example, we see how it consists of various activities. Some work focuses on theory, some on methods, and some on methodology, whereas the main body of work typically consists of constructive studies, reported in journals, conferences, and exhibitions. Also, we see how people take different roles in research.

Figure 3.1 Research runs in programs and has a past: research programs enable imaginative dialogs with the past[3].

3.1 Some Features of Constructive Research Programs

By now, there are several successful research programs in constructive design research. Interaction design in Eindhoven is certainly programmatic, and critical design in London has generated excess content over the years. Empathic design, co-design, and action research in Scandinavia have been programmatic, as have service design and design for sustainability in Milan. Research on user experience in Carnegie Mellon also belongs to this group.

In theoretical terms, the most influential work came from the Netherlands and from Pittsburgh. In this work, conceptual and theoretical development took several routes. In Delft, researchers first built on J.J. Gibson's ecological psychology, but soon they turned toward design issues like pleasure and emotions. A few years later, research focus in the Netherlands shifted to Eindhoven, where researchers were increasingly interested in emotions and experience. So far, these researchers have created several frameworks for designing interactive technology.[4] On the other side of the Atlantic at Carnegie Mellon, user experience became the new cornerstone, followed by an interest in social ecology and the concept of self.[5]

Initially these programs created little new theory. Instead, emerging interaction design borrowed theory from more established fields and researchers like the cognitive and ecological psychologist Don Norman.[6] However, recent work in places like the Netherlands and Carnegie Mellon University has clearly gone beyond cognitive psychology. Researchers are currently interested in issues like identity and how people function in the world with their bodies.[7] Constructive design research is gaining a theoretical core.

Some programs are also gaining a "hard core" of non-debatable beliefs—for example, the fate of "cultural probes" (see Chapter 6). Their main ideologist was Bill Gaver, a former cognitive scientist, who rejected scientific methodology and built an artistic methodology to replace it. His main inspiration was situationist "psychogeography," which urged artists to construct situations that would lead people to notice how their unthought-of routines restrict their lives.[8]

However, with few exceptions, designers and human–computer interaction (HCI) researchers who used the probes overlooked this artistic background and turned the probes into a data collection technique akin to diary studies. In 2008, Kirstin Boehner and her colleagues defended the original intentions of the approach against these "misuses."[9] They noted that cultural probes originally aimed to subvert or undermine traditional HCI methods, not supplement them. For them, the hard core of the probes lies in what they call the hermeneutic or interpretive methodology. The room for debate is in the details of probes, not in the basic approach.[10]

Cultural Probes

Cultural probes have become commonplace in European design research. Originally, they were developed at the Royal College of Art in the second half of the 1990s. A milestone article was published in 1999 by Bill Gaver, Tony Dunne, and Elena Pacenti.

As the name suggests, this method has a metaphoric basis. Quite simply, the idea is to send probes to culture, just as oceanographers send probes to the oceans or scientists send them to outer space. The probes gather samples from wherever they go, and send them back to researchers, whose job is to make sense of them.

A typical "probe" was a package of things like a disposable camera with instructions about what to shoot, postcards with provocative questions, diaries, metaphoric maps, and slightly later, all kinds of technological looking objects. Every package had instructions about how to do the tasks the researchers wanted (like photographing one's favorite place or the contents of the refrigerator) and about how to send the data back to researchers.

The social sciences have had a long and suspicious history of "diary studies." Researchers cannot control how and when people fill the diaries, which means that a sociologist or a psychologist does not know how to interpret these data.

Different from diary studies, from the beginning the probes were described as non-scientific instruments that did not collect representative and accurate data. This non-scientific tone extended even further; for example, to make sure that the probes were also interesting to the people who got them, researchers gave them to people personally. Also, the probes were to be projective and reflect the personality of the researcher rather than be a neutral instrument. Furthermore, the probes were built on artistic references. Finally, Gaver and others refused to give instructions about how to analyze the probes while vehemently denying that it is possible to analyze them scientifically since this was not their purpose.

The probes have gone through a long history of misunderstandings and misuses — some intentional, some unintentional. During the past decade, however, this methodology left a long mark on design research: it is playful and designers love its philosophy.

Gaver (1999).

Also, programs have a social organization. They have precursors, followers, and critics. When looking at empathic design in Helsinki, the precursors came from places like Palo Alto Research Center, the contextual inquiry of Hugh Beyer and Karen Holtzblatt, participatory design, SonicRim, IDEO, and Jodi Forlizzi's work on user experience.[11] However, theoretical work quickly took philosophical and sociological tones. Books like *Empathic Design* articulated the interpretive foundations of this work, but empathic design also built on pragmatist and ethnomethodological references.[12] Research methods were borrowed from other researchers and practice, but were used creatively. For instance, Tuuli Mattelmäki recast the cultural probes in interpretive terms.[13] Key case studies were done in several projects, including Väinö, which focused on senior citizens, and Morphome, which focused on proactive information technology. This work has influenced research in Scandinavia and in Delft, Carnegie Mellon, and Milan.[14]

3.2 Imagination as a Step to Preferred Situations

When Herbert Simon famously defined design as an activity that tries to turn existing situations to preferred ones, he pointed out a crucial feature of design — it is future-oriented. Designers are people who are paid to produce visions of better futures and make those futures happen.

However, although constructive researchers share Simon's general aim of improving the future, the way in which they work is different from what he proposed. Writing in the science-optimistic and technocratic post-world America, he was able to build on a very particular version of science. This is hardly viable in recent, more skeptical times in which research is tied to society in far more ways than during the era of Big Science. As the failure of the design methods movement suggests, design and design research will fail if they are reduced to a formula.

Constructive design researchers do not try to analyze the material world as Simon suggested, nor do they see design as an exercise in rational problem solving. Rather, they imagine new realities and build them to see whether they work. The main criterion for successful work is whether it is imaginative in design terms. Theirs is a science of the imaginary (see Figure 3.2).

Figure 3.2 A path to preferred states goes through imagination.

For designers, imagination is methodic work rather than a mental activity. They do not produce those futures by themselves, but as a part of a larger community of practitioners ranging from engineers to many types of professionals and other actors. This work takes place in a cycle that begins with an objective of some kind, and continues to user studies. These studies lead to concept creation and building mock-ups and prototypes that are typically evaluated before the cycle begins again.[15]

There is also another way in which imagination characterizes constructive design research. The things produced by researchers are seldom produced. Making them into commercial products would require the resources of major international corporations, which is clearly beyond most researchers' powers.[16] Evaluating constructive design research by whether it leads to products is unfair, especially when researchers are faced with "wicked" issues that can hardly be solved by anyone.

3.3 Making Imagination Tangible: Workshops and Studios in Research

Another design-specific characteristic of constructive design research is that it builds things, which is reflected in its infrastructure. Typically, this infrastructure consists of comfortable studio-like places that house discussions and create concepts and goes all the way to workshops with heavy machinery as well as computer and electronics labs.

In these places, ideas are made tangible, first with cheap materials like scrap wood, scrap metal, or foam, or in the case of software, programs in some test environment. Just as in any sandbox, iteration goes on until something survives critique. In this work, analysis and reasoning are important, but equally important is design experience, whether it is based on emotions, feelings, or intuition.[17] This work may start from theories, methods, and fieldwork findings, and just as often it begins with playing with materials, technology, and design precedents.

Over time, this culture creates a stockpile of concepts, designs, technologies, platforms, and stories that carry the culture and give it a distinctive flair. Without this culture of doing, many things of interest to designers would go unnoticed.[18] What would specifically be lost are those visual, material, and cultural and historical sensitivities Sharon Poggenpohl sees as essential to design.[19] Designers have to worry about things like how some material feels, how some angle flows gracefully over an edge, or how interaction works.

In an extreme form, this kind of culture has existed in places like the MIT Media Lab. In its hacker culture, doing has always been more important than reflection. This culture aims at pushing technologies to the extreme and finding ways to do things previously regarded to be impossible. However, the culture comes under various names such as innovation in Stanford's "d.school," the quality in interaction in Technische Universiteit Eindhoven, or simply education and teaching design skills in places like IO Studiolab at Technical University of Delft and Aalto University's Department of Design.[20]

Sometimes the culture is not bound to one place but to a regional network, as in Lombardy, where designers have explored design possibilities with industry through prototypes, one-offs, and limited editions.[21] Invariably, there is a "community of practitioners" with a variety of skills in doing, critique, and theory that keep the culture going (Figure 3.3).[22]

Workshops and studios are necessary, but are not the right condition for a healthy constructive design research program. A program may be successful for a few years if it hits the right technological or political gold mine. However, when returns from this mine get leaner, this model faces difficulties. For example, during research on tangible interaction the MIT Media Lab was followed globally, but now this following is far less extensive. Although researchers continue producing interesting prototypes, the Media Lab produces new thinking at a far slower pace.

3.4 How Constructive Design Research Produces Meaning

That constructive design research is grounded in imagination is also reflected in how researchers understand their contribution. Andrea Branzi wrote that the task of design research is to keep distance from the "pure practice of building."[23] For him, design in second modernity should offer alternatives rather than try to alter reality directly. No doubt, most constructive design researchers agreed with him when he wrote:

> *The architectural or design project today is no longer an act intended to alter reality, pushing it in the direction of order and logic. Instead the project is an act of invention that creates something to be added on to existing reality, increasing its depth and multiplying the number of choices available.*[24]

Here designers can learn from architecture. As Peter Hall notes following Cranbrook's Scott Klinker, architecture has a rich body of discourse based on hypothetical designs.[25] This is also the case with design, even though hypothetical products tend to

Figure 3.3 Downward: three pictures of studios; four of material-based workshops; three shops with industrial machinery. (Pictures from Helsinki, Bengaluuru, Borås, Pasadena, and Delft.)

play a less prominent role in it than in architecture, where most plans are never realized.[26] Plainly, if hypothetical designs are successful, they may change the ways in which people think about material and social reality. They can open up possibilities and prepare action.

Having a discourse based on hypothetical designs has several consequences: it enriches imagination and opens new ways of seeing and discussing opportunities.[27] It also provides exemplars and precedents that may be useful when new problems and opportunities emerge. This discourse may sound like art, but it may also provide important preparation for the future, much as a play prepares children for their later years.

Design has many types of hypothetical discourses, many of which have commercial roots. As Anthony Dunne and Fiona Raby wrote:

> *Critical design, or design that asks carefully crafted questions and makes us think, is just as difficult and just as important as design that solves problems or finds answers. Being provocative and challenging might seem like an obvious role for art, but art is far too removed from the world of mass consumption ... to be effective.... There is a place for a form of design that pushes the cultural and aesthetic potential and role of electronic products and services to its limits.... Critical design is related to haute couture, concept cars, design propaganda, and visions of the future, but its purpose is not to present the dream of industry, attract new business, anticipate new trends or test the market. Its purpose is to stimulate discussion and debate amongst designers, industry, and the public.*[28]

Not only critical designers propose alternatives to the present. When Philips hired Stefano Marzano to lead its design team in the mid-1990s, one of his first initiatives was a visionary process called Vision of the Future (Philips Design, 1995). The aim of the project was to re-imagine products rather than create science fiction like new worlds. It was design fiction, based on the idea that it is important not to accept existing economic and technical constraints. The results were a book, a Web page, and a series of traveling exhibitions focusing on themes like the kitchen. The aims of the project were very different from those of Dunne and Raby's critical design: Vision of the Future and several other projects re-imagined better futures instead of trying to disrupt existing ones. Still, for a company like Philips, this was an exceptional move. Since then, many companies have done projects like these. Perhaps most famous of these is Alessi.[29]

Needless to say, there are many ways to construct and understand such alternative discourses (see Figure 3.4). Some of these discourses try to alter and redo existing products such as concept cars, haute couture, or *Droog Design*. Some discourses take

Figure 3.4 Why not design for tormented *film noir* characters?

more critical overtones, providing designers not only with a mandate to think differently but also a mandate to think about what deserves to be created and what does not.[30] At the more radical end, such discourses aim at creating utopias. Most designers obviously fall in the middle of this scale. They want to make a difference but are far humbler about their powers than they were in the 1960s.[31]

From a bird's eye perspective, these differences are less important than the goal, which is to provide alternatives to deeply ingrained habits of thinking. If we say that since people have certain goods and they use certain technologies then they have to use them in the future as well, we have committed an error in judgment. Following the Cambridge philosopher G.E. Moore, philosophers call this error the "naturalistic fallacy": inferring from what is to what ought to be. Its consequence can be called the "conservative fallacy": thinking that what exists today cannot be improved. Wake-up calls are occasionally needed.

3.5 Toward Socially Robust Knowledge

Constructive design researchers are not alone in thinking about knowledge as statements in social discourse. As the sociologists of science Helga Nowotny and James Gibbons have noted, contemporary research is linked to society in many ways and faces many kinds of public and private scrutiny. The key questions most institutions that fund research ask are what kinds of applications research produces and what are its social, economic, and ecological implications. Research has to survive discussions in those boardrooms in which politicians and captains of industry decide where to allocate resources.[32] Many things in research have their

Mode 1	Mode 2
Expert-led science, production-oriented	Public-led, implication-centered research
Aim: reliable knowledge	Aim: socially robust knowledge

KEY WORDS:
DISCOVERY JUSTIFICATION APPLICATION IMPLICATION

Relationship to society:

Mode 1	Mode 2
Weakly contextualized, autonomous science	Strongly contextualized, research participates in society

Figure 3.5 The sociologist of science, Helga Nowotny, and her colleagues distinguish two "modes" of science: Mode 1 and Mode 2. Mode 1 is typical to first modernity and Mode 2 research is typical to second modernity.

origins outside research programs; social forces shape research agendas, priorities, topics, and methods (see Figure 3.5).[33]

This is where we need to revisit the notion of the research program. Lakatos was mainly interested in understanding how physics works; however, we need to keep in mind that he wrote in the 1960s. Back then, science was able to maintain a high degree of autonomy because governments, public monopolies, and oligopolistic companies funded it. Scientists worried about making discoveries and reliable explanations rather than about applications or implications, that is, what knowledge does to society. The ideal was to produce unbiased, freely shared knowledge among the community of peers.[34] How scientific knowledge was applied was another story. This was an era of knowledge transfer: what science discovered, society adapted.

Few constructive design researchers believe in the more authoritarian version of science. For them, research programs have to be in dialog with society. This dialog makes research socially robust. Whether it raises debate is more important than facts and knowledge; these are understood as temporary constructs. This is certainly the case in most parts of the constructive design research community. A successful constructive program participates in public discourse and interprets society rather than acts as a legislator.[35]

End Notes

1. Lakatos (1970).
2. We are not the first ones who have introduced Lakatos to design research. See also Glanville (1999) van der Lugt and Stappers (2006). Binder and Redström (2006) used the term in an architectural sense. Peter Downton proposed to rate programs in terms of how much danger to existing thinking its core idea posed. At the extremes are ideas that are capable of affecting personal practice and ideas that have power to invert existing knowledge. However, as Downton noted, it is too much to expect too much: most research programs "only contain small dangers" (Downton, 2005, p. 9).
3. As Juhani Pallasmaa notes, "the great gift of tradition is that we can choose our collaborators; we can collaborate with Brunelleschi and Michelangelo if we are wise enough to do so" (Pallasmaa 2009, p. 146).
4. Wensveen (2004), Frens (2006a).
5. Forlizzi and Ford (2000), Battarbee (2004). For social ecology, see Forlizzi (2007). For designing for self, see Zimmerman et al. (2009).
6. In historical contexts, interaction design has to be used cautiously. IDEO's Bill Moggridge (2006) claimed to have invented the term "interaction design" and, historical research pending, may be right. Along with IDEO, he certainly made it popular. For important textbooks on interaction design, see Schneiderman (1998), Preece (1990), and Sharp and Preece (2007).
7. For example, Overbeeke (2007), Forlizzi (2007), Zimmerman (2009).
8. Gaver et al. (1999), *Presence Project* (2000), Debord (2002). As Jappe (1999, p. 4) noted, the situationist notion of "spectacle" is indebted to commodity fetishism, as Karl Marx called the confusion of exchange value of a product with its value in use.
9. Boehner et al. (2007).
10. Boehner et al. (2007, pp. 1083–1084. In fact, Boehner et al. used the wrong terminology here. If the probes build on hermeneutic and interpretive thinking, they become humanistic and social science instruments rather than artistic expressions. For a balanced account of how the probes have been used and how tensions exist in the probing community, see Keinonen (2009).
11. Suchman (1987), Beyer and Holtzblatt (1998), Ehn (1988a), Forlizzi and Ford (2000).
12. Koskinen et al. (2003), Battarbee (2004), Kurvinen (2007).
13. Mattelmäki (2006).
14. For example, Forlizzi and Battarbee (2005), Sleeswijk Visser (2009), Rizzo (2009).
15. For example, see Szymanski and Whalen (2011, p. 12).
16. See in particular Joep Frens's thoughts about prototyping in research in Chapter 4.
17. Stappers (2007; see also Chapter 4). There is a lot of sandbox culture in science too. Again, Herbert Simon provides an example. After learning elementary programming and meeting Allan Newell in 1952, Simon and Newell decided to build programs that could play chess and construct geometrical proofs. They worked on what became the Logic Theorist, which was able to construct proofs from Russell and Whitehead's *Principia Mathematics* in 1955–1956, first in a sort of simulated computer, then in RAND Corporation's computers. Simon's excitement in finding an environment in which he could test his mathematical theories of human action is easy to sense from Hunter Crowther-Heyck's biography (2005, pp. 217–232).
18. In this section, we are influenced by Julian Orr's (1996) work on the work culture of copy machine repair men.
19. Poggenpohl (2009a, p. 7). See also Chapter 1.
20. For how the sandbox culture is integrated into research through teaching at TU/Eindhoven, see Overbeeke et al. (2006).

21. See Branzi's (2009) *Serie Fuori Serie* exhibition catalog from Triennale di Milano and Lovell (2009).
22. The notion of community of practice is from Brown and Duguig (2000).
23. Branzi (2006, p. 16).
24. Branzi (1988, p. 17).
25. Hall (2007). As innovation-focused schools, he classified IIT in Chicago and Stanford, while in the humanities camp he placed Philadelphia and Parsons after Jamer Hunt. On the art school route are the Royal College of Art in London and Cranbrook Academy of Art, which "have reputations for critical thinking and producing sexy imagery of objects — often more hypothetical than manufacturable," as Hall noted in his essay.

    However, some of the greatest revolutions in design have come from people like Ettore Sottsass, who described himself in a *Museo Alessi* interview in 2007 as a "theoretical designer; just as there are theoretical physicists who ... don't make plans for getting to the moon [but] think about what sort of physical laws a person going to the moon may encounter." This is just a metaphor, but there is a point in it. Many followed Sottsass; in effect, he became a theorist of design (see Museo Alessi design interviews, Sottsass, 2007, p. 24).
26. Dunne and Raby (2001, p. 59).
27. Molotch (2003). Andrew Abbott, a leading sociologist of professions, noted that there are professions like the military whose work almost totally consists of such hypothetical discourses (Abbott, 1988). Scenarios prepare for possible action.
28. Dunne and Raby (2001, p. 58). This quote is important because it shows many connections to practice. Indeed, quite often the best design ideas never enter the market but remain in the conceptual practices of designers.
29. For *Vision of the Future,* see Philips Design (1995). For other projects by Philips Design, see Philips bookstore at design.philips.com/about/design/designnews/publications/books/ (Retrieved August 11, 2010). *The New Everyday* was published not by the company, but by 010, an art and design publisher based in Rotterdam (Aarts and Marzano, 2003).

    Alessi's projects have been described by Robert Verganti (2009). Some examples done with design universities are *The Workshop* (Alessi and UIAH, 1995) and *Keittiössä: Taikkilaiset kokkaa Alessille — UIAH Students Cooking for Alessi* (Alessi and UIAH, 2002).
30. The quote about what deserves to be created is taken from the first paper written by Tomás Maldonado after he came to Ulm. This was the how he distinguished Ulm's education from that of Bauhaus. Bauhaus, he wrote, was "content ... to produce people who can create and express themselves," while "the Ulm school intends to mark out the path to the highest level of creativeness, but at the same time, and to the same extent, to indicate the social aims of this creativeness, i.e., which forms *deserve* to be" (Höger 2010, p. xvi).
31. For a design-focused analysis of these utopians, see Maldonado (1972, pp. 21–29). For art, see Bourriaud (2002, pp. 45–46), who noted that contemporary art mostly seeks to construct concrete spaces instead of utopias.
32. Nowotny et al. (2008) talked about "agoras" rather than marketplaces, stressing the political character of public places like the square where free men of Athens convened to decide the affairs of the city-state.
33. Nowotny et al. (2008, p. 131).
34. As a sociologist of science, Robert K. Merton idealistically formulated that science was characterized by the values of communitarianism, universalism, disinterestedness, and organized skepticism (see Merton, 1968). This formulation is from the 1930s.
35. The metaphors of "interpreter" and "legislator" are from the Polish-British social critic Zygmunt Bauman (Bauman and May, 2000).

4

LAB: CAN YOU REALLY STUDY DESIGN IN THE LABORATORY?

The sociologist Morris Zelditch, Jr., once published a paper called "Can You Really Study the Army in the Laboratory?"[1] Under this provocative title, he wrote about the limitations of studying large institutions in a laboratory. Zelditch's answer was yes, if the study is done with care. This chapter shows that this is true in design as well.[2] It is impossible to study a phenomenon like design in the laboratory in its entirety; design has many faces, only some of which are appropriate for laboratory studies. The trick, however, is to see which ones are.[3]

The historical foundations of this methodology are in the natural sciences, but it usually comes to design through psychology. The aim is to identify relationships designers might find interesting; for example, how the limits of human cognitive processing capabilities affect error rates in using tablet computers. The design justification for this methodology is straightforward: if such relationships were found, they could be turned into mathematical formulas that would provide a solid ground for design.[4]

This chapter is about the logic of laboratory studies.[5] Actual research tends to be impure in terms of logic; in particular, early stage user studies aiming at inspiration tend to be done with probes and contextual inquiries. They are qualitative and inspiration-oriented and are typically combined with laboratory-style studies. For example, Stephan Wensveen used cultural probes for inspiration in the early stages of his research.[6] Experimental work typically happens in concept testing and selection and in the evaluation phase of the prototypes. Although the ethos of this tradition comes from experimental psychology, researchers borrow from other ways of doing to complement it.

4.1 Rich Interaction: Building a Tangible Camera

Our example is from Technische Universiteit Eindhoven, where Joep Frens designed a camera with a rich interaction user

Figure 4.1 Joep Frens' rich interaction camera. (Picture by Joep Frens.)

interface and compared it to conventional cameras. The standard interaction approach in industry is based on a menu on a screen, which can be navigated with buttons. Frens aimed at creating an alternative to this standard approach.

While conventional digital cameras typically have controls based on buttons and menus on screen, rich interaction cameras had tangible controls. For example, with a rich interaction camera, the photographer could take a picture by pushing a trigger and save it by pushing the screen toward the memory card. To delete it, he had to push the screen back to the lens. Frens designed these unconventional forms, interactions, and functions so that the photographer could read the possibilities for action and function from the form (Figure 4.1).

Building on ecological psychology and literature on tangible interaction, Frens created a series of hypotheses for each camera variation to be able to compare user experience. Frens' main hypothesis was that a rich interaction camera is more intuitive to use than a conventional camera. Another hypothesis was that people think it is more beautiful. The cameras were stimuli in his study; measures for things like use and beauty came from Marc Hassenzahl, a German design psychologist.[7]

Frens' design process was driven by a wish to find alternatives for the prevalent industrial interaction paradigm for cameras. His inspiration came from his knowledge of trends in interaction design and from his background research, not from user studies. Research questions, hypotheses, and the rich interaction framework came after the first designs, and they were based on the insights gained during the design process (Figures 4.2 and 4.3).

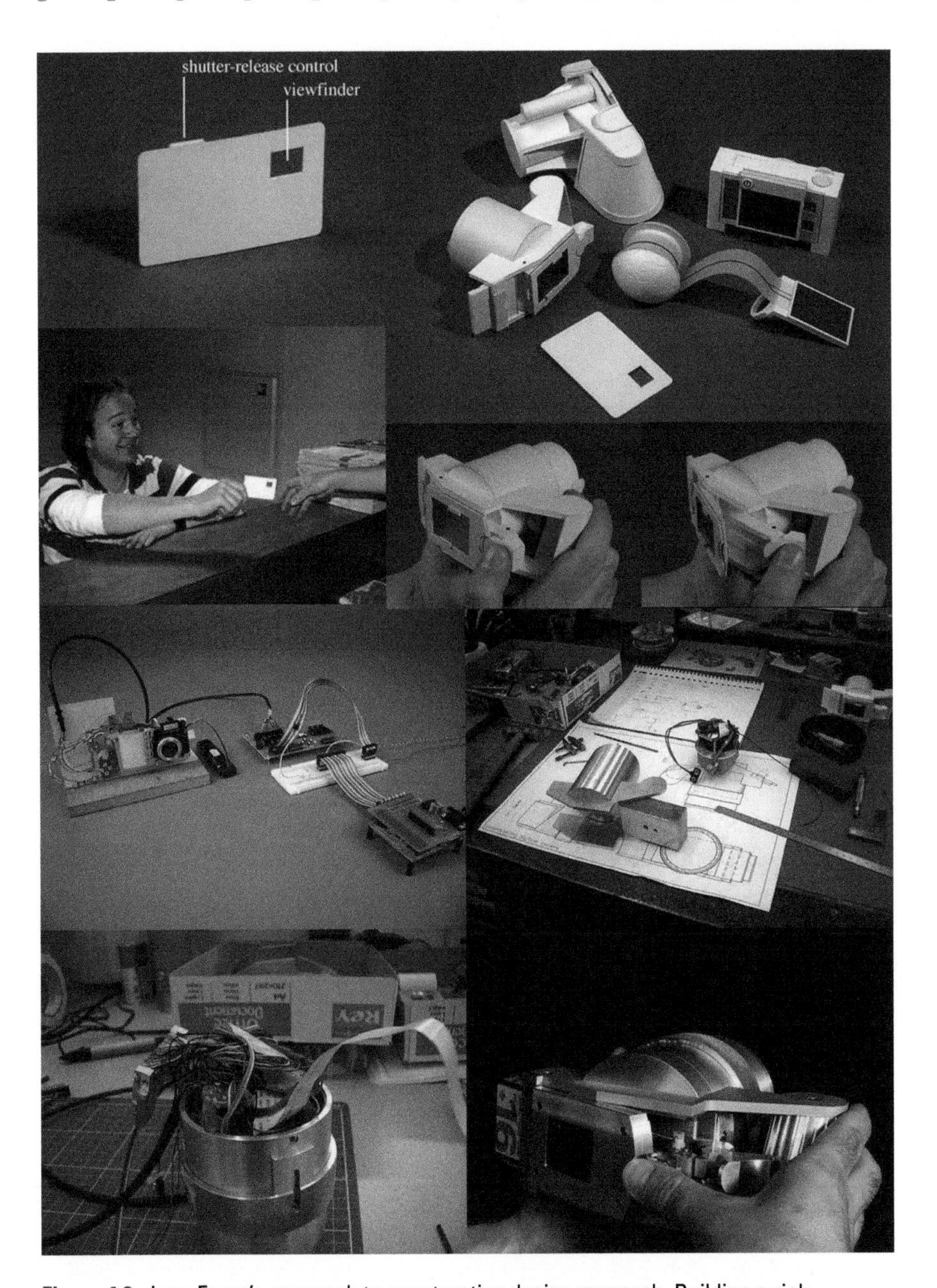

Figure 4.2 Joep Frens's approach to constructive design research. Building a rich interaction camera through mock-ups and prototypes. Top two left: details from a service scenario with a simple mock-up. Top three right: cardboard mock-ups from one camera variation. Below, clockwise from bottom left: fitting electronics into the cask, hacking existing technology; building a case, and final prototype of one camera.[8] (Pictures by Joep Frens.)

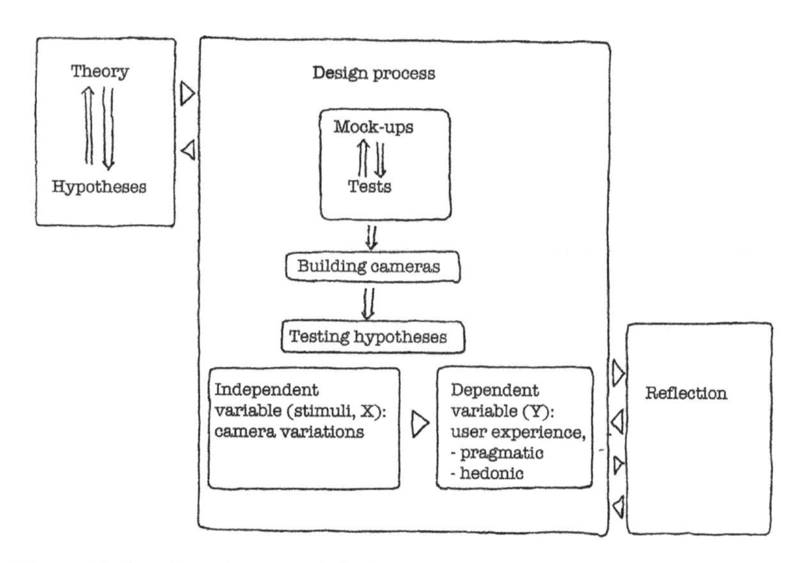

Figure 4.3 Joep Frens's research design.

Frens built several camera prototypes out of cardboard and tested these with students. Having a good idea of how to build a rich interaction camera, he built the body from aluminum. He also built several control modules that could be fitted to the body. The first module was with conventional controls; the second with light controls; the third with mixed controls; and the fourth with rich controls, all within the same form language. These designs formed a scale. At one end was an interface using conventional menus and buttons. At the other end was a radically reworked camera with tangible controls only.

He went on to test these cameras with 24 students of architecture in a laboratory setting. Each student received instructions, viewed the camera, and took photographs with it.[9] This study was repeated four times, once for each camera variation.[10] User experience was evaluated with a questionnaire. Afterward, the participants compared the cameras and completed a closing questionnaire.

From a cognitive psychology perspective one would expect that the rich interaction camera would do worse than a traditional one, as it breaks the user interface conventions of cameras. However, it did not, and it was appreciated by many of the participants. The rich interaction camera did not fare better than other cameras in aesthetic and practical terms. Still, Frens was able to say that his design was successful. At a more fine-grained level, the results were also positive. For example, saving images was found to be pleasing with the rich interaction camera, which participants also found more beautiful than other cameras.

4.2 Laboratory as a Site of Knowledge

Studying things in a laboratory means that something is taken out from its natural environment and brought into a controlled area where it can be subjected to experimentation. Almost anything can be studied in the laboratory: armies, design, chemical reactions, rich interaction, and so forth.

The trouble with studying a phenomenon in the real world is that usually many things shape it. This makes it difficult to find what causes something one sees; there are typically several possible explanations, and it is impossible to rule any of them out with a high degree of certainty. Research becomes an exercise in "what about if...."

Studying a phenomenon in a laboratory helps with this problem. The laboratory gives the researchers an opportunity to focus on one thing at a time. Most typically, this "thing" is a relationship, such as the relationship of rich interaction and user experience in Joep Frens' study. The laboratory also helps researchers study alternative explanations and competing hypotheses; doing this is far more difficult in natural settings. After researchers have eliminated alternative explanations, they are able to confidently say things about how rich interaction improves user experience in camera design. It is possible that the results are wrong, but this is highly unlikely.

Causes, Effects, and Variables

Scientists do not talk about "things" but use more specialized terminology. Things that exist before the phenomenon to be studied takes place are called "independent variables," which explain the behavior of "dependent variables." In addition, there are intervening, background, and consequent variables.

Ideally, a researcher should be able to state his hypothesis as a function $y = f(x)$, where y represents the dependent variable and x the independent variable, although this function is usually far more complex.

A hypothesis is an explanation based on theory: it is researchers' best guess about how the function works before they do a study. The hypothesis is not true before empirical proof, but there are theoretical reasons to think it will receive such proof.

Notice that the aim of experimental research is not to capture everything in a causal system; the aim is to focus on the key relationships.

When specifying causal systems, there are a few useful rules of thumb, such as supposed causes always ought to precede effects, and things that come first in time should precede things that follow. Perhaps most important, as the word "variable" tells, things in the system have to be able to vary. Other than that, specification depends on theory: theory should tell how x impacts y and how to work with other variables.

An alternative way is to talk about causes and effects, but social scientists usually avoid the language of causality. Talking about variables avoids confusing theoretical language with things this language describes.

In the social sciences, it is also not conventional to talk about the "causes" of what people or their social organizations do. Most social scientists prefer to think that people make sense of situations and act accordingly; whether these products of sense-making can be thought of as causes is a philosophical question.

For example, when Joep Frens built his rich interaction camera to enhance user experience, his independent variables were his cameras (x), while his dependent variable (y) was user experience measured with Marc Hassenzahl's scales. Frens did not study possible background variables like gender, which other researchers might have found interesting. He also left out consequent variables like the effect of his camera on users' satisfaction of life.

Such exclusions belong to any laboratory research: instead of studying everything, researchers have to decide which variables are relevant enough to be included in the research design. Specifying causal systems is a matter of judgment (Figure 4.4).

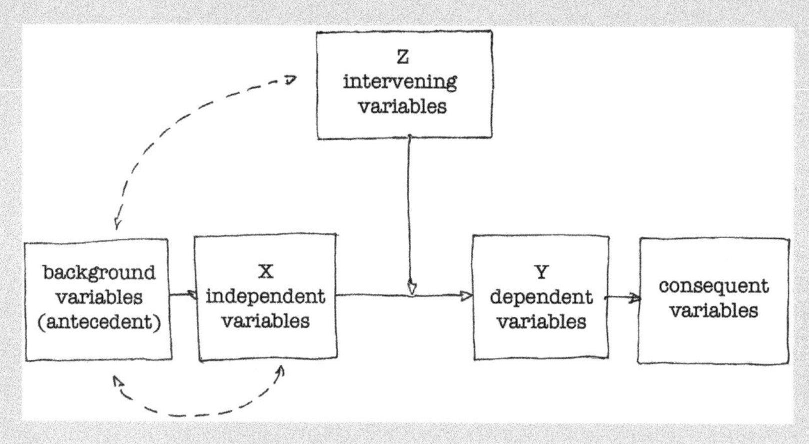

Figure 4.4 Specifying causal systems as systems of variables.

Working in a laboratory has many other benefits. For example, a laboratory can be equipped with instruments that help make detailed and accurate observations and measurements.

> *What is of the utmost importance, we think, when testing the variations, is that the user's actions on the prototype are recorded. We need a trace of the actual interaction, as it is done as soon as one stops to interact. The recordings of setting the alarm clock enabled us to reconstruct step by step how a, e.g., symmetrical pattern was constructed.*[11]

As the laboratory environment and experiments are typically documented in detail, it is also possible to replicate the study in other laboratories. This rules out errors coming from the setting and its research culture. This also applies to issues like "observer effects" — the researcher giving people cues about his intentions. If people understand a researcher's intentions, they may change their behavior to please or to confuse the researcher. There has to be a proper strategy to deal with these effects.[12] Most threats to validity are beyond this book. For example, to see how things like user experience develop over time, researchers often study the same people several times in so-called time series analysis. However, over time, people in the study learn about the study and change their behavior. There are ways to minimize such threats, but this complicates research design.[13]

Analysis in Nutshell

There are many statistical techniques to study how independent and dependent variables "covary."

To study covariation, researchers typically use some kind of linear model. These range from cross-tabulations to correlations, analysis of variance (ANOVA), and regression analysis. Non-linear techniques like logit and probit regressions are rare in design. Multivariate techniques like factor and discriminant analysis are normally used for pattern-finding rather than for testing hypotheses; they are non-linear and also rare.

For example, in studying whether there is a link between his cameras and user experience, Frens used the camera variations he built as his independent variable. Since he built four user interface variations, his independent variable got four values.

He hypothesized that as these cameras were different, people would experience (which was his dependent variable) them differently in ways that the theory of rich interaction can foresee. His null hypothesis predicted no change or a change so small that it could have been produced by chance.

Frens used several statistical techniques in his study but mostly relied on ANOVA to decide whether his camera variations led to predicted changes in user experience.

Statistical methods do not have to be complex and sophisticated. More attention should be placed on theory and identifying the underlying causal model. If there is no variation in data, it is impossible to find it even with the best statistical tools. As Ernest Rutherford — a physicist with several groundbreaking findings on his list of conquests — reputedly noted, "if your experiment needs statistics, you ought to have done a better experiment."

It is also good to keep in mind that even experienced researchers struggle to find the right model to describe the data. They routinely do dozens of analyses before they are happy with the results; patience is a virtue in statistical analysis.

Similarly, it is good to know that there are differences between methods preferred in different disciplines. For example, psychologists usually prefer some form of ANOVA.

4.3 Experimental Control

The crux of any laboratory study is experimentation.[14] The researcher manipulates the thing of interest in the lab to learn how people react to it while holding other things constant. Typically, he assumes a new design will improve things like user experience when compared to older designs. In research language, the null hypothesis predicting no change is rejected. Having established the basic relationship, researchers study other explanations to see whether they somehow modify results. Ideally, researchers vary one additional variable at a time to see whether it alters the basic relationship.[15]

For example, Frens studied user experience first by varying his camera designs and learned that a rich interaction interface improved user experience. He could have gone further; for example, he could have studied men and women separately to see whether gender somehow was relevant in explaining the link between rich interaction and user experience. However, he chose not to do these additional analyses, keeping his focus on the basic relationship only (Figure 4.5).

Research is successful when the basic relationship exists and the most important competing explanations are ruled out. Thus, if a rich interaction camera functions as expected and there are no serious alternative explanations, the theory about rich interaction ought to be accepted until a better theory comes along. If the first rich interaction camera of its sort is already about as good as conventional cameras, even though cognitive theory would predict otherwise, something must have gone right in the design process.

Selecting what to study and what to leave out is ideally a matter of theory, but equally often, it is also a matter of judgment. Many things influence human behavior, and it is impossible to study everything carefully. What is included is a theoretical question; for example, when Philip Ross selected people for studying his lamp designs, he selected university students with a similar value system in mind (see Chapter 8).[16] This limited his ability to generalize but also made his analyses easier. He would have gained little from knowing how people with different medical conditions would have reacted to his lamps. This might be an interesting question for another study but not for his.

There are also methodic ways to make research designs simpler. The most popular technique is randomized trial, in which

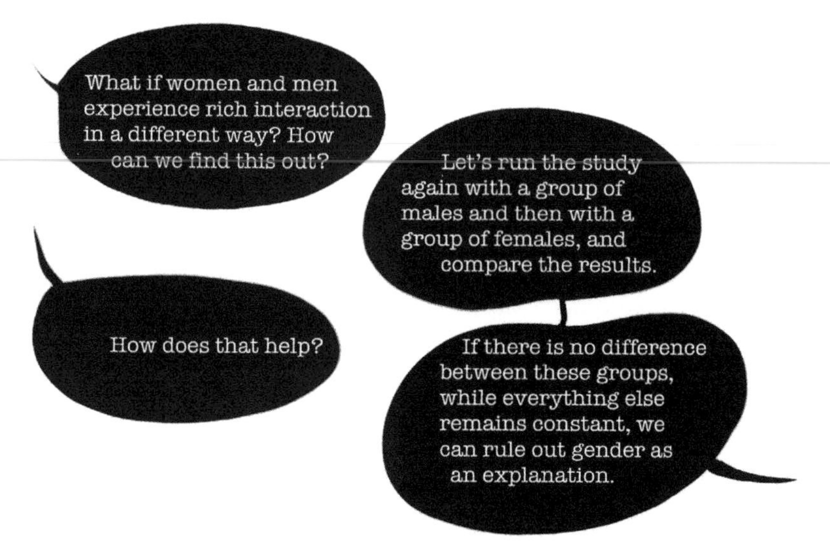

Figure 4.5 Ruling out alternative explanations.

researchers take one group of typically randomly selected people. Then they repeat the study with another randomly selected group. One of the groups is given a "treatment," for example, they have to use a rich interaction camera. The other group gets a placebo, for example, a conventional camera. Researchers measure things like user experience before and after the treatment in both groups, with the expectation that satisfaction has increased more in the treatment group than in the control group. Randomization does not eliminate variables like gender or horoscope sign, but in large enough groups the impact of such variables evens out.

Randomized Trials

The most typical research design, especially in medicine, is a randomized trial. In this research design, two groups of people are drawn randomly and allocated into a study group and a control group.

The study group gets a treatment; for example, in design research, they use the prototype. The control group does not receive this treatment.

A study begins with a measurement in which both groups fill out a questionnaire or do some other test. After the treatment, both groups are measured again. The thing to be measured can be almost anything, but typically it is user experience.

The hypothesis is that the treatment improves the study group's user experience, while the control group does not experience similar improvement. This set of expectations can be written more formally, for example:

1. $m^1_1 = m^1_2$
2. $m^2_1 > m^1_1$
3. $m^2_2 = m^1_2$

All of these conditions should to be compared with appropriate statistics, most typically with t-test or ANOVA.

The smart thing about this design is that it eliminates the need to conduct a new study for each possible alternative explanation, like gender or cognitive style. The number of observations, however, needs to be large enough (Figure 4.6).

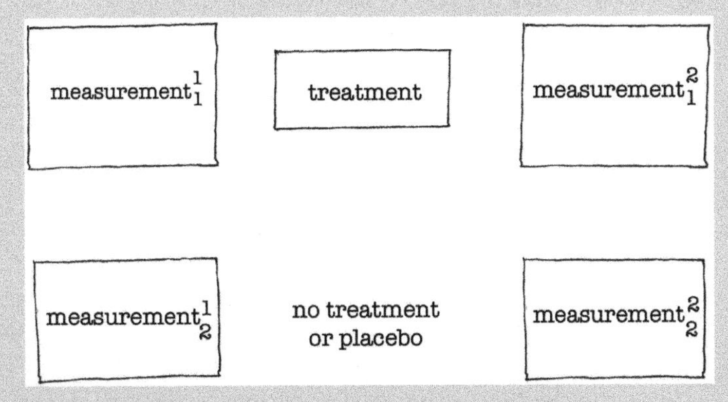

Figure 4.6 Simple randomized trial makes it possible to test whether a treatment leads to change.

4.4 Physical Hypotheses and Design

In constructive design research, the epitome of analysis is an expression such as a prototype. It crystallizes theoretical work, and becomes a hypothesis to be tested in the laboratory. For Stephan Wensveen, it was the alarm clock he built. For Ianus Keller, it was a cabinet for interacting with visual material. For Andres Lucero, it was a space he called the "funky-design-space" meant to support moodboard construction and browsing.[17] For Joep Frens, his camera variations are considered physical hypotheses.

However, adding the design phase to research also adds an important new ingredient to the soup — the designer's skill and intuition.

Stappers recently described some of the complexities involved in treating prototypes as hypotheses. In the design process, a prototype integrates many types of information. Theory is one component in the prototype, but not the only one. For example, ecological psychology tells us to build tangible controls that use human sensory motor skills to accomplish tasks like taking photos or setting the time for the alarm. However, it says little about many of the sensual issues so important for designers, including shape, colors, sound, feel, surfacing, and so on. Ideas for these come from the designer and the design process. As Stappers said:

> *Prototypes and other types of expressions such as sketches, diagrams and scenarios, are the core means by which the designer builds the connection between fields of knowledge and progresses toward a product. Prototypes serve to instantiate hypotheses from contributing disciplines, and to communicate principles, facts and considerations between disciplines. They speak the language of experience, which unites us in the world. Moreover, by training (and selection), designers can develop ideas and concepts by realizing prototypes and evaluating them....*
>
> *The designing act of creating prototypes is in itself a potential generator of knowledge (if only its insights do not disappear into the prototype, but are fed back into the disciplinary and cross-disciplinary platforms that can fit these insights into the growth of theory).*[18]

Elsewhere, Stappers listed some uses of prototypes. They can be used to test a theory, in which case they become embodiments of theory or "physical hypothesis."[19] However, they also confront theories: researchers, whose prototypes cannot hide in abstractions, have to face many types of complexities that working designers face. Similarly, they confront the world. When building a prototype, the researcher has to face the opinions of other people.

Figure 4.7 How a physical hypothesis emerges from various types of knowledge expressed as sheets on the floor. As understanding grows, more knowledge from other disciplines is drawn into the spiral. (Drawing by Pieter Jan Stappers.)[21]

Furthermore, they serve as demonstrations, provocations, and criticisms, especially to outsiders who have not seen their development from within (Figure 4.7).[20]

4.5 Design, Theory, and Real-World Relevance

As Stappers points out, prototyping is more than theory testing, it is also a design act. A design process may be inspired by theory, but it goes beyond it. A prototype is an embodiment of design practice, but it also goes beyond theory. For this reason, design prototypes are also tests of design, not just theory. Indeed, one of the most attractive things in research in Eindhoven has been the quality of craftsmanship. These designs can be evaluated as design statements. They are good enough to please a professional designer aesthetically, structurally, and conceptually.

Research sets some requirements for prototypes at odds with doing good design. Researchers almost invariably aim at simplification; for example, people bring in many types of aesthetic opinions to the laboratory and are barely aware of most of them. The way to control this is to eliminate clutter by keeping design simple. When the subjects' mind does not wander, changes in their behavior can be attributed to the designs. As Overbeeke wrote with his colleagues:

Design research resembles research in, e.g., psychology in that it has a minimum of controls built in when exploring the solution when testing variations of solutions. Therefore … "we have kept the devices simple, pure and with resembling aesthetic appearance." This makes it possible, to a certain degree, to isolate and even manipulate systematically critical variables.[22]

This is where there is tension. As Stappers noted, research prototypes are not pure expressions of theory; they also embody design values. The more they do, the more difficult it becomes to say with confidence that the theory that inspired design actually works. The secret of success, quite simply, may be design.

This is a catch-22. On the one hand, the more seriously researchers take design, the more difficult it becomes to draw unambiguous theoretical conclusions. On the other hand, when the theoretical frame and the aims of the study guide prototyping,[23] a good amount of design relevance is sacrificed. Ultimately, the way in which prototyping is done is a matter of the researcher's personal criteria for quality and taste. Most design researchers think design quality is more important than theoretical purity, but opinions differ.

Most design researchers, however, find it easy to agree that research prototypes differ from industrial prototypes. As Joep Frens noted, his cameras are finished enough for research but not production ready.

Moreover, the prototypes that are presented in this thesis are not products ready for production. The prototypes are elaborated to a highly experiential level so that they can be used in real life experiments to answer the research question ... The prototypes can be seen as "physical hypotheses" that have sufficient product qualities to draw valid and relevant conclusions from.[24]

As Frens related, prototypes are done to see where theoretically informed design leads. Issues like durability, electric safety, and the quality of computer code are in the background. In the foreground are things that serve knowledge creation; it is better to leave concern for production to industry.

4.6 From Lab to Society: The Price of Decontextualization

When things are taken from society to a laboratory, many things are decontextualized; however, this comes with a price. A laboratory is a very special place, and things that happen in the laboratory may not happen in society or may happen in a different way, as conditions are different. Do results of laboratory studies tell anything about real world?

There are several ways to answer this question, and sometimes this question is not relevant. Researchers may want to show that a certain outcome is possible by building upon it, and there is no need to produce definitive proof beyond the construct. This is called "existence proof."[25] This proof is well known in mathematics and is common in engineering but almost non-existent in empirical research. Sometimes, generalization happens to theory, and this is typical in many natural sciences — a piece of pure tin melts at the same temperature whether it is in Chicago or Patagonia.

Usually the jump from the laboratory to the real world builds on statistics. Many things in ergonomics may be universal enough for theoretical analysis, but it is more difficult to argue this in, say, aesthetics or design.[26] Researchers can calculate statistics like averages and deviations for those people they studied. They cannot, however, use these figures only as estimates of what happens in larger populations: it is always possible to err. The basic rule is that as sample size increases, confidence in estimates increases.

Finally, proof goes beyond one study. As Lakatos argued, there is no instant rationality in research.[27] Generalizing from individual studies is risky. However, if a program repeatedly leads to interesting results, it should be taken seriously. It was only after hundreds of studies that the world came to believe that asbestos and tobacco caused life-threatening illnesses. This logic also applies in constructive design research (Figure 4.8).

In actual research practice, these proofs coexist. Again, Frens provided a good example. In terms of an existence proof, his camera shows that it is possible to build rich interaction cameras. In terms of generalizing to theory, his research framework can be applied in many different circumstances. In statistical terms, his empirical results apply to people with a high level of aesthetic

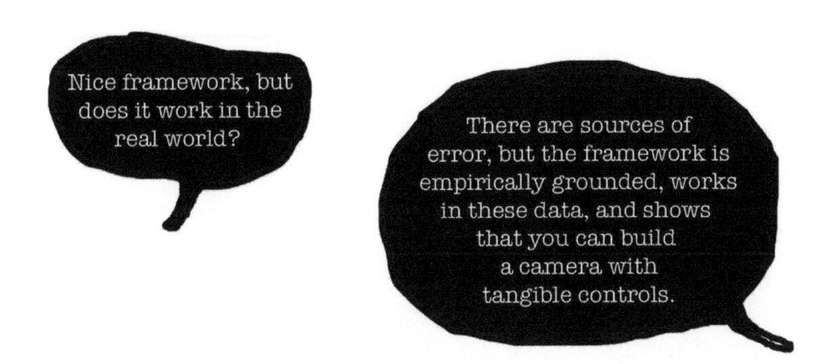

Figure 4.8 From laboratory to real world.

abilities and a great deal of experience in photography. Finally, by now dozens of designs coming out from the Netherlands show that ecological psychology can be fruitfully applied to designing interaction. The burden of proof does not lie on Frens only.

There is a margin of error in even the best of studies; however, after reading Frens, we know more about rich interaction in smart products than before. Researchers are skeptics and do not easily accept anything, but when they accept something, they stand behind it. Proving that a good study is wrong requires a careful study that shows in detail what was wrong.

4.7 Program at the Junction

Recent work in Eindhoven has taken a significant step away from its basis in ecological psychology. Earlier work built on J.J. Gibson's ecological psychology and aimed at formulating conditional laws and constructing mathematical models of actual interaction.[28] Since Kees Overbeeke's inauguration in 2007, however, research has turned to phenomenological and pragmatic philosophy.[29] Ecological psychology worked marvelously well when creating systems that can be used with one's body instead of cognition, but it gave few tools to see how things like social interaction and culture shape conduct. It remained limited in its ability to conceptualize reflection, thinking, and discourse, and these are just the things in the center of the most recent work coming out of the program.

For people trained in philosophy, this may sound risky. Phenomenology makes few claims about explaining human conduct. However, there is a tradition of experimental psychological phenomenology, and Maurice Merleau-Ponty, the key philosopher of psychological phenomenology, built many of his theories on reinterpretations of clinical and experimental studies.[30] Also, there are ways to combine careful measurement and phenomenologically informed theory.[31] William James, one of the founding fathers of the pragmatists, had a background in medicine, making him no stranger to experimental research. Here the line between philosophical thinking and experimental research is fine, but as long as a researcher keeps in mind that experiments are aids to imagination, he is on safe ground.[32]

The push came from Paris where philosopher Charles Lenay and his colleagues recently studied how we perceive other people's perception with our bodies. It is one thing to be alone somewhere and to see things; it is another thing to be there when others see me seeing things. I have to take into account other viewpoints and how they change as time goes by.[33] With his colleagues, Lenay studied Tactile Vision Sensory Substitution, a system developed by Paul Bach y Rita. This system transforms images captured by a camera into three-dimensional "tactile image," which is applied to the skin or tongue. It is meant to give blind people a three-dimensional perception of their surroundings. For Lenay and his colleagues, this commercial and prosthetic failure provided an opportunity to study how technology mediates perception. They showed what people are able to say when they interact with another person through the system. We give a body image to others, and others respond to this image. We can recognize this response. We know we do not deal with a machine.

This may sound like hairsplitting, but it has important implications for understanding many technologies that are specifically built on social assumptions. People do think about the image they give others because they know that others act on this image and that way affects them. Many "presence" technologies build on similar assumptions, and such considerations certainly shape behavior on social networks on the Web. This question is relevant in traditional design as well. For example, we dress differently for Midtown than we do for the neighborhood bar in Brooklyn because we know people will look at us differently in those places. It is much like looking into a mirror: you become more self-conscious.

This work has recently been picked up in Eindhoven. For example, in her master's thesis, Eva Deckers weaved a carpet that responds to movement of the hand, giving it the ability to perceive and react to people's perception. In her doctoral work, she focused on situations with multiple users.[34] Work like this is bringing the Eindhoven program to a junction. These studies promise a better understanding of many kinds of interactive technologies but also make research more difficult. Importantly, this new direction creates links to twentieth century Continental thinking in the humanities and the social sciences. Recent work is also bringing work in Eindhoven closer to interpretive sociology, ethnomethodology, and discourse analysis. This shift has certainly paved the way for more sophisticated research programs that may fill the promise of providing knowledge of "la condition humaine" — what makes humans tick.[35]

End Notes

1. Zelditch (1969).
2. For example, see Stanley Milgram's (1974) famous studies of obedience, which illustrated how easy it is to make people act against their will and ethics simply by giving them orders. Milgram's studies have been criticized for many problems, but his experiments provide a clear illustration of how one can take a key element of a place like the army — obedience to authority — and study it in isolation in a laboratory.

3. Thanks to Pieter Jan Stappers for some of the formulations in this paragraph, as well as pointing out the relevance of Milgram's work in this context.
4. See Overbeeke et al. (2006, pp. 63–64).
5. Lee (2001). There are many extensions of this methodology, like quasi-experimental studies and living labs, and many other methodologies emulate this model, including surveys based on questionnaires.

   For quasi-experiments, see Cook and Campbell (1979), and for living labs, see De Ruyter and Aarts (2010). Neither methodology has caught on. Quasi-experiments try to vary things like political programs, but as they take place in the open, not in a lab, control is barely more than a metaphor, and this needs to be taken into account. The problem with living labs like smart homes is that despite much of the rhetoric, they seldom combine the best of experimental laboratory work and working in real context, but tend to remain technological showcases or technical proofs of concepts (for a thorough study of smart homes, see Harper, 2003). An excellent introduction to survey methodology is De Vaus (2002).
6. Wensveen (2004).
7. Hassenzahl (2003, 2004).
8. Frens (2006a,b).
9. Technically speaking, these were not cameras but a body containing different interaction modules.
10. The order in which the cameras were given to the participants was varied to make sure that the order in which they were shown did not cause error.
11. Overbeeke et al. (2006, pp. 64–65). The reference to an alarm clock is from Wensveen (2004). Note that this is not always true. Ethnomethodologists have proven that one can use extremely fine-tuned audio- and videotapes for research (see Szymanski and Whalen, 2011). Importantly, this accuracy has a cost: compared to studies in natural environments, laboratory research is far less rich in terms of context. Accurate measurements may mean inaccurate rendering of the context.
12. There is practically a science on observer effects and how they can be controlled, starting from Robert Rosenthal's (1966) classic treatment of the topic. His work is still a standard reference and highly recommended reading.
13. The classic treatment of validity threats in psychological research — and, by implication, any work that involves experimenting and people — is referenced in Campbell and Stanley (1973). The main problem with this book is that it degraded non-experimental research unjustifiably; in particular, Donald Campbell revised his argumentation considerably in the early 1970s. In design research, the most comprehensive effort to minimize such threats is again done by Joep Frens (2006a, pp. 152–153), who showed statistically that the order in which he presented his cameras to participants did not affect the results.
14. As Pieter Jan Stappers noted in private, this is also why the lab is useful for validation studies of already fixed hypotheses but less suited for exploratory/generative studies where research questions evolve.
15. These additional studies help to elaborate analysis and rule out alternative explanations and competing hypotheses. These studies make the initial result more robust and defensible. They may also show that the basic relationship exists only for one group, or even remove the basic relationship altogether, in which case the original relationship is said to be spurious.
16. As Ross (2008, p. 196) wrote, "All participants were students at TU/e, from several departments or Fontys College in Eindhoven. None of these people had experience in interaction design. The advantage of having participants from the same social group (students) was that the factors other than values were more constant than they would be in a heterogeneous participant group."

17. Respectively, Frens (2006a), Wensveen (2004), Keller (2005), and Lucero (2009, pp. 17, 217).
18. Stappers (2007, p. 87). It is important to make a distinction between the prototype and the theoretical work that led into it. Occasionally, design researchers build marvelous prototypes even though their research shows that the reasoning behind the prototype is probably wrong. This was the case in Philip Ross' work, which produced marvelous lamps, but fairly inconsistent theoretical results. That his results were inconclusive and designs attractive suggest that the problem was not in the design process, but in the theoretical framework he used. More typically, researchers do solid theoretical work that leads to fairly awkward designs, at least when judged by professional standards. The reasons for this have been dealt with earlier in this chapter. Most constructive design researchers would probably side with Ross, and sacrifice some theoretical elegance to guarantee enough resources for design. Again, this is common in research: empirical researchers typically sacrifice theoretical sophistication if data so requires. Why not designers?
19. "... we use methods we borrow, mostly, from social sciences. The prototypes are *physical hypotheses* ..." (Overbeeke et al., 2006, pp. 65–66, italics in original).
20. Stappers, workshop Jump Start in Research in Delft, June 29, 2010. An updated list will reappear in 2011 in the PROTO:type 2010 Symposium held in Dundee, Scotland (Stappers, 2011).
21. Stappers (2007, p. 12). See also Horvath (2007).
22. Overbeeke et al. (2006, pp. 64–65, *italics* ours).
23. Overbeeke et al. (2006, pp. 64–65).
24. Frens (2006a, pp. 29, 185).
25. Our thanks go to Pieter Jan Stappers for pointing this out.
26. A researcher cannot take a result and say that he proved the theory at work behind the study without first checking his work. The main elements to check include things missing in theory, reliance on only one set of measures, overly simple measurements, the fact that people learn to respond "the right way," and the researchers' own expectations.
27. For Lakatos (1970), see Chapter 3.
28. Overbeeke et al. (2006, pp. 63–64). Caroline Hummels (2000, p. 1.27) talked about conditional laws in her thesis.
29. See Overbeeke 2007.
30. Merleau-Ponty's seminal works that continue to inspire psychological research are *The Phenomenology of Perception* (2002) and *The Structure of Behavior* (1963). Other key figures in phenomenological psychology include Albert Michotte. Also, many late Gestalt theorists like Kurt Koffka were influenced by Husserl's phenomenological philosophy.
31. The best recent example is probably Oscar Tomico's doctoral thesis in Barcelona, which built a method of measuring experience based on Kelly's (1955) personal construct theory. Tomico's thesis was a conscious attempt to combine elements from the empathic tradition of Helsinki with ecological tradition in Eindhoven. Today, Tomico works in Eindhoven.
32. As Overbeeke et al. (2006, pp. 65–66) wrote, their long-time hope is to discover conditional laws of human-machine interaction. However, they also tell that "the level of abstraction in our work is low. We almost argue by case. This is done by necessity; otherwise we would lose the rich human experience."
33. Lenay et al. (2007), Lenay (2010).
34. Deckers et al. (2009, 2010, 2011). See w3.id.tue.nl/en/research/designing_quality_in_interaction/projects/perceptive_qualities/.
35. These are words from Overbeeke et al.'s (2006, pp. 65–66) programmatic paper.

5

FIELD: HOW TO FOLLOW DESIGN THROUGH SOCIETY

Many design researchers have borrowed their methods from interpretive social science rather than experimental research. If there is one keyword to describe the field approach to design, it must be "context."[1] Field researchers work with context in an opposite way from researchers in a lab. Rather than bringing things of interest into the lab for experimental studies, field researchers go after these things in natural settings, that is, in a place where some part of a design is supposed to be used. Researchers follow what happens to design in that context. They are interested in how people and communities understand things around designs, make sense of them, talk about them, and live with them. The lab decontextualizes; the field contextualizes.

Field researchers believe that to study humans and their use of design they need to understand their system of meanings. Studying humans and studying nature differ in a crucial way because of these meanings. Simply, people make sense of things and their meaning and act accordingly. An apple falling from the tree does not care about the concept of gravity and cannot choose what to do. When the president declares war, he certainly knows what he is doing with his words and knows he has alternatives.[2] Even when people do something out of habit, they are selecting from alternatives and may always change their ways.[3] If researchers see society in these terms, they also think that searching laws that could explain human activity and society is misguided. Instead, they take even the goofiest ideas seriously if they shape human activities.

Design ethnography differs from corporate ethnography, an heir of studies in organizational culture, which focused on issues like management and how symbols integrate organizations. Design ethnography works with product design and is a way to handle cultural risks in industry.[4] Sometimes it is a separate front-end activity, and sometimes it is closely integrated into product development. Design ethnographers typically work in teams and use prototypes during fieldwork to create dialog with the people in the study. They communicate through formats accessible to engineers, and their fieldwork is measured in days or weeks, not months. For them, first-hand experience of context is typically more important than fact finding or even careful theoretically informed interpretation.[5] In this chapter, we use "design ethnography" and "field work" interchangeably.

5.1 Vila Rosário: Reframing Public Health in a Favela

Vila Rosário is a design project in a former village that is now a part of the vast metropolis of Rio de Janeiro. It is located about 15 kilometers north of the famous towns Corcovado, Ipanema, and Copacabana. Even though it is not among the poorest of Rio's areas, Vila Rosário is still a world apart from the glory of these famous neighborhoods (Figure 5.1). Its illiteracy rate is around 50%, sanitation is poor, and the poverty level is high. It suffers from high infant mortality and a high incidence of diarrhea, tuberculosis, and many tropical diseases, including yellow fever.

This was the playing field of two designers, Marcelo and Andrea Júdice, who set out to study the neighborhood and create

Figure 5.1 Views from Vila Rosário: (a) a health agent with one family, (b) the backyard of a poor home, (c) the clinic, and (d) the street in front of the clinic. (Photographers: Leila Deolinda, Figures (a) and (b), and Ilpo Koskinen, Figures (c) and (d).)

designs that would improve the town's public health. Initially, they were to introduce information technology into the village to improve the general living conditions of the inhabitants. However, after the first field studies, it became clear that it would not be a solution without considerable rethinking of the context. How could information technology help people who cannot read in a place where it is common to steal electricity?

The study began with cultural probes consisting of cameras, letters, diaries, and several tasks for volunteer health agents working in Vila Rosário.[6] After seeing the probe returns, the researchers realized that any attempt to make sense of Vila Rosário without visiting it would compromise a study aimed at improving health. So the researchers went to the village to do fieldwork and conduct a series of workshops with the locals to make sure they understood the probe results.

The study results identified hygiene and early diagnosis of tuberculosis as the main targets of design. Since it was beyond the means of the project to improve hygiene, the Júdices focused on improving awareness about the significance of hygiene, especially among children. The design hypothesis that evolved was based on this result. It became a combination of an IT-based information system and a low-tech approach. The aims were to raise awareness of how health and behavior are linked and to induce behavioral change among children and teenagers.

Design was started by creating a *telenovela*-like make-believe world with characters recognizable to the inhabitants in Vila Rosário. It was thought that these characters and their actions would stay in the minds of people better than mere health-related information. This world of characters had various types of individuals and families. Also, it had various types of professionals significant in terms of health, including doctors, nurses, nuns, and health agents. It did not, however, have characters like politicians, police, and gang leaders. The world reflected everyday life in Vila Rosário rather than its institutions, which locals did not trust (except the church and doctors).

Computers were pushed into the background. Essentially, IT became a Web connection helping nuns and local health agents (who are like paramedics, with some training in health care) to contact medical experts. Computers were placed in a local health clinic, Institute Vila Rosário, run by the church, which became the hub of the study.

The main effort was to put low-tech designs like comics describing safe ways to use water and cooking utensils (Figure 5.2). Other designs were posters pointing out key facts about hygiene, such as the importance of cleaning fingernails and kitchen knives, and there were also stories for children. The characters in these stories showed what happens to people who do not practice

Figure 5.2 (a) A tuberculosis booklet stressing the importance of paying proper attention to even mild symptoms, (b) an example of the characters created for the booklet, and (c) a poster linking hygiene to health and the logo created for the Institute Vila Rosário. (Artwork by Nestablo Ramos Neto.)

proper hygiene and do not see a doctor when they have symptoms of illnesses like tuberculosis. In addition, researchers created an identity for the program consisting of a series of accessories and company gift-like designs, such as folders, bags, and T-shirts. These were created to make the design program easy to identify and remember.

All these designs were cheap, colorful, relatively easy to produce, and did not produce anything valuable that could be stolen and sold on the black market. Furthermore, these designs fit into the social structure and cultural understandings of Vila Rosário. They were based on the probe returns as well as on ethnographic

Figure 5.3 Pictures from design tests: (a) evaluation in Vila Rosário, (b) studying designs in Helsinki, and (c) evaluation of designs in Namibia. (Pictures of Figures (a) and (b) by Marcelo Júdice and Figure (c) by Andrea Júdice.)

understanding. These sources provided the designers with a necessary understanding of themes important in Vila Rosário, which provided the information to create a local look and feel to the designs. The materials were produced locally, and distributed in Vila Rosário through health agents.

The designs were evaluated in three ways. In Vila Rosário, all of the main designs were evaluated with a variety of local participants in workshops. The focus was on whether people understood the design and whether they were enticing enough to produce. In Helsinki, a Brazilian expert specializing in public health in the tropics evaluated the design proposals. In this evaluation, the focus was on factual content and understanding the health care structure of the village. Finally, the design process was replicated in a two-week workshop in Namibia. Here, the question was whether it is possible to scale down the method developed in the study so that it could be used outside Rio de Janeiro (Figure 5.3).

The Vila Rosário study showed how a serious commitment to context may lead to a major redefinition of a design effort and how this commitment changed design from a technical exercise to a low-tech one. It also showed the importance of understanding the context in detail. The designs generated knowledge about the visible and material culture of the Vila as well as about its habits, beliefs, and social structures. When it comes to design ethics, the study showed serious commitment to poor people who do not usually get to enjoy good design. In terms of design research, it also led to questioning many first-world assumptions; for example, how can probe studies be done when people cannot read?

5.2 Understanding as the Basis of Design

Field research entered industry in the late 1970s and early 1980s mostly as a response to changes in computing.[7] In essence, it was a response to a failed case. When computers moved from universities, research institutes, and major corporations to homes and offices, users could not understand how these machines worked. The failure was obvious, but prevailing systems design methods were not able to explain why.

In response, researchers started to do fieldwork to see how computers were used in ordinary circumstances. This orientation primarily took place in countries with strong computer industries, with Silicon Valley leading the way. Field research proved to be especially useful for industry in the early phases of product design when requirements are specified. As design anthropologist Christine Wasson noted, "by 1997, every major design firm claimed to include ethnography as one of its approaches."[8]

This was certainly the case in Silicon Valley.[9] In the Valley's IT industries, ethnographic research was a response to the need to understand not only how people could use computers but also what they wanted from computing. Contextual design, in particular, became a business success.[10]

Silicon Valley also gave birth to a more design-led approach to fieldwork. Researchers like Jane Fulton Suri and Alison Black at IDEO and Liz Sanders at Richardson/Smith pushed designers out into the field to see what people do in real life.[11] The idea was to get designers out of the studio to bond with people and to focus on what they do rather than on what they say.[12] For skilled designers, insights drawn from observations are based on years of experience. Fulton Suri discussed about how a few successful designers do fieldwork:

> *Certainly ethnographic-style observation can provide inspiration and grounding for innovation and design. It increases our confidence that ideas will be culturally relevant, respond to real needs and hence be more likely to have the desired social or market impact. But for design and designers there's much more to observation than that.... Successful designers are keenly sensitive to particular aspects of what's going on around them and these observations inform and inspire their work, often in subtle ways. Firsthand exposure to people, places, and things seems to be key, but there is no formulaic method for observation of this very personal kind....*

But their approach was certainly not without discipline or rigor. Each case involved a similar pattern: a focused curiosity coupled with exposure to relevant contexts, attention to elements that invited intrigue, visual documentation and revisiting these records later, percolation and talking about what was significant with team members and clients, and storytelling and exploration of design choices and details.[13]

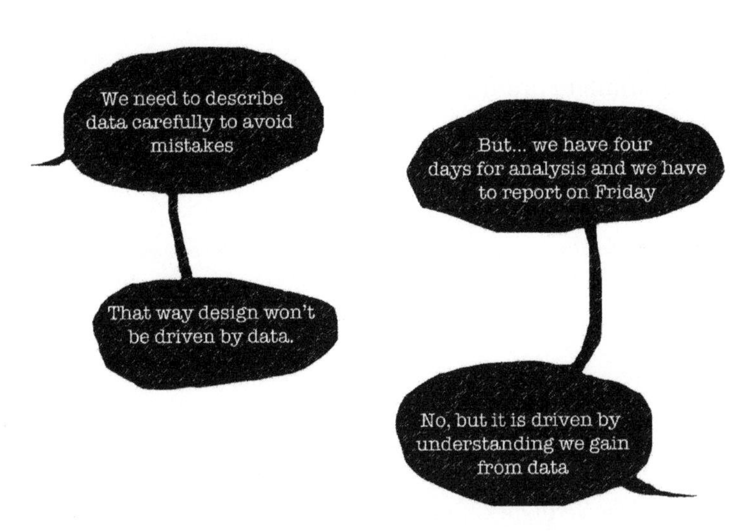

Figure 5.4 Two realities of fieldwork.

This kind of research goes far beyond tourist-like observation; it gains understanding of what goes on in people's minds in some instances. It also goes beyond mere analysis. Making a systematic description of data is a step in the process of gaining an empathic grasp, but research does not stop there. Good design research is driven by understanding rather than data (Figure 5.4).

Somewhere between these orientations were other earlier practices, such as in the Doblin group and later E-Lab.[14] Participatory design was a Scandinavian amalgam of computer science, design, sociology, and labor union politics.[15] It sought to battle deskilling, which the Marxist labor theorist Harry Braverman saw as the main aim of management in his book *Labor and Monopoly Capital*.[16] Instead of making workers replaceable by machines, participatory designers sought to empower workers.[17]

5.3 Exploring Context with Props

Field research methods in design are immediately recognizable to professional social scientists. They are also often taught to designers by social scientists. Still, design ethnography differs from ethnography as it is practiced in anthropology and its sister disciplines.[18] If there is something specific in design fieldwork, it is probably the focus on products and things and the use of mock-ups and prototypes.[19] Even more differences exist when design begins. Designers' analytic methods range from brainstorming techniques and future workshops to such co-design tools as "magic things," design games, video sketching, and using Legos to simulate products, interactions, and organizations.[20]

> *We put a large number of components together into "toolkits." People select from the components in order to create "artifacts" that express their thoughts, feelings and/or ideas. The resulting artifacts may be in the form of collages, maps, stories, plans, and/or memories. The stuff that dreams are made of is often difficult to express in words but may be imaginable as pictures in your head.*[21]

The aim is to turn fieldwork into an exercise of imagination rather than mere data gathering. In the tough time lines of design, it is hard to view "dreams" by observation alone. If researchers want to learn about things like dreams, people have to be invited to the dream during fieldwork. Sensitizers like Dream Kits are useful for this reason as they function to elicit people's projective fantasies.

For example, from 2008 to 2010, researchers from the Danish School of Design built a model to show how anthropology could be used in design. This model was developed in a book focusing on reducing garbage incineration in Copenhagen. The editor, Joachim Halse, opens the book by calling it a manifesto, stressing its political nature. For him, the book offers a participatory approach for creating design opportunities that evolve around life experiences. The spirit of the study was to lower the line between anthropological fieldwork and design, but there were other drivers as well. One driver was developed to get more and more diverse people involved in the process. In DAIM, shorthand for Design Anthropology Innovation Model, the researchers used mock-ups, acted out scenes, organized design games and workshops, and rehearsed service scenarios with people (Figure 5.5).

5.4 Generating Concepts as Analysis

One problem spot in fieldwork has been explaining synthesis — how design ideas emerge from fieldwork. Synthesis is a creative mash of common sense and research and stresses design opportunities rather than theory. This argument, however, puzzles non-designers, to whom this sounds mystical, to say the least. However, even though most designers avoid references to the social sciences, their methods are systematic.

Broadly speaking, there are two types of approaches that deal with synthesis. Some researchers borrow heavily from the social sciences. They search models from analytic induction, grounded theory, and thick description in symbolic anthropology.[22] Christine Wasson tells how at E-Lab ethnographic data were analyzed from

Figure 5.5 Rehearsing new practices at DAIM. In this project, many stakeholders are brought together to design and rehearse new relationships.

instances of data into patterns. These patterns were then turned into a model that interpreted ethnographic materials and envisioned a solution for the client.

> *The model offered a coherent narrative about the world of user-product interactions: how a product was incorporated into consumers' daily routines and what symbolic meanings it held for them. These insights, in turn, were framed to have clear implications for the client's product development and marketing efforts.*[23]

Most design researchers, however, avoid social science models altogether. They build on well-tried methods from design practice, including well-known models such as the workplace models and

Figure 5.6 (a) How affinity walls generate abstractions.[24] (b) Using affinity diagrams to analyze data to generate design ideas. (c) personas in an exhibition in Kone Corporation, a lift and elevator maker.[25]

affinity diagrams in contextual inquiry and personas in software development (Figure 5.6).

It is easy to add analysis to both procedures. If it is important to study gender, researchers simply analyze males and females separately and compare the results to see what kinds of differences exist. Adding age to this is also easy; researchers simply break the male and female groups into older and younger categories.

There are many overlaps between these two families; for example, working through data using affinity diagrams shares its underlying logic with analytic induction. Still, analytic induction is not always easy. Reflecting on her experiences on teaching ethnography in corporate settings, Brigitte Jordan noted how teaching data collection is easy, but the lack of tradition in analysis complicates analysis in design firms. Social scientists learn the craft of analysis through years of education and fieldwork that are almost impossible to convey "to non-anthropologists during a brief training period."[26] Seen from the other side of the fence, social scientists also fail: designers need more than verbal data and references from social science literature. When designers work with data, they make references to products, conceptual designs, and other pieces of design research rather than theoretical work in the social sciences.[27]

As Wasson noted, the association between ethnography and anthropology is little recognized in design, and the word "anthropology" is almost never heard.[29]An obvious exception is academic research carried out in universities, where it occasionally infiltrates into industrial practice. In particular, ethnomethodology has

Creating an Interpretation[28]

Most field researchers explicate patterns from fieldwork observations rather than analyze them statistically. This process does not have a mathematical basis but is systematic, and outsiders can inspect it to spot problems.

Practice

Practical designers have several terms for this process. The best known term is probably "affinity diagram." These diagrams cluster similar observations into groups, whereas other observations are in different groups. These clusters are then named. Analysis proceeds by grouping these clusters into still more abstract clusters. This process generates an abstract interpretation of data, and it is used as a starting point for design. This is done with Post-it® notes and whiteboards.

Analytic Induction

Social scientists call this kind of process "analytic induction." Just like affinity diagrams, analytic induction begins with observations with more abstract interpretation. The difference is that in analytic induction, researchers make sure that there are no negative cases that would question the interpretation. This interpretation may apply to other data; however, it is best treated as a separate question.

Parsimony

To provide clarity, researchers usually prefer interpretations that consist of only a few concepts. A good interpretation is parsimonious. This is known as "Occam's Razor," named after medieval philosopher Willem Occam. An interpretation that consists of 10 or 20 concepts is difficult to understand, remember, and communicate. Keeping Occam's Razor in mind helps to control this problem. Affinity diagrams and analytic induction lead to parsimony.

found its way into many types of software, design, and interaction design conferences, journals, and books.[30]

5.5 Evaluation Turns into Research: Following Imaginations in the Field

As the design anthropologist Dori Tunstall noted, any anthropologist studies the material world.[31] Constructive design researchers do this too; however, their interest is in a very special kind of make-believe world, which is partially their own creation. They introduce their design imaginations into the lives of people to be able to follow how these imaginations shape the activities, thoughts, and beliefs of these people. These imaginations are not treated as physical hypotheses like in laboratory studies; instead they are treated as a thing to be followed in context.[32]

These imaginations can be almost anything, such as a bottle refunding machine made of cardboard, but typically they are prototypes[33] as with Ianus Keller's attempt to build a tangible system for creating and browsing collections of pictures.[34] This was also the case in the project Morphome, which took a critical look at the idea of proactive technology — of using data from sensors to predict where human action is heading and adjusting things such as light and room temperature. Since there was no such technology on the market in 2002 when the project started, Morphome built proactive systems and devices, installed these systems into homes, and interviewed and observed people who used them.[35] These imaginations can also go beyond prototypes. For example, Andres Lucero simulated interactive spaces with design games by using objects like Legos as a tangible means to make people imagine what it would be to work and live in such spaces.[36]

Sometimes complex technological systems are needed to study designers' imaginations, as in two early studies of mobile multimedia phones, Mobile Image and Mobile Multimedia. In these studies, researchers in Helsinki followed how people sent multimedia messages by recording real messages.[37] A more recent example comes from Pittsburgh, where researchers have taken a service design approach to investigate service innovation for public services, in this case a transit service. Fieldwork with transit riders revealed that their greatest desire is to know when a bus will arrive at a stop. Commercial systems that provide this service cost tens of millions of dollars. So the researchers have taken a very literal approach to the idea of co-production of value. They have designed Tiramisu (means pick me up in Italian), a smart phone application that allows transit riders to share GPS traces while riding the bus. By combining the schedule from the transit service and GPS traces from a handful of riders, Tiramisu can generate real-time arrival predictions and make this available to riders over mobile phones or the web. In this design the riders literally make the service they desire. The researchers built a working system and initial field study indicates that riders will share traces and that these traces can produce accurate real-time predictions (Zimmerman et al., 2011).

To create proper conditions for using prototypes in research, some methodological decisions are needed. Esko Kurvinen argued with his colleagues that designers should place their imaginations into an ordinary social setting. They should also follow it in this setting using naturalistic research design and methods over a sufficient time span to allow social processes to develop. Kurvinen and his colleagues developed four guidelines for properly analyzing prototypes and other expressions as social objects.

1. *Ordinary social setting.* More than one person has to be involved in a unit of study to create the conditions for social

interaction. Social interaction has to take place in a real context to overcome studio-based contemplation.

2. *Naturalistic research design and methods.* People have to be the authors of their own experiences. They are involved as creative actors who can and will engage with available products that support them in their interests, their social interaction, and meaningful experiences. Data must be gathered and treated using empirical and up-to-date research methods.
3. *Openness.* The prototype should not be thought of as a laboratory experiment. The designer's task is to observe and interpret how people use and explore the technology, not to force them to use it in predefined ways.
4. *Sufficient time span.* The prototype ought to be followed for at least a few weeks. If the study period is shorter, it is impossible to get an idea of how people explore and redefine it.[38]

Designers usually prefer to work with rough models in order to not direct attention prematurely to design details. The last thing any designer wants is feedback focusing on surface features of the expression rather than the thinking behind it. Paradoxically, being too hi-tech and true to design leads to bad research and design.

5.6 Interpretations as Precedents

Field research has its roots in industry, where it primarily informs design. It has provided a solution to an important problem, understanding, and exploring social context. It has been useful, and it has turned into a standard operating procedure. Plainly, it is useful to know how people make sense of what they see and hear and how they choose what they do.

However, field researchers produce "local" understanding that describes the context that cannot be applied uncritically to other cases. It is also temporary rather than something long-standing.[39] This specificity makes it useful in industry, but it also raises the question of generalization, how to apply his knowledge to other cases.

There are several ways to respond to the question of generalization. Often generalization is irrelevant. Every designer studies the masters, whose works are always unique. Benchmarking looks at the top, not the average. At the top, the number of cases is by definition small. Also, studying a negative case may teach a lot; for example, even the best designers and companies fail occasionally, and these failures may be just as informative as the successes. Often, research generalizes through a program; instead of trying to describe

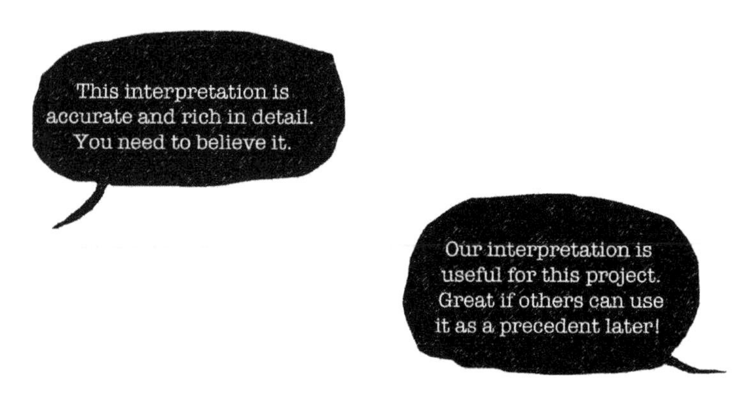

Figure 5.7 Field aims at precedents rather than knowledge.

universally applicable knowledge, it is often more useful to study one culture at a time. Finally, focusing on unique cases encourages creativity. Methods like cultural probes, experience prototypes, bodystorming, Magic Things, and role-plays came from individual projects.[40] Cultural probes would not have been seen if researchers in London had relied on well-proven scientific methods.

There is also a bigger picture. There are well-known and respected fields of learning that build on case studies. These include history and the humanities, clinical medicine, law, case-based business schools, and many natural sciences. Most good designers, design firms, and design schools work through precedents.[41] Whenever designers are faced with new problems, they study patents and existing designs to learn their logic. As a designer's stock of precedents grows, he is better able to respond to various demands, put problems quickly into context, and foresee problems.[42] Experienced designers know how to spot opportunities, because they know so much about existing products, materials, production techniques, trends, and human beings[43] (Figure 5.7).

5.7 Co-Design and New Objects

Field research has been an industrial success, and it is also alive and well academically. It flourishes in several niches and is done throughout the design industries in both big and small markets. There are people who build on the social sciences, collecting data carefully and processing it into "thick descriptions."[44] There are also people who stress the value of merely diving into society to gain an understanding of people for design. At advanced levels in design universities, it has become a default methodology: it is a conscious choice not to do any field-style research.

Over the past two years, some researchers in Northern Europe have started to talk about their craft as co-design or co-creation.[45] What is new here is that the design process is increasingly opened to people, whether stakeholders or users. When designers work as facilitators rather than detached observers, the last remnants of the idea that researchers ought to be detached, impartial observers — "flies on the wall" — disappear. What comes about is the idea that design is supposed to be an exploration people do together, and the design process should reflect that. Many designers doing fieldwork have taken this model to heart, sometimes making it increasingly difficult to draw a line between designers and non-designers.[46]

During the past few years, several researchers have also turned to action research, where the goal is to use knowledge gained by studying a group or community in order to change it. Particularly significant work has been done in Milan in conjunction with companies and communities in Lombardy. The Milanese approach to research is characteristically locally rooted and action-oriented, aiming to change local communities rather than creating new products. Around 2000, researchers were trying to improve service systems and concepts.[47] A few years later, this research evolved into studying how service design could be used to dematerialize society to make it ecologically and socially sustainable.[48] In terms of attitude, current Italian researchers are well in line with the ethos that drove their teachers' work but work far more methodically.[49] Also, researchers in Milan are learning from other parts of the world; for example, the best book about co-design is written in Italian.[50]

Prototyping Services: Nutrire Milano[51]

Figure 5.8 Shoppers in a sustainable service prototype at Largo Marinai d'Italia in Milan, Italy. Here people enjoy food they have just bought in the market "convivium." The market is a place to buy food but also a place to enjoy it, to meet friends, and to have a good time. (Picture undated, courtesy of INDACO, Politecnico di Milano.)

Maybe the best example of design tackling issues far larger than a product comes from Milan, Italy.

Under the leadership of Ezio Manzini and Anna Meroni at Politecnico di Milano, a service design group specializing in sustainability, studied the relationship between the city of Milan and Parco Sud, a vast agricultural area south of the city, for almost a decade. Combining three interests — sustainability, service design, and the Slow Food values (Slow Food is the main project promoter) — the group tried to create a business model that would keep alive small-scale food production in Parco Sud.

Manzini calls this approach "action research." The researchers worked with people trying to understand their hopes, needs, and worries. This research-based understanding was turned into projects that support the Parco Sud community. The aim has always been a permanent change to a common good.

This research illustrates the importance of fieldwork for design. Researchers have gone into Parco Sud and Milan, studying things like supply chains. They have ventured into co-designing business models through visual service design techniques. They also created a service prototype. There is a lively market every third Saturday of the month in Milan. The hope is that this prototype lives on and can be replicated elsewhere. Researchers have also built digital services to support their concept and continued designing new services for food production, provision, and consumption.

Key researchers in the group have mostly been trained in engineering, usability, and user studies. It is clear that in this study researchers had to work in the real world with people who have real problems and agendas. In trying to design viable business models, researchers do not have the luxury of going into a laboratory to build a model of research.

Through these developments, the designer's interest is shifting from individuals and systems to groups and communities. There is also a trend away from products, experiences, and even services toward communities and large-scale urban problems. Although field methodology has proved its value in product development, it is still expanding and finding new uses and opening up new kinds of design opportunities.

End Notes

1. See Wasson (2000, pp. 377–378).
2. Winch (2008, p. 119).
3. Winch (2008, pp. 86–87).
4. Salvador et al. (1999).
5. For some of these research practices, see Nafus and Anderson (2010). This synopsis is based on Koskinen's discussion with Ken Anderson, a veteran of design ethnography and the founder of the EPIC conference, Hillsboro, Oregon, August 19, 2010.
6. For cultural probes, see Chapters 2 and 6.
7. For example, see Hackos and Redish (1998).
8. Wasson (2000, p. 382).
9. For example, see Wixon and Ramey's (1996) collection. See Tunstall (2008). The *Ethnographic Praxis in Industry* conference occurred in 2005, providing a meeting point for the community. See Wasson (2000, pp. 384–385), Jordan and Yamauchi (2008), Jordan and Lambert (2009), Squires and Byrne (2002), and Cefkin (2010).

10. See Beyer and Holtzblatt (1998). For a guide to fieldwork based loosely on ethnomethodology, see Randall et al. (2007).
11. Fulton Suri still works at IDEO, but Black has her own agency in Reading, near London. Richardson/Smith was bought by Fitch, which Sanders left to set up SonicRim in 1999.
12. Segal and Fulton Suri (1997) and Black (1998). Perhaps the best example of such work is Fulton Suri's book *Thoughtless Acts? Observations on Intuitive Design* (Fulton Suri and IDEO, 2005), which consists of photographs of people's own design solutions without captions, and a short text that explains the intentions of the book. This text is at the end of the book and is meant to be read after watching the images because, as Fulton Suri noted, life comes without captions.
13. Fulton Suri (2011).
14. E-Lab was bought by Sapient in 1999.
15. See especially Ehn (1988a) who offers a first-hand account of participatory design, although years after the work was done. Also Greenbaum and Kyng (1991) and Schuler and Namioka (2009).
16. Braverman (1974). For example, Ehn (1988a) and Greenbaum and Kyng (1991). Some participatory designers flirted with activity theory, but this movement has no shared theoretical basis. See Kuutti (1996), Bødker (1987), Bødker and Greenbaum (1988), and Kaptelinin and Nardi (2009).
17. See especially Ehn (1998a).
18. Good and practical descriptions of fieldwork in design are Blomberg et al. (2009) and, for contextual inquiry, Holtzblatt and Jones (2009).
19. For a good example of systematic attention to products in fieldwork, see Jodi Forlizzi's (2007) work on the Roomba in senior citizens' homes.
20. For generative tools, see Sanders (2000), Stappers and Sanders (2003), and Sleeswijk Visser (2009). Magic Things are the brainchild of Iacucci et al. (2000), a good source for designing games is Brandt (2001), and a place to look at using video in design is Ylirisku and Buur (2007). A future workshop is from Jungk and Müllert (1983).
21. Sanders (2000).
22. For analytic induction, see Seale (1999), and for its application in design, see Koskinen (2003) and Koskinen et al. (2006).

    "Thick description" is how Clifford Geertz, the dean of American anthropologists, described how anthropologists try to unravel "complex conceptual structures … knotted into one another … that are at once strange, irregular, and inexplicit." Society is spaghetti, and the researcher's job is to do "thick descriptions" to make it understandable (Geertz, 1973).

    There is no shortage of good books on ethnography and fieldwork in the social sciences. To list a few, one can mention Lofland (1976) for fieldwork, Emerson et al. (1995) for writing field notes, Becker (1970) for a wide-ranging discussion on fieldwork and its problems, and Seale (1999) for analysis and quality control. The so-called Grounded Theory by Barney Glaser and Anselm Strauss has found its way into design more slowly than into fields like education (Glaser and Strauss, 1967; Strauss, 1987). If one builds on this "theory," one gets instructions on how to build an abstract framework from observations, but there is a price. Unwary reliance on it leads to theoretical commitments: the process relies heavily on symbolic interactionism (see Blumer, 1969). This same remark also applies to contextual inquiry, where the commitments go to work flow models rather than theory (Beyer and Holtzblatt, 1998).
23. Wasson (2000, pp. 383–384).
24. Holtzblatt and Jones (1990, p. 204).
25. Mattelmäki et al. (2010).
26. Jordan and Yamauchi (2008).
27. Aalto (1997), quoted in Pallasmaa (2009, p. 73).
28. See Koskinen (2003, pp. 62–64).

29. Wasson (2000, p. 385). As design ethnography mainly contributes to design rather than theory, the mother disciplines in the social sciences question its value. For example, as Tunstall (2007) related, the American Anthropological Association was then debating whether design anthropology is a worthy cause, or whether such a profit-seeking enterprise should be excluded from the scientific community.
30. In addition to researchers from Palo Alto Research Center, the most consistent ethnomethodologists writing about design have been former EuroPARC researchers Graham Button and Wes Sharrock and, later, Andy Crabtree (see Crabtree, 2004; Kurvinen, 2007). The Palo Alto Research Center has scaled down on ethnomethodology, but this work continues in several universities, mostly in the United Kingdom.
31. Tunstall (2008). However, there is a line here, which is well illustrated by Shove et al. (2007), who argued that designers should buy into "practice theory," as they called their approach. Their study shows how social scientists understand design: they focused on studying things that exist at homes and were content with it. Their study had no projective features, even though one of the editors of the book was a designer.
32. From a systems perspective, Keiichi Sato usefully talks about the knowledge cycle between artifact development and user. In his model, artifact development process, use and context of use are in a loop in which knowledge of use and use context feed the design of the artifact, and the artifact (or service) and design knowledge embedded in the artifact feed use and shape context of use (Sato, 2009, pp. 30–31).
33. See Säde (2001).
34. Keller (2005).
35. Koskinen et al. (2006), Mäyrä et al. (2006).
36. Lucero (2009).
37. Koskinen et al. (2002), Battarbee (2004), Kurvinen (2007), Koskinen (2007).
38. Kurvinen et al. (2008).
39. The expression of local knowledge is from the anthropologist Clifford Geertz (1983).
40. See Buchenau and Fulton Suri (2000), Iacucci et al. (2000), and the IDEO Card Pack.
41. Note that comparison to law cannot be taken literally. In law, precedents are not just aids to thinking but are binding. This is not the case in design, in which precedents in fact *have to* be surpassed. For this reason, Goldschmidt (1998) argued for discarding the notion of precedent and resorted to "reference" in her work on IT-based reasoning systems for architecture. However, as Lawson (2004, p. 96) noted, designers often refer to "whole or partial pieces of designs that the designer is aware of" as precedents. Like Lawson, we prefer to work with designers' own language but remind the reader about not taking the legal analogy too seriously.
42. Similar to Brian Lawson, a student of design cognition who notes about architecture, "one of the key objectives of design education is to expose young students to a veritable barrage of images and experiences upon which they can draw later for precedent" (Lawson, 2004, p. 96). For a discussion on references and precedents, see Goldschmidt (1998) and Lawson (2004).
43. Fulton Suri (2011).
44. Geertz (1973).
45. See Koskinen et al. (2003). Mattelmäki et al. (2010).
46. Speed dating is a technique to quickly decide which design concept works best: Davidoff et al. (2007), Park and Zimmerman (2010), and Yoo et al. (2010). This technique was first invented in a project reported by Zimmerman et al. (2003). Dream Kits are from Liz Sanders. Bodystorming and experience prototyping are from IDEO; cf. Buchenau and Fulton Suri (2000).

47. Pacenti and Sangiorgi (2010). For doctoral-level work coming from this work, see Pacenti (1998), Sangiorgi (2004), and Morelli (2006).
48. For system-oriented work, see in particular Manzini et al. (2004) and Jégou and Joore, (2004); also Manzini and Jégou (2003). For a shift in unit of analysis, see Meroni (2007) and Meroni and Sangiorgi (2011).
49. In particular, this goes for Ettore Sottsass, Jr. Penny Sparke (2006, p. 17) described his philosophy as a conscious antithesis to post-war modernism, which "in Sottsass' view, ignored the 'user.' His emphasis of the role of the user as an active participant in the design process, rather than a passive consumer, lay at the core of his renewal of Modernism. To this end, he experimented with a number of ways of bringing users into the picture while avoiding transforming them into 'consumers.'"
50. Meroni (2007), Rizzo (2009).
51. Thanks to Anna Meroni, Giulia Simeone, and Francesca Rizzo who helped to write this inset. For philosophy behind Nutrire Milano, see Manzini (2008).

6

SHOWROOM: RESEARCH MEETS DESIGN AND ART

The program we call 'Showroom' builds on art and design rather than on science or on the social sciences. When reading the early texts about research programs regarding showrooms, we were struck by critical references to scientific methodology. There is little respect for notions such as data and analysis, and it is possible to encounter outright hostility toward many scientific practices. Research is presented in shop windows, exhibitions, and galleries rather than in books or conference papers. Still, a good deal of the early work was published at scientific venues, most notably human–computer interaction (HCI). This work was aimed at reforming research, which it did to an extent.

Contemporary artistic practice is beyond the limits of this book, but it is worth noting that art went through many radical changes in the past century. While traditionally, art largely respected boundaries between painting and plastic arts, performing arts, and architecture, the twentieth century broke most of these boundaries. Contemporary art has also broken boundaries between art and institutions like politics, science, and technology. Although painting still dominates the media and the commercial art market, art has increasingly become immaterial, first exploring action under notions like happenings and performances, and then turning human relations into material.[1] With predictable counter-movements calling forth the return to, say, painting, art has moved out from the gallery and into the world at large (see Figure 6.1).[2]

Design has had its own radical movements.[3] Radical Italian designers of the 1960s and 1970s turned to art to create a contemporary interpretation of society. Thus, the Florentine group of Superstudio proposed cubic spaces that allowed the youth to wander in the city and claim possession of the city space.[4] Similarly, the Memphis movement from Milan changed design by turning to the suburbs for inspiration. They found traditional furniture, cheap materials, neon colors, and cheesy patterns and

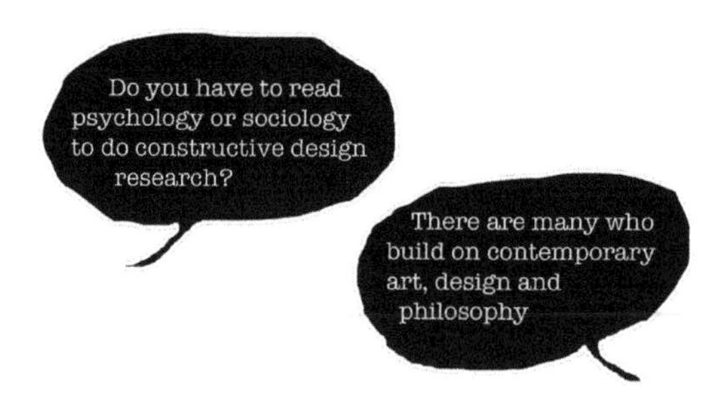

Figure 6.1 Research can build on a non-scientific premise.

built designs that challenged the high-brow aesthetic of modernism.[5] Designers like Jurgen Bey and Martí Guixé,[6] and groups like Droog carry the spirit to the present.[7]

For design researchers, contemporary art and design provide a rich intellectual resource. It links research to historically important artistic movements like Russian constructivism, surrealism, and pop art. It also links research to Beat literature, architecture, and music.[8] It certainly created links to radical writers and theater directors like Luigi Pirandello, Bertolt Brecht, and Antonin Artaud, who broke the line between the artists and their audience. Through these artistic references, design research also makes connections to some of the most important intellectual movements of the twentieth century.

6.1 The Origins of Showroom

The most influential program in Showroom is critical design, which has its origins in the 1990s in the Computer-Related Design program of the Royal College of Art (RCA) in London. Collaborations with Stanford's Interval Research and European Union pushed this famed art school into research. Key figures were Anthony Dunne and Fiona Raby, who coined the term "critical design" to describe their work. Above all, critical design was indebted to critical theory, but its debt to Italian radical design and radical architecture groups of the 1960s–1980s is also clear. These groups challenged the modernistic credo of post-war architecture and design with non-commercial conceptual and behavioral designs.[9] Building on this heritage, critical design tried to make people aware of the dangers of commercial design. The aim was to help people discover their true interests rather than accept things in shops as such.[10]

Early studies in critical design focused on people's relationships to electromagnetic radiation, building on those few artistic and design projects that had questioned commercial approaches to designing electronic devices.[11] Later, this work turned to exploring the impact of science on society. The main impetus was the debate on genetically modified food (GM), which came to the market from laboratories and agribusiness practically without debate, and raised a public outcry so loud that several European countries imposed limitations on GM products.[12] To avoid this mistrust and polarization of debate, critical designers today work with cutting-edge science, opening up science to debate before mistrust steps in.[13] Recent work has explored biotechnology, robotics, and nanotechnology. By building on science, critical design can look at the distant future rather than technology, which has a far shorter future horizon.[14]

Another track also came from RCA's Computer-Related Design program. Its main inspirations can be found in avant-garde artistic movements in post-war Europe rather than design. As the key early publication, the *Presence Project*, related, "we drew inspiration from the tactics used by Dada and the Surrealists, and especially, from those of the Situationists, whose goals seemed close to our own."[15] The situationists tried to create situations that lead people to places and thoughts that they do not visit habitually through *dérive* (roughly, drift) and *détournement* (roughly, turnabout).[16] In London, media embedded in ordinary objects like tablecloths provided these passageways.[17] Other artistic sources have been conceptual art, Krzysztof Wodiczko's "interrogative design," and relational aesthetics, in which the subject matter is human relations rather than situations.[18]

The turning point was the Presence Project, an EU-funded study that developed media designs for three communities: Bijlmer in Amsterdam, Majorstua in Oslo, and Peccioli in Italy. While its designs were typical media designs of the era, including things like "Slogan Bench" and "Image Bank," each was installed for brief field trials in Bijlmer. The main legacy of this project was the "cultural probes" that by now have become a routine part of design research in Europe.[19] Later, this line of work produced a constant stream of media-oriented design work, like Drift Table, History Tablecloth, and Home Health Horoscope.[20]

These prototypes became so robust that they could be field tested for months. The aim is to develop technology and find ways to create a "deep conceptual appropriation of the artifact."[21] Still, at the heart of this work is the situationist spirit. The task of design is to create drifts and detours, just like the Web does in making it easy to jump from one subject to the next.

6.2 Agnostic Science

Showroom had an agnostic attitude toward science in the very beginning. The sharpest formulation of the ethos can be found from the Presence Project, which studied three communities in Europe with cultural probes and then went on to do design for these communities. The project book provides a detailed description of the design process with a great deal of detail about the cultural probes, concept development, and how people in these communities made sense of the design proposals. In one of the project's key statements, Bill Gaver tells how "each step of the process, from the materials to our presentation, was designed to disrupt expectations about user research and allow new possibilities to emerge."[22]

The final section of the book draws a line between epistemological and aesthetic accountability. The former tries to produce causal explanations of the world and is epistemologically accountable. For example, "scientific methods must be articulated and precise ... [allowing] the chains of inference used to posit facts or theories to be examined and verified by independent researchers." Facts at the bottom of science also have to be objective and replicable, not dependent on any given person's perception or beliefs. By implication, these requirements severely constrain what kinds of investigations can be pursued.

Against this, the Presence Project constructs the notion of "aesthetical accountability." Success in design lies in whether a piece of design works, not in whether it was produced by a reliable and replicable process (as in science). Hence, designers are not accountable for the methods: anything goes. They do not need to articulate the grounds for their design decisions. The ability to articulate ideas through design and evaluate them aesthetically "allows designers to approach topics that seem inaccessible to science — topics such as aesthetic pleasure on the one hand, and cultural implications on the other."[23] Surrealism, Dada, and situationism provided ways to get into dream-like, barely worded aspects of human existence. Field research gives access to the routines and habits, but these art traditions focus on associations, metaphors, and poetic aspects of life.

There are many problems with this distinction. "Science" is characterized narrowly, and it sounds more like a textbook version of philosophy than a serious discussion. If one reads any contemporary philosopher or sociologist of science and technology, this description faces difficulties. For this reason alone, it is important to understand its polemic and provocative intent. For the philosophically unaware, it underestimates the power of science and overestimates the power of art and design to change the world. Another troublesome claim is the idea that science cannot access cultural implications. Believing this would delete the possibility of learning from the humanities and the social sciences, which are an important source of knowledge of culture and society. After all, design ethnographers do just that: study culture for design.

6.3 Reworking Research

The agnostic ethos is also reflected in the language used to talk about research. For example, instead of talking about "conclusions," researchers talk about disruptions and dialog. Also, the Presence Project talked about "returns" rather than data. Cultural probes were specifically developed for inspiration, and they were described as an alternative to the then prevailing methods of user research. These visual methods were inspired by psychogeography and surrealism, and they were described as "projective" in the sense of projective psychology.

Researchers have reworked research practices to reflect these beliefs. The purpose of the Presence Project was not about comprehensive or even systematic analysis. The project was happy to get "glimpses" into the lives of people from probe returns and use these glimpses as beacons for imagination.[24] Instead of analysis, "design proposals" are arrived at through a series of tactics rather than systematic analysis. Bill Gaver explained these tactics in the following manner.

Tactics for using returns to inspire designs

1. *Find an idiosyncratic detail. Look for seemingly insignificant statements or images.*
2. *Exaggerate it. Turn interest into obsession, preference to love, and dislike to terror.*
3. *Design for it. Imagine devices and systems to serve as props for the stories you tell.*
4. *Find an artefact or location.*
   - *Deny its original meaning. What else might it be?*
   - *Add an aerial. What is it?*
   - *Juxtapose it with another. What if they communicate?*[25]

As probe returns were mailed to London from research sites, they were spread out on a table. Researchers who came by simply discussed pieces people had sent them, trying to be like gossipers: creating a coherent story of what they saw, with some touches of reality, but only some. The instrument was the researcher, who neither analyzed nor explicated data as an outside expert. Instead, he filtered things he saw through his own associations and emotions.[26] As long as we accept the idea that people encounter the world with dreams, fable-like allegories, and moralities, this approach to analysis is justified. If parts of the human world are non-rational, methods should be too. It is difficult to select a word stronger than "gossip" to create distance to science.

It is also easy to imagine that "field testing" of the prototypes has artistic overtones. Ever since *Design Noir*, the Presence Project, and Static!, designs have been made public for longer

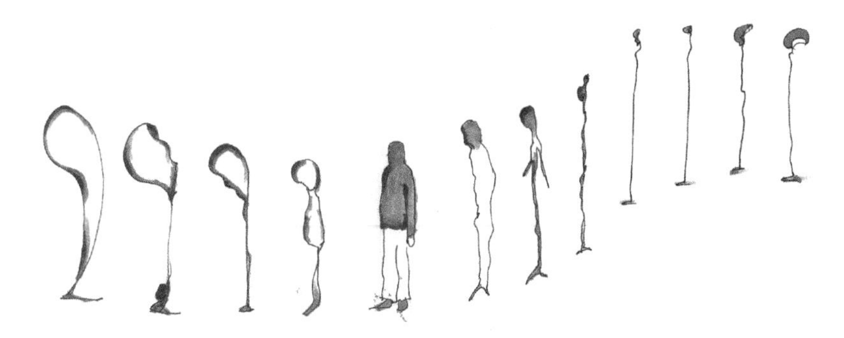

Figure 6.2 Interesting results build on humble beginnings.

and longer time periods; these are tests only in a nominal sense of the term. The aim of this fieldwork is to provide stories, some of which are highlighted as "beacons" that tell about how people experience the designs and what trains of thought they elicited. These stories are food for debate; they are not meant to become facts (see Figure 6.2).[27]

This research lives on in books, patents, and doctoral theses, as well as in exhibition catalogs and critical discussions in art journals, galleries, and universities. The outreach can be substantial, like in the case of the Design and the Elastic Mind exhibition in the Museum of Modern Art (MoMA).[28] As Dunne stated in *Objectified*, a documentary by Gary Hustwit, by going into places like MoMA, one can reach

> *hundreds of thousands of people, more than I think if we made a few arty and expensive prototypes. So I think it depends. I think we're interested maybe in mass communication more than mass production.*[29]

Still, one reason for why Showroom has a research following is because critical designers write about their work in ways recognizable to researchers. They tell the whole story from initial ideas to prototypes and how people understand them. The prototypes may be forgotten, but their message lives on in books.

6.4 Beyond Knowledge: Design for Debate

To go beyond individual projects, Showroom relies on debate rather than statistics, like Lab, or precedents and replication, like Field. It questions the way in which people see and experience the material world and elicits change through debate.

This goes back to the critical and artistic roots of these approaches. Design provides a "script" that people are assumed to follow, and they usually do.[30] If people follow these scripts, they become actors of industry and its silent ideologies. Design structures everyday life in ways people barely notice. Usually, these scripts give people simple and impoverished roles, like those of the user and the consumer.[31]

To give design more value, designers can adopt a critical attitude to make the public aware of their true interests. Critical designers look to shake up the routines of everyday life. Dunne summarized the primary purpose of critical design:

> *to make people think.... For us, the interesting thing is to explore an issue, to figure out how to turn it into a project, how to turn the project into some design ideas, how to materialize those design ideas as prototypes, and finally, how to disseminate them through exhibitions or publications.*[32]

The methods for making people think borrow heavily from art. The designs and the way in which they are explained lean toward *Verfremdung*, as in "estrangement," similar to critical theater by the German playwright Bertolt Brecht. For example, by adding inconvenient nooks into a chair, designers create distance from what people normally take for granted. Debate is a precondition to being critical toward the ideologies of design as usual as well as seeing poetry in ordinary things like Zebra crossings (see Figure 6.5).[33] Researchers get engaged with the world, taking a stance against its dominant ideologies. With hypothetical designs, research can explore technological possibilities before they happen.[34] Design works like an inkblot test on which people can project their questions and worries.[35]

6.5 Enriching Communication: Exhibitions

For many researchers in Showroom, exhibiting objects such as prototypes, photographs, and video are as important as writing books and articles. The exhibition format encourages high-quality finishing of designs over theory and explanation. At times, exhibitions may take the role of a publication. As Tobie Kerridge noted following Bruno Latour, exhibitions at best are *Gedankenausstellungen*, thought experiments that offer curators more freedom than academic writing.[36]

In research exhibitions, designs are exhibited in the middle of theoretical frameworks rather than as stand-alone artworks. Also, design researchers typically want to create distance from the art gallery format. They connect their work to the commercial roots of design with references to furniture shops and car shows. Tony Dunne wrote:

> *The space in which the artifacts are shown becomes a "showroom" rather than a gallery, encouraging a form of conceptual consumerism via critical "advertisements" and "products".... New ideas are tried out in the imagination of visitors, who are encouraged to draw on their already well-developed skills as window-shopper and high-street showroom-frequenter. The designer becomes an applied conceptual artist, socializing art practice by mobbing it into a larger and more accessible context while retaining its potential to provoke people to reflect on the way electronic products shape their experiences of everyday life.*[37]

Exhibiting in places like shops and showrooms also connects critical work to everyday life. In projects like Placebo and Evidence Dolls, Dunne and Raby gave their products to ordinary people[38] As encounters with everyday life become more important, this approach gets closer to field research.[39] The idea, however, is to use people's stories to create a rich understanding of the prototypes, not to gather detailed data for scientific research. Field studies and writing become a part of the Showroom format, but the aims are conceptual.

6.6 Curators and Researchers

There are also problems when research takes place in the exhibition context. Often, exhibitions are not solo shows but compilations of many projects collected under an umbrella envisioned by a curator.[40]

Typically, the curator places the work into a new framework by juxtaposing things that were not necessarily included in the original research projects. Some research concerns and knowledge might be present in the exhibition, but many are not, and yet others are typically rephrased or substituted. Further, most designs are ambiguous and often designed to prompt imaginative interpretation and interrogation.[41] This explanatory framework reflects the curator's interpretation of the research, which may differ significantly from the original goals of the researchers (Figure 6.3).

For example, the Energy Curtain from the Swedish Static! project has been used and showcased in diverse settings. Energy Curtain has been studied in several Finnish homes, it has been at energy fairs to represent a national research program, and it

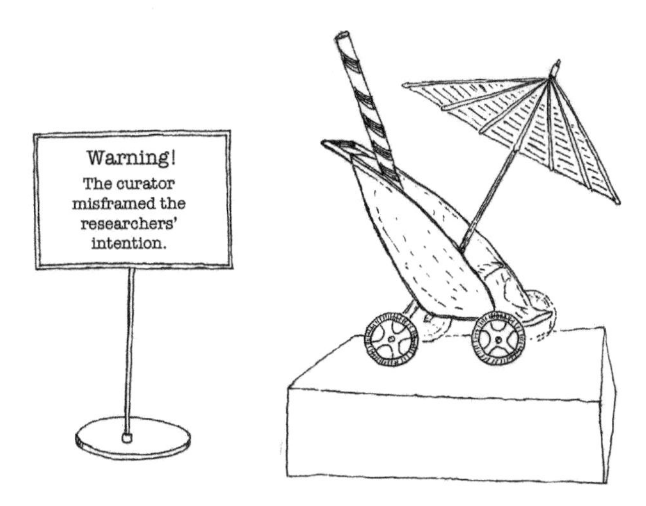

Figure 6.3 Research is exhibited in many frameworks.

has been in the touring exhibition Visual Voltage commissioned by the Swedish Institute. The exhibition has been in places as diverse as the Swedish Embassy in Washington, design exhibitions, expos and museums, and a luxurious shopping mall in Shanghai. It would be naive to think that the original research intent shapes how people look at design and read meaning into it in all of these places. When researchers' prototypes travel the world without the original theoretical context, they may even be treated like products. Approval is expressed through the question: Where can we buy this?[42]

Although exhibitions create many possibilities for communicating design research, they also create a need to carefully consider how other events, writings, and publications can be used to complement them to keep researchers' intentions alive. It is important to engage locally in staging further discussions and debate. For researchers, the attempt to control these meaning-making processes around design means extra work and traveling, which also makes research expensive.[43]

6.7 How Not to Be an Artist

When techniques and practices are borrowed from art, research may be labeled as art and treated accordingly — as political or social statements rather than serious design research. There are plenty of developments that push design to art. For example, curators find it easy to integrate conceptual design into art exhibitions, as in Hasselt, Belgium, where the art museum Z33 organized the 2010 exhibition Design as Performance as a sequel to its Designing Critical Design exhibition in 2008. Despite its name, the 2010 exhibition was framed explicitly as art, and most of the participants were artists.[44]

It is critical that designers fight being labeled as artists. Anthony Dunne explained how he draws the line:

> *What we do is definitely not art. It might borrow heavily from art in terms of methods and approaches but that's it. Art is expected to be shocking and extreme. Design needs to be closer to the everyday life, that's where its power to disturb comes from. Too weird and it will be dismissed as art.... If it is regarded as art it is easier to deal with, but if it remains as design ... it suggests that the everyday as we know it could be different, that things could change.*[45]

One way to distance design from art is to take discourse out into the real world. Much of the early work focused on changing design, but recently designers are getting engaged in larger societal issues.[46] We have already described how critical design has shifted its attention upstream from criticizing design to making science debatable.[47] The Stockholm-based project Design Act is another example. It discusses "contemporary design practices that engage with political and societal issues" by examining "tendencies towards design as a critical practice," which is ideologically and practically engaged in these issues.[48] If designers participate in dialog about the meaning of their work, it is not only curators, critics, and media who define it. A degree of control can be gained this way.

The main challenge of this tactic is to take debate to places where it matters. If researchers stay within the art world, it only strengthens the art label. To make debate meaningful, it ought to be organized in companies, government offices, malls, and community meetings, and face the questions contemporary artists face when they have turned human relationships into art. As the British critic Claire Bishop noted, the question for art is whether it ought to be judged by its political intentions or also by its aesthetic merits.[49] Is serious social content enough to justify a piece of design research, or should it also be judged on its aesthetic merits? Mere disturbance is easy, but is it enough (Figure 6.4)?[50]

Another tactic is to do design at a high professional level. This catches the attention of professional designers, who do not get to label researchers' designs as art, bad design, or simply not design. If researchers succeed in being taken seriously as designers, they may be able to direct attention to the intention behind the work.

The most eloquent articulation of this tactic comes again from Dunne and Raby. They stress that their conceptual products

Figure 6.4 Responding to the art label.

could be turned into products because they result from a design process, are precisely made, require advanced design skills, and project a professional aura. Fiona Raby, in an interview to the Z33 gallery in Belgium, said:

> *By emphasizing that this is design, we make our point more strongly. Though the shock effect of art may be greater, it is also more abstract and it doesn't move me that much. The concept of design, however, implies that things can be used and that we ask questions — questions about the here and now. What is more: all our works could actually be manufacturable. No one will of course, but as a matter of principle, it would be possible.*[51]

Here critical designers meet post-critical architects and many contemporary artists. The aim is to create ideologically committed but good, honest, and serious design work to make sure that attention focuses on design rather than labeling.[52] This is how many design revolutions have come about; for example, Memphis designs were mostly theoretical, but no one could blame them for bad design. They were taken seriously and, ultimately, conquered the world.

A third tactic is to study prototypes in real life. An early example of following what happens to design prototypes in society is Dunne and Raby's *Design Noir*, and another is the Finnish domestication study of two prototypes done by the Interactive Institute, Energy Curtain and Erratic Radio.[53] In London, Bill Gaver's group at Goldsmiths is also working on longer and more complex studies that move beyond notions of evaluation.[54]

Empirical research turns even very explorative designs into research objects. However, for Showroom researchers, fieldwork is typically not about issues around use but about issues like form. For instance, they may ask how static and visual notions of form are moving toward the performative and relational definitions. They also gather material that helps them to build better stories and concepts for their exhibitions.

6.8 Toward Post-Critical Design

Recent work at the Interactive Institute in Sweden shows how researchers can deal with these problems. This work has built on design, philosophical investigation, and more recently, critical discourse in architecture.[55] This work has explored computational technology from an aesthetic perspective and combined traditional materials with new technologies.[56] Its topic is how sustainable design may challenge thinking about energy and technology. Static! explored ways of making people aware of energy consumption through design. Switch! explored energy use in public life and architecture.[57]

Static! and Switch! consisted of several projects. Design examples were reinterpretations of familiar things. Throughout, the idea was to build new behaviors and interactions into old, familiar forms like radios and curtains.[58] The purpose was to create tension between familiar forms and unexpected behaviors to elicit new perceptions, discussion, and debate.

For example, one of the subprojects in Static! was Erratic Appliances — kitchen appliances that responded to increasing energy consumption by malfunctioning and breaking down. One prototype was Erratic Radio.[59] It listened to normal radio frequencies and frequencies emitted by active electronic appliances around the 50 Hz band. When the radio sensed increasing energy consumption in its environment, it started to tune out unpredictably. To continue listening, the user had to turn some things off. Erratic Radio has an iconic Modernist shape with a hint of classic Braun design, which gave it a persuasive and usable quality and underlined that the difference with normal radio was behavioral. Its inspiration was John Cage's Radio Music, but it took an opposite approach to Daniel Weil's Bag Radio, which broke the form of the radio but not its function. Prototypes like Erratic Radio were done in the spirit of the philosopher Ludwig Wittgenstein's thought experiments: they were aimed at questioning things we take as necessities even though they result from industrial processes.

Symbiots from the Switch! project at the Interactive Institute showed some artistic tactics at work. Inspired by notions such as symbiosis and parasitism in biology, Symbiots explored how these natural processes could be used to change ordinary forms into new ones. In Symbiots, graphical patterns, architectural configurations, and electrical infrastructure were turned into a photo series in the genre of hyper-real art photography. The intervention started with neighborhood studies. Residents participated in making the photographs, distributing posters, and discussions. The photo series were done in two different formats, art photographs and posters, to emphasize that there is more than one way to construct design objects.

This kind of work faces several problems. Most of this work is reported in scientific conferences and exhibited in contemporary design galleries. While it also may have some presence at expos and fairs and other venues closer to a commercial context, it is still clearly placed outside the market. If researchers want to show how design can make the world a better place, they have to go where people are. This does not happen through intellectual debates in galleries.

The pros of this step over the boundaries of the design world are obvious, but so are the cons. While fellow designers and critics may be able to pick up the intention behind the work and respect it, this cannot be taken for granted in a place like a shopping mall. Shopping malls place the work in a commercial frame in the original spirit of the Showroom metaphor, while an embassy places it into a political and national frame. This is unavoidable: design does not exist in a void. However, the key question is how to make sure that the research intention is not hijacked to serve someone else's interests (see Figure 6.5).

There are no easy answers to this question. Engagement and commitment have come to stay in constructive design research, but it is far more difficult today than it was in the 1960s and requires elaborate tactics. It is hardly possible to be counted as an avant-garde artist by emptying a glass of water into the North Sea, as Wim T. Schippers did in the 1960s, and shocking the audience has gone to such extremes that it has become very hard to continue like this.[60] Design has had its own share of failures, such as claims to solve the refugee crisis by building better tents.

Figure 6.5 Zebra crossings are graphical elements that become benches when they get a third dimension. Concept from Symbiots. Project team Jenny Bergström, Ramia Mazé, Johan Redström, and Anna Vallgårda. Pictures by Interactive Institute, photographs by Olivia Jeczmyk and Bildinstitutet.

In this case, anything does *not* go.[61] It pays to be careful with this type of claim or risk being dismissed as art.[62] Like artists and architects, designers today tend to make local rather than global commitments and exhibit doubts and controversies in their work. Showroom is about exposing, debating, and reinterpreting problems and issues. Ambiguity and controversy belong to it, just as they belong to contemporary art.[63]

End Notes

1. For a definition, see Bourriaud (2002). For an influential review, see Kester (2004). Bishop (2004, p. 62) lists as key sources Walter Benjamin's "Author as Producer," Roland Barthes' "Death of the Author," and Umberto Eco's *The Open Work.*
2. For example, see O'Doherty (1986).
3. John Thackara (1988, p. 21) once argued that "because product design is thoroughly integrated in capitalist production, it is bereft of an independent critical tradition on which to base an alternative." Design has had more than a few critical phases that have gained quite a following, including Victor Papanek's writings about ecology in the 1960s, and Italian radical design movements. Anti-commercial comments have been voiced even in the commercial heartland of design by people like Georg Nelson, who lamented Henry Dreyfuss for his commercialism after the 1950s; cf. Flinchum (1997, pp. 138–139).
4. Darò (2003). For Superstudio, see Lang and Menking (2003).
5. Radice (1985), Darò (2003).
6. See DAM (2007).
7. Betsky in Blauvelt (2003, p. 51). In another essay, he has characterized Droog as a "collection of detritus of our culture, reassembled, rearranged and repurposed ... they have institutionalized political and social criticism of a lifestyle into design and thus into at least some small part of our daily lives" (Betsky, 2006, pp. 14–15). Interestingly, most design researchers do create original designs rather than redo or remake things, even though this has been routine in the art world, especially in the 1990s (Foster, 2007, pp. 73–74).
8. Barbara Radice (1993) discussed at length Ettore Sottsass Jr.'s contacts to Beat poets and novelists in San Francisco, and how he introduced their work to Milan and Milanese designers.
9. See Parsons (2009, p. 143). For radical design, see Celant (1972, pp. 382–383); also quoted in Menking (2003, p. 63).
10. Dunne's quote is in Parsons (2009, p. 145). For another definition, see Dunne and Raby (2001, p. 58).
11. For example, Weil (1985); Dunne's (2005) *Hertzian Tales* is a virtual cornucopia on this work.
12. See Parsons (2009, pp. 146–147).
13. Dunne (2007, p. 8) and Kerridge (2009).
14. See especially Material Beliefs, a project in which Goldsmiths and the Royal College of Art collaborated. The best document is Beaver et al. (2009).
15. *Presence Project* (2001, p. 23). For situationism, see especially Debord (1955). Situationism shares a curious historical link to the Bauhaus (or more correctly, Ulm), which has been recently analyzed by Jörn Etzold (2009). The Danish artist Asger Jorn was a pivotal figure in early situationism. He was a founding member of the group CoBrA (Copenhagen, Brussels, Amsterdam). When he heard that Max Bill, a former student of Bauhaus, was building a

new design school in Ulm in continuation of the Bauhaus, he contacted him, arguing against Bill that the Bauhaus is not a doctrine with a place, teaching, and heritage, but artistic inspiration. Jorn founded a competing organization he called the Imaginary Bauhaus, which soon became the International Movement for an Imaginist Bauhaus (IMIB).

After learning about the Lettrists in Paris and establishing contact with Michèle Bernstein and Guy Debord, the two groups joined forces. One of its name proposals was IMIB, but it was discarded for the Situationist International, probably due to Deboard's negotiation skills. As years went on, Debord became the main figure. For him, the father to be murdered was Sartre rather than Gropius.

The connections of the situationists and design in Bauhaus style are distant. For Walter Benjamin, the sparse aesthetic of Bauhaus spaces opened materials for experience in ways in which there was no correct use anymore. The situationists tried to achieve something similar by opening the city with their *dérives* and *dépaysements* (disorientations). In this sense, the latter group shares a modernist credo, even though its materials, situation-changing aims and techniques could hardly be more different from the material and specific practice of the Bauhaus. Still, important differences remained:

> "*...whereas Bill's HfG in Ulm emphasized inheritance [from Bauhaus], doctrine, and continuity, Jorn and Debord's counter-effort was aimed above all at the intensification and consummation of disinheritance, as well as the affirmation of that absence of experience that Benjamin had identified as the impetus of modernity in the Bauhaus.*" (Etzold, 2009, p. 160).

16. Guy Debord's situationist notion of spectacle, from which he wanted to save people, is indebted to Marx's notion of commodity fetishism, and in particular, Georg Lukacs' Hegelian interpretation of Marx, which gave humans an important role in changing history instead of reducing human action to economic relationships alone. Other important sources of situationism were French existentialism, surrealism, and Antonin Artaud's theater; cf. Jappe (1999). See also Debord (1958).

17. See Debord and Wolman (1956). The situationists urged artists to place artistic work into everyday settings, where it matters to ordinary people. Nicholas Bourriaud (2002, pp. 85–86) noted that what is missing from this notion are other people: constructed situations derail people as individuals, but not direct them to see through those social relationships that define their habits. As such, the situationists were one group in a long list of twentieth century avant-gardists, including Dada and surrealism, but also Allan Kaprow's happenings, the Fluxus movement, Joseph Beyus' performance art, and Yves Klein's hard-to-classify work; cf. Bourriaud (2002, p. 95).

18. The notion of relational aesthetics is from Nicholas Bourriaud (2002), the French critic and curator. Gaver et al. (1999), Hofmeester and Saint Germain (1999, p. 22), Gaver et al. (2004). The reference to Calle and Wearing is from Gaver (2002). The *Presence Project* (2001, pp. 23, 82–83) also lists artists like photographer John Baldessari and filmmaker Cindy Sherman as sources of inspiration. For discussions on Calle's (2010) work, see *Sophie Calle: The Reader*. A good introduction to Wearing's work is Ferguson et al. (1999).

19. Cultural probes were introduced for the first time to an international audience in Gaver et al. (1999).

20. For Drift Table, see Boucher and Gaver (2007), History Tablecloth is from Gaver et al. (2006), and Home Health Horoscope is reported in Gaver et al. (2007).

21. Gaver et al. (2003, pp. 233, 235–236).

22. *Presence Project* (2001, pp. 22–23).

23. *Presence Project* (2001, p. 203).

24. *Presence Project* (2001, p. 24).

25. Gaver (2002, slides 78-79).

26. This tactic is reminiscent of psychoanalysis, where the analyst listens to the feelings that animate the patient's talk, and uses his own feelings to make sense of the patient's free associations. For a famously clear exposition of psychoanalytic technique, especially the interplay of "transference" (the patient's emotions) and "countertransference" (the analyst's feelings that respond to the patient's feelings), and how they are used in deciphering the patient's psyche, see Gaver et al. (2007).
27. For example, Gaver et al. (2007, pp. 538–541). There are precursors to all of this. In the humanities, this approach is called *explication du texte* or close reading. The difference is in the means: design is a material practice that aims at changing behavior through this material practice. Thus, rather than descriptive, the method is projective, done through design proposals.
28. Design and the Elastic Mind exhibit, 2008.
29. *Objectified*, 1 hour, 09 minutes, and 35 seconds – 1 hour, 10 minutes, and 03 seconds.
30. Akrich (1992) talks about the scripting and descripting that technology imposes on people.
31. As Dunne told to Parsons (2009, pp. 145–146). There are many ways to formulate this impoverishment in literature cited in this chapter. For example, existentialists like Jean-Paul Sartre would talk about bad faith, Nietzsche about slave morality, Marx about false consciousness, and Freud about neuroses. These concepts surface once in a while in design. For example, *Quali Cosi Siamo* — The Things We Are, an exhibition of Italian design curated by Alessandro Mendini for Triennale di Milano in Summer 2010, was partly based on psychoanalytic metaphors.
32. Parsons (2009, p. 145).
33. Bergström et al. (2009).
34. Seago and Dunne (1999, pp. 15–16), Dunne in *Design Interactions Yearbook* (2007, p. 8).
35. Beaver et al. (2009, pp. 110–111). The problem with staying within design and thus trivializing is pointed out by Jimmy Loizeau on p. 111.
36. Kerridge (2009, pp. 220–221). Design has been exhibited for decades. The past decade saw two developments: design was turned into art, which drove the prices of prototypes and one-offs sky high. As expected, there are already exhibitions mocking such ideology by celebrating ordinary industrial things, while simultaneously treating them as ready-mades (see Design Real, Grcic, 2010).
37. Dunne (2005) and Dunne (2005, p. 100).
38. Dunne and Raby (2001, p. 75).
39. See Dunne and Raby (2001); Routarinne and Redström (2007), Sengers and Gaver (2006), Gaver et al. (2007).
40. MoMA's exhibition Design and the Elastic Mind is a good example of the power of the curators. Critical design was only part of the exhibition, which also showed works from artists and scientists specializing in visualization and digital art.

    There are curators and critics who know the difference between art and design and take designers' reluctance to be labeled as artists seriously. The best recent example comes from Berlin's Helmrinderknecht gallery focusing on contemporary design. Sophie Lovell curated an exhibition called Freak Show: Strategies for (Dis)engagement in Design that ran in this gallery from November 13, 2010, and January 15, 2011. Exhibited was work from ten groups of designers, two of them coming from critical design. Each group challenged the prevailing ideas of design as usual, and explored ways in which design could become a life-serving force. These ways consisted of using bioengineering in James Auger and Jimmy Loizeau's work coming from Material Beliefs, and El Ultimo Grito's animalistic tables made of cardboard and artistic resin. The exhibition was a mélange of concepts, one-offs, small series products, and to-be production pieces.

41. See in particular Gaver et al. (2003, 2004).
42. Indeed, there is a market for prototypes by star designers like Philippe Starck and Ron Arad, whose prototypes may be valued at hundreds of thousands of dollars. This market is significant enough to have its own chronicler (see Lovell, 2009). To our knowledge, there is no market for design researchers' prototypes, but after institutions like MoMA have exhibited design research, the day will come when we will see research prototypes in auction houses.
43. For example, when Visual Voltage went to Berlin, the exhibition was expanded with local designers. There were events and a design research workshop around the themes of the project. See www.visualvoltage.se/.
44. For Design as Performance, see Z33 (2010); for one-offs and prototypes as art objects, see Lovell (2009); and for art exhibitions showing that industrial products are not art (*sic*), see Grcic's (2010) Design Real.
45. Anthony Dunne in *Design Interactions Yearbook* (2007, p. 10).
46. Redström (2009), pp. 10–11.
47. See Design and the Elastic Mind, *Design Interactions Yearbooks* after 2007, what Timothy Parsons (2009) says about design for debate, and Ericson et al. (2009).
48. See www.design-act.se/.
49. Bishop (2007, pp. 64–67) raised this question, suggesting that its history can be traced back to "Dada-Season" in Paris in 1921. She also suggested that relational art should somehow try to create "highly authored situations that fuse social reality with carefully calculated artifice" (p. 67). Art and by implication, design, can and perhaps even should disturb viewers, and learn from earlier avant-gardes like Dada, surrealism, or in America, Beat poetry. To promote change, one should not accuse art of mastery and egocentrism if it seeks to disturb rather than only something that emerges through consensual collaboration.

    The difficulty lies in negotiating the line between constructing a disturbance that evokes new thought models and shocking. As Grant Kester (2004, p. 12) noted in his study of dialog in art, much of the twentieth century avant-garde built on the idea that art should not so much try to communicate with the viewers, but rather seek to challenge their faith to initiate thinking. The premise was that the shared discursive systems (linguistic, visual, etc.) on which we rely for our knowledge of the world are dangerously abstract and violently objectifying. Art's role is to shock us out of this perceptual complacency, to force us to see the world anew. This shock has borne many names over the years: the sublime, alienation, effect, *l'amour fou*, and so on. In each case, the result is a kind of epiphany that lifts viewers outside the familiar boundaries of common language, existing modes of representation, and even their own sense of self. As Kester noted, recently many artists have become considerably sophisticated in defining how they work with the audience. Rather than shocking, they aim to create work that encourages people to question fixed identities and stereotypes through dialog rather than trauma. Prevailing aesthetics in such work is durational rather than immediate.

    Of course, this is the stance held by critical designers, as well as other representatives of Showroom, even though they have not been less vocal about their design tactics. The aim is to lead people to see that there are ways of thinking and being beyond what exists in the marketplace, but the way to lead people away from their habits is gentler and far less ambitious than in earlier avant-gardes that came from rougher times.

    Another problem with shocking is that contemporary art has gone to such extremes that it is increasingly difficult to shock. Shocking also leads to the problem of trivialization — something is shocking so it must be art and hence inconsequential. For good reason, critical designers try to avoid this tactic in their work as well as their discourse. A good discussion of the problems of shocking is den Hartog Jager (2003).

50. With the exception of critical designers, there are few debates in which designers study these questions. Andy Crabtree's (2003) advice is to think of technology as breaching experiments (see also Chapter 8), and Bell et al.'s (2005) argument is that designers need to make things strange to see things that are grounded in various "ethnomovements" of the 1960s, not contemporary art.

These movements argued for studying people from within, through their meanings, rather than using researchers' categories. One way to make the routine noticeable, unquestioned, and moral is to disturb and breach those routines. The reader can try this at the workplace by doing one of Harold Garfinkel's (1967) breaching experiments. Take any word people routinely use and press them to define it. Calculate how many turns it takes before people get angry at their friends, who should know what words like "day" or "flat tire" mean.

In critical design, as in contemporary art, disturbance is usually an opening into critical reflection rather than into studying the routine activities of everyday life. The difference may sound subtle, but it is essential.

51. Raby (2008, p. 65).
52. For post-critical architecture, see Mazé (2007, p. 215); for contemporary art, see Bourriaud (2002, pp. 45–46).
53. Routarinne and Redström (2007).
54. See Sengers and Gaver (2006), Gaver et al. (2007, 2008).
55. Mazé and Redström (2007), Mazé (2007).
56. See projects Slow Technology and IT + Textiles.
57. Mazé and Redström (2008, pp. 55–56).
58. See Ernevi et al. (2005).
59. First reported in Ernevi et al. (2005).
60. For Wim T. Schippers, see Boomkens (2003, p. 20).
61. For this example, and for discussion on designers using artistic tactics for photo ops, see Staal (2003, p. 144).
62. Dunne (2007, p. 10).
63. For a note on these doubts and commentaries on architect Rem Koolhaas' work, see Heynen (2003, p. 43).

7

HOW TO WORK WITH THEORY

This chapter looks at the theoretical background of constructive design research. When we look beyond individual studies, we find a few recurring theoretical sources. When we look at what inspired the selection of these sources, we see how most constructive design researchers have roots in twentieth century Continental philosophy, social science, and art. This chapter elaborates on the three methodological approaches outlined in Chapters 4–6. At the surface, the three approaches may seem like independent silos; if we go beyond the surface, we find a more common core. This shared core also explains why constructive design research differs from the rationalistic design methodologies discussed in Chapter 2.

Interaction design has inherited its methodological premises from computer science. Before that time, computers were in the hands of experts trained in rational systems development methodologies. When computers entered workplaces and homes in the 1980s, systems failed because people could not effectively use their new computers. Systems designers had a very different conceptual model of the system from the workers who used these systems to complete tasks.[1] Software developers turned to cognitive psychology for a solution: the driving design mantras became "ease of use" and "user friendly."

However, many products failed because they did not do what the users wanted or even needed them to do: no amount of massaging the details of the interface could address the fact that computers were often doing the wrong thing. First, the key notion of "task" tied it to behaviors and practices that exist but did not assist designers in imagining what should be. Second, there was a false universalistic belief that all people are the same, and it would be possible to find an optimal interaction solution that would persist forever. Third, this theoretical perspective implied that theory should guide design, which was a hard sell to designers.[2]

For reasons like these, new ways to bring research into design were needed.[3] There was a need to bring experimentation and "craft" into design research to more effectively imagine what could and should be. Researchers in the emerging field of interaction design turned away from cognition to post-Cartesian thinking: phenomenology, pragmatism, interactionism, and many strands of avant-garde art that connected designers to things like psychoanalysis and existentialism. These philosophies provided consistency and direction but encouraged exploration rather than prediction.[4] They encouraged using judgment and non-symbolic forms of intelligence. They also placed design in the center of research and saw theory as explication that comes after design. Finally, this turn connected design to the human and social sciences that had gone though a "linguistic turn" and "interpretive turn" two decades earlier.[5]

7.1 Acting in the World

In his inaugural lecture at Technische Universiteit Eindhoven, Kees Overbeeke, leader of the Designing Quality Interaction research group, argued that design researchers overrate cognitive skills. His lecture told how dissatisfaction with cognitive psychology drove him to J.J. Gibson's ecological psychology and more recently to phenomenological psychology and pragmatic philosophy.[6] His change of mind brought about an interest in people's perceptual-motor, emotional, and social skills.

> *Meaning ... emerges in interaction. Gibson's theory resulted from a long line of "new" thinking in Western philosophy, i.e., Phenomenology (Merleau-Ponty, Heidegger) and American Pragmatism (James, Dewey).... All these authors stress the importance of "acting-in-the-world," or reflection being essentially reflection-in-action.*[7]

In Overbeeke's vision, engineering and design join theorists in the humanities and the social and behavioral sciences. In these fields, researchers have grown disillusioned with studying people as mechanisms that can be manipulated and measured.

Showroom has followed a similar course, but it draws from a still wider swath of theory. In addition to philosophy, psychology, and the social sciences, Showroom also builds on art and design. Anthony Dunne's *Hertzian Tales* can be seen as a primary text for Showroom.[8] It offers a mesh of intersecting theories that is similar to the humanities of the 1990s. This text borrows from theories of post-modern consumption, phenomenology, French epistemology and semiotics, and product semantics. It also borrows from pragmatist philosophy, critical theory, and studies of material culture.[9] Italian *controdesign*, another important inspiration to critical design, built on post-war political sociology, urban studies, semiotics, and philosophy, as well as on futurists,

Dada, surrealism, and pop art. There are few scattered references to scientific psychology in *Hertzian Tales*, but scientific literature is simply yet another inspiration for design.

Field has arrived at the same destination by following a different route. Field researchers typically build on symbolic interactionism, symbolic anthropology, ethnomethodology, and Bruno Latour's actor-network theory rather than philosophy. However, when seen in the context of twentieth century thinking, there are significant affinities to Lab and Showroom. For example, the symbolic interactionism movements came to Chicago in the first part of the twentieth century, and its founding fathers listened to the lectures of pragmatists like John Dewey and George Herbert Mead. These two movements have clearly been conceived in the same intellectual climate.[10] A similar argument applies to ethnomethodology. It has roots in sociological theory, not philosophy, but it shares many similarities with phenomenology.[11]

These post-Cartesian philosophies gained more currency in the last three decades of the twentieth century; first in the humanities, then in the social sciences, and more recently in technical fields. By building on these traditions, designers are able to respond to more design challenges than by building on rationalistic and cognitive models only. These traditions have led constructive design researchers to see cognitive psychology and rationalistic design methodologies as special cases of a far larger palette of human existence. Seen through this prism, an attempt to see humans as information processing machines is not wrong, only a small part of the story. Research has become interdisciplinary, with ingredients from design and technology, and also psychology, the social sciences, and the humanities.[12]

7.2 Lab: From Semantic Perception to Direct Action

As the earlier quote from Overbeeke's inaugural lecture showed, recent work in Lab is interested in action and the body rather than thinking and knowing. Thinking and knowing are studied but from within action. Cognitive psychology has been pushed to the background; in the foreground are Gibson's ecological psychology and recently, phenomenological philosophy.[13] Eindhoven's Philip Ross makes a useful contrast between cognitive and ecological psychology and explains how they lead to different design approaches:

> *The semantic approach relies on the basic idea that we use our knowledge and experience to interpret the symbols and signs of*

> *products.... Products use metaphors in which the functionality and expression of the new product is compared to an existing concept or product that the user is familiar with. Emoticons in instant messenger applications are examples of emotionally expressive semantic interaction in the domain of on screen interaction.*
>
> *The direct approach is action based. It is inspired by Gibson's perception theory, which states that meaning is created through the interaction between person and the world.... Perception is action, which reminds us of the phenomenological concept of technological mediation.... It seems plausible that a device designed from the direct approach, which allows a person to actively create his own expression, would allow more emotional involvement. This approach would thus more likely allow a person to be meaningfully engaged with the activity of emotional self-expression and evoke an enchanting experience rather than a device that offers pre-created expressions.*[14]

While traditional user interface design works with symbols and proceeds to use through knowledge, research on tangible interaction focuses on how people interact with physical objects. The direct approach begins with action and proceeds to use through tangible interfaces and seeks design inspiration from action. Designers need to identify patterns of action that feed users forward naturally without a need to stop and think, which requires cognitive effort (Figure 7.1).

Philip Ross' work illustrates how the direct approach can be turned into a design tool. While ethics is usually the realm of the clergy and philosophers, Ross turned ethics into a source of inspiration. Nine designer/researchers from industry and academia convened around this challenge for a one-day workshop at the Technische Universiteit Eindhoven in the Netherlands.[16] The participants first learned about five ethical systems, Confucianism, Kantian rationalism, vitalism, romanticism, and

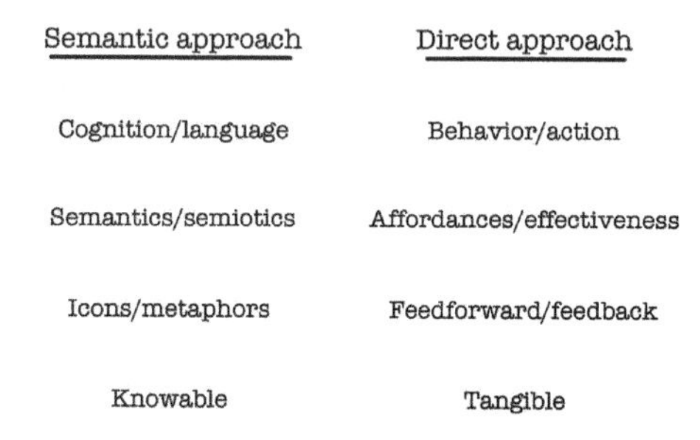

Figure 7.1 Two approaches used to create meaning in interaction design.[15]

Nietzschean ethics. They were then broken into three groups, and each group was given the task of building two functionally similar products that had to be based on two different ethical perspectives.

For example, one team was assigned the challenge of making two candy vending machines, one embodying Kantian ethics and the other embodying romanticism. They describe the "Kantian" machine in the following way:

> *The "Kantian" machine presents itself through a split panel with buttons and sliders.... On the left side of the panel, a person "constitutes" candy by setting parameters like for example the amount of protein, carbon and fat.... After adjusting the parameters, the machine advises a person to proceed or not, depending on his or her fat index.... After weighing the advice, the person proceeds to the right side of the panel. The machine asks for a credit card and determines whether the buyer's financial situation allows the purchase. If so, the machine deposits a round piece of candy with the requested constitution in the slot on the bottom right.*[17]

The Romantic machine, in contrast, displays dramatic emotions and incorporates elegant, grand gestures to treat people as sensuous beings. Its form language was non-utilitarian, it unleashed sugary aromas, it built anticipation through a slowed delivery of the desired product while using dramatic movements, and it required dramatic gestures before it accepted payment. While it is easy to see connections to the Kantian machine in many of the products and services people interact with every day, traces of the Romantic machine are harder to find. These romantic interactions, however, flourish in luxury spas, cruise ships, restaurants, and amusement parks (Figure 7.2).

As these workshops demonstrate, lab researchers in Eindhoven have turned away from semantics and symbols to direct action and beyond. They showed how design researchers can draw on highly abstract philosophy to spot design opportunities and process them into systems and objects. This work also asks a number of questions about implicit values in design, such as the hidden Kantian assumptions in so many products.

7.3 Field: You Cannot Live Alone

The approach of researchers in the field builds on theories of social interaction from psychology, sociology, and anthropology. This shift leads to a significant change in design. Cognitive psychology focused on the thinking process of an individual, and

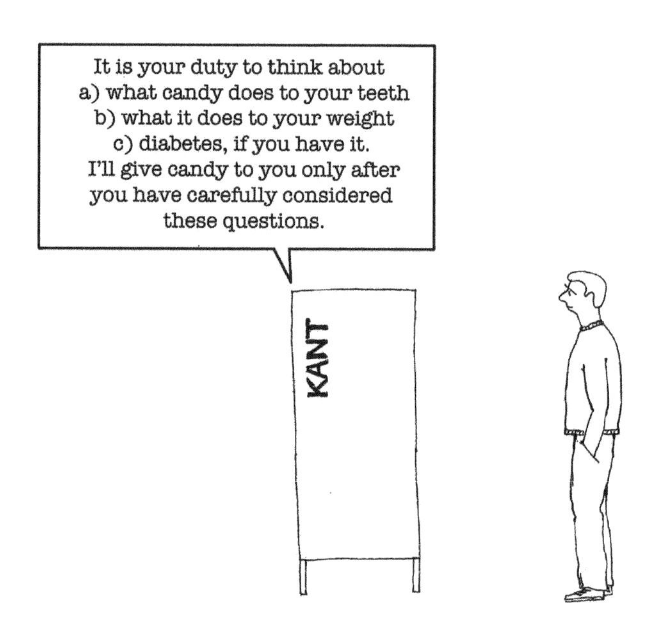

Figure 7.2 Duty-conscious candy machine, inspired by Philip Ross.

this was also true of Gibson's ecological psychology and Merleau-Ponty's phenomenology.[18] When field researchers began to study social action, they provided an important remedy for this individualistic tendency. People listen to other people, influence them, pay attention to things others see as important, and mold their opinions on things like ethics based on these social influences. Neglecting this social substratum is a risk for any ambitious researcher.

Designers and design researchers have always been able to bring social context into design. Many work with scenarios and storyboards that bring the context and the stories of people back into the ideation process. Interaction designers, in particular, have always worked this way. Their goal is to define the behavior of a product — generally a sequence of action and reaction that can best be captured in a narrative structure. They create characters who live in the context of use, and then they generate many stories about these characters in order to imagine new products and product behaviors that improve the characters' lives. Over the past few years, interaction design has increasingly focused on the social aspects of interaction: how products and services mediate communication between people.[19] However, unless these narrative methods are grounded in real data, they easily reflect only the wants and preferences of researchers. At worst, they become just devices of persuasion.

In contrast, field researchers have built on many kinds of sociological and anthropological theories to study people properly.

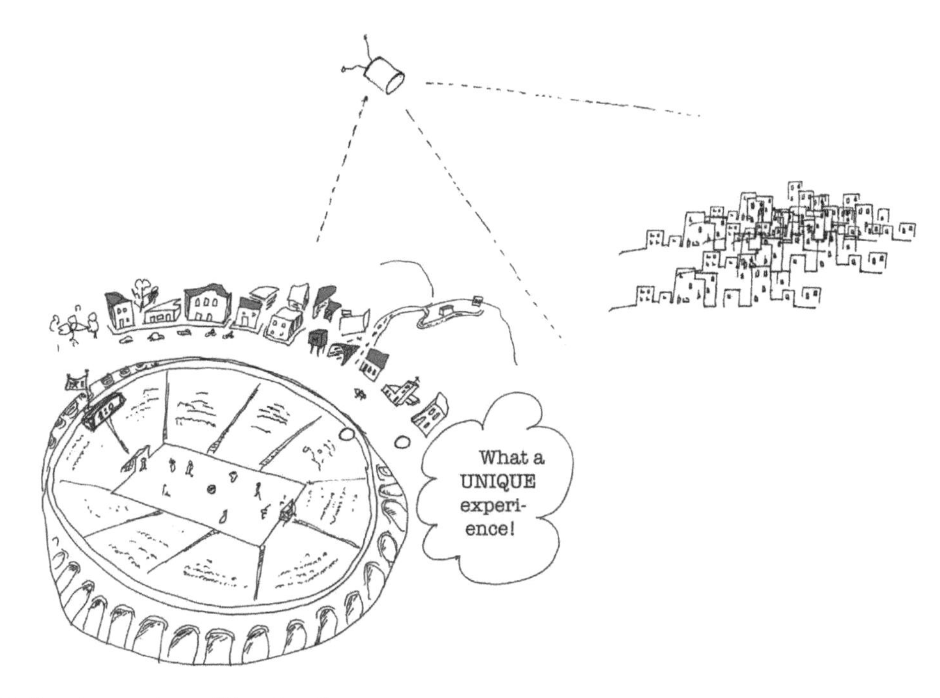

Figure 7.3 People experience things together.

The most popular theories in the field approach have come from symbolic interactionism, ethnomethodology, and symbolic anthropology. Interactionists describe how people define situations in order to take action, while ethnomethodologists describe "folk methods" (ingrained scripts of social behaviors) people use in organizing their activities.[20] Symbolic anthropologists, on the other hand, study how large systems of meaning play a part in what people do and how they think. Examples of such large systems are religion and beliefs about family (Figure 7.3).

One example of interactionist thinking is Battarbee's work on user experience as a social process.[21] Her work builds on the pragmatist look (from Jodi Forlizzi and Shannon Ford) on how some things become noticeable and memorable. People bring emotions, values, and cognitive models into hearing, seeing, touching, and interpreting the influence of artifacts. Social, cultural, and organizational behavior patterns shape how things are picked up from "subconscious" experience.[22] In contrast to the work of Forlizzi and Ford, for Battarbee, experience is a social process — hence, "co-experience" — for Battarbee. When people interact, they bring attention to issues, insights, and observations. In paying attention to things, and people make these things noticeable and sometimes memorable. Some things, on the other hand, are forgotten and pushed into the background.

Battarbee constructed her thinking during research on mobile multimedia. The path from a mere background possibility to an experience is social. She showed how communication technology can mediate this process. She investigated mobile multimedia in a real social context, focused on actual messages, and observed how people together pick up things and push them away from attention. Her work linked field observations with social theory. She also showed how designers can use these theories to generate design insights for new multimedia services.

Symbolic interactionism and ethnomethodology have their roots in sociology, but both traditions are distant relatives to the same philosophical traditions from which Lab seeks inspiration. Namely, symbolic interactionism came of age in the years between the World Wars in Chicago where an intellectual milieu shaped by the pragmatist John Dewey and the social behaviorist George Herbert Mead was created, and ethnomethodology had many affinities with phenomenology. It is important to understand, however, that these writers are not forefathers of these sociological traditions, which built on many other strands of thinking.

7.4 Showroom: Design and Culture Under Attack

Critical design focuses its attention on even larger things in society than field researchers. Its target of criticism is the way in which design supports consumer culture. Critical designers do not specify who they specifically blame and do not offer an alternative lifestyle. In this sense, research artifacts produced by critical designers are laden with many kinds of assumptions; viewers have to rely on their own background of culture, arts, and design to understand it. They have to make connections between the many theoretical perspectives at play to construct a rich understanding of this work.

In the preface to *Hertzian Tales*, Anthony Dunne told how "design can be used as a critical medium for reflecting on the cultural, social, and ethical impact of technology."[23] The basic objects of criticism are commercially motivated and human factor driven approaches at work in electronics; it is these electronics most people assimilate into their lives without thinking about how these objects shape their lives. In the preface to the 2004 edition of *Hertzian Tales*, Dunne looks back at 1999 when the book first appeared in print. He noted that little had changed in the design of electronics despite many calls for more creativity:

> *It is interesting to look back and think about the technological developments since [1999]. Bluetooth, 3G phones, and wi-fi are*

now part of everyday life. The dot-com boom has come and gone.... Yet very little has changed in the world of design. Electronic technologies are still dealt with on a purely aesthetic level. There are some exceptions, of course ... but still, something is missing. Design is not engaging with the social, cultural, and ethical implications of the technologies it makes so sexy and consumable.[24]

The critical design method builds prototypes and other artifacts based on "familiar images and clichés rather than stretching design language."[25] These designers investigate the metaphysics, poetry, and aesthetics of everyday objects to create designs that are strange and invite people to reflect on these qualities.[26]

The most difficult challenges for designers of electronic objects now lie not in technical and semiotic functionality, where optimal levels of performance are already attainable, but in the realms of metaphysics, poetry and aesthetics, where little research has been carried out.[27]

Clearly, this is an attack against the prevailing culture of design. But who are the "designers" under attack?

The answer lies in the theoretical background of critical design. As noted earlier, critical design builds on a wide array of sources. The main theoretical roots of critical design, however, can be found from twentieth century philosophy, humanities, and the social sciences. The original formulations of critical design borrowed heavily from post-structuralism, critical theory, post-Marxist interpretations of the material world, Italian radical design, and many kinds of avant-garde and contemporary art.[28] Some of the key targets of these writers were consumption, art, and everyday life. In particular, the all-pervasive media continually bombards people with images of art for commercial and political purposes. This seemingly endless cascade of images and sounds re-shapes people's desires, and it changes the processes and motives for the products and services that are made.[29] If designers build on this language of consumptive desire without trying to redirect it, they function like Hollywood film studios, looking for blockbusters and lucrative product tie-ins (Figure 7.4).

Such a culture of design goes beyond individuals and design institutions. For this reason, it makes little sense to directly criticize individual designers, design schools, or design firms. The proper place for criticism is language and visual culture, not any particular designer. To make critique meaningful, it has to be directed at what makes this culture possible — otherwise it becomes trapped within the same discourse. As always, stepping out of this culture is impossible. However, it is possible to work from within and create designs that extend the clichés and easy seductions into mainstream design.

Figure 7.4 Against men in brown suits doing design-as-usual.

There is considerable theoretical depth in critical design. The target of criticism is the very culture of design-as-usual. No one in particular is to blame: it is the background that makes this culture possible that needs to be questioned. Again, this is a premise that comes from Continental thinking.[30] Post-structuralists like Jean Baudrillard taught critical designers to focus on gaps in design practice, to seek ways to break it one small piece at a time. Practices like design are human achievements, but we tend to take them for granted, regardless of their historical character. Indeed, why not treat design the same way as philosophers Jacques Derrida treated literature and Michel Foucault treated the history of sexuality? Although theoretical references have largely dropped from critical design over its 15 years of existence, this background is still evident in its practices, aims, and critical ethos.

7.5 Frameworks and Theories

A rich array of theory gives constructive design research plenty of depth. It helps to raise interesting questions about ethics in design. It helps to see things like social interaction. It creates connections to other disciplines and forms of culture, deepening research and design. Finally, it also gives research consistency and a possibility to argue.

The question, then, is not whether theory is useful, but how should it be used. Design is not a theoretical discipline. Designers are trained to do things and are held accountable for producing stuff, to paraphrase the title of Harvey Molotch's book on design.[31] Designers are not trained to do product concepts and theories, nor are they held accountable for producing these abstract things. With few possible exceptions, design researchers have produced little theory that is used in other disciplines.[32]

To see how constructive design researchers use theory, it is useful to start from the frontline of research. The first frontline is design. In this book, we have seen several designs from product-like designs Home Health Horoscope and Erratic Radio. We have also seen artistic works like Symbiots. There are also service prototypes like Nutrire Milano and public interest prototypes like Vila Rosário. Researchers put most of their effort into developing designs and prototypes.

Also frontline are the frameworks that are generalized from these designs, such as Jodi Forlizzi's product ecology, Caroline Hummels' resonant interaction, and Katja Battarbee's co-experience.[33] Typically, these frameworks are reflections that come after designs. Their ingredients are theories, debates, and the design process. If design researchers want to contribute to theory, this is where they place their effort. Also, this is where constructive design researchers contribute to human knowledge at large. The best way to learn about how people interact with tangible technology is to read research coming from places like Eindhoven, Delft, and Carnegie Mellon University. The best way to see how to design large-scale services is to read work coming from Milan.

Even more abstract theoretical thinking keeps research programs going for years, creating consistency behind designs and frameworks. For example, J.J. Gibson's ecological psychology has been a constant source of inspiration in Eindhoven. To see how Tom Djajadiningrat's cubby, Stephan Wensveen's interaction frogger, Joep Frens' rich interaction, and Andres Lucero's intuitive interaction are related, it is necessary to read Gibson.[34] Symbolic interactionism has played a similar role in Helsinki, and situationism and *controdesign* in London. These references are abstract and as such, difficult to turn into design. Typically, they appear only in theoretical sections of doctoral theses and occasionally in conference papers. Constructive design researchers build on them but practically never hope to add to this knowledge. Martin Ludvigsen's collective action framework is built on Erving Goffman's sociology, but Goffman's theory is in no way tested by Ludvigsen.[35]

Explicit references to theory typically stop here. However, people like Gibson and the situationists have had their predecessors. Tracing back to these predecessors connects constructive design research with the most important philosophical and artistic movements of the twentieth century. These movements include phenomenology, pragmatism, Ludwig Wittgenstein's late philosophy, and also several artistic movements like Dada and surrealism, and through these, to existentialism and psychoanalysis. For

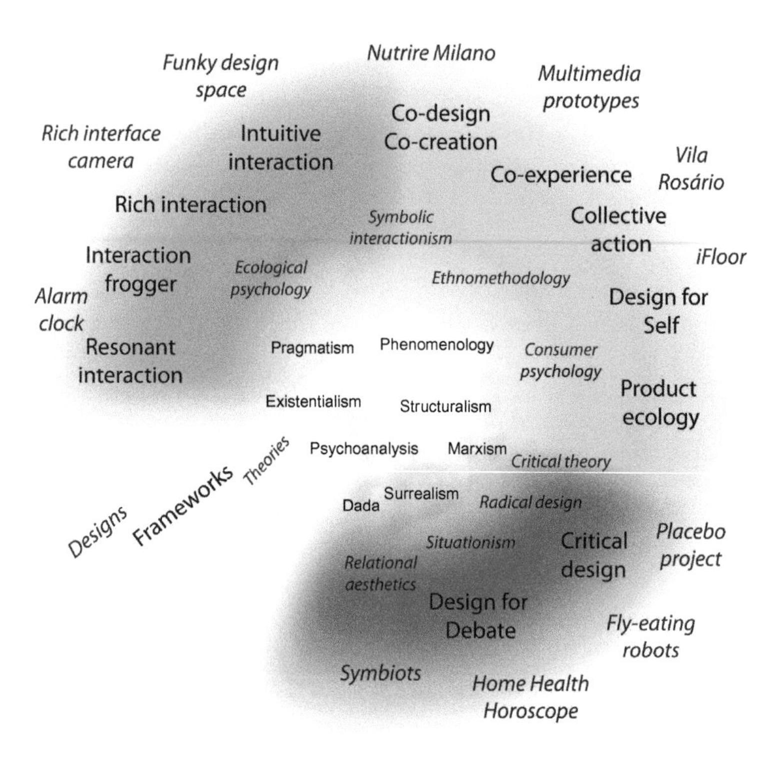

Figure 7.5 Designs, frameworks, theories, and philosophies.

example, in Field, these movements go back to pragmatism and phenomenology, and in Showroom to psychoanalysis, structuralism, and phenomenology (Figure 7.5).

In actual research, these philosophies and artistic movements remain in the background. Typically, only senior professors know the whole gamut. Even they seldom go to theoretical and philosophical discussions, and always cautiously, when rethinking something at the very foundation of the program. Knowing that some issues can be left to senior researchers makes life easier for younger researchers. Also, there are few direct links between philosophical and artistic thinking and actual designs. Going all the way to philosophy may even distract researchers. If a researcher wakes up every morning thinking that he must make a theoretical breakthrough, he fails, daily. There is no specificity in design research if it only focuses on philosophy: theoretical work is valuable but so is design and the creation of frameworks.

Although it may seem that constructive design researchers all have their own agenda, they converge at many points. Post-Cartesian philosophical and artistic approaches provide space for investigating materials, issues, and topics.[36] Among these issues and topics are things like the body, social action, or those unquestioned assumptions about "normality" that critical designers question.[37] Perhaps most important, these background philosophies and artistic traditions open doors for putting design into the center of research. Theory has a role in explicating why design works, but it does not tell how to create good design. This background, finally, explains why current constructive research looks so different from the rationalism of the 1960s — it comes from a different mental landscape.

End Notes

1. One of the most important voices in design at this time was the cognitive psychologist Don Norman, one of the early user interface researchers at Apple. In his view, human action proceeds in a cycle where people set goals, transform these goals into intentions and plans, and then execute these plans against a system. Following an action, people observe feedback from the system to assess how their actions change the circumstances; they evaluate whether their action advanced them toward their goal. In this classic feedback model, with a basis in information theory and cybernetics, humans functioned as information processors. To operationalize this model, interface designers needed to think about how a system could communicate its capabilities in a way that helps users generate appropriate plans, and they needed to provide feedback that clearly communicated how an action advanced a user toward a goal (Norman, 1988, pp. 46–49).
2. However, as John Carroll noted, this is not how human–computer interaction (HCI) or interaction design actually works. He described how the *thing* often precedes the theory (Carroll and Kellogg, 1989). Direct manipulation interfaces, as an advance to command line interfaces, appeared roughly 20 years before Schneiderman (1983) detailed the cognitive theory describing why this works. Xerox created the mouse as a pointing device before Stu Card performed the cognitive experiments that demonstrated this as an optimal pointing solution (Card et al., 1978). Bill Moggridge (2006, p. 39) relates that:

   > *Stu joined Xerox PARC in 1974, with probably the first-ever degree in human-computer interaction. Doug Engelbart and Bill English had brought the mouse to PARC from SRI, and Stu was assigned to help with the experiments that allowed them to understand the underlying science of the performance of input devices.*

   Examples of earlier direct manipulation interfaces were NLS (oNLine System), which was an experimental workstation design including a mouse and standard keyboard, and a five-key control box used to control information presentation. On December 9, 1968, Douglas C. Engelbart and the group of 17 researchers working with him in the Augmentation Research Center at Stanford Research Institute in Menlo Park, CA, presented a 90-minute live public demonstration of the online system, NLS, they had been working on since 1962. An earlier example is Ivan Sutherland's Sketchpad, which was one of the first CAD-like programs. It laid out the idea of objects and object-oriented programming. It was about touching "things" on the screen and motivated the development of NLS. As this history tells, theory came after the fact.

   Finally, it was increasingly clear that social aspects of work, including context and culture, play a significant role in how people use technology.

3. These frameworks, sometimes referred to as Design Languages (Rheinfrank and Evenson, 1996), attempted to explicitly document interaction conventions so other designers could more easily pick up and apply to their own designs. While similar to Christopher Alexander's (1968) concept of pattern languages, these were intentionally constructed conventions, not conventions arising from the longer process of social discourse between designers and users. They were similar to corporate style guides for printed/branded materials found in communication design, but they needed considerably more flexibility to allow for unanticipated future actions. Probably the best known of these frameworks was Apple's Macintosh Human Interface Guidelines. This was an early type of intentional design theory to emerge from the process of making new products and services.
4. The most important historical precursors came from the 1980s. Key writers in America were philosopher Hubert Dreyfus (1992), computer scientist Terry Winograd (Winograd and Flores, 1987; Winograd, 1996), and the social psychologist Donald Schön. In Europe, a similar push came from participatory designers (see Ehn, 1988a) and from Italians like Carlo Cipolla. For more contemporary criticisms and accounts, see Dorst (1997), Gedenryd (1998), and Dourish (2002).
5. Rorty (1967), Rabinow and Sullivan (1979). It is interesting to note that for many main proponents of rationalism like Simon, this philosophical critique was barely more than a form of religion, and therefore not worth replying to. Hunter Crowther-Heyck (2005, pp. 28–29 and 342, note 54) wrote in her biography of Herbert Simon how Simon, always eager to defend his views, had a prophet's difficulty in understanding why some people did not get his message: "He wrote many a reply to his critics within political science, economics, and psychology, but he never directly addressed humanist critics of artificial intelligence, such as Hubert Dreyfus and Joseph Weizenbaum because 'You don't get very far arguing with a man about his religion, and these are essentially religious issues to the Dreyfuses and Weizenbaums of the world,'" as he wrote in his private letters.
6. Interestingly, Norman sits in a pivotal position when it comes to the post-Cartesian turn. His scientific reputation was based in cognitive science, but he also popularized the notion of "affordance" from Gibson's ecological psychology through his 1988 book on design. Admittedly, he interpreted Gibson through cognition, talking about "perceived affordances" rather than direct perception, as Djajadiningrat (1998, p. 32) and Djajadiningrat et al. (2002) have argued.
7. Overbeeke (2007, p. 7).
8. Dunne (2005).
9. The main theorists were Jean Baudrillard in post-modernism and consumption, Paul Virilio in phenomenology, Gaston Bachelard in epistemology, Roland Barthes in semiotics, Klaus Krippendorff in product semantics, George Herbert Mead and John Dewey in pragmatism, Herbert Marcuse and Theodor Adorno in critical theory, and Arjun Appadurai and Daniel Miller in empirical research on material culture.
10. Joas (1983).
11. Dourish (2002); for ethnomethodology, see Lynch (1993).
12. Dourish (2002).
13. Djajadiningrat (1998); Djajadiningrat et al. (2002).
14. Ross et al. (2008, p. 361).
15. Djajadiningrat et al. (2002, p. 286).
16. Ross et al. (2008).

17. Ross et al. (2008, pp. 364–365). This simple workshop shows that many of the systems we engage in today channel Kant's strict, protestant, rationalistic ethic based on the idea of duty. Today you can even witness an increasing number of mobile applications that follow this line of thinking, helping people to track the details of their consumption including fat, carbohydrates, protein, etc. You can also see mobile tools like www.mint.com, which monitors electronic purchases, tracks personal finances, and visualizes how this impacts a user's explicitly set saving goals. It is not hard to then imagine a machine that begins to integrate these two streams and functions as a decision support tool in the way the workshop designers imagined.
18. For example, Lynch (1993, pp. 128–129).
19. Forlizzi (2007).
20. Ethnomethodologists talk about "ethnomethods," meaning those methodic procedures people use to organize their ordinary activities. The classic statement is Garfinkel (1967); a particularly clear exposition is Livingston (1987).
21. Battarbee (2004); Battarbee and Koskinen (2004).
22. Forlizzi and Ford (2000, p. 420).
23. Forlizzi and Ford (2000, p. 420).
24. Dunne (2004, p. xi).
25. Dunne (2005, p. 30).
26. *Hertzian Tales* distinguishes several classes of objects. "Post-optimal objects" provide people with new experiences of everyday life; "parafunctional" questions the link between prevailing aesthetics and functionality; while "infra-ordinary" objects to change concepts and probes how designers could author new behavioral and narrative opportunities. See Dunne (2005, p. 20).
27. Dunne (2005, p. 20).
28. This is not to imply that critical design is somehow Marxist. Dunne (2005, p. 83) distanced himself from Marxism and wrote: "Many issues touched on here, such as … the need for art to resist easy assimilation, overlap with those already addressed by the Frankfurt School and others…. The similarities between these issues and those addressed by Marxist approaches to aesthetics do not imply an identification with Marxism but are the result of seeing design as having value outside the marketplace — an alternative to fine art."
29. As the situationists noted, this mediascape is pervasive enough to be taken for reality (Debord, 2002). This was later one of the pet ideas of French philosopher Jean Baudrillard. As Chapter 6 showed, the situationists are particularly relevant to design through the early days of critical design and also to HCI through Bill Gaver's work.
30. In particular, Roland Barthes and Michel Foucault. This book is not a place to open conversation about their *oeuvre*. Readers are encouraged to read their original work.
31. Molotch (2003).
32. Leading candidates for such theorists are Tomás Maldonado and Klaus Krippendorff.
33. Forlizzi (2007), Hummels (2000), Battarbee (2004).
34. Djajadiningrat (1998), Wensveen (2004), Frens (2006a), Lucero (2009).
35. Ludvigsen (2006).
36. Including the leading writers from Ulm, like Otl Aicher (2009) and Tomás Maldonado (1972).
37. For example, see Overbeeke and Wensveen (2003, p. 96).

8

DESIGN THINGS: MODELS, SCENARIOS, PROTOTYPES

The Swedish computer scientist Pelle Ehn recently argued that design is "thinging."[1] This sounds mysterious, but the bottom line is that he describes a down-to-earth approach to design. It is his latest attempt to explain why designers get far better results with rough cardboard computers than using sophisticated systematic methods like flowcharts and simultaneous equations. In Ehn's opinion, the reason for the success of these rough "things" was that they brought people to the same table and created a language everyone could share.[2] Design things populate design studios and fieldwork. They range from quick black-and-white sketches on any piece of paper all the way to those skillfully finished prototypes that researchers construct in places like Eindhoven and London.[3]

The key point Ehn makes is that these things play an important role in keeping people focused on design. His argument is etymological. The English word "thing" has Germanic roots. This root is the word *ting*, which in Scandinavian languages still means an "assembly," where people gather to make decisions about the future of the community. If we accept an etymological argument like this, design things are like town hall meetings: places where people gather to decide collectively where to go.[4]

Design things are indispensable tools for transforming designers' intuitions, hunches, and small discoveries into something that stays — for instance, a prototype, product, or system.[5] They provide the means for sketching, analyzing, and clarifying ideas as well as for mediating ideas and persuading others.[6] In Bruno Latour's philosophical language, design things turn weak hunches into stronger claims. They also translate many types of interests into joined strongholds and provide tools that take design from short to long networks.[7] This ability to gather people to talk and debate without any command of special skills is what is needed to work with systems design methods. Flow diagrams and other rationalistic tools cut too many parties out from design, creating a caste system. Understanding these forms requires training, and the mere use of these tools tells non-experts to stay away (Figure 8.1).[8]

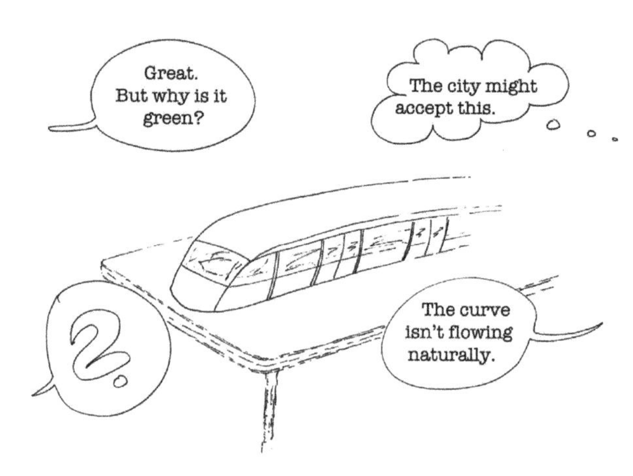

Figure 8.1 Design things bring people together and make conversation concrete.

Most writing about modeling and prototyping in design has been about the construction, technical qualities, and functions of prototypes and has typically tried to classify prototypes and other expressions by their function, technology, or place in the design process.[9] In contrast, writers like Ehn give a theoretical and philosophical grounding on design things and shift attention to what designers do with them.[10] To understand design properly, we need to look at design things in research practice.

8.1 User Research with Imagination

Many methods in constructive design research are immediately familiar to any social scientist, psychologist, or engineer. Researchers collect data at various phases of the design research process by doing interviews, making observations, administering questionnaires, and collecting many types of documents using textbooks from more established disciplines.[11] If there is something specific in how designers gather data, it is their frequent reliance on cameras and videos for data collection.[12] Another difference is that designers are not usually afraid of influencing people they study; they do not try to be flies on the wall.

More significant differences, however, go back to the imaginary nature of design. Designers are expected to imagine new things, not to study what exists today. In ordinary life, people are inventive but within the bounds of everyday life.[13] To get people into a more creative mood, constructive design researchers use several techniques that differentiate them from the social sciences. One technique is vocabulary, which often fails at crucial moments. Few people have an extensive vocabulary for describing things such as materials, colors, shapes, spaces, and other

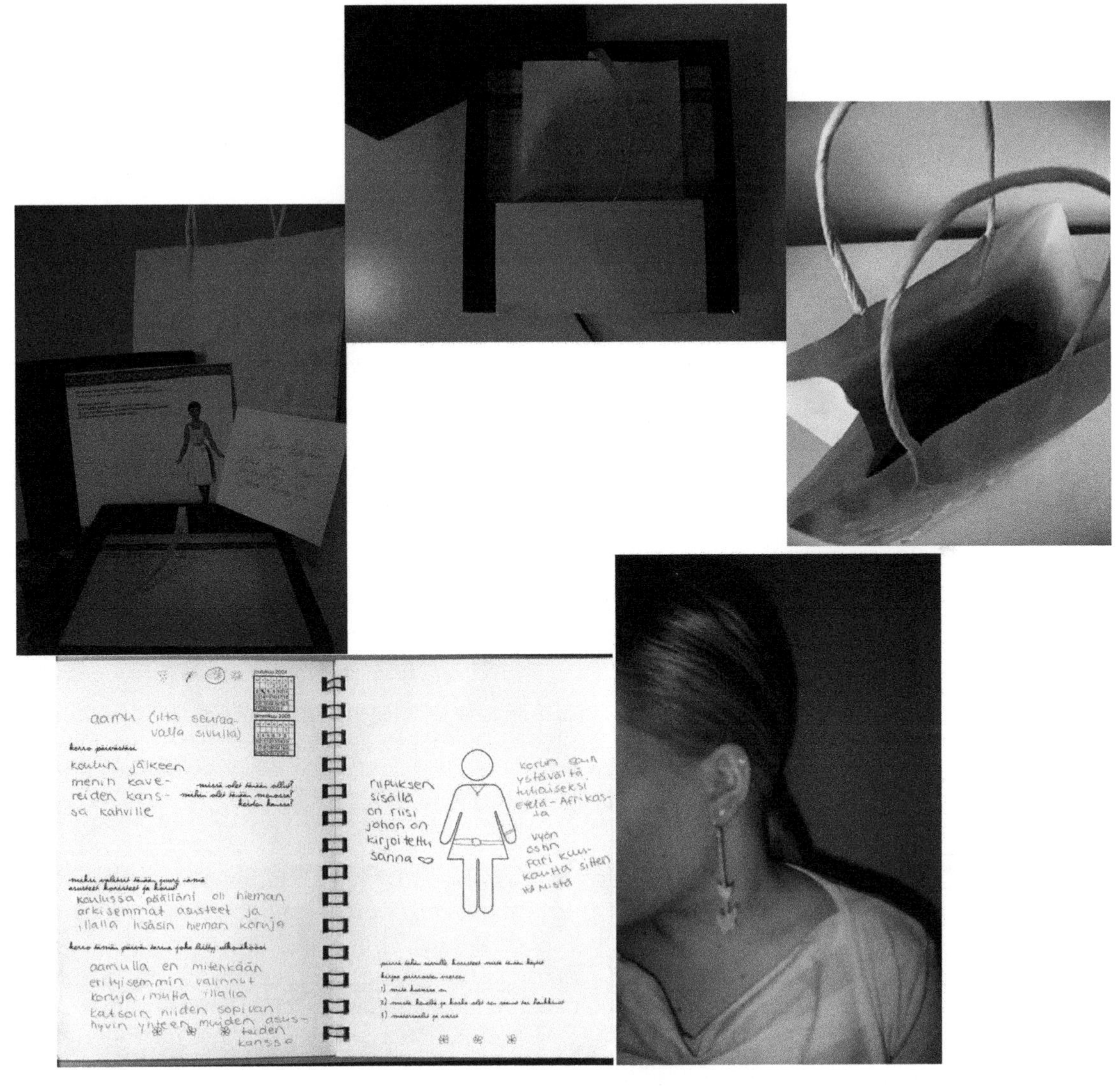

Figure 8.2 Probes and probe returns from a study of women's jewelry in Chicago (2009) and girl's jewelry in Helsinki (2006). (Pictures courtesy of Petra Ahde-Deal.)

things of immediate interest to designers. Designers have to find ways to make people imagine.

These inventive methods are heavily indebted to design practice; they try "stretching" the context rather than describing it in detail. With these methods, researchers try to get at "poetic" aspects of life: things that exist in imagination only or are unique. Among well-known examples are cultural probes and Make Tools that are routinely used in constructive design research (Figures 8.2 and 8.3).[14]

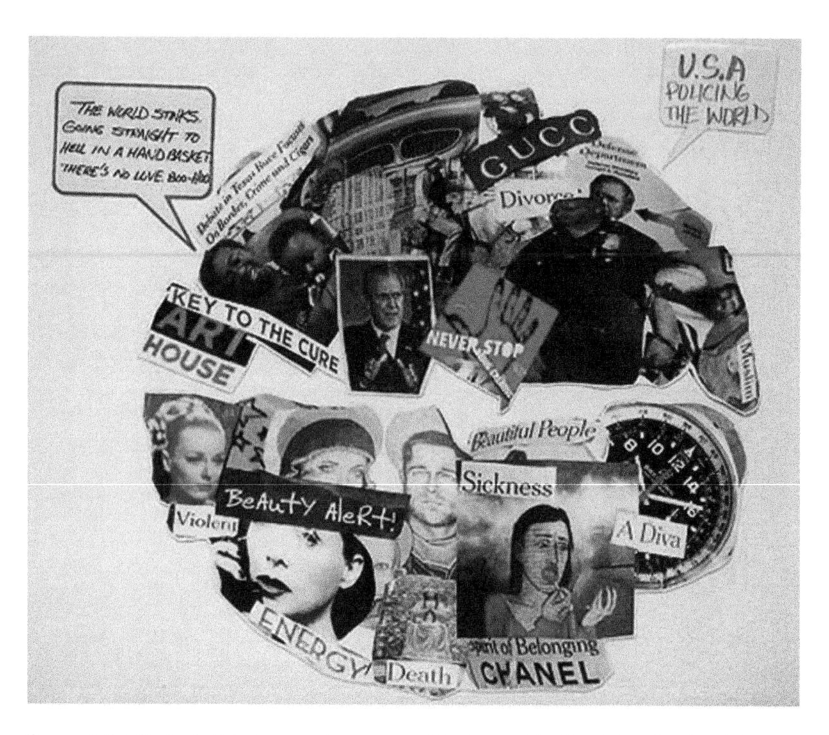

Figure 8.3 "Globe": this is a probe returned to Super Studio at Art Center College of Design, Pasadena, CA. This one collects adult and teen interpretations of what Earth would say to humans, if it could talk. Students: Yee Chan and Serra Semi. (Picture courtesy of Ilpo Koskinen).

For example, in a probe study in Pasadena in 2006, people were given empty globes and were asked questions like what Earth would say if it could talk. They did this by gluing clips from the *New York Times* on the globe.[15] Make Tools, on the other hand, were developed to capture people's imagination about how they make things rather than what they say or do. Make Tools were created to complement marketing research based on what people say in interviews and ethnography based on observations of what people do.[16] This logic also applies to many other methodologies, such as "magic things," which are used to capture sparks of imagination in those fleeting moments of life that usually disappear before anything valuable emerges (Figure 8.4).[17]

Also, designers regularly use things that force them to experience firsthand what it means to, say, have blurred vision, problems in hearing, or arthritis.[18] In the most extreme cases, researchers may even "go into a role" to see how people respond to old age, disease, and sickness. Here they follow the example of designers like Patricia Moore. Such firsthand knowledge is a way to gain empathy, sensitivity, and the ability to spot problems and identify opportunities.

Figure 8.4 Make Tools in design research. The toolkit is shown in the upper left corner. Then two seniors and one child are shown using Make Tools and imagining design solutions together with one user. (Pictures courtesy of Salu Ylirisku and Tuuli Mattelmäki.)

8.2 Gaining Firsthand Insights in the Studio

This lively imagined world has to be brought into the studio. The aim is to get firsthand insights into how people experience their environment.[19] Things like space, proportions, distances, weight, and proximity need to be made concrete so they can be discussed within the design group. For design researchers, this context has to be at their fingertips, not just in their minds: they have to be able to touch it and play with it.[20]

Studios are built to function as knowledge environments—a phrase designer Lisa Nugent used to describe research-oriented studio spaces.[21] There are several reasons for building knowledge environments and doing interpretation in workshops in these environments. First, they test ideas. Things that survive

Figure 8.5 Working in a knowledge environment in Pasadena. Here Yee Chan, Sean Donahue, and Lisa Nugent discuss observations about Angelinos' relationship to nature. (Picture courtesy of Ilpo Koskinen, 2006.)

these workshops are certainly robust because they are tested not only in talk but also through more rich bodily, social, and playful imagination. Second, they help to create joint understanding. They have an intensity that drives curiosity and creates a sense of accomplishment. This work often leads to rewriting research questions. Informed by field data, researchers are able to spot opportunities far better than before. In this early phase, researchers typically also start to create first design concepts (Figures 8.5 and 8.6).

Researchers typically play with these design concepts to gain insight into how people would experience them. Well-known practices are bodystorms, acting out scenarios, and role-plays in which participants switch roles to understand data from many points of view.

An iconic example comes from IDEO, in which bodystorming — the name refers to brainstorming — was once used to study the idea of placing sleeping facilities in airplanes under the seats. This idea might be economically viable but might not feel particularly good. There was a need to know what it would feel like to sit under other people in a small closed space and how it would feel to sit above people who are sleeping under the seat. No complex technology was needed for this exercise. The only props needed were chairs put into

FOR EMPATHIC DESIGNERS:

1. Spread data to the walls
2. Talk through data
3. Create quick concepts
4. Role-play these concepts to get them under the skin
5. What feels best?

Figure 8.6 Kitchen rules for empathic analysis.

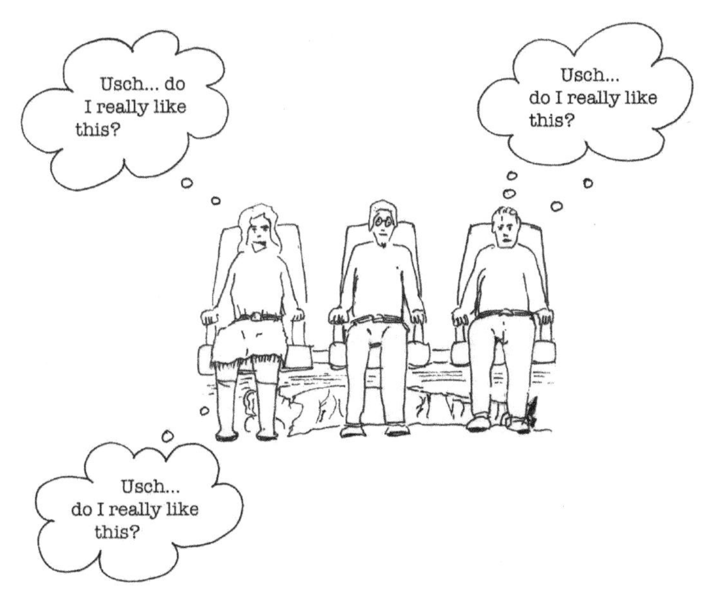

Figure 8.7 Maybe people would like to sleep under airplane seats? Bodystorming the idea.

a row and a few pillows and blankets. Some people sat on the chairs, while others tried to sleep under them (Figure 8.7).[22]

Even organizational simulations can be done this way. Researchers sometimes use humble things like matchboxes, paper cups, and Legos to stage organizational structures and processes. Again, these props are simple, but they generate a genuine feeling of excitement when they are used (Figure 8.8).

Like designers, design researchers prefer to work in multidisciplinary and multicultural workshops to quickly expose themselves to multiple perspectives. Usually, these workshops begin with presentations of data and go on in the classical

Figure 8.8 Snapshot from a design workshop in Design Factory, Helsinki, September 19, 2008. (Picture courtesy of Aalto University's Department of Design.)

brainstorming mode, typically into an open discussion in which criticism is not first allowed. It is only later that discussion points out problems in interpretations and possible design ideas emerge from these discussions. The preference for working together has its origins in design practice, where experience has shown that many eyes see more.[23]

Here, a firsthand sense of design things is particularly important. The work is experimental and playful, and firsthand bodily and social feelings are crucial. Partly for these reasons, most designers are wary of relying on technology only. Thus, even though the Web has extended the possibilities for design research with techniques like "crowdsourcing" and online testing of concepts, it has not caught on in design. Most likely the reason goes back to the disembodied nature of the Web.[24] Design research practice builds heavily on bodily and social interaction, which is difficult to do in the virtual domain.

8.3 Concept Design with Moodboards, Mock-ups, and Sketches

After studio work, constructive design researchers go on to design development, which begins with sketchy ideas and ends with prototypes. Previous phases of research have led to insights and design hypotheses, but many things such as forms, materials, look and feel, mechanic design, and interaction design are

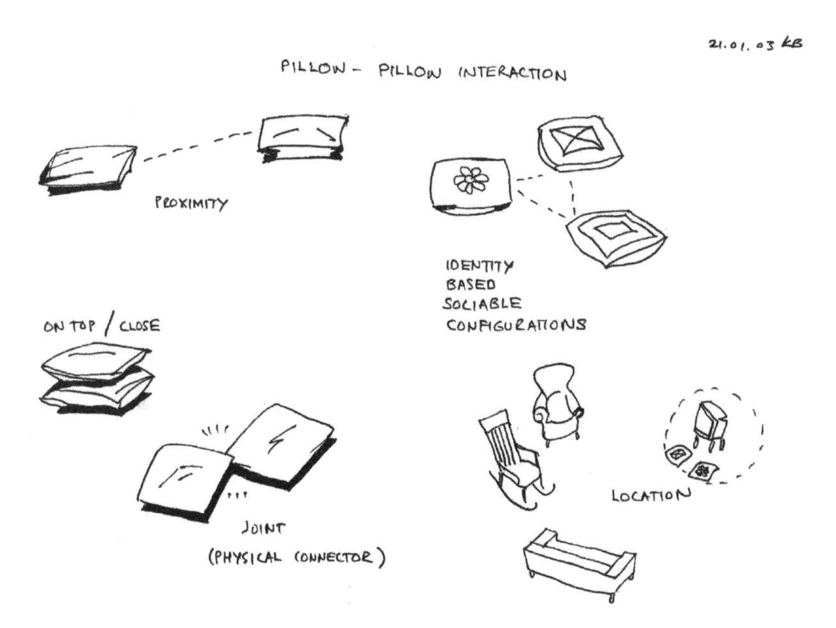

Figure 8.9 Sketches for interactive cushions by Katja Battarbee, January 21, 2003. (Redrawn by I. Koskinen, March 2011.)

still open. These issues are handled with methods borrowed from design practice, including moodboards from fashion design, storyboards from film making, and scenarios that have their origins in the military. With these methods, researchers are able to bring their design skills and intuition into the research process.[25] Up-to-date practice in scenarios starts with scriptwriting and ends with 3D animations, concept films, and virtual reality.[26]

For example, researchers explore how the design looks and feels; its color, light, and shade; surfaces; contrasts; and materials with sketches. They also explore structures and functions with these sketches.[27] Some sketches are 3D studies in clay and other cheap modeling materials like styrofoam. These sketches are done to study scale and feel in the hand and on the body, as well as mass, form, and composition. Later, they may also turn to studies of materials and mechanisms. It is important to choose the appropriate level of coarseness and not get into details before the basic idea is mature (Figure 8.9).

For studies of form and scale, researchers do mock-ups from cardboard, wood, cheap plastics, and other materials at hand. Mock-ups are simple and cheap, and they can be changed easily for feedback. Also, they facilitate communication, enable participation in the design process, and encourage imagination. As they are not limited to current technology, they unleash imagination.[28] Even though the past few years have seen a rapid technological

Figure 8.10 Sketches for an interactive robot from Carnegie Mellon's Snackbot study, which developed a mobile and autonomous robot for delivering snacks to people at Carnegie Mellon University.[30] (Picture by Eric Glaser, thanks to Jodi Forlizzi.)

development with 3D printers being used in design and design research, mock-up materials are typically low-tech (Figure 8.10).[29]

Sketches are helpful in nailing down design ideas; they also help to understand things like service flow, scale, form, and how people will interact with the concept. They are not meant, however, to study issues like technology, materials, the look and feel of the idea, details of user interfaces, or details of how the concept functions. For these studies, researchers use scenarios — often verbal, sometimes visual (Figure 8.11).

8.4 Prototyping

At this stage, design concepts are grounded in experience, but they still remain barely more than images. To get an idea of tangible things like mechanics, behavior, and materials and colors, researchers build prototypes. Prototyping is the only way to understand touch, materials, shapes, and the style and feel of interaction. It is also the only way to understand how people experience product concepts and how they would interact with them. As researchers in Eindhoven explained:

> *Design always goes through many explorations. The exploration within design research must be as abundant, but must also be more structured and systematic than in the normal design case. Reflection on a multitude of prototypes might, e.g., be done by trying to categorize them on dimensions of similarity and difference.*

The form theory course in [Wensveen's study] resulted in more than 100 models that could be categorized.... Reflection on this categorization informed the rest of the design process. This insight can only be gained by making all these prototypes, and not by thinking about them.[31]

Research prototyping shares these functions with industrial prototyping, but differs from it in several other respects.[32] For example, researchers are not usually interested in technical testing, robustness, safety, or manufacturability.[33] Also, they do not need to sell their ideas to product development, management, and customers. Prototyping has its share of problems. Since prototypes are future oriented, they often lack connection to the present. Also, there is a danger of "tunnel vision" in which researchers elaborate the prototype rather than question its premise. Finally, there is a danger of paying too little attention to social aspects of use, as technology development takes priority (Figure 8.12).[34]

Somewhere between mock-ups and prototypes are "experience prototypes," which Buchenau and Fulton Suri defined as representations designed "to understand, explore or communicate what it might be like to engage with the product, space or system we are designing."[35] Experience prototypes create a shared experience

Figure 8.11 Scenario studies of proactive information technology in everyday life. Top: lamps are brighter when they sense sound and dim slowly. Bottom: lamps react to the sound of other appliances at home. (From K. Kuusela, 2004.)

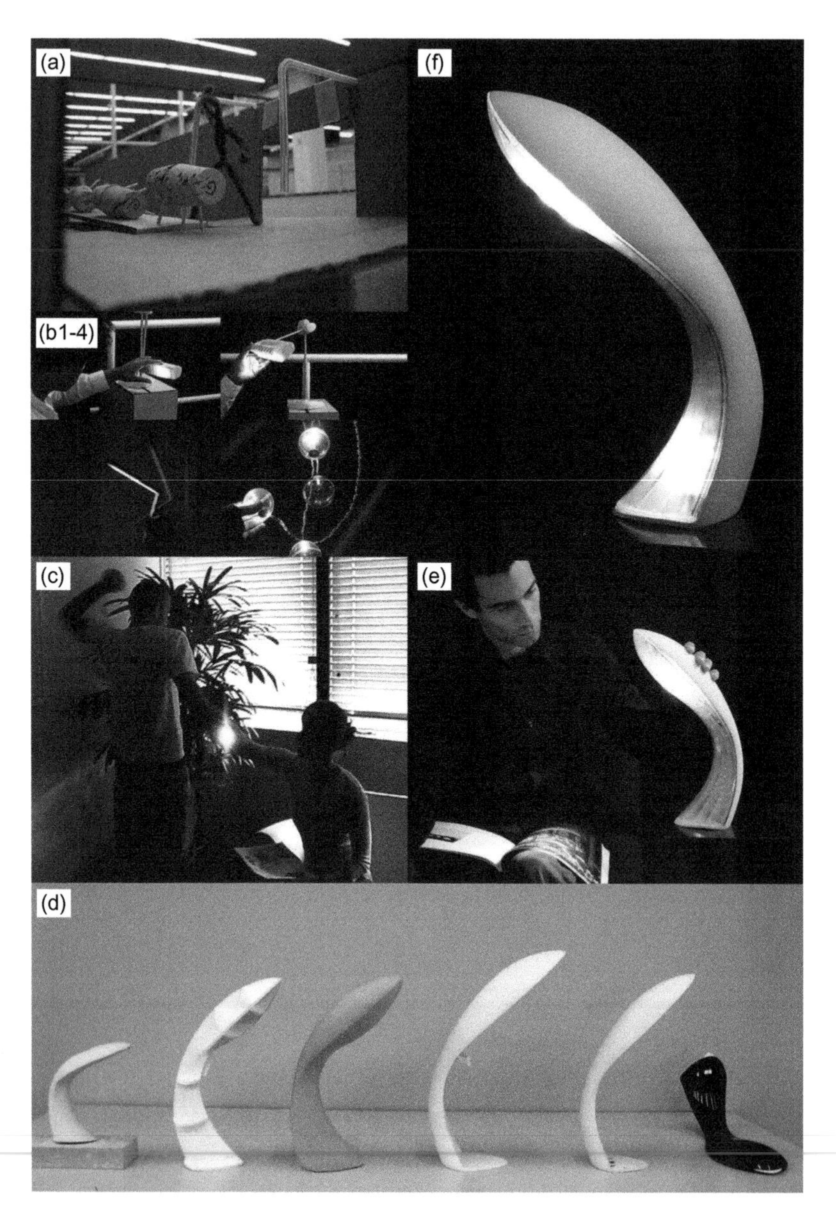

Figure 8.12 Building ethical lamps. (a) Nietzschean slaughter machine from an ethical workshop. (b1-4) Four lamp designs by TU/Eindhoven students (Rutger Menges, Ralph Zoontjes, and Lissa Kooijman). (c) Workshop on the aesthetics of interaction with dancers behaving as lamps. (d) Form studies. (e) Philip Ross using the AEI lamp. (f) Lamp prototype. (g) Philip Ross' industrial prototype. Sometimes research prototypes end up becoming industrial prototypes, but this requires extra work and funding. (Picture courtesy of Philip Ross.)

and provide a foundation for a common point of view in design teams. They are used to understand existing experiences and contexts, to explore and evaluate design ideas, and communicate ideas to audiences. With programmable toys like Lego Mindstorms it is also possible to build simple mechanisms and programs into the mock-ups to see how they function and what kinds of messages their behavior conveys.

8.5 Platforms: Taking Design into the Field

Prototypes may be ingenious and well made, but they remain researchers' guesses about a possible product unless they are somehow studied. Over the past few years, researchers have started to do increasingly ambitious research to see how their prototypes work. Research has recently gone beyond brief site visits, evaluation studies, and tests.[36] When working with new technologies that have little origin in current practices, the best way to follow these technologies and practices is to build them, hand them to people, and then study what happens.[37]

Researchers have increasingly given people freedom to do whatever they will with designs. For example, Ianus Keller gave his Cabinet design to several design studios for a month to see how designers interacted with it.[38] Another ambitious study was Morphome, in which all designs were repeatedly studied with people in everyday life for weeks and months.[39] The reasons are well explained on the Web site of Interaction Research Studio at Goldsmiths College, London:

> *Designing, building and testing prototype products is at the centre of our research.... We build our prototype products to a very high level of finish and technical robustness, which allows them to be tested for long periods in everyday life, and to be shown in lengthy exhibitions with minimal maintenance. Currently we are moving towards batch producing prototypes, so that we can disseminate 50–100 instances of a given design for extensive field trials.*[40]

In addition to field studies, many researchers have recently built platforms for observation. Radiolinja was a study about camera phones in Helsinki between 1999 and 2002. Researchers followed camera phone messaging through the network of Radiolinja, which was Helsinki Telephone Company's mobile carrier. In this system, people sent multimedia messages to the Radiolinja network, which distributed them to recipients' phones as well as a log site, where the message could be browsed through a Web link. Through the log site, researchers were able to follow

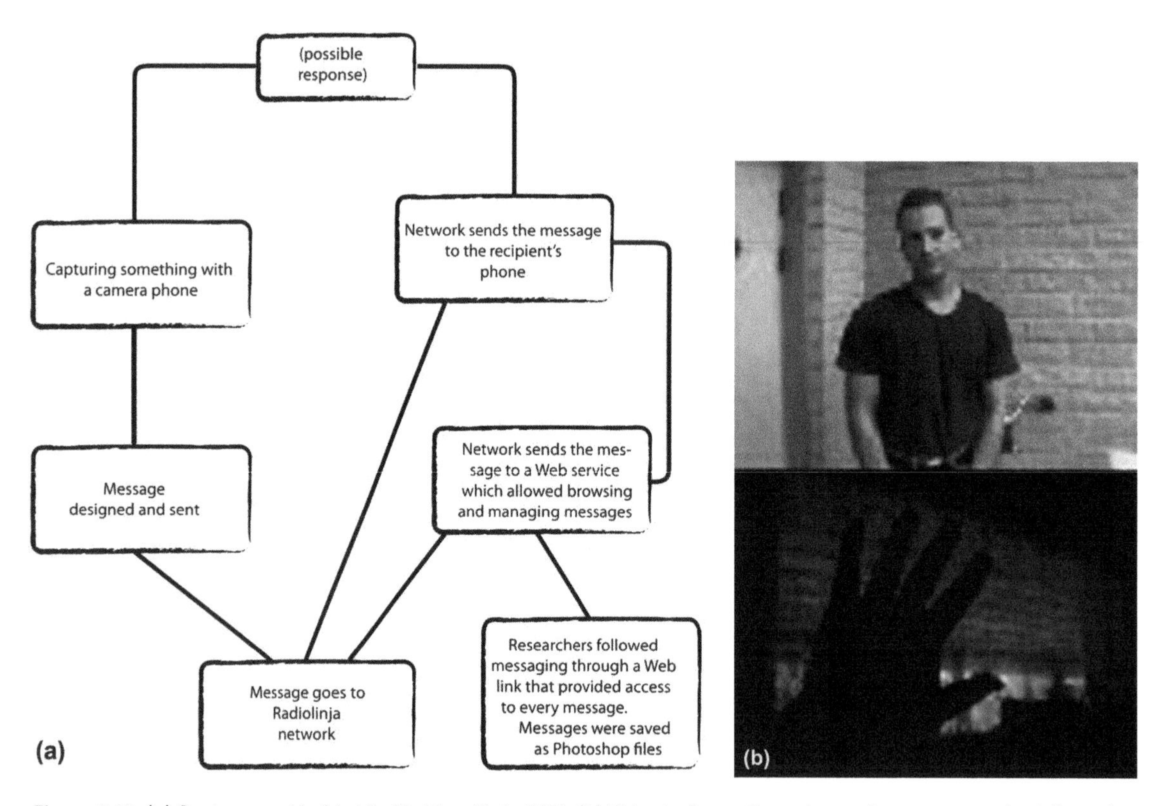

Figure 8.13 (a) System used in Mobile Multimedia in 2002. (b) This platform allowed actual messages to be followed. The first picture was sent to Anna with text saying "Greetings." Anna's response was a picture of a hand waving with the text "Greetings, also from Mama."

messaging. They followed it daily to see how people used this new technology (Figure 8.13).[41]

There is little new in these platforms. They have existed for a long time under various names, ranging from panel studies in the social sciences to field stations in agriculture, and field hospitals in medicine. In industry, the most comprehensive platform so far comes from Philips Research, which has developed an Experience Research Cycle for studying how ambient intelligence could be embedded into everyday life on a large scale. The cycle begins with a context study that maps context without technology, usually with observations. It continues to laboratory studies that test usability and user acceptance in controlled environments that enable detailed and accurate qualitative and quantitative studies. It ends with field studies that validate the results of laboratory studies and focus on the long-term effects of technology.[42]

Platforms like these enable many kinds of studies. For example, in Radiolinja the main focus was on how people design their messages and respond to them, but researchers also calculated statistics of traffic, message types and networks, and time series analyses.[43] Even more complex platforms for studying camera phones were built in Berkeley, leading ultimately to the redevelopment of services like Flickr.[44] With platforms, researchers can follow things over time and do comparisons between technologies and their variations. Another benefit of platforms is that they pave the way to more complex research designs, including doing quasi-experiments to compare different technologies and designs.[45]

8.6 Design Things in Research

Design things like moodboards and prototypes populate the spaces in which designers work. Likewise, they populate constructive design researchers' studios and the pages they write. The reasons for using them in research are the same as in design. They are an effective way to bring people to the same table to imagine better futures together. Most important, they make it possible to probe and discuss those sensuous, embodied and social things that are central to design — like colors, how materials feel on skin and the shapes of objects. Few people have a reliable vocabulary to talk about them. Inventive methods have a place in design for this reason alone. We do not know why these things work, only that they do work.[46]

This chapter looked at how design things are used over the design process. In early-stage user studies, these things are used to bring imagination and playfulness into these studies and to make imagination shareable. Later, when design enters a concept design phase, design things are used to develop concepts for products and systems. When research enters the design phase, researchers create models, mock-ups, and prototypes. Even later, with concepts and prototypes at hand, constructive design researchers usually study them with people to see how their ideas work. It goes without saying that for different types of research tasks, different methods are used. Also, there are few studies in which all of these steps are used; this is not a mechanical sequence, it is a creative process.[47]

Design things are colorful, playful, and usually projective: they illustrate future possibilities. They also fail occasionally. When the Presence Project asked people to imagine Biljmer in Amsterdam as a body, most participants were perplexed and did not know what to do.[48] This playful, exploratory, and projective stance made it difficult to think about these things logically. Design things are not traditional research instruments.

It is this richness, however, that creates touching points in life. Philip Ross did not need to be able to explain everything that happens in his clay models because people connected to them in many ways, not just intellectually; people can study and discuss these models. This is more important than whether or not design things can be explained in detail. In still broader terms, design things enable designers to capture Maurice Merleau-Ponty's "flesh" — that poorly understood netherworld in which humans meet things from which designers get much of their inspiration.[49] The specific skill of a designer is to be able to put a concept into a workable form. Ideas may fly in any conversation, but methods are needed to turn these ideas into prototypes, products, or systems.

End Notes

1. Ehn (2008, 2009).
2. Ehn (1988a,b), Star and Griesemer (1989).
3. There are a few precursors to this argument, most notably Henderson (1999; see also Kurvinen, 2005). Ehn's argument about design things is social institutional and, as such, an alternative to those explanations in which design is seen as primarily a cognitive activity (Lawson, 1980, 2004; Cross, 2007; Visser, 2006).
4. The link between using design things and making the design process more democratic is obvious and has been made by many writers, although usually in less colorful language than Ehn (see Muller, 2009; Säde, 2001; Shaw, 2007; Moon, 2005; Pallasmaa, 2009).

   Ehn's argument is similar to that of Bruno Latour and is also indebted to Martin Heidegger's philosophy. A member of the group led by Ehn, Giorgio De Michelis (2009, p. 153, italics added), wrote:

   > *In a short essay published in* Poetry, Language, Thought *Martin Heidegger recalls that the German word "ding" (sharing its root with the English word "thing") was used to name the governing assembly in ancient Germanic societies, made up of the free men of the community and presided by lawspeakers. It should be noticed that also the Latin word for thing, "res," occurs in "res publica" ("republic" in English).* So things are the issues governing assemblies take into consideration, the issues raising public concern. *The word "thing," therefore, does not indicate genericity, absence of specification, but impossibility of specification. Things are not without interest: on the contrary, they are what merit our attention. Things are matters of concern because they can't be reduced to any specification: Things exceed the way we classify them and are open to discovery and surprise.*

   From this perspective, as De Michelis noted, design appears as one of those elementary practices in which human beings experience not yet existing things.

   Similar semantics also works in Finnish, although etymology of the word "asia" is of course different.
5. Seago and Dunne (1999, p. 16).
6. For the politics of prototyping, see Henderson (1999). Juhani Pallasmaa (2009, pp. 58–60) wrote about models in architecture, but his description no doubt works in design too:

   > *Drawings and models have the double purpose of facilitating the design process itself and mediating ideas to others.... Even in the age*

of computer-aided design and virtual modeling, physical models are incomparable aids in the design process of the architect and the designer. The three-dimensional material model speaks to the hand and the body as powerfully as to the eye, and the very process of constructing a model simulates the process of construction. Models are used for a variety of purposes: they are a way of quickly sketching the essence of an idea; a medium of thinking and working, of concretizing or clarifying one's own ideas; a means of presenting a project to the client or authorities; and a way of analyzing and presenting the conceptual essence of the project.... The architect moves about freely in the imagined structure, however large and complex it may be, as if walking in a building and touching all its surfaces and sensing their materiality and texture. This is an intimacy that is surely difficult, if not impossible, to simulate through computer-aided means of modeling and simulation.

7. Latour (1987).

8. Models have received a lot of attention in architecture recently. Karen Moon (2005) wrote extensively about models in architecture, largely focusing on historical examples, but also on the likes of Eero Saarinen, Cesar Pelli, Norman Foster, Toyo Ito, Skidmore, Owings, & Merrill, and, of course, Frank Gehry.

Despite swings in popularity and purpose, architects still construct models mainly to develop their ideas and communicate them to clients and financiers. Models communicate a purpose, and often have a utopian character, and although for many architects, models are but stages in a process in which only the final product — usually a building or a plan — matters, they have recently achieved a celebrity status of sorts, having a market in which models are bought from studios sometimes at the cost of hundreds of thousands of dollars. Buyers are usually museums that have room for often precarious models.

Moon focused on architecture, where issues like scale, lighting, and photography are important, but some of her observations may also apply to design. In particular, the functions of models are largely the same. Designers face questions about the artistic and sculptural quality of their work just as architects do. Their models can also be expensive to build. In the main, however, design models are cheap, in-the-moment creations meant for critiques in the design process, and although there is already a market for design sketches and prototypes, the market for design models is less developed.

No doubt, this will change when design museums become more common and gain importance. After all, the key factor in developing a market for architecture models has been the rise of architecture museums. Design prototypes are also small, which helps in creating this market.

Another recent book on models in architecture is Morris (2006).

9. Säde (2001) is still a good introduction.

10. For recent discussion, see Zimmerman et al. (2007).

11. Sleeswijk Visser (2009).

12. Wasson (2000) and for E-Lab, Wasson (2002), Ylirisku and Buur (2007).

13. See Brandes et al. (2009), Fulton Suri and IDEO (2005).

14. For probes, see Gaver et al. (1999); for Make Tools, see Stappers and Sanders (2003).

15. Nugent et al. (2007).

16. Sanders (2000), Stappers and Sanders (2003).

17. Iacucci et al. (2000).

18. Fulton Suri et al. (2005).

19. See IP08 (2009).

20. See Poggenpohl (2009a, p. 7) and the reference to Maurice Merleau-Ponty in note 19 in Chapter 1.

21. Nugent et al. (2007).
22. Buchenau and Fulton Suri (2000).
23. Wasson (2000), Szymanski and Whalen (2011).
24. Dreyfus (2001).
25. For moodboards, see Lucero (2009); for scenarios, see Carroll (2000).
26. Raijmakers (2007).
27. Buxton (2007).
28. Ehn (1988a, pp. 335–336).
29. See Caption (2004). For lo-tech approach, see Ehn and Kyng (1991).
30. See snackbot.org and Lee et al. (2009).
31. Overbeeke et al. (2006, p. 12).
32. Säde (2001, p. 55). For differences between research prototypes and industrial prototypes, see Chapter 4, which quotes Frens (2006a, p. 64).
33. Ross (2008), Hummels and Frens (2008), and Frens (2006a). Some research groups, however, have gone into that direction, most notably researchers in Interaction Research Studio of Goldsmiths College, London. See gold.ac.uk/interaction/portfolio/, retrieved March 10, 2010.
34. See Mogensen (1992, pp. 5–6.
35. Buchenau and Fulton Suri (2000).
36. See Kankainen (2002).
37. Crabtree (2004).
38. Keller (2005, p. 119ff).
39. Mäyrä et al. (2006), Koskinen et al. (2006).
40. gold.ac.uk/interaction/portfolio/, retrieved March 26, 2011.
41. Koskinen et al. (2002), Battarbee (2004), Kurvinen (2007), Koskinen (2007).
42. De Ruyter and Aarts (2010).

    Some global companies have organizational models for achieving similar results. They have for so long placed their creative studios in fashionable places where designers can observe the world without effort.

    We have already mentioned Olivetti as a historical example in Chapter 2, but the practice still exists today; for example, one of Toyota's Creative Studios is in Chicago's fashionable Bucktown. Similarly, the car industry has long had its main design studios in the world's leading car culture, Los Angeles. Harvey Molotch (1996, pp. 257–258) wrote an elegy to Southern California:

    > *Those in California auto design disagree among themselves on what, if anything, may be the basis for the region's special design role. For Hiroaki Ohba, executive vice president of Toyota's Calty Design, the company's Orange County location is particularly stimulating, among other reasons because "Newport Beach is a museum for automobiles and an ideal place for the automobile designer.... We see many antique cars in Newport Beach." There are also "more exotic cars on the streets of a place like Newport Beach (Porsches, Ferraris), more, according to Ohba, than one would find in Germany or Japan. The youth of California have for generations been great style experimenters. One auto designer told me that the fashions on Melrose Avenue, a 1990s hot strip of boutiques and high-end junk shoppes for the affluent young, influence car design. The shapes and colors of jewelry, the textures and combinations of outfits, all may end up in design details.... Even if not consciously inventorying "the trends," designers are alert to such messages from the streets and shop windows. The GM California studio chef says he likes to take "a few of our guys and drive along the beach ... to see what people do on weekends with their vehicles." The Chrysler vice president for design explains his company's presence in Southern California as taking "advantage of the local culture there."*

There is also the notion of the "living lab," which we find confusing. Again, the idea here is to build environments in which people are free to do things, but which can be followed with permanent research instruments. This term gained some popularity in Europe from 2005 to 2008.

43. See Kurvinen (2007), Koskinen (2007). For other large-scale field studies in context, see Jacucci et al. (2007), who studied multimedia systems for rock and jazz festivals and even a massive, 400,000 participant World Rally Championship event in Finland.

44. van House et al. (2004, 2005).

45. For the "breaching experiment," see Crabtree (2004). For another approach, see Binder (2007) and Binder et al. (2011), who talks about design:labs.

46. However, see Kurvinen (2007) for a study of how people interact with design things in meetings.

47. But see Wensveen (2004) and Ross (2008).

48. Gaver (2002).

49. For this weight, see Chapter 1, and our inspiration, Maurice Merleau-Ponty (1968, 1970). See also Chapter 5 and the quote from Fulton Suri in that same chapter (Fulton Suri, 2011).

9

CONSTRUCTIVE DESIGN RESEARCH IN SOCIETY

Chapter 8 outlined the ways in which constructive design researchers use design things in their research process. Design things, we saw, gather people around actual design work.[1] Just as any research, however, constructive design research cannot stop there. Any research program worthy of its salt needs to function in society, not just during the project. Successful programs keep designers dialoging with society; unsuccessful ones are unable to keep this dialog going long enough.

This chapter reviews constructive design research in society. As soon as researchers leave the university, they face rationalities different from their own. Many of these rationalities are beyond their control; more often than not, researchers find themselves in a subordinate position in activities initiated and controlled by people who think differently.[2] In practice, constructive design researchers work in a network of contracts and overlapping commitments. As various partners come and go into the projects with varying agendas, it is difficult to predict what comes out. Projects like these are "garbage-cans," as Michael Cohen, James March, and Johan Olsen once famously called organizational decision-making processes.[3]

To keep research going, researchers have to understand the demands society imposes on them. To function, researchers need to understand some of the rationalities they face outside of the studio. This chapter explores some of these rationalities through the example of Luotain, a key project in Helsinki's empathic design program. Taking these demands into account improves the chances of success in research.

9.1 Luotain

Luotain ("probe" in English) was a design research project in Helsinki from 2002 to 2005. It was built around cultural probes that had been used in research in Helsinki since 1998. While the original British work on cultural probes sought to expand the mindset of human–computer interaction (HCI) researchers, Luotain took a step back and studied whether cultural probes work in company settings.[4] The practical goal was to improve product development in companies by introducing new, design-specific research methods. In practical terms, Luotain created concepts for companies. Product development, however, was left to the design firms.

The project had thirteen participants. The coordinators were industrial designers at the University of Art and Design Helsinki.[5] Originally, participants consisted of five pairs of companies. Each pair had a company and its design partner and brought a case for the project, which was run as a series of cases with seminars and workshops in between. Later, this setup expanded to include an extra design consultant and new companies. Funding came partly from companies, but the main funding came from the National Technology Research Agency.

The conceptual roots of Luotain were in an interpretive critique of emotions. By the end of the 1990s, the prevailing view in information technology was that emotions can and ought to be measured. Instead, Luotain turned to empathic, sociological, and interpretive theories of emotions. Emotions were seen as crucial to design and as social processes in need of empathic interpretation rather than directly measurable bodily processes (Figure 9.1).[6]

Figure 9.1 The structure of the Luotain project.

By any measure, Luotain was successful. It lasted about three years, and during this time it was able to attract company interest and funding. It also led to more than twenty scientific papers and Tuuli Mattelmäki's widely admired doctoral thesis "Design Probes."[7] Its later impact can be seen in numerous studies. It has influenced dozens of master's theses: some oriented to user research, some to concept development, and some to construction. For example, during Luotain Katja Soini was a doctoral student who went into organizational development and started to explore how design researchers can even participate in legislature. Another doctoral student, Kirsikka Vaajakallio, begun to explore how methods in Luotain were connected to participatory design; she first explored design games but later rediscovered the empathic roots of Luotain. Mattelmäki realized that through workshops many kinds of participants can be brought into design. Since then, this realization has led her to co-design.[8]

9.2 Researchers as Peers

Luotain found an audience in many research communities. The project plan in 2002 built mostly on literature in HCI, which was still fashionable after the dot.com bubble burst. The key papers in Mattelmäki's Empathy Probes from 2006 were published in human-centered computer science conferences. This work was based on earlier work in smart products — small software-intensive gadgets that had become an important part of the design business in the 1990s.[9]

The audience soon started to change. Luotain started to build on the notion of user experience, a term that had been introduced to design more than ten years earlier and had become popular after the turn of the century. For Luotain, this term opened doors to HCI and design research. By the end of the project in 2005, researchers were publishing in HCI conferences and journals as well as in more design-oriented conferences like the Royal College of Art's Include. Subsequent projects continue to be seen in all of these venues.[10]

For researchers, this is basically a safe world. Researchers may disagree on many things, but they share many goals. In this world, they are able to gain a high degree of control over their activities and ways of thinking, and they know a great deal about its ways of reasoning.

However, there are also differences. Interaction designers, for example, mostly build their research traditions on computer science and psychology. They favor theory building, experimental research, and statistical analysis. For empathic designers, this can be a hostile environment: there are few pockets of

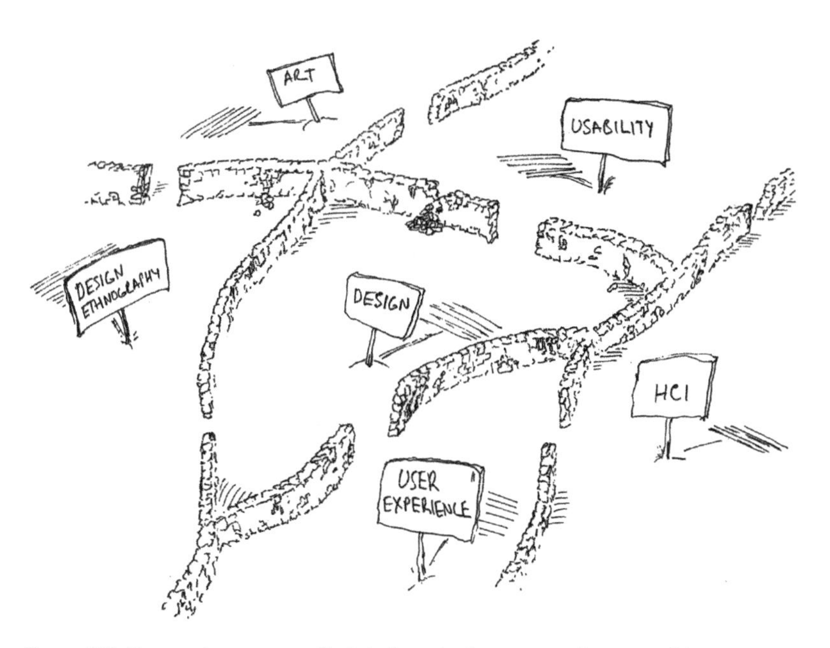

Figure 9.2 Research programs find their paths from several communities.

sympathetic reviewers. In ethnographic communities like the Ethnographic Praxis in Industry conference, empathic designers find people who understand interpretive research. Still, there are many dividing lines here too. For example, one issue is whether research should provide inspiration for design or whether it ought to be based on careful documentation, analysis, and theoretical work.[11] In artistically oriented communities, even interpretive research may be too analytical because it stresses writing at the expense of exhibitions (Figure 9.2).[12]

Constructive design researchers place their work on this palette of communities in several ways. For example, researchers in Eindhoven mostly publish in HCI conferences and journals but also find outlets in design. Critical designers publish in both places but have focused on HCI for most of the decade. They have only recently come back to design much like the participatory designer places in Scandinavian design universities and empathic designers in Helsinki.

As design research has matured and gained a degree of academic autonomy, there has been a marked trend toward design as a disciplinary base. Still, constructive design researchers keep publishing in several communities. Interaction designers have increasingly been interested in the material, cultural, and social sensitivities every good designer works with and are willing to learn from their practices. The scientific leanings of HCI occasionally clash with the creative leanings of designers, but the gap is far less pronounced than it was a decade earlier. The HCI community has become far more receptive to design, setting up a design subcommittee at its CHI conference in 2009.

Constructive design research has also found a home in many design schools. Often, however, design research in these schools focuses on history, aesthetics, and critical studies. Also, traditional design disciplines like ceramics and textiles define their future through art, not research. Perhaps for these reasons, constructive design research usually takes place in industrial and interaction design programs. Constructive research widens the research basis of art and design schools but may also create a split between the humanities. However, as most constructive design researchers build on interpretive thinking, art, and design, there are also many things that create bridges to the humanities.

9.3 Research Faces Design Traditions

Luotain was created after about ten years of work on smart products in Helsinki,[13] but it put methodology into a new theoretical context. The main research question was inspiration rather than usability: finding new design opportunities rather than optimizing products and product concepts. The leading idea was that designers need to understand people before they can start designing. This idea came to be known as "empathic design," even though "interpretive design" would have been a more accurate term. Innovative research methods, as Carnegie Mellon's Bruce Hanington has called them, quickly became a meeting point for researchers, companies, designers, and other stakeholders.[14]

In terms of design, these were not obvious steps. Language in design had few concepts with which to describe work that was interpretive, relied on post-Cartesian theory, and used methods that were often inspired by twentieth century avant-garde art.

Still, for many reasons, Luotain found support in industrial and interaction design. For some designers, Luotain was putting on paper what any good designer already knew. For others, it was a research community's answer to their interpretive self-image and that good design has to start from understanding people. Also, because Luotain borrowed many methods from design practice and its workshop-based methods of analysis were familiar to every designer, it was easy to integrate it into teaching and practice. Luotain's primary creator, Tuuli Mattelmäki, was named the industrial designer of the year in 2008.

A somewhat harder nut to crack was the workshop culture at the heart of design. Traditional design education is a hands-on education, and the dominant tradition of design education still uses the Bauhaus as its prototype.[15] The Bauhaus gave design education

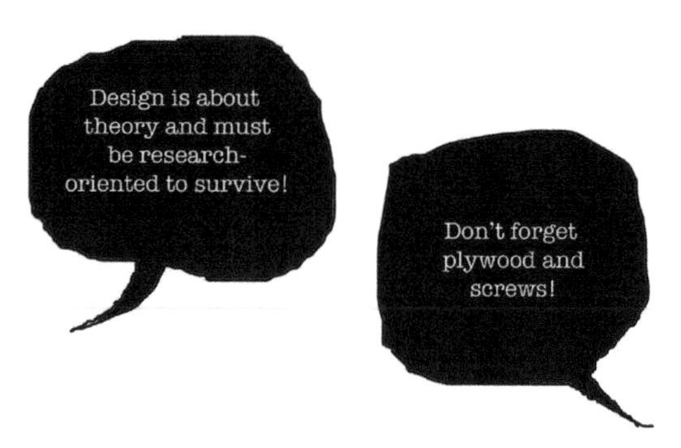

Figure 9.3 What designers tell researchers.

the idea of combining art, craft, and industry, as well as the idea of bringing the best from other fields of learning into design. However, empirical social science was not a part of its program.[16] In many programs modeled after the Bauhaus, user researchers have hit their heads against this heritage. They have usually been placed into separate research units, away from design.[17] Luotain's solution was to focus on the early-stage interpretive foundations of design work, concept search, and concept design, rather than plywood and screws. For practitioners, this is perfectly acceptable. Conceptual work belongs to good design, and many designers live by conceptual design rather than construction (Figure 9.3).

In broader terms, constructive design research has gained many sympathetic listeners in design. Since the 1960s, many things have been pushing design away from its practical roots.[18] Industrial design has made design a more abstract discipline, process-based rather than material- or form-based. CAD technologies have made the skills of the hand less important and pushed descriptive geometry to the sidelines. Design management has focused designers on brands, markets, images, and organizational processes. Interaction design had valued an ability to talk about behavior and meanings in the abstract and to think in terms of flows and logic rather than traditional design forms and materials. The media image of design has been conceptual and is on the verge of becoming artistic. Most recently, services and sustainability have pushed designers still farther into abstraction.

In this context, most practitioners have welcomed constructive design research. For them, its stress on doing has an air of familiarity. When they see researchers in studios and workshops, they find it easy to communicate with them on equal ground. Most ideologists of constructive design research are programmatically pushing into the heart of research. Some are even arguing for using research as a template for wider restoration of universities that have become dangerously scientific at the expense of practice.[19]

9.4 New Bauhauses: Digital and Electronic

Constructive design researchers face another type of environment in design programs at technical universities. Technical universities traditionally build design on science and engineering, not on art and craft. When designers in these environments turn to ubiquitous and tangible computing models, they often turn to industrial design as a model. At one extreme, the dream is to create a version of digital and electronic Bauhaus by merging technology and art.[20]

A recent example of this type of program is K3 at Malmö University in Sweden. This program combines art, cultural studies, and communication.[21] Its research side builds on media studies as well as on participatory design and computer science. Its founders' goal was to turn it into a digital version of the Bauhaus. For the program's founders, post-Cartesian philosophy and contemporary art provided useful arguments that justified building workshops to enable experimental work.[22] Here, they continued their earlier work from Sweden, where several researchers had defined electronics and software as design material.[23]

The reasons for bringing studios to technological research are well explained by Pieter Jan Stappers of Delft University of Technology:

Classically, design studios are known for their visual culture. Designers surround themselves with inspiring materials, sketches

Interactive Rear-View Mirror

IP08 was a nine-week design class given at the University of Art and Design Helsinki in spring 2008. In this class, master's level industrial design students went through user-centered design processes. Students had to create a design concept, learn the basics of microcontroller, learn some programming in C, and refresh the basics of electric circuits.

In 2008, the theme of the class was co-experience (Battarbee, 2004) in the car and safety while driving. Interaction between the front and the back seat at that time was a major road safety issue, taking people's focus away from what was happening on the road, causing potential hazards, and introducing risks into the driving experience. The class wanted to give students a firsthand bodily understanding of embedded technology, in our case how sensors and actuators work, and this was stressed throughout the class from the first user studies to the final testing of the prototypes.[24]

Kaj Eckoldt and Benjamin Schultz built an interactive rear-view mirror. Their work process is described in Figure 9.4.

In terms of process and the way in which the class oscillated between studios and workshops, IP08 is much like any typical design process. The difference is that the design came from theoretical reading, lectures, and the elaborate philosophy behind the class.

Figure 9.4 Constructive research in the classroom. (a) User studies in Lahti, Finland. (b) Concept creation. (c) Studio work. (d) An experience prototype of how screens could be used to mediate communication between parents and children. Eckoldt and Schultz rejected this concept and worked with real mirrors. (e) Eckoldt and Schultz are trying out early concepts with a Lego Mindstorms model in the workshop. (f) From the workshop. (g) They test another concept with Lego Mindstorms. (h) Mock-up of a child sitting in a baby chair.[25]

and prototypes; other designers in the studio absorb these visual sparks as well, and such visual outlets are known to set off unplanned and informal communications, and present people with unexpected inputs, which can serve as part of solutions and lead to serendipitous innovation.

In 2001, four research groups from our department started ID-StudioLab, in which staff, PhD students and MSc students on research projects worked in a studio situation to promote contact between different expertises and different projects.... It promoted the informal contact and sharing of ideas and skills, an undercurrent that can be as important for the dissemination of research findings as the official publication channels. Moreover, it formed a playground in which design researchers could "live with their prototypes," an important ingredient of "research through design"....

The "living prototypes" were part of the "texture" of StudioLab, influencing and being influenced by dozens of researchers, students and visitors who all brought and took away snippets and insights according to their specific background. This is why design studios are so important for growing knowledge.[26]

This setting keeps the distance between the source of inspiration and reasoning small. ID-StudioLab is also located close to Delft's workshops, and there is a small electronics lab next to the StudioLab. Proximity encourages researchers to explore their ideas not just through discussion, but also physically. However, StudioLab's researchers also have expertise in user studies and in field-based evaluation of their prototypes. It is not a laboratory in which researchers explore things sheltered from reality; its boundary is permeable.[27]

9.5 Meet the Business

Luotain was a novel experience to many company participants, just as it was for many designers. For instance, in Datex-Ohmeda, which General Electric bought during Luotain, the project was owned first by the company's usability group. Many suspicions were voiced because the project did not follow the group's standard practices and put many of them in doubt. When the upper management saw the value of the project, however, it began to be accepted. On the other hand, when Luotain worked with Nokia, it was not seen as a novelty. Nokia had been involved in European research projects that had used cultural probes, and many researchers working in the project had trained many Nokia designers.

With the exception of Nokia, Luotain prompted rethinking of products, product road maps, and in some cases product development as a whole as early as 2002. At the end of the project in 2005, companies were on the map. Former usability testing groups had by then evolved into user-centered design groups.

When Mattelmäki was writing her doctoral thesis, she interviewed companies that had been involved in Luotain. She learned that the main benefits of her "empathy probes" were that they provided inspiration and information on users' needs and contexts for company designers, they allowed users to express their idea to product developers, and they created a dialog between users and designers.[28]

There are other studies that show how constructive design research is attractive to industry and has been appropriated in businesses. When working with constructive design researchers, companies find research that helps them to identify opportunities. In addition, they provide concepts, prototypes, and well-crafted arguments that explain these. Constructive design research also prepares people who can go back and forth between theoretical ideas, studio work, and workshops, and who have the ability to plan and to work with materials and technologies. These are valuable skills.

There are some patterns in how research finds a place in business. With the exception of the smallest one-man firms, with few resources to buy research, several design firms have embraced design research, turning it into a strategic tool. On the one hand, research has helped design firms to diversify their offerings and to make long-term contracts with clients and land lucrative research contracts.[29] On the other hand, research adds value to the customer who does not want to buy research and prototypes from two different places. This business concept has been around since the early days of E-Lab and Cheskin and continues to thrive today.[30]

On the client side, there are also patterns. At one end are small companies with few resources to invest in design. At the other end of the business hierarchy are global companies like Intel, Philips, Microsoft, and Nokia that have resources for extensive research. Widely known research programs from these companies include Intel's former People and Practices Research group, Alessi's research programs, and Philips Design's vision projects.[31] Again, there are powerful economic reasons to invest in constructive design research. Failing in research is cheap compared to failing with a product (Figure 9.5).

The first markets for constructive design research were born in cities with sophisticated design markets, such as Silicon Valley, the Scandinavian capitals, Munich, Amsterdam, and London. These places have had markets for highly specialized design services for decades, and they continue to create demand for new openings. A city like London can support companies that specialize in using documentary film in user research.[32]

The Internet is currently creating a new interface between constructive design research and business. The cost of a startup on the Web may be little more than having time for research, a laptop, and an Internet connection. Testing concepts is also

Figure 9.5 Discussions about research in companies.

cheaper than testing physical products. Publishing on the Web is easy, and Web-based marketing is cheaper than traditional marketing. The differences in producing hardware are significant: a solid concept for a new umbrella has to be sold to business angels, risk investors, banks, manufacturers, wholesalers, and department stores. We believe that constructive work may provide IT start-ups with useful ideas and a relatively cheap way to test their ideas and strategies. In the world of bits, research gets a far more important role as the driver of innovation than in the world of atoms.

9.6 Embracing the Public Good

Design takes place in the market, but this is only one side of the story. The other side is the public sector. When funding comes from public sources, research is expected to produce something the market fails to do. Examples include plans and concepts for public spaces, new infrastructures, and for "special" groups too small to attract product development money from the private sector.

Again, Luotain is a good example. Although the public sector was not involved in the project, it made the project possible in several ways. It was mostly funded by public sources, and for this reason, it had to have several participants, and it needed to publish its findings to benefit society, not just participating companies. Besides, political considerations made the project possible in the first place. Funding for the project came from a government program, Muoto 2005!, which aimed at rebuilding Finnish industry through design.

Policy work that led to the Muoto 2005! program had been done in part by professors at Luotain's home department.

Local and national governments have funded many key constructive design research projects in Europe, and the European Union is another major source of funds.[33] Some of these projects have become important milestones on the road toward constructive research, like the Presence Project and Maypole.[34] Both were funded mostly by a consortium where part of the money came from industry seeking applications, but long-term continuity was built on funds from public sources.

Many European and Asian countries, such as the United Kingdom and the Scandinavian countries, and South Korea, New Zealand, South Africa, and India have similar design policies. The European Union was also preparing its design policy from 2008, building it mostly on experience and thinking from Denmark, Finland, and the United Kingdom. Small European countries, in particular, have integrated design and design research into their industrial and innovation policies.

Constructive Design Research in Innovation Policy

Constructive design research is a winner in many political discussions about what kind of research should be funded.[35] Its value proposal is flexible and robust. For companies with enough intellectual, technological, and fiscal resources, it leads to prototypes that companies may use in various ways, which is another promise field research can make. Like any research, it promises knowledge that is in the public interest. Profits from relatively small investments in research can be significant.

In particular, fieldwork is directly relevant for industrial interests. This is hardly surprising, given the roots of field research in industry and global companies' investment in it. The key word has been user-centered design. However, field research fits best under this concept. The word "design," for its part, creates the connection to industrial policy, which currently usually comes under the label of "innovation policy." Conveniently enough, "design" also has an air of creativity. This sounds like a marriage made in heaven.

The link between user-centered design and innovations has become the cornerstone in policies in Denmark, India, and more recently, the European Union. For example, the European Union has titled its design policy document as "Design as a Driver of User-Centered Innovation."[36] In this document, design is distanced from aesthetics and styling, and firmly situated in the realm of user-centered design. In these policies, design typically complements more traditional innovation activities such as research. Design and other non-technological innovation drivers like organizational development are less capital intensive and have shorter pay-back periods than, for example, technological research but still have the potential to drive competitiveness.

For example, the Muoto 2005! program in Finland aimed to increase the number of design graduates and to better connect design with industry.[37] It was surprisingly successful in both respects, but more relevant to our concerns is its conceptual structure. It consisted of concentric circles, with technology in the middle, business around this core, and social and cultural "factors" at the outer circles: design connected these circles. This delightfully simplistic model became the structure for both technological and social science and humanistic research. With the exception of a few theoretical studies, and some technology studies in industry, most research funded in this initiative was user-centered (Figure 9.6).

Designers have been more than passive partners in preparing these policies. A good deal of expertise for policy preparation came from the top of the design world, which had a plenty of resources needed to participate in the time-consuming and often tricky world of policy making.

In Muoto 2005!, most of the background preparation work was done in the country's largest design school and its design department. When the policy was running, management was delegated to business consultants. The university had expertise, money, and enough resources to participate in this work, which does not lead to billable hours. It was also sufficiently removed from industrial interests to be capable of articulating the larger interests of the design community.

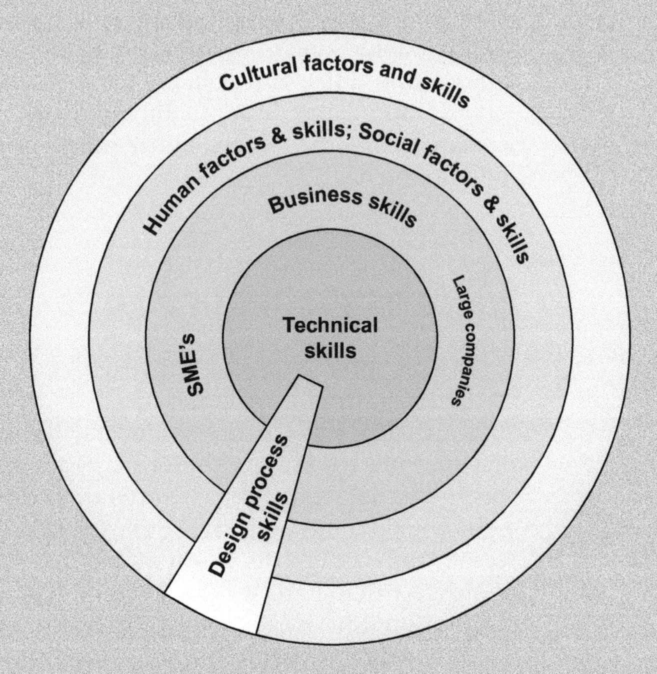

Figure 9.6 This was drawn in the preparation phase of Finland's design policy in 2000. Notice how it centers on technology. Despite its populist tone, this image lived for years, and it was used to explain design to engineers and technology policy makers. (Drawing by Juha Järvinen, original design by Juhani Salovaara and Ilpo Koskinen.)

The main exception is the United States. Although it has gone through several attempts to construct a design policy, little has been produced, and most funding is based on private funds.[38] America channels public funds to design, but usually through funding national security, which is impossible to track.[39] Other major stable sources of funding outside of the market are major foundations, but as far as we know, no systematic studies of how design has fared in their boards exist.[40] There is no way around the public good argument in America, although it does not work in the same way as in Europe.

Public funding introduces designers to partners they would not ordinarily work with. These include a host of engineering specialties but also several sciences, research institutions, service companies, public sector organizations, and non-governmental organizations. In this world, design researchers have learned to explicate their aims and methods with new types of arguments. The best recent example is probably Material Beliefs, a London-based project exploring potential implications of biomedical and cybernetic technologies. The project cooperated with engineers, scientists, and social scientists but aimed at producing prototypes, exhibitions, and debates rather than just scientific papers. It was funded by Britain's Engineering and Physical Sciences Research Council, which had a program about public involvement in science.[41]

9.7 Constructive Design Research in Society

This chapter reviewed constructive design research in society by illustrating it with Luotain, a study done in Helsinki from 2002 to 2005, with many spillovers that still continue. Luotain first oriented to HCI but later turned to design. Its home base was industrial design, but compared to design-as-usual, its aims were considerably abstract. Still, its methods were largely borrowed from design. Its business context was lively: eleven companies participated in the project. Luotain avoided product orientation but was business friendly. Finally, it had a public dimension through funding from the National Technology Research Agency. It was to produce knowledge for the public domain, which it did.

As Luotain illustrated, constructive design researchers face many types of rationalities. Some of these rationalities are close to home, such as in the research, design, and business worlds. Some others are distant such as the idea that public good seldom figures in designers' minds. It can be difficult to keep all of these rationalities in line, but Luotain managed to do that with design things and workshops. The project elaborated on the empathic design program a great deal, first by taking it into a more workshop-based methodology and, later, through co-design and service design. Projects that build on Luotain today seek inspiration from scenography and environmental art.[42]

How researchers face these rationalities depends on their positions in research and the social organizations that surround it. Researchers in Luotain concentrated on project work, published in conferences, and worked with businesses and occasionally in seminars organized by the National Technology Research Agency, where they saw a glimpse of technology policy. However, abstract arguments about public good were far from their minds; instead, they worried about design and conceptual frameworks, and tending to the public good was reserved for senior professors and university presidents. Indeed, many who inhabited these lofty heights were not from the design side; they were managers, industrialists, politicians, university presidents, and senior public servants.

Other programs relate to society in different ways. For example, research in Eindhoven has technical roots and builds on HCI, which is an accepted part of research in engineering and shares its mathematical beliefs. This is in stark contrast to research in art and design universities like the Royal College of Art, in which constructive design researchers share vocabulary, techniques, conventions, and methods for breaking social conventions with contemporary artists. Scandinavian research, on the other hand, falls in between. To make a constructive design research program socially robust, it has to respond to the demands of its local environment.[43]

End Notes

1. While Ehn primarily follows Bruno Latour's philosophy (especially Latour, 1987), this chapter takes most design readers to a more familiar terrain, pragmatism. In particular, Donald Schön (1983) did more than anyone in teaching researchers that design is a reflective dialog between designers and their materials. His perspective, building on pragmatism, was historically important in turning design research to post-Cartesian thinking, but it has its problems as well. In particular, it is too easy to misread Schön and exaggerate dialog at the expense of "design things." Here, Ehn's Latourian interpretation of design things comes in handy: it gives a far more important a place to those things that populate design practice. Precedents to this rehabilitation of material things are numerous; among writers we have referred to in this book, they most notably include phenomenologists and also Michael Lynch's reinterpretation of ethnomethodology (Lynch, 1993). One of the founders of pragmatism, John Dewey, has been another constant reference in Ehn's most recent interpretation of what makes design tools work (see Ehn, 2008, especially p. 99).
2. See Abbott (1988).
3. Cohen et al. (1972).

4. For original formulation of cultural probes, see Gaver et al. (1999); for defense of building ambiguity into design research, see Gaver et al. (2004).
5. The leader of the project was professor Turkka Keinonen and the main researcher was Tuuli Mattelmäki, who received her doctoral degree in 2006.
6. One issue in the study of emotions is how much interpretation there is in emotion. Roughly, the dividing line goes between the positivists, who see emotions as biological processes, and constructionists, who stress interpretation (Kemper, 1981). For positivists, stimuli leads to certain states in the body, and people understand these states as emotions (Kemper, 1981). For constructivists, stimuli leads to changes in the body, but these changes need interpretation before they become emotions (Shott, 1979). Some mediate between these views, usually on Darwinistic grounds: in some situations automatic emotional responses are the last resort to survival, and emotions like fear are for that reason beyond interpretation, while other emotions have an interpretive component (Kemper, 1981). Few claim that more complex emotions like enjoying good design belong to the automatic category.

   The details of this debate are beyond this book. It is important to note, though, that emotions are also used to make sense of ourselves, and they often function as tactical and even commercial devices (Rosenberg, 1990; Hochschild, 2003). These social uses of emotions are the ones researchers in Helsinki were after, not (possibly) measurable emotions like a fear of snakes; hence, interpretive (or constructive) theories of emotions.
7. Mattelmäki (2006).
8. This paragraph refers to several ongoing doctoral theses, built on Luotain, that are due to be published in 2011–2012. Workshops in the context of legislation have been explored by Katja Soini. Design games and their empathic roots are explored by Kirsikka Vaajakallio.
9. In Helsinki, Keinonen (1998) and Säde (2001).
10. Design conferences include the International Association of Societies for Design Research (IASDR), Nordic Design Research Conference (Nordes), Designing Pleasurable Products and Interfaces (DPPI), Design and Emotion (D + E), and Design Research Society in England (DRS). Popular journals are *Design Issues* and *Co-Design Journal*, among others. Popular human–computer interaction conferences like Computer-Human Interaction, and a host of smaller conferences like Designing Information Systems, Computer-Supported Collaborative Work, Participatory Design, and Mobile HCI.
11. See Chapter 5.
12. See the conference the Art of Research, the Design Research Society's Experiential Knowledge Special Group, and also the new *Craft Research* journal.
13. Around 1995 to 1999, smart products were much like computers had been 15 years earlier. Before 1995, few people carried complex electronic devices like mobile phones in their pockets and bags. With portable stereos and mobile phones, designers faced usability questions that were much like those met in Silicon Valley in the 1980s. Designers could not assume that the users were professionals or could even be trained to use products. Products had to be built for people, not the other way around.

   In research in Helsinki, usability became a research focus. While some work focused on consumer preferences, other pieces of work focused on developing methods for studying usability. Methods like paper prototyping were borrowed from computer designers, used in collaborative projects with industry, and then reported to HCI research communities.
14. Hanington (2003).

15. Why the Bauhaus has become a reference to design education is beyond the subjects covered in this book. It was only a small part of a much larger reform of design education in German-speaking Europe at the time (Siebenbrodt and Schöbe, 2009, p. 8ff). Also, its influence was, as Otl Aicher noted, felt more in museums than in actual life (Aicher, 2009).

    We believe the main reason it has become so prominent in historical writing goes back to the extraordinary talent from Weimar, Dessau, Berlin, and later, Chicago. With alumni like Paul Klee, Wassily Kandinsky, Marcel Breuer, Walter Gropius, and Mies van der Rohe, it obviously receives more attention than its competitors in early twentieth century Germany, Switzerland, and Austria.
16. The reasons are solid: empirical social science was in its infancy in the heyday of the Bauhaus and mostly built on history. Most of the tools of post-war social science were simply not available for people like Moholy-Nagy.
17. After all, it is easy to be romantic about handicrafts. However, it is also good to remember some of the problems in craft and workshops; they tend to be male-dominated, tradition-bound, and means-oriented. Also, history certainly tells a tale that questions any romantic call back to craft. It is industrialization that has lifted us from poverty and improved our life standards, not craft. Some of these critiques are discussed in Ehn (1988a).
18. This is the situation in architecture, too, as Pallasmaa (2009) noted.
19. Overbeeke (2007), Keitsch et al. (2010). For 50 years, industrial design turned to research to gain legitimacy at the face of the Bauhaus tradition, creating opportunities for researchers. See Valtonen (2007, p. 118 ff).

    It needs to be noted that departures from the Bauhaus tradition have happened in places in which design is business- and technology-oriented rather than artistic. There are exceptions, however. For example, critical design and the Presence Project both came out from Computer-Related Design, which was set up in the 1990s as a response to digital technology that had transformed design thoroughly in the previous decade. Computer-Related Design, headed by the graphic designer Gillian Crampton-Smith, was a multidisciplinary program from the very beginning but with roots in industrial design. It became the site for research after a research grant from Interval Research Corporation in 1994. Later, this program evolved into Design Interactions under Tony Dunne. For a brief history of Computer-Related Design, see Crampton-Smith (1997).
20. Ehn and Crampton-Smith (1998).
21. K3 stands for *konst, kultur,* and *kommunikation,* or in English, art, culture, and communication. For the original version in Swedish, see mah.se/fakulteter-och-omraden/Kultur-och-samhalle/Institutioner-och-centrum/Konst-kultur-och-kommunikation-K3/Om-Konst-kultur-och-kommunikation-K3/Design-pa-K3/, retrieved May 26, 2010.

    In his original manifesto for a digital Bauhaus, Pelle Ehn (1998, p. 210) wrote:

    > *What is needed is not the modern praise of new technology, but a critical and creative aesthetic-technical production orientation that unites modern information and communication technology with design, art, culture and society, and at the same time places the development of the new mediating technologies in their real everyday context of changes in lifestyle, work and leisure.*

    Nostalgic this may be, but this, indeed, is the Bauhaus applied to the digital domain.
22. In design in particular, Brown (2009) and Verganti (2009).
23. See Redström (2005).

24. See IP08 (2008). In 2008, the participants were Kaj Eckoldt, Thorsteinn Helgason, Riikka Hänninen, Jing Jiang, Ella Kaila, Timo Niskanen, and Benjamin Schultz. Funding for the project came from the Nordic Innovation Center's Ludinno project led by Tomas Edman. Instructors were Ilpo Koskinen, Jussi Mikkonen (electronics), and Petra Ahde (design).

25. Photos from the user study and experience prototyping are by Eckoldt and Schultz; others are by Ilpo Koskinen.

26. Stappers (2007, pp. 88–89).

27. IO StudioLab has been home to many of the best doctoral theses in the Netherlands, including Djajadiningrat (1998), Wensveen (2004), Keller (2005), and Sleeswijk Visser (2009).

28. Mattelmäki (2006, pp. 197–205).

29. This is especially true if they are able to link this new expertise to management consulting, as RED associates in Copenhagen. IDEO and previously E-Lab have provided important models for other companies.

At the small-business and craft-oriented end of the spectrum, researchers face some of the same tensions as artists. As Howard S. Becker (1982) noted in *Art Worlds*, craftspeople routinely complain about "bad craft" in seeing artists' craft objects. The complaint has institutional foundations. Art occupies a much higher position in society than art. When artists attempt pottery, for example, they are able to connect to media and wealthy clients in ways beyond reach by craftsmen, whose work, naturally, is technically much better. The strain is inevitable. No doubt, this is also the case with research. After all, research prototypes are barely ever meant to achieve a high level of craft, while research budgets can typically be only dreamt of by craftspeople.

30. For E-Lab, see Wasson (2000, 2002).

31. For Intel, see Intel's *Reassessing ICTs and Development: The Social Forces of Consumption* (Intel, 2010a), which presented a series of case studies of ICT use through a multi-site ethnography and contextualized these studies to social science literature on development. For Alessi, Verganti (2009) and Alessi and Zilocchi (2010); for Philips, for example, Aarts and Marzano (2003) and *Vision of the Future* (Philips Design 2005).

32. Like in Stbd, a design company based in Amsterdam and London that specializes in using documentary film for design. Its use of documentary partly builds on the doctoral thesis of one of its partners, Bas Raijmakers (2007). Companies like DesignIT in Copenhagen and Aarhus, Denmark, typically sell both research and design services. See designit.com/.

33. Many examples we have shown in this book, such as DAIM (Halse et al., 2010), Luotain (see Mattelmäki, 2006), and Switch!, received funding from national sources in their home countries. On the other hand, the EU funded the Presence Project and Maypole.

34. *Presence Project* (2000), Mäkelä et al. (2000).

35. Other winners are obvious: research in technology and business.

36. European Union (2009, p. 2).

37. For Muoto 2005!, see Saarela (1999).

38. For the latest effort, see designpolicy.org/from 2009. This effort came from the design world. In Europe, the main drivers have been people with power, usually either administration and politicians, or major corporations.

39. Historically, the military was an important source of revenue for design firms run by Henry Dreyfuss, Walter Teague, and even Raymond Loewy. Although the details still remain under the veil of secrecy, ergonomics is in debt to military spending that started during World War II. See Flinchum (1997, pp. 78–87).

40. To see how Herbert Simon connected with the Ford, Carnegie, and Rockefeller foundations to pool resources for psychology, management, and computer science at Carnegie Tech (now Carnegie Mellon University), see Crowther-Heyck (2005, pp. 149ff). Crowther-Heyck does not mention how design was progressing on Simon's agenda for the university. A more recent example is the now defunct Interval Research from Paul Allen, which funded what came to be one of the key projects in shaping constructive work, Presence.

41. See Beaver et al. (2009).

42. For workshops, see Soini and Pirinen (2005); for more artistic work, see Mattelmäki et al. (2010) and the Spice Project at designresearch.fi/spice.

43. "Socially robust" is from Nowotny et al. (2008).

10

BUILDING RESEARCH PROGRAMS

It is impossible to describe everything in constructive design research today, and we need more specific language to understand what is happening in this discipline. For us, this language has been methodology, which gives a simple enough yet informative storyline. As always in methodology, there is a fine line between aim, description, and prescription, which we wanted to avoid. We hope this book is not read as a manual. Having said this, this chapter gives a few tips for establishing and maintaining constructive design research programs.

We have located the origins of research from what Andrea Branzi called "second modernity."[1] In first modernity, design had few industries in which to work, consumer tastes were fairly homogeneous, and taste elites promoted sleek modernism in design. In second modernity, these certainties are not self-evident. Revolutions of taste have moved design from its modernist roots, and design has become a mass profession.[2] Also, the social base of design is far more diverse than before, and this gives design a better ability to respond to demands coming from all walks of life, however surprising these might be.

We have also seen how constructive design researchers have moved from product design to systems, services, organizations, technologies, and even the relationship of the city to the countryside.[3] Constructive design researchers may have changed the world only a little, but they have certainly seen what is happening around them and taken a stance. Society has changed, and so has design research. It does not have a simple objective anymore.

Almost a century ago, László Moholy-Nagy wrote about the need to bring many types of knowledge into design. In the same spirit, constructive design research has opened design for many new developments.

> *Human history is much too short to compete with nature's richness in creating functional forms. Nevertheless, the ingenuity of man has brought forth excellent results in every period of his*

history when he understood the scientific, technological, esthetic, and other requirements. This means that the statement, "form follows function," has to be supplemented; that is, form also follows — or at least it should follow — existing scientific, technical and artistic developments, including sociology and economy.[4]

Several people in this book are not designers by training. They have brought new skills, practices, and ideas into design and design research. It is hard to imagine the constant stream of innovative work coming from Eindhoven without Kees Overbeeke, a mathematical psychologist by training. Similarly, the psychologist Bill Gaver's contribution to interaction design and its research is undeniable. Many other characters in our story, however, are designers like Tom Djajadiningrat and Ianus Keller in the Netherlands, Simo Säde in Finland, and Anthony Dunne and Fiona Raby in England. Yet in other cases, we have been writing about designers whose roots are outside design, like Tobie Kerridge, whose first academic home was in English language, and Johan Redström, whose academic home was in music and philosophy. Research programs are rich creatures in which many kinds of expertise may be relevant.

10.1 Beyond Rationalism

If there ever was a paradigm in design research, it was during the 1960s. At that time, rationalism reigned in various forms. Herbert Simon tried to turn design into a science through systems theory.[5] For writers in the design methods movement, the aim was to turn design into a systematic discipline by making the design process methodic.[6] This was the dominant understanding of design methods in industrial design for a few years. Even though these writers aimed at rationalizing design and not research, many design researchers still built on their work.

This rationalistic ethos was paradigmatic. Its premise was accepted without asking if it was right or wrong. There was no need to question any premise in the post-war university, because it was dominated by one generation of white males with a background in engineering and the military, and with a small number of teachers coming from another generation. Practically everyone had similar values, and it was the *Zeitgeist*. Systems theory was growing in stature in the natural and social sciences, giving an air of legitimacy to the effort.[7]

However, this paradigmatic phase was short-lived. As we have seen, its main proponents quickly turned away from it[8] as well as practicing designers who found this effort impractical and unnecessary. Also, this paradigm failed in Ulm, as its long-term headmaster Tomás Maldonado noted (Figure 10.1).[9]

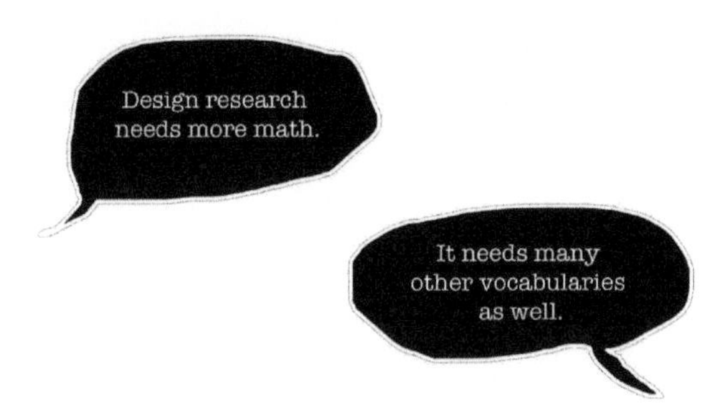

Figure 10.1 Contemporary design research has many rationalities.

During this time the intellectual climate changed. The rationalistic worldview was discarded in the humanities and the social sciences, at first for political reasons.[10] Some of the criticisms focused on its destructive force; it had created prosperity on an unprecedented scale, but also massive destruction, and others found problems with its conceptual and theoretical underpinnings.[11] When women, lower-middle class students, and new ethnic groups entered universities, the social basis of the rational paradigm was contested. For these critiques, rationalism was little more than a hollow claim to universalism by one demographic group.

As soon as we look at constructive design research programs, we find ourselves in a room familiar to any well-read philosopher, humanist, artist, or social scientist. From this room, we find J.J. Gibson's ecological psychology, which in turn builds on Gestalt psychology and is tied to phenomenology from many different directions. Similarly, there are references to symbolic interactionism and surrealism, and through them, to the very foundations of twentieth century thinking. These foundations include psychoanalysis, structuralism, phenomenology, and pragmatism.

Philosophers call these intellectual and artistic movements post-Cartesian. This word covers many things, such as the major differences between, say, phenomenology, structuralism, Dada, or Gestalt psychology.[12] Post-Cartesian philosophies importantly tell designers to approach the world with sensitivity by trying to understand it rather than by imposing theoretical order on it. They tell designers to become interpreters rather than legislators, and to use the metaphor of Zygmunt Bauman, a leading Polish-British social critic.[13] This quality is particularly important in design — a creative exercise by definition.

10.2 Contribution and Knowledge

Constructive design research creates many kinds of knowledge, and designs capture knowledge from previous research.

When researchers study these designs, they generate knowledge about design techniques and processes, as well as about how people understood and appropriated these designs.

Typically, however, the most important form of knowledge are the frameworks researchers build to explicate their designs. These frameworks vary from Stephan Wensveen's interaction frogger and Katja Battarbee's co-experience to Jodi Forlizzi's product ecology.[14] Even the frameworks may sometimes be unimportant: a good deal of critical design does not try to develop frameworks. Its contribution lies in debates raised by its designs. Constructive design research produces ways to understand how people interact with the material world. It also shows how to use that knowledge in design.

Constructive design researchers routinely build on theoretical and philosophical sources from older, more established fields of research, but few claim to contribute to psychology, sociology, philosophy, or the natural sciences. Knowing the theoretical background of a program helps to keep a program consistent and may help to take it forward at important junctions, but it does not help to make a better television, communication concept, or mouse.[15] Typically, only very experienced researchers go to philosophical heights. Even they take this step cautiously when settling controversies or breaking free from clichés of thought and not with the intention of contributing to philosophical discourse.

The word "knowledge" easily leads to unnecessary discussions that hinder research.[16] Chemists, after all, do not think they need to know how chemists think in order to do research or what kind of knowledge they produce. We believe that here, design needs to learn from the natural and the social sciences. It is better to go full steam ahead rather than stop thinking about knowledge in the abstract. When the volume of research grows, there will be milestones every researcher knows, refers to, and criticizes. Sociology may not have found any hard facts about society, but there is a tremendous amount of wisdom about society in that discipline.

Constructive design research probes an imagined world, not the real world of a social scientist. Although things that are often playful and sometimes disturbing populate it, it is a very useful world. It makes it possible to study things outside normal experience. For example, we learn how rich interaction might work by reading Joep Frens' work and how social media based on "self" might work by reading John Zimmerman's studies. Their research tells a tremendous amount about specifics like materials, forms, functions, user experience, software, and the social environment of design.[17] This knowledge is useful for the project at hand, and it may also end up being used in industry (Figure 10.2).

One implication is important. The "contribution" in constructive design research is not like in the natural sciences, where it is

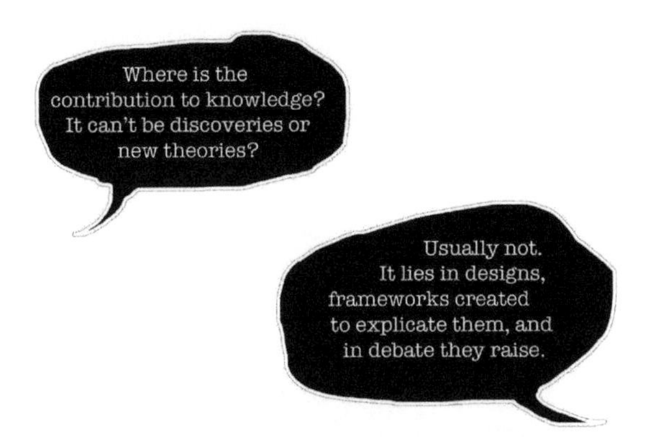

Figure 10.2 Ways to contribute to knowledge include designs, frameworks, and debate.

possible talk about "facts" as long as one remembers that most facts are contestable.[18]

With the possible exception of some researchers in Lab, most constructive design researchers work like the humanists and interpretive social scientists. They usually want to improve thinking and understanding, not to make discoveries, much like the humanities and the social sciences, where a new perspective or distinction can be an important contribution. Practically all contributions to knowledge of Shakespeare or Goethe come from improvements in discourse. This, however, is not a dramatic distinction. In the sciences, better explanations are welcomed even when little new data exist. Also, the main contribution of many scientific projects is an approach, method, or instrument. There is no one right way to do "science"; for example, to study bird migrations, researchers need different methods from astrophysics.

10.3 How to Build Research Programs

To anyone interested in entering constructive design research, the main advice from this book is to think in terms of programs. If we look at places in which constructive design research has taken shape, we see variety, but also many connecting dots. The key element is a community that is able to work with things we have talked about, including theory, many types of research methods, and imaginative design skills. Programs also need some infrastructure to make construction possible. What kinds of machinery and workshops are needed remains unanswered in this book, but for us it is clear that any design school, medium-sized design firm, and global corporation have everything necessary.

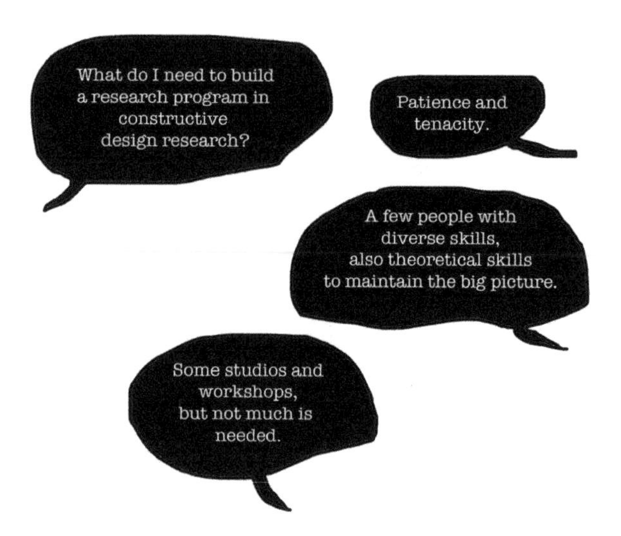

Figure 10.3 Things to keep in mind when building programs.

In design schools, the main difficulty is understanding how research works. Programs evolve and mature over time. What is important is typically seen only in retrospect and often years after the fact.[19] Few designers have enough patience to wait that long for results. It is easy to kill programs before they lead to success. In technical environments, the most difficult question is how to give enough space to design. As Kees Overbeeke noted in his inaugural lecture in 2007 at Technische Universiteit Eindhoven, universities tend to put too much value on cognitive skills at the expense of other human skills.[20] If the notions of science are narrow-minded, design may not get a fair chance to show its value (Figure 10.3).

Writing a successful program in a committee would require oracle-like abilities. Even though writing successful programs may be difficult, it is not difficult to create preconditions and make a good attempt. The risk is small if we look at the research described in this book. Major contributions often come from small groups, and these groups need to have theoretically knowledgeable senior researchers, young researchers, and designers, but they do not need dozens of people.[21]

Compared to these questions of ethos and managerial culture, some things are plain in comparison. In supervising research, it is important to build research on what others have done in the program. This is obvious for people in science universities, but clashes with the ethos of creativity that reigns in design schools, where originality and raising personalities are stressed. Also, research programs are not run by organizations. Every successful program has been open to change and has given things to other programs. For example, field researchers in Helsinki borrowed from cultural probes and from the Interactive Institute's artistic work. Larger organizations may run several programs, as in Sheffield-Hallam University in England.

Yet another observation is that it makes sense to build on one's strengths, whether design, science, social science, or contemporary art.[22] In places like Helsinki, one can work with complex technology, design, consumer goods, Web systems, and services simultaneously. All resources required are within a reasonable travel distance. With Philips Design nearby, it is natural for researchers in Eindhoven to focus on sophisticated interactive technology with a serious focus on process. London's art market accepts complex artistic argumentation that would raise eyebrows in Pittsburgh with its pragmatic culture valuing solid engineering.

However, this argument should not be stretched too far. It would be plainly wrong to say that the environment somehow dictates what researchers can do. Such a claim runs contrary to what we have just said about the relatively modest resources needed for a solid research program. Also, sometimes limits turn into opportunities; revolutions in thinking often come from surprising places. Why not art in Pittsburgh, which has some of the best art collections imaginable, but not the elite tastes of a New York or a Paris dictating what is interesting?

10.4 Inspirations and Programs

Our list of things that inspire constructive design researchers includes issues, ordinary things in society, research-related sources, and tinkering with materials.

Issues are funded by major corporations and the governments. The biggest issue lately has no doubt been climate and sustainability, but many other things on the design research agenda are also issues. Some issues come from technology policy and technology companies, as the steady stream of new technologies since the 1980s reveals. For example, one of the buzzwords of 2009–2010 was "service design," which initially had its origins in IBM's global strategy. It was later pushed into research and higher education as a novelty with little regard for the fact that most advanced economies have been service economics since the 1960s. Issues come and go. New issues emerge when governments and administrations change.

Behind these issues are the humbler sources in everyday life. These consist of ordinary activities, technologies, things happening on the markets, and all kinds of sources in culture, such as folklore, books, ads, and films.[23] Herein lies the charm of second modernity: it is manifold, consisting of many overlapping realities that inspire endlessly. Things closer to design research are scientific theories, frameworks, data collected in other studies, and the very history of design. Even closer to design is tinkering — work on structures and materials in workshops and laboratories. Interaction designers tinker with software rather than with materials and physical objects.[24]

As this offhand list shows, inspiration can come from anywhere. It is more important to look at how researchers turn these ideas into research questions and studies.

Here again, we meet research programs. Researchers turn what they see into research problems through conceptual analysis and theoretical work. In this work, they turn to their own program, look at what other researchers have done, and then decide what to do. The exact order in which these things are done varies and is less important than situating research into a program. Research programs have many ways to build on inspiration. Some stress artistic sources, while others turn to design history. Some turn to theory in psychology and sociology, while others start with user studies.[25]

Although sources of inspiration may change, programs have their histories, key members, methodological preferences, and tradition. These things give them identity but also an air of calmness. What may seem like rigidity is really a source of flexibility. Programs may change slowly, but they are repositories of expertise. Over time, successful programs provide referents and precedents.[26] For this reason, they are able to work on a wealth of inspirations. Thus, critical designers had no difficulties in going into the sciences, researchers in Helsinki switched from smart products to services and urban design effortlessly, and Danish researchers went from participatory design to co-design without missing a beat.

10.5 Research Programs and Methodologies

The first exemplary constructive pieces were done between 1998 and 2005. As often, the best formulations of central ideas are the first articulations. Some kinds of progress, however, are built into the notion of the research program. Where is research heading next? (See Figure 10.4.)

One thing to note is the difference between research programs and methodologies. Without a doubt, as constructive design research matures, several new research programs will emerge. They will find homes at art and design universities, technical universities, and in design practice.

Another thing of note is the difference between methods and methodologies. We will see new methods in the future.

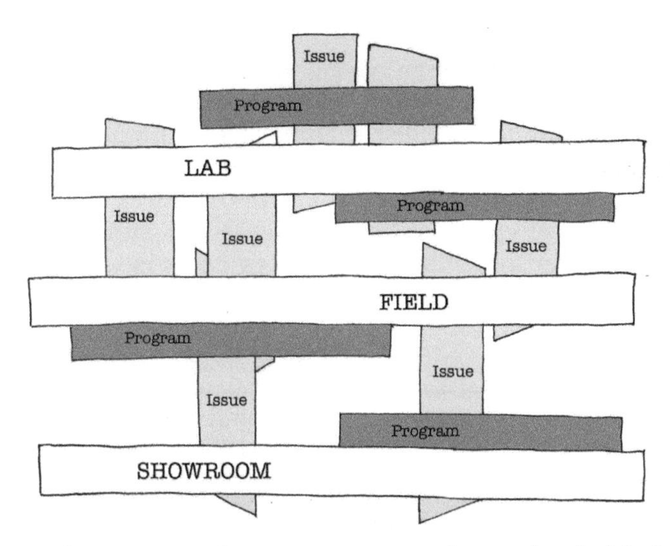

Figure 10.4 Issues come and go, programs are tenacious, and methodologies change slowly. Some issues come and go, some reform, reappear, and outlive the programs.

In inventing new methods, there is basically no limit, especially if we look at what Carnegie Mellon's Bruce Hanington once called "innovative methods."[27] We believe that the more methods there are, the better. Novelty in constructive design research has often been based on new methods rather than technologies, issues, or theories. There is far less room for methodological innovation. Here, constructive design research is in good company. The range of methodologies in the sciences is far smaller than the range of methods.

There are some directions to watch to foresee the future of constructive design research. There is a small step from some contemporary art and craft practices to research, and there are already good examples of turning craft into research.[28] Another likely breeding ground is engineering. This is well illustrated by places like the MIT Media Lab.

Also, social issues like climate change may be around long enough to feed research programs that bring more science into design research. In several universities, there are scientists who have become designers but who build their research programs on their scientific training. For example, there is only a short step from Carlo Vezzoli's work on sustainable design in Milan to constructive design research. In the near future, we will most certainly see constructive work based on his work.[29] Indeed, it is easy to imagine a chemist using her skills in design rather than doing technical or industrial applications.

There are also seeds of the future growing within existing research programs. With the exception of Lab, there has been little use of statistics in constructive design research, but there are several interesting openings. For example, Oscar Tomico combined statistics with George Kelly's personal construct theory to create a tool for capturing the sensory qualities of objects for design.[30] Similarly, Kansei engineers analyzed emotions and senses with multivariate statistics. Although the community has mostly influenced Japanese industry and technical universities, it has gained some following in Europe.[31] Furthermore, some recent work in Eindhoven has built on philosopher Charles Lenay's phenomenological work on sensory perception, combining sophisticated experimental work and statistical decision making to this ultimately descriptive philosophy.[32] Although phenomenology and symbolic interactionism are usually seen as qualitative traditions, this is a miscomprehension. There will no doubt be successful attempts to bring statistical analysis into design, and mixed methods approaches are certainly in the near future.[33]

One interesting trend is happening in Field. In Italy and Scandinavia, user-centered design has evolved into co-design and action research.[34] A step to organizational development and community design is not far, but this will further distance design from its base in products.[35] Another possible step is to study the business models in practice, which is happening in the SPIRE group in Sønderborg, Denmark, under Jacob Buur's stewardship. Here design research is intertwined in the policy sciences of the 1960s, but hopefully it avoids becoming overtly political and entangled in value discussions.

Finally, researchers need eclectic approaches to tackle "truly wicked problems" that require years of concentrated work with many stakeholders who often have contradictory agendas. Solutions to problems like climate change have to be particularly imaginative. Any solution has to survive the debate on a large and competitive "agora," where the audience consists of scientists, politicians, companies, and the general public.[36] There are several ways in which constructive design researchers are tackling these truly wicked problems, but are they satisfactory?[37]

10.6 The Quest for a Big Context

When Andrea Branzi was talking about second modernity, he put his finger on something every design researcher knows even though design researchers may not have the vocabulary to talk about it. Second modernity opens many kinds of opportunities for those designers who are willing to seize them.[38] They may be weak and diffuse rather than based on the sturdy realities of the past. For that reason, second modernity is difficult to grasp with concepts coming from first modernity. This applies to design research as well as to design.

Second modernity requires not only intellectual openness and curiosity but also modesty. We have seen how constructive design researchers have deliberately built on frameworks that encourage exploration. This echoes the opinions of some of the leading design practitioners. In an interview with C. Thomas Mitchell, Daniel Weil reflected on his experiences when studying at the Royal College of Art (RCA) in London in the early 1980s. He talked about how he was disappointed in designers' discourse and was attracted to contemporary art.

When Weil was talking to Mitchell, he had already left his professorship at RCA and was working at Pentagram. He wanted to gain a better grasp of "the big context": not just a product but also things around the product. He was worried about how industrial design in his day focused on products without context.

> *But there's nothing in three dimensions like that, no understanding of the big context, which is what architecture traditionally did. I believe that is the role of industrial design. The people who work in three dimensions need to move away from just being a service and understand the bigger picture. So it's all about understanding the context instead of just purely designing a solution according to what has been designed before in a similar area.... What has happened is that designers are accustomed to the one-to-one scale, but when it starts to go large, they're a bit lost. So it's quite important to work more conceptually on bigger pictures. Then they will find it a lot easier to discover more complexity in what they're doing. It's important that we put more complexity and a bit more intellect into the activity of designing, and the activity of encouraging other designers by doing so.*[39]

We see a revolution brewing here. Weil was among those young designers who grew up with Branzi's Studio Alchymia and was soon invited to participate in Memphis by Ettore Sottsass, Jr. The period he describes prepared him for new kinds of questions. Indeed, why does the radio have to be a box?

This quest for a bigger context later became the breeding ground for Showroom. It, however, can be observed elsewhere in constructive design research. For example, ergonomics taught how humans interact with their physical environment, interaction designers brought systems thinking to design from computer science, and design management introduced them to formal organizations and management, to take only three of the many examples available (Figure 10.5).[40]

Figure 10.5 Two attitudes to research.

Weil's generation, however, was looking for new vocabularies from design. His vocabulary of choice was design management, which gave him an opportunity to design in a strategic context. When constructive design research was created, it picked up many of the leads left by these designers but turned to research. In about ten years, constructive design researchers have given design ways to talk about issues, such as direct perception, social and cultural context, and the implications of top-notch science.[41] Design needs new vocabularies to work with the big context. The unique contribution of constructive design research is that it creates these vocabularies in a design-specific, yet theoretically sophisticated manner.

End Notes

1. Branzi (1988, 2006).
2. Branzi (2010).
3. For services, see Yoo et al. (2010), Mattelmäki et al. (2010), and Meroni and Sangiorgi (2011). For the garbage collecting case, see Halse et al. (2010); for community health see A. Júdice (2011) and M. Júdice (2011) and the relationship of the city to its surroundings in Meroni and Sangiorgi (2011).
4. Moholy-Nagy (1947) in *Vision in Motion*. We have avoided talking about "form" in this book for a reason, but since Moholy-Nagy's quote has a reference to Louis Sullivan's famous adage "form follows function," we need to add a note here.

   For us, it is not obvious that form is the main concern of design, and is far less a concern to design research: there are other concerns that are equally and more important. In Sullivan's cliché, "form" is also too easy to understand as information instead of chaos, whether the form is a thing, pattern, model, or service. Finally, it is already a cliché, and there is an industry of variations including titles such as *Less Is More, Less + More, Yes Is More,* and so forth.

Another word we have tried to avoid has been "complexity." It simplifies history into a process of increasing complexity and tends to lead to an idea that design needs to respond to increasing complexity by becoming more complex. Quite simply, this is not the way in which most designers prefer to work. Just as often, they describe their work using open-ended artistic terms like "intuition" and "inspiration." Given the well-known shortcomings of the design methods movement, this is understandable.

5. Simon (1996).

6. Jones (1992, 1984), Alexander (1968).

7. See Forlizzi (forthcoming). References to "paradigms" in this chapter are from Thomas Kuhn's (1962) *The Structure of Scientific Revolutions.*

8. For example, Alexander (1971) and Jones (1991).

9. See Chapter 2.

10. Marxism was important in European design schools, but as few schools did research in the 1970s, its impact on research was minor. In information systems design, the early 1980s saw several Marxist developments, in particular, in Scandinavia (see Lyytinen, 1982, 1983; Ehn, 1988a). The detailed history of Marxism in Western design is still unwritten.

11. These critiques were already voiced in Ulm in the 1960s (see the next note), and in the 1970s and 1980s software designers joined the chorus (see Dreyfus 1972, 1993; Winograd and Flores, 1987; Ehn, 1988a, b).

12. For example, see Aicher (2009) and Hoffman-Axthelm (2009, pp. 219–220) for accounts of the theoretical basis of design at the Ulm school.

13. Bauman and May (2000).

14. Wensveen (2004), Battarbee (2004), Forlizzi (2007).

15. See Carroll and Kellogg (1989).

16. Lawson (1980, 2004), Cross (2007), and Visser (2006). For an extensive discussion of knowledge in design, see Downton (2005).

17. In some cases, there are several environments, as our discussion of Nowotny et al. (2008) implies.

18. See Latour (1987). There was a long and once heated discussion in sociology about knowledge and whether even mathematical facts are social or not. In some sense, they are, because there would be no mathematics without people who agree to work with some conventions. Still, some conventions stay long enough to be treated as practically eternal facts. This happens in mathematics and logic, but also in some of the exact natural sciences.

19. Here we obviously follow Lakatos. See Chapter 3.

20. Overbeeke (2007). We must add that he specifically blamed the Greeks (the ancients, to clarify) for this cognitive bias and overvaluation of the written word over the bodily skills.

21. For good reasons. Large organizations get bureaucratic. They also increase the stakes so much that too many stakeholders get interested in protecting their investments and taking the credit for results.

22. See Molotch (1996).

23. Think about the film noir metaphor behind Dunne and Raby's Design Noir.

24. Wroblewski (1991).

25. *Presence Project* (2001); Intel (2010b).

26. See Goldschmidt (1998) and Lawson (2004). As Pallasmaa (2009, p. 146) noted, good architects collaborate not only with builders and engineers, but with the whole tradition of architecture: "Meaningful buildings arise from tradition and they constitute and continue a tradition.... The great gift of tradition is that we can choose our collaborators; we can collaborate with Brunelleschi and Michelangelo if we are wise enough to do so." No doubt, this statement has more than a hint of exaggeration, but the basic point is right and is also important for designers.

27. Hanington (2003), Stappers and Sanders (2003). For an empathic interpretation of some of these methods, see Koskinen et al. (2003).

28. For art, see Scrivener (2000). For craft, see Mäkelä (2003) and Niedderer (2004). *Craft Research Journal* started in 2010. Also, the first Craft Reader appeared in 2010 (Adamson, 2010).

29. See Manzini and Vezzoli (2002) and Vezzoli (2003).

30. Tomico (2007).

31. See, for example, Lévy and Toshimasa (2009).

32. Lenay et al. (2007).

33. Social scientists talk about "triangulation" when a study uses several methods simultaneously. The idea is that one can trust the results better when several methods point to the same results or interpretation. The origins of the word are in cartography and land surveying.

34. For example, Rizzo (2009), Meroni (2007), Halse et al. (2010), and Mattelmäki et al. (2010).

35. Meroni and Sangiorgi (2011).

36. Nowotny et al. (2008).

37. For example, see Beaver et al. (2009), Switch!, and the work of the Júdices in Vila Rosário, mentioned in Chapter 5.

38. Branzi (1988, 2006).

39. Weil (1996, p. 25).

40. The question of whether designers should be professional problem-solvers or do design in a broader context is one of the standing debates in design. Maldonado contrasted Ulm with Chicago's New Bauhaus:

> *The HfG that we are setting up at Ulm proposes a redefinition of the terms of the new culture. It will not be content to simply turn out men that know how to create and express themselves — as was the case with Moholy-Nagy in Chicago. The Ulm school intends to indicate the path to be followed to reach the highest level of creativity. But, equally and at the same time, it intends to indicate what should be the social aim of this creativity; in other words, which forms deserve to be created and which not. (Maldonado, quoted by Bistolfi, 1984, second page)*

For Maldonado, this was a call to reform Ulm's education to train designers who think about social content rather than think opportunistically about the market. His designers were to enrich cultural experience in addition to satisfy concrete needs in everyday life.

41. The references here are to Chapters 4–6.

REFERENCES

Aalto, A. (1997). Trout and the mountain stream. In G. Schildt (Ed.), *Alvar Aalto in his own words*. Helsinki: Otava.

Aarts, E., & Marzano, S. (Eds.). (2003). *The new everyday. Views on ambient intelligence*. Rotterdam: 010 Publishers.

Abbott, A. (1988). *The system of professions*. Chicago: University of Chicago Press.

Adamson, G. (Ed.). (2010). *The craft reader*. London: Berg.

Aicher, O. (2009). The Bauhaus and Ulm. In P. Oswalt (Ed.), *Bauhaus conflicts, 1919–2009. Controversies and counterparts* (pp. 174–186). Ostfildern: Hatje Cantz.

Akrich, M. (1992). The De-scription of technical objects. In W. Bijker & J. Law (Eds.), *Shaping technology/building society — Studies in sociotechnical change*. Cambridge, MA: The MIT Press.

Alessi and UIAH (1995). *The workshop*. Milano: Nero su Bianco. UIAH and Centro Studi Alessi.

Alessi and UIAH (2002). *Keittiössä: Taikkilaiset kokkaa Alessille — UIAH students cooking for Alessi*. Helsinki: UIAH.

Alessi, C., & Zilocchi, D. (Eds.). (2010). *Oggetti e progetti. Objects and projects. Alessi: History and future of an Italian design factory*. Milan: Electa.

Alexander, C. (1968). *Notes on the synthesis of form*. Cambridge, MA: Harvard.

Alexander, C. (1971). The state of the art in design methods. *DMG Newsletter*, *5*(3), 1–7.

Ambasz, E. (Ed.). (1972). *Italy: The new domestic landscape*. NYC: MoMA.

Anceschi, G., & Massimo, B. (2009). Hypermodern? Perspectives for the design education, research and practice. In M. Botta (Ed.), Multiple ways to design research. Research cases that reshape the design discipline. *Proceedings of the fifth Swiss design network symposium*, Nov 12–13 Lugano. Geneva: Swiss Design Network and Milano: Edizioni.

Archer, L. B. (1968). *Technological innovation: A methodology*. London, UK: Royal College of Art. Unpublished doctoral thesis.

Aspara, J. (2009). *Where product design meets investor behavior. How do individual investors' evaluations of companies' product design influence their investment decisions?* Helsinki: UIAH.

Banham, R. (1991). HfG Ulm in retrospect. In H. Lindinger (Ed.), *Ulm design: The morality of objects* (pp. 57–59) . Cambridge, MA: The MIT Press.

Bannon, L. (1991). From human factors to human actors. The role of psychology and human-computer interaction studies in systems design. In J. Greenbaum, J. Kyng & M. Kyng (Eds.), *Design at work. Cooperative design of computer systems* (pp. 25–44). Hillsdale: Lawrence Erlbaum Associates. Available also at <http://www.ul.ie/~idc/library/papersreports/LiamBannon/6/HFHA.html/>.

Bannon, L. (2009). Constructing utopia(s) in situ — Daring to be different. In T. Binder, J. Löwgren & L. Malmborg (Eds.), *(Re)searching the Digital Bauhaus* (pp. 62–77). London: Springer.

Battarbee, K. (2004). *Co-experience. User experience in interaction*. Helsinki: UIAH.

Battarbee, K., & Koskinen, I. (2004). Co-experience: User experience as interaction. *Co-design*, *1*, 5–18.

Bauman, Z., & May, T. (2000). *Thinking sociologically*. Oxford: Blackwell.

Bayazit, N. (2004). Investigating design: A review of forty years of design research. *Design Issues*, *20*, 16–29.

Beaver, J., Kerridge, T., & Pennington, S. (Eds.), (2009). *Material beliefs*. London: Goldsmiths, Interaction Research Studio. <materialbeliefs.com/>. Retrieved 05.03.2010.

Becker, H.S. (Ed.), (1970). Field work evidence. *Sociological work. Method and substance*. New Brunswick, NJ: Transaction Books.

Becker, H. S. (1982). *Art worlds*. Chicago: University of Chicago Press.

Bell, G., Blythe, M., & Sengers, P. (2005). Making by making strange: Defamiliarization and the design of domestic technologies. *ACM Transactions on Computer-Human Interaction, 12*(2), 149–173.

Berger, P. L., & Luckmann, T. (1967). *The social construction of reality: A treatise in the sociology of knowledge*. New York: Doubleday.

Bergström, J., Mazé, R., Redström, J., & Vallgårda, A. (2009). Symbiots: Conceptual interventions into urban energy systems. In: *Proceedings of the 2nd Nordic design research conference on engaging artifacts*. Oslo, Norway. Retrieved from <nordes.org/>.

Betsky, A. (2006). re: droog. In *Droog. Simply Droog* (pp. 14–22). Amsterdam: Droog.

Beyer, H., & Holtzblatt, K. (1998). *Contextual design: Defining custom-centered systems*. San Francisco, CA: Morgan Kaufmann.

Bill, M. (2009). What is industrial design? *Form, function, beauty = Gestalt*. London: Architectural Association. (Original essay in German in 1954.)

Binder, T. (2007). Why Design: Labs. Conference paper, *2nd nordic design research conference (NORDES)*, Konstfack, Stockholm, May, 2007.

Binder, T., & Redström, J. (2006). Exemplary Design Research. Paper presented at the *DRS wonderground conference*, November 1–4, 2006.

Binder, T., Brandt, E., Halse, J., Foverskov, M., Olander, S., & Yndigen, S. (2011). Living the (codesign) lab. In *Proceedings of fourth Nordic design research conference* (NORDES), Helsinki, May 2011.

Bishop, C. (2004). Antagonism and relational aesthetics. *October Magazine, 110*, 51–79.

Bishop, C. (2007). The social turn. Collaboration and its discontents. In M. Schavemaker & M. Rakier (Eds.), *Right about now. Art & theory since the 1990s* (pp. 59–68). Amsterdam: Valiz.

Bistolfi, M. (1984). The HfG in Ulm: Hopes, development and crisis. *Rassegna, 19*(3), 6–19. (Original in Italian: La HfG di Ulm: speranze, sviluppo e crisi.)

Black, A. (1998). Empathic design. User focused strategies for innovation. In *Proceedings of new product development. IBC conferences. Interactions*. Cambridge, MA: The MIT Press.

Blauvelt, A. (2003). *Strangely familiar: Design and everyday life*. Minneapolis, MN: Walker Art Center.

Blomberg, J., Giacomi, J., Mosher, A., & Swenton-Wall, P. (2009). Ethnographic field methods and their relation to design. In D. Schuler & A. Namioka (Eds.), *Participatory design principles and practices*. Boca Raton, FL: CRC Press. (Original in 1993 by Lawrence Erlbaum Associates.)

Blumer, H. (1969). *Symbolic interactionism*. Englewood Cliffs, NJ: Prentice-Hall.

Bocchietto, S. (2008). *Pop design: Fuori scala fuori lungo fuori schema*. Milan: SilvanaEditoriale.

Bødker, S. (1987). *Through the interface — A human activity approach to user interfaces*. Aarhus: Department of Computer Science, Aarhus University.

Bødker, S., & Greenbaum, J. (1988). A non-trivial pursuit — Systems development as cooperation. *Working Paper DAIMI PB*, nr. 268. Aarhus: Department of Computer Science, Aarhus University.

Boehner, K., Vertesi, J., Sengers, P., & Dourish, P. (2007). How HCI interprets the probes. In *Proceedings of CHI*, San Jose, CA.

Bonsiepe, G. (1999). The invisible facets of the HfG Ulm. *Design Issues, 11*, 11–20.

Bonsiepe, G. (2009). The Ulm School of Design (HfG) as an experiment of cultural innovation. In M. Carniel & L. R. Parker (Eds.), *Tomás Maldonado* (pp. 122–135). Milano: Skira.

Boomkens, R. (2003). Engagement *after* progress. In reflect#01. *New commitment. In architecture, art and design*. Rotterdam: NAi Publishers.

Borja de Mozota, B. (2003). *Design management: Using design to build brand value and corporate innovation*. New York: Allworth Press.

Borja de Mozota, B. (2006). The four powers of design: A value model in design management. *Design Management Review, 17*, 44–53.

Bosoni, G. (2001). *Italy. Contemporary domestic landscape 1945–2000*. Milan: Skira.

Boucher, A., & Gaver, W. (2007). Developing the Drift Table. *Interactions, January–February*, 24–27.

Bourriaud, N. (2002). *Relational aesthetics*. Paris: La presses du réel.

Brandes, U., Stich, S., & Weber, M. (2009). *Design by use. The everyday metamorphosis of things*. Basel: Birkhäuser.

Brandt, E. (2001). *Event-driven product development: Collaboration and learning*. Lyngby, Denmark: Technical University of Denmark. Unpublished doctoral dissertation.

Brandt, E. (2006). Designing exploratory design games: a framework for participation in Participatory Design? In: *Proceedings of participatory design conference* (pp. 57–66). Trento, Italy, August 1–5.

Branzi, A. (1984). *The hot house. Italian new wave design (nuovo design)*. Cambridge, MA: The MIT Press.

Branzi, A. (1988). *Learning from Milan. Design and the second modernity*. Cambridge, MA: The MIT Press.

Branzi, A. (2006). *Weak and diffuse modernity. The World of projects at the beginning of the 21*st *century*. Milan: SKIRA.

Branzi, A. (2008). *What Is Italian design? The seven obsessions*. Milano: La Triennale di Milano.

Branzi, A. (2009). *Serie fuori serie, series off series*. Milano: La Triennale di Milano.

Branzi, A. (2010). Design as a mass profession (*Design come profesione di massa*). In L. di Lucchio & A. Penati (Eds.), *Vitamins for design* (vol. 7, issue 42–43, pp. 32–43). Rome: Disegno industriale/industrial design.

Braverman, H. (1974). *Labor and monopoly capital. The degradation of work in the twentieth century*. New York: Monthly Review Press.

Brown, J. S., & Duguig, P. (2000). *The social life of information*. Boston: Harvard Business School Press.

Brown, T. (2009). *Change by design: How design thinking transforms organizations and inspires innovation*. New York: HarperCollins.

Buchanan, R. (1992). Wicked problems in design thinking. *Design Issues, 8*, 5–21.

Buchanan, R. (2001). Design research and the new learning. *Design Issues, 17*, 3–23.

Buchanan, R., & Margolin, V. (Eds.). (1995). *Discovering design. Explorations in design studies*. Chicago: The University of Chicago Press.

Buchenau, M., & Fulton Suri, J. (2000). Experience prototyping. In: *Proceedings of DIS* (pp. 424–433). ACM.

Bürdek, B. E. (2005). *Geschichte, Theorie und Praxis der Produktgestaltung*. Basel: Birkhäuser.

Burkhardt, F., & Morotti, C. (n.d.) *Andrea Branzi*. Paris: Éditions dis voir.

Butter, R. (1989). Putting theory into practice: An application of product semantics to transportation design. *Design Issues, 5*, 51–67.

Buxton, B. (2007). *Sketching user experiences: Getting the design right and the right design*. San Francisco, CA: Morgan Kaufmann.

Calle, S. (2010). *Sophie Calle: The reader*. London, Tilburg, and Copenhagen: Whitechapel Gallery, De Pont Museum of Contemporary Art, and Louisiana Museum of Modern Art.

Campbell, D. T., & Stanley, J. C. (1973). *Experimental and quasi-experimental designs for research*. Chicago: McNally. (Original 1957.)

Caption, J. (2004). *Trial-and-error-based innovation. Catalysing shared engagement in design conceptualisation*. Oslo: Oslo School of Architecture.

Card, S. K., English, W. K., & Burr, B. J. (1978). Evaluation of mouse, rate-controlled isometric joystick, step keys, and text keys for text selection on a CRT. *Ergonomics, 21*, 601–613.

Carroll, J. (2000). *Making Use. Scenario-based design of human-computer interactions*. Cambridge, MA: MIT Press.

Carroll, J. M. (1995). *Scenario-based design: envisioning work and technology in system development*. New York: Wiley.

Carroll, J.M., & Kellogg, W.A. (1989). Artifact as theory-nexus: hermeneutics meets theory-based design. In *Proceedings of conference on human factors in computing systems* (pp. 7–14). New York: ACM Press.

Castelli, C. T. (1999). *Transitive design. A design language for the zeroes*. Milan: Electa.

Cefkin, M. (2010). Introduction: Business, anthropology, and the growth of corporate ethnography. In M. Cefkin (Ed.), *Ethnography and the corporate encounter. Reflections on research in and of corporations*. New York: Berghahn Books.

Celant, G. (1972). Radical architecture. In E. Ambasz (Ed.), *Italy: The new domestic landscape* (pp. 382–383). NYC: MoMA.

Cohen, M. D., March, J. G., & Olsen, J. P. (1972). A garbage can model of organizational choice. *Administrative Science Quarterly, 17*, 1–25.

Cook, T. D., & Campbell, D. T. (1979). *Quasi-experimentation: Design and analysis issues for field settings*. Chicago: Rand McNally.

Cooper, A. (1999). *The inmates are running the asylum*. USA: SAMS.

Costa Gaspar da Pedro, M. (2003). *Cleaning marble, oolitic limestone and terracotta surfaces. A topographical assessment and comparison of the effects of conservation cleaning treatments on architectural materials*. London, UK: Royal College of Art. Unpublished doctoral dissertation.

Crampton-Smith, G. (1997). Computer-related design at the Royal College of Art: 1997 Graduation Projects. *ACM Interactions* (Nov–Dec), 27–33.

Crabtree, A. (2003). *Designing collaborative systems. A practical guide to ethnography*. London: Springer.

Crabtree, A, (2004). Design in the absence of practice: Breaching experiments. In *Proceedings of DIS 2004* (pp. 59–84). Cambridge, MA: ACM.

Cross, N. (2007). *Designerly ways of knowing*. Basel: Birkhäuser.

Crowther-Heyck, H. (2005). *Herbert A. Simon. The bounds of reason in modern America*. Baltimore, MD: Johns Hopkins University Press.

DAM, Designing critical design: Jurgen Bey, Martí Guixé, Dunne & Raby. *DAM Magazine, 33*.

Dandavate, U., Sanders, E.B.-N., & Stuart, S. (1996). Emotions matter. User empathy in the product development process. In *Proceedings of the human factors and ergonomics society*, 40th annual meeting.

Danish Design Centre, *Den danske designpris/The danish design prize 2004*. Copenhagen: Danish Design Centre.

Darò, C. (May 5, 2003). L'architetture radicale e la critica. *Arch'it* <architettura.supereva.com/files/20030505/>. Retrieved 15.08.2010.

Davidoff, S., Dey, A., & Zimmerman, J. (2007). Rapidly exploring application design through speed dating. In *Proceedings of the conference on ubiquitous computing* (pp. 429–446). New York: Springer.

Debord, G. (1955). Introduction to a critique of urban geography. *The situationist international text library* <library.nothingness.org/articles/SI/en/display/2/>. Retrieved 15.08.2010.
Debord, G. (1958). *Theory of the dérive.* Bureau of Public Secrets. <bopsecrets.org/SI/2.derive.htm/>. Retrieved 13.05.2010.
Debord, G. (2002). *The society of the spectacle.* (K. Knabb, Trans.) Bureau of Public Secrets. <bopsecrets.org/images/sos.pdf/>. Retrieved 13.05.2010.
Debord, G., & Wolman, G. J. (1956). *A user's guide to détournement.* Bureau of Public Secrets. <bopsecrets.org/SI/detourn.htm/>. Retrieved 13.05.2010.
Deckers, E.J.L., Westerhoff, J., Pikaart, M., van Wanrooij, G.A.F., & Overbeeke, C.J (2009). How perception gets emotional value through the use of an object. In *Proceedings of DPPI'09* (pp. 104–115). Compiègne, France.
Deckers, E., Westerhoff, Pikaart M., van Wanrooij, G., Overbeeke, C.J. (2009). How perception gets emotional value through the user of an object. *Proceedings of DPPI'09*, Compiegne, France. pp. 104–115.
Deckers, E.J.L., Wensveen, S.A.G., Overbeeke, C.J., PeR: Designing for perceptive qualities, *Proc. DeSForM* 2010, 68–70.
Deckers, E., Wensveen, S., Ahn, R., & Overbeeke, C. (2011). Designing for perceptual crossing to improve user involvement. In *Proceedings of CHI 2011*, Vancouver, Canada. pp. 1929–1937.
De Michelis, G. (2009). The phenomenological stance of the designer. In T. Binder, J. Löwgren & L. Malmborg (Eds.), *(Re)searching the Digital Bauhaus.* London: Springer.
den Hartog Jager, H. (2003). Always at a distance. Beyond the boundaries of engagement. reflect#01. *New commitment. In architecture, art and design.* Rotterdam: NAi Publishers.
De Ruyter, B., & Aarts, E. (2010). Experience research. In H. Nakashima, H. Aghajan & J. C. Augusto (Eds.), *Handbook of ambient intelligence and smart environments.* Dordrecht: Springer.
Design Interactions 2007–2009. *Yearbooks.* London: Royal College of Art.
Desmet, P. (2002). *Designing emotions.* Delft, the Netherlands: TU/Delft.
De Vaus, D. A. (2002). *Surveys in social research.* London: Routledge.
Dewey, J. (1980). *Art as experience.* New York: Perigee Books. (Original in 1934.)
Dilnot, C. (1989a). The state of design history. Part I: Mapping the field. In V. Margolin (Ed.), *Design discourse: History, theory, criticism.* Chicago: The University of Chicago Press.
Dilnot, C. (1989b). The state of design history. Part II: Problems and possibilities. In V. Margolin (Ed.), *Design discourse: History, theory, criticism.* Chicago: The University of Chicago Press.
Djajadiningrat, T. (1998). *Cubby: What you see is where you act. Interlacing the display and manipulation spaces.* Delft, the Netherlands: Technical University of Delft.
Djajadiningrat, T., Overbeeke, K., & Wensveen, S. (2002). But how, Donald, tell us how? On the creation of meaning in interaction design through feedforward and inherent feedback. In *Proceedings of DIS 2002* (pp. 285–291). London.
Dorst, K. (1997). *Describing design. A comparison of paradigms.* Delft, the Netherlands: Technical University of Delft.
Dorst, K., & Dijkhuis, J. (1995). Comparing paradigms for describing design activity. *Design Studies, 16*, 261–274.
Dourish, P. (2002). *Where the action is.* Cambridge, MA: MIT Press.
Downton, P. (2005). *Design research.* Melbourne: RMIT University Press.
Dreyfus, H. (1992). *What computers still can't do: A critique of artificial reason.* Cambridge, MA: MIT Press.

Dreyfus, H. L. (1972). *What computers can't do. A critique of artificial reason.* New York: Harper & Row.
Dreyfus, H. L. (2001). *On the Internet.* London: Routledge.
Dumas, J. (2007). The great leap forward: The birth of the usability profession (1988–1993). *Journal of Usability Studies, 2*(2), 54–60.
Dunne, A. (2005). *Hertzian tales.* Cambridge, MA: MIT Press. (Original as Dunne, A. (1999). *Hertzian tales. Electronic products, aesthetic experience and critical design.* London, RCA: CRD Research Publications.)
Dunne, A. (2007). Frequently asked questions. In *Design interactions yearbook 2007.* London: Royal College of Art.
Dunne, A., & Raby, F. (2001). *Design noir: The secret life of electronic objects.* Basel: August/Birkhäuser.
Ehn, P. (1988a). *Work-oriented design of computer artifacts.* Stockholm: Arbetslivscentrum.
Ehn, P. (1988b). Playing the language-games of design and use. On skill and participation. In *Proceedings of conference on supporting group work* (142–157). Palo Alto, California.
Ehn, P. (1998). Manifesto for a Digital Bauhaus. *Digital Creativity, 9,* 207–216.
Ehn, P. (2008). Participation in design things. *Proceedings of participatory design conference PDC'08,* pp. 92–101.
Ehn, P. (2009). Design things and living labs. Participatory design and design as infrastructuring. In M. Botta (Ed.), Multiple ways to design research. Research cases that reshape the design discipline. In *Proceedings of the fifth Swiss design network symposium,* Nov 12–13 Lugano. Geneva: Swiss Design Network and Milano: Edizioni.
Ehn, P., & Kyng, M. (1991). Cardboard computers: Mocking-it-up or hands-on the future. In J. Greenbaum & M. Kyng (Eds.), *Design at work: Cooperative design of computer systems* (pp. 169–196). Hillsdale, NJ: Lawrence Erlbaum.
Emerson, R. M., Frets, R. I., & Shaw, L. L. (1995). *Writing ethnographic fieldnotes.* Chicago: University of Chicago Press.
Ericson, M., Frostner, M., Kyes, Z., Teleman, S., & Williamson, J. (Eds.), (2009). *Iaspis forum on design and critical practice.* Stockholm: Iaspis and Sternberg Press.
Erlhoff, M. (1991). Ulm as a model of modernity. In H. Lindinger (Ed.), *Ulm design: The morality of objects* (pp. 51–55). Cambridge, MA: The MIT Press.
Ernevi, A. , Palm, S., & Redström, J. (2005). Erratic appliances and energy awareness. In *Proceedings of Nordic design research conference NORDES,* 2005, Copenhagen. <nordes.org/>. Retrieved 20.10.2010.
Etzold, J. (2009). Honoring the dead father? The situationists as heirs to the Bauhaus. In P. Oswalt (Ed.), *Bauhaus conflicts, 1919–2009. Controversies and counterparts* (pp. 152–170). Ostfildern: Hatje Cantz.
European Union (2009). *Design as a driver of user-centred innovation.* Brussels: Commission of the European Communities. <ec.europa.eu/enterprise/newsroom/cf/_getdocument.cfm?doc_id=2784/>. Retrieved 20.09.2010.
Fallan, K. (2010). *Design history. Understanding theory and method.* London: Berg.
Ferguson, R., de Salvo, D., & Slyce, J. (1999). *Gillian wearing.* London: Phaidon.
Findeli, A. (1998). A quest for credibility. Doctoral education and research in design at the University of Montreal. *Doctoral education in design,* Ohio, 8–11 Oct. 1998. <designresearchsociety.org/>. Retrieved 20.09. 2010.
Findeli, A. (2006). Qu'appelle-t-on "theorie" en design? Réflexions sur l'enseignement et la recherche en design. In B. Flamand (Ed.), *Le design. Essais sur des théories et des pratiques* (pp. 83–94). Paris: Editions de l'institut Français de la mode.

Fiz, A. (2010). *Mendini Alchimie. Dal Controdesign alle Nuovo Utopie*. Milano: Electa.
Flinchum, R.(1997). *Henry Dreyfuss, industrial designer: The man in the brown suit*. Washington: Cooper-Hewitt, National Design Museum, Smithsonian Institution & New York: Rizzoli.
Forlizzi, J. (2007). Product ecologies. *Understanding the context of use surrounding products*. Unpublished doctoral dissertation, Carnegie Mellon University, Pittsburgh, Pennsylvania.
Forlizzi, J. Exact reference not known in April 2011. Product Ecologies: A system approach to in process design.
Forlizzi, J., & Battarbee, K. (2005). Understanding experience in interactive systems. In *Proceedings of designing interactive systems DIS 2004*, 1–4 August, Boston, MA (pp. 261–268). New York: ACM Press.
Forlizzi J., & Ford, S. (2000). The building blocks of experience: An early framework for interaction designers. In *Proceedings of DIS2000, designing interactive systems*. New York: ACM.
Forlizzi, J., Stolterman, E., & Zimmerman, J. (2009). From design research to theory: Evidence of a maturing field. *Proceedings of IASDR*, Seoul, South Korea, 19–22 October, 2009.
Foster, H. (2007). (Dis)engaged art. In M. Schavemaker & M. Rakier (Eds.), *Right about now. Art & theory since the 1990s*. Amsterdam: Valiz.
Frayling, C. (1993). Research in art and design. *Royal College of Art Research Papers, 1*, 1–5.
Frens, J. (2006a). *Designing for rich interaction. Integrating form, interaction, and function*. Eindhoven, the Netherlands: Department of Industrial Design.
Frens, J. (2006b). Designing for rich interaction. Integrating form, interaction, and function. In *Proceedings of the* 3rd *symposium of design research: Drawing new territories* (pp. 91–109). Swiss Design Network. Zürich: Switzerland.
Fulton Suri, J., Battarbee, K., & Koskinen, I. (2005). Designing in the dark: Empathic exercises to inspire design for our non-visual senses. In *Proceesings of include 05*, Royal College of Art, London, England.
Fulton Suri, J., & IDEO, *Thoughtless acts? Observations on intuitive design*. San Francisco: Chronicle Books.
Fulton Suri J. (2011). Poetic observation: What designers make of what they see. In A. Clarke (Ed.), *Design anthropology*. Springer: Vienna.
Garfinkel, H. (1967). *Studies in ethnomethodology*. Englewood Cliffs, NJ: Prentice-Hall.
Gaver, B. (2002). Presentation about Cultural Probes. PowerPoint presentation, November, 2002, UIAH, Helsinki. <smart.uiah.fi/luotain/pdf/probes-seminar/GaverPROBES.pdf/>. Retrieved 18.04.2009.
Gaver, B., Dunne, T., & Pacenti, E. (1999). Cultural probes. *interactions, January–February*, 21–29.
Gaver, W., Bowers, J., Boucher, A., Law, A., Pennington, S., & Villar, N. (2006). The History Tablecloth: Illuminating domestic activity. *Proceedings of DIS*, June 26–28, 2006, University Park, Pennsylvania, pp. 199–208.
Gaver, W., Boucher, A., Law, A., Pennington, S., Bowers, J., Beaver, J., et al. (2008). Threshold devices: Looking out from the home. *Proceedings of CHI 2008*, April 5–10, 2008, Florence, Italy, pp. 1429–38.
Gaver, W., Sengers, P., Kerridge, T., Kaye, J., & Bowers, J. (2007). Enhancing ubiquitous computing with user interpretation. Field testing the Home Health Horoscope. *Proceedings of CHI 2007*, April 28–May 3, 2007, San Jose, California, pp. 537–546.
Gaver, W.W., Beaver, J., & Benford, S. (2003). Ambiguity as a resource for design. In *Proceedings of CHI 2003*, April 5–10, 2003, Ft. Lauderdale, Florida, pp. 233–240.
Gaver, W. W., Boucher, A., Pennington, S., & Walker, B. (2004). Cultural probes and the value of uncertainty. *interactions, September–October*, pp. 53–56.

Gedenryd, H. (1998). *How designers work: Cognitive studies.* Lund: Lund University. <lucs.lu.se/People/Henrik.Gedenryd/HowDesignersWork/>. Retrieved 10.08.2007.

Geertz, C. (1973). Thick description: Towards an interpretive theory of culture. *The Interpretation of cultures.* New York: Basic Books.

Geertz, C. (1983). *Local knowledge.* London: Fontana.

Glanville, R. (1999). Researching design and designing research. *Design Issues, 15*(2), 80–91.

Glaser, B. G., & Strauss, A. L. (1967). *The discovery of grounded theory: Strategies for qualitative research.* New York: Aldine de Gruyter.

Goldschmidt, G. (1998). Creative architectural design: Reference versus precedence. *Journal of Architectural and Planning Research, 15*(3), 258–270.

Gorb, P. (1990). *Design management. Papers from the London Business School.* London: Architecture Design and Technology Press.

Graves P., Ole Iversen, M., Gall Krogh, P., & Ludvigsen, M. (2004). Aesthetic interaction. A pragmatist's aesthetics of interactive systems. *Proceedings of DIS2004,* August 1–4, 2004, Cambridge, MA.

Grcic, K. (2010). *Design real. Exhibition curated by Konstantin Grcic.* London: Koenig Books and Serpentine Gallery. Serpentine Gallery, London 26 November 2009–7 February 2010.

Green, W. S., & Jordan, P. (1999). *Human factors in product design. Current practice and future trends.* London: Taylor & Francis.

Greenbaum, J. (2009). A design of one's own: Towards participatory design in the United States. In D. Schuler & A. Namioka (Eds.), *Participatory design principles and practices.* Boca Raton, FL: CRC Press. (Original in 1993 by Lawrence Erlbaum Associates.)

Greenbaum, J., & Kyng, M. (Eds.). (1991). *Design at work: Cooperative design of computer systems.* Hillsdale, NJ: Lawrence Erlbaum.

Greenson, R. (1967). *The technique and practice of psychoanalysis.* New York: International Universities Press.

Grudin, J. (2009). Obstacles to participatory design in large product development organizations. In D. Schuler & A. Namioka (Eds.), *Participatory design principles and practices.* Boca Raton, FL: CRC Press. (Original in 1993 by Lawrence Erlbaum Associates.)

Hackos, J. T., & Redish, J. C. (1998). *User and task analysis for interface design.* New York: John Wiley and Sons Inc.

Hall, P. (2007). Teaching the bigger picture. Design schools need to shift focus from the form of objects to understanding the systems that produce them. *Metropolis,* 18 April, 2007. <metropolismag.com/cda/story.php?artid=2595/>. Retrieved 20.05.2007.

Halse, J., Brandt, E., Clarke, B., & Binder, T. (Eds.), (2010). *Rehearsing the future.* Copenhagen: Danish Design School Press.

Hanington, B. (2003). Methods in the making: A perspective on the state of human research in design. *Design Issues, 19,* 9–18.

Hargadon, A., & Sutton, R. I. (1997). Technology brokering and innovation in a product development firm. *Administrative Science Quarterly, 42,* 716–749.

Härkäsalmi, T. (2008). *Runkokuituja lyhytkuitumenetelmin — kohti pellavan ja hampun ympäristömyötäistä tuotteistamista.* Helsinki: UIAH. (*Bast fibres by short-fibre methods – towards an environmentally-conscious productization of flax and hemp,* in Finnish.)

Harper, R. (Ed.). (2003). *Inside the smart home.* London: Springer.

Harris, C. (Ed.). (1999). *Art and innovation. The Xerox PARC Artist-In-Residence Program.* Cambridge, MA: MIT Press.

Hassenzahl, M. (2003). The thing and I: Understanding the relationship between user and product. In M. Blythe, K. Overbeeke, A. Monk & P. Wright (Eds.), *Funology. From usability to enjoyment* (pp. 31–42). Dordrecht: Kluwer.

Hassenzahl, M. (2004). The interplay of beauty, goodness, and usability in interactive products. *Human-Computer Interaction, 19*, 319–349.
Henderson, K. (1999). *On line and on paper. Visual representations, visual culture and computer graphics in design engineering*. Cambridge, MA: The MIT Press.
Heynen, H. (2003). Intervention in the relations of production, or sublimation of contradictions? On commitment then and now. In reflect#01 2003. *New commitment. in architecture, art and design*. Rotterdam: NAi Publishers.
Hirschheim, R., Klein, H. K., & Lyytinen, K. (1995). *Information systems development and data modeling. Conceptual and philosophical foundations*. Cambridge: Cambridge University Press.
Hochschild, A. R. (2003). *The managed heart. Commercialization of human feelings*. Berkeley: University of California Press.
Hoffman-Axthelm, D (2009). State-supported boredom. The distance of the 1968 student movement. In P. Oswalt (Ed.), *Bauhaus conflicts, 1919–2009. Controversies and counterparts* (pp. 212–223). Ostfildern: Hatje Cantz.
Hofmeester, K., & de Saint Germain, E. (Eds.). (1999). *Presence. New media for older people*. Amsterdam: Netherlands Design Institute.
Höger, H.L. (2010). Ulm: una morale raggiunta con metodi (Ulm: methodically drawing a moral). *Vitamins for design* (vol. 7, pp. 42–43) (Trans. Claudia Vettore). Rome: *Disegno industriale*.
Holt, S. S., & Skov, M. H. (2008). *Manufractured. The conspicuous transformation of everyday objects*. San Francisco: Chronicle Books.
Holtzblatt, K., & Jones, S. (2009). Contextual inquiry. A participatory technique for system design. In D. Schuler & A. Namioka (Eds.), *Participatory design principles and practices*. Boca Raton, FL: CRC Press. (Original in 1993 by Lawrence Erlbaum Associates.)
Horváth, I. (2007). Comparison of three methodological approaches of design research. *International Conference on engineering design ICED'07*, 28–31 August, Cité des sciences et de l'industrie, Paris.
Hummels, C. (2000). *Gestural design tools: Prototypes, experiments and scenarios*. Delft, the Netherlands: Delft University of Technology.
Hummels, C., & Frens, J. (2008). Designing for the unknown. A Design process for the future generation of highly interactive systems and products. *International conference on engineering and product design education*, 4–5 September, Barcelona, Catalunya.
Hustwit, G. (2009). *Objectified*. Documentary film, DVD, Swiss Dots Production, PLX-035.
Hutchins, E. (1996). *Cognition in the wild*. Cambridge, MA: MIT Press.
Iacucci, G., Kuutti, K., & Ranta, M. (2000). On the move with a magic thing: Role playing in concept design of mobile services and devices. In *Proceedings of DIS '00* (pp. 193–202), Brooklyn, New York.
Intel, *Reassessing ICTs and development. The social forces of consumption*. Portland: People and Practices Research, Intel Labs. <http://papr.intel-research.net/svm.htm/>. Retrieved 01.10.2010.
Intel, *The global aging experience project. Ethnographic research*. Portland: Product Research and Innovation. <ftp://download.intel.com/healthcare/telehealth/GAEbrochure.pdf/>. Retrieved 01.10.2010.
IP08 (2009). Hacking a car: Re-embodying the design classroom. Nordic Design Research Conference, Nordes, Oslo, Norway. (Koskinen, I., Mikkonen, J., Ahde, P., Eckoldt, K., Helgason, T., Hänninen, R., Jiang, J., Niskanen, T., & Schultz, B.) <nordes.org/>. Retrieved 15.08.2009.
Iversen, O. (2005). *Participatory design beyond work practices — Designing with children*. Aarhus: University of Aarhus.
Jacucci, G., Oulasvirta, A., & Salovaara, A. (2007). Active construction of experience through mobile media. A field study with implications for recording and sharing. *Personal and Ubiquitous Computing, 11*, 215–234.

Jappe, A. (1999). *Guy Debord*. Berkeley: University of California Press.
Jégou, F., & Joore, P. (Eds.). (2004). *Food delivery solutions. Cases of solution oriented partnership*. Cranfield, UK: Cranfield University.
Joas, H. (1985). *G.H. Mead, a contemporary re-examination of his thought*. Cambridge, MA: MIT Press. (Original in German, 1980.)
Johansson, M. (2005). *Participatory inquiry — Collaborative design*. Blekinge, Sweden: Blekinge Institute of Technology.
Jonas, W. (2007). Design research and its meaning to the methodological development of the discipline. In M. Ralf (Ed.), *Design research now. Essays and selected papers*. Basel: Birkhäuser.
Jones, J. C. (1984). *Essays in design*. New York: John Wiley and Sons.
Jones, J. C. (1991). *Designing designing*. London: Architecture Design and Technology Press.
Jones, J. C. (1992). *Design methods* (2nd ed.). New York: John Wiley and Sons.
Jordan, B., & Lambert, M. (2009). Working in corporate jungles. Reflections on Ethnographic Praxis in industry. In M. Cefkin (Ed.), *Ethnography and the corporate encounter. Reflections on research in and of corporations*. New York: Berghahn Books.
Jordan, B., & Yamauchi, Y. (September 2008). Beyond the university, teaching ethnographic methods in the corporation. *Anthropology News*, 35.
Jordan, P. (2000). *Designing pleasurable products*. London: Taylor & Francis.
Júdice, A. *Design for hope: Designing health information in Vila Rosário*. Helsinki: UIAH, in press.
Júdice, M. *You are important! Empowering health agents in Vila Rosário through design*. Helsinki: UIAH, in press.
Julier, G. (1991). *New Spanish design*. London: Thames & Hudson.
Julier, G. (2008). *The culture of design*. Los Angeles: Sage.
Jungk, R., & Müllert, N. (1983). *Zukunftswerkstätten. Wege zur Wiederbelebung der Demokratie*. München: Goldmann.
Kankainen, A. (2002). *Thinking model and tools for understanding user experience related to information appliance product concepts*. Espoo: Acta Polytechnical Scandinavica, Mathematics and Computing Series No. 118.
Kaptelinin, V., & Nardi, B. (2009). *Acting with technology. Activity theory and interaction design*. Cambridge, MA: MIT Press.
Keinonen, T. (1998). *One-dimensional usability. Influence of usability on consumers' product preference*. Helsinki: University of Arts and Design.
Keinonen, T. (2009). Design method. Instrument, competence or agenda? In M. Botta (Ed.), *Multiple ways to design research. Research cases that reshape the design discipline. Proceedings of the Fifth Swiss design network symposium*, Nov 12–13 Lugano. Geneva: Swiss Design Network and Milano: Edizioni.
Keitsch, M., Vavik, T., Morelli, N., Bolvig Poulsen, S., Koskinen, I., Holmlid, S., et al. (2010). *Ludinno — Learning labs for user-driven innovation*. Oslo: Nifca. Articles "Do Tank Helsinki" and "Reflections and Design Policy." <nordicinnovation.net/_img/ludinno_learning-labs_for_user-driven_innovation_web.pdf/>. Retrieved 10.05.2010.
Keller, I. (2005). *For inspiration only: Designer interaction with informal collections of visual material*. Delft, the Netherlands: Delft University of Technology. Unpublished doctoral dissertation.
Kelley, T. (2001). *The art of innovation. lessons in creativity from IDEO, America's leading design firm*. New York: Random House.
Kelly, G. A. (1955). *The psychology of personal constructs*. London: Routledge.
Kemper, T. D. (1981). Social constructionist and positivist approaches to the sociology of emotions. *American Journal of Sociology*, *87*, 336–362.
Kerridge, T. (2009). Does speculative design contribute to public engagement of science and technology? In M. Botta (Ed.), *Multiple ways to design research. research cases that reshape the design discipline*. In *Proceedings of the Fifth*

Swiss design network symposium, Nov 12–13 Lugano. Geneva: Swiss Design Network and Milano: Edizioni.
Kester, G. H. (2004). *Conversation pieces: Community and communication in modern art*. Berkeley: University of California Press.
Kicherer, S. (1990). *Olivetti. A study of the corporate management of design*. London: Trefoil.
Koskinen, I. (2007). *Mobile multimedia in action*. New Brunswick: Transaction.
Koskinen, I., Battarbee, K., & Mattelmäki, T. (Eds.), (2003). *Empathic design*. Helsinki: IT Press.
Koskinen, I., Binder, T., & Redström, J. (2008). Lab, field, gallery, and beyond. *Artifact: Journal of Virtual Design, 2*, 46–57.
Koskinen, I., Kurvinen, E., & Lehtonen, T. -K. (2002). *Mobile image*. Helsinki: IT Press.
Koskinen, I., Kuusela, K., Battarbee, K., Soronen, A., Mäyrä, F., Mikkonen, J., & et al. (2006). The home in metamorphosis: A field study of proactive information technology at home. *Proceedings of designing information systems, DIS*, Penn State University, 26–28 June.
Krippendorff, K. (1989). On the essential contexts of artifacts or on the proposition that "design is making sense (of things)". *Design Issues, 5*, 9–39.
Krippendorff, K. (1995). Redesigning design: An invitation to a responsible future. <asc.upenn.edu/usr/krippendorff/REDESGN.htm/>. Retrieved 15.10.2010.
Krippendorff, K. (2006). *The semantic turn. A new foundation for design*. Boca Raton, FL: Taylor & Francis.
Kuhn, T. (1962). *The structure of scientific revolution*. Chicago: University of Chicago Press.
Kurvinen, E. (2005). How industrial design interacts with technology: A case study on design of a stone crusher. *Journal of Engineering Design, 16*, 373–383.
Kurvinen, E. (2007). *Prototyping social action*. Helsinki: UIAH.
Kurvinen, E., Battarbee, K., & Koskinen, I. (2008). Prototyping social interaction. *Design Issues, 21*, 46–57.
Kuutti, K. (1996). Activity theory as a potential framework for human-computer interaction research. In B. A. Nardi. (Ed.), *Context and consciousness. Activity theory and human-computer interaction*. Cambridge, MA: MIT Press.
Lakatos, I. (1970). Falsification and the methodology of scientific research programmes. In I. Lakatos & A. Musgrave (Eds.), *Criticism and the growth of knowledge*. Cambridge, UK: Cambridge University Press.
Lang, P., & Menking, W. (Eds.). (2003). *Superstudio. Life without objects*. Milano: Skira.
Latour, B. (1987). *Science in action*. Cambridge, MA: Harvard University Press.
Laurel, B (Ed.). (2003). *Design research. methods and perspectives*. Cambridge, MA: The MIT Press.
Lawson, B. (1980). *How designers think*. London: Architectural Press.
Lawson, B. (2004). *What designers know*. Amsterdam: Elsevier.
Lee, K. -P. (2001). *Culture and its effects on human interaction with design*. Tsukuba, Japan: University of Tsukuba.
Lee, M.K., Forlizzi, J., Rybski, P.E., Crabbe, F., Chung, W., Finkle, J., et al. (2009). The Snackbot: Documenting the design of a robot for long-term human-robot interaction. *Proceedings of HRI 2009* (pp. 7–14). New York: ACM Press.
Lenay, C. (2010). "It's so touching": Emotional value in distal contact. *International Journal of Design, 4*(2), 15–25.
Lenay, C., Thouvenin, I., Guénand, A., Gapenne, O., Stewart, J., & Maillet, B. (2007). Designing the ground for pleasurable experience. *Proceedings of DPPI 2007*, Helsinki, Finland, pp. 35–58.
Lévy, P., & Toshimasa, Y. (2009). Kansei studies description and mapping through Kansei study keywords. *Kansei Engineering International, 8*, 179–185.

Lindinger, H. (Ed.), (1991). Ulm: Legend and living idea. In H. Lindinger (Ed.), *Ulm design: The morality of objects* (pp. 9–13). Cambridge, MA: The MIT Press.

Lippard, L. (1997). *Six years. The dematerialization of the art object from 1966 to 1972*. Berkeley: University of California Press.

Livingston, E. (1987). *Making sense of ethnomethodology*. London: Routledge & Kegan Paul.

Lofland, J. (1976). *Analyzing social settings: A guide to qualitative observation and analysis*. Belmont, CA: Wadsworth.

Lovell, S. (2009). *Limited edition. Prototypes, one-offs and design art furniture*. Basel: Birkhäuser.

Lucero, A. V. (2009). *Co-designing interactive spaces for and with designers: Supporting mood-board making*. Vaajakoski, Finland: Gummerus.

Ludvigsen, M. (2006). *Designing for social interaction*. Aarhus: Center for Interactive Spaces, University of Aarhus and Department of Design, Aarhus School of Architecture.

Lunenfeld, P. (2000). *Snap to grid. A user's guide to digital arts, media and cultures*. Cambridge, MA: MIT Press.

Lykke-Olesen, A. (2006). *Space as interface. Bridging the gap with cameras*. Aarhus, Denmark: Aarhus School of Architecture.

Lynch, M. (1993). *Scientific practice and ordinary action. Ethnomethodology and social studies of science*. Cambridge, UK: Cambridge University Press.

Lyytinen, K. (1982). *On information system development and its knowledge interests*. Göteborg, Sweden: Syslab Report 13.

Lyytinen, K. (1983). *Understanding language in information systems*. Jyväskylä: Computer Science Report. Working Paper 1.

Lyytinen, K. (1986). *Information systems developmena as social action. Framework and critical implications*. Jyväskylä: Jyväskylä Studies in Conputer Science, Economics and Statistics.

Mäkelä, M. (2003). *Saveen piirtyviä viivoja. Subjektiivisen luomisprosessin ja sukupuolen representaatioita*. Helsinki: Taideteollinen korkeakoulu. (*Lines Drawn in Clay. Representations of a Subjective Creative Process and Gender*, in Finnish.)

Mäkelä, A., Giller, V., Tscheligi, M., & Sefelin, R. (2000). Joking, storytelling, artsharing, expressing affection: A field trial of how children and their social network communicate with digital images in leisure time. *Proceedings of CHI 2000*, pp. 548–555.

Mäkelä, M., & Routarinne, S. (Eds.). (2007). *The art of research. research practices in art and design*. Helsinki: UIAH.

Mäyrä, F., Soronen, A., Vanhala, J., Mikkonen, J., Zakrzewski, M., & Koskinen, I., et al. (2006). Probing a proactive home: Challenges in researching and designing everyday smart environments. *Human Technology, 2*, 158–186.

Maldonado, T. (1972). *Design, nature, and revolution. Toward a critical ecology*. New York: Harper & Row.

Maldonado, T. (1984). Ulm revisited. In *Rassegna, Anno 19/3*, settembre 1984. (Frank Sparado, Trans.)

Maldonado, T. (1991). Looking back at Ulm. In H. Lindinger (Ed.), *Ulm design: The morality of objects* (pp. 222–224). Cambridge, MA: The MIT Press.

Manzini, E. (2008). Collaborative organisations and enabling solutions. Social innovation and design for sustainability. In F. Jégou & E. Manzini (Eds.), *Collaborative services. Social innovation and design for sustainability* (pp. 29–41). Milano: Edizioni Polidesign.

Manzini, E., Collina, L., & Evans, S. (Eds.), (2004). *Solution oriented partnership. How to design industrialised sustainable solutions*. Cranfield, UK: Cranfield University.

Manzini, E., & Jégou, F. (Eds.). (2003). *Sustainable everyday, scenarios of urban life*. Milano: Edizione Ambiente.

Manzini, E., & Vezzoli, C. (2002). *Product-service systems and sustainability: Opportunities for sustainable solutions*. Paris: UNEP-United Nations Environment Programme.
March, J. G. (1978). The 1978 Nobel Prize in Economics. *Science, 202*, 858–861.
Margolin, V., & Buchanan, R. (Eds.). (1995). *The idea of design. A design issues reader*. Chicago: The University of Chicago Press.
Mattelmäki, T. (2006). *Design probes*. Helsinki: UIAH.
Mattelmäki, T., Brandt, E., & Vaajakallio, K. (2010). Who are you? Designing interpretations for new interpretations. *Proceedings of design and emotion*, Chicago, 5–7 October, 2010.
Matthews, B., Stienstra, M., & Djajadiningrat, T. (2008). Emergent interaction: creating spaces for play. *Design Issues, 24*, 58–71.
Mazé, R. (2007). *Occupying time: Design, technology, and the form of interaction*. Stockholm: Axl Books.
Mazé, R., & Redström, J. (2007). Difficult forms: Critical practices in design and research. *Proceedings of the conference of the international association of societies of design research*. Hong Kong: IASDR, 12–15 November, 2007. <sd. polyu.edu.hk/iasdr/proceeding/papers/Difficult forms_ Critical practices in design and research.pdf/>. Retrieved 15.01. 2008.
Mazé, R., & Redström, J. (2008). Switch! Energy ecologies in everyday life. *International Journal of Design, 2*, 55–70.
McCarthy, J., & Wright, P. (2004). *Technology as experience*. Cambridge, MA: MIT Press.
McCoy, M. (1996). Interpretive design. In C. T. Mitchell (Ed.), *New thinking in design. Conversations on theory and practice* (pp. 2–11). New York: Van Nostrand Reinhold.
McDermott, C. (2008). The context of European design since 1985. In R. C. Miller, P. Sparke & C. McDermott (Eds.), *European design since 1985. Shaping the new century*. Denver and London: Denver Art Museum and Merrell Publishers.
Menking, W. (2003). The revolt of the object. In P. Lang & W. Menking (Eds.), *Superstudio. Life without objects*. Milano: Skira.
Merleau-Ponty, M. (1963). *The structure of behavior*. Boston: Beacon Press. (Original in 1942 in French.)
Merleau-Ponty, M. (1968). The intertwining—The chiasm. *The visible and the invisible*. Evanston, IL: Northwestern University Press.
Merleau-Ponty, M. (1970). *The concept of nature, I, themes from the lectures at the Collège de France 1952–1960*. Evanston, IL: Northwestern University Press.
Merleau-Ponty, M. (1973). *The prose of the world*. Evanston, IL: Northwestern University Press.
Merleau-Ponty, M. (2002). *The phenomenology of perception*. London: Routledge. (Original 1945 in French.)
Meroni, A. (Ed.). (2007). *Creative communities. People inventing sustainable ways of living*. Milano: Edizioni Polidesign.
Meroni, A., & Sangiorgi, D. (Eds.). (2011). *Design for services*. Adelshot: Gower Publishing.
Merton, R.K. (1968). Science and democratic social structure. *Social theory and social structure* (pp. 604–615). New York: The Free Press.
Milgram, S. (1974). *Obedience to authority: An experimental view*. New York: Harper and Row.
Mogensen, P. (1992). Towards a prototyping approach in systems development. *Scandinavian Journal of Information Systems, 4*, 31–53.
Moggridge, B. (2006). *Designing interactions*. Cambridge, MA: MIT Press.
Moholy-Nagy, L. (1947). *Vision in motion*. Chicago: Theobald.
Molotch, H. (1996). L.A. as design product. How art works in a regional economy. In A. J. Scott & E. Soja (Eds.), *The city. Los Angeles and urban theory at the end of the twentieth century*. Berkeley: University of California Press.
Molotch, H. (2003). *Where stuff comes from*. New York: Routledge.

Moon, K. (2005). *Modeling messages. The architect and the model.* New York: The Monacelli Press.

Morelli, N. (2006). Developing new product service systems (PSS). Methodologies and operational tools. *Journal of Cleaner Production, 14,* 1495–1501.

Morozzi, C. (2008). *Stefano Giovannoni.* Milan: Mondadoriarte.

Morris, M. (2006). *Models: Architecture and the miniature.* Chichester, UK: Wiley.

Muller, M. (2009). PICTIVE. Democratizing the dynamics of the design session. In D. Schuler & A. Namioka (Eds.), *Participatory design principles and practices.* Boca Raton, FL: CRC Press. (Original in 1993 by Lawrence Erlbaum Associates.)

Museo Alessi, *Ettore Sottsass. Museo Alessi Design Interviews.* Mantova: Edizioni Corraini.

Museum of Modern Art (2009). *Design and the elastic mind.* New York: Museum of Modern Art.

Nafus, D., & Anderson, K. (2010). Writing on walls. The materiality of social memory in corporate research. In M. Cefkin (Ed.), *Ethnography and the corporate encounter. Reflections on research in and of corporations.* New York: Berghahn Books.

Nelson, H. G., & Stolterman, E. (2003). *The design way: Intentional change in an unpredictable world.* Englewood Cliffs, NJ: Educational Technology Publications.

Niedderer, K. (2004). *Designing the performative object. A study in designing mindful interaction through artefacts.* UK: Plymouth University, Falmouth College of Art. Unpublished doctoral dissertation.

Nielsen, J. (1993). *Usability engineering.* San Francisco: Academic Press.

Norman, D. A. (1988). *The psychology of everyday things.* New York: Basic Books. New version as Norman, D.A. (1998). The design of everyday things. London: MIT Press.

Nowotny, H., Scott, P., & Gibbons, M. (2008). *Re-thinking science. Knowledge and the public in an age of uncertainty.* London: Polity.

Nugent, L., Donahue, S., Berberat, M., Chan, Y., Gier, J., & Koskinen, I., et al. (2007). How do you say nature. Opening the design space with a knowledge environment. *Knowledge, Technology and Policy, 20*(4), 269–279.

Nurminen, M. I. (1988). *People or computers. Three ways of looking at information systems.* Lund: Studentliterratur.

O'Doherty, B. (1986). *Inside the white cube. The ideology of the gallery space.* Berkeley: University of California Press.

Orr, J. (1996). *Talking about machines. An Ethnography of a modern job.* Ithaca: ILR Press and Cornell University Press.

Overbeeke, K. (2007). The aesthetics of the impossible. Inaugural lecture, Eindhoven, Technische Universiteit Eindhoven, 26 October 2007. <tue.nl/ bib/>. Retrieved 10.11.2007.

Overbeeke, K., & Wensveen, S. (2003). From perception to experience, from affordances to irresistibles. In *Proceedings of DPPI'03,* June 23–26, 2003, Pittsburgh, Pennsylvania, pp. 92–97.

Overbeeke, K., Wensveen, S., & Hummels, C. (2006). Design research: Generating knowledge through doing. In Swiss design network. Drawing new territories. state of the art and perspectives. *Third Symposium of Design Research,* 17–18 Nov, Geneva. Geneva: Swiss Design Network.

Pacenti, E. (1998). *Il Progetto dell'interazione nei servizi. Un contributo al tema della progettazione dei servizi.* Politecnico di Milano: Disegno Industriale. Unpublished doctoral dissertation.

Pacenti, E., & Sangiorgi, D. (2010). Service design research pioneers. An overview of service design developed in Italy since the '90s. *Design Research Journal, 1*(10), 26–33.

Pallasmaa, J. (1996). *The eyes of the skin: Architecture and the senses.* London: Academy Editions.
Pallasmaa, J. (2009). *The thinking hand. Existential and embodied wisdom in architecture.* Chichester, UK: Wiley.
Park, S., & Zimmerman, J. (2010). Investigating the opportunity for a smart activity bag. In *Proceedings of the conference on human factors in computing systems.* New York: ACM Press, pp. 2543–2552.
Parsons, T. (2009). *Thinking: Objects. Contemporary approached to product design.* Lausanne, Switzerland: AVA Publishing.
Penati, A. (2010). Education and design (Formazione e design). In L. di Lucchio & A. Penati (Eds.), *Vitamins for design* (vol. 7, pp. 32–43). Rome: Disegno industriale/industrial design.
Philips Design (2005). *Vision of the future.* Eindhoven, the Netherlands: Philips.
Poggenpohl, S. H. (2009). Time for change: Building a design discipline. In S. Poggenpohl & K. Sato (Eds.), *Design integrations. Research and collaboration* (pp. 3–22). Bristol and Chicago: Intellect.
Poggenpohl, S. H. (2009). Practicing collaborative action in design. In S. Poggenpohl & K. Sato (Eds.), *Design integrations. Research and collaboration* (pp. 137–162). Bristol and Chicago: Intellect.
Poggenpohl, S., & Sato, K. (Eds.). (2009). *Design integrations. Research and collaboration.* Bristol and Chicago: Intellect.
Preece, J (Ed.). (1990). *Human-computer interaction. Selected readings.* Hemel Hampstead: Prentice-Hall.
Presence Project. (2001). London, RCA: CRD Research Publications.
Rabinow, P., & Sullivan, W. M. (Eds.). (1979). *The interpretive turn: Emergence of an approach. Interpretive social science* (pp. 1–21). Los Angeles: University of California Press.
Raby, F. (2008). Interview in *Zoom in zoom out: Z33 design & art projects collected.* Gent: Z33 and MER. Paper Kunsthalle.
Radice, B. (1985). *Memphis. Research, experiences, results, failures and successes of new design.* London: Thames and Hudson.
Radice, B. (1993). *Ettore Sottsass. A critical biography.* London: Thames & Hudson.
Raijmakers, B. (2007). *Design Documentaries. Using documentary film to inspire design.* London, UK: Royal College of Art. Unpublished doctoral dissertation
Ramakers, R. (2002). *Less+More. Droog Design in context.* Rotterdam: 010 Publishers.
Ramakers, R., & Bakker, G. (Eds.). (1998). *Droog Design. Spirit of the nineties.* Rotterdam: 010 publishers.
Randall, D., Harper, R., & Rouncefield, M. (2007). *Fieldwork for design. Theory and practice.* London: Springer.
Redström, J. (2005). On technology as material in design. In A. M. Willis (Ed.), *Design philosophy papers: Collection two* (pp. 31–42). Ravensbourne, London: Team D/E/S Publications.
Redström, J. (2006). Towards user design? On the shift from object to user as the subject of design. *Design Studies, 27,* 123–139.
Redström, J. (2009). Disruptions. In T. Binder, J. Löwgren & L. Malmborg (Eds.), *(Re)searching the Digital Bauhaus.* London: Springer.
Rheinfrank, J., & Evenson, S. (1996). Design languages. In T. Winograd (Ed.), *Bringing design to software.* New York: ACM Press.
Rittel, H., & Webber, M. (1973). Dilemmas in a general theory of planning. *Policy Sciences, 4,* 155–169.
Rizzo, F. (2009). *Strategie di co-design. Teorie, metodi e strumenti per progettare con gli utenti.* Milano: FrancoAngeli.
Rorty, R. (Ed.). (1967). *The linguistic turn. Essays in philosophical method.* Chicago: University of Chicago Press.

Rosenberg, M. (1990). Reflexivity and emotions. *Social Psychology Quarterly, 53*, 3–12.

Rosenthal, R. (1966). *Experimenter effects in behavioral research*. New York: Irvington Publishers.

Ross, P. (2008). *Ethics and aesthetics in intelligent product and system design*. Eindhoven, the Netherlands: Technishe Universiteit Eindhoven.

Ross, P., Overbeeke, K., Wensveen, S., & Hummels, C. (2008). A designerly critique on enchantment. *Personal and Ubiquitous Computing, 12*, 359–371.

Routarinne, S., & Redström, J. (2007). Domestication as design intervention. Conference paper, *2nd Nordic Design Research Conference (NORDES)*, Konstfack, Stockholm, May, 2007. <nordes.org/>. Retrieved 10.08.2008.

Saarela, P. (1999). *Muotoilu 2005*. Kulttuuripolitiikan osaston julkaisusarja 3:1999. (*Design 2005*, in Finnish.)

Säde, S. (2001). *Cardboard mock-ups and conversations*. Helsinki: UIAH.

Salvador, T., Bell, G., & Anderson, K. (1999). Design ethnography. *Design Management Journal, 10*(4) Fall.

Sanders, E.B.-N. (2000). Generative tools for codesigning. In A. R. Scrivener, L. J. Ball & A. Woodcock (Eds.), *Collaborative design*. London: Springer-Verlag.

Sanders, E. B.-N. (2006). Design research in 2006. *Design Research Quarterly*, 1–8.

Sanders, E.B.-N., & Dandavate, U. (1999). Design for experience: New tools. *Proceedings of the first international conference on design and emotion*, Delft, the Netherlands.

Sangiorgi, D. (2004). *Il Design dei servizi come Design dei Sistemi di Attività. La Teoria dell'Attività applicata alla progettazione dei servizi*. Politecnico di Milano: Disegno Industriale. Unpublished doctoral dissertation.

Sato, K. (2009). Perspectives on design research. In S. Poggenpohl & K. Sato (Eds.), *Design integrations. Research and collaboration* (pp. 25–48). Bristol and Chicago: Intellect.

Schachter, S., & Singer, J. E. (1962). Cognitive, social and physiological determinants of emotional state. *Psychological Review, 69*, 379–399.

Schifferstein, H., & Hekkert, P. (Eds.). (2008). *Product experience*. San Diego: Elsevier.

Schneider, B. (2008). Le design comme science et comme recherché. In Swiss Design Network (Ed.) 2008. Focused — Current design research projects and methods. *Swiss design network symposium 2008*, 30–31 May, Mount Gurten, Berne.

Schneiderman, B. (1983). Direct manipulation. A step beyond programming languages. *IEEE Transactions on Computers, 16*(8), 57–69.

Schneiderman, B. (1998). *Designing the user interface. strategies for effective human-computer interaction*. Reading, MA: Addison-Wesley.

Schön, D. (1983). *The reflective practitioner. How professionals think in action*. New York: Basic Books.

(Original in 1993 by Lawrence Erlbaum Associates.)Schuler, D., & Namioka, A. (Eds.). (2009). *Participatory design principles and practices*. Boca Raton, FL: CRC Press. (Original in 1993 by Lawrence Erlbaum Associates.)

Scrivener, S. (2000). Reflection in and on action and practice in creative-production doctoral projects in art and design. *Working Papers in Art and Design 1*. <herts.ac.uk/artdes/research/papers/wpades/vol1/scrivener2.html/>. Retrieved 24.09.2008.

Seago, A., & Dunne, A. (1999). New methodologies in art and design research: The object as discourse. *Design Issues, 15*, 11–17.

Seale, C. (1999). *The quality of qualitative data*. London: Sage.

Segal, L.D., & Fulton Suri, J. (1997). The empathic practitioner. Measurement and interpretation of user experience. *Proceedings of the 41st Annual Meeting of the Human Factors and Ergonomics Society*, New Mexico.

Sengers, P., & Gaver, W. (2006). Staying open to interpretation: Engaging multiple meanings in design and evaluation. In *proceedings of designing interactive systems (DIS)*, State College, PA, 99–108.
Sharp, H., & Preece, J. (Eds.). (2007). *Interaction design. Beyond human-computer interaction.* Hoboken, NJ: Wilen.
Shaw, B. (2007). *More than the sum of its parts. Shared representations in collaborative design interaction.* London, UK: Royal College of Art. Unpublished doctoral dissertation.
Shedroff, N. (2001). *Experience design.* Berkeley, CA: New Riders/Pearson Education.
Shott, S. (1979). Emotion and social life. A symbolic interactionist analysis. *American Journal of Sociology, 84,* 1317–1334.
Shove, E., Watson, M., Hand, M., & Ingram, J. (2007). *The design of everyday life.* New York: Berg.
Siebenbrodt, M., & Schöbe, L. (2009). *Bauhaus. 1919–1933 Weimar-Dessau-Berlin.* New York: Parkstone.
Siikamäki, R. (2006). *Glass can be recycled forever.* Helsinki: UIAH.
Simon, H. (1996). *The sciences of the artificial* (3rd ed.). Cambridge, MA: The MIT Press.
Slate, R. (2002). *Autoreductive glazes: A systematic practical exploration.* London, UK: Royal College of Art. Unpublished doctoral dissertation.
Sleeswijk Froukje, V. (2009). *Bringing the everyday life of people into design.* Delft, the Netherlands: Technical University of Delft.
Soini, K., & Pirinen, A. (2005). Workshops — Collaborative arena for generative research. In *Proceedings of DPPI 2005, proceedings of designing pleasurable products and interfaces.* Eindhoven University of Technology, Eindhoven, the Netherlands. <taik.fi/images/stories/Future%20Home/dppi05_ks_ap_workshops.pdf/>. Retrieved 17.04.2011.
Sparke, P. (2006). Ettore Sottsass, a modern Italian Designer. In R. T. Labaco (Ed.), *Ettore Sottsass: Architect and designer.* London and New York: Merrell, and los Angeles: Los Angeles County Museum of Art.
Sparke, P. (2008). Design in Europe, 1945–1985. In R. C. Miller, P. Sparke & C. McDermott (Eds.), *European design since 1985. Shaping the new century.* Denver and London: Denver Art Museum and Merrell Publishers.
Squires, S., & Byrne, B. (Eds.). (2002). *Creating breakthrough ideas. The collaboration of anthropologists and designers in the product development industry.* Westport, CT: Bergin & Garvey.
Staal, G. (2003). Innocuous Involvement. The new legitimacy of a design profession. In reflect#01. *New commitment. In architecture, art and design.* Rotterdam: NAi Publishers.
Stappers, P.J. (2006). Designing as a part of research. In R. van der Lugt, & P.J. Stappers (Eds.), *Design and the growth of knowledge,* November 10, 2005. Delft, the Netherlands: Delft University of Technology, Faculty of Industrial Design Engineering.
Stappers, P. J. (2007). Doing design as a part of doing research. In R. Michel (Ed.), *Design research now* (pp. 81–91). Basel: Birkhäuser.
Stappers, P.J. (2011). PROTO:type 2010 Symposium held in Dundee, Scotland, exact reference not known April 2011.
Stappers, P.J., & Sanders, E.B.-N. (2003). Generative tools for context mapping: Tuning the tools. In *proceedings of the third international conference on design & emotion, Loughborough.* London: Taylor & Francis.
Star, S. L., & Griesemer, J. (1989). Institutional ecology, 'translations' and boundary objects: Amateurs and professionals in Berkeley's museum of vertebrate zoology, 1907–39. *Social Studies of Science, 19,* 387–420.
Strauss, A. L. (1987). *Qualitative analysis for social scientists.* Cambridge, UK: Cambridge University Press.

Suchman, L. A. (1987). *Plans and situated actions: The problem of human-machine communication.* Cambridge, UK: Cambridge University Press.

Svengren, L. (1995). *Industriell design som strategisk resurs. En studie av designprocessens metoder och synsätt som del i företags strategiska utveckling.* Lund: Lund University Press. (*Industrial design as Strategic Resource. A Study of the Methods of Design Process Seen as a Part of the Strategic Development of a Company*, in Swedish.)

Szymanski, M., & Whalen, J. (Eds.). (2011). *Making work visible. Ethnographically grounded case studies of work practice.* Cambridge, UK: Cambridge University Press.

Thackara, J. (Ed.), (1988). Beyond the object in design. *Design after modernism: Beyond the object* (pp. 11–34). New York: Thames and Hudson.

Thampirak, S. (2007). *Macro-crystalline glaze. Stable medium to low temperature investigation and development for domestic use in an industrial context.* London, UK: Royal College of Art. Unpublished doctoral dissertation.

Tilley, A. R., & Dreyfuss, H. (2002). *The measure of man.* New York: John Wiley & Sons.

Tomico, O. (2007). *Subjective experience gathering techniques for interaction design.* Barcelona: Technical University of Catalonia.

Tunstall, E. (2007). Will the NSF be the death of anthropology? December 16, 2007. Blog posting. <dori3.typepad.com/my_weblog/design_anthropology/>. Retrieved 14.01.2010.

Tunstall, E. (2008). Design anthropology: What can it add to your design practice? *Adobe tutorial.* Blog posting. <adobe.com/designcenter/thinktank/ tt_tunstall.html/>, 20 May, 2008. Retrieved 12.12.2009.

Turner, S. P. (1994). *The social theory of practices: Tradition, tacit knowledge and presuppositions.* Chicago: University of Chicago Press.

Valtonen, A (2007). *Redefining industrial design: Changes in the design practice in Finland.* Helsinki: UIAH.

van der Lugt, R., & Stappers, P.J. (2006). Introduction. In *Proceedings of design and the growth of knowledge,* November 10, 2005. Delft, the Netherlands: Delft University of Technology, Faculty of Industrial Design Engineering.

Van House, N., Davis, M., Ames, M., Finn, M., & Viswanathan, V. (2005). The uses of personal networked digital imaging: An empirical study of cameraphone photos and sharing. In *Proceedings of computer-human interaction CHI 2005,* Portland, Oregon. New York: ACM Press.

Van House, N., Davis, M., Takhteyev, Y., Good, N., Wilhelm, A., & Finn, M. (2004). From "what?" to "why?": The social uses of personal photos. *Proceedings of CSCW'04,* Nov 6–10, 2004, Chicago, Illinois.

Verganti, R. (2009). *Design-driven innovation. Changing the rules of competition by radically innovating what things mean.* Cambridge, MA: Harvard University Press.

Vezzoli, C. (2003). A new generation of designers. Perspectives for education and training in the field of sustainable design. Experiences and projects at the Politecnico di Milano University. *Journal of Cleaner Production, 11*(1), 1–9.

Vihma, S. (1995). *Products as representations. A semiotic and aesthetic study of design products.* Helsinki: UIAH.

Visser, W. (2006). *The cognitive artifacts of designing.* Hillsdale, NJ: Lawrence Erlbaum.

Wasson, C. (2000). Ethnography in the field of design. *Human Organization, 59*(4), 377–388.

Wasson, C. (2002). Collaborative work: Integrating the roles of ethnographers and designers. In S. Squires & B. Byrne (Eds.), *Creating breakthrough ideas. The collaboration of anthropologists and designers in the product development industry* (pp. 71–91). Westport, CT: Bergin Garvey.

Weil, D. (1985). *The light box.* London: A.A. (Architectural Association).

Weil, D. (1996). New design territories. In C. T. Mitchell (Ed.), *New thinking in design. Conversations on theory and practice*. New York: Van Nostrand Reinhold.

Weiser, M. (1991). The computer for the 21st century. *Scientific American, 265*, 94–104.

Wensveen, S. (2004). *A tangibility approach to affective interaction*. Delft, the Netherlands: Delft University of Technology.

Winch, P. (2008). *The idea of social science and its relation to philosophy*. London: Routledge & Kegan Paul.

Winograd, T. (Ed.). (1996). *Bringing design to software*. Reading, MA: Addison-Wesley.

Winograd, T., & Flores, F. (1987). *Understanding computers and cognition: A new foundation for design*. Reading, MA: Addison-Wesley.

Wixon, D., & Ramey, J. (Eds.). (1996). *Field methods casebook for software design*. New York: John Wiley & Sons.

Wood, G. (2007). *Surreal things. Surrealism and design*. London: V&A.

Wroblewski, D. (1991). The construction of human-computer interfaces considered as a craft. In J. Karat (Ed.), *Taking software design seriously. Practical techniques for human-computer interaction design* (pp. 1–19). San Diego: Academic Press.

Ylirisku, S., & Buur, J. (Eds.). (2007). *Designing with video: Focusing the user-centred design process*. London: Springer.

Yoo, D., Zimmerman, J., Steinfeld, A., Tomasic, A. (2010). Understanding the space for co-design in riders' interactions with a transit service. To appear in *Proceedings of the conference on human factors in computing systems* (pp. 1797–1806). New York: ACM Press.

Z33, *Zoom in zoom out: Z33 design & art projects collected*. Gent: Z33 and MER. Paper Kunsthalle. ISBN 9789074605007.

Z33, *Design by performance. Exhibition catalogue*. Hasselt: Z33.

Zelditch, M., Jr. (1969). Can you study an army in the laboratory. In A. Etzioni (Ed.), *Complex organizations. A sociological reader* (pp. 528–539) (2nd ed.). New York: Holt, Rinehart and Winston.

Zimmerman, J. (2009). Designing for the self. Making products that help people become the person they desire to be. *Proceedings of CHI 2009*, April 4–9, 2009, Boston, Massachusetts, pp. 395–404.

Zimmerman, J., Dimitrova, N., Agnihotri, L., Janevski, A., & Nikolovska, L. (2003). Interface design for MyInfo: A personal news demonstrator combining web and TV content. In *Proceedings of IFIP TC13 conference on human computer interaction* (pp. 41–51). New York: IFIP.

Zimmerman, J., & Forlizzi, J. (2008). The role of design artifacts in design theory construction. *Artifact: Journal of Virtual Design, 2*(1), 41–45.

Zimmerman, J., Forlizzi, J., & Evenson, S. (2007). Research through design as a method for interaction design research in HCI. *Proceedings of CHI 2007*, April 28–May 3, 2007, San Jose, California.

Zimmerman, J., Stolterman, E., & Forlizzi, J. (2010). An analysis and critique of research through design. Towards a formalization of a research approach. In *Proceedings of designing interactive systems, DIS 2010*. New York: ACM.

Zimmerman, J., Tomasic, A., Garrod, C. Yoo, D., Hiruncharoenvate, C. Aziz, R., et al. (2011). Field Trial of Tiramisu: Crowd-sourcing bus arrival times to spur co-design. In *Proceedings of Computer-Human Interaction, CHI 2011*. New York: ACM.

INDEX

CPI Antony Rowe
Chippenham, UK
2017-08-10 11:17

Preface and acknowledgements

Our account of modern Italian literature opens on the cusp of the eighteenth century when the practices, institutions and systems which constituted a recognizably modern literary culture began to take shape, in Italy as elsewhere. Starting here and not taking the 'modern' as shorthand for the twentieth century or the even more recent past has led to a deliberate chronological skew. By giving equal weight to the three past centuries, we have been selective in our treatment of the past twenty or thirty years in particular and correspondingly more generous in our coverage of the earlier periods, which are often marginalized or neglected in English-language treatments of Italian literature. We hope this book will enable readers to recognize the interest and importance of the pre-twentieth-century period, and see more clearly the continuities as well as the ruptures which have characterized the literary cultures of modern Italy.

Within this broadly chronological structure, the reader will find a variety of perspectives and complementary approaches to the literary and cultural history which is narrated and the literary texts which are highlighted. The overview which comprises our introduction allows us to take a step back from the detail of the individual chapters and to give some analytic shape to the salient arguments of the book. Readers who wish to focus on specific issues or moments of modern Italian literature will find it useful to consult this overview (as well as the index) in order to orient themselves with ease.

The successive parts and chapters of the book are the product of what we hope is a fruitful tension between literary and cultural history. The tension is real. Cultural history is concerned with 'culture' as a set of collective representations proper to a given society or, as it was put by the editors of the first book in English to adopt seriously a cultural studies perspective on Italy, 'a set of signifying practices and symbolic social forms' (Forgacs and Lumley 1996: 1). Literary historians are traditionally concerned with what they call the 'context' of the literary producers and production which they study, but remain wedded to an idea of the singularity and often exceptionality of the work, and are sometimes criticized by cultural historians for this. Pascal Ory, among other subtle discriminations, distinguishes cultural history from literary history by the former's concern with what surrounds the text, not only context but also paratext: only by stages, he points out, does a 'text' become a 'book', if indeed it ever does (Ory 2004: 14). The cultural historian, constitutionally resistant to the idea of singularity, emphasizes the complexity and multiplicity of individuals and texts, both of them the meeting point of many meanings ('polysemy'), and also the ideological folds and creases which live in any apparently smooth-surfaced representation. The literary historian, on the other hand, feels the obligation to give an account and to ferret out an interpretation of that particular text, that particular body of work, which has left a mark on the cultural life of a society, and, while far from rejecting ideas of polysemy or ideology, still has to confront what for him or her is the specificity, the uniqueness, of a given work.

The result, in this book, is a slalom between what Franco Moretti has called 'distant reading' ('in which the reality of the text undergoes a process of deliberate reduction and abstraction': Moretti 2005: 1) and the more traditional forms, at least in Anglo-American criticism, of 'close reading'. We are thus able to give some detailed attention to aspects of literary culture which are traditionally underrepresented – writing by women, still wilfully neglected or undervalued in much Italian criticism, popular fiction, forms of orality, the idea of a 'norm' or 'standard' within the literary culture at any given time, for example – while also analysing in depth particular works or bodies of work which transcend their value as evidence for wider trends and still have the power to arrest the reader. This is neither pure cultural history nor pure literary history, and it has not always been easy to distinguish between a cultural history of literature and a literary history of culture. What we have discovered in the writing of this book is that the relation between the terms varies over the course of the past three centuries, making both close and distant reading necessary at different moments.

We owe many debts of gratitude to friends and colleagues who have helped us and made suggestions, and particularly to the two anonymous Polity readers whose perceptive comments guided us towards some radical rethinking of parts of this text. We should also like to thank our three successive editors at Polity, Lynn Dunlop, Sally-Ann Spencer and Andrea Drugan, for their patient support, and with them the whole production team which has taken the book through to publication. Ann Hallamore Caesar wishes to thank the University of Warwick for granting study leave and the AHRC for a Research Leave award.

The authors and publisher are grateful to the following for permission to reproduce copyrighted material:

University of California Press for the translation in chapter 9 from Andrea Zanzotto's poem 'La perfezione della neve', translation originally published in L. R. Smith (ed. and trans.), *The New Italian Poetry, 1945 to the Present: A Bilingual Anthology*. © 1981 The Regents of the University of California. Published by the University of California Press.

Every effort has been made to trace copyright holders, but if any have been inadvertently overlooked, the publishers will be pleased to make the necessary arrangements at the first opportunity.

Introduction: an overview of modern Italian literature

As in the rest of Europe, the term 'literature' in Italy in the eighteenth century had a broader scope than that usually given it today. Its focus was on the written word and it covered almost anything written that had to do with the human or the natural sciences – in this broad sense 'literature' in English can still designate anything previously published on a given subject. To talk about what already in the nineteenth century was institutionalized as 'Literature' (something that might be taught in universities, something you wrote histories of), people in the 1700s used terms like 'poetry' (*poesia*) or 'belles-lettres' (*le lettere amene, la letteratura amena*). The *letterato*, the 'man of letters', was in effect a writer, without necessarily being a writer *of* any particular kind. To this generalized writer there corresponded a generalized reader, though how generalized depended on the circumstances. The members of a learned society (or *accademia*) might switch their attention in a single evening from a paper on economics to a paper on physics; the readers of journals or gazettes would let their eye wander over an even larger range of topics, but more rapidly and more superficially. The member of an academy and the reader of the newspaper might be, and often were, one and the same person, behaving differently as readers in different conditions. But the framework within which individual readers (or listeners) could act as a 'public' was already becoming firmly established in the eighteenth century – academies and the press being among its principal supports, as we shall see. Print-culture ensured the steady supply of written and visual materials suited to all tastes and pockets, particularly though not exclusively in the towns.

Against this general background, two broad features of Italian literary culture in the eighteenth century can be picked out. The first – something that concerns the culture as a whole ('literature' in the broad sense) – brings into play the complex interaction between antiquity and modernity in Italians' self-representation. The second is concerned with literature in the narrow sense, and has to do with the dominance of poetry and theatre in the Italian literary scene up until almost the end of the century.

Even at the beginning of the eighteenth century, Italian culture was 'old'. There was a written literature dating back, in unbroken sequence, at least five hundred years, and beyond that a classical tradition, particularly a Latin one, that was in the cultural DNA of every Italian writer. In the course of the century, inhabitants of the peninsula were increasingly brought face to face with their ambiguous classical heritage as the excavations of Pompeii and Herculaneum and the reorganized treasures of Rome and Florence opened the gates to generations of Grand Tourists, determined to see in Italy the very symbol of Europe's classical past and, in its present misery, the negative image of their own prosperity. The century opened with a determined effort, in Arcadia, to reappropriate and reinvent the past in a nostalgic spirit which nevertheless gave rise to particularly effective modern forms of association. But the experience of Arcadia showed that the collaborative sociability which was a feature of eighteenth-century cultural life could also be a means of defending particular interests, a form of complacency. By contrast, the more aggressive kind of classicism which emerged in the second half of the century – neoclassicism – could prove to have a revolutionary charge of its own, as in the playwright Alfieri, even if in due course it became a tiresome fashion worn out by repetition.

The notion of an Italy rooted in the past, or weighed down by the chains of its heritage, or 'sleeping' or 'dead', would return with renewed virulence in the nineteenth century and even enjoy a revival in the twentieth (it was fundamentally this stereotype that would be exploited in their own way by the Futurists). But eighteenth-century Italy also produced radical new ways of thinking about history (Muratori, Vico) and proposals for social change (including Beccaria's celebrated assault on judicial torture and the death penalty) which went under the general heading of 'reform'. Reform was a leitmotif of the century, not only in politics and governance, but also in the arts, and particularly in the theatre. Theatre was really the dominant literary form in eighteenth-century Italy, both musical theatre (Metastasio) and dramatic theatre (Goldoni in comedy, Alfieri in tragedy). Theatre was regularly seen throughout the century as the most 'social' of cultural forms mediated through the written or spoken language, and thus peculiarly sensitive to political circumstance and susceptible to technical change which could have meaningful effects, in terms of audience reception, in the short term. Theatre was the most reform-minded of cultural forms in an age of reform, and this is evident in the work of both Goldoni and Alfieri.

The poetry of the period, in the narrow sense of short compositions in verse, seems routine by comparison. It was by no means all bad, but it was sustained by a coterie culture which prized skill over originality and agreeableness over experimentation. The positive outcome of this was that much skilful, agreeable (and still readable) poetry got written, and that the pleasures of the language continued to be exploited and enjoyed by a wide circle of literate people: this is in fact the pulse of literature in any age – an average, medium, repetitive supply, poetry in the eighteenth century, perhaps fiction today – without which no other writing can be produced. Between poetry and the theatre, however, there was an absent third in eighteenth-century Italy: the novel. Despite the success of the genre in northern Europe, especially France and England, since early in the century, the novel struggled to establish itself in Italy other than as what was looked down on by the *letterati* as a cheap entertainment form for the lower classes: good only for 'our menservants' and 'the commonest little women', as Giuseppe Baretti irascibly declared of Pietro Chiari's highly profitable novels in 1764 (Baretti 1932: II, 31). The dominance of poetry and theatre in eighteenth-century Italy points perhaps to a public which was more collective and interactive than the 'individualistic' one habitually associated with the bourgeois form par excellence, the novel (though novels also live by being talked about among readers). In any event, it was the rise of a new, proto-Romantic, figure towards the end of the century, the poet or writer as exceptional individual whose writing was allowed to seem a reflection or extension of its author's life, which created the space in Italy both for the confessional novel and for a serious rethinking of the role and possibilities of poetry.

These are broadly the themes we shall explore in part I, beginning with the story of Arcadia, lyric poetry and the musical theatre (sec. 1.1), before turning to the wider political scene, reform and the comic theatre (secs 1.2–2.2), and the accelerating cultural changes which took place between the late eighteenth and early nineteenth centuries (secs 3.1–3.3).

The most startling event of the years that we review in part II was the transformation of Italy from a congeries of separate states, large, medium, small and minuscule, each with long and often antithetical traditions of civic independence but each more or less dependent on the patronage of a foreign power; its transformation from a 'geographical expression', in Metternich's sneering phrase, to a unitary and independent nation-state officially founded in 1861. This is one of the points in the cultural history of the past three hundred years where it is necessary to locate ourselves in relation to the political issues of the time, which we do here and in sections 5.3–5.4. The story of the Risorgimento ('resurgence'), as this process came to be called, is still a fascinating one, full of historical what-ifs and might-have-beens. Here we can only begin to sketch it very rapidly, in order to show where the literary-cultural chapters which make up part II fit into the broader picture.

Following the defeat of Napoleon and the Congress of Vienna (the peace conference dominated by the victorious anti-French forces) in 1815, Italy by and large was returned to the *status quo ante*, the map was redrawn, and the ruling families returned to their erstwhile kingdoms and duchies, this time, however, under the hegemony of Austria, which reintegrated Lombardy-Venetia as an Austrian province. The watchword was 'legitimacy', and the period of the Restoration (1815–48) was marked by a reassertion of conservative, authoritarian principles in both church and state, though these began to be challenged after the July revolution of 1830, which established a constitutional monarchy in France and re-established France on the international stage. The states were perpetually frightened by and on the look-out for subversive, insurrectionary or even revolutionary movements, and acted fast to repress them when they did break out in Naples and Palermo in the summer of 1820, in Turin in 1821, and in central Italy in 1831. The liberal opposition to the reactionary states had been driven underground and organized itself in secret societies, the most celebrated of which was the *Carboneria*, the sect of the 'charcoal-burners' (*carbonari*). They had to contend with a network of police informers and spies, who were largely successful during the 1820s and 1830s in preventing the spread of ideas and, more importantly, any large-scale political organization.

The Restoration period, in which the Italian states also suffered the consequences of a Europe-wide economic recession, was a period of intellectual and literary ferment. In Milan, a peculiarly Italian form of Romanticism, closely tied to the patriotic and democratic intelligentsia, was propagated and fiercely debated (sec. 4.1). Italy's two greatest writers of the early nineteenth century, Alessandro Manzoni and Giacomo Leopardi, each of international stature, completed their best work in the 1820s and 1830s. In section 4.2 we look at a moment when their paths crossed, emblematically in Florence, which, under the influence of Vieusseux's *Antologia*, had become the centre of liberal thinking in the peninsula. But they were two very different minds, and the following sections of chapters 4 and 5 examine their particular vision in detail, Leopardi in section 4.3 and Manzoni and his masterpiece *I promessi sposi* (*The Betrothed*) in sections 5.1 and 5.2. Both Leopardi and Manzoni were taken up in the national cause, though their own political positions were perhaps more nuanced than those of their admirers, as were those of the other great cultural hero of the Risorgimento, the composer Giuseppe Verdi. The tendency of contemporaries to read literary or musical works politically is a reminder, if one were needed, that the Risorgimento was a cultural as well as a political event. If the idea of national independence and unity spread from a small handful of intellectuals to large swathes of at least the urban population in the years leading up to Unification, it was a matter not simply of propaganda, but also of feeling and emotion. 'Popular' forms including historical novels, narrative verse *novelle* which could be memorized and recited, patriotic and sentimental poetry, and above all the opera (*melodramma*) carried situations, plots, characters and psychological states which added up to a national narrative (see sec. 5.3). Nor should we underestimate the importance of the fact that one essential building block of national unity was the language of the literary tradition, to be introduced to (or indeed imposed on) a population largely made up of speakers of very diverse dialects, which is almost to say that the literary tradition itself became *de jure* if not *de facto* part of the new national consciousness (see secs 5.2 and 5.4).

As Italy moved into the last third of the nineteenth century and the beginning of the next, the literary system as a whole took on an increasingly modern look, developing from the bases which had already been in place in the 1830s and 1840s. This modernization concerned both the place and function of literature in society at large and the contents and structure of the literary product itself. The terms 'modern' and 'modernization' here should not be understood in a teleological sense: we do not believe that literature follows a necessarily progressive path, onwards and ever upwards. The terms refer rather to a particular phase of cultural history, broadly corresponding to widespread industrialization in Europe and North America (rather than the initial pockets of industrial expansion which had characterized the 'industrial revolution' of the late eighteenth century in Britain), the multiplication of the effect of industrialization on a world scale thanks to imperialism (itself building on earlier colonialism), and periods of significant economic prosperity (alternating with recession) which allowed the bases to be laid of a mass market for consumer goods in the European and North American heartlands of capitalism, with incalculable consequences for the patterns of social behaviour (the invention of the department store, for example). Although Italy as a whole was behind the leading nations in terms of industrialization, certain regions, particularly in the north of the country, did not have so much ground to make up. The fact that the nation-state had been created on liberal principles, and that the newly constituted country found itself in a more fiercely competitive relation with its neighbours than hitherto, meant that much of the effort of the first fifty years of the kingdom's existence was devoted by liberals to maximizing the nation's economic capacity, and by many of the richest and most powerful people in the country to making sure that that did not happen at the expense of their own interests. Modernity was not just the site of economic growth and greatly expanded opportunities for many who had not previously had access to money or culture. It was also an almost permanent site of undeclared war, within countries and between them, marked by bitter class conflict between workers and the owners of the means of production, and eventually culminating in armed conflict between the European states.

In chapter 6, we pay particular attention to the ways in which literary texts themselves were implicated in the general economic and social developments which we have just outlined. As with other commodities, the demand for 'reading matter' – books, newspapers and magazines – was expanding rapidly (the number of periodical titles in Italy is calculated to have grown from 193 in 1846 to 1,120 in 1872: Ragone 1983: 711, n.1). More people were reading and people were reading more; they were also reading different things and in different ways: instalment novels appended to newspapers or magazines (the *romanzi d'appendice*), books about travel, descriptions of great exhibitions, catalogues of all sorts. Publishers had to cater for a public which was less 'intellectual' than the traditional market, and also more interested in writing that moved along fast and was exciting, and that reflected contemporary life (as Fogazzaro perceptively saw: sec. 6.3). But even this 'accelerated' reading (which might be done at home or in public, on trams and trains) depended on a level and spread of more than just a basic education which would have been inconceivable two generations earlier, both to impart the skill of reading in itself and to focus that skill on the national language, which, as we have already seen, was for many people not their native language. At the more advanced levels of instruction (from the secondary school onwards) the study of 'literature', meaning the Italian literary canon, was regarded as essential for learning how to write good Italian and later, in the 1880s, as central to the formation of the well-rounded future citizen (who, however, was being already distinguished from the 'technical' pupil, whose linguistic and literary prowess was not regarded as a priority). This focus on the literary tradition in the national education system shows in retrospect how important it was for a systemization of that tradition, such as the one that De Sanctis undertook, to be carried out. Sections 6.1 and 6.3 focus on this dimension of the literary system, and section 6.3 stresses the particular importance of the new market of women readers both as consumers of literature and as emerging subjects and producers of literary texts.

Following the broadly chronological order which we have adopted, our final three chapters deal with literature in the twentieth century and into the beginnings of the twenty-first. The continuing expansion in both the production and the consumption of literary material since the second half of the nineteenth century, and its increasing variety, make any pretence to comprehensiveness in our treatment of the subject even less plausible in these chapters than in the preceding ones. But in different ways the chapters which follow continue a theme which has been present in our analysis from the beginning: that of the hazy and shifting borderline between the private and the public in modern literature. Both the production and the enjoyment of literary objects have often been experienced in the modern world as essentially private experiences, conducted alone and taking place within the individual concerned, the lone creator, the solitary reader. There is an evident experiential truth to this perception, but it is equally evident that all writing, all reading derive from a series of interlocking cultural networks, starting with a shared natural language, and moving on through commonly understood rules of genre, reading practices and so on, mediated by schools, literary professionals, word of mouth. The Romantic view of the individual as inspired creator and privileged recipient of the inspired word was difficult to sustain other than in a nostalgic or parodistic mode when people's lives were increasingly organized on a mass scale according to industrial rhythms. At the same time, during the early twentieth century, the political connotations of the individual also came under strain. Individuals died in their millions in the First World War, and any sense of individuality amongst those numbers was lost. Participation in the political process, less and less a privilege of the few and wealthy, required a surrendering of at least part of one's identity to a greater whole, a process which might be unproblematic most of the time, but which could also take the form, as it did in Italy during the Fascist regime, of totalitarianism and mass mobilization. The ambiguities of the private–public boundary recur insistently in the work of twentieth-century artists and writers, whether it is because the contours of the self have themselves become indistinct or because social and political demands have at certain moments become particularly insistent. Implicit in any discussion of literature is the understanding that it does not simply 'reflect' reality, and its job is not merely to record or document something outside itself, supposedly more real than itself. Even the novels which came out of the Italian form of naturalism called *verismo* (discussed in sec. 6.2), which continued the mid-century tradition of 'documentary' narrative about working life but from a much more rigorously scientific, and totally non-moralistic, point of view, were as responsible for creating a reality through their representation of it as they were for reflecting one that already existed. In *verismo*, readers learnt to imagine a section of social reality, a part of their society and their culture, in a new way. Fiction was an agent in a construction of social and cultural facts in symbolic form, a form which was therefore communicable and interpretable, irrespective of how readily or how widely that particular construction might be accepted.

Bearing in mind the collective as well as individual dimension of the whole literary experience, and the fact that literary objects are active agents within a culture and not mere mirrors or sounding-boards, we can turn to the first of our chapters devoted to the twentieth century. Chapter 7 describes the challenge faced by the serious writer to define the position from which he or she speaks in the decades spanning the nineteenth and twentieth centuries during which the perception of the self, the status of the individual within a system which seemed designed to minimize if not to crush the individual, and consequently, from a literary point of view (both poetry and prose), the very idea of character and the integrity of the voice which says 'I', were all being called into question. The writers, texts and movements (like Futurism) which are examined in that chapter dealt with this challenge in many different ways, ranging from the superman voluntarism of a D'Annunzio to the modesty of a poet like Gozzano (the contrast is drawn in sec. 7.1) which is echoed in Saba's sense that the poet's loss of prestige was a liberation (sec. 7.2); from the overarching confidence of the Futurists that reality could be re-engineered with the help of the will and the imagination (a confidence which rested, however, on the guilty knowledge that it could also be destroyed: sec. 7.2) to the anti-heroic sense of a self disintegrating in the face of an outside which cannot be known scientifically (Svevo) or even accurately perceived other than as a reflection in a broken mirror (Pirandello) (sec. 7.3).

Chapter 8 is dominated by the Italian experience of Fascism, both during the regime and in the years immediately following it. Born indirectly from the trauma of the First World War, Italian Fascism retained a paramilitaristic ideology which was more or less apparent depending on events, though it was never a military dictatorship and its financial and technical preparation for the military enterprises in which it got regularly embroiled was generally inadequate. It was paramilitaristic to the extent that it stressed the virtue of obedience to a superior authority (the state or the leader), was prepared to use force and coercion as a form of political governance, resorted to war when the opportunity arose, and sought to organize the citizenry as far as possible in disciplined ranks in order to perform purposeful and visible tasks. It was a watchful regime, concerned above all to achieve conformity and consensus (whether forced or freely given, real or apparent). Its impact on culture was considerable. As the first totalitarian state in Europe, Fascist Italy was acutely conscious of the political need, and opportunity, to control the cultural sphere by all means at its disposal, both 'soft' (subsidies, prizes, promotions) and 'hard' (censorship, police repression, imprisonment and exile). At the same time, it learnt to recognize the limits of its power in the cultural sphere, or at least to prioritize its objectives: as far as possible to shape mass or popular culture (the equivocations between these terms run through the pages which follow), while leaving elite culture by and large to get on with its own affairs unless or until it offended the interests of the state or of public morality. Since in theory the state was all-encompassing in the Fascist conception of things, literature was potentially in a stranglehold; in practice, things were more flexible and there was during Fascism a surprising degree of openness to literary and artistic ideas and practices from elsewhere in Europe which were different from the preferred options of the regime, even if they were of interest only to a tiny minority.

It is important to stress that in many ways the mental framework established under Fascism, with which sections 8.1–8.3 are concerned, did not entirely go away when the regime crumbled in 1943–5. Indeed, Fascism itself was part of a larger pattern. Twentieth-century Europe was dominated for at least seventy years by political ideology which directed attention, whether from the left or the right, to the organization of the state and the role of the citizen (including the intellectual) within it. This was a situation fraught with tension and real danger in the central years between the mid-1930s and the mid-1940s and again during the Cold War. We trace this continuity through to post-war neo-realism (sec. 8.4) and, perhaps rather more surprisingly, to the neo-avant-garde of the 1960s, which in section 9.1 we suggest was as much concerned with political, or cultural-political, questions as it was with aesthetic ones, though these were also of great importance for the subsequent development of literary forms in Italy.

Probably the single most important issue for literature in the second half of the twentieth century was the need to renegotiate the relations between elite and popular (or mass) culture (secs 9.1–9.2). However successfully this was done, or not, there is no doubting that the cultural scene today, including what we think of as literature, would be all but unrecognizable to a cultural actor of a hundred or even fifty years ago (though some foresaw it in part). 'Culture' has become a massive industry, which is marked above all by hybridity. At its centre, which is in one sense everywhere like the medieval God, it appears crowded and undifferentiated in terms of value, level, genre, product. But its shifting circumference is occupied by any number of niches, cults, specialist interests, carefully targeted products, which are renewable and substitutable. What has disappeared almost entirely is the idea of a hierarchical cultural whole, guided from the top down, with many of its potential participants at the bottom of the pyramid effectively excluded – the model which, with all its nuances, had been inherited by the eighteenth century and passed on to survive well into the twentieth.

Within this shifting panorama we focus on two other aspects of post-war culture: the problematic category of 'women's writing', which is raised by the emergence of a strong and confident canon of writing by women (sec. 9.2), and, by contrast, the characterization of what we call a 'minimalist postmodernism' through a close textual analysis of work by three of Italy's most interesting male writers of narrative fiction towards the end of the twentieth century (sec. 9.3). The final section (sec. 9.4), putting aside strict analysis, delves into the pages of the cultural weeklies to offer a snapshot of the literary market-place in the spring of 2006.

PART I

The Long Eighteenth Century (1690–1815)

1

Cross-currents of modernity

1.1 This is Arcadia

In the eighteenth century Italian culture was known abroad for many things – its classical heritage, its theatre, music and opera and the supposed musicality of the Italian language, its interesting sexual mores, the generally doleful effect of the Counter-Reformation church on its intellectual life – and high on the list were its academies. These *accademie* were the principal medium of artistic, scientific, literary and cultural exchange. Every urban centre, down to the smallest, in all the various states and statelets of the peninsula and the islands, had its academy, sometimes comprising only a few members and lasting only a few years, a constellation of intellectual life which led D'Alembert to declare in the *Encyclopédie* that 'Italy alone has more academies than the rest of the world put together' (Quondam 1982: 823). D'Alembert, in common with the most advanced Enlightenment thinking of the middle of the century, was not tender towards the Italian academies with their 'funny' (*bisarres*) names, their occasional fancy dress and Byzantine rules. He had his own agenda, arguing for the creation and maintenance of strong, centralized, national academies on the French model to act as the engines of scientific endeavour at the national and international level. But Italy was not a centralized nation-state at this time, and the diversity D'Alembert described, however condescendingly, matched the reality on the ground. Amidst this plethora of academic activity, however, one academy stood out: the Accademia degli Arcadi, or 'Arcadia' for short. Founded in Rome in 1690, it was the first Italian academy to acquire a national character and it dominated poetic style for at least half a century (Felici 1999: 130).

Arcadia was formally established by a group of fourteen *letterati* on 5 October 1690 in the gardens of the church of San Pietro in Montorio, on the Janiculum Hill overlooking the city. In choosing the name of their academy, the founders, amongst whom were Giovanni Mario Crescimbeni (1663–1728) and Gian Vincenzo Gravina (1664–1718), had at the back of their minds the classic of late fifteenth-century Italian literature which had founded the pastoral genre in Europe, Jacopo Sannazaro's *Arcadia* (published 1504), and the wealth of not only pastoral but also mythological associations which were conjured up jointly by the poem and the geographical name. 'Arcadia' was thus an allusion both to a classicist agenda – one in which respect for the achievements and values of Greek and Latin literature would be prominent – and to an idealized notion of the simple life of the countryside, removed, even if only temporarily, from the cares and pressures of the city, in the present.

As with other academies, the act of foundation entailed first and foremost the choice of an emblem (an *impresa*), in this case a pan-pipe crowned with laurel and pine, and the drawing up of rules. Each member took an Arcadian identity, comprising a first name which he or she chose from the pastoral tradition, and a second which was chosen by lot and represented a place drawn from the literary tradition, over which this newly ordained shepherd or shepherdess ideally held sway: thus Crescimbeni chose the proper name Alfesibeo (from the *Aeneid*) and was given the surname Cario, from Caria, a region on the coast of Asia Minor, while Gravina became Opico Erimanteo (from a character in Sannazaro's poem and the river Erimanthus where Hercules hunted down the wild boar) (Bellina and Caruso 1998: 249). In this way, the Arcadians sought to create a kind of ideal republic, in which each member was nominally equal, made uniform by their assumed name, which thus functioned also as a mask, whatever its owner's actual social origin or rank. Time was measured in Olympiads (the foundation of 1690 occurred in the second year of the 627th Olympiad in Arcadia-time). Its spiritual home, wherever members might actually be meeting, was the Bosco Parrasio. The membrane between fantasy and reality was not watertight. Mercifully for later historians, the Arcadians did keep a record of who was who, so it is easy to check who the mythical Alfesibeo Cario and Opico Erimanteo were in real life (Giorgetti Vichi 1977). There was also an internal hierarchy for organizational purposes, with day-to-day affairs being run by the custodian general (*Custode Generale*; Crescimbeni from 1690 to his death in 1728) and his deputy (Gravina up until 1711, when he fell out with Crescimbeni and quit Arcadia) and a council of fourteen. And, this being Rome, the classical disguise was not entire: the academy was put under the protection of the Child Jesus (*Gesù Bambino*), the pope was given the honorific title of Great Shepherd (*Pastore Massimo*), and the question of the relation between Arcadia and the Roman hierarchy of the church remained an important one. Even so, the third of the laws of the academy, drawn up by Gravina in 1695, was unchallenged: 'Patronus nullus esto', there shall be no ruler.

The cosmopolitan, or at least supra-regional, character of the new academy was reflected in the diverse provenance of its founding members – from Macerata, Spoleto, Roggiano in Calabria, Civita Latina, Imola, Turin, Genoa, Florence, Siena, Rome, Orvieto and Spello – and, most of all, in the rapid spread of its 'colonies' (*colonie*) all over Italy. This was the decisive factor in the success of Arcadia: the creation of new academies which took the name, rules and practices of the mother academy in Rome but were largely autonomous; they often absorbed some of the older, smaller, local academies in the process. In addition to geographical spread, the Accademia degli Arcadi also achieved durability, for it still exists today. In its prime, during the first half of the eighteenth century, literary activity was the cement that held it together, but its meetings were varied affairs, often including musical recitals and the reading of learned dissertations on philosophical and scientific subjects in addition to literary ones, as well as the performance and exchange of poetic compositions. A meeting of the academy was a social as well as a cultural or intellectual event, and Arcadia had a membership that was both 'representative', including numerous members of the nobility and the clergy, in effect the ruling class of the *ancien régime*, and 'aspirational', people drawn from the third estate of doctors, lawyers, state employees, professors, painters, architects and musicians, the professional strata of the newly emerging bourgeoisie. Another important feature of Arcadia was the growing presence of women, who had habitually been excluded from the academies of the seventeenth century as part of the general exclusion of women from public, or semi-public, spaces on moralistic grounds. Arcadia did not exclude women, even if the take-up was initially slow (only 74 of the 2,619 *arcadi* accounted for up to 1728 were women). Their number increased as the century progressed, though there was clear discrimination in the conditions for entry: while men were expected to be learned in at least one of the principal sciences, women were asked 'also' to be actively engaged in poetry ('di più, che attualmente professino la poesia'); but the 'also' was effectively an 'only', since it was not until well into the century that women, and then very few, were able to accede to university-level education (the first and most famous was Laura Bassi (1711–78), who graduated from Bologna in 1731 and taught there, becoming professor of physics; she was a member of Arcadia between 1728 and 1743) (Graziosi 1992: 325; the source is a letter from Crescimbeni written in 1700).

There is a strong current in Italian cultural-historical opinion which regards Arcadia as being more concerned with cultural politics than with an intellectual agenda. Born in the shadow of the Roman Curia, it reproduced some of its structures (the organization of the *colonie* recalls in part that of episcopal sees or monastic orders), benefited from the patronage of the senior cardinals in that same Curia, and took a stance on trends and tendencies in contemporary culture which were supportive of orthodoxy. Arcadia's internal and local autonomy protected it against direct political influence, but at the price of its members restricting their activities, and perhaps their thinking, to the limited, self-contained sphere of their own devising. They could not, by definition, take an anti-ecclesiastical or a secularist stand and remain members of Arcadia. From the statistics that he was able to derive from Arcadia's records, Amedeo Quondam concluded that the recruitment from different social classes to Arcadia was backed up by an idea of the neutrality of culture, in the light of which intellectual activity was thought to be different from and divorced from the conflicts, tensions and divisions in society. Thinking (and writing, creating), according to this model, was something that went on elsewhere, in an ideal, even magical setting governed by harmony and sociability, in which the welcoming of new talent (entailing the process of social promotion which the statistics reveal) and the ability to get on with one's peers, the lure of good taste and pleasantness, were more important than confronting difficult problems. The upshot was to give powerful and widespread support to a moderate conservatism, and already in the eighteenth century the pastoral refuge that was Arcadia could be seen as a more or less willing instrument in the hands of a Curia bent on fending off modernity.

A more benign view of Arcadia was expressed by Mario Fubini, the leading literary scholar of the period in the middle of the twentieth century. His preoccupation was not so much the shadow of the church as the academy's poetic concerns, to which we now turn. Poetry was at the centre of the Arcadians' programme. They perceived themselves as returning to the true path of Italian poetry after the excesses of the Baroque and of the brash and innovative manner known as 'marinismo' after the name of its greatest exponent, Giovanbattista Marino (1569–1625). Disagreements about what that true path was were one of the factors which led to the split between Crescimbeni and Gravina. Both agreed that the seventeenth century (the *Seicento*) had to be liquidated by seeking models further back in the past. Gravina championed a mythical and didactic poetry whose models were to be found in the Greeks and in Dante. Crescimbeni, on the other hand, always more moderate, more prudent, more conscious perhaps of what was effectively possible, argued for a return to the more recent Italian tradition, the Petrarchism of the sixteenth century, the Anacreontic verse practised by Gabriello Chiabrera (1552–1638), a quiet, light kind of poetry-making, whose hallmark would be simplicity, clarity, elegance. Crescimbeni's, by and large, was the winning card. The poetry that resulted was marked by moderation – the objects of this verse were familiar, realistically reproduced, in clear language and balanced diction, without surprises or disturbance. The classics were re-examined critically, but the outcome was often no more than imitation, and this was the limit of Arcadia: it produced a style of poetry which was easily reproduced, and was so endlessly, but left little scope for originality. The rationalism underpinning it, however, was not what Quondam called a 'degraded rationalism', but rather a style which set the agenda for much of the rest of the century. The values of the Enlightenment, from this perspective, were not at odds with those of Arcadia, but simply a more decisive, a more engaged, a more determined kind of rationalism. Arcadia and Enlightenment both stemmed from the same source, but evolved in different directions and at different speeds. Thus, far from being an exercise in nostalgia or in pure escapism, Arcadia, in Fubini's view, was a typically eighteenth-century organism which brought literary people together on a more democratic footing than the courtly structures of the sixteenth century (the *Cinquecento*) had allowed.

Arcadia signalled the triumph through most of the eighteenth century of the lyric genre. The lyric is a relatively short and, at least in its eighteenth-century guise, a sociable form. Poems following well-understood rules and adhering to clear structures could be exchanged as gifts, recited in public, applauded by a like-minded and mutually admiring audience, collected into multi-authored *raccolte* (anthologies) which underlined their function as the threads of a social web (the archetype of which were the successive volumes of *Rime degli Arcadi* published between 1716 and 1722). Such poetry became also a means whereby an elite though not exclusively aristocratic society (aspiring professionals could enter it through intellectual and artistic endeavour) mirrored itself and, by and large, liked what it saw. Even when the verse was not so complaisant and cast a critical or satirical eye on its rites and customs, the impression left was of a world that was at ease with itself and hedonistic, and, where there was trouble, inclined to confront it in a spirit of rational judiciousness, for example through the studied contemplation of conflicting passions, the tension between which was often left hanging, deliberately unresolved. It was also a society in which appearance and decorum were important; thus, within the confines of good taste, public performance was an indispensable part of getting on in polite society. It is no surprise that under the auspices of 'Arcadia' in the widest sense (understood as the touchstone of a cultural climate as well as a specific institution or network of institutions) regulated, and sometimes virtuoso, oral exchange should flourish: recital, conversation, formalized discourse and debate, verbal game-playing and the peculiarly Italian skill (as it was seen by European contemporaries) of improvised poetry.

At the same time, the lyre in the lyric suggested a connection with musicality and song, and often in social situations the pre-eminent form of the eighteenth-century lyric, the *canzonetta*, would be set to music, accompanied by an instrument, and/or sung. The *canzonetta*, which generally consisted of linked pairs of four-line strophes made up of relatively short lines of seven or eight syllables, reflected the dominant canons of the age in the simplicity of its structure and its invitation to a minimalist and gracefully deployed vocabulary as well as in its musicality, as in the example which follows, the beginning of 'L'isola amorosa' ('The amorous isle') by Carlo Innocenzo Frugoni (1692–1768; he served as court poet in the Duchy of Parma): 'La bella nave è pronta: / ecco la sponda e il lido, / dove nocchier Cupìdo, / belle, v'invita al mar. // Mirate come l'ancora / già dall'arena svelsero / mille Amorin, che apprestansi / festosi a navigar' (Gronda 1978: 108: 'The fair ship is ready: / Behold the shore, fair ladies, / Where the love-god at the helm / Bids you to the water's edge. // See how a thousand cupids / Loosen the anchor from the sand / and how they laugh and hurry / To put the ship to sea'). The attraction of this relatively new form was its immense adaptability: it could vary in length, in metre, in rhyme-scheme, and be used for any number of purposes and subjects, intimate and gossipy as well as mythological or sententious. In this it had an advantage over the other popular short form, the sonnet, which, however, continued to be widely used, and indeed so overused as to become a term of abuse: in its honour, the eighteenth century came to be derided as good for nothing but sonnets, Italy as a country of sonneteers. The first half of the century was a laboratory of metrical experiment and invention, as well as creative exploitation of the flexibility of the *canzonetta*. In a climate in which participants in the cultural game were both allowed and encouraged to compose in verse, poets proliferated, few stood out. But among the names which one should at least mention, all of them members at one time or another of Arcadia, are those of the most accomplished female poet of the early part of the century, Faustina Maratti Zappi (?1680–1745), whose poems were published together with those, mainly sonnets, of her husband, Giambattista Felice Zappi (1667–1719), in Venice in 1723; Petronilla Paolini Massimi (1663–1726), author of a number of *canzoni*, some of which dealt with painful personal experience, including the murder of her father and the death of her son; Pier Jacopo Martello (1665–1725), who was a playwright above all and whose name is preserved in the *verso martelliano*, a fourteen-syllable line named after him which sought to achieve the effect of the French alexandrine; Eustachio

Manfredi (1674–1739), mathematician and, in poetry, a strict Petrarchist; Tommaso Crudeli (1703–45), a poet who became the first Italian to be persecuted for being a Freemason; and Paolo Rolli (1687–1765), who spent much of his career in London as a prolific librettist and the first translator of Milton's *Paradise Lost* (1733).

Rolli, though older, shared a part of his road with the most notable poet to emerge from Arcadia in the first half of the eighteenth century, Pietro Metastasio (1698–1782). Like Metastasio, Rolli was a native of Rome and a pupil of Gianvincenzo Gravina, and both of them achieved precocious fame as improvisers (indeed, improvised together). Both of them also achieved fame and fortune as 'poets for music' and entered prestigious employment abroad. Rolli from 1716 was tutor to the children of King George II and librettist to the Royal Academy of Music, where he wrote for Handel among others. Metastasio, much more gloriously, was court poet (*poeta cesareo*) at the court of the Austrian emperor Charles VI, to which post he was appointed in 1729 in succession to Apostolo Zeno (1668–1750); Metastasio remained in Vienna, with occasional sorties to other parts of the empire, for the rest of his long life.

Metastasio had already published a volume of *Poesie* (*Poems*, 1717) and a tragedy when he moved to Naples after Gravina's death, became involved with the vibrant musical life of the city, and had an immediate triumph with the production of his first melodrama, *Didone abbandonata* (*Dido Abandoned*, 1724, music by Domenico Sarro). This, and the *intermezzo* which accompanied it, *L'impresario delle Canarie* (*The Impresario of the Canaries*) – an *opera buffa* subject which convention, mainly led by Zeno, now separated from the main *opera seria* action – established Metastasio's reputation as a musical poet, and a string of compositions followed during the next few years spent in Naples and back in Rome. It was not long before the call came from Vienna, and for the next ten years, from 1730 to the emperor's death in 1740, Metastasio continued to write with confident regularity in the very different context of a proud and moralistic court. For the emperor's name-day (4 November) he wrote five heroic libretti between 1731 and 1736, all set to music by Antonio Caldara, and in due course by others: *La clemenza di Tito* (*The Clemency of Titus*, 1734), for example, was set some sixty times during the eighteenth century by composers who included Gluck (1751), Domenico Scarlatti (1757), and later, with a much altered text, in its most famous version, Mozart in 1791. The Empress Elizabeth's birthday (28 August) was also celebrated, with more sentimental compositions. When Maria Theresia came to the throne, and the War of the Austrian Succession began (see sec. 1.2), the atmosphere at court became more sombre, and Metastasio's operatic production slackened. He did, however, write some interesting reflections on Aristotle's *Poetics* (as well as translating Horace's *Ars poetica*), from which he drew his conviction that the modern melodrama could trace a direct lineage back to Greek tragedy (which was sung or chanted), with the dialogue-based recitatives recalling the ancient 'scenes of action' and the arias echoing the strophes of ancient tragedy (Kimbell 1999: 365). But he begged to differ from Aristotle as to the means whereby tragedy may gain its effect: fear and pity are neither sufficient nor necessary to the moral outcome, when 'the admiration of virtue' and 'horror in the face of the evil dispositions of the human heart' are 'effective and laudable means by which to give delight as well as benefit' ('Estratto dell'"arte poetica"', in Metastasio 1947–54: IV, 1075).

In Metastasio's *drammi per musica* complications and obstacles abound as the drama tacks between the spoken recitatives and the musical, sung, parts which interrupt the action, to be resolved by heroic or generous deeds or through the expedient of recognition scenes in the third act. His natural poetic gifts came through particularly in the arias, in which he carried the implicit Arcadian poetic of rationally balanced emotional tension and non-resolution expressed in a sonorous, metrically inventive, crystal-clear yet always not quite satisfied display to its elegant and sweet-sounding best. The same qualities may be found in his *canzonette*, some of which, like his verse written expressly for music, had a long afterlife in both poetry and music. One example is the poem 'La libertà' ('Freedom'), written in Vienna in 1733, whose opening double-strophe reads: 'Grazie agl'inganni tuoi, / al fin respiro, o Nice, / al fin d'un infelice / ebber gli dei pietà: // sento da' lacci suoi, / sento che l'alma è sciolta; / non sogno questa volta, / non sogno libertà' (Gronda 1978: 16–17: 'Thanks to your cheating, / Nice, I breathe at last, / The gods at last took pity / On an unhappy man: // I feel that my soul / Is freed from its bonds; / This time I am not dreaming, / I am not dreaming of freedom'). The poem, which goes on for another twelve double-strophes, was repeatedly set to music during the eighteenth century, as, according to Metastastio's biographer, the English musicologist Charles Burney, 'a Venetian Ballad, a Canzonet, a Duo, and a Cantata' (Burney 1971: I, 127), and by many famous musicians, including Rousseau, Paisiello, and Metastasio's lifelong friend, the *castrato* Carlo Broschi, known as Farinello, as well as by Metastasio himself to a melody which, says Burney, 'compared with airs of the same period and kind, will be found superior to most of them in elegant simplicity'(I, 127). Although it is difficult to reproduce the sensation now, Metastasio was for many years, and even into the nineteenth century, regarded as a very great poet, and this alone is testimony to the extent to which an Arcadian taste had penetrated not only Italian but European sensibility.

1.2 New states, new thinkers

The heyday of Arcadia coincided with a period of continuous warfare which engaged the Italian peninsula both militarily and diplomatically. The end of the Habsburg line in Madrid with the death of the emperor Charles II in 1700 created a potential power vacuum in Italy which other major continental powers, notably France and Austria, were keen to exploit. The Spanish empire, including its Italian possessions (Lombardy and the Kingdoms of Naples and Sicily), passed by inheritance to the grandson of Louis XIV of France, who, as Philip V, established a new Bourbon dynasty in Spain. This did not please the Habsburg emperor of Austria, Leopold I. The first of three consecutive wars, known as the Wars of Succession (Spanish, Polish, Austrian), saw Austria invade Lombardy, defeating the French in the north of Italy in 1706. A year later an Austrian army marched into Naples. The treaty of Utrecht, signed in 1713, ratified these Austrian conquests, but it did not produce lasting stability in Italy. For the next twenty years, Philip V manoeuvred by diplomatic and dynastic means to reassert Spanish ascendancy in the peninsula. Events precipitated in 1733 when a dispute over the succession to the throne of Poland led to the French attacking the Austrians in Italy. Allying with Spain, France promised the Kingdom of the Two Sicilies (comprising southern Italy and Sicily) to Philip's son, Don Carlos, who had already inherited the Duchy of Parma by marriage in 1731. Naples was conquered in 1734, and a new settlement began to take shape, helped by the passing of the last of the Medici, Gian Gastone, who died childless and heirless in 1737. Don Carlos was recognized as king of the Two Sicilies, Austrian rule was restored in Lombardy, and the Medici Grand Duchy of Tuscany passed to Duke Francis Stephen of Lorraine, whose former domains were ceded to France. Since he had recently married Maria Theresia, heiress to the Habsburg empire, Tuscany now came under indirect Austrian rule. The final twist in this three-act drama began four years later. With the outbreak of war over the Austrian succession, the Bourbons launched an attack on Maria Theresia's Italian possessions, hoping to make a settlement for the Spanish emperor's younger son, Don Felipe. After Don Felipe had occupied Milan and then been forced out (1745), peace was finally signed at Aix-la-Chapelle in November 1748.

In retrospect, this turned out to be a momentous date, for the new treaty brought peace to Italy for nearly half a century, until the violence of the

1790s sparked by Napoleon's Italian campaign and the political and military reactions to it. It did so 'by establishing Italy as a separate state system, insulated from the rivalries of the great powers. The Italian branches of the Habsburg and Bourbon dynasties were severed from their parent houses. Milan remained a province of the Habsburg empire, but Tuscany was constituted as a separate sovereignty under Maria Theresia's second son, Peter Leopold. Likewise sovereignty over the Two Sicilies and Parma was vested in the junior branches of the Bourbon dynasty' (Symcox 2002: 118).

Something else had also shifted in the peninsula during the previous fifty years, apart from the marching and countermarching of the armies of the continental powers. The Savoy dynasty, rulers in Piedmont and, after 1720, Sardinia, had steadily exploited and enhanced its usefulness to the other powers as the controller of the strategic northwestern passes into the peninsula, and by virtue of this geographical advantage and its own increasingly professional military expertise, had expanded its territory eastwards into Lombardy as well as obtaining its long-sought-after royal title: the duke of Savoy was now the king of Sardinia. The Italian states managed to stay out of the Seven Years' War of 1756–63, no less bloody and disease-ridden than its predecessors, but their elites were painfully aware that this was thanks to the way the competing dynastic interests in the peninsula played at that moment rather than to any effort or achievement of their own. The presence of foreign government ministers was resented; the sense of Italy, in the shape of its various states, being no more than a pawn in the hands of foreign powers scarcely abated. Nevertheless, there was an equilibrium of a sort, there was peace and a breathing-space, and in those conditions the possibilities for reform opened up. Although the reform movements of the middle of the century associated with Enlightenment ideas will be described in the next chapter, this is a good moment to consider some of the earlier signs of change.

In the area of public administration, the most rapid steps in the first half of the century were made by the Duchy of Savoy. During the 1710s and 1720s the nobility was integrated into the state service, local administration was reorganized, laws were recodified, land tax registers were revised, the fiscal immunities of the church were restricted. All these were harbingers of things to come in other Italian states later in the century, but they took place within the specific circumstances of the Savoy polity and with a clear purpose: to enhance the military power and effectiveness of the state (Symcox 2002: 119–20). Elsewhere, the opportunities for reform were slim as yet, but that did not mean that a sense of intellectual challenge was absent or non-existent. In Venice, for example, the patrician Scipione Maffei (1675–1755) made his mark with a treatise on the aristocracy, *Della scienza cavalleresca* (*On the Science of Chivalry*, 1710), in which he argued that the nobility should play an active role in the governance of the state according to modern criteria, freeing itself from superstition and prejudice and, above all, from all feudal pretensions. He used his social position and his money to promote cultural forms that reached out beyond the elite to a more broadly educated public. In this role as 'cultural organizer', he was co-founder with Apostolo Zeno of the *Giornale de' letterati d'Italia* (1710–40), which aimed to keep Italian literati in touch with all that was going on in contemporary Europe. Having also written a tragedy of his own (*Merope*, 1713), he edited a collection of Italian tragic plays to which he prefaced a useful *Discorso storico sul teatro italiano* (*Historical Discourse on Italian Theatre*, 1723): he emphasized the longstanding perception of the theatre as the most 'social' of literary forms and asserted the standing of Italian tragedy compared to French. Maffei's openness to European currents of thought, a feature of the more lively strand of Italian intellectual life which was already establishing itself in the late seventeenth century and would increase during the eighteenth, was shared by his fellow northeasterner and near-contemporary, Antonio Conti (1677–1749), who was from Padua. Conti also wrote classical tragedies, but is particularly well known for his translations, notably of Pope's *Rape of the Lock* (published posthumously, in 1751). As a scholar and philosopher, and a reader of Locke, Conti became convinced of the irreconcilability of science and theology; his increasingly heterodox views brought him a ban on publication after his return to Italy from his many foreign travels in 1726, and much of his work was left in manuscript and in a haphazard state.

Conti's fate reminds us that it was impossible to be thinking, writing, speculating in eighteenth-century Italy without taking account of the Catholic church, without indeed, in the vast majority of cases, professing or at least conforming to Catholic orthodoxy. The two centuries after the conclusion of the Council of Trent (1563) and the papal edicts which followed it during the late sixteenth century have been described as 'featuring a process of confessionalization and social discipline', in which both ecclesiastical and secular authorities 'sought to make their inferiors understand and conform to directives from on high': 'Prelates and rulers aimed to form clerics and layfolk well-informed about the tenets of the faith adopted by their rulers, readily inclined to conduct correctly and take part regularly in all mandated religious observances, alert and willing to denounce deviations from orthodoxy' (Jacobson Schutte 2002: 125–6). Although this process of socialization and internalization can be misrepresented as all one way, and there is evidence, throughout the period, of people not only resisting unwelcome pressure but also exercising agency of their own 'in the development of early modern Christian spirituality and religious practice' (2002: 125–6), Jacobson Schutte concludes that 'without questioning its genuineness, one might characterize Italian religion of the eighteenth century as normalized, routinized, and conformist' (2002: 139). With a slightly different emphasis, Gregory Hanlon declares that 'Counter-Reformation devotion reached its peak intensity around 1700' (Hanlon 2000: 310). This meant both a papacy which 'trumpeted its certitudes, its traditions and its jurisdictions to ward off encroachment by princes north of the Alps' and a church which 'sponsored innovative scholarship, primarily in the domain of religious history, but more generally in philology, classical history and literary criticism' (2002: 310).

One outstanding product of this environment was Ludovico Antonio Muratori (1672–1750), who was born in Modena, ordained priest in 1695, went to Milan in the same year to become librarian at the Biblioteca Ambrosiana, and returned to Modena in 1700 as court librarian to the Este family, in which post he remained until his death. A polymath whose interests ranged from jurisprudence and religion to philosophy, literature and history, Muratori began (1703) by calling for the formation of a 'republic of letters' conceived differently from that of Arcadia (though he was an Arcadian himself), one founded on the search for 'the true' and subject to serious critical reflection. Underpinning this was the idea of poetry which he expounded in *Della perfetta poesia italiana* (*On Perfect Italian Poetry*, 1706), based on the conjunction of imagination and intellect, of images that in some way impress themselves on our mind and a truth that they teach, whether this truth be concrete and real or, more appropriately in the case of poetry, possible and resembling the real. The imagination is fired by enthusiasm or *estro* or *furor poetico*, which is nothing other than a necessary and, in poets, natural, but not 'divine', Muratori insists, 'lively excitement' of the imagination (Muratori 1971–2: 218); the operations of the imagination are in turn governed, regulated, by judgement, intellect and 'good taste'. This last was the guiding category of his subsequent book, *Riflessioni sopra il buon gusto nelle scienze e nelle arti* (*Reflections on Good Taste in the Arts and Sciences*, 1708), where it took on a wide meaning as a form of social regulation informing any intellectual activity. At a certain point, however, Muratori's literary interests give way to a passion for historical erudition, which produced the truly monumental achievements of the twenty-five-volume *Rerum italicarum scriptores* (*Writers on Italian Matters*, 1723–51), the six-volume *Antiquitates italicae medii aevi* (*Italian Antiquities of the Middle Ages*, 1738–42), and the twelve volumes of the *Annali d'Italia* (*Annals of Italy*, 1745–9), written in Italian on the same medieval theme for a wider reading public.

Although his researches touched on delicate matters of state–church relations, Muratori remained prudently within orthodoxy when discussing the historical role of the church. His contemporary, the Neapolitan Pietro Giannone (1676–1748), who was a layman, lawyer and historian, was less respectful. In his *Istoria civile del regno di Napoli* (*Civil History of the Kingdom of Naples*, 1723), he too went back to the Middle Ages in order to trace the origins of and to try to unravel the innumerable legal and jurisdictional disputes which pitted state against church. This was a radically new way of writing history, distilled in the slow and tortuous evolution of institutions rather than the clash of battle, but it was also a fierce denunciation of ecclesiastical abuse of power. The reaction from the Curia was not slow in coming. Giannone had to flee to Vienna, where he lived for ten years on a modest imperial pension before being expelled; when he was tricked back into Italy in 1736, he was arrested and remained a prisoner of the Savoy duke Carlo Emanuele III until his death. In the view of some modern readers, his masterpiece is the autobiography he wrote in prison, *Vita di Pietro Giannone* (1736–7), which, though he calls it the story of a 'shipwreck', is a testament to his intellectual and moral integrity.

Unlike Giannone, his fellow Neapolitan Giambattista Vico (1668–1744) steered well clear of political questions and never challenged the church head-on. In fact, Vico was on the surface distinctly uncontemporary in everything he did. Holder of a low-prestige and low-paid chair of rhetoric at the University of Naples from 1699, he did not enjoy an upwardly mobile career, although he was given an honorary appointment as royal historiographer by the new Bourbon king Charles in 1735. The sources of his thinking as revealed in his *Autobiografia* (1725) – Tacitus, Plato, Francis Bacon, the legal philosopher Grotius – were perceived as unfashionable, and the very structure of his masterwork, the *Scienza nuova* (*New Science*) – is 'baroque' in its liberal use of metaphor, its abrupt changes of direction, its encyclopedic omnivorousness, its construction of Chinese boxes, its sometimes impenetrable language; it certainly does not conform to eighteenth-century standards of taste or decorum. But, if it made little impact on Vico's contemporaries, its brilliance and originality have ensured it a long afterlife from the nineteenth century to the present, among philosophers, historians, creative writers (notably James Joyce) and general readers.

The *Scienza nuova* – first published as *Principj di una scienza nuova intorno alla natura delle nazioni* (*Principles of a New Science Concerning the Nature of Nations*, 1725), revised and added to as *Scienza nuova seconda* (*Second New*

Science, 1730), and this version further revised for the posthumous and definitive edition of 1744 – is divided into five parts. In the first, Vico imagines the scene after the Flood, when Noah's three sons, scattered about the earth, and their descendants, having lost all sense of religion, became a bestial race of giants. How, from this barbarism, Vico wants to know, did civilization arise? In the second book, it is made clear that the origins of humanity were not a golden age or a blissful state of nature (by starting his narrative after the Flood, Vico skilfully avoids having to deal with the problem which this view would pose about the Garden of Eden). They were brutal, and dominated by violence. Man had no reasoning, but he did have imagination. Sensitized to his environment, he could imagine (fearfully, very often) something outside it. This capacity was symbolized by his reaction to thunder, which evoked the presence of gods: thanks to this 'poetic' imagination, with its connotations of creating, fashioning, man literally 'made' his gods. As the poetic imagination took hold, men moved from a guttural, gestural, 'silent' language to 'poetic language', which enabled them to conceptualize what Vico calls 'universali fantastici', fantastic universals, to imagine and verbalize abstract entities in concrete personifications: the gods got a name. Religion was reborn, rites and rituals were established, families and clans were formed, brutes became men. In the third book, 'Discovery of the true Homer', the *Iliad* and the *Odyssey* are read as an expression of the foundation of the Greek nation. They held no secret or recondite meaning, as scholars had speculated, but were the voice of a whole people, 'still immature and violent, heroic in the *Iliad*, but already seeking more articulate forms of knowledge and social life in the *Odyssey*' (Fido 1999: 350). As such, they could not have been written by a single individual (Vico here connects with a controversy about the authorship of 'Homer' that had first surfaced in 1664 and which in one form or another continued well into the twentieth century). Book Four summarizes the pattern of human development. First there was the 'age of gods', that to which man's 'poetic nature' corresponded. This was followed by the 'age of heroes' and the corresponding 'heroic nature' of man. Force was used to curb violence, to establish rules and territory. Finally, there is the 'age of men', and here 'human nature' governed by reason is the order of the day. In the fifth book, Vico reveals that the process does not reach an end, but recurs (thus giving rise to perhaps the best-known formula of the book, that of the *corsi e ricorsi* of history). These recurrences (*ricorsi*), however, are not identical repetitions: every time that society heads back towards barbarism, it carries with it some imprint of the previous age of men. Modernity is seen as a resurgence from the Middle Ages, conceived by Vico as 'tempi barbari ritornati' after the decline of the civilization of antiquity.

The guiding principle of Vico's reinterpretation of human history is that of *verum est ipsum factum*: the human race can only know what it itself does, or makes. The divine plan is hidden, and although Providence moves mysteriously through the argument of the *Scienza nuova*, it is not for human beings to try and decipher it. Paradoxically, this voluntary renunciation gave Vico extraordinary freedom. He did not have to try to make all the evidence fit what can only be assumed to be a divine plan (since the divine mind is so far out of the reach of our own). He could ridicule those who did precisely that and who conceived of the world allegorically, as a realization or materialization of some superhuman idea. Neither did he have to apologize to God (or the church): what he saw and tried to make sense of was strictly manmade. But it was *everything* manmade: monuments, languages, myths, fables, institutions, artefacts, rituals, tropes – the list is endless (to our human eyes), and not surprisingly Vico is sometimes thought of as the father of cultural anthropology. There is a fundamental pragmatism about Vico's thought, despite the extraordinary inventiveness and metaphorical élan of his language: the *Iliad* was not composed to convey an esoteric meaning, it was composed as the voice of the entire Greek people of that time (and only that time). Pragmatic, but also challenging. The method we are asked to adopt is that of looking at the past on its own terms, without preconception or prejudice. But by the same token, we are asked to look deep into the past, that is to say into our own civilization, to understand the process of self-construction by which we have emerged to our present (not eternal) state, and to understand the primacy of language and symbolic representation in the making of human culture.

2

Enlightenment and the public arena

2.1 Journalism, theatre and the book trade in Venice

The diplomatic settlement of 1748, once all the cards had been shuffled and dealt on the international gaming board, left the Italian states in the hands of their absolute rulers, three of them holding significant regional power (the house of Savoy in the northwest, the Habsburgs in Lombardy and Tuscany, the Bourbons in the south). The republic of Venice, an oligarchy in its form of government, continued its slow if splendid decline. The other surviving maritime republic, Genoa, sold the island of Corsica to the French in 1768 and turned increasingly in on itself. Rome's absolute ruler was the pope, who, however, did not have territorial ambitions beyond maintaining his Italian possessions curving across the centre of the peninsula. But alongside the affirmation of absolutism there was in many parts of Italy, as in much of northern Europe, a widening of civil society beyond the nobility (itself in numerical decline in some states) to include an emerging professional class of doctors, lawyers, scientists and engineers: a social opening which paralleled that which we have already noted in the membership of Arcadia, and which often involved the same people. An increasing professionalization of important state functions is noticeable in the second half of the century. Military training became more technical and noblemen competed for entry into the new technical schools. The appointment of permanent, professional judges replaced the previous rotation of untrained patricians in the role of magistrates. After 1770, according to Hanlon, 'non-nobles dominated every sector of the administration, and reduced the nobles to an honorific elite' (Hanlon 2000: 322).

The access being gained by wider sections of society, with different experiences and preparation from those of the traditional nobility, though still relatively limited in scope, went hand in hand with the emergence of a new 'public space'. This process had already begun in the seventeenth century, but it accelerated in the eighteenth and assumed forms which were to shape the modern state in Europe and the West, and are still recognizable today.

The process was not uniform either in Europe as a whole or specifically in Italy, but where it happened it entailed apparently unstoppable trends towards an accelerating exchange of ideas and information, especially through the medium of print, and multiple, intersecting forms of association between people (freedom of the press and freedom of association, already fundamental principles of the English Revolution of 1688–9, were even more forcefully reiterated in the American and French revolutions of 1776 and 1789).

Already by the end of the seventeenth century in Italy, as in France and England, a recognizable newspaper culture had been established; in the course of the eighteenth, it has been estimated that some 2,200 periodicals were published in over fifty locations all over Italy (Dooley 2002: 213). There was a distinction, maintained for at least the first half of the eighteenth century, between *gazzette* and *giornali*. The *gazzette* were printed in the various cities with government permission and under government control. They carried foreign reports (commercial, political, arrivals and departures) and news of court ceremonies, public festivities and theatre programmes. The *giornali*, on the other hand, were devoted to 'literary' matters in the broadest sense, dealing with the arts and sciences as well as poetry and drama, but also with matters of public debate. As Scipione Maffei put it in his introduction to the pioneering *Giornale dei letterati d'Italia* in 1710, *giornali* are to be understood as 'quell'opere successive, che regolatamente di tempo in tempo ragguaglio dànno de' varj libri, ch'escono di nuovo in luce, e di ciò che in essi contiensi: notizie accoppiandovi delle nuove importanti edizioni, degli scoprimenti, delle invenzioni e di tutte quelle attività finalmente, che alla repubblica letteraria in qualche modo possono appartenersi' ('those successive works which at regular intervals provide information about newly published books and their contents, accompanied by news concerning important new editions, discoveries, inventions and in short all those activities which may be said in some way to belong to the republic of letters'; quoted in Natali 1929: I, 38). The 1760s saw a flurry of innovative campaigning *giornali* – Gasparo Gozzi's *Gazzetta veneta* (1760–1; the editorship passed to Pietro Chiari for the second and final year of the periodical's existence) and *Osservatore veneto* (1761–2), Giuseppe Baretti's *Frusta letteraria (The Literary Scourge)*, also published in Venice (1763–5), and the Milanese *Il Caffè* (1764–6) (see below, sec. 2.2). Though generally short-lived, these publications signalled a shifting of the ground. By the second half of the century, the literary journalism which had dominated previously seems to be following two divergent paths. One led to increased sectoral specialization with more restricted readerships. The other broadened the appeal of the journal beyond the traditional *letterato* to a readership made up of 'the educated public in an ever widening arc of civil society' (Ricuperati 1976: 350: 'il pubblico colto in un arco sempre più vasto della società civile'). A striking example is *Europa letteraria*, edited in Venice between 1768 and 1773 by Domenico Caminer, his daughter Elisabetta Caminer Turra, and Alberto Fortis, which then metamorphosed into the *Giornale enciclopedico* (1774–81) and continued as *Nuovo Giornale enciclopedico* under the sole editorship of Elisabetta from 1783 to 1787. The 'encyclopedic journal' was to evolve into a staple crop of nineteenth-century journalism, covering everything from scientific discoveries to gardening tips and – following a trend already well established in the eighteenth century – cramming increasing amounts of information onto densely printed, and thus relatively economical, pages.

The role of Venice for much of the century as the engine of innovative journalism extended to innovative theatre in the person of Carlo Goldoni (1707–93) and to taking the lead in the peninsula's burgeoning book trade. The thread that unites these three activities is the presence in the Serenissima and its territories of an energetic and entrepreneurial mercantile middle class.

The young Carlo Goldoni was destined for a legal career, and did indeed practise as a lawyer in the mid-1740s in Pisa. But though he was not in any sense born into the theatre, his passion for the theatre was intense. His meeting with the actor-manager Giuseppe Imer in 1734 gave him the opportunity to write for two theatres in Venice, the San Samuele and the San Giovanni Grisostomo, both owned by the patrician Michele Grimani. Most of what he wrote between 1737 and 1743 was libretti and tragicomedies. But he was also coming to grips with the challenge of writing comedy. The tradition was that of the *commedia dell'arte*, where the 'characters' were fixed roles (Arlecchino, Pantalone and so on) represented visibly by the masks the actors wore, and there was no script, only *canovacci* or *scenari*, which were scene-outlines to which the actors improvised. In Goldoni's view, this form of theatre was becoming shopworn, blocking off the possibilities of theatre by only offering the public what it was accustomed to and often pandering to the lowest common denominator of taste. But the tradition was deep-rooted and popular, and many actors were resistant to the idea of abandoning their masks in favour of roles based more on character. Goldoni tried gradually to introduce the idea of character acting and in 1738, in *Momolo cortesan*, he introduced a written part into a scenario-based comedy, using the personal skills and characteristics of the actor who played Pantalone, Francesco Golinetti, to craft a script for this character – the other parts remained unscripted. But these years, up to 1748, were generally a period of familiarization with the medium, of experimentation and testing, of feeling his way towards the language which would become a hallmark of Goldoni's comedy: switching between Italian with a strong 'northern', rather than Tuscan, inflection and a Venetian dialect which was no longer simply 'comic', but which reflected the regional language as it was variously spoken through all classes of Venetian society.

The second phase which now opened (1748–53) saw Goldoni writing indefatigably – for one season (running from October 1750 to Carnival 1751) he promised to write no fewer than sixteen new comedies, and kept his promise – and producing some of his best early plays, including *La bottega del caffè* (*The Coffee Shop*, 1750), set in a Venetian *piazzetta* and tracing the confrontation between the honest coffee-house-keeper Ridolfo and the intriguingly malicious Don Marzio, and *La locandiera* (*The Innkeeper*, 1753), where the seductive Mirandolina, the innkeeper of the title, in the end renounces her aristocratic catch and society returns to normal. During this period too, Goldoni began to put some theoretical flesh on what he calls his reform, his 'riforma'. The preface to the first volume of his plays, which appeared in 1750, told the reader that the 'books' from which Goldoni had learnt were those of 'the world' and 'the theatre': from the first he had learnt the 'natural characters' of people, from the second the techniques whereby these could be rendered on the stage and made understandable to an audience. Comic effect is attained by us seeing 'effigiati al naturale, e posti con buon garbo nel loro punto di vista, i difetti e 'l ridicolo che trovasi in chi continuamente si pratica, in modo però che non urti troppo offendendo' (Goldoni 1969: 1312: 'the failings and absurdities that can be found everywhere and in everyone, drawn naturally and presented to the public with wit, but in such a way as not to jar by being offensive').

His second great period of theatrical writing, beginning with his return to the Teatro San Luca in 1759, was also to be his Venetian swansong. A number of the plays of this period home in, always in comic vein, on the tensions, self-deceptions, concern with appearances, petty tyrannies and deceits of the bourgeois, mercantile and professional class, of which he was a part. Three of the best, *I rusteghi* (*The Rustics*, 1760), *La casa nova* (*The New House*, 1760) and *Sior Todero brontolon* (*Todero the Grouch*, 1762), were written in dialect and pitted the values of the older generation (the 'rusteghi') – hard work, thrift, following the rules – against the desire of the young for greater freedom: Goldoni, in the true spirit of comedy, favoured the young, but not without some nostalgic yearning for those 'rustic' values. With the so-called *Trilogia della villeggiatura* (*The Holiday Trilogy*, 1761), the feisty young heroine Giacinta proves her moral superiority by remaining faithful to her half-ruined fiancé Leonardo – holidaying in the country is a wastefully expensive business – and giving up the more appetizing Guglielmo. And with *Le baruffe chiozzotte* (1762), Goldoni returns, in Chioggia dialect, to the world of the working people who might also be the audience of the play (this too was written for the end of Carnival). The lives of the women left behind in Chioggia while their men are off fishing are not idealized: they are full of anxiety and tensions, and that is when the fights (the *baruffe* of the title) break out. But they have a vitality and spontaneity which is recognized, and a little envied, by Goldoni's semi-autobiographical representative, the magistrate's assistant Isidoro, who sorts matters out in the end.

In addition to the four Venetian theatres Goldoni worked in (in 1762 he left for Paris, where he remained for the last thirty years of his life) there were three others in the city, and all seven were thriving and in sharp competition with each other. In Venice more than anywhere else in Italy, the commercial theatre, the model for the future, dominated the scene, in contrast to the private theatres in patrician houses or colleges or (sometimes) ecclesiastical buildings in which most written theatre was performed in the seventeenth or early eighteenth centuries. The 'reform' of comedy was in a sense a merging of the popular tradition of improvised *arte* and the written texts of the elite, but in a context that was essentially bourgeois and market-oriented. Audiences were numerous, vociferous and fickle, broadsheets kept up a running commentary on what was on in the theatres, often critical if not openly offensive. Goldoni's 'realism' was a theatrical realism, which put on stage, often very funnily, the whole gamut of contemporary Venetian society talking its own language, and living out its tensions and hostilities, albeit 'without offence'. But it existed within this wider realism, the realism of the theatre itself, where reputations were made and broken, money was made and lost, success and failure shared the same bed. And it is perhaps this combination which still gives Goldoni's comedies their edge: the stage itself is in the end a continuation, or a small fragment, of the world it represents.

This Venice also remained for decades the centre of Italian book production in the peninsula, though by the end of the century other important urban centres were catching up. Producing fifty or sixty titles annually around 1700, we are told, Venetian presses printed more than five hundred in 1790 (Hanlon 2000: 318). A substantial proportion of these (one in six, according to a conservative estimate; ibid.) were publications in the original French, and translations, especially from French, also made up a significant part of the total. These publications, in both book and periodical form, were destined for a reading public that was clearly growing during the century, but which it is difficult to put figures on. How far did it reach beyond the elite? One characteristic of early modern Italy which always has to be borne in mind is that it was a territory which (for the Europe of the time) included an unusually large number of large and medium-sized cities, which were accustomed to acting as cultural, political and economic centres. During the eighteenth century, the population of Italy rose from 13.4 million in 1700 to 18 million a hundred years later, a one-third increase that was actually slower than the two-thirds average increase over the same period registered by Europe as a whole. Some cities registered a spectacular increase in population: in the second half of the century alone, Palermo grew by 30 per cent, and Naples by a staggering 40 per cent (to a total of 427,000 in 1800). Others showed more modest growth in the same fifty years, ranging from 9 per cent (Milan) to 18 per cent (Rome), or remained stable (Venice). If literacy increased to any significant extent during the century – and anecdotal and inferential evidence makes clear that it did – it is likely to have happened more rapidly in the cities, where an ability to read was a desirable skill for much of the population, the ability to write was needed in certain kinds of employment, and the opportunities to learn, especially through articulated educational structures, were greater than in the countryside.

While for the majority of the population, especially in the rural areas, access to the printed word remained geographically patchy and often defective in practice (a notional literacy often signified no more than semi-literacy, or an ability to sign one's name), and would continue to do so at least until the unified nation began to tackle seriously the provision of universal primary education in the 1870s, the newly emerging 'civil society' described above saw its opportunities expand and grow. Almost by definition, it could count on access to literacy and to education at all levels up to and including an already generous provision of university-level teaching (there were fifteen universities in Italy at the beginning of the eighteenth century, as against England's two) which was modernized and expanded, particularly in the last quarter of the century. But other factors contributed to the enrichment and fertilization of intellectual life. The many academies already discussed, both generalist and specialized, were an indispensable setting for association and exchange. The first salon on the French model was established in Milan during the War of the Spanish Succession (Hanlon 2000: 319). Here men and women could meet on equal terms for entertainment and to debate a wide range of topics in the semi-formalized setting of the *conversazione*. By later in the century, the role of the *salottiera* as the organizer of cultural exchange in a convivial setting was well established, though women, however powerful and respected, increasingly appeared as hostesses rather than participants, and, unlike in France, the *salotto* developed as one of several overlapping social circles in which men (predominantly) moved, especially in the nineteenth century (Palazzolo 1985: 24–31). The first Freemasons' lodge was established (by English residents) in Florence in 1731; as the century progressed, the lodges tended to radicalize their secretiveness and exclusiveness, and became increasingly oppositional. By the middle of the century, the café, the coffee shop on the English model, was well established, and gave its name both to one of Goldoni's best-loved plays and to the Verri brothers' Milanese journal fourteen years later.

Nor should we underestimate the opportunities for travel, both national and international. Some Italian intellectuals lived abroad, often for long periods at a time, and Italy itself became the principal destination of the Grand Tourists of the northern European aristocracy, especially in times of peace and after the uncovering of Herculaneum (1738) and Pompeii (1748), which persuaded travellers that a journey to Italy was also a journey towards antiquity. But the journey could also be much more. Although few travellers left the well-worn path which took them from Turin or Milan down through Florence to Rome, and thence to Naples to admire both Vesuvius in eruption (a frequent occurrence in the second half of the eighteenth century, as many visual as well as written records attest, most notably Sir William Hamilton's *Campi Phlegraei* of 1776–9) and the ruins it had left behind, and then back up to Venice and on perhaps to Austria or Germany and home, the improved roads allowed them also to visit smaller centres. If they were interested, they were generally welcomed to the academies and to the *conversazioni*, and some used their diaries to note not only the splendid antiquities, the natural marvels, the Italian love of spectacle, music, theatre and poetic performance, but also their encounters with Italian scientists and men of ideas. Conversations were held, letters were exchanged (assisted by an improving postal service); travel, talk, letters (often written with half an eye to subsequent publication) were all forms of association which multiplied the opportunities, and the outcomes, of personal exchange.

2.2 Enlightenment and reform from Naples to Milan

The relative social mobility described in the preceding paragraphs, the causes of which were complex, gave rise to pressure for cultural and social reform, and reform in turn was associated with many of the principles of the Enlightenment. These bald statements at once need qualification. The expansion of civil society in Italy was modest compared to that in the most advanced countries in the Europe of the time: Italy had not yet developed the solid, numerically strong, middle class that already existed in Britain, while France was very much seen as the leader in culture and ideas. The disparities between the states which occupy the territory of present-day Italy always had a part to play, as did the vagaries of succession and personality in their absolutist leaderships. In the view of Gregory Hanlon, 'Enlightenment Italy was a rarefied elite living primarily in Lombardy, Emilia-Romagna, the Veneto, Tuscany and the Marches; Rome and Naples were isolated southern outposts' (Hanlon 2000: 318); for other writers, the reforms associated with Enlightenment ideas had an even more restricted geographical and chronologically variable reach.

Then there is the question of the Enlightenment itself. The Enlightenment is rare amongst intellectual movements in having baptized itself with a name that has stuck. This was the *siècle des lumières*, the *secolo dei lumi*, shining its mental light into the shadowy recesses of superstition, feudal and ecclesiastic privilege, judicial torture and administrative malpractice, but also into the secrets of nature and the human mind. Enlightened minds shared a belief in the need for humanity to take hold of its own destiny on earth (in this respect, the works of Vico and even a historiographer like Muratori can be seen as one of the currents which fed enlightened ideas); for some, but not all, this conviction led not just to criticism of the earthly institutions of organized religion, but to profound religious scepticism, or denial, as well. There was a shared belief too in the possibility of progressively enhancing the public good, a commitment to the incremental advance of greater happiness for the many. Both of these negative (critical) and positive (reformist) faces of what in Italy is known as *Illuminismo* were shared and disseminated, however, with varying degrees of radicalism and conviction, depending on local circumstances. In the case of Italy, constraints included the relatively narrow social base from which the reformers were drawn and into which they reached, reflected in the low levels of literacy, and thus openness to new ideas conveyed in print, already discussed, and by the censorship of printed matter which continued to be exercised by the church and, increasingly, by the states (though there were ingenious ways of getting round it, and the censors themselves sometimes turned a blind eye). Conversely, suggestions for reform did not all come from those who were sympathetic to Enlightenment ideas. Indeed, some came from those hostile to these ideas, particularly from different, and conflicting, currents within the church itself. The 'disciplined devotion' promoted by Muratori, whose ideas were strong in Lombardy, was pitted against the austere piety of the Jansenists, and the Jesuits' influence continued even after they had been expelled from successive states and their order had been formally suppressed by Pope Clement XIV in 1773.

Looking more widely, beyond the confines of Italy, it is clear that in Europe as a whole, the Enlightenment was not a single thing, however much its propagandists saw it as the foundational moment of all that is good – progress, reason, tolerance, etc. – about the modern West, and its opponents all that is bad, from the mechanistic and 'inhuman' organization of the modern state to its blindness to the victims of rational, ordered economic progress, whether peasants in Northamptonshire forced off common land by enclosures or the dispossessed and enslaved of eighteenth-century Europe's global colonial expansion. Or more precisely, the Enlightenment cannot be seen as a single, coherent set of ideas which set a programme for 'enlightened' reform. Yet, in the same way as, throughout this chapter, we can still talk of 'Italy' while all the time reminding ourselves that this was not like 'our' Italy, but was territorially divided and largely ruled by outsiders, so, beyond all the differences and distinctions, it is still possible to hold in mind an idea of the Enlightenment, to acknowledge its variety while at the same time recognizing a family likeness in its manifestations. So perhaps the best way to describe the complex interweaving of Enlightenment and reform in eighteenth-century Italy is to situate a few specific cases. These are selective, but important, and they concern two major centres in the peninsula: Naples and Milan.

In the south, the interests of the reformers did not immediately follow the path mapped out by Vico (who in any case, as we have seen, abstained from pronouncing on contemporary affairs), but addressed more directly the huge financial and social problems all too evident from the vast and often unproductive feudal estates which dominated the regional economy. Despite the apparent openness to reform of the new dynasty after 1748, and the presence of a sympathetic minister in the figure of the Tuscan Bernardo Tanucci, who ran the government up until 1776, the conservative interests and instincts of the landowning aristocracy ensured that little real progress was made.

Antonio Genovesi (1713–69) is sometimes seen as a precursor of the free-market economist Adam Smith. His best-known work, *Lezioni di commercio o sia di economia civile* (*Lectures on Commerce or Civil Economy*), was published in 1765. It derived from the lectures he gave at the University of Naples, where in 1754 he had been appointed to the first chair of 'meccanica e commercio' (political economy) to be created in Europe. His detailed analysis adopted a free-trade perspective and identified in feudalism and the privileges and protectionism associated with it the biggest obstacle to the expansion of wealth, the levelling of social inequalities and the reduction of poverty. In practice, he was looking to the creation of a dynamic middle class on the model of others emerging elsewhere in Italy and Europe. A more radical, but also more caustic and ultimately disenchanted and conservative figure was Ferdinando Galiani (1728–87), a gifted intellectual who made a name for himself at an early age with his 1751 book on the theory of value, *Della moneta* (*On Money*), which explained how money is the 'representation' or 'sign' of wealth. He was sent as secretary to the Neapolitan embassy in Paris, where he met and mixed with many of the protagonists of the French Enlightenment. Diderot published Galiani's *Dialogues sur le commerce des bleds* (*Dialogues Concerning the Trade in Wheat*) in 1770; here Galiani argued that the trade in wheat cannot be left to the market alone, as was being argued at the time by the extreme free-trade theorists known as the Physiocrats. His work, which included an interesting study on Neapolitan dialect, *Del dialetto napoletano* (*On the Dialect of Naples*, 1779), seems to offer a model of penetrating insight combined with pessimistic realism which would be repeated in many southern writers of the nineteenth and twentieth centuries, from De Roberto to Tomasi di Lampedusa.

In the meantime, a younger generation of reformists built on Genovesi, but also looked back to Vico. Prominent amongst them was Gaetano Filangieri (1753–88), whose major work, *La scienza della legislazione* (*The Science of Lawmaking*), composed between 1780 and 1783 and left incomplete, proposed a systematic and 'rational' framework of legislation as the basis of a reformed society. The same years in the mid-1780s also saw the publication of Francesco Maria Pagano's (1748–99) *Scritti politici* (*Political Writings*, 1783–5), which again looked to Vico for an understanding of the roots of contemporary oppression and constituted another call for political reform in the south. Unlike Filangieri, however, Pagano lived long enough to draft a constitution for the short-lived Repubblica Partenopea of 1799 (cf. sec. 3.1), for which he was executed the same year.

Alongside this ferment of ideas (but limited practical application) in the Bourbon south, there were important foci of Enlightenment thinking elsewhere in the peninsula. Tuscany under the grand duke Peter Leopold, for example, built up a tradition of attention to agrarian reform with its intellectual leadership in the Accademia dei Georgofili, founded in Florence in 1753. The brief flowering of the so-called Milanese Enlightenment, however, had a particular impact, both at the time, and in the memories of future Lombard and, more generally, Italian writers. The mid-1760s saw three significant achievements in the broad field of Milanese writing: the emergence in 1764 of the new journal *Il Caffè* from the ambience of the Accademia dei

Pugni, which had been founded in 1761; the publication, also in 1764, of Cesare Beccaria's landmark treatise on penal reform, *Dei delitti e delle pene* (*Of Crimes and Punishments*); and, intersecting with these, from a position slightly to one side, the publication in 1763 and 1765 of the first two parts, *Il Mattino* (*Morning*) and *Il Mezzogiorno* (*Midday*), of Giuseppe Parini's satirical poem *Il Giorno* (*The Day*). This flurry of activity coincided with a renewal of reformist initiatives in the Austrian-dominated (Habsburg) region of Lombardy, following the conclusion of the Seven Years' War in 1763.

Pietro Verri (1728–97) founded the Accademia dei Pugni after some years spent in the service of the Austrian army. His dissatisfaction with the premier academy of the Milanese cultural elite, the Accademia dei Trasformati, made him determined to create an institute that would focus on knowledge that was useful to society, pursued in a critical spirit and with an open mind, drawing on ideas and experience from across Europe, and not bogged down in the kind of formalistic rules and rituals which characterized many of these gatherings of cultured people, starting with Arcadia, the length and breadth of Italy. Verri published his first important book, *Meditazioni sulla felicità* (*Meditations on Happiness*), in 1763, where he argued that it was man's inbuilt dissatisfaction with things as they are that led to progress, a fundamental idea, grounded in empiricist thinking, which he elaborated on later in his *Discorso sull'indole del piacere e del dolore* (*Discourse on the Nature of Pleasure and Pain*, 1773). Here, pleasure is seen essentially as the momentary cessation of pain or sorrow (*dolore*); its being something that is in reality an absence, whether a release or an aspiration towards or expectation of future happiness, is an idea which was extensively mined and reworked by Leopardi in his own 'theory of pleasure' (*teoria del piacere*). Verri also wrote on political economy, and his 'meditations' on the subject (*Meditazioni sull'economia politica*) were published in 1771.

One of the first products of the Accademia dei Pugni, and by far the most important, was *Dei delitti e delle pene*. Cesare Beccaria (1738–94) prefaced his treatise with an epigram from Bacon (in Latin translation) which seemed to suggest a reformist prudence as well as steadiness: 'In all negociations of difficulty, a man may not look to sow and reap at once; but must prepare business, and so ripen it by degrees.' With the caution shown by many Italian reformers, Beccaria acknowledges the distinct spheres of religious law, sanctioned by Christian revelation; 'natural law', the law of nature, which would be there for all to see 'if the imbecility or the passions of men did not obscure it'; and law created by social custom. It is the last which is at the heart of the argument around the fundamental questions which Beccaria proposes to address (his emphases): 'La morte è ella una pena veramente *utile* e *necessaria* per la sicurezza e pel buon ordine della società? La tortura e i tormenti sono eglino *giusti*, e ottengono eglino il *fine* che si propongono le leggi? Qual è la miglior maniera di prevenire i delitti? Le medesime pene sono elleno ugualmente utili in tutti i tempi? Qual influenza hanno esse su i costumi?' (Beccaria 1958: I, 47). Or, in English: 'Is death a punishment which is really *useful*, and *necessary* for the security and good order of society? Are torture and instruments of torture *just*, and do they attain the *ends* propounded by law? What is the best way of preventing crimes? Are the same penalties always equally useful? What influence have they on social custom?' (Foster and Grigson 1964: 13). Although *Dei delitti e delle pene* is primarily, and rightly, remembered for its arguments for a limitation of the death penalty (allowable in conditions of civil strife), and the abolition of judicial torture, and, nearly two hundred and fifty years later, has lost none of its relevance, its true scope extends further than this very important focus of its 'business'. With a Vichian sense of the 'barbarism' from which men emerge and the rule of force which governs early societies, Beccaria argues that people sacrifice a part of their liberty in order to guarantee the rest; within a society, society as a whole must be protected from the egocentric ambitions of each individual. In summary: people are induced to cede part of their liberty by necessity; each individual cedes as little as possible; the aggregate of these ceded parts forms the right to punish; everything beyond that is abuse, not justice. Four consequences flow from this argument: no punishment can be greater than that stipulated by law; legislative power must be separated from judicial power; punishment is to be judged by its usefulness; and finally, the judge must interpret the letter, not the 'spirit' of the law (for this to happen, and to prevent judges from making up the law as they go along, the laws should be clear, written down, and written in the native language, not Latin). Beccaria's work was an immediate success, translated very quickly into the principal European languages, its author lionized in Paris; it was placed on the church's *Index of Prohibited Books* with no less despatch (1766).

The second important product of the deliberations of the Accademia dei Pugni was the magazine *Il Caffè*, which was edited largely by Pietro Verri and his brother Alessandro (1741–1816). *Il Caffè* appeared every ten days in Milan between June 1764 and the spring of 1766. It was modelled on Addison's *Spectator*, from which it borrowed the fiction of the coffee house, in this case run by a certain Greek called Demetrio. In keeping with the spirit of the coffee house, the contributors maintain a joshing kind of *esprit de corps*, which manifests itself more seriously in a commitment to 'lo spirito filosofico' combined with an interest in practical problems and issues close at hand.

One area of considerable interest concerns language and literature. In what is perhaps the most famous article ever published in *Il Caffè*, the 'Rinunzia avanti notaio degli autori del presente foglio periodico al Vocabolario della Crusca' ('Renunciation of the Crusca Dictionary by the authors of the present periodical before a notary'), written by Alessandro Verri, the journal launches its campaign for a modern, flexible language untrammelled by the pedantic rules of the sixteenth-century grammarians represented by Pietro Bembo (*Il Caffè* 1993: 47–50). Many other articles support the call for a reformed class of *letterati*: it is characteristic of *Il Caffè*, and perhaps particularly of Pietro Verri's tireless moral vigour, that the first target of reform is those who are calling for reform, the intellectuals themselves, as exemplified by his essay 'Gli studi utili' ('Useful studies'), whose keynote is that intellectual work should be useful to society at large (1993: 311–18). *Il Caffè* practised what it preached by devoting a large amount of space to scientific articles on physics, meteorology, medicine and statistics, and to social studies, agriculture (including various schemes for the introduction of new products into the Lombard and Italian economies: cocoa, coffee, tobacco, flax), and political economy and its moral context. Also of great interest are the various articles on social custom and social psychology, in particular Alessandro Verri's 'Digressioni sull'uomo amabile, sulla noia, e sull'amor proprio' ('Digressions on amiability, boredom and self-esteem': 1993: 677–85). And it was in the pages of *Il Caffè* that what came to be widely seen as a precocious call for the unity of the Italian people was published: 'Sono Italiano' was the proud declaration of the Istrian-born author of 'Della patria degli italiani' ('On the homeland of the Italians'), Gianrinaldo Carli (1720–95) (1993: 421–7).

Giuseppe Parini (1729–99) did not fit easily with the young nobles and rising bourgeois who constituted the most advanced wing of the reformers in Lombardy. Parini was born in Bosisio, in the rural region of the Brianza, where his father was an agent in the silk trade. He was educated by the Barnabites in Milan and was ordained a priest in 1754. He had already shown his keen interest in the classics and in poetry and in 1752 had published a 'sample' of his poetry under a pastoral pseudonym, *Alcune poesie di Ripano Eupilino*. It was at this time that he began to make his way in Milanese literary society, becoming a member of the Accademia dei Trasformati in 1753 and being employed as the children's tutor in the Serbelloni family the following year; in 1763 he took on the same role in the family of Giuseppe Maria Imbonati, the principal animator of the Trasformati. In the late 1760s, he was briefly the official poet at the Regio Teatro Ducale and editor of the weekly *Gazzetta di Milano*. In 1769, he began his long public teaching career, as professor of belles-lettres. He took on various bureaucratic roles in the reformed educational system in Milan and, in failing health, served the city administration for the three years of French control (1796–9). He died four months after the return of the Austrians in April 1799.

The persona that Parini created in his writing depended to some extent on the intermediate position in which he found himself in Milanese society. At least until his change of career direction in 1769, he was conscious of his humble background, and of being in the service of an aristocracy about which he felt ambiguous; intellectually, he committed himself early on to a Horatian view of poetry, looking to create a poetry which was useful as well as pleasurable, but he found himself rubbing shoulders with a cultural elite whose approach, at least in the 1760s, was ruthlessly utilitarian. In his loyalty to the Accademia dei Trasformati, he was choosing a more remote, more cautious way of making himself useful to his fellows, one that was more consensual than what a Verri or a Beccaria might allow themselves, but which was also likely to harbour frustrations and resentments. In this light, we may better understand why Parini, somewhat unexpectedly, decided to launch a frontal attack on the mores of the aristocracy in his big satirical project, *Il Giorno*, and why, despite the brilliance and enjoyableness of many passages, he failed. In the end, the more telling moments of criticism, and the more poetically effective, come in the numerically small but fertile collection of his *Odi*.

The central figure of *Il Giorno* is a fatuous 'giovin signore' ('young lord'), the undeserving heir of ancient ancestors' achievements, whom we see in *Il Mattino* (1763) at his toilet, preparing fastidiously for the day ahead, and in *Il Mezzogiorno* (1765) at large in the wider world, with the lady to whom he acts as *cavalier servente* (or *cicisbeo*) and her entourage of fops and hangers-on. The glittering paraphernalia of luxury is described by Parini with a rococo love of detail. But it made Pietro Verri complain that 'il solo sentimento che da pitture sí ben espresse può nascere è il desiderio di poter fare altrettanto' ('the only feeling that can arise from such well-expressed depictions is the desire to do likewise'). Verri went on to suggest that if Parini really wanted to ridicule the young man he should show him talking to his creditors, plotting and scheming to maintain his false appearance, being outdone by an *homme d'esprit* ('Sul ridicolo' ('On ridicule'), in *Il Caffè* 1993: 560–6, esp. 562). Verri wanted a narrative and a programme and, in the context of his argument, he wanted the author to flatter the self-regard of his readers (they should feel superior to the target of the satire). But if *Il Giorno* does not satisfy these demands, what does it do? What does it say?

Parini's satire took two principal forms. One is that of antithesis, emphasizing the gap that exists between the young lord and the common people who serve and service him. The other is conveyed by the rhetoric of accumulation, for example the articles of the young man's clothing or his armoury of watches, lorgnettes, canes and so on, which are exhaustively described, especially in *Il Mattino*, and the ultimate effect of which is a certain dispersiveness. The two apparently contradictory rhetorical strategies – antithesis and accumulation / dispersiveness – are juxtaposed in the question of the *giovin signore*'s relations with his ancestors. There are two distinct moments of Parini's thinking on this question. On the one hand (see also his dialogue between a nobleman and a poet who happen to find themselves in the same grave, entitled *Dialogo sopra la nobiltà*, 1757), the so-called nobility is created by force or fraud on the part of cruel and greedy men dominating their weaker fellows and enslaving them; nobility is itself corrupt. On the other, it is the modern aristocracy that is degenerate, the decadent descendants of an original nobility that had notable, if rough and simple, virtues. In *Il Giorno*, Parini was content to place these two very different views of the matter side by side, and then let them wend their way through the poem autonomously. This works well enough within the terms of the poem, for here everything depends on the effectiveness of the description of the moment. But as soon as the reader starts trying to relate it to the social reality which is supposedly being described, she or he is confused. The two failings of the poem are really the same thing, and are at the same time its greatest strength: the absence of connections, the reliance on the immediate impression (or sensation). It was a way of writing, or seeing, which was also a source of ideological uncertainty.

If the *Odi* were, as a whole, more successful than *Il Giorno*, it was not only because they were closely studied, and had an important message for the great poets of the next two generations (Foscolo, Manzoni and Leopardi were all admirers), but also because they were more made to Parini's measure, relatively short, highly focused, allowing room for dramatic effect, but not requiring the long narrative haul of the satirical *poemetto*. The poems were composed in two broad periods of Parini's life: 1758–69 and 1783–95. As far as theme is concerned, all the poems of the early period concern 'social issues' (in the modern sense): agricultural techniques, public health, corruption, need, colonialism, the castration of young male singers; in most cases, the poet is appropriately angry. Parini could not be more explicit at this stage about what poetry is for: 'Va per negletta via / ognor l'util cercando / la calda fantasia, / che sol felice è quando / l'utile unir può al vanto / di lusinghevol canto' ('La salubrità dell'aria', 'The cleanliness of the air', 1759, ll. 127–32: 'Down a neglected path / Always searching for the useful / Goes excited fantasy, / Which is only happy / When it can unite the useful / To the gift of charming song'). The second period did not include any poems of the thematic type of the first. Rather than with 'issues', the poet was more concerned with 'manners', and some erotic poetry made an appearance. There is more reflection on art and poetry, which is consonant with a change in the self-projection of the poet. In general, the individual figure of 'Parini' came into greater prominence, and if one can say that the earlier poems were designed, at least in theory, to shake the readers into action, these seem intended more to nudge them into reflection. This development involved a stabilization in Parini's social outlook: there is no longer any vital relationship between one social class and another, and the critique of society as a whole pales in consequence. In the later poems, his targets are boorish or selfish or stupid, but the poet's consciousness of the cruel and oppressive nature of the grandees' greed, exploitation and complacency, which animated the early poems and the first two parts of *Il Giorno* (as in the classic episode of the 'vergine cuccia' in *Il Mezzogiorno*, ll. 517–56, where the lady's dog bites the leg of a servant who 'audace / con sacrilego piè lanciolla' ('boldly / with sacrilegious foot despatched it': ll. 522–3) and, with his entire family, loses his livelihood as a result and any hope of employment elsewhere), has faded. Corresponding to this stabilization of the social dialectic is the emergence of more intimate themes that come increasingly to the fore during the poet's later years.

Parini's self-projection as a (or The) Poet was an important dimension of the *Odi*. This was not a boastful gesture; on the contrary, he took his calling seriously and tried to live up to it. There were two constants to his image as a public figure which carried right through the *Odi*. There was, first, the Celebrator, whose function was to eulogize or to lament some beneficial person or institution or invention. The second constant was that of the Good Man, and particularly the man of moral dignity and courage, who would not prostitute his talent; this was a feature which became more marked in the second period, notably in 'La caduta' ('The fall') and 'La recita de' versi' ('Reciting poetry'). The two aspects are combined in 'La laurea' ('The university degree', 1777), celebrating the law degree awarded to a woman, Maria Pellegrina Amoretti from Oneglia, where the poet asserts that he will not be cajoled or bought into celebrating someone who is not worthy of the honour; only true worth will break his silence. And at the end of the poem he explicitly compares the new laureate with the ancient *victor ludorum* and himself with Pindar, composer of 'gl'inni alati' ('the wingèd hymns'). Despite the changes from the more utilitarian poetic of the early poems to the later neoclassical compositions and the shifts in emphasis inherent in the thematic developments over the forty years, Parini's self-projection is essentially consistent. The *precettor* (the tutor), who both extols and warns, is equally coherent, notwithstanding the changes of emphasis, in *Il Giorno*.

Parini had been a talented young man from up near Lake Como who wanted seriously to be a poet in the classical mode, a Horatian poet. He observed the metres and the conventions of the Italian tradition – many of his *odi* recall in form or style the Arcadian *canzonetta* – and his language was selected and deployed with the greatest care. But, himself in need of a place and a role in a hierarchical society, he lived in times of intellectual challenge and change, and his critical and sometimes contrary nature and the subject matter which he chose or was given somehow always drew him back to the issues that mattered in his day. These he addressed solemnly, quizzically, sometimes humorously, but always with dignity. It was the dignity of a poet who stretched the traditional forms to question the values of the new world around him, without trivializing either the language or the issues themselves, that has ensured his enduring reputation. He is, in the best sense of the term, a poet's poet.

Parini's contemporaries evolved in their own way too. The men who had edited and contributed to *Il Caffè* were radical in their approach to cultural and political issues, polemical in their denunciation of wrongs, injustices and anachronisms, exploratory in their attempts to understand the mechanisms of the mind and the imagination on a 'sensationist' basis, level-headed in their practical approach to understanding how things worked and how they might be improved, and realistic about the prospects for reform at the level of the state. A number of them, nevertheless, including Pietro Verri and Cesare Beccaria, found their way into the state administration at the end of the 1760s; the slowness and innate conservatism of the bureaucratic machine took its inevitable toll on the proponents of the Milanese Enlightenment as it did on like-minded reformers in other Italian states. Indeed, in retrospect, it seems almost as though the Italian Enlightenment, and the reform movements associated with it, followed a three-stage parabola: there was an increasing awareness of Enlightenment ideas, and excitement about the possibility of their practical application, in the 1740s and 1750s, followed by a period, roughly between the late 1750s and the mid-1770s, during which, in some states and at certain moments, there were effective opportunities for reform-minded intellectuals to contribute in some capacity to reform-minded administrations. It ended, however, in disillusionment on the part of many writers and thinkers, and a more autocratic attitude on the part of the states, in the years leading up to the upheavals of 1789 and the decade that followed.

3

Literature and revolution

3.1 Italy and France

Throughout the eighteenth century, the dominant cultural influence in Italy, as in the rest of Europe, was France, the source not only of powerful philosophical and political ideas, but also of a rationalistic way of thinking and writing, which some Italian commentators deplored as alien to the ways of their own literary tradition. What was done and said in France, however, became even more important in the wake of the Revolution of 1789, and it is legitimate to ask how this cataclysmic event affected cultural and intellectual life in the peninsula, and literature in particular. In order to address this question, we must first take a step back.

The high water mark of reform in the Italian states arrived, as has already been noted, in the 1770s and 1780s. It was during these decades that, at least in some states, new legal codes, often inspired by Beccaria, were promulgated, feudalism was abolished, there was a push towards greater administrative centralization (and less local autonomy based on custom), and economic reforms ushered in a regime of expanding free trade. Such reforms as these were authorized by absolute rulers who sanctioned them for a variety of motives, which included genuine intellectual conviction, a judicious assessment of the pressures for reform coming from below, the power of others' example or the desire to score a propaganda point of their own. But, for all its achievements, there were two structural weaknesses in the process of eighteenth-century reform which quickly began to make themselves visible. First, the driving force of reform lay in the relative handful of intellectuals (philosophers, government ministers, sometimes both combined in the same person) who had the ear of the princes, but did not have a substantial social base to support them. They spoke on behalf of a middle class which seemed throughout the century to have been permanently 'emerging'. It is true that as a result of reform itself the number of property-owners increased (thanks indirectly to the abolition or reduction of feudalism and the rationalization of tax systems), as did the number of literati, who were the product of an enlarged education system and found gainful employment in the growing number of cultural institutions such as colleges and universities, scientific academies, museums and galleries. But this social class carried little numerical or (as yet) economic weight. The weakness of the middle class invariably ran up against the inertia of established bureaucracies, the lack of adequate funding and the resistance of conservatives in the clergy, the nobility or the magistracy. The years just prior to the French Revolution did not produce a radical shift in the realities of a society (with regional variations across the peninsula) divided between the inordinately wealthy and the desperately poor.

The second structural weakness of reform lay in the fact that the rulers who promulgated it were absolute rulers: the fact of absolutism in itself was the weak link in what the historian Ettore Passerin d'Entrèves called the 'golden chain' of enlightened reform. If at any time the princes' own interests were threatened they could turn off the tap of reform at will. This fact, along with events overseas, particularly the winning of independence from the British king by the American colonies in 1776 and the drafting of a republican constitution in 1787, led some people in Italy to start thinking about more radical kinds of change. While reform was taking place, with all its limitations and the disillusionment which it engendered, during the 1770s and 1780s, Gaetano Filangieri in Naples (see sec. 2.2) was proposing the complete dismantling of the structures of the *ancien régime*, and there was a simultaneous growth of utopian movements, some of which sprang out of Freemasonry while others linked with movements of popular protest against the consequences, intended or not, of economic liberalism. By the end of the 1780s, there was real tension in many parts of Italy between opponents of reform, amongst the rural masses as well as the privileged classes of society who felt that reform had already gone too far, and reformers themselves, who were convinced that it had not gone far enough.

Thus, when the Revolution came in 1789, 'it did no more than confirm the belief shared by most Italian rulers and their ministers that the reform movement had been the portent of revolution' (Rao 2002: 252). It also generated vigorous counter-revolutionary propaganda: for the church in particular, the revolution in France was 'the perfect opportunity for launching a massive propaganda campaign against the Enlightenment and reform' (2002: 252). Over the next few years, events in France itself shook up the Italian scene even more vigorously. The ascendancy of the Jacobins in Paris signalled a radicalization of the Revolution, and the coming of the Terror in 1793–4 completed the alienation of the more moderate among the intellectuals. It also emboldened the rulers in their repression of oppositional voices within their own states. Even in progressive Tuscany, the death penalty was reinstated, secret police agents were everywhere, censorship was reintroduced, the Freemasons were persecuted. In 1792, the French government annexed Savoy as part of its policy of completing the country's 'natural frontiers', and by 1793 the principal states of Italy were committed to an anti-French coalition with Britain, Austria and Prussia.

In the spring of 1796 a foreign army, under the command of the 26-year-old general Napoleon Bonaparte, whose task was to take pressure off the French armies on the Rhine, crossed into Italian territory for the first time in nearly fifty years. Napoleon made rapid progress, occupying Piedmont and Lombardy in twenty days (April–May 1796), then turning his attention to Romagna. Whatever hopes Italian supporters of the French government, the so-called *giacobini*, might have had of political reforms following in the wake of the republic's military advance were quickly dashed. Although Napoleon had his own differences of view with the Directoire in Paris, he toed the line to the extent of exacting from the occupied territories fiscal penalties rather than political change, and limited his political dealings to 'moderate' rather than 'radical' reformers. In any case, Napoleon was manoeuvring on a much wider stage in the winter of 1796–7. Having settled a territorial compromise with Pope Pius VI, he turned his attention to negotiating with Austria. The outcome of this diplomacy was the treaty of Campoformio, signed in October 1797, whereby Austria ceded to France the Rhineland and various Italian territories in the peninsula, in the Adriatic and in the Aegean, and was given in return Dalmatia and Istria, the Veneto stretching as far as the Po and the Adige rivers, and the city of Venice itself. Napoleon had begun his carve-up of Europe, and the cynicism with which the centuries-old history of the Serenissima, the independent republic of Venice, was brought to an end with the stroke of a pen astonished even the most battle-hardened among European observers. The wider significance of Napoleon's first Italian campaign, it has been observed, was that 'France was now no longer fighting for its "natural frontiers", but was engaged in a war of expansion and conquest from which it would be unable to extricate itself' (Duggan 1994: 91).

The events already described and those which followed – the establishment of a Repubblica Cisalpina on the French model with its capital in Milan (1796–9), the short-lived Repubblica Partenopea in Naples, bloodily suppressed by Nelson on behalf of the ousted Bourbon king Ferdinand in 1799, the brief return of Austrian rule in northern Italy (1799–1800), and Napoleon's decisive victory at Marengo in June 1800, leading to more than a decade of French hegemony in the peninsula – had a powerful and often personal effect on writers at the time. Their impact on the emerging national question in Italy will be explored in chapter 4, and the remainder of this chapter will dwell on three of the most visible writers of the Napoleonic years, people whose work struck a chord with the educated public and seemed to suggest answers – not on the whole very comforting ones – to the anxious questions readers asked themselves during those politically and socially turbulent times. In two of them, Vittorio Alfieri (1749–1803) and Ugo Foscolo (1778–1827), there is a strong oppositional streak, though the reality of their political and philosophical positions was more complex, as we shall see in the second and third sections of this chapter. Alfieri, a product of the *ancien régime*, imagined in both his autobiography and his highly wrought tragedies of the 1770s and 1780s an old order which was stretched to breaking point. Foscolo, born on the Aegean island of Zante and a citizen of the Venetian republic, aged nineteen at the moment of its demise, offered in his novel *Ultime lettere di Jacopo Ortis* (*Last Letters of Jacopo Ortis*) the intoxicating image of a Romantic hero who loves his homeland, loves life, loves love, but is fatally crushed by history.

But we start (briefly) with the third, who tells us something about the difficulties of negotiating revolutionary times. Vincenzo Monti (1754–1827) was a poet who, like Alfieri and Foscolo, wanted to be present through his work in the public arena, but who believed that the way to achieve this was by accommodating himself and his work to whoever was in charge at the moment. This at any rate was the view that contemporaries formed of him, and that was transmitted to later generations: a man for all seasons, or worse. More recently, a case has been made for a fundamental coherence underlying Monti's position as a moderate reformer, which was shaken only by so traumatic an event as the French Revolution (Timpanaro 1969: 12, cited in Cerruti and Mattioda 1998: 352–3). It was almost for his simply 'being there', his omnipresence and visibility, that Mme de Staël called him 'le premier poète de l'Italie' ('Italy's foremost poet').

Although he was born and brought up in the Romagna region, Monti's adult life revolved around two poles: Rome, where he lived for nearly twenty years from 1778 to 1797, and Milan, which was to be his base for the remainder of his life. Rome was dominated by the court of the Romagna-born pope Pius VI, who reigned from 1775 to 1799. Pius was a generous patron of the arts, the founder of the Vatican Museum (the Museo Pio-Clementino), and celebrated by Monti as the new Pericles. The city was one of the two centres of neoclassicism in Italy, the other being Naples. The archaeological discoveries and excavations of the remains at Pompeii, Herculaneum and Paestum from the late 1730s on had prompted new interpretations of classical art and architecture. The German art historian and archaeologist J. J. Winckelmann (1717–68) had argued that the 'ideal' beauty achieved by classical, and particularly Greek, artworks was attained not by imitating natural beauty, according to the dominant poetics of the day, but by achieving a higher synthesis of the separate aspects of the beautiful which are present in nature. The grace, simplicity and serenity of these ancient artefacts not only represented an aesthetic standard to which to aspire, but were also a model of civilization. The idea of a continuity between the values of the ancient world whose artefacts were increasingly being brought to light and those which might be aspired to in the contemporary helped foster the myth of Rome as the 'eternal city' in the second half of the eighteenth century, as the place where that continuity was immediately visible to the naked eye. Rome was already the magnet for painters and sculptors from all over Italy and Europe, amongst whom Jean-Louis David, Antonio Canova and many others were setting a new pace in the neoclassical style. And during the years that Monti lived there, the city fostered the illusion that it was undergoing a second renaissance, as though the court of Pius VI were set to re-enact the glories of Julius II and Leo X, celebrated patrons of the arts and poetry nearly three centuries earlier.

Poetry, of a largely Arcadian variety, fuelled the social engagements of this well-to-do and privileged society. In this environment Monti proved his versatility. Having published a large selection of his previous work in a *Saggio di poesie* (1779), he turned out a great variety of poetic work in different genres. His most famous poem from the Roman period was the ode in Dantesque terza rima *In morte di Ugo di Bassville* (*On the Death of Bassville*), known universally as the *Bassvilliana*. Four cantos were completed and published in 1793; the poem remained unfinished. The political climate in Rome had changed in 1789 with the Revolution and the head-on attack it had brought on the privileges of the church, a threat that was passionately resisted by the Roman people, traditional supporters of the courtly structures on which the economy of the city depended, as well as by the many intellectuals who also owed their living to the patronage of the Vatican establishment. In 1792 the unfortunate Bassville had been sent to place the arms of the republic on the door of the French consulate, a provocative act which was resisted by the secretary of state, Cardinal Zelada. Bassville was set upon by the mob in the Corso in the afternoon of 13 January 1793, was stabbed in the stomach and died the following day. There was much spinning and speculation about the actual sequence of events, and the responsibilities of individuals, in the days that followed, along with an alleged deathbed conversion on the part of Bassville himself, as a result of which his funeral was funded by the pope. Monti's poem seizes on this anti-revolutionary propaganda opportunity and imagines the soul of Bassville rising to heaven and seeing the horrors that the revolution has unleashed, beginning with the guillotining of Louis XVI a week after Bassville's murder. The moderation of the Christian princes would be the only bulwark against the evil spreading out from Paris.

As the 1790s progressed, and the Italian peninsula became directly involved in the fortunes of France, even Monti's moderate progressivism began to look suspect in the eyes of the defensive and reactionary papal court, and in March 1797, he left Rome, threw in his lot with the emergent Repubblica Cisalpina, and moved to Milan, where, apart from a spell in Paris between the collapse of the republic in 1799 and the restoration of French hegemony after the battle of Marengo a year later, he remained for the rest of his life. In the early years, he had to work hard to neutralize the memory of the *Bassvilliana* and establish his revolutionary and republican credentials. Monti came into his own with Napoleon's ascendancy after 1800 and proclamation as emperor in 1804; acting as in effect a court poet and as a cultural spokesman for the regime right up to the fall of Napoleon and the Restoration in 1815, Monti was able to exercise considerable influence and power. His propensity for the 'Napoleon solution' – combining a tiredness with the extremes of Jacobinism, particularly after the setbacks of 1799, with a desire for an orderly and moderate continuation of the reforms which had already been achieved – were expressed in the terzine of another poem 'on the death of', this time in honour of the poet and mathematician Lorenzo Mascheroni, also known as the *Mascheroniana* (three cantos published in 1801). During the following years, Monti wrote numerous celebratory verses, and was able to adapt to the return of Austrian rule in northern Italy after 1815 without any apparent strain. But he was also very active as a translator during these years, his free-verse translation of Homer's *Iliad* (1810) attracting particular attention.

Not all of this attention was welcome. Foscolo, who prided himself on his own (native) mastery of Greek and on his philological attentiveness to the nuances of the ancient language, derided Monti's version as 'a translation of translations'. Monti's Homer indeed summarized his strengths and weaknesses as 'the foremost poet of Italy'. Schooled in neoclassicism, he was an eclectic poet who possessed amazing powers of assimilation. Both politically and emotionally he was unsure of himself and highly adaptable; he was less interested in transferring his human feelings into his poetry than in trying out different literary forms. In making the *Iliad* accessible to his contemporaries, and in mounting a late defence of the use of mythology in poetry

(*Sermone sulla mitologia*, 1825) against the strictures of the Romantics, he created a kind of classicism which would be within reach of and acceptable to a middle-class readership whose acquaintance with the classical world and languages was not profound, a classicism for modern tastes.

3.2 Alfieri: life and drama

Vittorio Alfieri was born into an aristocratic family which was well integrated into the power structures of his native Piedmont, but he was in important respects a self-made man. In his youth he travelled widely, liked fast horses and high living, began to read widely, and at the same time craved order and discipline in his haphazard studies. He was among the first of his generation to mount a frontal attack on the very principle of absolutism, while remaining reticent about the practical alternatives to it. He set about reinventing the genre of Italian tragedy and committed himself to systematic and dour self-criticism. In a gesture of personal independence, which would free him from his obligations as an aristocrat to the king of Sardinia, he made over his possessions to his sister Giulia in return for an annuity in 1778. An admirer of both the American and the French revolutions, he became increasingly conservative in the wake of the Terror, which did not stop his name from being revered in the years following his death in 1803 as a patriot and scourge of tyranny, celebrated in patriotic hymns such as Foscolo's 'Dei sepolcri' ('On tombs', 1807) and Leopardi's 'Ad Angelo Mai' (1820).

The form in which Alfieri conveyed his proud image to posterity most durably proved to be that of autobiography. His *Vita di Vittorio Alfieri da Asti scritta da esso* (*Life of Vittorio Alfieri of Asti Written by Himself*), published posthumously in 1806, had an enormous impact on the Romantic generation, because of both the story it told and the way in which it was told. This was the first modern autobiography to be published in Italian – both Goldoni's *Mémoires* (1784–7) and Casanova's *Histoire de ma vie* (1791–8) were written in French – and it very consciously set out to tell the story of how its remarkable subject had become who he was. The reasons that Alfieri gave for this exercise in self-portraiture were correspondingly modern and knowing. His *Vita* was justified, first of all, as the product of 'self-esteem' (*amor proprio*), a psychological motivation which he believed to be common to all humanity. Through self-analysis, furthermore, he could pursue the more general aim of 'studying humanity' at large. Less high-mindedly, he also recognized a demand from his public. Readers of his tragedies demonstrably wanted to know more about the author, a demand Alfieri was willing to satisfy. At the same time, the author had an interest in managing as far as possible his own reputation: knowing that his tragedies would be republished after his death with a biographical introduction, he preferred, he tells us, to set his own version of his life on the record first.

The discovery of his literary vocation is at the heart of the *Vita*, and much of the preceding narrative of his childhood and youth really leads up to this point: the features of his character discernible from his earliest years will find their fullest expression in the tragedies which he will write; his calling as a tragedian is the fulfilment of his earlier self with all its mistakes and disappointments. Alfieri's *Vita* is not strictly an intellectual autobiography, nor is it primarily an attempt to recapture time past. It is the story of a self as it is being formed, as it becomes what it will be, and as it is affirmed. These strong representations of the self explain much of the book's fascination for Romantic readers. But as well as self-creation, the modern reader might ask how far the *Vita* is also self-justification. Alfieri was a nobleman who rejected the normal career opportunities available to him as well as his social role; his choice of literature as a way of life required him to be completely independent. But he was the first to recognize that that independence was only guaranteed by the privilege (and particularly the financial privilege) into which he was born. Alfieri never seriously questioned the values or actions of his own class, and that may in turn have affected the kind of tragedy which he wrote, a kind of family tragedy of the aristocracy. It may also have lent a certain artificiality to the idea of tragedy itself, as though the genre were only possible in the modern age in very select and carefully nurtured circumstances. In the *Vita* and in other prose writings which he composed in order to try and fix in his own mind the relation between literature and political power (*Della tirannide* (*On Tyranny*, 1777) and *Del principe e delle lettere* (*On the Prince and Letters*, 1778–86)), the result was that a powerful, rhetorically supercharged denunciation of tyranny, the abuse of power and the terrible effects it has on its victims runs alongside a much less convincing portrayal of how this power might be countered. The form of the tragedies allowed this contradiction to fester creatively; in his discursive prose it was a weakness.

For an idea of what Alfieri was aiming at, very deliberately, in his tragedies we can turn to the reply which he wrote in 1783 to an appreciative letter from the librettist and opera reformer Ranieri de' Calzabigi (1714–95). Calzabigi was commenting on the first four plays – *Filippo, Polinice, Antigone* and *Virginia* – included in the Siena 1783 edition; the whole correspondence was later used to introduce the complete Paris edition of 1787–9. With fourteen approved plays behind him, Alfieri had solid ground on which to base his conception of the genre. What he hoped to achieve, he told Calzabigi, even if perhaps he had not attained it, was:

> La tragedia di cinque atti, pieni per quanto il soggetto dà, del solo soggetto: dialogizzata dai soli personaggi attori, e non consultori o spettatori: la tragedia d'un solo filo ordita, rapida per quanto si può servendo alle passioni, che tutte più, o meno pur chiacchierano, semplice per quanto uso d'arte il comporti, tetra, e feroce, per quanto natura lo soffra, calda quanto era in me. (Alfieri 1978, 'Risposta al Calzabigi')
>
> (The five-act tragedy, each act filled only with the subject so far as possible, the whole play spoken only by characters involved in the action, not by confidants or lookers-on, a tragedy with a single plot-line, moving as swiftly as possible while allowing for the passions which always chatter on to a greater or lesser extent, as simple as the custom of art allows, dark and fierce as far as nature might permit, as ardent as I could make it.)

The five-act structure and the implicit observation of the Aristotelian 'unities' of time, place and action confirm that Alfieri was working within the 'classical' conception of tragedy theorized by the Italian humanists and practised by the leading dramatists of the French stage in the seventeenth and eighteenth centuries (Corneille, Racine, Crébillon and his rival Voltaire). But Alfieri went further even than the very taut constructions of these models. He wanted no spare characters who were there just to move the action along (confidants, messengers), and no sub-plots, no deus ex machina, no coincidence, nothing 'unnatural'. What he sought, within the bounds of verisimilitude and theatrical decency, was the primacy of actions over words, especially in the first-act exposition and the 'catastrophe' or denouement of the action: intensity, focus, concentration, squeezing the maximum amount of dramatic and emotional force from the characters and the situation, these were the guidelines of his writing.

Calzabigi had raised questions about the style of Alfieri's writing. Although the Piedmontese seemed 'nato da sé', he was perhaps inclined to adopt too much the harshness and hardness that he had learnt from the old masters like Dante and Michelangelo. Here Calzabigi scored a point: from the *Vita* we know that, far from being 'self-born', Alfieri was above all self-taught and had schooled himself in the language of the Italian tradition once he had recognized that 'ogni qualunque autore sopra il Metastasio mi dava molto imbroglio ad intenderlo' ('any author earlier than Metastasio I had real trouble in understanding': *Vita* III, 12, in Alfieri 1951: I, 125). But it was precisely the lesson of Metastasio and countless others that Alfieri was urged to take on board: Metastasio's was the more fluent, elegant style that was required by modern sensibilities.

Alfieri's response was telling. First, if harmony of language is an objective of tragic verse, it is not the same as that of epic or lyric poetry. One must remember, he told his correspondent, that theatre is dialogue: thus the lover on stage is not reciting a sonnet, but *talking* to his loved one. Such a case would need a style halfway between lyric poetry and everyday speech, and is best achieved by adopting an unusual word-order. What must be avoided above all on stage is the sing-song effect, *la tiritera*. Sing-song leads to inverisimilitude, and thence to boredom. Secondly, he responded to Calzabigi's charge of 'obscurity', the accusation, one that was often repeated, that Alfieri's lines were difficult for the audience to follow. To be energetic in the way that he wants tragedy to be, Alfieri countered, you must be brief, concise. This sometimes means using forms which are not obscure to anyone who is familiar with the properties of the language, but which might sound strange to Italy's uneducated public. The answer is that the public must learn. The problem with Italian is its excessive fluidity, or the danger that it becomes too fluid; his own aim, Alfieri repeats, has always been 'sfuggire la cantilena e la trivialità' ('to get away from sing-song and triviality').

The exchange is fascinating because it shows Alfieri in effect turning his back on what had ensured the huge success and popularity of Italian as the language of theatre, at any rate the musical theatre, throughout the eighteenth century. It was precisely its lightness, its elegance, its musicality, its singability that now seemed to stand in the way of a drama aiming at a whole different range of sensations (energy, force, intensity) and at a darker and more demanding vision of the world. The starting point for this vision, as already intimated, was the reflection on power and freedom which obsessed Alfieri from the mid-1770s on, both existentially and in his reading of contemporary political philosophers, like Montesquieu, Helvétius, Voltaire and Rousseau, and ancient history, mediated particularly through Plutarch's *Lives*. The drama of absolute power, the effect it has on those who wield it and on those who suffer it, the themes of manipulation, deception, self-deception and fear, are the single most consistent thread running through the nineteen verse tragedies Alfieri composed between 1775 and 1788. Different aspects of this tragic vision are evident in three of his most interesting creations. *Filippo*, which was reworked over a long period (1775–81) and was the earliest of his 'approved' tragedies, explores tyranny as itself a kind of theatre. In *Saul* (1782), the tyrant is explored as the victim of his own tyranny. *Mirra* (1784–6) returns to a theme which is strongly present in *Filippo*, the impossibility of concealment, but in a very different context.

Filippo took as its subject the paranoid sixteenth-century court of Philip II of Spain and the legend surrounding the death of his son Don Carlos, whose former fiancée Isabella was married instead by the king and thus became his stepmother. The same story attracted the attention of Schiller, whose *Don*

Carlos was first performed in the Mannheim National Theatre in 1784. Neither playwright was particularly exercised by historical accuracy in his reconstruction of this period, and in Alfieri in particular the climate of oppression is heightened still further by the very limited number of characters and scene-changes. This enclosed and claustrophobic atmosphere reflected not only the structural spareness which Alfieri believed to be essential to the new tragedy, but also the fact that characteristically what he wrote was a kind of chamber drama, for a small and restricted audience, for performance in a private house rather than a public theatre.

The play echoed *Della tirannide* in allowing a sense of oppression to predominate. The stage is overwhelmed by the 'reggia', the court, which seems alternately monster and machine. It is a place governed by envy, hate and above all fear, peopled by an 'aulica turba' ('courtly throng') of flatterers and placemen, who have hypocritically appropriated the name of friendship to describe their relations with each other and the king, so that true friendship can scarcely exist or be recognized, as Carlo tells his only friend Perez: 'Nome ognor dalle corti empie proscritto / Bench'ei spesso vi s'oda' ('A name that is always banished from wicked courts / Though it is often heard there': act I, scene 3, ll. 181–2). Everybody watches everybody else, and the unwary, such as Isabella, are doomed. The court is actually a kind of theatre, with the tyrant Filippo as the proprietor, stage-manager and director. Indeed, the whole action of the play, up to but excluding the vital last scene, is in the hands of Filippo. In a sense it is by his will that we have a play at all. For he is all along aware of the budding affair between Carlo and Isabella, his son and his wife, and he quite literally plays all the others along until the stage is perfectly set for the denouement which he has decided on. He cruelly teases the disingenuous Isabella with barely concealed plays on words; spins a web of half-truths and falsehoods around Carlo and the servile members of his own privy council, in order to disguise his personal vendetta as husband and father in the more becoming garb of *raison d'état*; and allows only Gomez to spy out the secrets of the king's heart, that he may the more efficiently work as the king's instrument: a privilege which makes Gomez dangerously exposed, as he is brutally reminded at the end of the play.

It is true that Filippo also has his moment of victimhood. At the end of the last scene, as he surveys the carnage – Carlo and Isabella dying innocent by his hand – there comes the moment of doubt: 'Ma, felice son io?' This question – 'But am I happy? – and this theme were to be developed to an extreme degree in *Saul* (1782), where the figure of the Old Testament king was depicted as both tyrant and victim. Basing his action on events narrated in the First Book of Samuel, and exploiting to the maximum the poetry of the Old Testament and the patriarchal awesomeness of the rulers and chieftains whose stories it tells, Alfieri focuses on Saul at a moment of profound despair which coincides with the vital battle which the Israelites must shortly fight with the Philistines. The courtier Abner attributes the king's misfortunes to political intrigue and malice on the part of Samuel and Saul's former champion David. But Saul, in a moment of rare lucidity early in act II, knows that the cause of his despair is deeper and 'più terribil' ('more fearful') than politics. He has lost his youth and confidence, he terrorizes the children whom he loves, he has lost David and he has lost God. His inner world is in melt-down. He veers between strong affection and suspicion towards the family circle closest to him; any confidence he has in his own judgement is constantly undermined by Abner; he is prone to visions, dreams and the apocalyptic predictions of prophets; he seems at times close to insanity; he is terrified of mortality and the judgement of God. But what is brilliantly done in the play is the way in which this Lear-like sense of loss of power, prestige, possession, of everything which constitutes the king's identity, is combined with the portrayal of sheer aggression, as Saul turns against his helpers, his people, and above all David (and behind David, as he understands all too clearly, God, whose servant David is). Saul rages, magnificently and impotently. His rages wreak destruction around him, particularly amongst those closest to him. He makes it impossible for those who would help him to approach him. Pinioned between destruction and self-destruction, he is undoubtedly Alfieri's finest and most complex tragic creation. The author himself seems to have identified with this character (whose part he took in the first performance of the play in Florence in 1793, ten years after it was first read in public), in whom the explosive mixture of melancholy and anger echoes characteristic states of mind which, as recounted in the autobiography, were Alfieri's own.

In counterpoint to the dominant figures in Alfieri's tragedies around whom the tragic action and denouement revolve are the weaker characters who are very often the innocent victims of the tyrant's paranoia: the 'children' Carlo and Isabella in *Filippo*, or Gionata and Micòl in *Saul*, the 'friends' or would-be helpers like Perez or the prophet Achimelech. Later in his life, Alfieri turned increasingly to these figures, in the *Rime* and in some of the later plays. His masterpiece in the exploration of the 'pathetic' was the figure of Myrrha (*Mirra*, 1784–6). The play is a rare example in Alfieri's work of a tragedy which took its name from the victim rather than the tyrant, in part because there is no real tyrant in the play. The story was drawn from Ovid's *Metamorphoses* (Book X) and tells of the incestuous passion which Myrrha conceives for her father, the king Cinyras. In the *Vita*, Alfieri wrote that what most moved him in Ovid's account was 'la caldissima e veramente divina allocuzione di Mirra alla di lei nutrice' ('Myrrha's intense and truly divine speech to her nurse': *Vita* IV, 14, in Alfieri 1951: I, 259), the part of the story in which Myrrha does everything possible not to reveal her secret. This reticence is at the heart of the Italian poet's treatment of the theme, and it is not until the very end of the play, in the fifth act, that the fatal words are wrenched from her and her father knows the truth (in Ovid, the incest is consummated, with the connivance of the nurse, and Cinyras only learns the truth when he calls for a light to see the face of his new lover). Myrrha's parents, up to that point, have behaved with the concern of the most respectable bourgeois couple, seeing their daughter in great and inexplicable distress and desperate to find the cause. The action of the play is drawn along by Myrrha's absolute need not to confess, even, or especially, to herself. At times she seems almost to convince herself of the illusions with which she convinces others; at others, dropping her guard, she lets slip revealing words. The others half-know what is going on: her mother Cecri, and later Ciniro, that she is the object of divine wrath; her suitor Pereo, that she *wants* to die and might yet make him, despite her protestations, the instrument of her death. But they too seem unable to resist the drag of Myrrha's inner compulsion. The most interesting aspect of the play, in fact, is the way in which the heroine is torn between her conscious desire to conceal and her unconfessed desire to reveal. Everything depends on her image of her father, as supremely loveable and as supremely to be feared, which is entirely at odds with the 'reasonable' (and asexual) image which he projects of himself, at least until the moment when the power of the taboo, whose infringement is finally revealed, makes any less than absolute judgement unthinkable.

The subjects of Alfieri's tragedies were all drawn from written sources: Roman and modern European history, Greek and Roman mythology and theatre, the Bible. The majority of them, thirteen in all, harked back to the classical world. Classicism provided a guideline for Alfieri in his composition of the tragedies: he adapted the criteria of rationality, regularity and simplicity from the French dramatists of the seventeenth century (and behind them, Descartes), while his insistence on the systematicity of dramatic composition echoed the priorities of Italian neo-Aristotelian theorists in the late sixteenth. But the greatest importance of the classical heritage for Alfieri lay in its political dimension. Roman history in particular supplied models of heroes, and heroines such as Virginia and Octavia, whose resistance to tyranny was exemplary. The classical world was made contemporary, but it was also, by its very distance, 'other', suggesting a set of values and a strength of character which the modern world, more complex, more divided, more unsure, could not reproduce. Alfieri's aristocratic conception of the ancient world, tinged with nostalgia, also had room for the common people defending their right to liberty. In the ode he wrote on the storming of the Bastille in 1789, 'Parigi sbastigliato' ('Paris un-Bastilled'), it was the proud independence of the populace of ancient Rome that he saw brought back to life in revolutionary Paris. If a few years later he denounced the Revolution and all its works in his 'French-hating' pamphlet, the *Misogallo*, a patchwork of verse and prose written between 1793 and 1799, it was because in his view that populace had become a mob, and freedom had given way to terror.

3.3 Foscolo: between classicism and romanticism

Descriptions of Ugo Foscolo during his life and after emphasized his restlessness and volatility. These were not just features of his personality, but characterized his writing too; in fact, the two sides of Foscolo are difficult to keep apart. He was extremely busy and energetic as a poet, playwright, translator, but was inclined to revise constantly. He was a perfectionist, who left much unfinished, but at the same time his work conveys a sense of urgency and of having something important to say which gives it an authority unmatched by any of his contemporaries in Italy.

Foscolo was born to a Greek mother and Venetian father on the island of Zante (then a Venetian possession) in 1778. Five years after the death of his father, he rejoined his mother in Venice in 1793. The little family unit, which included a brother who committed suicide in 1801, lived in very straitened circumstances; contemporary accounts record that the young poet did nothing to try and hide his poverty, indeed that he rather gloried in it. He quickly developed revolutionary sympathies, and began to establish himself in the literary and social world of Venice. In 1796 he took refuge in the Euganean hills on the mainland to escape the surveillance of the Venetian authorities, and the following year his tragedy *Tieste* was performed in the Teatro Sant'Angelo in the city, to great acclaim. It was an Alfierian sort of a piece, with a tyrannical father opposed by a freedom-loving son. In the spirit of the latter, Foscolo composed an ode 'A Bonaparte liberatore' ('To Bonaparte the liberator'), also in 1797, the year that began amongst the radical intelligentsia with great hopes for the liberation and independence of Italy and ended with Bonaparte's ceding of Venice and much of its mainland possessions to Austria. Foscolo, now without a homeland, remained loyal to the cause of freedom through the next seventeen years, with varying degrees of enthusiasm, exasperation, commitment, criticism and despair. For several years he was a serving army officer and was assigned to the forces massed on the Channel coast for an eventual invasion of England between 1804 and 1806. His military career was in part a means of distancing himself from a literary establishment that was being forced into ever greater conformity in the Napoleonic Kingdom of Italy, with whose administration and its supporters he came into frequent and accelerating conflict. He was not afraid to assert his independence: in his *Orazione a Bonaparte pel congresso di Lione* (*Oration to Bonaparte for the Congress of Lyons*, 1802), he adopted a critical stance towards the proposed constitution for northern Italy (though flattering Napoleon at the same time); and there is a famous passage in 'Dei sepolcri' (1807) which celebrates the 'britanne vergini' ('Brtish virgins') mourning their fallen hero Nelson (ll. 131–2).

The novel with which his name was most often associated, and with whose hero he sometimes allowed himself to be confused, *Ultime lettere di Jacopo Ortis*, was first published in full in Milan in 1802; Foscolo embarked on a definitive edition in 1816–17. He published a slim volume of *Poesie* in 1803; apart from these works, he devoted himself to commentary and translation (the first and third books of the *Iliad*, 1804–6, and Laurence Sterne's *Sentimental Journey* during the same period). From the latter he derived a new alter ego, Didimo Chierico, based on Sterne's Yorick, a disenchanted, ironic, worldly observer and the supposed translator of the book, to balance the fiery and passionate Jacopo Ortis. On long leave from the army, he was briefly appointed professor of eloquence at Pavia University in 1808–9; although the post was suppressed almost immediately for political reasons (November 1808), he did manage to deliver a memorable inaugural lecture, *Dell'origine e dell'ufficio della letteratura* (*On the Origin and Function of Literature*), which would continue to resonate with the Romantic generation a decade later. In the 1810s, as well as completing two more tragedies, Foscolo began work on an ambitious, unfinished, poetic project, *Le grazie* (*The Graces*), which remains important even in its fragmentary state.

With the impending collapse of the Napoleonic system and the Kingdom of Italy, Foscolo sought ways, in vain, to preserve the independence of the latter; as the leading intellectual critic of the Napoleonic regime, he was eagerly sought out by the Austrians when they reoccupied Milan. He turned down the invitation to edit the government-backed journal *Biblioteca Italiana*, and chose instead to go into exile, finally arriving in London in September 1816. He was initially well received by admirers grouped around Lord Holland and his set. But it was not long before his flamboyant personality and his inability to control his spending or repay his mounting debts began to jar with the more restrained not to say puritanical nature of his British hosts, and over the following years he gradually found himself frozen out of the company of the social and cultural elite in the capital. Two further elaborations of his complex public persona evolved during these last years. First, to the Romantic generation back in Italy, he came to embody the figure of the exile, a political type with strong Dantean overtones, which grew increasingly numerous and visible as the Restoration set in and was accompanied in the early 1820s and 1830s by a series of failed insurrections and rebellions. And secondly, for British audiences first and in due course for Italian ones too, he became the author of a new and persuasive kind of literary history of Italy with a series of masterly essays published initially in the literary reviews of the time. Foscolo died in poverty in 1827. His remains were exhumed in 1871 and reburied in the church of Santa Croce in Florence, which he had celebrated in 'Dei sepolcri'.

Foscolo acknowledged two models in particular for his one novel, *Ultime lettere di Jacopo Ortis*. In *Julie, or The New Heloise* (1761), Jean-Jacques Rousseau had told the story of the love between a young man of humble origins and a young woman who is married off by her father against her wishes; the novel played on the conflict between the demands of nature and the constraints of society. *The Sorrows of Young Werther* (1774) by Johann Wolfgang von Goethe follows the stages by which a young man, thwarted in his career ambitions and frustrated in love, comes to the decision to take his own life; here too the heroine (Charlotte, or Lotte) is put out of the hero's reach by her engagement to another man. In this case, however, Foscolo was at pains to point out the differences as well as acknowledging the similarities. One of the major differences from Goethe was the centrality of politics in Foscolo's novel, which, if anything, was accentuated as the novel went through its various revisions, particularly in the second half of the book.

The novel, an epistolary novel of the kind that, following Samuel Richardson's *Pamela* (1740), had become popular in the eighteenth century, consists almost entirely of letters written to Lorenzo, Jacopo's closest friend, who has remained in Venice, although it includes some written to the woman he loves, Teresa, and towards the end Lorenzo emerges as the narrator of events as well as the editor of the letters he has received. The timespan it covers is October 1797 to late March 1799. The novel opens with Ortis escaping from Venice to the Euganean hills; the betrayal of Campoformio has taken place, but Ortis rejects any servile role in the new order; Italy seems destined to more internecine strife. Ortis despairs of the situation, but affects a certain aloofness from the political disaster; amongst his own peasant folk in the hills he is nobly paternalistic. Enraptured by feminine beauty (Teresa), his is an 'anima perpetuamente in tempesta' ('a soul perpetually in torment': letter of 26 October 1797), in contrast with his rival

Odoardo, all reason and calculation. The sequence of letters in the first part of the novel traces Jacopo's intensifying love for Teresa and the contrasting emotions which it arouses in him, and, as far as he can judge, in her too. Nature is experienced as mirroring the emotional states of the protagonists, as their story progresses through its phases of sunshine, storm and nocturnal gloom.

The second part of the novel finds Jacopo in self-imposed exile, moving with increasing desperation from one part of the Italian peninsula to another: from Bologna, where, horrified, he witnesses public executions and begging in the streets, to Florence, where he worships at the tombs of great Italians in Santa Croce and muses on the renaissance of Italian art to which the city gave birth, to Milan, having been refused a passport for Rome. In Milan, he sees signs of the lack of freedom and a climate of non- or anti-Italianness in the new Repubblica Cisalpina, but has a moving meeting with the ageing Parini: 'Scrivete a quei che verranno,' the poet tells him, 'e che soli saranno degni d'udirvi, e forti da vendicarvi' ('Write to those who are to come, for only they shall be worthy of hearing you and have the force to avenge you': letter of 4 December 1798). From Milan he goes to Genoa and then strikes westwards along the Ligurian coast, heading for the French border. At Pietra Ligure he encounters an old schoolfriend, an ex-lieutenant in the Cisalpine artillery, now reduced with his wife and infant child to extreme poverty and hopelessness: this letter (15 February 1799) is a meditation on the pain and injustice of exile. It seems to fuel his despair further. Five days later, he is at Ventimiglia, and his thoughts turn definitively to suicide. Here at the frontiers of Italy, he reflects on how Italians are powerless to resist the constant violation of those frontiers. But are the terrible events of the years through which he and his contemporaries live not just another manifestation of a universal destiny repeating itself over centuries, and enacted by individuals of a given historical moment 'orgogliosamente e ciecamente' ('proudly and blindly')? Nations and empires rise and fall; history is the long story of one people devouring another and being devoured in its turn – 'La Terra è una foresta di belve' ('the Earth is a forest of wild beasts'). So-called 'heroes' are mere instruments of destiny. True virtue, Jacopo concludes, resides 'in noi pochi deboli e sventurati; in noi che dopo avere sperimentati tutti gli errori, e sentiti tutti i guai della vita, sappiamo compiangerli e soccorrerli. Tu, o Compassione, sei la sola virtù! tutte le altre sono virtù usuraje' ('in us few who are weak and unfortunate; in us who have experienced all the mistakes and felt all the troubles of life and are able to sympathize with them and bring them comfort. Compassion, you are the only virtue! All the others are virtues to be bought and sold'; letter of 19 or 20 February 1799). In the course of his meditation at Ventimiglia, Ortis has become aware that nothing is to be gained by endless flight, and has resolved to return to his 'are domestiche' ('domestic altars'), where he will find pity beyond the grave. Once Jacopo has made his decision to return to the Euganean hills, events unroll steadily, even predictably. His mind is made up, he is calm; there is now a kind of precipitation towards the conclusion in contrast to the hesitancy of the first part of the novel.

Jacopo Ortis is a novel of high passion, seen almost exclusively from a single point of view which brings the epistolary novel close to the fluid form of the diary. It is a deeply pessimistic book, politically and historically, but one which seeks compensation in a potentially compassionate and tender view of human relations. It is a novel which also recounts a search for identity, and the fashioning of Ortis, in the mind of his creator and in that of his readers, is particularly complex. The first print run of 1,600 copies sold out immediately. Ortis became a cult figure among young Italian patriots, though suggestions at the time that the character spawned a rash of copycat suicides were off the mark. Jacopo was widely seen as a self-portrait on the part of the author, in keeping with his practice of experimenting in his writing with self-representations. But a self-portrait should not be confused with a representation of the 'real' Foscolo. Behind Jacopo's instinctive and spontaneous personality lay a literary character who had been brilliantly created by his author in a language that was imbued with residues of other famous writers. Jacopo's letters are a mosaic of half-remembered quotations, references and allusions to great poets and patriots, which, in their turn, make Jacopo a part of the literary firmament that he represents. The hero is nevertheless the product of a specific historical moment. In common with the novel's readers, his life is subject to historical events that are not within his power to control: a seismic story of invasion, occupation and war. But if he does not contain history, neither, it seems, does his history contain him. The conflict he represents, between the absolute desires of the subject and the inexorable laws of history, is such that no political or historical event would ultimately be able to resolve it. Only death – the death prefigured from the very first lines of the novel – will 'compose his features' or, as Foscolo put it in his self-portrait sonnet 'Solcata ho fronte' ('My brow is furrowed'), 'Morte sol mi darà fama e riposo' ('Death alone will give me rest and fame'). Jacopo Ortis's preoccupation is not with living, but, as Norbert Jonard once perceptively remarked, with surviving himself: how he will look, how he will be remembered *after* he is dead.

By contrast with the high-octane prose of the *Ultime lettere*, Foscolo's poetry was marked by classical restraint, in search of a form of expression in which the tensions to which he gave voice could be resolved. There is powerful autobiographical material in the dozen sonnets and two odes which he published in their final form in 1803, and sometimes the sonnet form which he inherited from Petrarch and which he was almost the last poet in Italy to practise with any degree of seriousness is unable to contain that material comfortably. But in the best of his poems from this period – the ode 'All'amica risanata' ('To his friend returned to health'), for example, or sonnets like 'Alla musa' ('Pur tu copia versavi alma di canto': 'Yet you poured a living stream of song') or the beautiful homages to his home island ('Né piú mai toccherò le sacre sponde': 'Nor shall I ever touch again the sacred shores') and his dead brother ('Un dí, s'io non andrò sempre fuggendo': 'One day, if I am not for ever fleeing') – he takes the reader into a calm and luminous world of myth and ideal emotional balance with unmatched harmony and authority. The hopes he put in the civilizing and saving power of art and literature take form in the fragments for the poem *Le grazie* on which he began work in *La chioma di Berenice* (*Berenice's Hair*) in 1803. *Le grazie* was never completed, editors have struggled in vain to suggest a definitive order to the fragments, and indeed it has been argued that the fragmentary form was precisely the one that Foscolo, a master of the unfinished, but also a representative of an age which cherished ruins and remains, had in mind.

One poem which Foscolo did not revisit, and which, along with *Ortis*, defined him in the minds of his contemporaries and right through the Risorgimento, was 'Dei sepolcri', published in 1807. The immediate occasion was the Napoleonic edict, issued in 1804 and extended to Italy two years later, prohibiting new burials anywhere except in cemeteries outside inhabited areas, but it tapped into a much wider discussion about the role of burial in the later eighteenth century and into a taste for graveyard poetry which can be traced back to the English poets Thomas Gray and James Hervey. At moments there are even macabre elements in the gothic fashion of the time, but none of this was central to Foscolo's poem. It was not intended as a meditation on the theme of death or the afterlife, nor were death and burial seen as the great levellers in the 'democratic' English mode of Gray's 'Elegy Written in a Country Churchyard' (1750). Rather, 'Dei sepolcri' was all about the living, and the challenge of death is how it can be overcome, how the dead may be remembered and through that memory still be active in and for the living. A poem that begins 'All'ombra de' cipressi' ('In the shade of the cypress trees') ends 295 lines later with a grand vista onto the future, 'finchè il Sole / Risplenderà su le sciagure umane' ('as long as the Sun / Shall shine on human woes'). Tombs and monuments are meaningless to the dead, but they have a value for the living. Even though any idea we might have that we are communicating with the dead when we visit their grave is an illusion, it is a noble illusion, evoking a 'corrispondenza d'amorosi sensi' (a 'correspondence of loving feelings') which is on the side of life and virtue. Beyond the individual enrichment it bestows, the tomb has an educative function in the wider society: it is the link between the present and the past and at the same time points to the future. Most importantly, through his meditation on burial, on its real and symbolic role in the foundation of civilization (Vico is present here), on its conceptualization in myth and poetry, Foscolo is able to reposition himself in relation to history and to actualize in the poem the compassion for what has happened and for those who are lost which in *Ortis* was only a pious hope.

Foscolo was the most visible and most distinguished poet of the generation born in the 1770s which grew up reading Ossian and the English graveyard poets, inherited the classical models of Horace and Pindar, but was also open to a new kind of poetry coming from north of the Alps, spiritual as in Klopstock, sentimental and idyllic as in Gessner, thanks to the mediation with the German-speaking countries of Italian *letterati* such as Aurelio de' Giorgi Bertola (1753–98). Goethe and Schiller also made their mark among young writers of this generation, in which the seeds of Romanticism were sown. Some very good poets emerged from their number, among them Ambrogio Viale, 'the solitary of the Alps' (1770–1805), and, particularly, Diodata Saluzzo Roero (1775–1840), whose *Versi* (1792), varied and deeply felt, were one of the best products of late eighteenth-century pre-Romanticism and were singled out by Di Breme (see sec. 4.1) as a model of lyric poetry in his defence of Romanticism in 1816. Though never achieving the same recognition, she continued to write, working notably on her philosophical novel in terza rima centred on the ancient Egyptian philosopher Hypatia (*Ipazia, ovvero delle filosofie*, 1827). Above all, Foscolo's remarkable generation was alert to the swirl of political and historical events around it, was excited by them, participated in them, was more or less exalted or damaged by them, but was never able to escape the world-changing experiences that had shaped these future writers in their youth.

PART II

Literature and Unification (1816–1900)

4

Romantic Italy

4.1 Milan 1816

Just as Italy had been a 'classical' destination for Grand Tourists in the eighteenth century, so it became a 'Romantic' one for nineteenth-century travellers attracted by the combination of extraordinary art (now from the Christian, as well as the classical, age), warm sun and wild scenery, a hint of mystery and danger, and in some cases by the ideals of Italian patriotism that were emerging into the great adventure of the Risorgimento. But how 'Romantic' was Italy itself, in the sense of its culture, its literary culture in particular, embracing features which in northern Europe, Germany and England especially, since the 1790s had become known as 'Romantic'? The answer is that Romanticism in Italy took on a particular form, that of a provocative and polemical, self-conscious movement. It lasted a very short time and was limited essentially to a single place (Milan, 1816–21), but it had substantial repercussions for the cultural life of the rest of the peninsula.

For all but two of the previous nineteen years northern Italy had been governed directly or indirectly by post-revolutionary France. The experience marked those who lived through it and those who grew up in it. These generations internalized the idea that governments should work for the general good, that they had a legitimate interest in all aspects of public life, and that culture in general and literature in particular also had a social responsibility. The Napoleonic regime recruited cultural support through its distribution of patronage (posts, prizes, subsidies for publishing and so on), with a distinct preference for work which was demonstrably 'useful' in the public domain. Napoleon's successors in the reconstituted Austrian province of Lombardy-Venetia were also quick to grasp the importance of culture for the consolidation of power. As the Austrian chancellor Prince Metternich put it when recalling his authorization of funds for a new 'independent' Milanese journal to be called *Biblioteca Italiana* in 1816, literature, whose moral influence had become so powerful a lever for governments in his time, seemed to him the best way of bringing the two nations closer together.

The first issue of *Biblioteca Italiana* opened with a prestige article by the celebrated Mme de Staël on 'the manner and utility of translations' (Bellorini 1943: I, 3–9). At first sight the choice of author and subject seemed an inspired one. Germaine de Staël had maintained a dignified opposition to Napoleon from her exile on the shores of Lake Geneva. She was not Austrian. Her European bestseller, *Corinne, or Italy* (1807), a dramatic and moving romance, had offered a sympathetic portrait of Italians in general while serving as a handy guide to the innumerable artistic and natural marvels of the country. Translation did not seem to be a particularly contentious issue; indeed, it was a commonplace of post-Enlightenment discourse that the 'commerce of ideas' was as desirable and beneficial as the trading of material goods. Staël in her article was not insensitive to the national feelings that could be aroused by her topic. She tried to be even-handed. Who better than the Italians, she asked rhetorically, could translate the Greek of Homer, Monti's example to hand? But she was also insistent about the defamiliarizing effect of translation: only by translating from other languages and cultures do we allow new ideas, new images, new myths and fables, even new words into our own. So the Italians would do well to translate 'assai delle recenti poesie inglesi e tedesche' ('plenty of recent English and German poems'). She noted that Shakespeare had been translated with great success into German; interestingly, she did not suggest that the Italians should instantly open their doors too to the barbarian genius, but she did suggest that drama from the French might go down well, especially if accompanied by some of the stupendous Italian music.

The article provoked a conservative and nationalistic backlash which discomfited the administration of the multinational Austro-Hungarian empire, not least because it conjured up a cultural division between southern and northern Europe, a Mediterranean culture steeped in classical antiquity and one more attuned to northern mists and gothic superstition. But then, between June and December 1816, something unexpected happened. In response both to the article and to the virulent attacks on it, a number of Milanese literati began to make a different kind of case. Taking their cue from Staël's attention to the refreshing of national cultures by translation, but sidelining the question of translation itself, these young critics focused on the need for Italian culture to renew itself from within. Lodovico Di Breme (1780–1820) argued that the enemy of good literature was not one kind of writing or another ('classical' or 'Romantic' – terms not used by Staël in her article, but immediately deployed by her detractors), but pedantry, rule-making and mechanical imitation (*Intorno all'ingiustizia di alcuni giudizi letterari italiani*; *Concerning the Injustice of Some Italian Literary Judgements*: Bellorini 1943: I, 25–56). Pietro Borsieri (1788–1852), a lawyer by profession, assumed the role of a non-professional but sincere booklover in his pamphlet *Avventure letterarie di un giorno* (*One Day's Literary Adventures*: Bellorini 1943: I, 85–178) and argued that the quality of a nation's culture must be judged by the number of middling works it produced as well as the few good ones. He urged that the genres Italy had most need of cultivating at the moment were the novel, comic theatre and 'buoni giornali' ('good newspapers'). Giovanni Berchet (1783–1851), the only one of the three to make a career as a poet, also stressed the new, 'middling' audience of literature. Poetry must not be the property of an elite, but be 'popular', *il popolo* being specified as that soberly named middle class located between the effete, aristocratic 'Parisians' and the cloddish 'Hottentots' who dwell in 'le ultime casupole della plebe affamata' ('the lowliest hovels of the famished plebs') (*Lettera semiseria di Grisostomo al suo figliuolo*; *Half-Serious Letter from Grisostomo to His Son*: Berchet 1972: 460).

The exchanges of 1816 served to draw up the main lines of the debate about renewal which would continue for much of the next five years. In the short term, the most effective, but also easiest, rallying point for the 'Romantic' (as they were now seen) modernizers was the attack on arbitrary authority: Berchet saw the year out with the rousing slogan 'Al diavolo colle Poetiche!' ('To hell with poetics!') In the longer term, something that was hardly touched on openly at this stage, but which was implicit throughout, was the consciousness of *history* as a method and as a theme. The growing interest in history accommodated both the assertion that there are no eternal laws of poetry, no perceptions of the realities of this world that are not subject to the laws of time, and the conviction that only in its own history will a nation, a 'people', find its own identity.

Milan in the late 1810s was a cosmopolitan city. There was a post-war atmosphere around. People were travelling across Europe in ways that had not been possible for more than a decade. Di Breme had Byron at his dinner table; Stendhal, a fascinated observer of the 'Romantic' debate (see Stendhal 1959), was another frequent visitor. Artists and writers from other Italian states also came (when they could get a passport). Milan had taken over from Venice as the most energetic publishing city in Italy, with a flourishing trade in books and periodicals and the emergence of new, enterprising, publisher-booksellers like Anton Fortunato Stella, with whom Leopardi was to work in the 1820s (see below, sec. 4.2). The city also had a strong theatrical culture, centred on the Teatro alla Scala. Theatre, in fact, became the main battleground of the polemic between Romantics and anti-Romantics in Milan. The year 1817 saw the first Italian translation, by Giovanni Gherardini, of a fundamental text of European Romanticism: A. W. Schlegel's *Corso di letteratura drammatica* (lectures delivered in Vienna in 1809–11 and translated into English as *A Course of Lectures on Dramatic Art and Literature* in 1815). Schlegel had gone far beyond his brief to produce a complete theory of literary history, in which there figured prominently a famous distinction between the classical and Romantic 'genres', the former being defined as 'statuesque', solid, lucid, formally perfect, tending to express serenity, the latter as 'picturesque', fluid, colourful, heterogeneous, tending to express melancholy. His main thesis on the theatre concerned the ineptitude of modern classicist drama (French and especially Italian, a pale imitation of the ancient Greek tragedy) when compared to the 'authentic' (Romantic) modern drama of Calderón and Shakespeare. Gherardini's translation, and the popularization of Schlegel's theses in Milan, upset the diplomatic applecart carefully kept upright by Mme de Staël in her remarks on Italian theatre.

The principal forum for Romantic attacks on the classical theatre was the twice-weekly 'foglio azzurro' (the 'blue sheet', so called from the colour of its paper) *Il Conciliatore*, edited by Silvio Pellico (1789–1854) between September 1818 and its closure by the Austrian censors just over a year later. Not as conciliatory as its title intended it should be, this magazine, like its illustrious predecessor *Il Caffè* in the 1760s, focused on the social and the immediate (Branca 1953–65). Its articles were devoted to political economy, to history, and as far as literature was concerned almost exclusively to the theatre. The theatre – rather than the novel, still as yet relatively unestablished in Italy – continued to be seen as the social medium par excellence, the place where a common, 'popular', cultural identity might be forged. There was a distinct progression in the drama theory expounded in the thirteen months of *Il Conciliatore*'s existence. Initially it took the form of a straight attack on the convention of the theatrical unities (whereby the action of a drama must be restricted to twenty-four hours, one place and a single 'action') on the grounds of the arbitrariness of the rule and more importantly the distortions (to factual or psychological truth) which the rule forced the poet to make of his material. The issue would have seemed old hat to a northern European observer familiar, for example, with Samuel Johnson's *Preface to Shakespeare* (1765). But in Italy the most revered modern playwright, and one greatly admired by this Romantic generation too, Vittorio Alfieri, had built his theatrical practice, and his reputation, on the most severe application of the unities in the modern theatre (see sec. 3.2) – it is interesting that Alfieri himself, the embodiment of liberty, was never directly attacked in the course of these arguments. Gradually, however, and not without reservations, the championing of historical drama in the manner of Shakespeare for reasons of content rather than form predominated, that is to say, the championing of a drama that would deal with the national history of the Italian people and serve to awaken its national consciousness. With this, the political implications of the Romantic movement rose dangerously close to the surface.

The tendency towards direct involvement in politics led to personal disaster for many of the contributors to *Il Conciliatore*. Pellico and others were implicated in the abortive *carbonaro* uprising of 1820–1 in Piedmont; he and Borsieri were given long prison sentences and despatched to the Slovak fortress of Spielberg in Brno. Pellico was released in 1830 and wrote the best-selling *Le mie prigioni* (*My Prisons*, 1832) as an account of his experiences; Borsieri came out in 1836 and was deported to America. Berchet managed to escape into voluntary exile before being brought to trial, living first in London and then in Belgium; he did not return to Italy until 1845.

Already in 1820, however, the literary dispute had entered a new phase with the emergence of Alessandro Manzoni (1785–1873) as the leading figure of the Milanese 'Romantic school'. His already considerable reputation (based partly on the *Inni sacri* (*Sacred Hymns*) first published in 1815, partly on his defence of Catholic morality in *Osservazioni sulla morale cattolica*, 1819) was further enhanced by the publication of his first historical tragedy, *Il conte di Carmagnola* (*The Count of Carmagnola*), and by the swingeing attack on the dramatic unities contained in the preface to the play (1820). Manzoni's commitment in turn was of prestigious value to the Romantic case, which was further strengthened by the appearance of his second tragedy, *Adelchi*, two years later. He dealt with the question of the unities at length in a private letter to a French critic, Victor Chauvet, who had generously undertaken to rewrite *Carmagnola* according to the established conventions. While Manzoni deployed the familiar arguments against the rules (arbitrariness; psychological and aesthetic distortion) he also elaborated his own characteristic perspective: the assertion that the rules cause *moral* distortion. The arbitrary restriction on timespan meant that the poet must invent causes for known effects, thus destroying the basic moral value of history and the justification for using history in poetry, namely the necessary combination of known causes and known effects. Further distortions occur at the level of dramatic 'commonplaces'. Manzoni, echoing French Jansenist moralists of the seventeenth century such as Bossuet and Nicole, cited as examples of this the glorification of suicide in classicist drama (a 'solution' imposed by the need to keep within the time constraints) and the excessive prominence given to erotic love, being a 'rapid' and therefore (according to the conventions) easily dramatized passion.

Manzoni's placing of this and other questions arising from the Romantic controversy in an ethical and religious perspective proved immensely attractive to a generation discouraged by the failure of short-term political 'adventurism'. The national struggle, though never lost sight of, as the first chorus in *Adelchi* bears witness, took second place to 'truth' and to the search for a literary form that could express truth without falsification. The search would lead to Manzoni's most successful fusion of the 'truth' of history with the 'invention' of fiction in the historical novel for which he is famous, *I promessi sposi* (*The Betrothed*: first complete edition, 1827), but also to his recognition of the obstacles to any meaningful uniting of the two in the essay *Del romanzo storico* (*On the Historical Novel*), which he began immediately afterwards and published in 1850 (see sec. 5.2).

In 1823, in another private letter (the document known as *Lettera sul romanticismo* (*Letter on Romanticism*), published without authorization in 1846 and republished, with certain important modifications, in 1870), Manzoni gave a retrospective summary of the Romantic controversy. He saw its 'tendenza cristiana' ('Christian tendency') as the most positive aspect of the movement; while this emphasis reflected Manzoni's own religious commitment, it was also true that the Italian Romantics did regard themselves as *Christian* intellectuals, even if only (as in some cases) in the sense of identifying themselves with a Christian (modern) as opposed to a pagan (ancient) civilization. He regarded the principal 'negative' victories of the movement as its rejection of classical mythology as the stock-in-trade of the imaginative artist, its ending of servile imitation of the classics, and its abolition of 'rules founded on individual cases rather than general principles, on the authority of rhetoricians rather than on the basis of argument'. A further positive achievement he saw as poetry's commitment to depict 'il vero storico e il vero morale' ('historical and moral truth') directed towards a popular rather than an elite audience; the Romantics, he wrote (in the revised edition of 1870), were unanimous 'that poetry should aim for the true, since the true is the sole source of a delight that is both noble and enduring'.

Manzoni, in his understated way, described his letter as 'the recollection of a moment in Italian literature which is over now, though it certainly did not leave things as it had found them, and was not without some effect, even outside Italy' (1981: 158).

4.2 Florence 1827

In the late summer of 1827, Manzoni took his family down to Florence, where they would stay until October. The publication of *I promessi sposi*, which had begun in 1825 in instalments, was nearing completion. In revising the novel from its first, unpublished, version, titled *Fermo e Lucia* (*Fermo and Lucia*), written between 1821 and 1823, Manzoni had paid particular attention to the language. In order to communicate to the widest possible number of readers (and 'second-order' readers, those who we know had parts or all of the novel read to them), the novel had to be written in accessible Italian. And this was no easy matter in Italy, where the written language, based on fourteenth-century literary Tuscan, was quite distinct from the great variety of dialects habitually spoken in the different states and regions of the peninsula and the islands. In *Fermo e Lucia* he had used what he himself called 'an indigestible mash of a bit of Lombard dialect, a bit of Tuscan, a bit of French, even a bit of Latin'; indigestible perhaps, but also rather effectively expressive. In the 1827 edition of *I promessi sposi*, he opted for a more consistent linguistic formula, which was a kind of Tuscanized Lombard, an educated Lombard idiom that would present no insurmountable difficulties to a Tuscan reader. His stay in Florence in 1827 persuaded him that he was on the right track but also that he should go further; the definitive edition of 1840–2, the one we generally read today, was effectively recast in the language of the Florentine middle class of the day, with no non-Tuscan elements admitted unless they could be made compatible with the now standardized language of the novel as a whole. Given the immense reach of *I promessi sposi* before and after Unification (and, thanks to its place in the school curriculum, through most of the twentieth century), and given also Manzoni's role in old age as chair of the parliamentary committee which recommended the use of Tuscan as the common language of the nation (*Dell'unità della lingua italiana e dei mezzi di diffonderla*; *On the Oneness of the Italian Language and How to Bring It into Common Use*: 1868), the linguistic decisions Manzoni made in the 1820s and 1830s were of fundamental importance.

But in Florence in 1827, Manzoni was not only on a mission of his own, he was also welcomed as perhaps the greatest, certainly the most talked-about, Italian author of the day. Among the social gatherings he attended, those held at the Gabinetto di lettura in Palazzo Buondelmonti were particularly stimulating. The reading room (*gabinetto*) had been founded by Giovan Pietro Vieusseux (1779–1863) in 1819 (its successor library still bears the name of Gabinetto Vieusseux) and it quickly became a meeting place for artists and intellectuals from all over Italy and Europe. Vieusseux was also the founder and editor of one of the most influential periodicals in 1820s Italy, *Antologia* (1821–33), and was someone who had the ability to attract the brightest contemporary minds both to his journal and to his salons. One of those whom he had wooed, unsuccessfully, as a contributor to *Antologia*, Giacomo Leopardi (1798–1837), was also in Florence that summer.

Leopardi – for many readers the greatest Italian poet after Dante – was not yet the literary monument he was to become, slowly and tortuously, after his death. But even during his lifetime, and still in his twenties, he was respected among the *letterati* for his learning, intellectual integrity, and poetic power. He was also rather feared, and distrusted, because he was known to hold unorthodox opinions and to be often scathing and intransigent in his judgements. From these nuclei of contending reactions his later reputation would grow.

Alessandro Manzoni was pathologically shy and up to the last moment it was not known whether he would accept the invitation to Vieusseux's soirée on 3 September 1827. In the end he did go and, according to his daughter, actually enjoyed himself. Giacomo Leopardi was no less reserved and while his atheist friend Pietro Giordani hogged the limelight and boldly asked the Catholic Manzoni whether he believed in miracles, to Leopardi's embarrassment, Leopardi himself kept well in the background, and not more than a few words of formal introduction were exchanged between the two men. But Manzoni, or at least the aura of the author and his celebrated novel, left a trace in Leopardi, thirteen years his junior. At the very least, Leopardi seems to have felt, in an anxious sort of way, that this was somebody against whom he would have to measure himself.

Leopardi too was on the cusp of a productive wave, albeit not a particularly creative one. Although in Florence he was drafting two more prose 'operette' to add to the twenty he had composed during 1824 and had just published, he had written only two poems of note since the autumn of 1823 and would not write another until the following spring, while entries in his notebooks, the *Zibaldone di pensieri*, had almost dried up after the more than three thousand pages of continuous writing committed to them in the three years from 1821 to 1823. Since 1824, however, the reclusive Leopardi, who Vieusseux thought might like to do a column for him as 'the hermit of the Apennines', had been making a name for himself. His first collection of poems, which he titled *Canzoni*, had been published in Bologna in 1824 and had been read, by some at least, such as the classicizing Francesco Orioli, in an Alfierian vein, displaying all the masculine virtues ('tutte forti, e severe, e maschie', 'all strong, severe and manly': Bellucci 1996: 42). Others suspected them of harbouring subversive political opinions or views not compatible with morality and religion. Nearly all readers found them difficult, demanding. A different image was created by the publication of a collection of *Versi*, also in Bologna, two years later, shorter poems which included two of the most famous of Leopardi's early career, 'L'infinito' ('The infinite') and 'La sera del giorno festivo' (later 'La sera del dì di festa', 'The holiday evening'). Giuseppe Montani (1789–1833), one of the most perceptive of Leopardi's early readers, described these poems, in a review he wrote for *Antologia* (Montani 1827), as seeming to come from a brother of Werther, but whom he now realized to be unique – 'buono', 'dolce', 'infelice' ('good', 'gentle', 'unhappy') were the adjectives Montani used. Given the date of publication, it is highly probable that Montani wrote this review after getting to know Leopardi personally in Florence. By 1827, Leopardi's reputation was beginning to be cast in both 'masculine' and 'feminine' terms, as befitted a poet ('il buon Leopardi', 'good Leopardi') whom his admirer Pietro Giordani (1774–1848) had described in 1825 as 'sdegnoso altamente e del pari affettuoso' ('highly disdainful and loving in equal measure'), like Dante (Gussalli 1857: 121). At the same time Leopardi was working more directly for the publishing industry.

Leopardi's was an unusual case. He was the eldest son of an aristocratic, landowning family from the Marche (then in the Papal States) which would have been content to maintain him at home as an independent scholar, or better still, place him in a dignified librarianship or similar role in a prestigious ecclesiastical foundation, perhaps the Vatican itself. Not feeling the call to either of these careers, Leopardi had to try and make his own way in the literary market-place, with varying degrees of success and varying degrees of dependence on subsidy from one source or another, including his family, throughout his life. In the mid-1820s he was working flat out on commission from the Milan publisher A. F. Stella, who seems to have taken a (for him) unusually benign attitude to his highly vulnerable employee. In 1826, Stella published Leopardi's commentary on Petrarch's *Canzoniere* in his 'Biblioteca amena' series, which was specifically aimed at a female readership. A year later, Leopardi delivered his remarkable anthology of Italian prose, the *Crestomazia italiana della prosa* (1827), which Stella destined for the schools market, followed in 1828 by the less successful and for Leopardi even more burdensome *Crestomazia italiana poetica* (*Anthology of Italian Poetry*). Stella would have been prepared to dole out as many more commissions (editions, translations, commentaries, introductions) as Leopardi could cope with, had he been willing to continue toiling, like so many others, in the literary vineyards of Milan.

During these same years, Stella also published the first edition of Leopardi's most important original work in prose, the *Operette morali* (*Moral Tales*), the book which, Leopardi told him, was more precious to him than his eyes. Interestingly, on this occasion, Leopardi as an author rather than an editor exercised some autonomy in relation to his publisher. He did not want the *Operette* published in the 'Biblioteca amena' and he refused to let it come out in instalments, despite Stella's (correct) assertion that the public found it perfectly acceptable to buy new books in parts (as indeed was the case with *I promessi sposi*) (Berengo 1980: 155–6). The volume came out in June 1827, in a more than respectable print run of 1,250 copies. It was thus as the published author of the *Operette morali*, as well as the *Canzoni* and the *Versi*, that Leopardi met the author of *I promessi sposi*.

What made him anxious? There are only glancing references in letters to guide us, but they are indicative (for the references below, see Leopardi 1998a). On 23 August 1827 he wrote to Stella from Florence that people of taste in the Tuscan capital found the novel much below expectations (he himself had only heard a few pages read). This was Leopardi's usual defence mechanism when a neighbouring reputation appeared to be glowing too warmly for comfort. The comments on Manzoni were followed immediately by a weary defence of the supposed 'negativity' of the *Operette* discerned by a critic whose words had been reported to him by Stella, and the claim that here in Florence he had heard the work praised to the skies by certain foreigners. In December he complained to Vieusseux about the 'adulation' bestowed on Manzoni in an article in the last issue of *Antologia*, the Lombard writer's 'deification' as he called it (letter from Pisa dated 31 December 1827). Two months later, it appeared that he had read the novel, or at any rate 'looked at' it. Characteristically, his apparent (grudging?) admiration for the novel was enveloped in, perhaps justified by, his indubitable respect for the man: 'I've seen Manzoni's novel, which in spite of its many faults I like very much, and it is certainly the work of a great mind; which is what I found Manzoni to be in several conversations I had with him in Florence. He is a truly amiable and estimable man' (Leopardi 1998b: 214). And finally, in another letter to Vieusseux, from Recanati, dated 12 April 1829, he revealed the sore that was being rubbed: he had heard that, specifically not to award its quinquennial prize for Italian prose style to the *Operette morali*, the prestigious Accademia della Crusca (founded in Florence in 1582 and responsible for the authoritative dictionary which bore its name) was intending 'spontaneously' to offer the prize to Manzoni's novel even though it had not been entered. Leopardi was wrong about the novel; no such plan was afoot. But he was right about the *Operette morali* (in fact the desired prize, worth 1,000 *scudi*, went to the historian Carlo Botta (1766–1837) for his *Storia d'Italia dal 1789 al 1814*; *History of Italy from 1789 to 1814*, published in 1824). Underlying Leopardi's less than wholehearted admiration for Manzoni there was a degree of competitiveness, and perhaps a sense of hurt.

4.3 Leopardi: the challenge of poetry

Leopardi's was the strongest and most uncompromising voice to emerge from nineteenth-century Italian literature. More than any of his contemporaries, at least in Italy, he embodied and expressed a supremely modern sense of being cast into the world without reason or discernible purpose, other than to leave it again. This condition of being an unwanted guest in a dwelling that, superficially at least, seems to beckon and offer comfort gave rise to a body of work, in prose and in verse, which is both insistent in the recurrent themes of loss, denial and exclusion that run through it like a drumbeat and varied in its explorations of the ramifications and implications of human life on the brink of modernity. Leopardi worked through these themes and implications in terms of the individual human subject, of the historical moment in which he and his contemporaries found themselves, and of what could be discerned or understood of humanity's (infinitesimal) place in the wide panorama of existing things, from stones to animals to stars. He was a poet and a moralist and a philosopher, and he was an unparalleled master of the Italian language.

Leopardi was shaped in his teens, between the ages of eleven and eighteen (1809–16), by the 'seven years of mad and desperate study' which he spent in the library in Palazzo Leopardi, which his father, like other booklovers with money to spare, had accumulated on the huge market created by the suppression of monasteries and convents in 1808–9 at the time of the French occupation. This library was his gateway to the world of classical 'literature' in the widest sense, that is, the written culture of antiquity, Greek as well as Latin (and some Hebrew), science, philosophy, ethics and history as well as poetry. It also gave him access to more recent writings, including many of the philosophers of the previous century, which religious establishments had acquired in order better to combat their rationalistic and anti-religious ideas. As a beginner in the art of writing verses (his earliest surviving efforts date from 1809), Leopardi inherited the received culture of Arcadia. But whereas classical motifs were used in eighteenth-century poetry largely for decorative purposes, and to reinforce the sense of comfortable familiarity which its users (poets and audience) enjoyed, Leopardi's immersion in the world of the ancients was total. Classical literature revealed a world so full, so vigorous and energetic, so *human*, that the meanness and inconsequentiality of the present were thrown into stark contrast. The sense of the present as a hostile environment was reinforced by Leopardi's personal unhappiness, to which the permanent damage done to his health and his physical constitution by his unrelenting dedication to study had certainly contributed. At the same time, however, his reading of more recent literature helped to develop the spirit of observation and curiosity about life which were never to leave him.

By 1816, Leopardi had begun to occupy himself more intensively with the writing of poetry (translations and original compositions, for the most part later rejected by the author). His 'conversion to literature' was accompanied by a decisive phase in the development of his ideas which is generally referred to as 'historical pessimism'. Human history is seen as a process of decline or decadence: contemporary society and culture are a deliberate, or more often thoughtless, turning away from the values of antiquity, a rejection of the origins, an abandonment of a more happy and more worthwhile time. Human understanding has been corrupted by an excess of 'reason', whereby every action must be weighed in the balance of profit and loss, and perpetual analysis forestalls genuine commitment and involvement. In this Rousseau-like spirit, Leopardi weighed into the debate about Romanticism between 1816 and 1818 with two unpublished articles (see sec. 4.1). The second of these, *Discorso di un italiano intorno alla poesia romantica* (*Discourse of an Italian concerning Romantic Poetry*), was written in response to an article by Di Breme which used Byron's *Giaour* as a platform to reflect on the 'pathetic' strain in modern poetry, by which he meant 'depth and vastness of feeling'. This was a sufficient provocation to the classicist in Leopardi to stimulate an impassioned, but closely reasoned, demonstration that 'feeling' was no invention of the moderns in general, or the Romantics in particular, but was manifest in classical literature, indeed was all the stronger and more authentic in as much as those feelings were close to nature, still linked to the origins, while the 'feeling' of the Romantics was an artificial construct. The moderns should therefore value that poetry above all, and try to approximate to it as much as possible, for poetry understood in this 'classical' way was the last redoubt of nature in the modern, civilized, scientific world. The poetry of the ancients was in the fullest sense a poetry 'of the heart', unlike the 'sentimentalism' of the Romantics, which was affected, narcissistic and exhibitionist, the poetry of a heart worn on the sleeve. The *Discorso* stands out as a declaration of faith in poetry, a defence of poetry, to which, although his ideas changed radically over the years, Leopardi remained faithful. It ended with a rousing call to Leopardi's peers, his generation of 'giovani Italiani', offering himself as a spokesman in defence of the national culture.

This was Leopardi's coming-out, his determination to reach an audience as he would speak of doing in his correspondence with Pietro Giordani and Giuseppe Montani in these years. Just after the drafting of the *Discorso*, and immediately following Giordani's visit to Recanati in September 1818, Leopardi wrote the first of the two poems which were to become known as the *canzoni patriottiche*, 'All'Italia' and 'Sopra il monumento di Dante', which were published early the following year in Rome (but with the date '1818'). The same impassioned patriotic theme was reiterated, so much so that some of the members of the local secret societies in the Marche (the *carbonari*) thought the poems were written for them or that their author was a fellow member. In reality, Leopardi's poetics evolved rapidly over the years between 1819 and 1823. With the so-called *idilli* ('idylls', short lyrics which recall some versions of ancient Greek pastoral poetry), written between 1819 and 1821, Leopardi found a space for a more personal poetry which could explore states of mind, feelings of loss, memory, sadness and melancholy, with a lightness of touch which he was to theorize as the essential propensity of modern poetry to express the 'vague' and the 'indeterminate'. The most famous of them is the earliest, 'L'infinito' ('The infinite'), written in 1819. It is 'almost a sonnet', fifteen lines long rather than fourteen, and while the *canzoni patriottiche* are a call to arms, 'L'infinito' is like a beginning, an inauguration:

> Sempre caro mi fu quest'ermo colle,
> E questa siepe, che da tanta parte
> De l'ultimo orizzonte il guardo esclude.
> Ma sedendo e mirando, interminati
> Spazi di là da quella, e sovrumani
> Silenzi, e profondissima quiete
> Io nel pensier mi fingo; ove per poco
> Il cor non si spaura. E come il vento
> Odo stormir tra queste piante, io quello
> Infinito silenzio a questa voce
> Vo comparando: e mi sovvien l'eterno,
> E le morte stagioni, e la presente
> E viva, e il suon di lei. Così tra questa
> Immensità s'annega il pensier mio:
> E il naufragar m'è dolce in questo mare.
> (Leopardi 1984: I, 131–2)

(Always dear to me was this lonely hill, / and this hedge, which from so great a part / of the furthest horizon excludes the gaze. / But sitting and looking, boundless / spaces beyond that, and superhuman / silences, and

> profoundest quiet / I fashion in my mind; wherefore / my heart almost takes fright. And as the wind / I hear rustle through these plants, I that / infinite silence to this voice / compare: and I recall the eternal, / and the dead seasons, and the present / and living, and the sound of it. So in this / immensity my thought is drowned: / and shipwreck is sweet to me in this sea.)

Even in the literal English translation the reader, we hope, can sense the boldness of this poem, the use of enjambment and breaks in the middle of the line so that the fifteen lines become almost twice as many or simply merge into one uninterrupted flow, the sheer excitement of the poem's spaces and times, which bring into one line or one phrase eternity and the present, the leaves rustling and the superhuman silences, the 'this' (which is close and here and now) and the 'that' (which is distant and there and other) of existence. 'L'infinito' stands at the extreme of an important distinction which Leopardi made in his notebooks: that between imagination and feeling. Emblematic of Leopardi's lyric power, it is also unique, in that it does not address the theme of *dolore*, suffering. It is one of the very few in which the act of speaking (or uttering) is not represented as such. Leopardi is not describing a feeling but a transcendent experience, or sensation, one at the very limits of expression. It is the nearest thing to a poem of the imagination that he ever wrote.

But the poem is written as a memory (the first line is echoed in a later remark in the notebooks: 'the infinite can only be expressed when it is not felt': Leopardi 1991: 714–17: these, as is customary, are Leopardi's own page numbers). What is remembered, what is recorded is the moment at which something that was there before language – a sensation? – becomes language (or, as the poem puts it, is fashioned in thought, which for Leopardi is the equivalent of language). The spaces, the silences, the peace are the names given to what was without name. The poem enacts the verbalization of the preverbal and as such returns us also, individually and collectively, to a state of infancy.

'L'infinito' is a last evocation of the beginnings of language at a point where Leopardi's work takes him increasingly and rapidly to a period of comprehensive and independent reflection on human destiny, the relationship between man and nature, and the conditions of modern life, in his poems (both *idilli* and *canzoni*, which we shall consider in a moment) and in the increasingly systematized writing, on an almost daily basis, of his notebooks. Leopardi was conscious of a 'total change' in his outlook, which he described as a 'conversion to philosophy':

> The total change in me, my passing from the ancient state to the modern, took place, you might say, in a single year, that is, in the course of 1819 when, deprived of the use of my sight and the continual distraction of reading, I began to feel my unhappiness in a much darker way, I began to abandon hope, to reflect deeply on things [. . .] to become a professional philosopher (instead of the poet I had been), to feel the certain unhappiness of the world, instead of knowing it, and all of this thanks also to a state of bodily languor, which led me even further away from the ancients and brought me closer to the moderns. (Leopardi 1991: 144)

The two *canzoni patriottiche* were followed by further important experiments in the *canzone* genre. Unlike the *idilli*, which were relatively short and written entirely in hendecasyllables, the ten *canzoni* which were included in the Bologna edition of 1824 had an average length of 115 lines; they contained a mixture of hendecasyllable and seven-syllable lines (*settenari*), with a preponderance of the former, with in most cases the same number of lines and the same rhyme-scheme in each strophe. In general these *canzoni* preserved the aura of measured regularity which had characterized the two *canzoni patriottiche*, which was used, however, to articulate a radical and evolving chain of thought. While 'Ad Angelo Mai' ('To Angelo Mai', early 1820) reiterated the themes of 'historical pessimism', but this time with specific reference to the Italian, rather than the Latin, cultural tradition, 'Bruto minore' ('Brutus Minor', December 1821) staged the titanic rage of Brutus defeated by Mark Antony at the battle of Philippi (Brutus' monologue occupies almost the whole poem) against the emptiness of the concept of 'virtue' and against the 'putridi nepoti' ('stinking grandchildren') who are destined to follow him. The hollowing-out of virtue, in a bleak and barren landscape, is a substantial devaluation of the natural 'illusions' which Leopardi had seen as so vital and beneficial to the world of antiquity in its proximity to nature. The poem is a high point in a kind of battle which runs through the *canzoni* written from 1820 to 1822, between the desire to hold on to those illusions and to find ways of reinventing them in modern poetry. From the strained optimism for the future expressed in 'Nelle nozze della sorella Paolina' ('On the marriage of my sister Paolina', which did not actually take place) and 'A un vincitore nel pallone' ('To a victor in the ball game'), both written in 1821, it moves to the now nostalgic revisiting of foundational myths the following year in 'Alla primavera, o delle favole antiche' ('To spring, or concerning ancient fables') and 'Inno ai patriarchi' ('Hymn to the patriarchs') and the recognition of their ineffectiveness, with different tonalities, angry and embittered as in 'Bruto minore', bemused and melancholic, almost tender, as in the other great masterpiece of these years, 'Ultimo canto di Saffo' ('Sappho's last song', May 1822).

Both Brutus and Sappho, these heroes (or anti-heroes) of disillusionment, it will be noted, are figures from classical antiquity, and in allowing the 'rot' of civilization to reach these hallowed creatures, Leopardi was signalling the radicalization of his reflection on existence, which became known as 'cosmic pessimism'. The progression of this mode of thought can be traced in the pages of the *Zibaldone* in the period of its most intensive composition between 1821 and 1823. What Leopardi was now realizing was that there had never been a period in human history when nature was maternally benign and human beings had lived in harmony with it: nature was fundamentally hostile, or at best indifferent. This evolution of his thought in a materialistic direction was accompanied by his increasing distance from even the exterior signs of religious observance (maintained to some extent in order not to worsen even more the strained relations with the pious household of his parents). The question which was left open, the tension traced in the *canzoni*, was whether, even so, all semblance of illusion, ideals, fiction should be abandoned in favour of 'the truth', or whether some semblance of it might still be held on to, particularly in the form of poetry. The chronologically 'detached' *canzone*, 'Alla sua donna' ('To his lady'), written unusually quickly (six days) in September 1823, after Leopardi's return from his first extended visit away from Recanati, to Rome, seemed to give the possibility of a positive answer, but in a teasingly ambivalent way. It was a love-poem, Petrarchan in tone, suffused with a subtle neo-Platonism, a love-poem for a 'donna che non si trova'. Love, it seemed, retained all its allure and vitality, but with the lover's gaze turned upon a love object which was defined by its 'not being there'.

Nevertheless, the possibility of poetry, in the way that he had written it up to now, seemed all but exhausted. In due course, an alternative view of poetry, in which poetry would not be the last redoubt of illusion, the enemy of philosophy, but its ally in the revelation of 'truth', would take shape. A halfway house was announced in the one poem Leopardi wrote between 1824 and 1828, the *epistola* 'Al conte Carlo Pepoli' ('To Count Carlo Pepoli'), recited aloud by the poet in Bologna in March 1826: when none of his familiar things could move him any more, he would elect 'altri studi men dolci' (l. 138: 'other studies less sweet'). Instead, Leopardi turned in 1824 to a project he had long nurtured, the writing of satirical dialogues in the model of Lucian and other fantastical prose pieces which would become the twenty *Operette morali* written during that year. It was in the *Operette* that the principal themes worked out in the notebooks over the previous four years would find a suitable 'fictional' form, a form in which they could be presented to the public not as dry philosophy, not as a 'scientific' discourse freighted with technicalities and specialist language, but as trains of thought that were approachable and even entertaining, sometimes humorous, in the form of dialogues or fables. There was nothing simplistic, however, about either the ideas or the language in which they were expressed; the language, utterly different from the sort of populist idiom commonly used in early nineteenth-century dialogues, was precise, taut and syntactically complex. Like the poems, Leopardi's prose demanded attention from its reader. In both cases, the author played a risky game. His desire to communicate was (and remained) extremely strong: the repeated initiatives he took to have his work published, the concern with which he followed the stages of publication, his anxiety about the reception of his work were enough to show that Leopardi was no literary recluse. On the other hand, *what* he wanted to communicate was exactly what he wanted to say (he was aware too that *how* the work appeared affected the communication of its message). On this basis of amicable intransigence Leopardi could hope to engage with his readers on such topics as the futility of the present, the unimportance of human beings in the natural order of things, the impossibility of achieving pleasure, the indifference or hostility of nature to all things human, the supremacy of death over life, the phenomenology of *noia*, the illusoriness of literary or any other kind of fame, and above all the right of the writer to say things which go against the grain of public opinion or common sense (but which are true).

His hopes were not fulfilled: the *Operette*, like the *canzoni* before them, were perceived as 'difficult'. On 1 August 1827, his publisher Stella wrote to the author diplomatically: 'I hear your *Operette morali* spoken well of by everybody, even though Italy is not yet accustomed to that kind of reading.' Some reactions, such as that of Tommaseo, who thought that the style of the prose pieces was admirable but not their negativity, were a good deal harsher. Publication, essential to Leopardi's sense of himself as a writer, brought with it its inevitable baggage of incomprehension, misunderstanding, distortion and downright hostility. Perhaps it was no accident that the years in which Leopardi had made his greatest effort towards the public (1824–7) merged quite rapidly into a period of radical withdrawal, one in which he described himself, using the English word, as 'absent', before he began to find a way back again in the later 1820s.

The route back led through poetry. When Leopardi began to write verse again in Pisa in the early months of 1828, 'in the old way', as he wrote to his sister Paolina, it was something of the style and ambience of the early *idilli* that seemed to revive in him, at least at the beginning. (Paolina Leopardi (1800–69), the closest of Giacomo's siblings with his brother Carlo, born a year after him, was the right person to send this message to; she was particularly sensitive, so Giacomo thought, to matters bearing on the feelings; educated alongside her brothers, she was an attentive and intelligent reader of French literature and published a translation of Xavier De Maistre's *Nighttime Journey Around my Room* in 1832.) The first two poems in this new phase of creativity, apart from the short 'Scherzo' written in February, were both written in Pisa in April 1828. 'Il risorgimento' ('The resurgence', with no political connotations) was written in a style unusual for Leopardi, that of the Arcadian *canzonetta*, which allowed him to combine a tripping musicality with a measured artifice, as though he were keeping his newfound feelings at a distance. The poem is strictly constructed, describing the decline of the poet's capacity to feel in the first ten strophes, and the 'resurgence' signalled in the poem's programmatic title in the other ten. 'A Silvia' ('To Silvia'), on the other hand, written almost immediately afterwards, is much freer, as the poet glides from the poem's celebrated opening ('Silvia, rimembri ancora / Quel tempo della tua vita mortale, / Quando beltà splendea / Negli occhi tuoi ridenti e fuggitivi, / E tu, lieta e pensosa, il limitare / Di gioventù salivi?': 'Silvia, do you still recall / That time in your mortal life, / When beauty shone / In your laughing, glancing, eyes, / And you, happy and full of thought, were stepping / Across the boundary of youth?'), from stanza to stanza, from room to room, the dead girl's workroom and the poet's study, evoking the memory of her truncated life and his abandoned hope.

Memory, the interplay between present and past, meditation on lost youth and lost hope and the contemplation of non-existence and death, provided the creative urge for the poems with a Recanati setting, which Leopardi wrote for the most part in Recanati itself during what was to be his last visit to his native town (November 1828 to April 1830): 'Le ricordanze' ('Memories'), 'La quiete dopo la tempesta' ('Calm after the storm'), 'Il sabato del villaggio' ('The village Saturday'), and possibly 'Il passero solitario' ('The lone song-thrush'; its dating is uncertain). But the greatest of the poems of this period (with the possible exception of 'Le ricordanze'), 'Canto notturno di un pastore errante dell'Asia' ('Night song of a wandering shepherd from Asia', 1829–30), abandons the familiar setting to imagine the most fundamental, the most essential questions about the nature and the meaning of existence put in the mouth of a nomadic shepherd in the desert singing, or chanting, his despairing utterances to the brilliant, virginal and silent moon. In a final stanza of great dignity, the shepherd/poet acknowledges and accepts how circumscribed and limited his own earthbound condition is while not flinching from his radical pessimism ('Forse s'avess'io l'ale . . .': 'Perhaps if I had wings . . .').

In 1830, Leopardi returned to Florence, and it was there, in 1831, that he published a new edition of his poems. It included all of the *canzoni* published in 1824, some of the shorter poems included in the *Versi* of 1826, and the new poems which had been written between 1828 and 1830. This edition was the first to be given the title of *Canti*, and the order in which it put the poems provided the template for all subsequent editions, in Leopardi's lifetime and after. The choice of title for the 1831 edition was extremely suggestive, as well as being unusual if not unique as the title of a collection of poems at the time. It echoed the titles of two of Leopardi's most moving poems ('Ultimo canto di Saffo' and 'Canto notturno di un pastore errante dell'Asia'), poems in which the poet's bleak vision of human existence was mediated through the vulnerable figures of two speakers who were forced to confront the implications of humanity's solitude in their own person. A 'canto' suggested musicality, underlining Leopardi's expectation of poetry that it should convey the vague and indefinite as music does and his conviction in the 1828–30 period that the lyric – literally, poetry that is sung with the lyre – was the only true poetry. Because it also implied voice – a 'canto' is in principle sung, or perhaps chanted – the title drew attention to the special nature of the utterance, something heightened, intense, out of the range of ordinary speech, and to orality itself, making of the poem something which harked back to the earliest origins of thought and speech. A song in that tradition is never something purely individual, it is always addressed to, or in some instances even produced by, a collectivity, and perhaps Leopardi also wanted to signal that his *Canti* were songs to be shared and internalized by others. Finally, it is worth noting that in the Italian tradition of literary genre names, a *canto* was normally a part of a whole, especially in narrative poetry, as in the 'canti' of each of the three parts of Dante's *Commedia*, or those of the Renaissance epics of Ariosto, Tasso and others, or, close in time to Leopardi, the 'Canti quindici', which was the subtitle of Tommaso Grossi's verse narrative *Ildegonda* (1820): maybe the title *Canti* also pointed to the fragmentary status of each of the components of the volume. Leopardi's new title was overdetermined, but it stuck, and with it he seems to have found the right formula for the publication of his lyric verse.

The subsequent editions of Leopardi's poetry (Naples 1835 and Florence 1845) included the poems commonly known as the Aspasia cycle, written in the course of an unhappy infatuation with Fanny Targioni Tozzetti between the early and mid-1830s. They include perhaps the bleakest poem Leopardi ever wrote, 'A se stesso', 'To himself', another near-sonnet (sixteen lines), but with a very different sense of the infinite from 'L'infinito': 'Or poserai per sempre, / Stanco mio cor [. . .] / Omai disprezza / Te, la natura, il brutto

/ Poter che, ascoso, a comun danno impera, / E l'infinita vanità del tutto': 'Now you shall rest forever, / My tired heart [. . .] / Now despise / Yourself, nature, the ugly / Power which, hidden, rules over our common harm, / And the infinite vanity of everything'). They also included two 'sepulchre' poems written on the theme of youth and death, his final meditative statement on the relation between man and nature ('La ginestra, o, il fiore del deserto'; 'The broom, or the flower of the desert'; written 1836 and published posthumously) and the extraordinary 'farewell' poem 'Il tramonto della luna' ('The setting of the moon'), also published after his death. During the last years of his life, spent between Florence and Rome (1830–3) and Naples (1833–7), Leopardi also turned his attention increasingly to contemporary events and to what he called 'social Machiavellianism' (*machiavellismo di società*), themes which emerged not only in poems such as 'Palinodia al marchese Gino Capponi' ('Palinode to Marquis Gino Capponi') and 'I nuovi credenti' ('The new believers', which was not included in the *Canti*) and in the two new *operette morali* written in 1832, but also in new forms. Among these was the mock-epic in *ottava rima* used for a disenchanted but not unsympathetic satire of the liberal movements of the previous fifteen years, *Paralipomeni della Batracomiomachia* (*Matters Omitted from the War of the Mice and the Frogs*, early 1830s; this 'libro terribile' ('shocking book') was first published in Paris in 1842), and the 111 aphorisms, mainly on social life and mainly drawn from the *Zibaldone*, which he intended to publish under the title of *Pensieri* (*Thoughts*, published in 1845).

We started this section by talking about Leopardi's uncompromising stance. It goes without saying that he was uncompromising with himself, driven by a view that literature ('poetry') might still in the modern world have some residual power to make us, or enable us to, confront the truth about ourselves and the conditions of our existence, while still, also residually, legitimizing our regret at what is lost, in our own lives and in the life of the world: lost innocence, lost beauty, lost youth, a lost sense of oneness with the world. 'Truth' became the stated object of his poetic inquiry, but no less important was the value of 'truthfulness' in ourselves. In consequence, readers too have felt compelled to test the poet's assumptions and assertions, to 'learn his song', not necessarily to identify with it, but to understand and perhaps to challenge it. Leopardi's radical pessimism has not always made his readers feel comfortable, but it has never left them indifferent.

5

Writing the nation

5.1 Manzoni: the responsibility of the writer

The early years of Alessandro Manzoni (1785–1873) were unsettled. The relations between his parents were strained: his mother, Giulia Beccaria, daughter of Cesare – see section 2.2 – had married the much older Pietro Manzoni for financial reasons; they legally separated in 1792, but it was already rumoured that Alessandro's real father was Giovanni Verri, younger brother of the two Verris who had edited *Il Caffè* back in the 1760s. This reconstituted Enlightenment family circle was completed when Giulia moved in with Carlo Imbonati in Paris in 1796; Imbonati had had Parini as his tutor. Manzoni's education was also affected by the uncertain political situation on the ground. The religious order of the Padri Somaschi, with whom the young Alessandro had been sent to study, moved its school from Milan to Lugano, just across the Swiss border, when the French marched in in 1796; later he returned to Milan and was educated by the Barnabites; in 1803 Pietro Manzoni, keen to keep his son away from the liberal influences of reoccupied Milan, sent him off to Austrian-governed Venice. Finally, in 1805, Alessandro was able to join his mother, in mourning for the loss of Imbonati, in Paris; it was an opportunity for him to consolidate a close relationship which they sustained for the rest of Giulia's life, and to reconnect with the freethinking environment of her household.

It was in Paris in 1810 that Manzoni underwent the profound spiritual crisis which led to his wholehearted embracing of the Catholic faith. He was influenced by the classical French moralists of the seventeenth century and his faith took a strongly ethical, Jansenist direction. This enabled him, throughout his long life, to maintain an independent attitude towards papal authority and a generally liberal position in politics. He was firmly in favour of the independence and unity of an Italian state which had every right, in his view, to incorporate the former Papal States. From the 1810s on, however, his religious conviction informed everything he wrote, though other factors also shaped the aesthetic and artistic ideas which he developed at the time.

The Romantic debate (described in sec. 4.1) fell in the middle of Manzoni's most creative period as a writer, stretching roughly from 1805 to 1830. Already in 1809, he had undergone something of a *poetic* conversion. After finishing the last of the neoclassical odes of his youth (the poem 'Urania'), he wrote to one of the closest and most influential of his Parisian friends, Charles Fauriel (1772–1844): 'I am very dissatisfied with this poem of mine, mainly because of its complete lack of interest. From now on I'll write poetry that may be uglier, but never again anything like that' (letter of 6 September 1809, in Manzoni 1986: I, 95). The 'new poetry', written between the 1810s and the early 1820s, took religious and political themes, radically simplified the language, aiming at comprehensibility without sacrificing complexity, and became epic in scope, taking on great sweeps of human, moral and social history, within a relatively brief span of verses; the subjective, individual voice was rigorously excluded. Between 1812 and 1815 Manzoni composed four 'sacred hymns' (*inni sacri*): 'La Risurrezione' ('The Resurrection'), 'Il Nome di Maria' ('The Name of Mary'), 'Il Natale' ('Christmas') and 'La Passione' ('The Passion'), to which 'La Pentecoste' ('Pentecost') was added in 1822 (earlier drafts in 1817 and 1819). His most accomplished 'political' poem was the ode written on the death of Napoleon in 1821 ('Il Cinque Maggio', 'The Fifth of May'), the same year in which he composed 'Marzo 1821' ('March 1821') in response to the failed insurrections of the early part of the year in Lombardy and Piedmont.

Manzoni's two verse tragedies, *Il Conte di Carmagnola* (1820) and *Adelchi* (1822), were also produced during this intensely creative phase, along with critical and theoretical reflection on the nature of tragedy and on the dramatic function and use of history, which was deepened over many years from 1816 on in private letters (one of Manzoni's most important media of communication and reflection) and essays or prefaces for publication. *Il Conte di Carmagnola* (which was published with an important preface) focuses on the dignified self-defence of a fifteenth-century mercenary captain (*condottiere*) wrongly accused, on the basis of the historical evidence as Manzoni interpreted it, of treachery by his paymasters, the republic of Venice. The theme of betrayal was to be a recurrent one throughout the mythography of the Risorgimento. Between the second and third acts Manzoni introduced the device of the chorus, which he regarded as a 'little corner' for himself, but which is also a device allowing the spectator (or more probably the reader) to step back from the action and to think about what is going on. The chorus in *Carmagnola*, following on from Carmagnola's victory at the battle of Maclodio, dwells on the horror of the bloodshed and laments the fratricidal war in which Italian slaughters Italian for no better reason than that he is paid to, while the ravenous foreigners bide their time and wait for the moment to come down into an exhausted Italy and divide the spoils among themselves. From that remote historical setting the author draws a lesson full of resonance for his contemporaries. The choruses in the second tragedy, *Adelchi*, are even more radical. The first, 'Dagli atrii muscosi, dai Fori cadenti' (act 3: 'From the mossy atriums, the ruined forums'), describes the advance of the Frankish army led by Charlemagne and laments the fate of the mass of the populace in an Italy which has no name or nation of its own. The action of the play is set in the eighth century; it tracks the displacement of the former rulers of northern Italy, the Longobards, and the doomed attempts of the tragic hero, Adelchi, co-ruler with his stubborn father Desiderio, first to negotiate with Charlemagne, then to resist, and then to save what is saveable. The second chorus is quite different from the first but is equally 'eccentric' to the main tragic action: in 'Sparsa le trecce morbide' (act 4: 'Her soft hair falling loosely'), the dying Ermengarda, Adelchi's sister and Charlemagne's rejected wife, is hymned to her rest by her attendants in an intimate and elegiac aria.

Manzoni's use of history in these plays was accompanied, as has been said, by much thought on the subject, and there is a clear continuity between those reflections and the groundwork laid in the early 1820s for what will become Manzoni's masterpiece, the historical novel *I promessi sposi*. But before looking at the novel in more detail, let us pause for a moment on why and in what way history was so important to the author.

No nineteenth-century Italian writer was more concerned than Manzoni about the reader's wellbeing. His attitude may have been protective, even paternalistic at times, but it is striking how consistently, when he thought about literature, Manzoni put himself in the position of the audience. It was a way both of registering the importance of reading for him, and of acknowledging, even soliciting, the responsibility of the writer. Manzoni's most thoroughgoing account of what he called 'the historical system' was contained in his *Lettre à Monsieur Chauvet sur l'unité de temps et de lieu dans la tragédie* (*Letter to M. Chauvet on the Unity of Time and Place in Tragedy*; originally written in 1820, it was revised and published in Paris in 1823; see also above, sec. 4.1). In the *Lettre* he described the special pleasure, the attraction, for an audience, of knowing that a certain plot was derived from history, and that the connections between its various parts were therefore real. But he also stressed, and it was no contradiction, that historical accuracy in drama, fidelity to the facts as given, did not inhibit but rather enabled and legitimated the exercise of the creative imagination. For Manzoni, at least in 1820, conceived of the historical event, or action, or person, as something that stood out against a relatively undifferentiated background, and which at the same time was incomplete, in the sense that history records only the externals of what has happened. The historical event, therefore, as considered by the poet, was something that needed to be explained, developed, disentangled, explored, for its true meaning to become apparent. It was the completion, the restitution to history of its 'lost part', that was the creative task facing the poet of the present day. History provided the poet with enormous spaces for his or her imagination to fill: indeed the *Lettre* might be read as saying that the whole of the past – admittedly excluding those parts of it that were 'undramatizable', but including far more extensive areas than those that could be adapted to the conventions of the unities – was properly open to exploitation by the dramatic poet. But their historicity guaranteed that the 'inventions' with which the poet peopled these spaces were real, discoveries rather than inventions, and not figments of his own mind, not 'individual fictions', as Manzoni called them.

That 'part' of history which in the *Lettre* Manzoni spoke of as missing, and to be supplied by the poetic imagination, was the inner lives of the protagonists of history, their thoughts and feelings, their means of self-expression, all that which made up their human reality, the individuality concealed behind the 'outside' which historical events presented to posterity. In due course, and in practice, this hidden side of history would come to include subject peoples (*Adelchi*) and the lower classes (*I promessi sposi*), and this extension of the concept would in turn bring the 'system' of the *Lettre* into crisis (see below, sec. 5.2). But in *Il Conte di Carmagnola* the furthest that the idea ventured sociologically was to introduce the count's family (wife and daughter) in the final act of the play as a means of confirming his transcendence of the historical limitations of his time. The *Lettre*, which we recall was a by-product of *Carmagnola*, also saw the 'lost part' of history as an essentially psychological entity, identified with the intentions, motivations and desires underlying the dramatically interesting actions preserved by history or the characters who performed these actions. The historical character himself acted as a signal; perceived as an 'imposing character', he 'arrests' and 'invites' the poet to probe further, to develop this character on the basis of the information which history provided. Thus, the 'character' stood beckoning as a kind of outpost ('Observe me, I will teach you something about human nature': Manzoni 1981: 114) at the entrance to a territory which was real (based on history) but unknown (unrecorded). Such a character is, for example, the Napoleon of the ode *Il Cinque Maggio*.

For the composition of the historical tragedy *Adelchi*, Manzoni selected a period of Italian history (the eighth century, the demise of the Longobard hegemony) that was obscure, poorly documented and, in his view, superficially treated by previous historians. The filling-in of the immense gaps included, on the historical side, a revaluation of the role of the papacy, and of the relations between the oppressor race, the Longobards, and the conquered Latins. But Manzoni was also to profess himself embarrassed by the absence and inaccuracy of historical information in so far as it affected the shaping of his principal character: 'I imagined the character of my protagonist on the basis of historical evidence which I believed to be well-founded,' he wrote to Fauriel on 3 November 1821, 'at a time when I was not yet sufficiently aware of the carelessness with which history is handled; I built on that evidence, I expanded it, and I realized that there was nothing historical about it when my work was already well advanced' (Manzoni 1986: I, 248). But in any case, the play was not designed only to illuminate the 'beautiful soul' of a historically outstanding character, that is to say, to fill out what in recorded history is only sketched in or hinted at; it was designed also to correct error. Or, put more accurately, the concern of Manzoni's poetic was to take things from being not known, or only half-known, to being known, and from being obscure or confused to being clear (as it was to 'develop' them from the hidden to the manifest). At the other end of the telescope, so to speak, there was reckoned to be a spectator or reader of clear vision and balanced judgement. One of the functions of the first chorus of *Adelchi* was to demonstrate and embody the process of clarification, which was at the same time the keystone of Manzoni's moral conception of the drama.

The concern with judgement derived from Manzoni's overriding concern with the *effect* of drama on its audience, which was why in his theoretical writings he devoted considerable attention to analysing the kind of response that plays expected to generate in the spectator, what he called, in the conventional language of dramatic theory of the day, the 'interest' of a play. He distinguished between two kinds of response, two kinds of interest. There was, first of all, the kind of play in which the spectators felt themselves caught up with and bound up in the actions and passions of the characters on stage: in which their feelings were swayed between one character and another or according to the progress, for better or worse, of the protagonist, and in which they suffered (or enjoyed) the anxiety of suspense as they awaited the outcome of the drama. And then there was another kind of play in which the spectators were not held in suspense, in which they were not so much moved by the passions enacted on the stage as removed from them, at a distance from which they could contemplate and reflect upon them, and in which, if there was a mystery to be unravelled, as Manzoni noted in his *Materiali estetici* (*Aesthetic Materials*), it was not that of the plot, but 'the mystery of ourselves'.

As a minimum position, Manzoni merely argued that both kinds of interest be acknowledged, and that the hegemony of the first, at least in France and Italy, should not be allowed to obscure the claims of the second. But behind this apparently equanimous stance lay a firm moral commitment to a poetic which valued the spectators' 'judgement' on the action much more highly than their 'complicity' with it, and regarded it as the business of dramatic art to excite not 'sympathy' but what he called 'felt reflection' ('riflessione sentita': Manzoni 1981: 339). Spectators should not be a part of the drama, as it were an extension of the feelings played out on stage, but detached and critical, though necessarily 'interested', observers capable of exercising reflection and judgement on what they saw before them.

The function of the first chorus in *Adelchi* is to provide a concentrated illustration of the process of judgement taking place. Confusion, misapprehension and disillusion are dramatized in a striking way before the eyes of the spectator/reader. There is an element of real surprise in the first reading of the chorus as the report of what seems like liberation (the advancing armies of Charlemagne) gives way before the stern authorial warning ('Udite!', 'Hear!') not to be deceived by appearances (the oppressed Latins, themselves like human ruins of the fallen empire, will be no freer under the Franks than they were under the Longobards: 'Il forte si mesce col vinto nemico, / Col novo signore rimane l'antico', ll. 61–2: 'The strong man mingles with the beaten enemy, / The old master stays beside the new'). And because of this element of surprise, the chorus works in part as a commentary on events, but even more importantly as a process, or something that initiates (and controls) a process in the mind of the reader/spectator: the process whereby we consciously distance ourselves from the drama and pass judgement on the action we see taking place before us. The kind of judgement involved in this case may be a very simple one involving a general political know-how, though it has very specific analogies with the current political situation of Restoration Italy. But it does work precisely for the reader/spectator (contemporary to Manzoni) as a means of establishing the right relationship (judging the right distance) between himself or herself and the material of the drama: she or he both sympathizes with the despised *latini* and takes a wider, wiser, more knowledgeable view of their predicament – he or she possesses, or acquires, the experience of history.

5.2 History and fiction

Even before publishing *Adelchi*, Manzoni had begun working on the novel which was to become recognized as his most important achievement. The first draft, *Fermo e Lucia*, was more schematic in structure than the later version, and as we have already seen (sec. 4.2) regional and local dialect forms played a larger part in the language of the narrative than was subsequently the case. Manzoni was never a specialist 'dialect writer' like his brilliant friend Carlo Porta (1775–1821), who inherited the stock Milanese character Meneghin from his seventeenth-century predecessor Carlo Maria Maggi (1630–99) and revitalized the tradition of the stubborn, bloody-minded, resilient, wisecracking Milanese urban poor as a vehicle of satire on the powers of the day and as a statement of basic human values. Porta's huge repertoire ranged from 'El lava piatt del Meneghin ch'è mort' ('Dead Meneghin's dish-washer', 1792) and the first ever dialect translation of parts of Dante's *Inferno* to late poems like 'La nomina del cappellan' ('Nominating the chaplain', 1820) and 'La guerra di pret' ('The war of the priests', 1821), written during the heyday of the Restoration. As well as being a friend and sponsor of the Milanese Romantics, Porta was also an inspiration to the great Roman poet Giuseppe Gioacchino Belli (1791–1863), whose sonnets in *romanesco* (Roman dialect) captured the voices of the Roman populace as they expressed their grievances, prejudices, erotic longing and satirical contempt with telling precision. Belli was very well known in his day; his poems circulated in manuscript and were occasionally published in periodicals, but a complete edition did not appear until 1896. Both Porta and Belli demonstrated through their work that there was nothing marginal about dialect poetry and that on the contrary it could have a more immediate and communicative effect than much that was written in literary Tuscan.

Despite Porta's example in Lombardy, however, there was also a countermovement away from dialect to Italian. A case in point was another close friend of Manzoni's, Tommaso Grossi (1790–1853), who began by collaborating with Porta, translated his dialect narrative poem *La fuggitiva* (*The Fugitive*, 1816) into Italian, and then concentrated on writing, mainly on medieval themes, in the national language (*Ildegonda*, 1820; *I Lombardi alla prima crociata* (*The Lombards at the First Crusade*), 1826; and the historical novel *Marco Visconti*, 1834). One reason for this countertrend may have been that dialect was seen as especially effective in certain kinds of verse, notably satirical and scurrilous writing: another example of a famous satirist of the day drawing extensively on colloquial speech if not dialect in the strict sense was the Tuscan poet Giuseppe Giusti (1809–50), noted in his early days at least for his republicanism and anti-Austrianism.

Traces of the Milanese 'popular' tradition remain in Manzoni's novel – in the peasant wisdom of Lucia's mother Agnese, for example, or in some of Renzo's encounters in Milan at the time of the bread riots – and the novel has an undoubted satirical edge which is directed particularly against the political class. Nevertheless, it is clear that Manzoni in what was to become

I promessi sposi was aiming at a broader, more comprehensive, 'higher' perspective which would encompass the 'knowledge' of history and even, in Manzoni's case, tentatively approach the viewpoint of Providence. Satire was not sufficient to his purpose (or particularly congenial to his nature), and the language had to be correspondingly flexible, allowing the view from below to be accommodated with the view from above.

In reworking the novel from *Fermo e Lucia* Manzoni not only revised the language, but removed a lot of historical information and digression and made some structural alterations to the central part of the novel in order to give the narrative more suspense. He firmly established his narrative voice, that of a wise, humane, benignly amused uncle, who can use sharp words when he needs to. The narrator is omniscient (except when it suits the author to pass something over in silence) and Manzoni establishes a distance from the seventeenth-century material through the device of an anonymous original manuscript which he begins by quoting from, only to abandon it on the grounds of its impossibly flowery and dated language. The action of the novel takes place over three years, 1628–30, in Spanish-dominated Lombardy. The thirty-eight chapters can be divided into six or seven blocks. In the first eight chapters, the two betrothed lovers of the title, Lucia Mondella and Renzo Tramagliano, are prevented from marrying because the local lord, Don Rodrigo, has his eye on Lucia. The parish priest, Don Abbondio, is threatened and frightened, but a Capuchin monk, Fra Cristoforo, helps the 'little family' (which includes Lucia's mother, Agnese) to escape across Lake Como. On the other side they separate. In chapters 9 and 10, Lucia finds refuge with Gertrude, the 'nun of Monza', in her convent. Gertrude, from a proud aristocratic family, had been forced to take the veil as a young girl; she has become bitter and corrupt, and will betray Lucia. In the meantime (chapters 11–17), Renzo has made his way to Milan, where there is a food shortage and he witnesses and gets caught up in a riot; he is arrested and briefly detained, but makes his escape and eventually finds his way to the banks of the river Adda, which he will cross into the relative safety of Venetian territory. The focus returns to Lucia in chapters 19–24. She has been turned over to the wicked Innominato ('the Unnamed'), a feared warlord, much more powerful than Don Rodrigo, who will sell her on to the latter. But the Innominato, who like Gertrude has a troubled past, is ready for conversion, and in this essentially inner process he is helped both by the saintly behaviour of Lucia, who makes a vow of lifelong virginity to the Virgin Mary, and by the providential arrival of the (historical) cardinal archbishop of Milan, Federico Borromeo. Lucia is released and taken under the wing of a well-to-do Milanese family; Borromeo proceeds to the lovers' village, where he has a serious conversation with Don Abbondio (chapters 25–6). But now history intervenes on a massive scale (chapters 27–35). War comes to the area, and with it rape and pillage, famine and plague. Renzo returns to Milan, where the plague rages, in search of Lucia. In the final chapters (36–8), the lovers are reunited, Lucia is absolved of her vow by Fra Cristoforo, Don Rodrigo dies, and the marriage is celebrated.

Manzoni ends his novel with a moral. But that moral ('they came to the conclusion that troubles often come to those who bring them on themselves, but that not even the most cautious and innocent behaviour can ward them off; and that when they come – whether by our own fault or not – confidence in God can lighten them and turn them to our own improvement': Manzoni 1997: 550) is not the whole of the story. It is not even the whole of the conclusion. The whole of the story consists in our arriving at that conclusion, and we get there not by a straight line, but via a series of contradictions and convolutions.

The experience of the novel is based on an unceasing equivocation between appearance and reality. Its action springs from a single act of *prepotenza* (arrogance) committed by the apparently strong against the apparently weak. In the course of the novel, the humble are sustained in their attempts to undo the effects of that action by faith in a transcendental justice willing and able to intervene on their behalf in the world. That intervention is in fact seen to take place, but it is also seen that it is dependent on the action of the characters themselves within the human world, which is the realm of contradiction and equivocation – the ambiguities of human actions and human power are detailed in a careful historical and sociological narrative. The truth concerning man's *reality* (the relationship between human action and divine, as Manzoni sees it) is known instinctively by and embodied in Lucia, and is learnt gradually and painfully by Renzo. At the end, death (in the form of the plague) forces all the protagonists to face up to that truth (or to continue to ignore it, as Don Abbondio does), and the effects of the initial act of injustice are eliminated. But that is as far as it goes: there is no great settling of accounts. After the pestilential drought, the revivifying rain; after the massacre, life begins again. A truth has been arrived at through the experience of all these characters, but there is no final solution. Life continues to be lived with all the ambiguity which is proper to life itself. The constant oscillation between ambiguity and clarity is what sustains the novel and what confers on the book itself a persistent ambiguity.

All that can be said is that by the end of the novel, the reader is more aware; he or she understands more clearly the machinery of Manzoni's world, at one with Renzo and Lucia's greater understanding of God's world.

It is a consciousness that we acquire step by step through the novel, moving from a vague presentiment in the first eight chapters (the sense of a power beyond that of the individual actors) to the dramatic choices presented by the conversion and the plague. But the biggest step forward comes not with these two great events, but with that which prepares them and makes them comprehensible (if not subjectively acceptable): the journey of Renzo. He is the traveller of the novel, its Ulysses. He is open to new experiences, he sees the world and learns, and for a significant part of the novel (the bread riots, the night at the inn, his flight from Milan) he is the medium through which we as readers see the world and enact, through empathy, our own experience in the world. The position of Renzo, as he is initially presented, is supremely ambiguous. He is a representative of the people (unlike Lucia's house, which is at the end of the village, Renzo's is specifically described as being in the middle of it), yet he is a man without any family. As a worker, he is both a peasant and a skilled silk-weaver, alternating, according to circumstances, between the land and his trade, midway between the peasant Tonio, worn down with hunger and a family, and cousin Bortolo, ensconced in his silk factory at Bergamo. Overall, this is a position which confers on Renzo extreme *mobility*: he has no ties or responsibilities (except to Lucia, who is distant); he is servant to no man; with his work he can find employment either at home, where emigration has wiped out the competition, or abroad, where they are crying out for workers with his skills.

Renzo is the character in *I promessi sposi* who most threatens to undermine its author's control of the novel. He is in fact brought rather severely into line by Manzoni. Once he has escaped Milan and spent his purificatory night by the banks of the river, he virtually disappears from the story and only re-emerges when his presence is strictly required by the exigencies of the plot: he has to find, and then marry, Lucia. In order to understand the troublesomeness of Renzo one must remember the scale of the task with which Manzoni chose to grapple. In what was the first serious attempt to write a large-scale historical novel in Italian, Manzoni not only set out to supersede what he saw as the limits of the existing models, particularly the scarce adherence to historical accuracy which he discerned in Walter Scott, but was morally impelled to redefine the rules of realist fiction from first principles. This may help account for the sense the reader has of the controlling hand of the author over material that resists control. If we ask ourselves, 'What is the narrative motor of *I promessi sposi*? What makes the novel tick?', we have to conclude that it is nothing specifically in the novel itself. It is not the love-story of the young couple, or their personal growing into consciousness of the world, though this element is certainly present, particularly in Renzo, and the famous 'sugo' (the 'juice', the moral of the tale) is the conclusion appropriate to that kind of novel; neither is it the history; nor is it entirely the religious and social message of the book. Rather, the catalyst of the novel lies outside, in the overseeing eye of the author, who is attempting to hold all these elements together in an all-embracing vision of human life, which is always beyond his grasp because no human can grasp life in its entirety, being part of it and embedded in it himself. And this is the drama of fiction, at least as Manzoni conceptualized it: the novel is a modelling of reality, an always defective approximation to reality whose value and achievement are always in question.

I promessi sposi enjoyed immediate success. The first print run was quickly sold out and the readership extended well beyond the first purchasers: Lapo Ricci described reading the novel to an awed group of Tuscan peasants in a letter to Gino Capponi right at the beginning of 1828 (Capponi 1882–90: V, 326) (in a scene consciously or unconsciously echoing one of Jacopo reading to 'his' peasants near the beginning of *Ultime lettere di Jacopo Ortis*). The immediate reception of *I promessi sposi* – transmitted to us in private letters and memoirs and in periodical reviews – was enthusiastic but critically mixed and tended to take apart what Manzoni had so painstakingly put together. Amongst the *letterati*, there was some persistent unease about the low life depicted in the novel; it was criticized on the grounds of slowness and prolixity; there were complaints that there was 'too much history' and the middle class of readers who were accustomed to the passionate and exotic in the novel were disappointed; for some readers there was too much religion and a feeling that the author's patriotism was equivocal. But there was also a powerful feeling about the deep emotional effect of the novel, which was testified to by many of its first readers.

In general, one's impression is that nearly everyone was thrown off guard by the newness of the work, which often gave rise to contradictory judgements in the same person. Professional critics in the 1820s had the greatest difficulty in coming to terms with the combination of 'history' and 'romance' (*romanzo*) in the historical novel (*romanzo storico*) and, true to a classical tradition of rhetorical analysis learnt in their schooldays, still sought out the defining genre to which the individual work belonged. Any given work could only be 'about' one thing at a time, or, to put it another way, every work of imagination (since here we are concerned with literature) was directly referential to reality in a one-to-one relationship. Thus, a *romanzo* referred to 'private', therefore fictional life, while history referred to 'public', that is, documented life. *I promessi sposi* is either 'Renzo-and-Lucia' or it is the history of seventeenth-century Milan; in the first case, the history is digressive, in the second, the love-story is a pretext. Paride Zajotti (1793–1843), who was a high-ranking official in the Austrian administration of Lombardy-Venetia as well as a literary critic, hit on an ingenious solution whereby he could praise Manzoni and condemn the historical novel in the same breath, and that was to call *I promessi sposi* 'descriptive', though he admitted that it was 'historical' in parts. Either way, the conclusion as to what the novel was 'about' was no less selective: 'What befalls Renzo and Lucia may seem to be the main concern only to those who wish to apply the usual norms to this novel: but careful reflection will show that its first objective is to describe the course of civil society in the Duchy of Milan at the beginning of the seventeenth century' (Manzoni 2000: 186). This idea that the love-story, that is to say, the 'novelistic' part, was merely a pretext for the description of historical events was shared by one of the leaders of the rising generation of critics, Niccolò Tommaseo, who affirmed 'without doing the book an injustice [. . .] that the episodes are what is important here, and the main plot is the least of it' (Tommaseo 1827: 108).

There was, astonishingly perhaps, only one critic of *I promessi sposi* who managed almost entirely to escape from this need to select the most important amongst the component parts of the novel and who put his finger on what he saw as the inspiration and the 'spirit' of the novel, and this was Giovita Scalvini (1791–1843), who was in exile at the time. In Scalvini's eyes, what mattered in the book was the contrast between the blackness of this life and the promised joy beyond, its Christianity, its Catholicism (Manzoni 2000: 241–69). Scalvini paid little attention to the question of whether the book was a history or a romance; he was concerned essentially with the feel, the message it conveyed beyond the form. He ignored the parts, the components of the novel, and returned to this one general aperçu again and again. In other words, he set about *interpreting* the novel rather than simply analysing it, and in this he seems to have achieved what had been an ambition of the *conciliatori*: to write criticism which would catch the 'spirit' of a work, something rarely achieved in practice by the Romantic generation itself. Manzoni noticed Scalvini. 'He has read between the lines', he remarked (Bacchelli 1919: 62).

But despite this endorsement, Manzoni – characteristically – was torn himself and in *Del romanzo storico e, in genere, de' componimenti misti di storia e d'invenzione*, drafted in the immediate aftermath of publication of the novel, between 1828 and 1831, revised between 1848 and 1850 when it was published, he let all his doubts about the historical novel as form out into the open, in much more sophisticated terms than those of his critics, but in substantial agreement with them. A central term of his argument – *il verosimile* – links *Del romanzo storico* to the most substantial spin-off from the novel, an account of the judicial persecution of people suspected of spreading the plague by smearing the walls of houses with an ointment, which was too long to be kept in the novel itself and appeared with the title *Storia della colonna infame* (*History of the Column of Infamy*) in 1842 alongside the final edition of the novel. The word 'inverosimile' is the one more laden with threat than any other in the prisons of Manzoni's plague-stricken Milan. If the interrogator tells the prisoner that his story is 'implausible', 'unbelievable', it means that the prisoner is shortly going to be submitted to even more extreme torture, until he produces a story which is more plausible. The shadow of plausibility falls over another level of the judicial process as well: the judges, having extracted their confessions, need to find a way of making the various stories compatible with one another for the purpose of their judgement. The *verosimile*, in short, that which is like truth but is not necessarily true, may just as well be the seat of coercion, error and downright falsehood.

The term may not take on such lurid colours in the more abstract argumentation of *Del romanzo storico* (whose composition ran for a time in parallel with the second version of *Storia della colonna infame* in the early 1830s), but there are connections between the two uses. In *Del romanzo storico*, Manzoni made a stark distinction between the kind of 'historical' assent which a reader accords those things which are positively the case and the 'poetic' assent which he or she gives to the *verosimile*, the true-like. His argument was that the two kinds of truth should not be mixed in any composition – it is a rejection *a posteriori* of the historical novel – because to do so would be to muddy the reader's perception. The hypothetical reader is at the centre of the essay, and the key word is 'assent' (*assentimento*). Sandra Bermann, in the introduction to her 1984 translation (Manzoni 1984: 35), rightly spoke of Manzoni's 'extraordinary solicitude' for the reader. But this concern for the reader – a crucial ingredient of Manzoni's whole literary project, which we discussed at the beginning of section 5.1 – also goes further than solicitude. The reader portrayed in *Del romanzo storico* is a moral agent, with moral rights and responsibilities. The responsibility of an author, almost like that of a judge, is not to put the reader in a false position. The responsibility of the reader, thus unmolested by the author, is to recognize the appropriate kind of truth and respond accordingly. But Manzoni stopped short of defining quite what the truth of poetry, verisimilitude in the affirmative, might be.

5.3 Literature and the people

Readers between the 1820s and the 1840s developed a seemingly insatiable thirst for historical subject matter, and if critics like Zajotti and Tommaseo agonized about the nature and function of historical novels it was in part because so many of them were beginning to appear and they were so popular. Amongst the many that were published almost contemporaneously with or in the wake of *I promessi sposi*, we will mention *Il castello di Trezzo* (*The Castle of Trezzo*, 1827) by Giovanni Battista Bazzoni (1803–50), author also of two collections of *Racconti storici* (*Historical Tales*, 1832 and 1839); the first novel by the Livornese republican democrat Francesco Domenico Guerrazzi (1804–73), *La battaglia di Benevento* (*The Battle of Benevento*), which he followed up in 1836 with *L'assedio di Firenze* (*The Siege of Florence*), published in Paris under a pseudonym; the novel by Manzoni's friend Tommaso Grossi already mentioned, *Marco Visconti* (1834); and the two novels actually published (a third was left unpublished) by the writer, painter and later diplomat Massimo Taparelli D'Azeglio (1798–1866), *Ettore Fieramosca* (1833) and *Niccolò de' Lapi* (1840). Among the direct spin-offs from *I promessi sposi*, in addition to Manzoni's own *Storia della colonna infame*, we should note *La monaca di Monza* (*The Nun of Monza*, 1829) by the Pisan writer and art historian Giovanni Rosini (1776–1855), who wrote two further historical novels in the 1830s, and the historian Cesare Cantù's (1804–95) *Ragionamento sulla storia lombarda del secolo XVII* (*Essay on Lombard History in the Seventeenth Century*, 1833), republished as a companion piece to the 1842 edition of the *Sposi*; from this work were derived the 'Illustrazioni sopra li Promessi Sposi di Alessandro Manzoni' ('Notes for *The Betrothed* by Alessandro Manzoni') which were frequently appended to editions of that novel in the nineteenth century.

The passion for history was by no means limited to the novel, but was evident in the theatre, in music, in opera especially, and in the visual arts throughout the years leading up to the failed but exhilarating insurrections of 1848–9. But before exploring this passion in greater depth, some further detail about the political development of the Risorgimento itself is necessary.

The defeat of the insurrectionary movements in 1831 led patriots of different shades of opinion to reflect on what had happened over the previous fifteen years and to review options for the future. Although Piedmont was one of the most reactionary and authoritarian of the states, it was also the most independent because of its geopolitical role as a buffer state (see above, sec. 1.2). There, moderate 'liberal-Catholic' writers were trying to imagine top-down solutions to the 'Italian problem', normally involving an accommodation between the existing rulers, some kind of confederal arrangement, and a 'neutral' monarch. Of these the most ambitious was conceived by Vincenzo Gioberti (1801–52), a Catholic priest then in exile from Piedmont, who in a nostalgic cultural-nationalist exaltation of the supremacy of Italian civilization proposed a confederation of the states ruled by the pope (*Del primato morale e civile degli Italiani* (*On the Civil and Moral Pre-eminence of the Italians*), 1843). Such schemes were proposed at least in part by way of resistance to the ideas coming forward from the 'democratic' wing of patriotic thinking, which were wider and more radical in their ambitions. The most prominent of the 1831 exiles was Giuseppe Mazzini (1805–72), founder of the *Giovine Italia* ('Young Italy') movement. *Giovine Italia* retained some of the paraphernalia of the earlier secret societies, but its style was quite different. Mazzini believed that one reason for the failure of earlier movements in Italy had been the lack of decisive leadership on the part of individuals; he himself adopted the role of a prophet and an educator (he had strong views on literature and music, as we shall see in sec. 5.3), and stressed the moral imperative of commitment and self-sacrifice in the name of the cause. The movement, which gave rise to imitators in other aspiring nations and a *Giovine Europa*, had a mission to free the oppressed peoples of Europe and to realize a democratically governed nation guided by the true principles of religion. Politically too, Mazzini went further than he or others had done in the past: Italy should be a unitary state, not a confederation; it should be a republic, not a monarchy; its future was in its own hands and would be settled by propaganda, education and insurrection, not by diplomacy and the patronage of foreigners.

One of the people that Mazzini inducted into Giovine Italia in Marseilles in 1833 (Mazzini subsequently moved to London and spent most of the rest of his life in exile there) was Giuseppe Garibaldi (1807–82). Garibaldi, born in Nice, at that time part of Piedmontese territory, was to become the heroic embodiment of the Risorgimento. He was a man of action, red-haired, red-shirted, a guerilla fighter, a military leader of genius, a troubleshooter, courageous but also cautious and, as events showed, ready to compromise; a man of sorrows too, the tragic death of whose young *guerillera* wife Anita immediately became a Risorgimento legend, a man who had his fair share of rejection, abandonment, exile; and finally a man of words and images, a novelist in his spare time and a canny manager of his own persona in the rapidly expanding world of the popular press at home and abroad. Garibaldi was the ultimate Romantic-Risorgimento icon.

The revolutionary movements which spread across Europe in 1848, which included a significant socialist strand for the first time, put the various patriotic ideas in Italy to the test. Events favoured two alternatives above the others. Gioberti's vision of a federal Italy governed by the pope collapsed as Pius IX, whose remarks after his election in 1846 had raised hopes amongst Italian patriots, became increasingly fearful of socialistic insurrection and fled from Rome. An alternative, republican form of confederation drawing on the Swiss model, proposed by the Milanese economist Carlo Cattaneo (1801–69), came up against the unyielding rock of local rivalries in Lombardy and Venetia. As constitutions were granted up and down the peninsula under popular pressure and then revoked when it subsided, revolutionary governments held out for as long as they could in Milan, Venice and Rome until foreign armies (Austrian in the north, French in Rome) forced them to decamp. Mazzini's democratic constitution for the short-lived Roman republic, promulgated as it fell in July 1849, invoked the principles of popular sovereignty and the values of equality, liberty and fraternity. By contrast, the constitution which Carlo Alberto of Piedmont had been forced to subscribe to in March 1848, while establishing a parliament, did not specify the powers or duties of the prime minister and made it clear that 'the King alone possesses executive power' (see Duggan 1994: 121). But Piedmont, which prided itself on its military tradition, suffered humiliating defeats at the hands of the Austrians in 1848–9; the king abdicated in favour of his son, Vittorio Emanuele II.

The passion for history was certainly one of the principal vehicles, though not the only one, for the formation of a national consciousness in the crucial decades leading up to the unification of Italy. It fulfilled an educative function – as Manzoni and the Romantics hoped – though what it taught might be selective – as Manzoni feared. It could also serve as a cipher for the present, a means of commenting indirectly on contemporary affairs without falling foul of the censor. But most importantly, as A. M. Banti has argued, it was motivating. History, along with a widely shared religious culture, became a potent force in making people want to recognize and fight for a common national identity. Banti reconstitutes a canon of what might be called Risorgimento literature, music and painting (it is obvious that themes, images, emphases, interpretations migrate without hesitation between one art-form and another, then as now), what he describes as 'a series of works of many different kinds [. . .] which reworks the myth of the Italian nation, its past history and its recent experiences in a variety of ways and creates a compact and coherent narrative around specific themes and figures' (Banti 2004: 54). Among the authors and texts which we have already encountered, he includes Berchet's poetry (*Poesie*, fifteen editions between the early 1820s and 1848), Leopardi ('All'Italia'), Pellico (*Le mie prigioni*), Manzoni (*Adelchi*), Guerrazzi (*L'assedio di Firenze*), D'Azeglio (*Ettore Fieramosca*), as well as the composer Giuseppe Verdi (1813–1901) and many others. In this canon he discerns 'a coherent picture of what the Italian nation is and why people should fight for it'. There is first an emphasis on the ties of blood that link the national community together, the present generation with itself and with the past and future; the imagery of family relationships helps in turn to define the nation: the nation is a mother, the members of the nation are brothers and sisters, their leaders are fathers. The nation is further held together by culture: a common language, a common religion, and a common past. This past is not one of happy memories, but one marked by oppression, humiliation, foreign occupation and internal division, a historical past that weighs on the present.

Within this 'deep conceptual nucleus' and amidst all the variety of stories and representations which draw on it, Banti identifies three principal figures and a highly charged plot dynamic. There is, first, the hero, the brave soldier ready to lead his community against the foreign oppressor (less frequently, the single tyrant or tyrannical regime, inherited from Alfieri), noble but nearly always doomed to defeat and death. The second stock figure is that of the traitor, who is motivated by ambition or greed, and who is responsible for both the death of the hero and the defeat of the national community. The third is the national heroine, who shares with the hero an absolute loyalty to her community, but who is otherwise marked by specifically gendered traits: she is virtuous, a loving wife and mother, blameless, chaste and pure, but her sexual integrity is threatened by the traitor and/or the foreign enemy. If and when her honour is taken, she faces either death or exclusion from the community.

Banti points out that these three figures map rather precisely onto models which were extremely familiar to Italians of the early nineteenth century from the holy scriptures: the Christ-like hero, whose death and (potential) resurrection are the focal point of the story, the traitor Judas, the immaculate virgin-mother. These religious connotations overlapped with the ethics of honour, which was played over again and again (the virtues of loyalty, defending the honour of the nation and/or the heroine): the duels and battles which have to be fought to that end become 'holy', the dead are 'martyrs' and must always be remembered. The combination of religion and honour, the interweaving of anxiety about sexual purity and an almost obsessive return to narratives of battle ('war stories'), in a highly gendered context which was scarcely challenged by women themselves (and indeed was constantly reinforced in narratives and poems written by women), produced a supercharged rhetoric which played a considerable part in fuelling patriotic enthusiasm in the Risorgimento.

It did so through the production of prose fiction, *novelle* in verse and patriotic and sentimental poems, which had two characteristics as far as their reception and dissemination were concerned. First, they sold well (narrative, as usual, more than poetry): publishers could rely on certain plot-formulae and the pressing of identifiable emotional buttons to ensure at least steady sales. These works were 'popular' in the sense that Berchet and the Romantics understood the word 'il popolo': comprising essentially the middle and lower-middle classes of the towns and cities and those small parts of the rural population who had contact with and were visible to the upper classes. In other words, the majority of the population was still out of the reach of the written word, though the numbers of people who bought or borrowed books to read was increasing through the century. And secondly, these products were recyclable, or reusable. In the case of poems, in the nineteenth century, people did not just hear poems, or read them, they very often memorized them and repeated them, reciting them to themselves and others. But scenes or characters from novels or *novelle* too which were particularly liked could be lifted out of context, re-elaborated, become themselves the subject of new work, set to music and so on. The diffusion of a popular genre or text did not just depend on direct sales, but took place in a capillary, almost underground way as well, in directions which are not easy to track. And this seems to have happened regardless of the literary quality of the work in question. Most of what was produced in the first half of the nineteenth century did not have much intrinsic merit, but it appears to have performed an invaluable function in providing its readers (and listeners) with an unlimited and reliable supply of sensations, emotions, ideas, positions in which they could recognize themselves.

Poetry was probably never so 'popular' in this sense as it was in the mid-nineteenth century. There were of course the overtly patriotic compositions which stirred the heart, like 'Fratelli d'Italia' ('Brothers of Italy'), written in 1847 by Goffredo Mameli (1827–49); it was to become the Italian national anthem after Unification. Romantic poetry of this period deals sometimes in dangerous places, female longing, poverty, loss, sadness and depression, a certain languor, death, gothic fantasy, but is generally also reassuring, not least because of its underlying Christian piety. Both of the two most representative poets of these years, Aleardo Aleardi (1812–78) and Giovanni Prati (1814–84), experimented with variations on these themes, Prati scoring a notable success with his scandalous *novella in versi* called *Edmenegarda* (1841), supposedly based on a real-life case of adultery. Both poets, who were friends, naturally wrote patriotic and Risorgimento poems and both achieved respectable positions in newly united Italy.

Coincidentally, this was also the period during which serious attempts were made to uncover the poetic traditions of the mass of the people, particularly in the countryside. A substantial contribution was made to the collection and description of folk-poetry by Niccolò Tommaseo, the Italian part of whose *Canti popolari toscani corsi illirici greci* (*Popular Songs from Tuscany, Corsica, Illyria* [= Dalmatia] *and Greece*, 1841–2) was the product of fieldwork done in the Apennines in the 1830s. In part, this interest stemmed from a desire inherited from the eighteenth century to find continuities between the earliest traditions of Italian (especially Tuscan) verse and the remoter corners of the modern countryside (and Tommaseo was excited to have found shepherds who read Tasso in the Pistoia hills: Tommaseo 1841–2: I, 6), and in part from the felt need to carry out a pedagogic mission, to rescue and in some cases to sanitize traditional songs which were in danger of being lost. An interesting case of a poetry-prospector of this kind was the priest Pietro Paolo Parzanese (1809–52), who graduated from writing songs *for* the people with moral intent in his *Canti popolari* (*Popular Songs*) of 1841 ('Songs for the people should be used as an enjoyable means of civil and Christian education': Parzanese 1856–7: II, 8) to collecting songs *by* the people and rewriting them for wider consumption (*Il Viggianese*, 1846; the Viggianesi came from a village in the Basilicata and were well known as seasonal migrant singers and musicians).

The years leading up to 1848 in particular were ones during which personal emotions and political and patriotic sentiment intertwined, especially among the young generation, and where the national and political question, overtly or covertly, absorbed a good deal of attention and energy. The theatre was the place where potentially this double helix of strong emotion and patriotic fervour could come closest to the surface, but it was also the place where the public authorities could most easily exercise control, with severe sanctions for owners or actor-managers who overstepped the line. As a result, writing for the theatre was less exciting than one might have expected during the Risorgimento. The gap was filled, or perhaps was created, by the success of the musical theatre, the opera, which was the one genre in which Italy had recognized cultural authority on an international scale.

A cultural history of literature is concerned with opera at two levels. First, opera depended on a close relationship with the literary world. Like film-makers a century later, composers and librettists plundered the literary storehouse for themes and texts, with Shakespeare, Walter Scott, Victor Hugo and many others all supplying material for some of the greatest operas of the time. In addition, a number of very able writers wrote libretti, among them Felice Romani (1788–1852) for Rossini, Bellini and Donizetti, while Francesco Maria Piave (1810–76), Temistocle Solera (1815–78) and Salvatore Cammarano (1801–52) all collaborated with Verdi. Secondly, it was through opera, which reached tens of thousands of people every year, and many others beyond the audience through the sale of sheet-music and the work of popular musicians, that the primary themes and motifs of Romantic-Risorgimento literary culture reached the public.

In 1836 Mazzini (who could not abide Leopardi because of his standing aloof, as Mazzini saw it, from the national struggle) wrote an essay on the 'philosophy of music' (*Filosofia della musica*), in which he paid particular attention to the potential of the choral moments in opera. In a way not dissimilar to Manzoni's (and A. W. Schlegel's) reflection on the chorus in drama, Mazzini seized on this collective moment in the action as one where a national and patriotic consciousness could be instilled. His insight seemed to be verified with the patriotic success of the chorus of the Hebrew slaves in Verdi's *Nabucco* (1842). A song of exile and yearning, 'Va' pensiero' became imbued with patriotic meanings (although not as rapidly, it appears, as subsequent legend suggested). But opera reached its audience in many other ways as well. It had subjects which dealt, in an Alfierian way, with tyranny and oppression or the conflict between two peoples (which has echoes of *Adelchi*) – though, always mindful of the censor and the police, composers and librettists would keep these subdued and well away from the Italian context; powerful emotional and interpersonal situations, such as the relation between father and daughter several times revisited by Verdi; spectacular scenery and theatrical effects; and above all the power of the music and the uniqueness of the human voice. It has also been suggested recently, in an intriguing essay, that there is a link to be explored between the aesthetics of longing, which might have a personal or a patriotic content; the commodification of patriotic emotion – something that you pay to go and have provided for you; and urban consumption itself, which by the 1850s and 1860s was beginning to expand in the major Italian cities as elsewhere (Sorba 2002: 149–50).

5.4 Memory, monuments and the national past

In this final section, anticipating in miniature what is more fully analysed in the next chapter, we consider three instances in which the attempt is made to construct memory, both personal and national, in the late 1850s and the 1860s.

In national terms, the 1850s had seen the gradual emergence of Piedmont as the leading player on the Italian scene, thanks in considerable measure to the systematic pursuit of a policy of economic and political liberalism, a combination of free-market trade and constitutional reform, by the prime minister Camillo Benso di Cavour (1810–61). Cavour turned himself into the spokesman for Piedmontese leadership of a future Italian state and manoeuvred skilfully on the international stage, engineering his country's involvement on the side of Britain and France in the Crimean War (1854–6). His policies succeeded in enabling a crucial political alliance in 1857 between moderates and democrats, including Garibaldi, on the basis of an acceptance of the role of the house of Savoy in the national independence struggle – much to the chagrin of intransigent republicans like Mazzini. It was in the spirit of the 'Political Credo' of the *Società nazionale italiana* ('Italian National Society'), written by the Sicilian exile Giuseppe La Farina (1815–63), that Garibaldi famously shook Vittorio Emanuele's hand at Teano on 25 October 1860. The previous months had brought about the unity of Italy in ways that nobody had quite expected. Cavour hatched a plot with Napoleon III in 1858 to drive the Austrians out of northern Italy and for Piedmont to take over, leaving the other states as they were. France backed out at a point which left Piedmont only in control of Lombardy, having ceded Nice and Savoy to the French (1860). Garibaldi, smarting at the loss of his home town, accepted a request to come to the aid of a peasant uprising in western Sicily. The upshot was the 'expedition of the Thousand', sailing down the western coast of Italy, and landing at Marsala. After only a few weeks this tiny force of mainly untrained and inexperienced young volunteers had routed the Bourbons in Sicily and crossed the straits of Messina; by 7 September 1860, Garibaldi was entering Naples in triumph. Cavour had to block Garibaldi, about whose intentions he was uncertain, but without seeming to, because his exploits had aroused such popular enthusiasm. The Piedmontese army pushed south; at Teano (north of Naples) Garibaldi surrendered his powers to the king and the handshake took place. Suddenly, Italy (with the exception of the Veneto, Rome and part of the surrounding Papal States) was a united country.

In strictly literary terms, the historical novel has run its course by the time of the final achievement of United Italy, although the idea that emblematic figures from the past still have an exemplary role in the present survives. In the wake of the final battles of the Risorgimento, there is a spate of autobiographical memoirs, and there is a strong sense now that the past that really matters is the recent past, the one that is within living memory. But at the same time the new nation needs to systematize its own past, and that includes its literary past. It is during the 1860s that the foundation stones are laid for a canonical history of 'Italian' (that is, national, unitary) literary history. In the remainder of this section we shall be looking in turn at Ippolito Nievo's *Confessioni d'un italiano* (*Confessions of an Italian*), written in

1857–8, at the celebrations in 1865 for the sixth centenary of the birth of Dante, and at Francesco De Sanctis's *Storia della letteratura italiana* (*History of Italian Literature*), first published in 1870–1.

Ippolito Nievo (1831–61) wrote prolifically during his short life. The idea for his *Confessioni* may have come from the first instalments of Giuseppe Rovani's *Cento anni* (*One Hundred Years*), which appeared in 1857 (see sec. 6.1). The two novels share the basic idea of a very old man looking back on his life, although Rovani rather quickly loses track of his near-centenarian. Nievo's novel is finished but unrevised: he died at sea on 4 March 1861 in the wreck of the *Ercole*, during a mission to recover documents from Palermo to counter charges of maladministration during Garibaldi's rule of the island the previous year. His hero, Carlo Altoviti, born in the time of the *ancien régime*, 1775, is an orphan who has been brought up in a castle in Friuli, in the extreme northeast; everything there is full of life, sensuality and irrational fears. His mother's sister has taken him in, and of course he falls in love with his cousin, la Pisana. Pisana has become a kind of archetype in Italian literature, an eternal rebel, both impulsive and reflective, a 'seductive demon', as she has been called (De Ceccatty 2006: 3), who will pursue Carlo nearly all his life. Their passion is mutual but they will never marry. She marries an old codger whom she leaves to rejoin Carlo. Carlo marries another young woman, on her instructions. 'What do they want?' the reader asks helplessly – perhaps 'a woman (or a man) who cannot be found', in Leopardi's words, but actually who is there, in flesh and blood. In Stendhalian manner, they get caught up in the events of history, Napoleon's invasion of Italy, and there are some wonderful scenes of the Napoleonic spin-machine at work: 'The hour of liberty has sounded,' the general informs Carlo, 'the time has come to rise up and fight to conquer it, or be crushed. The French Republic stretches out its hand to all peoples that they may regain their liberty [. . .]. Liberty is well worth some sacrifice. One must accept that' (Nievo 1999: I, 674). The novel tacks between the crazy, 'impossible' passion of Carlo and la Pisana and the Napoleonic wars, with many adventures in other parts, including long years spent in London. La Pisana eventually returns to care for Carlo during a long illness, but dies herself of consumption; only after her death does he discover himself as a mature and complete individual.

The novel was published in 1867 with the title *Confessioni di un ottuagenario* (the intrusion of an octogenarian into the title was said to have come about because the portrayal of the 'italiano' in the original title could open up recent wounds), but did not have much success. Twentieth-century readers, perhaps influenced by Proust, have generally much preferred the opening chapters, which deal with the narrator's childhood and establish the structure of his deliciously frustrating relationship with his cousin. But the novel may also be read as the conflicted attempt by a man who was in the thick of the events leading up to Unification to order a recent past, and having recourse to fantasy, fable and the deus ex machina of death as a means of beginning to come to terms with it (and with himself).

What for centuries had been an essentially literary idea of Italian nationhood, tracing its origins back to Dante, had become a political idea and, in due course, a political reality. In the early 1860s the new state had many immediate and practical problems to deal with, not least the fact that some territories were still not incorporated into the national whole and the fact that the peoples which had been united politically were by no means united socially or economically, an asymmetry brutally symbolized by the new government's ruthless repression of peasant rebellion, or as they preferred to call it 'brigandage', in the south of the country from the mid-sixties on. Some of the cross-currents and contradictions of the new Italy came to the fore in 1865, the sixth centenary of the birth of Dante, 'father' of the nation, its language and literature, symbol of its unity and stern admonisher of its shortcomings, now to be officially recognized by an Italian government for the first time.

On the face of it, the celebrations held in Florence in May 1865 should have been the natural culmination of the literary and patriotic exaltation of the poet that had been going on for the previous forty years at least. In reality, it was left to an obscure Florentine journalist, Guido Corsini, to take the initiative and do most of the organizational legwork for the three days of national festivities (originally intended to be eight) to happen at all. As a working journalist, Corsini was aware of the need to 'prepare' the public for the event. To this end, he created two journals. The *Giornale del Centenario* was distributed every ten days to subscribers only from 10 February 1864 to 31 May 1865. In addition to carrying the texts of decisions or recommendations by the Festival Committee, the Municipality, the Provincial Council and other official bodies, the *Giornale* also had a substantial 'unofficial' section. Long-running items such as a date-chart, articles on the 'moral and political conditions of Italy in relation to Dante's teaching', and the first Italian translation of Charles Fauriel's lectures on Dante (first published in Paris in 1854) betray the strongly didactic orientation of the journal. But it also made room for reviews and critical articles and, considering the pressure under which it was produced, maintained a consistently high level.

But Corsini also had a less sophisticated audience in mind. Convinced of the duty of journalism to explain the necessity and importance of the festival to 'the people' – that is, the working classes, artisans, small shopkeepers and peasants – and to stimulate their interest in it, he brought out once a week a four-page paper which he called *La Festa di Dante*. Here the intention to instruct and, in a general way, to 'do good' was more explicit and more central than it was in the *Giornale*, as might be expected from a journal very definitely written *for* the people, 'in a popular idiom', and not by the people. The language more often than not was schoolmasterly; while the didacticism of the *Giornale del Centenario* went hand in hand with a commitment to scholarship and criticism, *La Festa di Dante* underlined the moral and edifying aspects of Dante's teaching. Continuing series spelt out the 'catechism' of Dante and summarized the content and moral lessons of the *Commedia*, or discoursed upon Dantean virtues such as 'jealously guarded honour' or 'love of country'; there were also encyclopedia-type guides to the people and places of the poem, and their historical background.

La Festa di Dante belonged in a tradition of populist journalism, associated with educational reform movements, that had flourished in Tuscany in the 1820s and 1830s. The liberal spirit of the movement, though battered by the ideological reaction that characterized the last fifteen years of the grand duchy, had not succumbed altogether. In the 1860s, as it had been in the 1830s, its principal message was a call for social peace. Unity was the great theme of the *Festa di Dante* and especially civil unity: it was after all the very absence of that unity which had brought his exile and all his subsequent misfortunes upon the head of Dante. In reality, rather than a time of social peace, these first years of the united Kingdom of Italy were ones of growing tension, economic hardship, unemployment – especially in Tuscany, which under the old regime had been relatively protected from the industrial competition of the north. We do not know how real a financial loss was concealed behind the brave but disappointed voice of the director of the *Giornale del Centenario* when he reported in November 1864 that the sales of *La Festa di Dante* had been less than expected. It was not for want of trying.

The political and ideological, more than literary, significance of the anniversary was clear from the start, at home and abroad. As early as 1860, *Le Charivari* of Paris, welcoming the idea of countries making the memory of their great men flower every hundred years like aloes, observed that if Florence were to do likewise for Dante, it would be above all to 'honour the politician'. An unsigned article in *Il Giornale Illustrato* sang the virtues of centenaries as a way of emphasizing tolerance and brotherhood in a nation, enhancing patriotism and educating the people to faith in progress and the cult of genius. Under the rhetorical cloak of unity, the different post-Risorgimento political currents interpreted the Dante festivities in different ways. Those Catholics who wanted to see the pope retain temporal power in Rome were on the defensive, but determined to invoke Dante's authority in their cause. Against them, the most intransigent republicans found it infuriating that at this very moment the new Italy should be kissing the slipper of 'Boniface VIII's successor' in Rome and seeking a negotiated settlement to the discord between the two powers. But for the moderates in charge of the proceedings, the major gain was to be a display of national unity around the person of the king. With the flags of the as yet unliberated territories draped in mourning, the stage (Piazza Santa Croce) was set for a ritualistic enactment of centralism: all eyes focused on the king and the statue rising totemically from the middle of the theatrical space (it has since been shifted to the side). In the words of Britain's official representative at the celebrations, Henry Clark Barlow:

> The speech ended, the King shook hands with the Gonfaloniere, and said a few words himself, there was a grand flourish from the orchestra, the veil of the monument parted at the top then lay in folds on the ground, and the majestic figure of Dante stood revealed before us – in marble, looking, as in life, the man – then off went all hats, and there arose a shout – 'Onorate l'altissimo Poeta!' – such as fair Florence had not heard before, and never will again, that rent the air, it was so loud and long. (Barlow 1866: 29–30)

Barlow caught well the sense that this had to be understood as a unique, and never to be repeated, occasion.

The theme of a unified identity of Italian literature stretching from the past to the present, and its oneness with the nationality so recently achieved, was reiterated in its own way by another great monument of united Italy, the *Storia della letteratura italiana* published by Francesco De Sanctis (1817–83) in 1870–1. De Sanctis was the finest critic of the nineteenth century; after the publication of the *Storia* he went on to publish his lectures on the modern writers, including Leopardi and Manzoni, whom he had not had space to fit into the earlier work. He was also an outstanding teacher and a man very much involved in public affairs, being five times minister of education. His *Storia* focused on the many contradictions and discordances in the history of Italian culture. He was intrigued by the mismatch between cultural and political leadership and the contrast between Dante, whom in some ways he saw, romantically, as a barbarian genius, and his anti-artistic age. He saw Italian culture as beset by a fundamental weakness which in effect he laid at the feet of Petrarch and subsequently humanism: the primacy given to a kind of art for art's sake, a preoccupation with form over content, a lack of interest in the real world, the consequent gap between writers and the people, a detachment from intellectual and artistic movements in the more advanced parts of Europe which was only beginning to be narrowed in the eighteenth century by Goldoni, Parini and Alfieri. De Sanctis's history did not tell a seamless story, but it discerned an overall pattern linking century to century, artist to artist. He created a synthesis which his readers could see in the round, even though, with the rise of positivism, De Sanctis himself was aware that the 'age of synthesis' – like the 'grand narratives' displaced a hundred years later by postmodernism – was giving way to an 'age of analysis'. In the later years of the nineteenth century, readers and critics of Dante, for example, would be once again aware of the gaps and distances between verifiable historical fact and the legendary or poetic elaboration of it, between the experience and consciousness of the creator and the achieved creation which is before the reader, between 'poetry' and 'structure', 'allegory' and material reality, and would prefer to focus with extreme caution on the 'positive' study of the texts, the documents, and the themes and topics of the 'world of Dante' or any other author, in a spirit hostile to all aestheticism, all subjectivism, all construction of grand and comprehensive systems. But De Sanctis's 'synthesis', mediated by Croce, Gramsci and a stream of academic critics, was to be extremely influential through much of the twentieth century as well. What is perhaps most attractive to us still today in De Sanctis's writing is its humaneness and directness, along with a critical acumen from which we can still learn.

6

Making the nation

6.1 The literary culture of Unification

Unification was to have a significant impact on the cultural life of the peninsula, but because of widespread moral and ideological disquiet at the events that led to the creation of a unified Italy, not helped by the political machinations of monarchy, state and church in the years that followed, its effect is often underestimated. The uneven progress towards recovering the territories left out of the national picture by the formal Unification of 1861 was underlined in humiliating fashion by the new kingdom's defeat by the Austrians on land at Custoza and by sea off the coast of Dalmatia at Lissa in June–July 1866 (the surrender of Austrian control of most, but not all, of the northeast was achieved instead by diplomatic means), while the annexation of Rome in 1870 came about almost by accident as a result of Napoleon III's defeat and withdrawal from Italy. The early years of united Italy failed to match up to the ideals.

The Italy that was born in 1861 was a constitutional monarchy under a king who enjoyed powers that far exceeded those of any other monarch in Europe, and, with 98 per cent of the population lacking voting rights, it could hardly be considered a democracy. Patriots who had fought long and hard found themselves immediately disenfranchised. It was only with the introduction of reforms in 1882, which extended the right to vote to all male citizens over the age of twenty who were able to read and write, that the number of those entitled to vote rose to 7 per cent of the population. It was this new electorate that sent the first socialist, Andrea Costa, to parliament. But in the years immediately following Unification most citizens who had contributed actively and creatively to the building of a unified state found themselves excluded from the processes of decision-making, leading, inevitably, to a climate of cynicism, hostility and distrust. Different regions of Italy experienced the rapid centralization of administrative power that came with Unification in very different ways. In Sicily, for example, the first decade was marked by a bitter and violent struggle between the peasantry and what it saw as an army of occupation, made up mostly of young men for whom compulsory military service meant they were for the first time in their lives far from home. In Lombardy, such was the obtuse process of 'Piedmontization', which took away the more autonomous and liberal conditions the region had previously enjoyed under Austrian rule, that Cavour drew on it as a textbook example of what not to do in the case of Tuscany.

With the annexation of Rome in 1870, the Catholic church's temporal power became purely symbolic, although the church mobilized its own networks and strengthened its influence in the field of education, above all primary education. Pope Pius IX retreated still further into a doctrinaire intransigence, forbidding participation in elections, which may help explain why, of the 2 per cent of the population entitled to vote, only half of that exiguous proportion took up the option. The publication in 1864 of the papal encyclical *Quanta cura*, along with its 'Syllabus of errors of our times', caused uproar by its outright condemnation of various currents of contemporary philosophy, including liberalism, democracy and socialism, press freedom and the secular nature of the state. Papal opposition politics continued unabated through the decade, culminating in the death sentence passed and carried out on two Italian patriots in 1870, the king's personal plea for clemency going unheeded; in that same year the (first) Vatican Council proclaimed the doctrine of papal infallibility.

The cultural impact of Unification did not make itself felt overnight, but over a period of several decades. The most immediate matters of concern were education and the question of the language. The pressing need for a common national language arose directly out of the creation of a united Italy, although many would claim that it took almost a century and the arrival of the television era to attain it. A command of written and spoken Italian carried no cultural kudos, the first king of Italy did not speak Italian, and the first government that met in Turin used French as its lingua franca. What one spoke was the product of where one came from, and outside Tuscany and some strata of Roman society where Italian was spoken, dialect continued to be the most usual form of expression and communication among all sectors of the population, both in the countryside and in the towns and cities. The question of a common national language was bound up with that of literacy. It has been estimated that at the time of Unification about 75 per cent of the population as a whole over the age of six had no literacy skills at all, a figure which concealed sharp regional variations, with an estimated 86 per cent illiteracy in the south as a whole as against 37 per cent in Tuscany. Education became a battle zone between liberals, conservatives and Catholics, who were divided over what children should be taught to make Italians of them. The Casati law of 1861 introduced compulsory state education for two years for girls and boys, but the law allowed for many exemptions and little was done to enforce it. Single women made up the majority of teachers in these schools, often living in remote communities very far from home, where they were the victims of prejudice and in some cases assault.

Unification helped propel Italy towards joining the Europe-wide process of the modernization of infrastructures. Railways were built linking towns as well as town and country, and railway stations, the new cathedrals, brought about the destruction of entire districts in city centres. The enormous cost of these new railways contributed to the financial overload that brought down the left under Depretis and returned the right to power in 1876. Civic building included the creation of shopping and leisure arcades, such as the elegant *gallerie* that still today are a hub for street life in Milan, Genoa and other cities, alongside places of official culture – museums, theatres, universities. Towns witnessed the greatest building and demolition programme to have taken place in the history of the peninsula – not only Turin and Milan, but also Rome, which on becoming the capital in 1871 saw an army of office workers and their families advance on it, leading to the creation of an entire new *quartieri*. Italy, unlike France or England, had never experienced the hegemonic pull of a single city; there was nowhere that had a comparable influence to that of contemporary London or Paris over the rest of the country. Italy did have a relatively large number of towns (twenty Italian cities at Unification had a population of over 50,000, although only about 20 per cent of Italians lived in towns with populations over 20,000), so the changing cityscapes were evident wherever one went. Never was the absence of one hegemonizing centre more marked than in the first decade of unified Italy, when the nation's capital relocated twice in ten years: from Turin to Florence in the middle of the decade, and finally to Rome. Industrialization got under way considerably later in Italy than in England and France, and it is only in the 1870s that it made its presence felt in Lombardy and around Milan. It is therefore not surprising that the effects of Unification on social and cultural life across the country were so much more marked in some cities than in others.

It was Milan that was to be initially the centre for the revitalization of Italian culture. A fervent patriotism attenuated by the experience of life in a unified Italy, exhilaration at the speed of the growth and transformation of the cities combined with a nostalgic backward glance at rural life and family values, a need to deprovincialize and to shake off the constraining hand of the previous generation, all contributed to the arrival of Italy's first self-consciously literary movement. The *Scapigliatura*, like the French *bohème* that it was loosely modelled on (the word means 'dishevelled'), linked art and an anti-bourgeois lifestyle that often translated into real poverty. The name comes from Cletto Arrighi's novel of 1862, *La scapigliatura e il sei febbraio* (*Scapigliatura and the Sixth of February*), where the author identified a group of young patriots, independent in thought and lifestyle, restless, living in the heart of a city from which they felt excluded but of which they form the cultural vanguard. Avant-gardes see no mutual exclusivity between the public and the private, and in life as in art the *scapigliati* chose to go against the status quo. The main figures in this loosely knit and fluctuating group, in addition to Arrighi (1830–1906), were Iginio Ugo Tarchetti (1839–69; 'Ugo' was adopted in homage to Foscolo), Emilio Praga (1839–75), Camillo Boito (1836–1914) and Arrigo Boito (1842–1918), with, a few years later in Turin, Giovanni Faldella (1846–1928), Roberto Sacchetti (1847–81) and Achille Giovanni Cagna (1847–1931), and, sharing the same interest in linguistic experimentalism as the Piedmontese group but standing apart, Carlo Dossi (1849–1910). They wrote novels, short stories and poetry; Arrigo Boito was a librettist for Verdi; and they were all journalists. The mentor of the movement was Giuseppe Rovani (1818–74), author of the five-volume historical novel *Cento anni*, first published in serial form in 1857–63, whose open-air lessons in aesthetics at an inn in Milan were a rallying point for the group.

This was the start of a period of rapid expansion in print-culture, books, periodicals and newspapers, to meet the growing appetite for entertainment and, increasingly, education. The journals the *scapigliati* contributed to and sometimes edited rarely circulated much beyond the town of origin and often had a life of no more than a few months. The most successful of those associated with the Milanese circle between 1860 and 1880 were *Cronaca grigia* and *Figaro*. The *scapigliati*'s receptiveness to literary cultures outside Italy, combined with their drive to deprovincialize their own culture, took Tarchetti and Boito to Edgar Allan Poe, Mary Shelley, Hoffman and Gautier (among others) and through them to the introduction of the fantastic to Italian readers. They turned to Charles Dickens and Eugène Sue for models of the social humanitarian novel, while Heine and Baudelaire offered Praga a poetics which mixed realism and the macabre. One much-hated manifestation of the new Italy was the conscript army, and I. U. Tarchetti drew on his experiences as a volunteer officer between 1859 and 1865 for *Una nobile follia* (*A Noble Madness*, 1867), a novel which provided a powerful denunciation of the conscript army at a time when the armed forces were a potent, if fragile, symbol of Italy's unification.

Often written hurriedly, the work of the *scapigliati* continues to communicate the sense of personal and artistic adventure and excitement which came from testing the limits of the acceptable. Only Carlo Dossi eschewed the cultural market-place; at eighteen he published in an elegant limited edition an autobiographical narrative, *L'altrieri* (*The Day Before Yesterday*, 1868), followed by the equally experimental *Vita di Alberto Pisani* (*Life of Alberto Pisani*, 1870). Where the first makes no reference at all to the public or political domain, the second work offers a reading of the protagonist as representative of his age, but representing the negative consequences of history, the psychological scars that historical events had left on the generation that came of age after Unification.

Independently of the *Scapigliatura*, a group of mainly Tuscan painters known as the *Macchiaioli* – from the stain or blot of colour ('macchia') which they used to emphasize luminosity and contrast – used to meet regularly at the Caffé Michelangelo in Florence in the 1850s and 1860s. Their work had a strong visual impact, almost pre-Impressionist in some cases, and at the same time a clear social message. Dramatically composed canvases highlighting some of the 'hidden' moments of the wars of independence (field hospitals, a desperately wounded cavalryman being dragged along the ground by his runaway horse, sentry duty at some hot and dusty outpost) reminded the viewer of the sacrifices made by ordinary volunteers for the cause, and made the *Macchiaioli*'s depiction of provincial life in post-war Italy all the more poignant. These paintings of street scenes and ordinary people, often women, engaged in their daily work, were a reminder of the gulf that had opened up between the 'paese reale' and the 'paese legale', between the non-enfranchised people of Italy and the tiny percentage already mentioned with the legal right to participate in the construction of the new Italy.

No writer of the post-Unification period can be claimed as the single voice of the new Italy. Manzoni, whose *I promessi sposi* probably contributed more to the creation of a sense of national culture than any other individual work since Dante's *Comedy*, found a different outlet for his patriotism when he was asked in 1868 to preside over a committee whose task it was to find ways to encourage the diffusion of a common language throughout the peninsula. It gave rise to the publication nearly thirty years later of a dictionary of contemporary spoken Florentine. At the same time his novel became a central plank in the national school syllabus (see above, sec. 5.2). The only poet to be seen as part of the establishment was Giosuè Carducci (1835–1907), one of three whose collective importance gave them the soubriquet 'le tre corone' ('the three crowns'); the remaining two were Pascoli (1855–1912) and D'Annunzio (1863–1938). By age and outlook Carducci was the most firmly rooted in the nineteenth century, and, perhaps unjustifiably, he came to be the poet that other writers rebelled against. Known for his public, oratorical and anti-Romantic poems, he continued in his poetry with the forms of civic and ideological commitment that had been articulated at the time of the struggle for Unification. Although there was another side to him, he gradually came to be seen as an unofficial poet laureate with a poem for every public occasion. After the 1880s, however, he found the contradictions of his role too difficult to accept and his poetry broke up into two spheres – the private world of childhood in the Maremma, which shows a clear disillusionment with history, and the poetry that belongs to the public voice which speaks for the nation.

The sense of estrangement between writers and the new Italy is particularly pronounced in the case of Giovanni Pascoli. The second 'corona', he saw history in an entirely negative light, believing, perhaps not mistakenly, that the course of history seemed to be preparing for a new barbarism, a terrible catastrophe. Personal tragedy underpinned ideology. A happy rural childhood was destroyed at the age of twelve when his father was accidentally shot dead on the way home from work; soon afterwards his mother died, followed by five of his siblings. Such a brutal entry into the adult world could well have contributed to his identification of all that is positive with the family, the countryside and, above all, the child. In each of us, he suggests, there coexist the adult who is aligned with history, society and all that he finds abhorrent, and the child, who embodies the rural and poetry. In his essay *Il fanciullino* (*The Little Child*, 1897) he argued that we all carry the child within us, but the poet is unique because only the poet has the capacity to think back into the intuitive understanding of reality that belongs to the child and that is so much more insightful than anything provided by the intellect. This working through leads us back to the essence of things. It creates a 'poetica degli oggetti' ('poetics of objects') which is not all that dissimilar to T. S. Eliot's objective correlative, and leads in Pascoli's poetry to a correspondence between state of mind and the natural world. In his first and most compelling collection, *Myricae*, which was published in 1891 and reappeared in a definitive edition in 1903, the poet's wish to represent the objects of rural life as accurately as possible puts pressure on a literary language that did not have the lexicon to articulate the concerns of daily life. This non-elitist poetics is created through the omission of the realities of contemporary Italy with its rapidly developing industries and its migration to the cities. Pascoli was equally at ease writing in Latin, and his collection of Latin poetry, *Carmina* (1914), reminds us of the continuing cultural importance of that language.

6.2 The artist as observer: *verismo* and the social

Before Unification the poor infrastructures that impeded travel within the country, the customs posts that had to be negotiated, and the expense all contributed to people travelling little, other than out of necessity. After 1861 the sense of not knowing the country that they were now citizens of, combined with increasing ease of travel, led Italians to want to see their country for themselves. The Grand Tour favoured particularly by the English and Germans began to be emulated in a much more modest form by Italians in, for example, the growing popularity among the middle classes of honeymoons which combined visiting some of Italy's most famous sights with an opportunity to meet relatives. Such was their popularity that the realist writer Matilde Serao (1856–1927) advised against them on the grounds that the tour simply led to exhaustion and misunderstandings between the newlyweds.

Photography and a magazine culture contributed to the curiosity and encouraged the spread of new genres of writing which set out to explore life in present-day Italy. Investigative journalism into the lives of the urban poor, generously spiced with a dash of sensationalism, gave rise to collections of campaigning essays such as Serao's on poverty in Naples, *Il ventre di Napoli* (*The Belly of Naples*, 1884), or essays that lifted the lid on the *bassifondi* ('lower depths') of some of Italy's major cities, such as the journalist Paolo Valera's (1850–1926) *Milano sconosciuta* (*Unknown Milan*, 1879) or the two-volume, multi-authored *Ventre di Milano: Fisiologia della capitale morale* (*The Belly of Milan: Physiology of the Moral Capital*, 1888). In a typical example of a new book hoping to capitalize on the success of its predecessors in the genre, the title of this one quoted both Zola's *Ventre de Paris* (*Belly of Paris*, 1873) and Balzac's *Physiologie du mariage* (*Physiology of Marriage*), which had already been adapted by the bestselling doctor, senator and positivist scientist Paolo Mantegazza (1831–1910) for his own *Fisiologia dell'amore* (*Physiology of Love*, 1873). Alongside the 'ventri', the bellies of the cities, another more fictionalized form of writing, the 'misteri', which derived from Eugène Sue's bestselling *Les mystères de Paris* (*The Mysteries of Paris*, 1843), spread through Italy. Social humanitarian, melodramatic and, as time went by, increasingly sensationalist, these stories provided cliffhanging adventures in settings as various as Palermo, Rome, Florence, Livorno and Genoa, together with investigative journalism. An early and witty example of the genre was provided by Carlo Lorenzini (1826–90), who broke off his *I misteri di Firenze* (*The Mysteries of Florence*, 1857–8) at the end of what was intended to be the first volume on the grounds that it was impossible to write in this genre in a town where everybody knew everybody else's business. Under the pseudonym Carlo Collodi, he later created in Pinocchio one of the most popular children's characters of all time (see below, sec. 6.3).

Other forms of evidence were also being gathered through the work, for example, of Giuseppe Pitrè's (1841–1916) monumental twenty-five-volume collection making up the *Biblioteca delle tradizioni popolari siciliane* (*Library of Sicilian Popular Traditions*, 1870–1913). Whereas collections of folk-songs such as Tommaseo's *Canti popolari toscani corsi illirici greci* (see sec. 5.3) had begun to appear in the first half of the century, Pitrè's anthology was part of a new move to collect and preserve regional folk-tales, in this case in the original dialect. Grazia Deledda (1871–1936), the Sardinian writer who won the Nobel prize in 1926, produced in 1895 a remarkable study of the popular traditions of her home town Nuoro. New disciplines in the social sciences, such as ethnography, anthropology and, early in the twentieth century, sociology, contributed, as well as investigations commissioned by the government.

Prose fiction offered another, often more entertaining way for Italians to learn more about their country and its inhabitants. A tradition of writing about rural life had developed in the years leading up to Unification. Caterina Percoto (1812–87) was a daughter of the impoverished nobility from near Udine, who combined the struggle to keep on the right side of destitution with her work as a writer of short stories about peasant life in Friuli, some of which she wrote in dialect. Sympathetic to the characters in her stories, whose lifestyle she shared and whom she saw as embodying virtues that the aristocracy were noticeably deficient in, she wrote in a manner that was never sentimental. In this she differed from other contributors to what a contemporary critic, Cesare Correnti, described in a piece written in 1846 for one of the leading periodicals of the day, *Rivista europea*, as 'letteratura rusticale' ('rural literature'), and which was gradually to feed into the kind of rural realism which became known as *verismo* in Italy between the 1870s and 1880s. After the high moment of *verismo* had passed, representations of rural life became the preserve of the short story or sketch (*bozzetto*). The link between form and subject matter had economic advantages for the writer in that the press was keen to publish stories and payment came sooner. Gabriele D'Annunzio's *Novelle della Pescara* (*Stories from Pescara*, 1902) owe much to Verga's tales, and many of the stories that make up the 200 or more of Luigi Pirandello's *Novelle per un anno* (*Stories for a Year*) use incidents of Sicilian rural life.

Verismo developed out of French naturalism attenuated with elements of French realism, the 'mirror held up to life', and reworked to address a very different reality. In Italy it concerned itself particularly with rural life, often in the South, a topic that was also much discussed in the Rome-based journal *Rassegna settimanale*, edited by the conservative liberals Leopoldo Franchetti (1847–1917) and Sydney Sonnino (1847–1922) between 1878 and 1882. Although Italian writers shared with their French colleagues an ambition to be all-inclusive in their representations of contemporary life, both Giovanni Verga (1840–1922) and Federico De Roberto (1861–1927) stalled when they tried to write cycles of novels that would take in the full sweep of Italian society. While Verga has no problems with fashionable stories about conspicuous consumption, sex, poverty and art among the upper-middle classes in Milan, he was to find the *verista* depiction of Sicilian nobility so problematic that he ended up abandoning *La duchessa di Leyra* (*The Duchess of Leyra*), the third volume of his novel-cycle *I vinti* (*The Defeated*), which was to be about the nobility of Palermo.

Verismo had a significant impact on the development of the novel in Italy, more so than any other movement since the historical novel of the 1820s, but it was short-lived and by the end of the 1880s its moment had passed. Where the historical novel was influenced primarily by Scottish and English novels and reworked their aesthetics to accommodate an Italian reality, *verismo* looked to France. Its decisive moment came in 1878, when the Sicilian writer and journalist Luigi Capuana (1839–1915) joined his friend and fellow Sicilian Giovanni Verga in Milan, bringing with him Zola's just-published *L'Assommoir*, a novel that traces Gervaise Macquart's descent into alcoholism and the accompanying dissolution of a family in the slums of Paris. The book made a lasting impression on the two Italian writers. Zola's aesthetics had developed out of his fascination with the sciences and combined a commitment to empirical observation with evolutionary biology. In their own fiction Verga and Capuana would share the pessimism of naturalism, and its commitment to empirical observation, but not always the indebtedness to modern science. At the same time they were as different from each other in their work as it is possible to be.

Giovanni Verga was one of a group of Sicilian writers, which included Pirandello and, in the twentieth century, Sciascia, who wrote about the south while living at a distance on mainland Italy. It is a curious irony that until Unification the history of Italian writers is also a story of displacement (for some anti-Fascist writers it recurs in the form of 'internal exile' in the late 1920s and 1930s), and after that for many it takes the form of voluntary exile. Born into a wealthy family in Catania in 1840, Verga's literary life began in the salons of Florence during its brief period as artistic and political capital of Italy. In 1872 he settled in Milan, where he had a successful career writing fictions about femmes fatales, indigent artists and doomed affairs, which show the influence of his *scapigliati* friends. The turning point, precipitated by Zola's novel, is illustrated in a short story about a Sicilian fishing community that Verga published the following year, 1879. 'Fantasticheria' – shortly afterwards the opening story in Verga's first collection of Sicilian tales, *Vita dei campi* (*Life in the Fields*, 1880) – opens with a train journey in the company of the author and narrator of the tale and the addressee, his elegant travelling companion, a thinly disguised portrait of the contessa Paolina Greppa, whose literary salon in Florence was frequented by Verga. The community they encounter is utterly foreign to his uncomprehending friend (as she is to them) and the novelist tries in these few pages to explain in retrospect their 'religione della famiglia' ('religion of their family'; Verga 1987: 11) and their tenacious clinging, like molluscs, onto the rock face where they were born. On this occasion the narrator is a go-between, attempting the hopeless task of mediation between two worlds whose distance is emphasized by the fact that the only words the contessa speaks are in French.

For one of his rare statements of his poetics, one has to turn to the preface to another story, 'L'amante di Gramigna' ('Gramigna's lover', 1880), where Verga suggests that the work of art should appear '*essersi fatta da sè*, aver maturata ed esser sorta spontanea come un fatto naturale, senza serbare alcun punto di contatto col suo autore' ('*to have created itself*, to have grown spontaneously and come to fruition as though it were a part of nature, without preserving any point of contact with the author'; Verga 1987: 92). This is achieved by maximizing speech and minimizing any descriptive or third-person passages. Given that, unlike the case in other cultures with a realist tradition, the gap between written and spoken, regional language and Italian, was unbridgeable, the only way to achieve impersonality was to adopt free indirect speech and lend a collective voice to the community. This is the strategy which Verga adopts in his first 'Sicilian' novel, *I Malavoglia* (later translated as *The House by the Medlar Tree*, 1881). The seeing eye has now joined the community it speaks about. It is a brilliant paradox that Verga's writerliness creates a richly oral language on the page. The novel shows the hollowness of the myth of progress by telling the story of a family's decline brought about partly through natural disaster, partly by corruption and partly by usury. Where family values, hard work and honesty still reassert themselves in *I Malavoglia*, *Mastro-don Gesualdo* (1888), the second of what Verga intended should be a cycle of five novels, is far darker. A builder grows rich and marries into one of the many destitute aristocratic families, only to lose touch with the community he has left behind while being humiliated and falling victim to the scheming and snobberies of the milieu he thought he would be accepted into. Where *I Malavoglia* is a choral work, *Mastro-don Gesualdo* alternates scenes of isolation and solitariness with great collective set pieces. In both the novels and the collections of Sicilian tales, economic considerations and 'la roba' ('stuff', the accumulation of money and goods) remain paramount, but as D. H. Lawrence, Verga's first English translator, noted, the storytelling is epic, and within the weave particularly of the tales are fables, myths and legends. Verga's contemporaries enjoyed and appreciated most warmly his early fashionable writing; these later masterpieces of *verista* narrative only began to be appreciated after 1918 when, among others, fellow Sicilian Luigi Pirandello wrote in praise of them.

It was Federico De Roberto (though born in Naples, De Roberto was, like Verga and Capuana, brought up in Catania on the east coast of Sicily) who completed at least the first part of an epic narrative of the Sicilian aristocracy. The two-volume *I vicerè* (*The Viceroys*), which was published in Milan in 1894, follows the story of a rapacious and corrupt aristocratic dynasty, the Uzedas, descendants of the Spanish viceroys, who try to hold on to every aspect of their political and economic power during the succession of historical events which occurred between 1855 and 1894, from the Bourbons through Unification to a nascent democracy, assisted by the cowardice and connivance of the people. Its successor, *L'imperio* (*The Empire*), which follows the protagonist, Prince Consalvo, to Rome as a parliamentary deputy, remained unfinished. Such was the historical negativism, so strong the conviction that change for the better was a benighted illusion, and so wholeheartedly did De Roberto buy into scientific determinism that the narrative was left at a standstill.

In 1891 Matilde Serao published the definitive realist novel of Neapolitan life, *Il paese di cuccagna* (*The Land of Cockaygne*), which shows how for the poor and not so poor in Naples life revolves around the weekly lottery, while a year later Remigio Zena (1850–1917) published a realist novel located in the rabbit warren of dank, dark alleyways that made up the *bassifondi* around the port of Genoa. Milan was the location for Emilio De Marchi's (1851–1901) best-known novel, *Demetrio Pianelli* (1890), about an office worker in Milan who bravely tries to protect his widowed sister-in-law from her dead husband's former boss. Grazia Deledda published, after her move to Rome in 1900, a series of harsh, uncompromising novels about life in her native Sardinia, including *Elias Portolu* (1903), *Canne al vento* (*Reeds in the Wind*,

1913) and *L'edera* (*Ivy*, 1908). In a geography whose wildness D. H. Lawrence would compare to that of *Wuthering Heights*, her protagonists struggle with a corrosive guilt imbued with a strong sense of being in the grip of destiny. Pirandello was later to write a rather cruel *roman à clef* called *Suo marito* (*Her Husband*; the title was later changed to *Giustino Roncella nato Boggiòlo* (*Giustino Roncella Born Boggiòlo*)) satirizing the relationship between Deledda and her husband, who worked as her press agent in the period immediately after she had left Sardinia for a Rome where a new relationship was being forged between art, commerce and the press. Both Marchesa Colombi (1846–1920) and Matilde Serao adopted realism to write stunning denunciations of the exploitative conditions of women workers. Colombi's *In risaia* (*In the Rice Fields*, 1878) is a novella about women who work in the rice fields (it was these women workers of the Po valley, working up to their knees in water in extremes of heat and cold, who later took the first industrial action in Italy), while Serao wrote stories about women who worked in the telegraph service or as primary school teachers – work that they had, of course, to relinquish if they married.

Where the *verismo* of Verga, Serao, De Roberto and Deledda had a strong regional component, Luigi Capuana's descriptions of milieu were more markedly informed by naturalism's indebtedness to the medical sciences; the position adopted by the writer in regard to his subject matter is analogous to that of the surgeon – both engaged in the task of opening up, revealing and recording their subjects' entrails, The eponymous protagonist of *Giacinta* (1879), a novel dedicated to Zola, marries the man she loathes only to take the man she loves as her lover as a way of getting her own back on a society that rejected her because she was raped in childhood. Her life descends into madness and suicide. A later novel, *Il marchese di Roccaverdina* (*The Marquis of Roccaverdina*, 1901), focuses on the irrational violence of a Sicilian marquis who, after killing his mistress's husband in a fit of jealousy, is driven insane by guilt.

6.3 Domesticity and the literary market

The critical reception of Zola in Italy was a microcosm of the establishment's views of French culture and its influence on the Italian public in general. He was held in high esteem by literary critics and was a literary model for writers who later acquired a canonical status in Italy. But at the same time he was the scourge of clerics and commentators, who felt that he and alongside him many other French writers were a nefarious influence on susceptible readers, and he would corrupt women and the young and impressionable.

In her epistolary novel *Prima morire* (*Die First*, 1887), Marchesa Colombi explores the pressures that city life and the world of business and entrepreneurialism bring to bear on marriage and domesticity. It opens with a letter sent by Eva, the protagonist, to a friend together with a copy of Zola's *Une page d'amour* (*A Page of Love*), which she has out from her lending library. In the letter she argues in mock self-defence that the dishonesty of sharing a book borrowed on the one subscription is trivial alongside the condemnation she would receive from her priest if she confessed to having ever read such a novel in the first place.

While a post-Unification generation of writers brought rural life to the attention of a mainly northern, urban readership, closer to home a more attenuated realist fiction was developing that focused on domestic life and whose radicalism was to be found more in its choice of subject matter than its literary aesthetics. Middle-class women like the protagonist of Colombi's novel, with limited direct experience to draw on and who gained much of their knowledge of life from fiction, became themselves the focus of attention in a new tradition of fictional narrative that set out to address in the first instance a female readership. The rise in female literacy was one of the most marked and far-reaching of social trends in post-Unification Italy, although literacy rates remained significantly lower than in many other European countries. According to the national census taken in 1871, 76 per cent of women were illiterate, a figure which by 1881 had fallen to 69 per cent and by 1901 to 54 per cent. The press responded to the new opportunities this offered by becoming more sectorialized. The earliest publishing venture directed at a female market had been in 1822, when Giovanni Pirotto launched a 'Biblioteca amena ed istruttiva per le donne gentili' (a 'Pleasant and Instructive Library for Gentlewomen') specializing in translations of fashionable foreign novels. He failed, however, to recruit the 900 subscribers needed to make the enterprise economically viable, and so it folded.

Until the 1870s there was little for the adolescent girl to read. The novelist Neera, born in 1846, describes in her memoir *Una giovinezza del secolo XIX* (*A Youth Spent in the Nineteenth Century*, 1919) how, after finishing school at fourteen, she returned to her home in Milan, where she led a lonely life deprived of cultural activity. When asked in later years how she prepared for her future as writer, she would reply: 'calze e camicie, camicie e calze' ('stockings and shirts, shirts and stockings'). She read whatever she could find – St Augustine, Foscolo, some Balzac, Sterne's *Sentimental Journey*, even some Byron – claiming that she was fortunate in that, although her father was alarmed by her passion for books and urged her to desist at least from reading novels, he did not intervene or monitor her reading directly. The eponymous heroine of her best-known novel, *Teresa* (1886), on the other hand, is not depicted as so fortunate. She is not allowed into her father's meagre library, which is housed in his study and is out of bounds to the female members of the household with the exception of her mother, who is permitted to enter the room to dust it first thing in the morning. In the 1870s the rapid expansion of the print market and readership and the corresponding rise in the number and range of publications led to a more targeted press. Periodicals and *collane* (book series) intended specifically for women were accompanied by another new phenomenon: fiction written for, by and about women.

The 1870s saw the rise of a genre of domestic realism which was associated primarily with the names of three women writers and journalists, Neera (1846–1918), Marchesa Colombi (1846–1920) and Matilde Serao (1856–1927), who, unlike preceding generations, were not operating from the protected space of the salon, but as working professionals in a developing cultural market. Both Colombi and Serao were separated from their journalist husbands, Eugenio Torrelli Viollier and Edoardo Scarfoglio, and were bringing up children on their own; as a consequence, money but also social respectability were crucial. Their novels cover all aspects of domestic life from a female perspective, but whereas in England a few decades earlier there was a particular concern for the difficult life of the governess, here it was for the spinster (*zitella*), who often endured the same precarious status and economic deprivation. Neera's *Teresa* is a study of a young girl growing up in a small provincial town, her hopes finally dashed by the realization that the time for marriage has passed and she is destined to a life of spinsterhood caring for a father, a brother and, at the end of the book, in a fit of independence, the man she loved. Whatever their differences, the three men share an almost sublime disregard for anything other than their own welfare and creature comforts.

By making women the protagonists, and by deploying irony or the art of saying what you do not mean as a covert form of attack, Neera, Colombi and Serao led the way in creating a female subjectivity that had been absent in Italian literature. The relationship of the readership to these narratives is very different to that described in the *verista* fictions above. Here the reading public is often following stories about its own milieu, gender and social class, and in periodicals which either address a specifically female readership, as in Colombi's *Vita intima* (*Intimate Life*), or have sections which are concerned with matters that fall within a female ambit, such as Serao's newspaper columns. Their authors are also leading contributors to the growing field of conduct literature, advice columns, writings on pedagogy and health, so that they are embedded in a circuit of information directed at women. It is a period when the relationship between journalism and literary writing is so close as often to overlap.

Outside the home, theatre was one of the few public venues that middle-class women were permitted to frequent and where they could meet and talk among themselves or in mixed company. The transition from pre-Unification to post-Unification theatre had seen it move away from historical plays to contemporary domestic dramas which focused on the home, daily life and bourgeois values. Novelists including Verga and Capuana wrote for the theatre as a way of making some money out of literature, but the period of realist prose drama is associated primarily with playwrights including Marco Praga (1862–1929), Giuseppe Giacosa (1847–1906) and Achille Torelli (1844–1922), who, through plays that were often witty but also moralistic, contributed to the ongoing task of offering Italian role models and sturdy middle-class values for the new Italy.

The novels for a female readership, like the leading realist works, did not acquire large readerships, and we have to turn elsewhere to find the Italian bestsellers in Umbertine Italy (the name given to the period that coincides with the reign of King Umberto I, who remained on the Italian throne from 1883 until his assassination in 1900). On 21 May 1872 Antonio Fogazzaro delivered a lecture called 'Dell'avvenire del romanzo in Italia' ('On the future of the novel in Italy') at the Accademia Olimpica of his home town of Vicenza in northern Italy. There were still few widely read Italian novels beyond *I promessi sposi*, and Fogazzaro used the lecture to appeal to Italian writers not to dismiss the novel as 'letteratura leggera' ('light reading'; Fogazzaro 1983: 56) but to adopt it as a way to write about contemporary life, claiming that 'il posto del romanzo contemporaneo psicologico e sociale è vuoto' ('the place of the contemporary social and psychological novel is vacant'; Fogazzaro 1983: 56) in Italy. The lecture was a breath of fresh air in the often stultifying, moralistic debate that had been waged over the novel in Italy. It belongs to a tradition of liberal writing on the novel which can be traced back to the Risorgimento journalist and critic Carlo Tenca (1816–83), who called for writers to abandon rural, paternalistic writing in favour of novels that could act as 'lo specchio e l'anatomia dei corpi sociali' ('the mirror and anatomy of social bodies'), in an unattributed essay published in 1853 in the Milanese journal *Crepuscolo*. Other contributions include Ruggero Bonghi's fine book *Perchè la letteratura italiana non sia popolare in Italia* (*Why Italian Literature is not Popular in Italy*, 1855), where the future minister of education argued for a more accessible and approachable Italian. In some ways Fogazzaro's intervention can be seen as a natural successor to I. U. Tarchetti's 'Idee minime sul romanzo' ('Minimal ideas on the novel', 1865), for although Fogazzaro did not share the *scapigliato*'s anti-Manzonianism, he would not have disagreed with the need to reconcile the social marginalization of the writer with the social and ethical importance of the novel itself in modern times. The public, Fogazzaro suggests, is more educated than ever before, but readers of novels no longer have the classical knowledge of a traditional culture, and this means that novelists have to engage in a complex task of drawing together new and emerging fields of knowledge for a differently formed reading public.

'Dell'avvenire del romanzo in Italia' is also written from the point of view of the reader (nearly a decade was to pass before the publication of his own first novel *Malombra*), and Fogazzaro describes how the multifaceted, chameleon-like novel with its 'fascino irresistibile del divieto' ('irresistible fascination of the forbidden') has held him in thrall: 'Noi abbiamo divorato [quei romanzi] nelle notti insonni con ansia febbrile come se ci venisse incontro il soffio di quel mondo sconosciuto che indarno ci si dipingeva infido e pauroso' ('We used to devour [those novels] through sleepless nights with feverish anxiety as though we had been touched by the breath of that unknown world which in vain they had shown us as frightening and untrustworthy'; Fogazzaro 1983: 52). Where others might consider its social levelling dangerous, for Fogazzaro the novel's appeal lies in its inclusivity – it can be consumed both by the seamstress and by the lady of the house. Writing a novel is intellectually and artistically difficult precisely because the finished product must make it appear easy. Living in a practical and down-to-earth age, people none the less want to know more about themselves; they are possessed by the 'passione di ritrarsi e vedersi ritratti' ('passion for self-portrayal and seeing oneself portrayed'; Fogazzaro 1983: 64). In short, Fogazzaro's prescription for the novel was much like the one that Henry James was later to suggest – it must be interesting, it must be involving, and it must be original enough to catch the imagination.

Just under a decade later, the year 1881 seemed to be 'the year of the novel', with the publication of Verga's *I Malavoglia*, Fogazzaro's *Malombra*, Neera's *Il castigo* (*Punishment*), Serao's *Cuore infermo* (*Sick Heart*) and Oriani's *No*, to name only a few from that year's remarkable crop. It was also in the 1880s that writing for children (with more than half an eye to an adult readership) became a lucrative source of revenue. Carlo Collodi's *Le avventure di Pinocchio* (*The Adventures of Pinocchio*) was first published in instalments in a children's periodical before appearing as a book in 1883. The story, which straddles different genres, is about a rebellious wooden puppet who is caught up in all sorts of adventures until he finally learns how to behave, and only then is he transformed into a real little boy.

It was, however, Edmondo de Amicis's (1846–1908) *Cuore* (*Heart*, 1886) that was to top the polls in a piece of research conducted by the Bibliographical Society of Italy in 1906 into what they called *Libri più letti in Italia* (*The Most Read Books in Italy*); it had sold over 330,000 copies in twenty years (and later in 1923 was the first novel to reach over a million sales). To put this into perspective, D'Annunzio's *Il piacere* (*Pleasure*, 1889) registered 17,000 copies sold, and Verga's *I Malavoglia* 5,000. *Cuore*'s sales were helped by its patriotism and a pedagogical imperative that ensured that it was soon to become a compulsory school text across the nation. De Amicis had previously published a glowing collection of sketches of *La vita militare* (*Military Life*, 1868), which had provoked I. U. Tarchetti's powerful indictment of the introduction of compulsory military service in his novel *Una nobile follia*; De Amicis was also popular with his contemporary readership for his very fine travel writing.

While *Cuore* remains a popular if dutiful read today, Carlo Collodi's wooden puppet Pinocchio enjoys an almost iconic status and has been reproduced in every conceivable way. By the end of the nineteenth century children's literature was firmly established in Italy, but a new indigenous genre of adventure stories also developed which blurred the division between adult and childhood reading. Emilio Salgari (1862–1911), some of whose books continue to be widely read today, led the way with his novels, written for serialization, of adventures on the high seas and in tropical lands. His output was formidable; he was also a travel writer and edited a newspaper for children.

Antonio Fogazzaro's reputation has been built on *Piccolo mondo antico* (*Small World of Days Gone By*, 1895), a novel of provincial life in northern Italy in the 1850s with, at its centre, the marriage of its two middle-class protagonists, Luisa and Franco, after their daughter is drowned and they have to pick up the pieces of their shattered lives. Much of Fogazzaro's writing was informed by his own struggle as a practising Catholic to reconcile his religious and social beliefs in face of a church that had resolutely rejected the new state and any manifestation of liberalization. His bestselling *Il Santo* (*The Saint*) of 1905 with its honourable struggle to reconcile spirituality, Darwinism and science was, to his horror, put on the Index, the register of proscribed books, two years later. But recently it has been his first novel, *Malombra* (1881), that has enjoyed a resurgence of interest, in part because it is a singular example of an Italian novel of the period whose inspiration comes primarily from the English Victorian novel and the late gothic.

Fogazzaro's own interest in spiritualism has been traced back to 1869 and should be seen in part as an expression of his aversion to materialism and positivism. By turning to the supernatural and the gothic the point is made that realism can never give us the complete story.

The death of her father and the revelation of his parlous financial position mean that the beautiful young marchesina Marina di Malombra has no choice but to exchange the social whirl of Paris for the sombre *palazzo* overlooking a lake in northern Italy where her uncle on the maternal side, the count Cesare d'Ormengo, has offered her a home. Some months later, she discovers in a secret recess the relics of an ancestor, the 'infelice prigioniera' ('unhappy prisoner') Cecilia, her grandfather's first wife, who died some sixty years earlier after a long period of being isolated in the house by her jealous husband, who believed that she had deceived him. Marina soon becomes convinced that she is the reincarnation of Cecilia. Among the other guests at the *palazzo* is a young writer, Corrado Silla (author of one, unsold, novel, *Il sogno* (*The Dream*)), who Marina now believes is the reincarnation of Cecilia's lover. Gradually the *palazzo* acquires an uncanny aura as it becomes less and less part of the present and more and more part of the past. By the time the novel ends Malombra, now possessed with the spirit of her ancestor, kills the count by appearing before him as Cecilia and inducing in him a fatal stroke, and then shoots Corrado dead for refusing to accept that he is the reincarnation of her former lover. She then vanishes in her boat into the night.

The supernatural expresses itself in the novel through metempsychosis, whereby the spirit of Marina's dead ancestor Cecilia passes into her after the discovery of the relics. The plot is imbued with a strong sense of predestination, as if what happens is a playing out of what has already been decreed. This suggests that there is no living human agency behind the events and so absolves any one individual of responsibility, including the murderer herself, Marina. To borrow from Clara Reeve's formula for the gothic, *Malombra* has 'a sufficient degree of the marvellous to excite the attention; enough of the manners of real life, to give an air of probability to the work; and enough of the pathetic to engage the heart in its behalf' (Reeve 1999: 742). It was this recipe that also made it a successful film in 1917 with the diva Lydia Borelli playing the part of the fated Marina.

Women become increasingly aberrant in Italian literature – possessed as in the case of Malombra, sexually predatory and hysterical as in Tarchetti's Fosca, sick as in Capuana's Giacinta, rapacious as in the protagonist of Oriani's *Gelosia* (*Jealousy*). Women's susceptibility to music, to literature and to the theatre was initially seen as a cause of disorder and waywardness and ended as evidence of it, while medical and moral discourses permitted the representation of women as erotic and sadistic. Men by contrast become increasingly helpless or hopeless and the relationship between the sexes becomes one of predator (female) and prey (male).

PART III

From Modernism to the Market (1900 to the Present)

7

Modernism and the crisis of the literary subject

7.1 The search for identity

Throughout his life Gabriele d'Annunzio (1863–1938) did all he could to ensure that his life and his writing were so closely bound up that to know the one is to know the other. From his teens on D'Annunzio systematically set out to break down the divide between private (itself a far remove from the world of domestic realism) and public life. His flair as self-publicist first showed itself when as a 16-year-old schoolboy he sent a collection of poems, *Primo vere* (1879), to the press with a cover note under another name informing them of the tragic death of its young author; the volume received excellent coverage and reviews. His second volume, *Canto novo* (*New Song*, 1882), is an account of his seduction of the young daughter of a duke followed by kidnapping and shortly afterwards, against her father's wishes, marriage. She was abandoned a few years later, the first in the long line of women who contributed to the creation of a scandalous private life. The story of the seduction followed by a collection of erotic poetry cleverly exploits the running together of fact and fiction that the presence of the first person encourages. But D'Annunzio's main poetic achievement was *Alcyone*, one of the three volumes that were published of the ambitious and unfinished seven-volume cycle of *Laudi* (*Praises*) which appeared in 1904. Of the other two volumes, *Elettra* (*Electra*) is imperialistic and anti-democratic, and *Maia* exalts the aggression of the ruling class in its capacity both to dominate the masses and to drive forward technological progress; *Alcyone*, however, though it shares the same ideology, focuses on nature and landscape and bypasses the historical. Put at its simplest it is the story of summer; described by one critic as 'a lyrical diary of a summer by the sea', the collection has a marked mythological dimension. The poems focus on a relationship between the protagonist and the elements that is of such intensity that the human subject and the landscape fuse together in a process of continuous metamorphosis. In a poem such as the superb 'La pioggia nel pineto' ('Rain in the pine forest'), where the poet and his lover, the actress Eleonora Duse, walk through the woods, a very delicate balance between signifier and signified is sustained with a musicality typical of the finest of decadent writing. Where in naturalism identity is fixed and things are what they seem to be, here the opposite occurs and the poem is orchestrated around the dissolving of self. By breaking up traditional syntax the poet creates an endless play on sound.

Between 1889 and 1910 D'Annunzio was to publish seven novels, of which the first, *Il piacere* (*Child of Pleasure*, 1889), remains the best-known. Here the regional realism of his tales of the Abruzzi, *Novelle della Pescara* (1902), and the best of his work for the theatre, *La figlia di Iorio* (*Iorio's Daughter*, 1903), is left behind. The novels share with the poetry a love for incantatory, unusual language, a 'poetica della parola' ('poetics of the word') whose celebration of art for art's sake will ultimately lead nowhere. While Umbertine Italy under 'left' governments led by Agostino Depretis and then Francesco Crispi had been slowly democratizing itself in the 1880s and 1890s – male suffrage was trebled in 1882, for example, although it still only reached two million – the novels' elitism expressed itself in a hatred of mediocrity, a sadistic eroticism and an exotic cult of beauty. In the decadent novel *Il piacere* (1889), the adoption of a first-person narrative perspective ensures slippage between the amoral and narcissistic protagonist Andrea Sperelli and the author. A poet and connoisseur of beauty, Sperelli operates against the furnishings, fabrics and fittings of a Roman aristocracy that Verga was unable in the end to write about. In 1904 D'Annunzio published *Il fuoco* (*Fire*), the barely fictionalized account of his eight-year affair with Eleonora Duse, the greatest Italian actress of the nineteenth century. When Italy entered the war in 1915 the now 52-year-old D'Annunzio, ardently in favour of Italy's intervention, achieved the rare feat of joining all three of the armed services and went on to fight his own war when, disgusted by the terms of the armistice in 1919, he led a contingent of men to capture Fiume (now Rijeka in Croatia) and occupied it until 1921. In the same year he retreated to Lake Garda, where he lived on until his death in 1938. Faithful to his interpretation of the Nietzschean superman, he created a grandiose residence to which he gave the patriotic name *Vittoriale degli italiani*, a home that was also a monument to his life (and to kitsch) and a shrine to his name. It remains one of the places in Italy most visited by Italians.

It was the Sicilian writer and leading critic of the day Giuseppe Antonio Borgese (1882–1952), whose own underrated novel *Rubé* (1921) presents the ideological climate of the lower-middle classes in the period between the end of the First World War and the rise of Fascism, who pointed to the change in mood when he used the collective term 'crepuscolari' to identify a group of some six poets, among whom were Guido Gozzano (1883–1916) and Sergio Corazzini (1886–1907), both of whose short lives were lived in the shadow of tuberculosis. The *crepuscolari* were not a movement, they had no journal and they did not operate as a school. What immediately strikes one, on the contrary, is their negation of the role or persona of the poet as being either a voice speaking for the nation or a solitary genius. With the figure of the poet cut down to size, it is not surprising that Gozzano expressed few illusions about poetry. His point that literature has an inbuilt obsolescence – 'i versi invecchiano prima di noi' ('verses grow old before we do') – is a radical departure from the profoundly Romantic view that poetry speaks across time and culture. The epithet *crepuscolare,* with its reference to twilight and gloaming, picks up instead on the tone of their poetry – off-centre, minor, modest (one critic unkindly referred to it as a poetry of 'vegetables and vacillating lovers'), but in an ironic, tongue-in-cheek key. Their subject matter is *noia*, mundanity, the tedium of life; their poetics, in keeping with this, is prosaic without being prose, anti-rhetorical and discursive. Their poetry and their self-representation as poets are deliberately and provocatively set up in opposition to D'Annunzio's ornate, grandiloquent decadence but equally against Pascoli's anti-historicism and humility. Where D'Annunzio's city is Rome, rich, decadent and aristocratic, Gozzano's is industrious, provincial, unshowy Turin. Similarly, where D'Annunzio's retreat from Rome is the *Vittoriale degli italiani*, for Gozzano it is the *Melèto*, a house which takes its name from its apple-orchard, private, modest, filled with the clutter of ornaments and knick-knacks of fifty years earlier (and he did grow vegetables in the garden). Gozzano, who believed it was disastrous not to be able to separate life from art, once wrote in an article that he felt that D'Annunzio was fatally intoxicated with the 'tabe letteraria', the disease of literature.

Gozzano thought of his poetry as being concerned with the 'vita piccola e borghese' ('modest bourgeois life') and it is in keeping with the climate of his day – imperialism's moment has passed, the invasion of Libya is yet to come, the first stage in the industrialization of the country is over, but Italy has serious social and economic problems to face up to. Gozzano's verse often turns to the past, evoked through an object such as a photograph album whose images reconstruct a world that has gone. Clutter, much of it kitsch, the 'buone cose di pessimo gusto' ('good things in terrible taste'; Gozzano 1981: 99), has an important place in his poetry; it is through the concatenation of objects linked by half-rhyme and internal rhyme and always with a self-conscious mockery that the past is brought back.. His poetry is peopled by women: energetic and independent young women, but also often celibate aunt figures. In a letter he wrote on 5 June 1907 to his lover, the poet, novelist and feminist Amalia Guglielminetti (1881–1941), whose own personal life too often overshadowed her artistic one, he picked up on the figure of the 'spinster' (*zitella*) whose circumstances had been such a subject of concern in women's writing of the 1870s and 1880s, complaining that 'signorina' was a 'nome brutto' (an 'ugly name'; Gozzano 1987: 100), a bourgeois version of the earlier 'virgin'. In one of his best-known poems, 'La signorina Felicita, ovvero la felicità' ('Miss Felicita, or felicity'), he wrote that in his protagonist he wanted to idealize a figure that is 'oppressa, ambigua, derisa, spesso' ('oppressed, ambiguous and often derided'; Gozzano 1983: 187), the figure precisely of the 'spinster'.

With the opening up of the intimate space of the home, everybody from doctors and scientists to lawyers, politicians, clerics and educationalists seemed to want to have their say on family life in the late nineteenth century. But the most remarkable account of a girl's coming of age, marriage and motherhood, and a *cause célèbre* in its day, was to appear early in the twentieth century. *Una donna* (*A Woman*, 1906) is an autobiographical novel written after its author had fled to Rome leaving behind a despised husband and oppressive home-life, but also her much-loved young son. Without ever claiming to be an autobiography – indeed, the book's subtitle is 'Un romanzo' – Sibilla Aleramo's *Una donna* played on the confusion between the first-person voice of the narrator and the empirical writer much as Gabriele D'Annunzio had done.

In first-person narration, with no narrator writing from outside the story frame, the real author can exploit the pretence that there is only the protagonist's point of view to go on, and build into the narrative gaps born of ignorance, blind spots, occlusions and misunderstandings which the reader may then either share or choose to interpret independently of the narrator. This is not to suggest that only first-person narratives are capable of representing an individual psyche. Realist fiction is also about psychology and the establishing of character, and the narrator has the technical means to enter a character's mind at will: free indirect speech and stream of consciousness are just two of the vehicles available. But in the interests of verisimilitude, readers of third-person narrative need to feel that the character conforms to a recognizable type. First-person narrative offers the reader other possibilities. Sibilla Aleramo's own literary career was a continuing experiment in self-representation through poetry, letters, journalism, diaries, the first-person novel, the epistolary novel and the literary fragment.

The claustrophobia first felt by the protagonist when she moves with her family south to a small town on the Adriatic near Ancona, and which later becomes all the more suffocating after her marriage, is reinforced stylistically by the total omission of proper names – all the characters are presented in terms of their relation to the protagonist (my father, mother, son, husband, mother-in-law) or, very occasionally, in terms of their profession (doctor, bookkeeper etc.). The protagonist never introduces herself by name, nor is she addressed by name, so that the main marker of an individual identity is missing. Even the empirical author's name, Sibilla Aleramo, is a pseudonym (her name by birth was Rina Faccio), proprietorially created by fellow poet and lover Giovanni Cena, as he reminds us in a sonnet from *Homo* (1909): 'io la scopersi e la chiamai Sibilla' ('I discovered her and called her Sibilla'). This (auto)biography without names stands in marked contrast with a writer we shall come to shortly, Luigi Pirandello, where the proper name is the one certainty his protagonists have in an otherwise ontological mess. The title of *Una donna* suggests any and every woman, and although the heroine's exceptionality makes her an exemplary figure, the circumstances that make the novel a *roman à thèse*, a work of social protest, are ones with which many of her female readers would identify.

The protagonist's story, in all but the ending, runs parallel to the author's own past. The family moved in 1884 when her father became technical director of a glass factory belonging to a wealthy Milanese family. The place had been chosen as a site for the factory because cheap labour and primary materials were available locally. As recompense for taking her out of school (she was fourteen and there was no further schooling available for her in the Marche) her father gave her a job as clerk and bookkeeper in the factory. Her parents' marriage disintegrated under the burden of her father's persistent infidelities and in 1892, when she was fifteen, the protagonist herself was raped by a fellow worker, whom a year later she married. Her mother's mental and physical health steadily deteriorated and eventually she was interned in a mental asylum. After a miscarriage associated with her distress at her mother's state of mind, the heroine gave birth to a son in 1895. Her husband lost his job in the factory and for a period they lived in Milan, where she earned a living as journalist. After an unhappy period back in the Marche, the discovery of a letter by her mother firmed up her resolve to leave her husband and therefore her son and move to Rome. In the embedded narrative that is dedicated to her mother's life the author traces the processes whereby a woman is trapped by motherhood, and her own story becomes an example of how the pattern of self-sacrifice is handed down from mother to daughter. The protagonist presents her relationship with her young son as one of mutual love and understanding, but into this she injects the argument that it is these self-same bonds that become the source of the woman's own oppression. The last section is taken up with her heartwrenching decision to leave the marital home in the knowledge that under Italian law – the Pisanelli code introduced in the wake of Italian Unification – she has no legal entitlement to her child, so that her departure means that she is leaving her son to his father. Her decision is her response to the example set by her mother's life, and underpinning it is her conviction that women, trapped by maternity, simply transmit to the next generation those very structures that have been the source of their own oppression.

The ending of *Una donna*, with the protagonist's journey north and her definitive rupture with her young son, draws together two of the narrative skeins: autobiographical fiction and the narrative as *roman à thèse*. A part of the novel's strength rests in the way it challenges the criticism that writing by women is too caught up in the private and the domestic, by offering a compelling example of the inseparability of the two realms, the private and the public. *Una donna* was a new departure in writing by women. Mixing autobiography and manifesto, the author created a self-portrait that was without precedent in Italy. It drew on the tenets of autobiography which emerged in the late Middle Ages and early Renaissance, where the concept of selfhood promoted the individual over the collective. It encouraged a sense of separateness, of individual and public achievement, in short a quintessentially masculine self, and accommodated this to the conditions of a woman's life. By choosing the first person Aleramo invited her readers to link author and subject; she put herself to some extent on trial and challenged her public to take a long, hard look at the legal subordination of women.

Among those who disliked Gabriele D'Annunzio and all he stood for was Luigi Pirandello, who in a book review of *Le vergini delle rocce* (*The Virgins of the Rocks*, 1895) noted acidly that such was D'Annunzio's carelessness that he even misremembered his protagonist's name. Pirandello was born in 1867 in the hamlet of Kaos, not far from Agrigento (formerly Girgenti) in Sicily, and died in 1936. He was the author of over 200 short stories known collectively as *Novelle per un anno*, several volumes of poetry, seven novels, forty-four plays, essays including an important treatise on humour and aesthetics, *L'umorismo* (*Humour*, 1908), film scripts and articles. The breadth of his literary interests is remarkable; not only did he write for the stage, he also set up his own theatre company. His thoughts on the moving image and his experiences of scriptwriting gave rise to *Si gira!* (*Shoot!*, 1915; later retitled *Quaderni di Serafino Gubbio* (*The Notebooks of Serafino Gubbio*)). This novel was the first to take cinema as its subject, and features in Walter Benjamin's groundbreaking essay 'The Work of Art in the Age of Mechanical Reproduction'

(Benjamin 1973). Although Pirandello's international reputation comes in large part from his work as a dramatist, he saw himself as a novelist whose move into theatre was intended to be temporary.

Although better known outside Italy as a playwright, he was also a distinguished novelist. His works include *L'esclusa* (*The Outcast*), a novel which turns on its head the classic late-nineteenth-century European tale of adultery where the guilty heroine either dies by her own hand or sees her child suffer horribly. It helps explain why this otherwise conservative writer on matters sexual wrote in Sibilla Aleramo's defence after she left her husband and child.

In 1904 he began work on what was to be one of the great European modernist novels, *Il fu Mattia Pascal* (*The Late Mattia Pascal*), working under very difficult circumstances, for the flooding of the family's sulphur mines and the consequent loss of his wife's dowry had left the family without any income other than his own earnings. He and his wife had moved to Rome after their marriage, but after the birth of their three children, Antonietta's mental health deteriorated rapidly, and she fell victim to an acute paranoid jealousy that would later lead her to believe that there was an incestuous relationship between one of her daughters and her husband, and that attempts were being made to poison her. In 1918 she was confined in a private asylum outside Rome, where she died in the 1950s. The impact of this tragic experience on Pirandello's writing was to be profound.

Given the pressures he was up against it is unsurprising that *Il fu Mattia Pascal* begins with an escapist fantasy which sees the hapless protagonist walk out of an unhappy marriage, win a small fortune at the roulette table in San Remo, return home only to discover that his wife has conveniently identified the corpse of a drowned man as being his, and promptly leaves again to start a new life under an assumed identity. The fantasy, though, proves unrealizable, and after a feigned suicide Mattia returns home. On learning that his wife has remarried, he takes up residence on the outskirts of the community, where he spends his days as a librarian in a deconsecrated church. It is here that he writes the memoirs that make up the book. The narrative mixes realism and the picaresque, the fantastic and the comic. The adoption of a first-person perspective allows the protagonist to tell his life-story from his own viewpoint uncontested by others. It is a privilege that some of the characters in his plays would dearly like to share.

The germ of Pirandello's most famous play, *Sei personaggi in cerca d'autore* (*Six Characters in Search of an Author*, 1921: extensively revised in 1925), can be found in a letter he wrote to his son in 1917 where we learn that his intention had been to write a novel. Unable to make progress with the project, he tried to put it to one side, but the group of characters at the centre of the story had so completely taken hold of his mind and imagination that he could not escape them. To release himself from their hold, he devises a strategy whereby they are let loose on the stage, where they try to persuade the theatre company to adopt them and the story they have to tell. The Characters make up an extended family dominated by a Father and his Stepdaughter, who is the eldest of three children of his former wife's new family. The Mother is also present. Each of the Characters is fixed in a single familial role by which she or he is known; they have no other name or role. When they invade the stage where a theatre director and his company are involved in a lacklustre rehearsal of another of Pirandello's plays, *Il giuoco delle parti* (*The Rules of the Game*, 1919), they try to persuade the company to abandon the script they are working with and replace it with their own story. In a powerful mix of tragedy and melodrama whose motors are poverty, sex and perversity, they re-enact the story of the Mother, who, driven by poverty, becomes a seamstress in the establishment of a certain Madama Pace. What she does not know is that her employer has also taken on her schoolgirl daughter as a prostitute to compensate for her substandard needlework, until, that is, the dramatic occasion when she bursts into a room where her daughter is about to have sex with a man the woman recognizes as her former husband and her daughter's stepfather.

Sei personaggi in cerca d'autore was the first of a trilogy of plays within a play and was followed by *Ciascuno a suo modo* (*Each in His Own Way*, 1924) and *Questa sera si recita a soggetto* (*Tonight We Improvise*, 1929), which between them explore every aspect of the theatrical event. Pirandello proceeds by identifying the point of tension and applying pressure until it explodes into conflict. In the first play of the trilogy, there is a three-way conflict (between actors, characters and director), as there is in the second, except that here the tension is between the audience, the actors and the playwright. In the third, the director is in conflict with everybody. Despite these structural overlaps, each play is self-contained, with its own 'characters, circumstances and passions', as Pirandello wrote shortly before his death ('Premessa', in Pirandello 1936: 1). Contributing to Pirandello's experimental approach to the stage as physical space and performance were his formative experiences as director of his own theatre company, the Teatro d'Arte, which he established in 1924 with financial help from the Fascist Party. It survived until 1928 and during that time was often innovatory in the plays it chose, premiering some twenty-four new ones, and in introducing radical new lighting techniques and striking sets.

The idealist philosopher and critic Benedetto Croce (1866–1952), who held to the conviction that reflection damages the spontaneity of creative intuition and the imagination, was severe on Pirandello, whose writing he described as being 'taluni spunti artistici, soffocati o sfigurati da un convulso inconcludente filosofare' ('some artistic bursts, suffocated or disfigured by a fitful and inconclusive philosophizing'; Croce 1974: 362). Pirandello had indeed classed himself in the preface to *Sei personaggi* as belonging to the category of 'scrittori più propriamente filosofici' ('writers who are more properly philosophical'), even though at the same time each character carries their own specificity and their own story, and the experiences which they depict are unique to them in all their extraordinariness. In other plays, key themes take on different configurations. Identity, for example, is explored in *Così è (se vi pare)* (*Right You Are (If You Think You Are)*, 1917) through the persistent, inquisitorial grilling a family of three is subject to when they arrive in a new town after their home town has been razed by an earthquake. The well-heeled, complacent circle they meet is ready with its sympathy, but as soon as the citizens realize that there is a mystery at the heart of the family that gentle probing will not prise open, the questioning descends into an interrogation and the drawing room into what the critic Giovanni Macchia described (1981: 107) as a 'torture-chamber'. The protagonist of *Enrico IV* (*Henry IV*, 1922) is an anonymous aristocrat of the present day who, while participating in a cavalcade some years earlier in the role of the German emperor, had fallen from his horse. He had come round with the certainty that he was the man whose role he had been playing and with no memory of his 'true' identity. The stage set is made up of the carefully created court of the eleventh-century emperor, the carers and companions dressed in the costume of the day. The title Pirandello gave to his collection of plays, *Maschere nude* (*Naked Masks*), refers to the masks we don to confer on ourselves an identity in the eyes of others; the disturbing part of the title is contained in the adjective, with the implication that far from there being a true, authentic self concealed behind the mask, there is nothing. We are the masks we wear.

7.2 War, technology and the arts

Technology had a very significant impact on daily life between 1880 and 1910. Gas and then electricity brought lighting to some homes and streets, and the invention of the telephone meant that the human voice could be 'moved' from one place to another without the body accompanying it.

Gramophones and wirelesses were likewise to bring the disembodied voices of strangers into the home. The year 1895 marked the arrival of the first silent cinema followed in 1927 by the 'talkies'. Daily urban living became more tolerable and often healthier, with sewers, running water and public transport. Cars appeared – Giovanni Cena's *Gli ammonitori* (*The Forewarners*, 1903) was the first novel to be published in Italy which involved a death (a suicide) under the wheels of a car. The growth of the middle class led to increased consumption, while at the same time eight million Italians, mainly from the south, left the country as economic migrants in search of work elsewhere. New technologies and new patterns of communication combined with a rejection of the past and its values gave rise to Italy's avant-garde movement, Futurism, which was to be active between 1909 and 1940 but whose heyday was over by 1925.

In keeping with the Futurist imperative to deprovincialize, the 'Fondazione e manifesto del Futurismo' ('The Founding and Manifesto of Futurism') which launched the movement in 1909 first appeared in *Le Figaro* in Paris, then in London in the *Daily Mail*, and only afterwards in Italy's Futurist capital, Milan. At the helm was the 32-year-old Filippo Tommaso Marinetti (1876–1944), born like the poet Giuseppe Ungaretti (1888–1970) in Alexandria in Egypt, a city which at the time had a large Italian community. The family later moved to Europe and Marinetti was educated in Paris and Genoa. The founding manifesto is a celebration of the city – modern, industrial, mechanized, with its electric light ('let us kill the moonlight'), cars, factories, smoke, metal – the city is relished with sexual passion as a living, pulsating being. The world in which 'i miei amici ed io' ('my friends and I'; Hulten 1986: 311) live is simultaneously animal and mechanical; machines are 'belve sbuffanti' ('snorting beasts'), the driver is a 'leone' ('lion'), the car becomes a shark and people machines. There is no room for the single individual, for feelings, rationality or humanity. People are crowds, feeling is sexual energy, the only reason is unreason.

From this dramatic beginning Futurism attracted a group of young artists, painters, sculptors, musicians, architects and writers who, with an unrelenting barrage of manifestos, public meetings, events and exhibitions, maintained a constant assault on the public. They used all possible means of communication available to them to maximize their impact, conducting themselves at times like a commando group or an extremist political party. The manifesto itself was a form of urban advertising, which could be printed in newspapers in an eye-catching layout, but also plastered on walls in the streets. They staged outrageous events, including the celebrated Futurist evenings ('serate futuriste') at which the audience was likely to be harangued, get caught in the crossfire between performers and hecklers, or find themselves glued to their seats (literally). In artistic terms the Futurists' prime target was representational realism, whether it be the conventions of three-dimensional painting and mimetic representation in art or those of discursive narrative bound by the laws of syntax in writing.

Two manifestos on painting rapidly followed the founding manifesto. In 1910 Umberto Boccioni, Carlo Carrà, Gino Severini and Luigi Russolo published the 'Manifesto dei Pittori futuristi' ('Manifesto of Futurist Painters'), followed a few months later by the 'technical' manifesto 'La pittura futurista' ('Futurist Painting'), and in 1914 Antonio Sant'Elia produced a manifesto for 'L'architettura futurista' ('Futurist Architecture'). In response to the rapid expansion of towns (Milan's population had doubled between 1881 and 1914), Sant'Elia designed multilayered structures intended for high-density living with walkways, railways and even aircraft landing strips in the heart of the city. In these futuristic cityscapes, there was no place for nature. The Futurists caught the dynamism, the kaleidoscope of modern, urban perception on their canvases, while in writing a predilection for nouns and verbs in the infinitive to denote action and immediacy led to experiments with 'words in freedom' and the 'wire-less imagination'. Syntax, punctuation, adjectives were all perceived as slowing down the action and therefore to be jettisoned. Poetry became an 'uninterrupted sequence of new images', but the visual appearance of the word on the page, exploiting new printing techniques to the maximum, breaks through the barriers of traditional printed literature to achieve a multimedia effect.

One of the most significant aspects of the writing was the desire to destroy the 'io' (selfhood) and with it all moves in the direction of psychological representation of character. Rubbing down the boundaries between art and life, there were few areas of cultural life in the broadest sense which the Futurists left untouched, and thus they left their mark, at least temporarily, on practices as diverse as fashion (when it appeared in 1914 that Italy would not be intervening in the war, they demonstrated in pro-interventionist uniforms designed by themselves) and cuisine (the doyenne of fine cooking in the mid-twentieth century, Elizabeth David, included several of the more feasible recipes from the Futurist cookbook in her own publications).

In the narrower context of literature and art, Futurism was the first avant-garde movement of the twentieth century to move with ease, and to encourage such movement, between genres and media, and in that it set a pattern for other avant-gardes to come. Marinetti published an infamous novel, *Mafarka le futuriste* (*Mafarka the Futurist*), in 1909. They made films, all of which were sadly destroyed in a fire. The painter Luigi Russolo recycled himself as a musician, or rather a noise-artist, with his elaborate stage contraptions known as 'noise-intoners'. Artists, poets and musicians also exhibited and performed throughout Europe and established contacts with artistic and literary circles in Paris, Brussels, London, Munich and Amsterdam. Futurism never intended itself to be seen as a school, but rather as a global experience transcending divisions between life, art, culture and politics. It wanted nothing less than to 'change life'; its call was for complete and violent renewal. Its founders wanted to break down the divisions between life and art, and to take their work into the infrastructures of the city itself – the music hall, the cinema and above all the streets.

Its militaristic rhetoric, its ideology which linked virility with violence, its celebration, in an extreme form of social Darwinism which events would prove was no joke, of war as 'the hygiene of the world' – all of these might suggest that this movement would hold little for women. But while the vanguard, the 'io e i miei amici' of the founding manifesto, was male, the forms of artistic expression and the anti-bourgeois, anti-Catholic message drew women writers and poets from all over Italy. This convergence gave rise at times to works that were deeply ambiguous, as in the case of Valentine de Saint-Point, whose manifesto on lust, 'Manifesto futurista della lussuria' (1913), presented rape as a natural and spontaneous part of the regeneration that follows a bloody battle or war. The document is a sharp reminder, if one is needed, of the murkiness of Futurist sexual politics.

The history of the Italian Futurist movement is closely bound up with war. The Libyan war of 1911 saw Marinetti celebrate the battle of Tripoli with 'Guerra sola igiene del mondo e sola morale educatrice' ('War the only hygiene of the world and the only morality that educates'), and one can still hear a 1935 recording of his radio performance of the long poem 'Zang Tumb Tumb' (1914) about the siege of Adrianopolis (in the Balkans). During Italy's period of neutrality at the start of the First World War, the Futurists were vociferously pro-interventionist, and were eager volunteers as soon as the fighting started. Marinetti was wounded and two of the leading figures, Boccioni and Sant'Elia, were killed during the hostilities. After the war a short-lived Futurist Political Party which was closely aligned to Mussolini's Fascist Party came into existence, and one can see how Futurist manifestos prefigured the Fascists with their nationalistic, militaristic and colonialist rhetoric. Marinetti and Mussolini stood on the Fascist-led list for Milan in the general elections of 1919 and both were soundly defeated. Marinetti and Futurism enjoyed a sometimes close relationship with Mussolinian Fascism, drawing away when Fascism became less radical in the early 1920s. Later

Marinetti was to dissociate himself entirely from the anti-Semitic legislation introduced in the late 1930s.

When Italy entered the war on the side of England and France on 23 May 1915, polls taken earlier in the month suggested that most Italians were against intervention, but strong pressure to enter came from politicians, political groupings of the left other than the Socialist Party, the right, and also much of the intelligentsia. The left saw intervention as a way of creating the right conditions for a socialist revolution while prominent figures on the right like Vilfredo Pareto, one of the founding fathers of sociology, saw it as a way of setting the socialist cause back half a century For others it was seen as a way of 'completing' Italy's own recent history: 'the fourth war of Independence' or 'the last battle of the Risorgimento'. *Lacerba*, the once avant-garde magazine, came out in favour of intervention on 15 August 1914 with an issue where the typeface was changed from black to red. It was clear from the editorial that the editors' decision had been guided by their awareness that, whereas during the Risorgimento the writer might have had a civic role as a spokesperson, culture now had little or no impact on the nation. There were different ways of responding to the marginalization of the writer, as we have seen in the case of both D'Annunzio and the Futurists, who saw war as a way of breaking through the barrier between 'life' and 'art'.

The poets Giuseppe Ungaretti and Umberto Saba (1883–1957) supported the war by enlisting as volunteers, and where they could have joined the officer rank they opted instead to be 'soldati semplici' ('common soldiers'). The horror of it all was no less terrible for Italians than it was for any other nation, but it did not produce so much a poetry of war as a poetry where the horror of war speaks to the poet's own condition. Ungaretti, an anarchist when he enlisted, on being asked later about how he reconciled politics and war said that at the time he was convinced that victory would mean victory for the people – the slogan 'guerra o rivoluzione' ('war or revolution') would become 'guerra e rivoluzione' ('war and revolution'). Ungaretti fought the war on what was to be one of the most terrible fronts in Europe – along the river Isonzo on a bare, waterless, limestone escarpment called the Carso where, as in France and Belgium, an entire generation was wiped out. In the first seven months alone 6,000 men were killed and 190,000 wounded.

As a child in Alexandria, Ungaretti had grown up on the edge of the city where town and desert meet, and later he was to claim that the desert landscape and the Bedouin songs that he heard were an important influence on his poetics. The harsh, direct way in which the songs evoke reality contributed to his own 'poetica della parola' ('poetics of the word') the 'parola gridata' ('shouted word'), while the Bedouins reinforced his own sense of being nomadic, rootless, belonging nowhere. Alexandria itself was a city that was constantly being eaten into by the desert, a city without monuments. This sense of a landscape without defining features, of a poetry that is all sound and no colour, of the awareness that everything crumbles and yields to the onslaught of time, is at the heart of Ungaretti's poetry.

He had spent several years in Paris, a meeting place for the avant-garde, where he became a good friend of the poet Guillaume Apollinaire, among other French writers, and where the first Futurist exhibition was held in 1912. The collection of his war poetry, *L'Allegria* (*Joy*), was referred to by him in his 1931 preface as a 'diary'; it was composed initially of thirty-three poems, each one carefully dated, written in a period of ten months. The title refers to a kind of mirthless joy, an appetite for life that is all the stronger because of the proximity to death. These poems jotted down in the trenches were new and direct; they set out to illuminate the single moment. Ungaretti's language isolates elemental words like 'sasso' ('stone'), 'acqua' ('water') or 'sole' ('sun') so that the historical specificity of the events is extracted from the poetic discourse and carried by the dates of the diary entries. Like the Futurists he suppresses the connections between the words and the feelings, creating brief, terse poems (in his most famous, 'Mattina'('Morning'), just four words), but more marked are the influences of Rimbaud's *Une saison en enfer* (*A Season in Hell*) and Mallarmé's poetics. The impact of the word is heightened by the visual effect of the layout on the page, where the amount of blank paper in relation to words communicates silence and frames off the spoken. It is far more important than punctuation. His poetry of this period marks out something quite new in Italian work.

Umberto Saba, who on enlisting was given a clerical post, never wrote war poetry because he felt that it was wrong to write literature or poetry about a tragedy of such proportions; it was a position that he later shared in relation to the Second World War with Eugenio Montale (1896–1981) and Salvatore Quasimodo (1901–68). In 1914 Trieste was still under Austro-Hungarian rule and it was a cruel irony that the Italy Saba identified with and fought for was later to persecute him; the Fascist anti-Semitic legislation introduced in 1938 resulted in his having to hand over his antiquarian bookshop to his assistant. He took refuge in Paris but he was unhappy there and moved to Rome, where Ungaretti, who had first met him in Paris, was able to help him find some protection. After the Nazi occupation of northern and central Italy in 1943 he went into hiding in Florence, where friends, including Montale, helped him.

An outsider like his fellow Triestine Italo Svevo (see below, sec. 7.3), Saba was what he called 'un periferico' ('marginal'), someone on the edges of the

Italian literary establishment. Just as Trieste, referred to by Italians according to Saba as 'laggiù' ('out there'), formed the cityscape of Svevo's novels, so it was to be the protagonist of much of Saba's poetry, in particular the *città vecchia* which, with its narrow, untidy, cobblestone streets and alleyways, had a very Italian feel to it. Montale later described Trieste as a 'città di traffico ma anche città d'anime, città simbolica non meno della Praga di Kafka e della Dublino joyciana' ('a city of trade, but also a city of souls, a city no less symbolic than Kafka's Prague and Joyce's Dublin') (Montale 1996b: II, 2505). But far from the frightening, alienating city of modernism, this was where one could be a human being among other human beings, where one could live 'la vita / di tutti' ('the life / of all'), where the poet could be 'come tutti / gli uomini di tutti / i giorni' ('like all / men all / days'). For Saba the loss of privilege as a poet is liberating. The language he uses is ordinary, if not banal; rather than the single climactic moment, it was the overall effect that he aimed for; he insisted that popular language is no less resonant than literary language and where he uses metaphor and analogy it is as discursive as possible. In 'Meditazione' he summed up his strengths in these lines: 'però che in questo è tutta / la mia forza: guardare ed ascoltare' (Saba 1988: 37; 'for in this is all / my strength: to watch and to listen'). Lines that are not perhaps as modest as they sound, for they are an adaptation of Nietzsche, taken from his *Gay Science*: 'superior beings distinguish themselves from the inferior [. . .] because they look and listen contemplatively'.

Through the collection called *Il Canzoniere* (*The Songbook*), first published in 1919 and added to until the definitive edition appeared in 1961, Saba tried to give a meaning to existence, and the poems themselves interrelate through a web of echoes and recalls, moving from poetry of youth and adolescence through to old age. Poetry was for Saba, like prose for Svevo, a kind of personal therapy which could be achieved if the writer were absolutely honest with herself or himself. In his poetry the 'malessere' ('malaise') which is a constant of modern poetry is neither metaphysical nor spiritual but rather psychological. As this all suggests, he was an assiduously autobiographical writer focusing first and foremost on direct personal experience both in the individual poems and in the structure of his work, the *Canzoniere*, as a whole. It was written to be understood, aiming to rescue the integrity of the individual against a cultural climate which was high on rhetoric.

Saba, like Italo Svevo, enjoyed the benefits of a central European culture which was quite foreign to Italy. Both men, for example, were deeply interested in psychoanalysis and in Freud's work long before it was known in most of the rest of Italy. Saba was indeed psychoanalysed by a former pupil of Freud's, Dr Weiss. Unlike Svevo, whose dream of going to Florence was not realized until late in his life, Saba had long periods there between 1905 and 1908 when he had contact with the Florentine literary circle that gathered around *La Voce*, a cultural journal which in 1914 had become purely literary. Although they published his poetry from time to time, they were highly critical, one claiming that the poems lacked 'virility' and 'moral vigour'. A fine article he wrote in 1911, 'Quello che resta ai poeti' ('What remains for poets to do'; Saba 2004: 72), arguing against aestheticism and the 'letterato di professione' ('the professional man of letters') and concluding with the simple comment that the poet should write poetry that is honest, was promptly returned with a rejection note. On the other hand *Solaria*, which also celebrated Italo Svevo's writing, dedicated an issue to his work in 1928 (see below, sec. 8.3). After the war Saba published the prose work *Storia e cronistoria del Canzoniere* (*History and Chronicle of the Songbook*), where, using the third person, he describes and explains his life and his poetry. He left unpublished and unfinished a childhood memoir that he had abandoned in 1953, published posthumously in 1975 as *Ernesto*, where he traces an early homosexual relationship. It is the first work in twentieth-century Italy to represent homosexuality subjectively, normalizing it rather than codifying it as an expression of moral and political corruption.

7.3 Narratives of selfhood: the subjective turn in fiction

After *verismo* writers often adopted the first person, as the seeming stability and reliability of third-person narrative, based on the tacit understanding between the real author and the reader as to what constitute reality, time and identity, began to break down. But where Aleramo invited identification of author and subject, in a letter written on 17 February 1926 to the poet Eugenio Montale, Italo Svevo (1861–1928) recommended that his novel *La coscienza di Zeno* (*Zeno's Conscience* – or 'consciousness': for the ambiguities of the title, see below) should be read as an autobiography, but not its author's. The self-consciousness and experimental forms of literary modernism, its concern with the layerings of consciousness and subjectivity, the loosening of narrative unity and structure, were all features common to two of the major novels of the early twentieth century.

Italo Svevo's *La coscienza di Zeno* and Luigi Pirandello's *Uno, nessuno e centomila* (*One, No One and a Hundred Thousand*) were published within three years of each other, in 1923 and 1926 respectively, by writers who were both born in the 1860s, the one in a Trieste that, as we have seen, was part of the Austro-Hungarian empire until the post-First World War peace settlement when it was annexed to Italy, the other at the diametrically opposed corner of the country in southwest Sicily. For Italo Svevo (whose real name was Ettore Schmitz) *La coscienza di Zeno* followed two unsuccessful novels that he had published privately at his own expense. His first novel, *Una vita* (*A Life*), appeared in 1892. It tells the story of a bank clerk with literary ambitions who seduces and then abandons the daughter of a wealthy banker. His second, *Senilità* (1898), is a brilliant study of the psychological impotence of its 35-year-old protagonist, Emilio Brentani, whose life is on hold, his will paralysed, his one claim to artistic fame a small book now yellowing in a bookseller's window. A daydreamer who lives with his sister Amalia, he meets and falls in love with Angiolina, a young woman who makes ends meet as an escort girl. The two women represent opposite poles – life and death. His error is to believe that life and literature are interchangeable; as long as he has never known a woman he can fantasize an ideal based on novels, but he cannot transfer the woman he has known back to literature – she simply will not fit. He discovers that life and literature are separate universes. *Senilità*, which appeared in English as *As a Man Grows Older*, the Italian title being untransferable to English, recapitulates many of the preoccupations of the novel in preceding decades.

The hero of *La coscienza di Zeno*, Zeno Cosini, also hopes that writing will be a way of resolving the dilemmas thrown up by life, but in his case the narrative is demanded of him by his psychoanalyst, whom he has consulted in order to stop smoking. He is a married man with children and the 'perfect' wife. He is also a *malade imaginaire* and a smoker who spends much time and effort trying to give up. As a young man he was a disappointment to his father, whose death, however, leaves him rich and with little to occupy his time, for his father has ensured that the management of the family business is in the hands of a loyal administrator, Olivi. Zeno had hoped to marry the beautiful Malfenti daughter, Ada, but careful manipulation by his future in-laws ensured that he got the cross-eyed Augusta. Ada goes on to marry his arch-rival Guido Speier, a man who despite his accomplishments, which include the playing of the violin and an enviable command of Tuscan, will end up a failure and will ultimately kill himself. Zeno's own happy marriage is, he feels, only enhanced by the extramarital affairs he enjoys, including one with the impoverished piano teacher Carla, who, having extracted all she needs financially from him, goes on to make a suitable marriage for herself. The novel ends with Zeno's own financial speculations during the war, the success of which lead him to fire his psychoanalyst. The novel's orbit is the daily, the domestic, the mundane; its protagonist suffers no existential crises.

Zeno has put pen to paper in response to his psychoanalyst's suggestion that he record his dreams, memories and thoughts as they come into his mind in a flow of free associations in an effort to get to the root of his attachment to smoking. The organization of time is therefore determined by the vagaries of the protagonist's memory. As chronology and causality have been replaced by the mental association of ideas, the five chapters which make up the novel are arranged thematically. Chronological time, where it is represented, is usually bizarrely random because all the significant dates – such as the birth of a child or the death of a pope – revolve around the one non-event in his life: giving up smoking. These dates are registered by Zeno all over the place – in margins of books, on pictures, on the wallpaper. Zeno himself notes that the calendar is arranged so oddly that it is difficult to have an ordered and regular 'risoluzione', for no two months are the same: 'Un vero disordine nel tempo!' ('A real muddling of time!'). History, the succession of public events, makes only offstage appearances, its relationship to the rest of the narrative much like Trieste's to the rest of Italy – tangential.

A diary entry in the fifth and final chapter of the book dated 26 June 1916 (but referring back to the events of 23 May) records his encounter with history when he learnt that that Italy had entered the war, but while the dates of the occasional diary entries in this last chapter – 3 May 1915 to 24 March 1916 – associate in the reader's mind with the First World War, the title of the chapter, 'Psico-analisi', keeps it firmly within the ambit of Zeno's own personal drama. As it turns out, it is the war and not a doctor that will 'cure' Zeno; the war energizes him, and while the young and the fit die at the front, and the administrator of the family firm has taken refuge in Switzerland, Zeno, now a man in his sixties, becomes a highly successful speculator and entrepreneur, and has never felt better. His personal success in the context of a European catastrophe is, as the closing pages of the novel make explicit, a triumphant if ironic vindication of social Darwinian theory.

Three of the five chapters, 'Prefazione', 'Preambolo' and 'Psico-analisi', provide the framework to the two long chapters that contribute the bulk of the narrative. The novel has two introductions. It opens with the brief 'Prefazione', which stands on the threshold outside the body of the narrative. Written by Dottor S., it is the only occasion in the book when the reader has access to a voice and a point of view that is not Zeno's. Its position and authorship therefore give it a particular status and authority. In what Philippe Lejeune has described as 'the ambiguous game of prefaces' (Lejeune 1975: 29), the doctor, 'di cui in questa novella si parla talvolta con parole poco lusinghiere' ('who is occasionally talked about in this story in not very flattering terms'; Svevo 1972: 599), tells readers that what follows has been written on his instructions; we also learn that the doctor is publishing these records (what he calls a 'novella') 'per vendetta' ('in revenge'), without his patient's knowledge or consent, after an irrevocable breakdown in their relationship led Zeno to abandon the treatment. His reference in his concluding words to the 'tante verità e bugie ch'egli ha qui accumulate!' ('so many truths and lies that he has gathered together here!'; Svevo 1972: 599) alerts the reader to the potential duplicity of the narrative she or he is about to begin; at the same time as it unintentionally reveals that the doctor himself lacks the professional discretion that a patient has the right to expect, it also effectively drives a wedge between reader and narrator. It destroys the trust and intimacy that should be the effect of a first-person narration and encourages in its place an attitude of scepticism. By reminding us that our understanding of Zeno comes from how we read him, the slippery words of Dottor S. shepherd in a revolution in understanding character.

Svevo himself was very well read in the European novel – Zola, Maupassant, Verga, Turgenev were among his preferred writers – and his decision to return to fiction after the critical failure of his first two novels and the twenty years' silence that fell between *Senilità* and *Coscienza* may itself have been stimulated by his friendship with James Joyce, who between 1904 and 1914 lived in self-imposed 'exile' in Trieste. But it was Svevo's engagement with Freud – he even claimed in a letter to Jahier that *La coscienza di Zeno* was born of the experience of reading Freud – that was decisive in the shaping of the novel. Svevo's interest, which began in 1908, led him to work on a translation of *The Interpretation of Dreams* with his nephew during the war years. Svevo was always to claim, however, that he considered Freud to be more interesting from a literary standpoint than from a therapeutic one: '*Letterariamente* Freud è certo più interessante [. . .]. Magari avessi fatto io una cura con lui, il mio romanzo sarebbe risultato più intero' ('Freud is certainly more interesting *from a literary point of view* [than a clinical one]. If only I had been treated by him, my novel would have been fuller'; Svevo 1966: 857, letter to Jahier, 27 December 1927).

In the novel too Svevo's protagonist does not feel that psychoanalysis has helped much with his condition; indeed it would be fair to say that the analysis never really gets under way. Zeno begins the final chapter with the words 'L'ho finita con la psico-analisi' ('I am finished with psychoanalysis'), explaining that having practised it for six months he is now more 'squilibrato e malato' ('unbalanced and ill') than ever, even though with the diagnosis made, the treatment should be at an end. If anything shows the distance that has been covered from the Romantic hero of the Risorgimento, Foscolo's

Jacopo Ortis, to the anti-hero of *Coscienza*, it is to be found in Zeno's response to the diagnosis of his condition. Although flattered, even enchanted, at the idea that his is the self-same condition that Sophocles attributed to Oedipus, he pragmatically settles for an illness that can be identified empirically, in his presence, from a urine sample. (The diagnosis turns out to be wrong.)

While we cannot pronounce on whether Zeno has diabetes or not, many readers will have seen the Oedipus complex at work long before the final chapter, in the rivalry and hostility that characterizes all Zeno's male relationships – those with his father, father-in-law, Guido, and his doctors – and the uxorious love for his mother that repeats itself in his relationship with his wife. It is also the very failure of the transference with Dottor S. that gave rise to the publication of the narrative. But while the Oedipus complex provides an explanation for Zeno's behaviour, it remains none the less curiously tangential to the knowledge that readers have acquired for themselves of the protagonist from an attentive reading of his narrative.

This is because the significance of Freud for Svevo is not to be found in the therapeutic aspects of his work so much as the processes by which the diagnosis is reached. Although Freud had rejected the written word in favour of a 'talking cure' – the immediacy of the spoken word reduced the patient's opportunities for self-censorship – the role that *La coscienza di Zeno* creates for the reader is not dissimilar to that of the Freudian analyst. Both introduce a revolution in our understanding of reading character by foregrounding the role of language in the making of subjectivity. Apart from the preface, the novel is written entirely from Zeno's point of view, but the reader learns to read for the latent content behind the surface, reading between the lines to tease out the contradictions, repetitions and inconsistencies of the text, that is, the repressed thoughts that have escaped the censor and made their way to the surface, albeit in disguised form. The novel's title, *La coscienza di Zeno*, where 'coscienza' could refer either to 'consciousness' or to 'conscience' or to both, demonstrates the ambiguity of language even before the reader has turned to the opening page.

Zeno himself, like his author, is haunted by his inability to write literary (Tuscan) Italian and having to settle instead for a Triestine, middle-class Italian, a language that is much more closely tied to the private and intimate, to the realm of the family. This is far from being an affectation on the part of Svevo, who was snubbed by *letterati* for writing what they considered to be a syntactically awkward, Germanic and cumbersome Italian. Trieste itself was a commercial town, very much on the perimeters of Italy's high culture, where the influences were Italian and Slav, Germanic and Slovene and, as in Svevo's case, Jewish. Zeno may be presented by his author as lacking in self-knowledge, but in other ways he is shown to be very knowing, and he plays the language card for all it is worth. As Zeno points out, his life-story written in dialect would look completely different, and the more Zeno insists on his own linguistic inadequacy, the more the reader is reminded that the words he writes can be as much alibi and subterfuge as channel of communication.

Luigi Pirandello, author of the mock autobiographical narrative *Uno, nessuno e centomila*, was, like Svevo, bilingual. His earliest literary activity was as translator of classical Greek theatre into Sicilian dialect for a modern audience, and his own writing for the theatre would include plays in dialect. But for Vitangelo Moscarda, the protagonist of his novel *Uno, nessuno e centomila*, what is at issue is neither the choice of language nor his own linguistic limitations, but language itself. In the extract below from chapter 4 of the novel, Vitangelo has just told us, his audience, that while we may think that after an hour or two in each other's company we understand each other, we are in fact victims of the deception perpetrated by language. Words delude us into believing that we have understood what he describes as the other's 'reality', but in practice the language we share is just a cover to conceal the incommunicability of individual experience:

> Il guaio è che voi, caro, non saprete mai, né io vi potrò mai comunicare come si traduca in me quello che voi mi dite. Non avete parlato turco. Abbiamo usato, io e voi, la stessa lingua, le stesse parole. Ma che colpa abbiamo, io e voi, se le parole, per sé, sono vuote? Vuote, caro mio. E voi le riempite del senso vostro, nel dirmelo; e io nell'accoglierle, inevitabilmente, le riempio del senso mio. (Pirandello 1973: II, 769)

> The problem is, my dear friend, that you will never know, and I will never be able to tell you, how what you say is translated inside me. You haven't talked in Turkish. We've both used the same language, the same words. But what fault is it of ours if words, in themselves, are empty? Empty, my dear chap. And you fill them up with your meaning as you're speaking to me; and I when I receive them inevitably fill them up with mine.

The individual subject can speak but cannot be spoken; Vitangelo's story in the mouth of another would be another story. Unable to cross the barriers that divide us and that hold us back from other realities and other psyches, we are stopped short at the threshold and from there we apply labels to each other with devastating effect, as an anguished Vitangelo comments: 'Eh, ma si formano pure così le cosidette opinioni correnti! E guai chi un bel giorno si trovi bollato da una di queste parole che tutti ripetono. Per esempio: *usurajo*! Per esempio: *pazzo*!' (Pirandello 1973: II, 814: 'Yes, but that's just how so-called current opinion gets formed! And woe betide the man who finds one fine day he is stamped with one of those words which are repeated by everyone. For example: *usurer*! For example: *madman*!'). Where in Svevo's novel Zeno struggled with a language unsuited to his purposes and over which he claimed he had an imperfect mastery, Vitangelo's crisis is born of the realization that a common language hides from its users the hideous consequences of the impossibility of ever reaching a common understanding. Unlike the other novels in this chapter, where first-person narration is accompanied by a *mise en abyme* of the scene of writing to increase the aura of authenticity, *Uno, nessuno e centomila*, appropriately for a novel that aspires to a state of pure disembodied voice, carries the markers of orality. An interesting tension exists throughout the novel between word and image.

Uno, nessuno e centomila was the last of Pirandello's seven novels and, in common with *La coscienza di Zeno*, it has the quality of a work in progress. It was written over a period of sixteen years, so that what the author had originally envisaged as being an introduction or prologue to his plays turned out in the end to be closer to an epilogue. Divided into eight 'books', the first five, possibly six, were written between 1909 and 1916, while the seventh and eighth belong to the period 1919 to 1925. Between them, these 'libri' contain sixty-three often unconnected chapters, many no longer than a couple of pages and some as short as a paragraph. The episodic quality of the plot increases the novel's fragmentary nature, while the many extracts included by Pirandello from his own essays and plays heightens the impression of a writer's diary or notebook; he also returns to plots that he first experimented with in short stories such as 'Stefano Giogli, uno e due' ('Stefano Giogli, one and two') and 'Quando ero matto' ('When I was mad'). The whole work was finally published in instalments in *La Fiera Letteraria* between December 1925 and June 1926.

The novel opens with a flashback to a short conversation between the narrator and his wife. As she watches him scrutinize his reflection in the mirror she comments on his crooked nose, and then does not improve matters by listing other physical defects that had so far escaped his attention. While this comes as a blow to the personal vanity of a man who had always considered his nose to be 'se non proprio bello, almeno molto decente' ('if not exactly beautiful, at least pretty decent'), far more seriously it puts in train a series of observations that make him realize that the man he thought he was and the man friends and acquaintances 'knew' are not one and the same person. As in a *Bildungsroman*, everything turns on the self-awakening of the protagonist, but where in the one coming to awareness leads to a shaping and deepening of character, here it is reversed and Vitangelo sets out to divest himself of all the attributes of selfhood; the 'dati di fatto' ('factual data') that make him what he is in the eyes of everybody else. He begins with the name, Vitangelo Moscarda, which gives him an identity, but one of his father's making. Just like the irritating house fly (in Italian, *mosca*) with which he shares his surname, he finds that multiplying under the name is an ever-proliferating number of selves. 'Ma presto l'atroce mio dramma si complicò: con la scoperta dei centomila Moscarda ch'io ero non solo per gli altri ma anche per me, tutti con solo questo nome di Moscarda, brutto fino alla crudeltà' ('But soon my atrocious personal drama got complicated: with the discovery of the one hundred thousand Moscardas that I was, not only for others, but also for myself, all with this one name of Moscarda, so ugly as to be cruel'; Pirandello 1973: II, 741). At the same time he has to contend with his wife's emasculating, childish sobriquet Gengé.

Where Pirandello's first first-person novel, *Il fu Mattia Pascal*, rewrites the eighteenth-century picaresque novel of chance, as a win at the roulette table gives the narrator the opportunity to live out the fantasy of a new life under an assumed identity, *Uno, nessuno e centomila* transforms the customary battle between self and society that we find in nineteenth-century literature into a struggle within his psyche to eliminate the myriad social selves that have accrued over the years. Vitangelo's journey is psychological, not physical, and it is a journey inwards, but far from being a journey of discovery to a self, it is to a loss of self as conventionally understood, into an opening out into and participation in the flux of experience. By dis-identifying himself with all those statutes of selfhood, he enters a realm of non-history, aphasia and silence. In the final chapter, called appropriately 'Non conclude' ('It doesn't end'), the protagonist's non-identity shuts down any possibility of development in the narrative. Freed from the constraints of the social, what for onlookers looks like a gesture of self-destruction along the 'high road to madness' is for Vitangelo an act of liberation, of release. The outcome has nothing to do with spiritualism or mysticism, both of which Pirandello felt offered false solutions, but with a 'vital energy' (*élan vital*) whereby Vitangelo has reached a beyond – an *oltre* – where instability and inconclusiveness hold sway. Such an experiment in the systematic dismantling of selfhood is also inevitably a literary experiment with narrative and its procedures. There are no markers of time in the novel; we cannot, for example, work out how much time has elapsed between the opening and the ending, nor do we know what distance in time lies between the events described and the moment of describing them. The last chapter of the novel slips into a timelessness where the narrative accompanies the flux of a ceaselessly changing world of pure consciousness.

Uno, nessuno e centomila is a remarkable feat, for it creates and describes a personal identity which is soon dismantled as the narrator journeys into a pre-linguistic state of pure being. In *Uno, nessuno e centomila* the indefinite article in the title denotes a negation of selfhood, whereas in *Una donna* it was just the opposite: an affirmation of selfhood. What Vitangelo describes is a philosophy and what he seeks to attain is a state of pure being, but the route leading to its successful enactment is through the psyche. Like Svevo, Pirandello was writing during an extraordinary time in Italian history – the Great War, the Russian Revolution, the March on Rome and the rise of Fascism (with which in the early 1920s he was to have close links), among others. No reference is made at any point within the narrative to any contemporary event beyond the small town of Girgenti. Zeno, who it has to be admitted was unsuitably dressed for the occasion, does nevertheless accidentally wander into war. Vitangelo and Zeno come from markedly different backgrounds, the one Catholic and the other Jewish, the one Sicilian and the other Triestine, but their material circumstances reveal interesting similarities. Both live off inherited wealth; neither is obliged to work in the family business, and indeed their respective fathers have taken measures to ensure that they do not work by giving the management of the family businesses over to a trusted administrator. Vitangelo's wife seems to have much the same fondness for her husband as she does for the family dog in whose company he appears to spend much of his time, while Zeno's wife is presented as the backbone of the family and shows little curiosity about her husband's whereabouts. The two anti-heroes are excellent examples of a much wider malaise, a crisis of masculinity that one can find outside Italy as well. There is a term in Italian cultural history for these male figures: *inetto* – a word used to describe literary anti-heroes who, while alienated from the society they are part of, none the less do not follow a course of open rebellion. Detached, they feel equally dissociated from the world of politics and the ideals of the Risorgimento for which their fathers fought.

8

Literature, Fascism and anti-Fascism

8.1 Writing and the regime

What difference did Fascism make to culture in general, and literature in particular? The answer to the question lies partly in the question itself: the idea that a particular government or regime makes any substantial difference to cultural life presupposes a political order that is inclined to intervene and impose its will in cultural affairs, and runs contrary to the liberal certainty, authoritatively represented by the leading intellectual Benedetto Croce (1866–1952) during the Fascist years, that politics and culture are separate spheres (see sec. 8.2). In the specific case of Fascism, two factors, which also apply elsewhere, need to be borne in mind. The first is that while the regime may have served very specific interests in the country, starting with the conservative groups within the economy and society who abhorred the idea of socialism, it did emerge from a popular base and pursued a populist agenda. Fascism came into being at a time when large swathes of the population had been and were continuing to be made conscious of themselves as in some degree actors in the political affairs of their country (a process accelerated by the experiences of the First World War). The second is that the administration of the twentieth-century state was becoming increasingly centralized and, in the case of Italy, this tendency was accelerated under Fascism. It follows that there is an unavoidable overlap between politics and culture in the modern state, between the organization of the state and the means at its disposal for ensuring a broad coincidence between its own objectives and those felt subjectively by individual citizens (what is sometimes thought of as the 'manufacture' of consensus).

The second part of this section will indeed detail some of the ways in which the Fascist political order tried actively to shape the cultural life of the country over which it had assumed authority. But the situation was quite nuanced. Alongside the directive instincts of a totalitarian regime we must set the calculation made by Mussolini and his associates that the traditional separation between elite and mass or popular culture was useful to the purposes of the regime; if anything, it was widened and institutionalized during the more than two decades of Fascist rule (known in Italy as the *ventennio*). The Fascists also concluded that it would do more harm than good to interfere too much with the work of writers and artists, scientists and philosophers, whose audience was restricted to relatively small numbers of readers, viewers and listeners. On the whole, the cultural elite could be left in its ivory tower, though here too there were subtle differences in practice, and the situation changed significantly when, in addition to the political opposition, Jewish intellectuals began to be targeted with the introduction in 1938 of anti-Semitic race laws on the Hitlerian model.

A second qualification which needs to be made to the assumption that the regime would naturally want to take a degree of control of cultural life is the observation that many of the structures and processes which underlay the modern, increasingly industrial production, transmission and consumption of culture had been developing over many decades, were already in place, were developing further under their own momentum, and were delivering or would soon deliver outcomes which would have happened anyway, Fascism or no Fascism. In many ways, what emerged in the broad cultural sphere in Italy in the 1920s and 1930s simply replicated what was happening in other relatively advanced economies in Europe and North America. The question was how Fascism would interact with structures and processes which were not of its making or strictly in its power to control. To take a first sounding of this question, we can look at the substantial 'popular fiction' market, which still included successful reprints of novels by nineteenth-century figures like Fogazzaro and Invernizio. Print runs over successive editions could, in a few cases, reach six figures (between 100,000 and 400,000), though the average initial run was 2,000 and an edition of 20,000 could be regarded as a substantial success. This was an important area of the literary market where the authorities could intervene both negatively and positively. A good deal of this fiction, ranging from the romantic to the pornographic, concerned itself in a whole variety of ways with sensitive subject matter like marriage, adultery and sexual relations in general, which could easily fall foul of moral censorship, especially as the regime during the late 1920s worked hard to reach the settlement with the Catholic church which would result in the Concordat of 1929.

The basic formula of the 'romantic' genre, as it was known by the publishers, is that of two people of the opposite sex who are deeply in love and whose desire to realize their hopes is thwarted by a third; the struggle between the two protagonists and the antagonist tends to boil down to a struggle between good and evil. In the 1920s there is an interesting evolution of the genre with the triumph of the happy ending. The lovers can finally get together, and this is not entirely a sentimentalization of the genre; rather, as Michele Giocondi pointed out, it is a sign that the virtue of renunciation in a spirit of either self-sacrifice or ethical resistance to extramarital relationships was now 'out of fashion' (Giocondi 1978: 45–6). Guido Da Verona (1881–1939) took the aristocratic erotic and superman themes of Gabriele D'Annunzio and reworked them for a lower-middle-class readership. *Colei che non si deve amare* (*She Who Must Not Be Loved*), first published in 1911, was about an incestuous affair; *Mimí Bluette, fiore del mio giardino* (*Mimi Bluette, Flower of My Garden*, 1916) told the story of a prostitute redeemed by love and was a favourite in the trenches; both novels sold in excess of 300,000 copies in the 1920s. The bestselling 'pornographic' genre, though far from twenty-first-century standards of explicitness, was enjoyed by its readers both for its predictability and for its intimations of another sexual-familial reality which it made legitimate to fantasize about; its undisputed king was Pitigrilli (1893–1975), editor in the 1920s of *Le grandi firme*, in which many of his own short stories appeared. All of these productions trod a fine line between risking prosecution for offending public morals – a threat which 'high' literature could also fall foul of (Giocondi claims that many of the 70,000 purchasers of Moravia's first novel, *Gli indifferenti* (*Time of Indifference*) bought it mainly for the sex; Giocondi 1978: 13) – and reinforcing in the end conventional family structures (something of which Moravia's novel could not be accused: see sec. 8.3).

This large market of 'popular' readers could also be targeted, from the regime's point of view, with more overtly propagandistic publications. In the wake of D'Annunzio, nationalist and patriotic fictions poured off the presses in the years following the war and during the early years of Fascism. Later on, there was a substantial production of novels presenting a lightly fictionalized account of the achievements of Fascism and the evil of its enemies, especially communism and socialism. As the regime was consolidated, a distinct genre began to make its appearance: the official Mussolini biography. The first, and perhaps most famous, was written by the Duce's mistress at the time, Magherita Sarfatti (1880–1961), in 1924 and translated into English the following year; an accomplished journalist and art critic, she fled to Argentina after the promulgation of the race laws (other Jewish writers who were faced with harsh choices at this time were Da Verona, who committed suicide, and Pitigrilli, who converted to Catholicism). But the bestselling example of the genre was Giorgio Pini's *Mussolini*, which was published in 1926 and went on to sell 400,000 copies in the next fifteen years. Early editions of this book are priceless for their gallery of photographs of the Duce literally wearing a series of different hats corresponding to his various governmental and military responsibilities.

At the same time as both the narrative structures and the production techniques of popular fiction were proceeding along lines already mapped out in the nineteenth century, new media were establishing themselves in the public domain and in people's private lives. The Fascist regime was good at exploiting traditional opportunities for reaching 'the masses' in what was still a largely rural population: local papers and specialized publications (geared, for example, to farmers or to serving soldiers), agricultural shows and travelling theatre (the popular *carri di Tespi*, 'Thespe's wagons', which toured the country in the 1930s). But already in the 1920s, and even more after the introduction of sound in 1927, the cinema was a mass medium, particularly in the cities, but capable of being extended to much smaller population centres as well, and one which could serve many different social purposes, from entertainment and escapism to exhortation and outright propaganda. The regime took a very close interest in the production and distribution of films, both Italian and foreign, as did other Western governments in the interwar period. Another important innovation of the period was radio. It should be mentioned here in passing that like cinema, and like television later, radio was to provide a valuable source of income and varied career opportunities for writers, in the same way as mass journalism had done in the nineteenth century and continued to do in the twentieth. Regular broadcasting, by a private company under government licence, began in Italy in late 1924. By 1939 there were 1.17 million private sets and another 40,000 in schools; the 1938 broadcasting level of some 65,000 hours per year was ten times more than a decade earlier. About a third of these hours were devoted to political programmes, reflecting the spread of direct or indirect state ownership and control of the broadcasting network from 1933 onwards. The spread of radio constituted a significant penetration of this medium, but in European terms the 1939 figure compared unfavourably with the 13.5 million sets that were owned in Nazi Germany in the same year (Cannistraro 1975).

Popular fiction, cinema and radio were all important genres or media which continued their development in Italy, as in other countries between the wars, in many ways irrespective of the political ideology or system in power. At the same time, it is difficult to talk about them, as it is about elite cultural forms in the same period, without alluding to Fascism as a force which directly or indirectly affected contents and structures. It is time to see a little more closely how the relationship between politics and culture worked in Fascist Italy.

Introducing a London exhibition devoted to *Art and Power: Europe under the Dictators 1930–1945* in 1995, the historian Eric Hobsbawm identified three 'primary demands that power usually makes on art, and which absolute power makes on a larger scale than more limited authorities'. The first two have to do with the glorification of power itself in the form of monumental, celebratory architecture, sculpture and painting, of which there was a fair amount in Fascist Italy, and the formal organization of power as public drama, ritual and ceremony, as in the mass rallies orchestrated by the Nazis and the military parades and huge sporting events which were a feature of all the totalitarian regimes of the 1930s. The crowd was itself enrolled in these performances as more or less conscious participant. There is a hilarious scene in Silone's *Fontamara* (see sec. 8.3) in which the assembled villagers, ordered to chant the name of the Duce, dutifully obey but get the rhythm slightly wrong, so that their hymn to the leader comes out as a meaningless chant of 'ce-du! ce-du!' The third service art performed for power was, Hobsbawm states, 'educational or propagandist: it could teach, inform and inculcate the state's value system' (Hobsbawm 1995).

The purpose of using art in these ways was to secure public consent through, at its simplest, the spectator's identification with awesome spectacle or his or her internalization of what 'officially' he or she needed to know, think and feel. The regimes were not democratic, they were often very conservative, but they were populist. It was therefore important that these functions be performed in ways that people could understand. Fascism, Nazism, Stalinism all in their different ways institutionalized the gap that had been emerging and becoming ever more apparent since the French Revolution, the gap between the culture reserved to a highly educated and sophisticated few and that which came to be described, not without much confusion of terminology, as mass or popular culture (on the confusion of terminology, and the different connotations of 'mass' and 'popular' in Italy and Britain, see Lumley 1988). In both Nazi Germany and the Soviet Union this process had a dark and violent side: 'decadent' work was systematically destroyed, non-conformist artists, writers and intellectuals could be tortured and murdered or simply 'disappear'. Persecution did not on the whole take these forms in Fascist Italy once the regime was established, though individuals were driven into exile and the introduction of the race laws in 1938, even beyond their immediate effect on the lives of thousands of people, was an ugly sign for the future.

But the attitude to art of many functionaries in the higher echelons of the Fascist Party was eclectic. Futurism, the most exuberant of the pre-war avant-gardes, was after all politically sympathetic to Fascism, sharing many of its values, and the initial anti-bourgeois, revolutionary spirit of the Fascist movement had a modernist ring to it. Even violence against its political opponents could be experienced as an act of Futurist-like bravado in the name of vigorous and masculine self-assertion against socialistic collectivism. Even as the regime consolidated and focused on remodelling the nation rather than overturning the old order, there was still space for echoes of the avant-garde and a judicious modernism to find expression in architecture, in the visual arts and, as we shall see, in literature. In other words, the regime never imposed a single style on Italian culture; it was not the case that all sculpture had to be pseudo-Roman. But this eclecticism institutionalized the separation between the different 'levels' of culture in its own way. Modernist exploration and experiment were permissible, within a limited circle.

The basic policy has been outlined in an excellent essay on the topic by Lino Pertile. Describing the situation as it evolved after the March on Rome (1922), Pertile writes:

> While the regime dealt ruthlessly with political opposition, it adopted a much more lenient and sophisticated attitude towards hostility from the literary world. In practice it allowed high culture to live undisturbed at the margins of society, as a privilege of the small liberal elite, while attempting to create through the mass media a popular subculture over which it could exert total control. In other words, the Fascists quickly recognized that the traditional separateness of high and mass culture in Italy could be useful to a totalitarian project. (Pertile 1986: 170–1)

There was of course a price to be paid for this leeway. Since for a writer the principal link to the public authority was his or her publisher, most writers had to go along with what the publishers deemed best, or even possible, in their own interest, and primarily their commercial interest, on which their very existence depended. This was a question not only of what the market would take, but of what would be acceptable to the censor. As the regime consolidated, so writers and publishers became more adept at gauging what could safely be published. This was helped by a system of 'pre-censorship' (*censura preventiva*), whereby books could be submitted to the censor in pre-production form, saving the publisher the costs of printing and distribution if the text should prove unacceptable (Forgacs 1990: 61). People also learnt the art of self-censorship: anything openly critical of the regime was unthinkable; care had to be taken with anything that might offend public, and especially Catholic, morality; but, beyond that, at least until the mid-1930s, publishers could navigate with a certain sense of security (Forgacs 1990: 61–2). A degree of conformity with the generally understood rules did not of course guarantee sales. The alternatives to accommodation with the system were to publish clandestinely or abroad (with all the attendant risks) or not to publish at all.

8.2 The social condition of intellectuals

In 1923 Mussolini put the philosopher Giovanni Gentile (1875–1944) in charge of his government's first major piece of social legislation, a reform of the education system which confirmed and reinforced the central role of the humanities in the formation of future public officials, at the expense of technical and scientific teaching. The Gentile Act began by making the administration of educational establishments more authoritarian while introducing a degree of liberalization in teaching methods – no contradiction in the eyes of Gentile, who believed that 'the objective existence of freedom' was in the state. Two years later Gentile was the leading signatory of the 'Manifesto degli intellettuali fascisti' ('Manifesto of Fascist intellectuals'), which was published in Italian newspapers on 21 April 1925, three months after Mussolini had assumed dictatorial powers and created a one-party state. The same fundamental idea which had guided the education reform was present in the manifesto: the individual pursuing his or her interests outside or against the state is a perversion; the only true liberty is found in the adherence of the individual to an idea, specifically that of the Patria, embodied in the state; the individual realizes his or her true strength in a collective consciousness guided from above in the name of a higher purpose. These intellectuals therefore enthusiastically welcomed the triumph of Mussolini's Fascism. It was against this argument that Benedetto Croce and others published a 'Manifesto degli intellettuali antifascisti' ('Manifesto of anti-Fascist intellectuals') in *Il Mondo* on 1 May 1925. Against the Gentilian idea of the individual being submerged in the state, with the consequence that all his or her activity is at least consonant with the priorities of the collectivity, Croce argued that, while what intellectuals do as intellectuals (the highest calling, in his view) is in the disinterested service of humanity at large, their political choices are their own affair. The latter should never interfere with the former. The key passage from the anti-Fascist manifesto reads as follows:

> Intellectuals – those who cultivate art and science – may exercise their right and perform their duty as citizens by joining a party and serving it faithfully. But as intellectuals their sole duty is to concentrate on raising all men and all parties equally to a higher spiritual sphere, through research, criticism and the creation of art, thus enabling them to fight the necessary battles with ever more beneficial results. To overstep these limits of the

> task assigned to intellectuals, to mix politics with literature, politics with science, is a mistake. (Original text in Papa 1974: 212–14)

With this formulation, Croce provided intellectuals in general, and literary people in particular, with a kind of let-out clause. It was not only prudent, but also intellectually respectable, to get on with one's own work and keep silent about political or more generally public matters. In exchange – this was how the regime interpreted this 'abstentionist' option – the state would by and large leave you in peace. On the basis of this understanding, sociologists and social historians of literature have described 'the new social condition of the intellectuals' (Luperini and Cataldi 1999: part 6, vol. 1, 23–8) as it took shape in the 1920s and particularly the 1930s in broadly binary terms. On the one hand, the *letterati-letterati* ('pure writers') opted for the Crocean solution and pursued their intellectual interests in a kind of ivory tower. On the other, the *letterati-ideologhi* ('ideological writers') chose a more public stance, working within the political and ideological apparatus of the state to support, but also later, in the thirties, to question them from within, and, with the fall of Fascism, maturing into the largely left-wing 'engaged' or 'committed' literature of the post-war period. The broad distinction between these two kinds of writer is helpful provided that it is understood that what it describes is not individual writers in absolute terms, but possible, and variable, positions which writers might take up. An individual might veer in different circumstances and at different times between the 'ivory-tower' and the 'activist' position, but it is accurate to say that these positions, with all their internal nuances, do help to describe the parameters of what was possible during this period. The apparatus erected by Fascism was complex: it created prestige organisms like the Reale Accademia d'Italia, founded in 1925, and high-profile projects like the Treccani *Enciclopedia Italiana* (1929–39), which included contributions from non- and anti-Fascist as well as Fascist experts, and it set up an elaborate system of honours, subsidies, stipends and prizes as well as the various levels of censorship and control already described.

With these general considerations in mind, it is now time to turn to the work of individual writers. In the remainder of this section, we shall look at trends in the 1920s and early 1930s, starting with the poets. The next section will be concerned with the emergence of critical voices in the mid- to late 1930s, particularly from the ambit known as 'left-wing' Fascism. And in the final section we shall be concerned with the impact on writing of the Resistance and civil war of 1943–5, and the relation between the political and economic Reconstruction period and the approach to narrative representation, particularly in film and fiction, known as 'neo-realism' (roughly 1945–55).

Poetry, especially lyrical poetry, was the genre which, during Fascism, most lent itself to the 'abstentionist' position described above, and indeed this trend was accentuated and codified in the poetic style known as hermeticism in the 1930s. But the tendency of the lyric to look in on itself was not only a product of the political moment and individual choice. It was a feature of much of twentieth-century Italian literature that while narrative fiction struggled to establish itself, and never seemed quite to find a form with which its practitioners and its public could be satisfied, lyric poetry had the confidence born of a continuous tradition of Italian verse stretching over seven centuries, a rich humus for future poets. We shall return to this distinctive feature of twentieth-century Italian literature in chapter 9.

Confidence born of a long tradition does not of course mean that any single poet can simply start to speak (or write) unreflectingly. Having already discussed in chapter 7 two major poets, Ungaretti and Saba, who published innovative volumes in 1916 and 1921 respectively, we can now introduce the third, Eugenio Montale (1896–1981), whose debut volume, *Ossi di seppia* (*Cuttlefish Bones*) was first published in 1925. Montale, who was awarded the Nobel Prize for Literature in 1975, was an unmistakable voice in twentieth-century Italian poetry, and his first book illustrates brilliantly both the wealth of the tradition on which he was able to draw with inventiveness and relish, and the typically early twentieth-century unease of a subject assailed by existential doubt and feelings of negativity. The collection (to which some more poems were added in 1928) is organized around two central sections: the thirteen untitled 'fragments' of 'Ossi di seppia' which then gave its title to the book as a whole, and the long poem in nine parts called 'Mediterraneo' ('Mediterranean'). They are surrounded by a number of other poems which, however, broadly share the same landscape and the same concerns as the central ones. The speaker of the poems moves and watches in a dry, harsh landscape which corresponds (imaginatively) to the eastern Ligurian coastline around the Cinque Terre where Montale (who was born in Genoa) spent the summers of his childhood and adolescence. It is a landscape already established in the earliest poem included in the collection (1916), which begins 'Meriggiare pallido e assorto / presso un rovente muro d'orto, / ascoltare tra i pruni e gli sterpi / schiocchi di merli, frusci di serpi' ('Sit the noon out, pale and lost in thought / beside a blistering garden wall, / hear, among the thorns and brambles, / snakes rustle, blackbirds catcall'; Montale 1996a: 30; 1998: 41). The sound qualities of these lines, to which Montale pays great attention, will distinctively mark the whole collection: the use of alliteration, assonance, rhyme and half-rhyme, the hint of onomatopoeia, and Montale's already assured control of metre (echoing if not always reproducing exactly the established metres of Italian poetry) and the rhythm of the verse. Frequently this speaker observes some movement or other of animal life, something that is just scurrying away or disappearing, which stands for a reality that seems graspable but remains just out of reach and from which he is excluded; the moment passes, the 'inganno consueto' ('normal illusion') returns.

Often the poems are addressed to another person, a 'tu', who can perhaps do something that the poet cannot. In the one which opens the volume, 'Godi se il vento . . .' ('Be happy if the wind . . .'), the speaker enjoins this other: 'Cerca una maglia rotta nella rete / che ti stringe, tu balza fuori, fuggi! / Va, per te l'ho pregato, – ora la sete / mi sarà lieve, meno acre la ruggine' ('Look for a flaw in the net that binds us / tight, burst through, break free! / Go, I've prayed this for you – now my thirst / will be easy, my rancour less bitter'; Montale 1996a: 7, 1998: 5). Not only is this sun-drenched, baking world ungraspable in its secrets, it is also hostile, communicating a fundamental badness, a 'male di vivere'('an evil or a sickness of living'), a negativity. This hostility is barely attenuated by the other major feature of the landscape in *Ossi di seppia*, the sea and the points where the sea meets the land. The cuttlefish bones themselves seem to be like something reduced to the essential, washed clean and white as they are. Their skeletal form is the bare essence of the living cuttlefish, to which it bears no discernible resemblance; the thing that has disappeared returns unrecognizable. But it also attests to the constant, rhythmic cleansing of the sea, whose embrace, in the 'Mediterraneo' sequence, is sometimes maternal, sometimes paternal: a comforting, if mysterious, presence.

The 'perilous law' of the sea in 'Antico, sono ubriacato dalla voce' ('Ancient one, I am drunk with [your] voice'), 'to be vast and different / and one and the same' ('la tua legge rischiosa: esser vasto e diverso / e insieme fisso'), is reduced in hopeless, almost parodistic, human form in the 'troppo noto / delirio, Arsenio, d'immobilità' ('the too well-known / delirium, Arsenio, of immobility') addressed to an alter ego on a rain-lashed urban seaside afternoon ('Arsenio'). It is a poem which encapsulates Montale's negative stance. In keeping with this stance, it is not the task of the poet to speak on behalf of others or to lead others, as a moralist or an opinion-former. In perhaps his best-known statement of this position, which opens with the words 'Non chiederci la parola' ('Do not ask us [i.e. the poets] for the word'), the poem closes, echoing Leopardi, with the assertion that all we can tell you today ('oggi') is 'ciò che *non* siamo, ciò che *non* vogliamo' ('what we are *not*, what we do *not* want', emphases Montale's; compare Leopardi's 'Altro dirti non vo'', 'I do not want to say anything more to you', in the conclusion of 'Il sabato del villaggio', 'The village Saturday').

Despite their evident differences, an influential anthology of post-war poetry also drew attention to points in common between the language of Montale's *Ossi* and that of Ungaretti's *Allegria* and Saba's *Canzoniere*. There is, rather surprisingly, a common realist root in the vocabulary of all three of them which allows them to call on different linguistic registers. At the same time, there is a clear intention in each of them to work out a lyric code, the complexity and variety of whose materials are designed to safeguard its independence (from other linguistic codes) and its inner coherence: 'a search [. . .] whose purpose is to absolutize the lyric code and make it all the stronger and more independent of any other context the more complex and heterogeneous the linguistic materials which make it up' (Cucchi and Giovanardi 1996: xv). This is not exactly 'poetry for poetry's sake', nor is it the intention to create a secret language strictly for the initiated, and Giovanardi is at pains to distinguish this search from the emergence in the 1930s of poetic hermeticism, which, whatever its origins, risked with time becoming mannered and repetitive. In Montale's next collection of poems, *Le occasioni* (*The Occasions*), published in 1939 (shortly after he had been dismissed from the directorship of the Gabinetto Vieusseux in Florence because he would not join the Fascist Party), there is a clear working out of a language which is tighter, more allusive, more puzzling to the reader, and altogether more difficult than was the case with the finely wrought but generally accessible idiom of *Ossi*.

In retrospect, Montale distanced himself from the idea of 'pure poetry', but did make it clear that he aimed to create a poetry which would contain its meanings without laying them out on a plate. 'Admitting that in art there is a balance between the outside and the inside,' he wrote in an 'imaginary interview' in 1946, 'between the occasion and the object-work, it was necessary to express the object and to suppress the occasion or impulse' (Montale 1976: 567). These epiphanies do not exclude a 'realist' language, as in this example from the sequence 'Mottetti' (evoking the musical form of the motet): 'Addii, fischi nel buio, cenni, tosse / e sportelli abbassati. È l'ora. Forse / gli automi hanno ragione. Come appaiono / dai corridoi, murati!' ('Farewells, whistling in the dark, waves, coughs, / and lowered windows. It's time. / May be the robots have it right. See how they look / from the corridors, walled in!'; Montale 1996a: 143; 1998: 197). But from a generic opening suggesting closure and departure which readers can elaborate in their own way, we come up against a dubitative 'Forse' (in contrast with the affirmative 'È l'ora') and the appearance of objects ('automi', 'corridoi') and conditions ('murati') to which we do not have an immediate key. T. S. Eliot's theory of the 'objective correlative', which Montale endorsed, guides us away from the specific reference of the objects which are named and towards the emotion that is expressed or signalled by their correlation within the poem: that is where the deep meaning of the poem may be found. A poetry then in which the signs of the objects speak, not their external referents or motivations, and speak in relation to each other – like a language. As in the example given, the language is far from abstract, and the poems of *Le occasioni* are given a further dimension by the introduction of 'real' women, lovers in real life, in the poetry shadowy figures who nevertheless acquire shape and personality in the poet's and the reader's mind and replace the more generic 'tu' of *Ossi*.

In practice, Montale's second collection does have much in common with the hermetic poetry being written in the 1930s, particularly by poets associated with Florence, which acted as a kind of non-Fascist cultural capital at the time. The term 'hermeticism' suggests mystery and secrecy, and it was first used pejoratively by the critic Francesco Flora in 1936 to describe the poetry of Ungaretti (particularly in the wake of his challenging second collection, *Sentimento del tempo* (*Sentiment of Time*), published in 1933), Montale and the Sicilian poet Salvatore Quasimodo (1901–68). After the war, it continued as a term of abuse among anti-Fascist intellectuals who deplored its introspection, its inaccessibility and its alleged indifference to the real world outside. In poetic terms, it was a development of French symbolism and was interested in verbalizing inner experience not through metaphor or metonymy but through 'analogy', the superimposition of different orders of experience to produce a unitary meaning. This means of proceeding became increasingly interesting to young poets desperate to find a way to escape the ever-proliferating and, as they saw it, contaminating presence of public discourse in the 1930s, whether propagandistic, journalistic or materialist. The motivation was frequently spiritual or religious (though there was no religious impulse in Montale's case) and a search for authenticity. As well as the poets mentioned, others who were later to become significant poets in their own right followed this path, at least in part and for a time. They included Leonardo Sinisgalli (1908–81), Alfonso Gatto (1909–76) and Mario Luzi (see sec. 9.1); an essay by the critic Carlo Bo, 'Letteratura come vita' ('Literature as life', 1938), underlines the spiritual ambitions of 'hermetic' writing.

8.3 Testing the limits of the novel

It proved to be more difficult for prose writers, and particularly the writers of fiction (novels and short stories), to find an adequate language during and in the immediate aftermath of Fascism. There was of course an already-made language, that which was routinely adopted in popular fiction, some of whose themes and formulae we have described above. There also continued to be, during the 1920s, a market for the so-called *prosa d'arte*, the refined, deliberately precious and intricate style used to effect in short, fragmentary prose pieces which had originated with the writers of the magazine *La Ronda* (1919–22), notably the poet and journalist Vincenzo Cardarelli (1887–1959) and the critic, journalist and art historian Emilio Cecchi (1884–1966), who had a particular interest in English and American culture. But *prosa d'arte* achieved its best results in forms like the essay or the prose poem, while amongst serious writers of fiction, the naturalism which had served the novel well since the 1880s and continued to do so at the popular end of the market seemed to have run out of steam.

Why should this be? In very broad terms, we can point to two important factors. First, writers were very exposed to the idea of modernity in general. Both the Europe-wide impact of the First World War and, in Italy specifically, the rise of Fascism and the inauguration with much fanfare of a new era in the history of the Italian nation made writers understand that they had been and were living through times of great change. The change was not only political, but also technological, cultural and moral. The problem for the novelist was, as always, to find the language and style appropriate to these changes; a language that would not only describe but in some way embody and express the transformations taking place. Secondly, the most promising source for the new writing lay in the European avant-garde, whether in the lesson of established or emerging models of literary modernism like André Gide, James Joyce (who had a direct impact on Svevo), Franz Kafka, Katherine Mansfield, Marcel Proust and Virginia Woolf, or in the experience of the radical experimentation being carried out in the 1920s by the Surrealists, particularly in Paris (which, throughout the first half of the twentieth century, remained the cultural beacon for Italian intellectuals).

At this point in its history, Italian culture was in two minds: in pursuit of the new, within the limits of research allowed it, but conscious too of the growing call for a return to order, a return to rationality. The outcome was, in the twenties at least, a rather hesitant relationship with the new, programmatically bold – we must bring ourselves up to date with the most advanced European culture – but often timid in practice: psychoanalysis, for example, an important and indispensable component of Surrealism, had hardly any audience in Italy before the 1930s. (The notable but ambiguous exception was Svevo's Trieste; the first practising psychoanalyst in Italy, Edoardo Weiss (1889–1970), who had trained with Freud, published his manual

Elementi di psicoanalisi (*Elements of Psycho-analysis*) in 1931. He was another victim of the race laws in 1938 and emigrated to the US.)

An interesting representative of this period of Italian cultural life was the highly talented and versatile Massimo Bontempelli (1878–1960). Bontempelli was a poet, fiction writer and playwright, as well as a composer and literary journalist. He took a leading role in supporting Fascism, joining the party in 1924 and being appointed to the Reale Accademia d'Italia six years later. In 1926 he and the politically maverick Curzio Malaparte (1898–1957) founded the journal *'900* (*Novecento*), which continued until 1929. The journal was a vehicle for Bontempelli's self-imposed mission to deprovincialize Italian culture and to open it to wider European influences, but in a way that was appropriate to the kind of mass civilization being built in Italy. To this end he also championed a vague movement known as *stracittà*, which, as its name suggests, highlighted the urban dimension of the new social reality, as opposed to *strapaese*, headed by the journalist and engraver Mino Maccari (1898–1981), intended to defend the values and culture of rural Italy (the rival tendency to which Malaparte characteristically defected: see his *L'Arcitaliano* (*The Arch-Italian*), 1928). It was in the pages of *'900* that Bontempelli developed his theory of 'magic realism' (*realismo magico*), a theory that has nothing to do with the Latin American use of the term in the 1970s. Bontempelli was trying to adapt Surrealism to Italian tastes and Italian reality. His was not a systematic pursuit of analogy, free association or, still less, 'automatic writing'. There was a more mystical streak to his programme. He thought of the way in which fifteenth-century painting like Mantegna's gave the viewer a precise delineation of reality, yet pointed to another, dreamlike state behind it. This was the effect he recommended writers to seek out in the very different context of modern urban, and suburban, life. The surreal is not the product of the apparently arbitrary (unconsciously guided) conjunction of disparate elements of perceived reality; it is something that is hidden within the real.

Bontempelli was one of a number of writers who were experimenting on the boundaries of realism and fantasy, the rational and the irrational, at this time. His best works can still be read with pleasure as examples of this quest: from the dramatic dialogue *Eva ultima* (*Last Eve*, 1923) and the stories of *La donna dei miei sogni* (*The Woman of My Dreams*, 1925) and *Mia vita morte e miracoli* (*My Life, Death and Miracles*, 1931) to the more directly 'magic realism'-related works *Il figlio di due madri* (*The Son of Two Mothers*, 1929) and *Gente nel tempo* (*People in Time*, 1937). But they lack the bite that tells the reader they really are dealing with a new insight into human nature or the human condition. They protect themselves with a veil of irony or playfulness which says 'please do not take me too seriously', and which insulates the reader too against the implicit cruelty and bleakness of many surrealist images. The same criticism, to a greater or lesser extent, may be levelled against two other prominent writers of the period who explore fantasy, metamorphosis and other forms of non-empirical reality: Alberto Savinio (1891–1952), the brother of the leading metaphysical painter Giorgio De Chirico, who had already overlaid classical mythology with bourgeois convention in an early but accomplished novel, *Hermaphrodito* (1918), and Antonio Delfini (1907–63), whose best work includes the stories of *Il ricordo della Basca* (*Memory of the Basque*, 1938). Tommaso Landolfi (1908–79) was influenced by Surrealism in his early collections of stories, *Dialogo dei massimi sistemi* (*Dialogue of the Grand Systems*, 1937 – the title echoes one by Galileo) and *Il mar delle blatte* (*Cockroach Sea*, 1939). Landolfi, a celebrated gambler in his lifetime, was particularly adept even in his early work at bringing out the processes of obsession, challenge, chance and loss in his protagonists' interaction with the world.

In the late 1920s and the early 1930s, however, there were several independent attempts to find an alternative to the domesticated avant-garde propagated by Bontempelli and *'900*, which in one way or another drew on the realist tradition but were also marked by the uncertainties of recent years, particularly as concerned the voice and tone of the narration. In 1929 the young Alberto Moravia (1907–90) published his debut novel, *Gli indifferenti*. It was a hard-hitting depiction of the shallow lives of an upper-middle-class professional Roman family, of which even the younger members, Carla and her brother Michele, are resigned to realigning their lives in conformity with the imperatives of social hierarchy (represented by the cynical triumph of the older male) and 'reality'. Moravia succeeds in painting an extremely convincing portrait of this society, and the effect is soberly realistic. Yet there are also notable elements of performance in the writing style; for example, the parody of Lucia's 'Addio' speech in *I promessi sposi* in Carla's farewell to her familiar life on the night she is due to be 'seduced' by her mother's lover Leo ('Farewell streets, deserted neighbourhood lashed by rain'; chapter 8), and the theatricality of the way in which the action of the novel is presented, from the famous opening scene (a more appropriate word than 'chapter'), 'Entrò Carla' ('Carla entered'), to the structuring of the plot in sixteen chapters over two days mainly in the Ardengo family's apartment. The realism is thus combined with a heightened sense of artificiality, which coincides with the pasteboard world of the characters themselves. In stylistic terms, a tragedy in the form of a novel ('una tragedia in forma di romanzo') is exactly what the young writer was aiming at.

The early 1930s saw the appearance of three strong novels which drew directly on the naturalist tradition, but again with a difference. *Gente in Aspromonte* (*People in Aspromonte*, 1930), by Corrado Alvaro (1895–1956), was an uncompromising look back at the harsh landscape and pitiless social relations of his native Calabria, narrated through the figure of an adolescent encountering the hostility and injustices of the real world, on the part of an author now firmly ensconced in the cosmopolitan worlds of Milan and Rome, where he collaborated on *'900* and became an intimate of Pirandello. This, his best novel, may stand for the tension in his work between a deep understanding of his origins and the sense that he has no choice but to enter modernity.

The year 1930 was also when Ignazio Silone (1900–78), a Communist Party militant in exile in Switzerland, began his masterpiece *Fontamara*, which was eventually published there in 1934 and became an international bestseller (not in Italy, where it was banned). The novel tells, in fabulatory vein, of how the peasants of Fontamara in the Abruzzi, already the lowest of the low, are tricked out of their water supply by a speculator (one of the newly arrived 'new men' of Mussolini's Italy), how they resist, the forces ranged against them, their defeat and dispersal but refusal to surrender (represented by the Leninist slogan 'Che fare' ('What is to be done'), which is the title they give the newspaper they attempt to produce). What is striking about this novel, beyond the precision and humour with which the social relations are depicted – writing it, Silone once suggested, was like writing a party report plus the things that party reports left out (interview in Virdia 1967: 4–5) – is the freshness and inventiveness of the mode of narration itself. The events are recounted by three escaped villagers telling their story in turn, weaving their accounts together in the way the oral storytellers of the Abruzzi do, so their amanuensis, the narrator who introduces the story, tells us. Part of the drama of their experience is their transition from oral to written communication (the smashed-up printing press) and their being forced back to oral transmission, which will in its turn be written (the novel). But other forms of communication are also present. One of the most harrowing scenes in the novel, the rape of Maria Grazia in chapter 5, is narrated in long-shot, so to speak, and the narrative focus swiftly switches to the terrorized and traumatized reaction of its innocent witness, Elvira; the effect is a cinematic one. In short, *Fontamara* has a political and social point to make and sets out to do so in the most inventive and at the same time most appropriate form that the author can manage.

Perspective is also important in the third of these 'realist' novels of the early 1930s, *Tre operai* (*Three Workers*, also 1934) by Carlo Bernari (1909–93).

The novel describes the lives of three working-class people, two men and a woman, in a dull and rainy Naples; the anti-picture-postcard aesthetic is a direct quotation of Verga's 'Fantasticheria'. As Silone's was for the destitute of the countryside, Bernari's was the first modern novel to present the lives of the urban working-class poor from their own perspective and with a use of indirect free speech which aims to capture the cadences of their own words; in both respects it was an important point of reference for the development of neo-realism.

In all of these cases – Moravia, Alvaro, Silone, Bernari – there seems to be an effort on the part of writers to find a fictional language and form (different in all four novels) which can deal more directly with the sense of immobility and, increasingly, threat and dread that hangs over the collective consciousness both at the beginning (the Wall Street crash and the depression that followed) and towards the end of the 1930s. A sense of foreboding may also be discerned in the most successful novels in the surrealist, or at least fantasist, vein by Dino Buzzati (1906–72), *Bàrnabo delle montagne* (*Bàrnabo of the Mountains*, 1933) and *Il deserto dei Tartari* (*The Tartar Steppe*, 1940), in both of which the protagonists wait a lifetime for the moment of redemption, which never comes. In reality, Italian fiction was looking for ways in which to accommodate both the realist and the surrealist strands in its recent tradition.

Nowhere was this more the case than in the Florentine journal *Solaria*, which was founded by Alberto Carocci (1904–72) in 1926 and was finally forced to close in 1936 (with an issue dated '1934'). *Solaria*, whose title was a utopian allusion to the 'city of the sun', aimed, like *'900*, to Europeanize Italian culture, but also to recognize the contribution to European modernism of writers like Svevo (to whom an issue was dedicated in 1929) and the Sienese novelist Federigo Tozzi (1883–1920). It was influential in transmitting the lesson of Proust as a model of a fiction structured around memory which began to be pursued in Italy in the 1930s and 1940s, by writers such as Gianna Manzini (1896–1974); for the pleasures of reading Proust, see Natalia Ginzburg's autobiographical memoir, *Lessico famigliare* (*Family Sayings*, 1963), which introduces the figure as a young man of the most influential critic and champion of contemporary literature in mid-century Italy, Giacomo Debenedetti (1901–67). *Solaria* published and encouraged some of the most important poets (including Ungaretti, Saba and Montale) and fiction writers of the day: amongst the latter, in addition to Gadda and Vittorini, whom we shall consider shortly, Giovanni Comisso (1895–1969), Alberto Loria (1902–57) and Alessandro Bonsanti (1904–83), who later became a co-editor of the magazine, should be mentioned. *Solaria* was attentive to both the 'deep historical and moral sense of life found in the novels of Manzoni, Balzac and Dostoevski' and 'the sense of deep human structure owed to the modern discovery of the unconscious' (Dombroski 1999: 524). This heady mix of the structure and concerns of the nineteenth-century European novel and psychoanalysis, combined with a particular interest on the part of writers in adolescence as a period of transition and formation, may help perhaps explain the later preoccupations of a great novelist not directly connected with *Solaria*, Elsa Morante (see sec. 9.2).

Solaria also published two of the most important narrative voices to emerge in the 1930s, those of Carlo Emilio Gadda (1893–1973) and Elio Vittorini (1908–66); indeed the serial publication, which was halted, of the latter's novel *Il garofano rosso* (*The Red Carnation*) was the last nail in the magazine's coffin. To these we shall add, in the paragraphs that follow, the name of Cesare Pavese (1908–50). These three writers between them gave particular impetus to the elaboration of new narrative forms in the 1930s and early 1940s, forms run through with tension and difficulty. Their work has a strong autobiographical dimension, often painful in content, and transposed more or less successfully, more or less completely, into some kind of fictional shape. Gadda published two books under the *Solaria* imprint, in 1931 and 1934, and contributed to the magazine, but it was in the pages of its successor, *Letteratura*, also published in Florence, that he began to publish the chapters of his masterpiece, *La cognizione del dolore* (*Acquainted with Grief*, 1938–41; an edition in book form was published in 1963, and an expanded and definitive one in 1970). Set in a thinly disguised South American dictatorship, it foregrounds the neurotic figure of the *hidalgo* Gonzalo Pirobuttiro d'Altino and his relationship with his mother and the villa she inhabits. Intertwined with a tale of political thuggery, criminality and murder is a catalogue of the obsessions, fears, pet hates and outbursts of anger which make up Gonzalo and constitute his image to the outside, unsympathetic, world; a choral network of opinion, judgement, impulse and desire which, together with Gonzalo's own reinternalization and reimagining of it, constitutes the perspective from which the 'events' of the novel unfold. 'Events' is put in inverted commas because, although climactic events do occur – the old woman is found dead in her villa, but killed by whom? by Gonzalo himself? or by the gang of self-appointed nightwatchmen he refuses to pay off? or by someone else? – there is no logical sequence which produces them, and it cannot be said that anything is resolved, or even really changed, by their occurrence. The novel, even in its final form, is open-ended, leaving the reader still grasping for an order in the universe which simply is not there. Gadda, whose resemblance to Gonzalo is attested by many of his other writings, private notes and diaries, which together seem to make up a single narrative text, was denied, or denied himself, any sense of closure. In choosing to work with the novel, which in its simplest form might expect a story with a beginning, middle and end in that order, he revealed the intractable nature of life and the impossibility of containing it within a neat structure. Its uncontrollability is reflected not only in the anti-narrative perspective of his books, but also in the extraordinary linguistic creativity which is his hallmark, jumbling the standard language together with archaic literary language, dialect, foreign and even invented languages in a mix which reveals, and revels in, the bottomless wealth of language and its essential self-referentiality. Gadda subverts the narrative form and thwarts the reader's desire for completion – not only here, but also in his other acknowledged masterpiece, *Quer pasticciaccio brutto de via Merulana* (*That Awful Mess on the Via Merulana*, published in book form in 1957; see sec. 9.1) – and yet that same reader cannot help coming back for more, re-reading, trying again.

Elio Vittorini also wrote his most accomplished work of fiction, *Conversazione in Sicilia* (*Conversation in Sicily*), during the late thirties, and this too was first published in *Letteratura* in instalments in 1938–9. It was written at a time of political and existential crisis for Vittorini. The formative experiences of Gadda, fifteen years his senior, had taken place during the First World War (*Giornale di guerra e di prigionia* (*Days of War and Imprisonment*), first published in part in 1955) and, as a professional engineer, Gadda kept a critical distance from the regime which he satirized indirectly in his novels and openly and vehemently in a tract like *Eros e Priapo* (*Eros and Priapus*, written at the end of the war, published in 1967). By contrast, Vittorini belonged to the generation which had virtually grown up with Fascism; he was fourteen at the time of the March on Rome. Like many other young people, he enthusiastically embraced the more revolutionary and anti-bourgeois aspects of Fascist ideology and was correspondingly disappointed as he became aware that these were no longer the priorities of the regime. The conflict between the adolescent impulse towards life, love and liberty and a hard political reality is already evident in *Il garofano rosso* (instalment publication in *Solaria*, 1933–6; in book form, 1948, with a self-justificatory preface). Vittorini was part of a generation which, even as Mussolini embarked on his imperial adventures in East Africa in 1936, was looking for a way in which Fascism could be brought back to its more radical social roots, and in which they themselves, young but in many ways marginalized by an increasingly conformist society, could do something. This was the so-called 'left-wing Fascism' which fed into significant parts of the internal opposition within the country, the Resistance during the final stages of the war, and the emergence of the Communist Party and other left-wing groupings after the war.

More than the attack on Abyssinia, which led to failed League of Nations sanctions and defensive patriotic sentiments, it was the involvement of Fascist Italy alongside Nazi Germany in the Spanish Civil War, on the side of Franco's rebels against the republican government, which crystallized the harsh and dangerous realities of European politics for the young Fascists of Vittorini's generation, as it did for other young people elsewhere in Europe. Spain is the ghost at the feast in *Conversazione in Sicilia*, where Silvestro, who has moved to the city and works as a typesetter, is assailed by the trumpetings of war from the newspaper hoardings and, haunted by 'abstract furies', is rendered almost unable to speak: his language has become like the words of a dictionary, empty, heavy, without resonance. He is saved by a summons home: his father suggests he visit his mother Concezione back in Sicily. The novel traces the five stages of this return to Silvestro's origins, during which he meets emblematic figures along the way, has lengthy conversations with his mother; with a child, perhaps his earlier self; with the memory of his 'Shakespearean' father, who, like Vittorini's own, was a station-master who staged plays in makeshift venues in the surrounding villages; with older inhabitants of the village, who are variously deluded or defeated in a scene which is staged like a descent to the underworld; and finally, in the cemetery itself, with the dead. It is here that Silvestro learns that his brother has been killed in battle, and he prepares to return to the mainland and the north. The whole novel is cast in a mythical and lyrical mould; the language is elevated, seeming always to strain for the expression of an essence. That may be the reality of poverty, in the figure of the orange-seller who has no choice but to feed himself and his companion on the oranges he cannot sell, contrasted to the image of safety conveyed by the smell of the herrings his mother cooks and the memory of the melons she used to hide when they were children, or the constant appeal to 'other duties' and to a reality that is 'twice real', as though beyond this reality it might be possible to reach a higher state of being. The amazing thing about this novel is that Vittorini succeeds, through his sustained lyrical prose, in convincing the reader that this shimmering 'other' has a real presence, even though Silvestro's return to the humdrum yet threatening reality of everyday life (a job, a family) is inevitable.

Though less obviously experimental and innovative than either of these two, Cesare Pavese's debut also marked out new paths. A graduate of Turin University, Pavese first made his mark as a critic writing about English and particularly American literature and as a translator. He was prominent among a group of young intellectuals, including Vittorini, who cultivated a deep interest in American writing in the 1930s, both for the stylistic innovations wrought by contemporary American fiction writers such as John Steinbeck, William Faulkner and Ernest Hemingway, some of which would be echoed in Italian fiction, and for a sort of 'myth of America' which these and other writers created in their work, or at any rate which their Italian readers read into it: an America that was huge, open, young and full of possibility in contrast to their tired, narrow and self-destructive Europe. This very positive image of America, which perhaps signalled the beginning of the mid-century shift of cultural hegemony from Paris to New York, was doubtless reinforced by the success of American cinema, even in an Italy whose authorities tried to regulate the influx of foreign-made, essentially Hollywood films. The love-affair was temporarily suspended during the war itself, particularly after the United States' entry into the war in 1941; Vittorini's extensively annotated anthology, *Americana*, published by Bompiani, was confiscated, and most of the notes replaced by a much less sympathetic commentary by Emilio Cecchi (cf. above), whose travel reportage, *America amara* (*America the Bitter*, 1939), had presented a more critical view of American society more in keeping with the perspective of the Fascist regime.

Pavese's essays were collected and published posthumously in 1951 as *La letteratura americana e altri saggi* (*American Literature and Other Essays*) by Einaudi, the Turin publishing house regarded with suspicion by the Fascist authorities, whose staff he joined in 1942. He was sent into internal exile in a remote village in Calabria in the mid-1930s because of his association with members of the anti-Fascist 'Giustizia e libertà' movement. This moment of his life was recorded in *Il carcere* (*Prison*, written 1938–9), but his most interesting work during this period – apart from the working diary which was published posthumously as *Il mestiere di vivere* (*The Business of Living*, 1952) – were the poems of *Lavorare stanca* (*Work Tires*, 1936) and the novel *Paesi tuoi* (*Your Places*, 1941). The poems, which were published under the *Solaria* imprint, were unusual for their time: narrative rather than lyrical, and employing a correspondingly long line, they aimed for an objective representation of working-class people in both town and country. The basic theme – the encounter between town and country, usually a conflictual one made up of fear and misunderstanding – is pursued in *Paesi tuoi*, where some of Pavese's strong themes and approaches begin to be apparent: ritual and myth, linked here to Talino's incestuous passion for his sister Gisella culminating in the latter's killing, the threat of savagery, but also, more accentuated in his later work, the story of the country-born lad who has become urbanized and needs to find his way back into the country and his own childhood through memory and the wise counsel of those who have remained. The existential and fictional drama of the clash between town and country, already adumbrated in Alvaro, is given universal resonance in Pavese's often mythopoeic writing, in which he combines an autobiographical quest for origins with a highly developed interest in anthropology and ethnography (sciences whose growth he helped to promote through his editorial work).

One final point to reiterate here is that the poets and novelists discussed in the previous two sections were not generally reaching very many readers (*Gli indifferenti* was an exception; see sec. 8.1). *Solaria* never printed more than 700 copies of an edition in the ten years of its existence (Pertile 1986: 177). Yet it was precisely the small magazines, continuing the pre-Fascist tradition, that had a disproportionate importance for both readers and authors. They functioned as meeting places, a turntable for the exchange, spread and circulation of ideas, a laboratory for literary experiment. When one was suppressed, or ran out of money, or simply expired, another quickly took its place. Some, like Ugo Ojetti's (1871–1946) *Pegaso* (1929–32) and *Pan* (1931–5), were much like house-magazines for the regime and espoused conservative values; later, the technically Fascist *Primato* (1940–3), founded by Giuseppe Bottai (1895–1959), who was a leading cultural spokesman throughout the Fascist regime but was by now leaning towards left-Fascist positions, was open to a variety of opinions and styles. (Elsa Morante, however, was later to claim that Bottai refused to publish her work because she was a woman.) The small magazines, sometimes backed up by small publishing operations of their own, were the lifeblood of serious literature during the Fascist period.

8.4 Resistance, Reconstruction and neo-realism

From the title of this section, it might appear that historical events, and the ideology of 'realism' that goes with them – the social call, the need for literature to focus on things that matter to large numbers of people, the need to respond to the immediate environment – once again take primacy in our cultural history of modern Italian literature. But this is only partly the case. It is certainly true that the violence, destruction and disruption of war and civil war fought across much of the national territory in 1943–5 brought about conditions that were new to the majority of writers, and that the overthrow of a regime and the construction of a new order along with the material rebuilding of the country were necessarily felt as an inaugural moment. But, in strictly literary terms, the experimentations of the previous twenty years, both in poetry and prose, were not lost or forgotten.

Let us begin with beginnings. In 1964, Italo Calvino (1923–85) republished his first novel, *Il sentiero dei nidi di ragno* (*The Path to the Spiders' Nests*), set in the backstreets of his native San Remo and the mountains behind the city during the Resistance, a novel which had first appeared in 1947. He introduced it to a new public with a long preface which described, among other things, the difficulty of getting the novel started, of finding the right theme for it, the right characters, the right narrator, the right plot devices, the right tone. The preface itself is a series of false starts, doublings-back, reruns, not unlike the series of beginnings which go to make up the much later novel *Se una notte d'inverno un viaggiatore* (*If on a Winter's Night a Traveller*, 1979). It is, in other words, a characteristically Calvinian exercise, but like all Calvino's exercises it has a point, for this reiterated attempt to explain helps to evoke, far better than mere argument could, a moment of extraordinary communicativeness in Italian life:

> The return of free speech was experienced by people to start with as an urgent desire to tell each other stories: in the trains which began to run again, packed with people and sacks of flour and cans of oil, every traveller told strangers about the things that had happened to him, and so did every customer who ate at the 'people's canteens' and every woman queuing at the shops; the greyness of daily lives seemed to belong to another era; we circulated in a multi-coloured universe of stories. (Calvino 1978: 7–8)

Such a diffusion of narrative is a common experience to all survivors of dramatic or tragic events, great or small. It does not last long. But what did it mean to the writer? The moment Calvino described endured a few months, perhaps only a few weeks. Indeed, its transience was of the essence. Liberation was like a moment suspended in time, a huge party, a carnival, which was bound to end, but not yet. The stories swapped in café, tram and office were a way perhaps of prolonging the moment, and in order to do that they had to retain the freshness, spontaneity and immediacy of stories told as if for the first time – they must reject any suggestion of being recorded and made permanent. The stories of the Liberation were a genuinely oral repertoire which resisted writing – and the writer – however rich a pool of tales and however eager an audience they seemed to promise. Then, later, with the euphoria passed and people picking up the threads of their lives again, the writer could begin to draw on that material, but it was as something to which he or she, as a writer, was extraneous and subsequent.

There was at the same time a kind of writing which, rather than drawing on the oral repertoire, was its written equivalent. Already in the closing months of the war, the anti-Fascist underground press was publishing brief accounts of incidents of partisan life and pen-portraits (or obituaries) of comrades-in-arms. At the end of hostilities, numerous small publishing houses came into being and survived on the publication of diaries, memoirs and re-evocations of life in the Resistance movement. Larger publishers and the cultural pages of newspapers continued to print such documents through 1945 and 1946, and after a time the flood of Resistance stories was swollen further by the memories of war veterans and survivors of the concentration and extermination camps. These memoirs included Primo Levi's masterpiece *Se questo è un uomo* (*If This is a Man*), published by a small house (De Silva of Turin) in 1947 and little noticed at the time (Einaudi in fact turned it down), but one of the first attempts to confront at all, and even more to confront without rhetoric, the experience of Auschwitz. Levi and a few others aside, most of the kind of writing alluded to in this paragraph is documentary in nature, and it should be noted that the purpose of such writing was diametrically opposed to that of the oral narrative discussed above. People wrote down their experiences precisely in order to remember, to draw to the attention of others, and very often to point a moral or political lesson. But it may be considered as a written equivalent to the oral repertoire for the simple reason that it presented itself as a direct representation of lived experience and had no doubts about the immediacy and directness of its contact with its audience. Writing as a means of preserving what might otherwise quickly be forgotten was also, in the eyes of the veterans who practised it, a means of carrying on the struggle in which hitherto they had been engaged militarily or politically, and it was very definitely not 'literature'. It was, if anything, a kind of anti-literature: events followed on paratactically one from another; there was minimal characterization; moral choices were posed in black-and-white terms; the mimetic capability of language was unquestioned; language itself was made to approximate as closely as possible to the spoken norm.

There is undoubtedly a continuity, in terms of literary history, between this 'naïve' writing of war and Resistance and the more formal literary (and cinematic) tendency known as neo-realism (Corti 1978). But, in the immediacy of events, it seemed for the post-war writer of fiction, faced with the ineluctable demand to take 'reality' as one's subject matter, meaning the political and social reality of the immediate past, as if there was not only a superabundance of reality to write about, but a superabundance of narrative too, from the oral anecdote to the written document. And it seemed also that this reality and this narrative had a privileged relation to each other in a closed circle that excluded the professional writer, the serious writer, and perhaps the writer of fiction. Initially at least, the writer was more blocked than liberated by the end of dictatorship and foreign occupation. He found himself in the situation of the young intellectual locked in a cell measuring three metres by one-and-a-half with four other prisoners, in the SS headquarters in Via Tasso in Rome, described by Guglielmo Petroni in his memoir published in 1948 with the title 'Il mondo è una prigione':

> Then I began to undergo a new torment. I found peace, sometimes an infinite serenity, lazy and unthinking, in silence. But it was different for the other four. Silence was their worst enemy. [. . .] 'Someone say something!' went up the cry, and then someone would talk. [. . .] They talked, yet I could find nothing to say except a few sentences. In fact, I realized that when *I* said something, it was like writing a page of a book. [. . .] *They* talked; every word was an image, every speech a world swarming with characters, emotions, children, mothers and lovers. (Petroni 1948: 52–3)

This passage, and the context of psychological and ethical discomfort in which it is placed ('You never say anything!' Petroni's cellmates accuse him), does not conceal the fact that the unease experienced by the writer in the presence of the uninterrupted flow of words is part of a wider sense of social and moral inadequacy: that of the 'aesthete' confronted by the 'working man', that of intellectuality confronted by the world of experience. With this, the problem posed to the writer by the superabundance of speech is linked to the sense of guilt which lacerates some post-war intellectuals. Another accusation: 'You know so many things, Corrado, and yet you do nothing to help us.' The speaker: Cate, anti-Fascist activist, working mother, ex-lover of the schoolteacher protagonist, who does not defend himself against the accusation. The book: Cesare Pavese's *La casa in collina*, published in 1949 (Pavese 1972: 215). The 'house in the hills' of the title is Corrado's family home, where he will escape all active responsibility in the remaining months of the war. The theme: failure and betrayal, one of the reiterated themes of the fiction of the late 1940s and early 1950s, and a variant of the larger social theme of the disappointed (or defeated) revolution which recurs in neo-realist texts. Near the centre of the nexus writer–people–politics–present stands the anxiety-figure of the intellectual who let the side down, or could not rise to the occasion, or who remained, whether through his own fault or not, marginal to the situation which demanded by every means and at every opportunity his active participation. This dramatic, even tragic theme is grist to the mill of guilt, and represents an extreme and depressive solution to a problem which lies at the heart of post-war narrative. To examine this problem, we should like to remain within the space opened up by the writer's relation to narrative and to the real.

The narrative of the war and the Resistance began in the closing stages of the war itself with the publication of real-life stories, eyewitness accounts and some fictional stories in the pages of the underground press, and continued after the war with a large and increasing quantity of diaries, memoirs, reports and stories. The emphasis was always on the notion that what the readers had before them was a true account of what actually happened, that it was the facts that mattered, that the job of the writer – in this case the person who went through the experience – was simply to put down in words the events through which he or she lived or which he or she witnessed. Very often this kind of writing, which was frequently produced by people who had never set pen to paper in their lives, was posited as a kind of anti-novel, meaning that it was not invented and it was not written *up*: 'this is not a novel, and it is not an exaltation of the partisan war,' affirms one typical preface (Pierro Carmagnola, in Falaschi 1976: 28).

Once this factual content was established, however, different options as to *how* to relate the story became available. The stress might fall on the autobiographical nature of the account, which seemed to guarantee its authenticity. This was a path which in its turn forked in two: along the first, the collective subject is brought into focus by the author stressing his ordinariness, his typicality, while along the second, it is the individual that is brought into focus by the author emphasizing his own spiritual and personal development. Other narratives made less play of their autobiographical origin, while still keeping it in view, and stressed instead the factual nature of the account, deliberately presenting a succession of events recorded with the chronological order, restraint of style and lack of literary pretensions of a report. Others again had much more of an eye to literary effect (even in a purely factual, autobiographical, account) and exploited the dramatic possibilities inherent in the Resistance story, especially the element of suspense associated with the adventures of escape, chase, unexpected confrontation, trying to cross the lines, the frontier, the river, the open space without any cover, to get from A to B. But even one of the most effective, precisely, of such adventure narratives, Pietro Chiodi's *Banditi* (*Bandits*, 1946), begins with the ritual recital 'This book is not a novel.' The prime purpose of these accounts of wartime experience was to convey information, information that had hitherto been unavailable and which the public (or a certain public) demanded in order to answer the question 'What really happened?' and to complete its picture of the recent past.

Alongside this memorialistic writing, and to some extent growing out of it, there are those books which looked back on the war and the Resistance commemoratively, even nostalgically, as a moment of national tragedy or achievement and pride that had been lived and should be remembered collectively. Although such feelings were sometimes expressed in the more factual, memorialistic kind of writing, their tendency towards a choral form and epic dimensions was more easily realized in the novel. One of the better examples in terms of narrative quality, written by Renata Viganò (1900–76), was *L'Agnese va a morire* (*Agnese Goes to Die*), which won the Viareggio Prize in 1949. Viganò herself had been a partisan and part of her narrative at least was based on personal experience. But in the figure of Agnese, the peasant woman who devotes herself body and soul to the Resistance when her husband is killed by the Nazis, the author sought to create an outstanding, exemplary figure, a positive hero with whom, because of her own simplicity and natural goodness, ordinary people could identify.

In both these kinds of narrative, the memorialistic and the epic-celebrative, the latter (generally) fictional and the former not, the relation of the narrator to her material is one of humility: here is the story, my writing is the medium through which events speak for themselves, the story tells its own tale. Quite the opposite effect was achieved in what was, chronologically, the very first novel of the Resistance, Vittorini's *Uomini e no* (*Men and Not-Men*), written during the author's involvement in the Milanese underground movement and published in June 1945. While the hero is an intellectual who succeeds, to a certain extent, in combining theory and practice at the level of his militancy in the Resistance, the novel (in its original edition) is predicated on a split between this intellectual activist and a shadowy figure who appears from time to time, in italicized sections of the text, to give voice to another reality, essentially that of memory, nature, the imagination, which is not realized in what we must call the main parts of the novel (the italicized sections were deleted by Vittorini from the third edition of 1949; all but two were restored for the sixth edition, in 1965). This figure is identified with the writer, and what Vittorini was doing with this metafictional device, borrowed from Faulkner and, further back, Gide, was to establish that separate identity for the writer or, more exactly, the act of writing, away from the flow of reality for which other authors of his generation felt a particular need: Anna Banti (1895–1985), for example, who in the marvellous novel *Artemisia* (1947) took advantage of the biographical accident of the loss of her original manuscript about the sixteenth-century painter Artemisia Gentileschi to interweave the rewritten version with reflections on the novel and on the battle for Florence in 1944; or Elsa Morante (1912–85), in *Menzogna e sortilegio* (*Lies and Magic*, 1948, translated as *The House of Liars*), with her juxtaposition of the writer Elisa and the family history which she relates on different planes of narration.

If we can momentarily take Viganò and Vittorini as emblematic of two different sorts of post-war writing, we can see that the relation between writing and the real was conceived in radically different ways. The subordination of the narrator in Viganò, who limits her active intervention at most to the celebration of qualities already inherent in the object of her narration and brought out by her, gives way in Vittorini to a separation between the narrated and the narrator which is potentially destructive. The spirit of division persisted in writers of a younger generation, those whose earliest work began to appear after the war. But the division took on a different, less dramatic, configuration. A writer like Calvino, for example, was not interested in exposing his consciousness to the public gaze, even if in oblique or symbolic form. Perhaps what *he* learnt from the war writers was a certain modesty, even a certain shyness, about writing. But the problem of relating writing to reality remained urgent: while for Viganò and the memorialists, the world presented itself as rich and full, though perhaps morally simple (good and evil are easily identified and distinguished by political, even national traits), for Calvino the world presented itself as rich and confusing, and morally complex. His narration must allow the reader to see both what is and what is not, the other-than-the-narrated, and this without drawing attention to the author. The child's-eye view adopted in *Il sentiero dei nidi di ragno* was perfect for his purposes: the view of a knowing child who sees the world as a series of adventures, who is both attracted and repelled by the adult world, and through whom the adult reader also perceives a reality which has few of the charms it possesses for the boy Pin.

Thanks to this variation of narrative perspective, Calvino also put himself in a position to be able to reinterpret the Resistance 'from below': it reveals itself as the scene of heroism but also of cowardice, purposeful but also muddled, hopeful but also a lost cause for some – a perspective that demanded personal honesty and some courage in 1947, in the midst of hagiography and mythmaking. And in this connection we should mention finally the name of Beppe Fenoglio (1922–63), who devoted almost the whole of his short writing career to an exploration without sensationalism of the Resistance and its aftermath during the period of post-war reconstruction. His was the world of the partisans of whom, in the opening words of the title-story of his collection *I ventitre giorni della città di Alba* (*The Twenty-Three Days of the City of Alba*, 1952), 'two thousand captured Alba on the tenth of October and two hundred lost it on the second of November 1944' (Fenoglio 1976: 3). What happened to the other eighteen hundred and how the Resistance managed to snatch defeat from the jaws of victory as well as vice versa were valid starting points for Fenoglio's revision of wartime myths.

We are now talking about writers who were writing in the heyday of literary neo-realism (roughly between 1945 and 1955), but who were removed from it. It is obvious that certain themes and certain stylistic devices were common at this stage to anyone who took recent or contemporary history as their subject matter. At its best, for example in *Le terre del Sacramento* (*The Lands of Sacramento*, 1950), a historical novel by Francesco Jovine (1902–50) set in his native Molise in the years leading up to the triumph of Fascism in 1922, the neo-realist novel succeeded in depicting a wide spectrum of society, but it empathized in particular with the poor majority, urban or more usually rural, which is exploited and oppressed, and it told a complex story, sometimes of epic proportions, in direct and relatively simple language. But while it could represent the hierarchy and interplay between social classes and social actors effectively, it was not able to take that distance from itself which would in any way allow it to question its own procedures.

Perhaps these qualities were necessary in a period of ideological confrontation, such as that which led to the defeat of the political left in the 1948 elections and the institutionalization on a global scale of the Cold War between 'the West' and the Soviet Union. But it was a period too in which, for those same political reasons, the relation between politics and culture was up for redefinition. Already in 1946–7, Vittorini, then editor with Franco Fortini (1917–94) of the left-wing journal *Il Politecnico* (a 'continuation' of the secular cultural journal of the same name founded by Carlo Cattaneo in 1839), clashed with the leadership of the Italian Communist Party (PCI) over what appeared to be differences of policy detail, but in reality was an unacknowledged struggle between Vittorini's belief in the intellectual's freedom of action and the tendency of the party to want to 'manage' culture politically. And it cannot be denied that neo-realism had a tendency to sentimentalize the working classes, something, for example, of which Vasco Pratolini (1913–91) was accused in his hugely successful chronicle of Florentine working-class life *Cronache di poveri amanti* (*Chronicles of Poor Lovers*, 1947) and, with rather more justice, in *Metello* (1955), a historical novel set at the turn of the century. The oral historian Luisa Passerini observed acutely in this regard: 'After listening to many working-class people talking about themselves, we can recognize their sentimentality as it appears in literature but not the laughter which follows it, the false bravado but not the self-irony, the high-minded tone but not its deflation' (Passerini 1987: 25). Younger writers like Calvino and Fenoglio would be more interested in the laughter, the self-irony and the deflation.

9

From the avant-garde to the market-place

9.1 The last avant-garde?

Throughout this book we have used dates, decades, centuries as convenient markers for change in literary culture. These markers can be both arbitrary and misleadingly precise, but they can also be dictated by convention. Datings change, and so it is with the period after the Second World War. For the generations immediately affected the decisive date was the end of the war and the defeat of Nazism-Fascism, and so 1945 was seen as a turning point for all aspects of cultural and social life, including literature. In reality, there were significant continuities between the writing of the thirties and the forties, and historians starting with Romano Luperini (Luperini 1981: I, xv–xx) have proposed 1956 as the start of a distinctive phase in modern Italian literary culture. In reality, this date too was determined by non-literary criteria. It was at or close to the beginning of a period of astonishingly rapid and intensive economic growth in Italy (what at the time was called the 'economic miracle' is usually dated to the years between 1958 and 1963), the acceleration of the trend away from agriculture to industry, the movement of more than a million workers from the countryside to the cities, and the creation of an expanding market for consumer goods. It also had political significance as a particularly tense moment in the Cold War, when Soviet troops moved into Poland and Hungary just a few months after Stalin's crimes had been denounced, in very guarded terms, by his successor in Moscow. The political events had repercussions in the Italian intelligentsia – a number of writers and other intellectuals left the Italian Communist Party (PCI), which they had joined after the fall of Fascism and identified with since then. The economic, social and cultural changes which were taking place in the country during the late fifties and early sixties had an even more profound, and more lasting, impact on the literary scene, and writers watched and tried to understand them with great care.

An important attempt to mark out a new position, mainly from the point of view of poetry, was the work of the Bologna-based magazine *Officina*, edited by Francesco Leonetti (1924–), Pier Paolo Pasolini (1922–75) and

Roberto Roversi (1923–). It mounted a vigorous campaign against the decadentist tradition in Italian poetry and distanced itself from both hermeticism and neo-realism. In order to forge a different poetics, which would be neither withdrawn as the hermetics were alleged to be nor 'committed' and beholden to a political agenda, Pasolini looked to the poetry of the late nineteenth and early twentieth centuries, the civic poetry of Carducci and Pascoli's *Poemetti*, as the basis for a distinctively contemporary experimentalism, a vein which he continued to mine in his own poetry through the 1960s and into the anti-lyrical polemics of his final published collection, *Trasumanar e organizzar* (*Transhumanize and Organize*, 1971). Franco Fortini (1917–94), a Marxist poet and critic, who was associated with *Officina* although he quarrelled with Pasolini, developed a prophetic and warning tone with a similar sense of civic responsibility. A number of writers, however, continued to build on their hermeticist foundations, notable amongst them Giorgio Caproni (1912–90), Vittorio Sereni (1913–83) and the prolific Catholic poet Mario Luzi (1914–2005). All of them, however, shifted noticeably towards a more conversational and accessible language in the course of their long post-war careers.

A more radical attempt to break with the traditions of the recent past occurred with the publication of a selection of the work of five young poets in an anthology called *I novissimi* (1961, reissued with a new preface in 1965), whose title was a programme in itself: nothing could be newer than the super-new. The five poets – Alfredo Giuliani (1924–), Elio Pagliarani (1927–), Nanni Balestini (1935–), Antonio Porta (1935–89) and Edoardo Sanguineti (1930–) – had come from the stable of *Il Verri*, a distinguished poetry review founded by Luciano Anceschi (1911–95) in Milan in 1956. What was even more important was the active involvement of Giuliani, Balestrini and Sanguineti in the debates and polemics of the Gruppo 63, which came into being at a new music festival in Palermo in October 1963 and published theoretical essays and interventions for a number of years before being submerged by the protest movements of 1968–9. *I novissimi* became something of a beacon for the Gruppo 63; together they represented what came to be referred to as the neo-avant-garde (*neoavanguardia*). The self-proclaimed status of these writers as a new avant-garde had a very specific resonance. They too were trying to claim a portion of the early twentieth-century, pre-Fascist, poetic heritage, though a different part from that claimed by Pasolini (who detested them). This was the 'historic' avant-garde of the Futurists and the Surrealists, who were appreciated for their generic non-conformism, for the fundamental avant-garde mission to break with the past, and for their openness to the modern in the case of the Futurists and their interest in language and psychoanalysis in the case of the Surrealists.

The interlocking groups which formed in the 1960s around the idea of the avant-garde were in fact probably the last to be able to lay claim to that name. The radicalism of some of their ideas was matched by a strong ideological and political motivation which was overtaken by events at the end of the decade. Both the radicalism and the politicization alienated many of their contemporaries, while if a literary avant-garde is to function today it must do so in very different material circumstances from those of the 1960s (it will happen online, for example, and involve many more people, undermining the idea of small, exclusive groups and demonstrative actions which the militaristic idea of a 'vanguard' necessarily connotes). The *neoavanguardia* continues to be snubbed by influential sections of the Italian literary establishment, but what it had to say about both poetry and the novel remains an incisive point of reference for the period.

At the heart of the poetics of the neo-avant-garde lay a radical distrust of language, both the reified language of mass communication and the illusion that language 'reflects' or 'expresses' an external reality. On the contrary, the content of poetry is not what it says, but what it does; it is a critical experience of reality. The importance given to 'things' and to 'experience' in the poetry of the neo-avant-garde was partly in opposition to what Antonio Porta called the 'ostentation' of the self. The ideal is a 'poeta-oggettivo' ('objective-poet') rather than a 'poeta-io' ('I-poet'). The poet 'descends' into reality, with an attitude of openness, engaged in discovery or research, establishing a contact which may at first be difficult or painful. The idea is to get reality to reveal itself, beyond the deception of appearances (see Caesar 1999: 571 for more detail on this point). The poem thus becomes a journey for the reader as well. The radical disruption of language and the critical demands on the reader which were entailed by this project were perhaps best exemplified by a slightly older poet, Andrea Zanzotto (1921–), who had nothing to do with the Gruppo 63. Following the itinerary of a Zanzotto poem, the reader may achieve a provisional meaning, not by straining to see the impossible match between the words and the real world they express or represent, but by participating in the disintegration of words in a centrifugal movement away from apparent meaning, as in these lines from 'La perfezione della neve':

> Quante perfezioni, quante
> quante totalità. Pungendo aggiunge.
> E poi astrazioni astrificazioni formulazione d'astri
> assideramento, attraverso sidera e coelos
> assideramenti assimilazioni

> (So many perfections, o so many totalities. It adds, stinging. And then abstractions starfactions the making of stars frost-bite across sidera and coelos frost-bites assimilations) (from *La beltà* (1968); tr. Smith 1981: 213)

The neo-avant-garde became concerned with experimentalism in the novel in the mid-1960s. The debate was more bitter and more personalized than it had been on the subject of poetry. Once again we discover one of the fault-lines of the Italian literary consciousness. There was an authority and self-confidence in the internal discussions about poetry that was lacking in those about the novel: Italian poetry rests on a tradition stretching back centuries which is constantly revisited; at the same time it is refreshed by its international links, moves confidently in the multinational environment of poetry and is respected in it; it has a small and dwindling audience – sometimes it seems made up mainly of other poets – but a sophisticated one; there is a sense that poets are speaking the same language even when they are violently disagreeing. Discussion about the novel, on the other hand, was seared by an anxiety of backwardness, the sense that Italy did not have a tradition of the novel comparable to that of the more 'advanced' nations and languages, that it desperately had to modernize and get up to date.

Behind this real anxiety there lay the persistent sense of the 'particularism' of Italy in the post-war period: the idea that Italian culture was specifically, even uniquely, marked by the (normally creative) tension between tradition and modernity, between a vernacular culture of the highest quality dating back seven centuries, and a religious and classical culture much older than that, and a process of economic and social modernization, conducted at breakneck speed, which was in part a catching up with the more advanced economies of neo-capitalism and in part a leapfrogging of competitors. It is worth mentioning here that today the situation is quite different, and the question of Italy's modernity does not arise, whatever 'modern' means in the global, postindustrial, twenty-first century. 'Culture' too occupies a much more substantial place in the economy than it did in the 1950s or 1960s. It is a different kind of culture, of course (see sec. 9.2).

Part of the anxiety about backwardness lay in the very difficulty of constructing a heritage. The avant-garde reacted virulently against the work of writers like Giorgio Bassani (1916–2000), Carlo Cassola (1917–87) and the Pasolini of his 1950s Roman novels (*Ragazzi di vita* (*The 'Ragazzi'*, 1955) and *Una vita violenta* (*A Violent Life*, 1959)), all seen as embodying, though in different ways, the sentimentalism, provincialism and misguided narrative realism attributed by the neo-avant-garde to the fiction of the previous decade. Bassani had committed the additional crime of recommending Feltrinelli to publish Giuseppe Tomasi di Lampedusa's (1896–1957) historical novel *Il gattopardo* (*The Leopard*, 1958), regarded as conventional and reactionary by many on the left but a huge bestseller. The avant-garde was ideologically sympathetic to, but did not have much to say about, the linguistic or stylistic achievements of the numerous fictions which tried to get to grips with the alienating realities of the rapid industrialization and urbanization of the early 1960s. Among these were works by contemporary writers such as Luciano Bianciardi (1922–71), Lucio Mastronardi (1930–79) and Ottiero Ottieri (1924–2002), although *Il padrone* (*The Boss*, 1965), a savage satire by Goffredo Parise (1929–86), and the first two novels by Paolo Volponi (1924–94), *Memoriale* (*Memorandum*, 1962) and *La macchina mondiale* (*The Worldwide Machine*, 1965), did excite the attention of the innovators. To some extent a native lineage for a non-realist or non-mimetic novel could be constructed using the achievements of Svevo, Pirandello and Gadda (this last republished in 1957 and 1963/1970; see sec. 8.3); otherwise, the appeal was back to the modernist giants of European literature who were already being held up as examples in the 1920s and 1930s.

What is striking, looking back at the fiction published in the 1960s and 1970s, is how good a lot of it was. Experimentalism played a part, from Balestrini's *nouveau roman*-style endeavour *Tristano* (1966), which already used the characteristic cut-up technique which he would deploy to great effect in *La violenza illustrata* (*Violence Illustrated*) ten years later (Balestrini was also working with computer-generated sequences for his poetry in the 1960s) to Sanguineti's *Capriccio italiano* (*Italian Caprice*, 1963) and *Il giuoco dell'oca* (*The Goose Game*, 1967), which, like his poetry, drew on the resources of multilingualism and the unconscious, and from the 'surrealist' *Signorina Rosina* (1959) by Antonio Pizzuto (1893–1976) to the rebarbative essay-novels of Giorgio Manganelli (1922–90). But pure formal experiment tended to be sidelined, or at any rate judged unreadable, and many authors were canny enough to work their interest in point of view, plot manipulation, metalinguistic and metaliterary play into narrative forms and language with which an averagely educated but alert and interested audience could engage. Chief amongst these was Italo Calvino. First with the fabulatory trilogy *I nostri antenati* (*Our Ancestors*, 1951–8), then with the 'fantastic' *Cosmicomiche* (*Cosmicomics*, 1965) and *Ti con zero* (translated as *Time and the Hunter*, 1967), which integrated literature and science, and finally with the minutely plotted structures of *Il castello dei destini incrociati* (*The Castle of Crossed Destinies*, 1973, begun in 1969) and *Le città invisibili* (*Invisible Cities*, 1972), followed after a long silence by the metafictional and parodic *Se una notte d'inverno un viaggiatore* (1979), he set a model of lucid and controlled prose which many of his contemporaries would try to emulate (see also secs 8.4 and 9.3).

The language was of crucial importance here: it was in this period that Italian became a 'standard' language, a language of normal communication rather than one reserved for the higher reaches of culture. The reasons were obvious, chief among them the extension of the school-leaving age and the opening of the universities to all qualified students in the 1960s, the spread of television with its standardized, national speech understood by everyone, and greater physical mobility for many people. The standardization of Italian impacted on the written word in different ways. For some it signalled the trivialization of the language of culture; amongst other things, the language could no longer be policed as effectively as in the past by purists or the defenders of 'good' Italian. Montale for one responded by joining them rather than trying to beat them: his last, epigrammatic, collections of poems in the 1970s expressed his pessimism by deliberately abjuring any elevated, 'poetic' style. Amongst both poets and novelists, however, it made possible a much more communicative relationship with the public.

There was also a greater readiness to engage with popular forms which previously might have seemed to be beneath the serious writer, or at any rate something to be put into a separate category. Science fiction, romance, but most importantly the crime novel – forms that were largely alien to the strong Italian tradition of realist and regional writing – were forms nevertheless that novelists in the 1960s and 1970s looking to modernize the Italian tradition found useful to exploit. Gadda had given an authoritative demonstration of the possibilities of the crime format (known as *il giallo* in Italian) in *Quer pasticciaccio brutto de via Merulana*, but others were also exploring this vein. Nearly all the fiction written by Leonardo Sciascia (1921–89) can be described as an investigation of one sort or another, from the Mafia-centred novels of the sixties (*Il giorno della civetta* (*The Day of the Owl*, 1961) and *A ciascuno il suo* (*To Each His Own*, 1966)) to his more darkly political work such as *Il contesto* (1971, translated as *Equal Danger*) and *Todo modo* (*One Way or the Other*, 1974). The detective may be read as an alter ego of the first-person researcher who appears in other works, in which, on the basis of scanty and often incomplete documents, and usually not more than circumstantial evidence, Sciascia seeks to put together again a long-neglected historical event or chain of events involving a mystery or an injustice. The usual situation is that the patient investigator comes up against a wall of silence, *omertà* or blankness.

Among the many other writers who could be mentioned as exponents or exploiters of the *giallo* format in the novel, Luigi Malerba (1927–) wrote a prose that was both entertaining and provocative in *Il serpente* (*The Snake*, 1966), the dubious confession of a Roman stamp-dealer who claims to have eaten his lover, and *Salto mortale* (*Somersault*, 1968), a *giallo* within a *giallo* where it is left to the reader to decide whether what is written is true or false. The publication of *La donna della domenica* (*Sunday Woman*) in 1972 inaugurated a string of successful novels co-written by the Turinese authors Carlo Fruttero and Franco Lucentini which was interrupted only by the death of the latter in 2002. We should add at this point that the use of genre fiction, and particularly the detective story or thriller, grew exponentially in the 1990s to the extent that another Sicilian writer, Andrea Camilleri (1925–), who had spent his career in television and the theatre, could become one of Italy's bestselling authors with his fictional detective Montalbano (a homage to the Catalan author Manuel Vázquez Montalbán), a success replicated by many younger writers, from Carlo Lucarelli (1960–) to Gianrico Carofiglio (1961–), a working anti-Mafia judge.

One of the things that is interesting in Camilleri's work is that he uses a demanding but entertaining mix of Italian and Sicilian. The fact that he can do this, and that this is one of the attractions of his prose for many readers, may be connected with the revival of dialect as a literary, and in some cases an invented, language by a number of poets in the last quarter of the twentieth century, as well as its more frequent use in the mass media. Pasolini had used a reinvented Friuli dialect in his poetry of the 1940s and Roman dialect in his novels; Zanzotto has made consistent use of his Veneto dialect as part of the linguistic tissue of his work; among poets who have written mainly or exclusively in dialect are another Veneto poet, Biagio Marin (1891–1985); Albino Pierro (Lucania, 1916–95); Tonino Guerra (1920–) and Raffaello Baldini (1931–), both of whom use a Romagna dialect; Franco Loi (Milan, 1930–); Franco Scataglini (1930–94) whose composite language draws heavily on his native Ancona dialect; and Franca Grisoni (Sirmione, 1945–). The public which learnt to read Italian with pleasure in the 1960s and 1970s is now willing to grapple with the other languages of the country (the same phenomenon can be observed in the UK), although there is a difference between poetry and fiction: while in fiction the reader is expected to glean the meaning from the general context, in poetry it is normal to provide a translation for the Italian-speaking reader so that he or she can concentrate on the play of linguistic difference. This public does not only read its poets, it hears or sees them too: the return of oral performance was one of the notable features of poetic production in the last quarter of the twentieth century.

9.2 The widening of culture

In the previous section, we looked at the neo-avant-garde as a source of ideas, polemics, poetics and indeed original work, and worked out from there to some of the significant developments in Italian literary culture between the late 1950s and the late 1970s, with occasional glances forward to the near-present. But now we need to look more closely at what lay behind the positions taken up by the vanguardists and at their implications for the future.

The impulse to reflection came from the perceived need to reposition the left in relation to the realities of post-war neo-capitalism which were now beginning to make themselves acutely apparent in Italy, a little later, but not so much later, than elsewhere in a Europe materially devastated by six years of war (in Britain, 'austerity', complete with ration cards and bread and jam for dinner, only ended in 1952). The 'left' here needs to be understood in cultural as well as strictly political terms. The PCI had sought to lead progressive and anti-Fascist opinion in the post-war years; defeated politically in the 1948 election (along with the Socialist Party, which would take fifteen years to get back into government in coalition with the ruling Christian Democrats, while the Communist Party would be excluded from power as long as the Cold War lasted), it nevertheless strove to hang on to its cultural hegemony among many parts of the intelligentsia. An important factor in this struggle was the posthumous publication between 1948 and 1951 of the prison notebooks (*Quaderni del carcere*) of the founder-leader of the party, Antonio Gramsci (1891–1937), which revealed both an original analysis of the origins and rise of Fascism and a coherent policy for a counterbalance to future threats from the right, and included two important messages for the cultured classes. First, the left should seek to promote a 'national-popular' literature, a literature which had a popular base with a national reach: the relation of the nation to the people should be bottom-up, not follow the Risorgimento tradition of top-down. Secondly, the intellectual of the future, favoured by the specific conditions of industrial proletarian life, would be an 'organic intellectual', somebody who emerges from the working class and remains linked to it. Gramsci's principal concern was the achievement of hegemony, leadership, on the part of the working class, and this entailed a close attention both to cultural factors (such as had been given in the past by the Catholic church, an institution from which Gramsci thought the left had much to learn) and to the need for alliances. But if the Resistance and neo-realism had been the domain of the cultural left (neo-realism in particular being imbued with Gramscian ideas), the economic boom of 1958–63 very definitely was not. What had enabled that was the Christian Democrat government's total subservience to the United States on the one hand, and its broad (though not wholehearted) acceptance of the principles of open markets on the other.

The neo-avant-garde was in fact a battlefield within the left, broadly defined. One should not underestimate the impact of anti-capitalist and anti-American sentiment on the cultural left, parts of which conducted a coherent and courageous battle against what it saw as the discriminatory and damaging effects on the working class of rapid industrialization, migration and wage-pressure. The step from this to the condemnation of 'mass' culture, widely seen as 'American' (cinema, music, food, clothes), as opposed to 'popular' culture (local, regional, of the people) was a short one. It was one that was easily taken within the PCI by intellectuals who did not or could not recognize the implicit cultural elitism they were defending. The neo-avant-garde was in part a testing-ground of a new left, which was also a new generation, for whom the idea of mass culture, which could easily be recodified as popular culture, did not necessarily signify that the end of the socialist dream was in sight or that it was not worth fighting for.

In reality, the economic and social changes taking place in Italy during the 1960s would lead, as one of their major consequences, to the inclusion of ever greater numbers of people, and an ever wider spectrum of the population, in what can broadly be called 'culture' in the context of advanced capitalism: education, mobility, travel, aspiration and the cultivation of aspiration. As a not insignificant part of this culture, given its propinquity to the language and its role as a powerful source of thought, image, emotion and ideals, literature was coming within the reach of a hugely expanded proportion of the population. As it reached a new audience, and became a new target of the aspirations of those who had formerly been excluded, or who had excluded themselves, it would itself change, to meet both those aspirations and the effective capacities of those who aspired. It was not the first time this had happened. Already in the nineteenth century there had been a significant expansion of the reading public amongst, primarily, the urban middle classes, an expansion which had, decisively, crossed the gender divide (see secs 6.1 and 6.3). But now it was happening on a greater scale and at a greater speed.

There were not many in the new left, which broadly clustered around the neo-avant-garde, who understood the process which was under way. The avant-garde was critical of the PCI, but there was ambiguity in their criticism. The tired old (neo-)realism favoured by the party bosses was also something that was familiar, and in some degree reassuring, to the party cadres. They might also actually enjoy Hollywood movies, but the avant-garde was not in the business of promoting Hollywood movies over neorealism. Its concern, on the whole, was with producing a more incisive, a more critical writing, that would strip away all illusions, and all self-delusion, that would penetrate the screen of writing and reveal all reality as constructed. Umberto Eco (1932–), in the seminal essays collected in *Apocalittici e integrati* (1964), lambasted equally both the 'apocalyptics' who saw in mass culture the end of civilization as we know it and the 'integrated', those whose optimistic acceptance of the 'invasion' of mass culture (almost as though they were wartime collaborators) was often a life-choice. It is worth quoting at some length Eco's description of the rather slippery notion of 'integration' and the basis on which he contrasts it with the splendid isolation of the apocalyptic position (and/or its pale petty-bourgeois imitations):

> The combined efforts of TV, newspapers, radio, cinema, comic-strips, popular novels and the *Reader's Digest* have now brought culture within everybody's reach. They have made the absorption of ideas and the reception of information a pleasurable and easy task, with the result that we live in an age in which the cultural arena is at last expanding to include the widespread circulation of a 'popular' art and culture in which the best compete against each other. Whether this culture emerges from below or is processed and packaged from above to be offered to defenceless consumers is not a problem that concerns the integrated intellectual. Not least because, if apocalyptics survive by packaging theories on decadence, the integrated intellectuals rarely theorize. They are more likely to be busy producing and transmitting their own messages in every sphere, on a daily basis. The apocalypse is a preoccupation of the dissenter, integration is the concrete reality of non-dissenters. The image of the Apocalypse is evoked in texts *on* mass culture, while the image of integration emerges in texts which *belong* to mass culture. (Eco 1994: 18)

Eco, who had been boning up on recent American cultural theory, took this situation as the cue to develop a theory which would give an account of the 'culture industry' as a whole, and his involvement in semiotics over the next few years stemmed in some considerable measure from the need to develop a theory of how messages were constructed, transmitted and received, without regard to their aesthetic value (though he soon realized also the necessity of developing an account of the specificities of the 'aesthetic message').

In charting his middle way between apocalyptics and the cheerful, or at least dutiful, managers of whatever happened to be there (the 'integrated'), Eco may have foreseen one of the most important consequences of the arrival on the Italian scene of mass culture in the modern sense: the process of hybridization. He certainly produced his own version of it in his first novel, *Il nome della rosa* (*The Name of the Rose*, 1980), which has enjoyed a worldwide and continuing success. The plot of the novel centred on a murder investigation carried out in 1327 by an English Franciscan who resembles Sherlock Holmes, with his Benedictine assistant, in a remote Italian mountaintop abbey, which is also the scene of violent theological disputes spiced with more than a touch of heresy. Although the novel has a firm and persuasive narrative focus, ensuring that its readers read from beginning to end, it accommodates time-slippages and anachronisms (including a medieval quotation from the twentieth-century philosopher Ludwig Wittgenstein towards the end), the daunting use of Latin phrases, many teasing intertextual references to other books (thus the novice Adso, and the novice reader, learn that 'books are made of other books'), and a good deal of erudite philosophical discussion which probes some of the cognitive issues raised by semiotics, all within the more familiar surroundings of the historical novel (familiar to an Italian public raised on *I promessi sposi*, whose ironic tone can sometimes be heard in this novel's pages too), combined with the universally recognizable structure of the detective novel (though the library which Guglielmo and Adso explore is a rather more serious and complex one than will be found in the average English country house).

Eco is quite explicit about the different 'levels' of reader at which the novel is aimed: those who will be quite content with the crime story part, those who are fascinated by the clash of ideas, and finally those who will delight in its metaliterary qualities. There are critics (among them one of the authors of this book) who have found Eco's threefold definition of the reader disingenuous and insufficiently respectful of the sophistication and versatility of real-life readers. But looked at from the point of view of hybridity, Eco's partitioning of his readership is understandable, for it emphasizes the many different ways in which any text can be approached and therefore its availability in principle to the widest possible range of readers (but not of readings: see Eco 1990: 44–63). Though there is something of the pedagogue that is emerging in Eco's stance here, it does show that he is one person, perhaps one of the few, associated with the Gruppo 63 who has consistently taken an optimistically democratic view of the hybridization of literature which has inevitably arisen from the impact of mass culture in the last forty years.

We recalled above how the expansion of the reading public in the nineteenth century had crossed the gender divide and encompassed women. The assumption underlying that observation was that up until a certain point the core constituency of literature was male, of a certain class and a certain age, presumably heterosexual. The male hegemony did not totally exclude women, as we have made clear in our chapters on the eighteenth and early nineteenth centuries, but it is manifestly the case that women have become actors in the literary scene in the past hundred and fifty years or so in a way that would have been inconceivable in the past. Middle-class women and some working-class men were the first beneficiaries of the expansion of education and literacy in the nineteenth century; in the latter part of the twentieth century almost all sectors of the population have had access to books (whether or not they choose to take that option). From the point of view of writers, however, the post-war period was also a golden age of fiction written by women, to the point, it has been suggested, that '(paradoxically) the literary market at the end of the century was all but gender-blind' (Gordon 2005: 127).

It therefore seems a reverse paradox to segregate women writers into a subsection of their own in this chapter, but in the huge expansion of writing (as well as reading) that has characterized the last decades, it is one way of highlighting the phenomenon and of reflecting on it in general (more than analysing the work of single authors). The not-so-distant history of the exclusion of women from literature has led women themselves to seek to recover lost voices from the past and to highlight the problems that beset the woman who wants to write (Elisa in Morante's *Menzogna e sortilegio*, mentioned in sec. 8.4) or the liberation it affords her, as in Maraini's *La lunga vita di Marianna Ucrìa* (*The Long Life of Marianna Ucrìa*, 1990). Poets such as Maria Luisa Spaziani (1924–) and Biancamaria Frabotta (1947–) have highlighted the distinctiveness of poetry written by women, and there is now a clear lineage of poetry not only written but published by women which makes up a significant part of the post-war poetic canon. Elsa Morante's most important output in the 1960s was her poem-cycle *Il mondo salvato dai ragazzini* (*The World Saved by Children*, 1968). Positioned between her mythopoeic novel of lost innocence, *L'isola di Arturo* (*Arturo's Island*, 1957) and her epic story of the struggle of a woman and her child to survive in the last years of the war in Rome, *La Storia* (*History*, 1974), *Il mondo* gave Morante the opportunity to speak directly her most cherished political and moral beliefs, some of which, such as her trust in a vulnerable and threatened 'happy few' carrying the hopes of mankind, were echoed in *La Storia* but all but abandoned by the time of her despairing last novel, *Aracoeli* (1982). Amelia Rosselli's (1930–96) poetry draws on the resources of English and French as well as Italian to deal with the breakdown of language as a means of understanding the world, in an almost hallucinatory discourse of rare power. Giulia Niccolai (1934–) also drew on a multilingual background for the wordplay of her poems of the 1970s published in *Harry's Bar* (1981), and with her partner Adriano Spatola (1941–88) she was active in the advancement of 'total poetry' in their review *Tam tam* (founded 1971). The work of Alda Merini (1931–), which draws heavily on her own psychiatric experiences, has been widely acclaimed, thanks in part to her many public appearances in recent years. Among the post-war generation of women poets, substantial and interesting work has been done by, among many others, Vivian Lamarque (1946–), Patrizia Cavalli (1947–), Patrizia Valduga (1953–) and Antonella Anedda (1958–).

The notion of a distinct lineage of women's writing, up until at least very recently, has found substantial evidence in the history of the twentieth-century novel in Italy. As has been pointed out, with the exception of Viganò and Giovanna Zangrandi (1910–88), women played very little part in the literature of the Resistance (as opposed to the Resistance itself) or neo-realism. The women who had been born between the 1890s and the 1910s had often cut their literary teeth on the modernist canon that was championed by *Solaria* in the 1920s and 1930s. In addition to the names of Morante, Banti and Manzini (see sec. 8.3 and above), this catalogue also includes Fausta Cialente (1898–1993), Maria Bellonci (1902–86), Lalla Romano (1906–2001), Alba De Cespedes (1911–97), Anna Maria Ortese (1914–98) and Natalia Ginzburg (1916–91). The work which they wrote after the war continued to pursue the high literary ideals of modernism (which for some included a principled resistance to the political demands of parties or organized feminism and a lack of interest in mass culture) and to work on some of the favoured subject matter of the modernist novel: the exploration of subjectivity, memory and sensation, the course of individual lives. Several of these writers also drew on their own experience during the war years and after as women, often with families, in very difficult circumstances (Hallamore Caesar 2000).

With rare exceptions such as the Swiss novelist, journalist and translator Alice Ceresa (1923–), the Gruppo 63 and the wider neo-avant-garde were also a largely male affair. A focus on women's lives continued to dominate much of the narrative fiction produced by women in the 1970s and 1980s, a substantial body of work which included novels by Gina Lagorio (1922–2005; *La spiaggia del lupo* (*Wolf Beach*, 1977)), Francesca Sanvitale (1928–; *Madre e figlia* (*Mother and Daughter*, 1980)); Rosetta Loy (1931–; *Le strade di polvere* (*The Dust Roads*, 1987)), Francesca Duranti (1935–; *La casa sul lago della luna* (*The House on Moon Lake*, 1984)) and Fabrizia Ramondino (1936–; *Althénopis*, 1981). Some of these women absorbed the quest of 1970s feminism to recover women's writing from the past – Sanvitale, for example, edited an important anthology of nineteenth-century women writers (Sanvitale 1995) – others made quite clear their lack of connection with political feminism.

Feminism impacted more directly on the novelist and poet Dacia Maraini (1936–), who, in a prolific output of work which includes documentary reportage as well as novels, poetry and theatre, has tirelessly anatomized the condition of women in the present and in the past: paternal repression in the eighteenth century (as in *La lunga vita di Marianna Ucrìa*, 1990, already mentioned) and male violence at the beginning of the twentieth century in *Isolina: La donna tagliata a pezzi* (*Isolina: The Woman Cut into Pieces*, 1985). Giuliana Morandini (1938–) compiled influential anthologies of documents relating to female madness (*. . . e allora mi hanno rinchiusa* (*. . . And Then They Shut Me Up*, 1977)) and earlier women's writing (*La voce che è in lei* (*The Voice Which is in Her*, 1980)). Both she and Maraini have been, and Maraini continues to be, effective and active publicists for women's writing in general and for their particular causes, a style of public presence which has been embodied with particular tenacity and courage by the actress Franca Rame (1929–). The authorship of her dramatic monologues is problematical, because they continue to be co-signed by her husband Dario Fo (1926–) and are included in the Einaudi edition of his collected works. They usually take the form of hard-edged satire but also include *Lo stupro* (*The Rape*), a detached, dignified and very moving account of her kidnap and rape at the hands of neo-Fascist thugs in 1973.

The novelists, poets and performing artists were joined in the 1970s and 1980s by a new generation of feminist critics and of critic-writers such as Elisabetta Rasy (1947–; *La lingua della nutrice* (*The Nurse's Tongue*, 1978), *Le donne e la letteratura* (*Women and Literature*, 1984), and *Ritratti di signora* (*Ladies' Portraits*, 1995)) and Sandra Petrignani (1952–; *Le signore della scrittura* (*The Ladies of Writing*, 1984, revised edn 1996)) – titles which attest to a growing market during the 1980s and 1990s for a critical, documentary and historical writing specifically to do with women as writers. Since the 1990s, writing by women has tended to follow different paths. The novels of fantasy written in the early stages of her career by Paola Capriolo (1962–) revealed the emergence of an exceptional and quite individual talent. Some younger women have tended to merge with the trends and styles of their own generation, male or female, before striking out on their own paths: an example is Silvia Ballestra (1969–), whose early work, notably *Gli orsi* (*The Bears*, 1994), echoed the colloquial, in-your-face style of youth writing pioneered by Pier Vittorio Tondelli (1955–91) in his *Altri libertini* (*Other Libertines*, 1980) and subsequent novels, and promoted by him in three anthologies of young unknowns published between 1986 and 1990. Elena Stancanelli's (1965–) *Benzina* (*Petrol*, 1998), subsequently made into a successful film, was a rare account of a lesbian relationship, this too perhaps made possible by the increasing openness and confidence about homosexuality in Italian literature, reflecting the wider culture, in the 1990s (here again Tondelli had been an important pioneer).

The reality, then, for most of the post-war period seems to have been that women as writers have assumed a distinctive voice that sometimes seems almost to amount to a separate tradition, or what we have described as a 'lineage', of female writing, but at the same time, in contrast to the nineteenth or even much of the earlier twentieth century, women writers have been able to assume femaleness as part of their identity without having to apologize for it or make jokes about it or defer to their male readers about it. It is nevertheless the case that in a culture dominated by ideology from the 1920s to at least the 1970s male writers hogged the limelight: theirs were the 'movements', the 'groups', the 'programmes' (neo-this or neo-that) which were pronounced, proclaimed, amplified and repeated ad infinitum by the custodians of the culture, the critics and literary historians. A strong tradition of writing by women has emerged, one that is evidently capable of renewing itself, but perhaps it owes more to readers than to critics and more to informal networks of communication than to 'official' ones. Despite the great changes of the last fifty years, is the literary culture now really gender-blind, or is that an illusion? And how far do literary productions, particularly those that are popular, necessarily make an appeal to identity (gender, race or other)? In the complex literary market of today, is it the market which determines the match of text and target audience?

9.3 A minimalist postmodernism: the poetics of attention

The last book published by Italo Calvino in his lifetime, *Palomar* (1985, translated as *Mr Palomar* in the same year), opens to the movement of waves and the look of a solitary observer whose gaze attempts to follow the progress of one single wave in its passage, separated and isolated from that of all the others, from open sea to shore. Mr Palomar, the observer, is a nervous man, living 'in a frenzied and congested world': congested not only with other humans like himself, crowding preferably into places which seem to reflect back at them mute incomprehension of their triumphant ubiquity (the zoo, the garden of rocks and sand of the Ryoanji of Kyoto), but crisscrossed furthermore with signals and signs, simultaneously requiring and resisting interpretation. Palomar's attempt to isolate the wave is a difficult and repeatedly unsuccessful one. But where does the difficulty lie? In the things themselves? In Mr Palomar? Neither of these, strictly, is the territory of Calvino's fiction, which focuses rather on the relation between the two. Mr Palomar is aware that the words we use to ask the questions and phrase the answers determine the very reality which they are intended to interrogate. The little waves 'strike' the shore, the high part of an advancing wave is a 'hump'; looking to another portion of creation, it would surely be better, but impossible, just to 'observe' the behaviour of migrating starlings than to try to understand it through the conflicting 'explanations' that have been proposed for it. Visiting the ruins of Tula in Mexico, Palomar is torn between interpretation and non-interpretation, between the explanations of his knowledgeable friend, who transforms each mysterious stone into 'a cosmic tale, an allegory, a moral reflection', and the attitude of the teacher with his little party of schoolchildren who resolutely refuses to speculate on meaning, preferring simply to show his pupils the thing that is there. Not knowing whether to interpret or not, and trying to decide between two impossible alternatives, is a characteristic problem for the 'nervous' Mr Palomar, who, 'to defend himself against the general neurasthenia [. . .] tries to keep his sensations under control insofar as possible' (Calvino 1985b: 4).

In his precisely delineated observation of the world, Calvino's Palomar was an emblematic figure of postmodern Italian fiction. Neither a sociological nor a psychological type, he represented an assemblage of mental attitudes, providing a kind of vade mecum and at the same time an ironic counterpoint to the anxieties of a public that was presumed by the book itself to have lost faith in totalizing explanations and all-encompassing narratives. Stefano Tani pointed out at the time that Calvino's idea of observation, within his wider poetic of 'seeing', was a different matter from 'the impassive and indifferent, basically *blind*, gaze that we have inherited from the *nouveau roman* [of the 1960s]' (Tani 1986: 122). Calvino's, and Palomar's, gaze, on the contrary, was interrogatory, teasing out the meaning of things, impartial but never impersonal or 'inert'. In the work of some of Calvino's younger contemporaries – Andrea De Carlo (1952–), for example, whose first novel, *Treno di panna* (*Cream Train*, 1981), was warmly praised by Calvino

– the registration of detail and the reproduction of objects, gestures and expressions are conscripted into a form of obsessive and narcissistic display on the part of the observer. By contrast Calvino, for all his hero's doubts and self-irony, still has his Palomar wanting to penetrate the secrets of the world and, to this end, what is seen acts only as a means of activating the thoughtfulness of language. Whether the explorations of language, with all their risks of being self-defeating, are successful is another question. But compared with the world of De Carlo's first novel, set in Los Angeles, where the information garnered by the eye leads to no critical interrogation of reality, Palomar's, and Calvino's, project seemed almost hopeful.

Palomar can be read as a series of representations of the world, attempted reproductions and descriptions of the out-there being constantly modified in the light of new experience and new information. The observer's readiness to modify is admirably honest and ultimately exhausting: the process of adjustment can go only so far before atrophy threatens. Each of Palomar's observations is a quest and each, in itself, a failure (even though the book, taken as a whole, conveys a sense not of waste or disappointment but, on the contrary, of something rather noble and achieved).

Quests and questions of a distinctly Calvinian kind were the stuff of the two very intelligent novels published by Daniele Del Giudice (1949–) at the beginning of his career, *Lo stadio di Wimbledon* (*Wimbledon Stadium*, 1983) and *Atlante occidentale* (*Western Atlas*, 1985), both of which also had a metaliterary dimension which linked them to Calvino's other influential late novel *Se una notte d'inverno un viaggiatore*. The first follows the attempts by the first-person narrator to reconstruct the life and inner motivation of the Triestine man of letters Roberto ('Bobi') Bazlen (1902–65), whose literary ambitions were realized solely through the promotion of other writers and never through a completed work of his own. From the tracking of this 'non-writer', Del Giudice went on, in the second novel, to the portrait of a fictional novelist who, on the brink of receiving the Nobel Prize, acknowledges with joy that he has passed beyond writing, emphasizing at the end of this passage two key words in the Del Giudice vocabulary, 'waiting' and 'transparent':

> I do not think that I am claiming any particular credit if it seems to me that I have traversed writing in all forms, as best I could. Now I have emerged from it, just as happy. I have always been waiting, all my life, for writing and storytelling to be transparent to me as well; that moment has arrived. (Del Giudice 1985: 30)

The metaliterary component is not so much in the existence of characters who discourse on the state of the art, even obliquely, through the exploration of writing's other – non-writing or no-more-writing – as in the project of the central characters, which is the essentially dramatic one of trying to imagine themselves into the world of another. In *Lo stadio di Wimbledon*, the young researcher is drawn in search of his elusive quarry by the few traces that remain: the occasional photograph; a few letters and other writings; the memories of surviving contemporaries. The effect of his successive encounters and discoveries – which are very sparse – is that things become more complicated, or rather, that they become increasingly difficult to describe, to 'capture'. The narrator gradually comes to recognize that he is 'passing through', as a mariner passes through the waves, and that the truth of which he is in pursuit is not an object fixed in time and space. He cannot approach it by superimposing successive and ever more accurate (more informed) mental approximations to the real thing; he cannot name it, like an object, without fear of equivocation; but rather it lies here, in the moment through which he is passing, and the important thing is to see that.

The dialectic between 'passage' and 'approach' is played subtly in both novels. Simply to pass risks a sense of purposelessness; but the purposefulness of approach requires delicacy and tact. In *Atlante occidentale*, the writer Ira Epstein meets the particle physicist Piero Brahe after a near-collision in midair between their two light aircraft in the skies above Geneva. Brahe works on the CERN accelerator (assumed already in the novel to be completed and working); his experiment involves close and constant watching of the monitor which will tell him when the 'event' has taken place. This is not, however, a novel about two cultures (literature and science are well integrated in Del Giudice's interests and his writing, as is the hands-on experience and the metaphor of flying light aircraft: see his later *Staccando l'ombra da terra* (*Lifting Off*, 1994)); it is a novel rather about two people, and about friendship between an older man and a younger. The approach of the two men to each other is conducted like a ritual, a crucial moment of which comes when they go up in a plane together for the first time. Brahe 'shows' Epstein his work – that is, he flies him around the thirty-kilometre circumference of the accelerator which is buried deep underground, pinpointing the surface features and describing their relation to the features concealed below the surface. Epstein then insists that Brahe should 'tell' him about his work, but that he must use the right words, the words that he would use with his scientific colleagues. Brahe complies, and they enter into a description of the accelerator and the experiment, the details of which are covered for the reader (not for the protagonists) by the engine noise:

> Epstein as he listened leant towards Brahe, and Brahe as he spoke leant towards Epstein, and they were so involved with each other, and in any

> case the engine noise was so continuous and enveloping, like the air, that no one, behind them, could have heard anything! (Del Giudice 1985: 120)

This small but central incident might serve as a model for Del Giudice's representation of knowing – the broad sweep, an outline superimposed on a subterranean reality; the naming of things in a concentrated and satisfying way; these as the preparation for meetings that are both intellectually passionate and composed, without possibility or need of further elaboration.

There is a passage in *Palomar* which plays on the dialectic between speech (or sound) and silence and which might be taken to foreshadow the structure of the book as a whole. Every summer Palomar listens to the birds in his garden, and this is a part of what he observes:

> After a while the whistle is repeated – by the same blackbird or by its mate – but always as if this were the first time it had occurred to him to whistle; if this is a dialogue, each remark is uttered after long reflection. But is it a dialogue, or does each blackbird whistle for itself and not for the other? And, in whichever case, are these questions and answers (to the whistler or the mate) or are they confirmations of something that is always the same thing (the bird's own presence, his belonging to this species, this sex, this territory)? Perhaps the value of this single word lies in its being repeated by another whistling beak, in its not being forgotten during the interval of silence.
>
> Or else the whole dialogue consists of one saying to the other 'I am here' and the length of the pauses adds to the phrase the sense of a 'still', as if to say: 'I am here still, it is still I'. And what if it is in the pause and not in the whistle that the meaning of the message is contained? If it were in the silence that the blackbirds speak to each other? (In this case the whistle would be a punctuation mark, a formula like 'over and out'.) (Calvino 1985b: 22)

These reflections encapsulate the essential spirit of this and many other episodes in *Palomar*. Observation is at a certain point self-effacing; interrogations cancel each other out. Inquiry arrives at a point of maximum tension, then cannot proceed further. Impasse is reached. The tension is resolved, the impasse broken, by pushing on, to the next moment, the next story or reflection. But there is no interconnection between these moments: although there is a recognizable Mr Palomar throughout, operating in a recognizably similar environment from one piece to the next, there is no attempt to construct a coherent and consistent account from his scattered observations.

What the reader comes across are events, flashes, brief encounters, steps on a journey, though what the shape and direction of the journey itself might be it is hard to say.

A similar structure may be discerned in Del Giudice's novels (which tend to the episodic), but was decisive in another important book of the mid-1980s, Gianni Celati's (1937–) *Narratori delle pianure* (*Voices from the Plains*, 1985), a book with which Celati returned to writing after seven years of 'silence' and critical and theoretical reflection. The 'pianure' in question were the flatlands of the Po valley, stretching from the region around Milan in the west to the river-delta in the east, and the 'narratori' are the anonymous sources of the tales which Celati relates. Each of the thirty stories in the book bears a relation, sometimes strong, sometimes tenuous, to a place on the schematized map with which the reader is presented when he or she opens the volume (not, alas, in the English translation). This map and the sense of movement from one place to the next form the frame of the book, and it ensures that *Narratori delle pianure* is read not as a collection of stories, but as a succession. That said, it is also true that each of these stories is self-contained and, like each of Palomar's two- or three-page reflections, intimates concentration. The stories read as distillations of the life or experience of ordinary people (working people, the lower middle class, and also the 'emarginated', the young, the unemployed, the old) plucked from a grey background where nothing appears to be going on.

The stories themselves do not, however, recount an exceptional event, indeed they seldom focus on a single event at all. Rather, they represent (in very few pages) the continuities of people's lives through and beyond the ordinary accidents of birth, marriage, death, fortune and misfortune. A hairdresser believes he sees the ghost of a fellow soldier; spends some years in a mental hospital; on his release is rejected by his wife, who he believes is 'denying him his existence'; begins to think that everyone else is denying him his existence, perhaps because he was once shot at by a German and they all think he is dead; spends his Sundays looking into the river for the bullet which missed him; after his death, his wife discovers she is pregnant; she lets it be known that the hairdresser has spoken to her by night and told her 'he was very happy that she had recognized the child as his, because that way she had stopped denying him his existence'; when eventually she moves away from Piacenza, the hairdresser stops speaking to her by night. A woman spends many years doing domestic work in Cremona; she saves all her money to buy an apartment for her son when he gets married; her no-good husband, the boy's father, reappears after years and demands assistance; she refuses; when the son is engaged, she relents and negotiates subsidies to her ex-husband, for a suit, a car, a wedding present; she organizes a big reception to which she invites all her former employers; nobody comes except a tennis-star; there is no sign of the husband; her lawyer tells her that the girl her son is marrying is her husband's mistress and that he had already taken over the apartment; she reflects a moment and decides to carry on with the reception, everything is all right, 'if no one notices anything, it is as though nothing has happened'; passers-by are invited to join the wedding-party, which they happily do because the tennis-star is present; the husband turns up in his new car; no one takes any notice of him because no one knows who he is, except for the car-dealer he sometimes does jobs for, who tells him all new cars lose half their value as soon as they are bought and end up on the scrap-heap anyway.

These tales are related with an extraordinary lightness: the frequency of the present or the perfect as narrative tenses; the adoption of a simple but precise vocabulary; the sparing use of adjectives; the composition of short, essential paragraphs added one to the other, not like bricks, in the conventional metaphor of story-building, but more like transparent balloons lifting the story off the ground – with all of these techniques, Celati created a mode of storytelling which shook off the weight of narrative, in what was a conscious and consistent effort to pare away the superstructure of ideology and 'that homogeneous and totalizing continuity that is called history' (Celati 1975: 14). In his travels across the plains, Celati imagined a space which may be filled with meanings, but where no single or definitive meaning could be imposed. Neither origins nor ends predetermine meaning, which for the reader may rest as much in the gaps between the stories as in the stories themselves, in their continuity and succession as in their uniqueness and completion. Indeed, at a certain point the stories come to seem almost like pauses, moments of reflection perhaps, in a wider discourse that envelops the written word, so as to make the readers of Celati's narrative acknowledge something in common with Palomar listening to his blackbirds, uncertain which part of their communication is language, which silence.

What these texts have in common, it seems to us, is a quality of attentiveness which has different layers of meaning. There is the attentiveness of the professional writer doing his job: Calvino, the finest Italian prose stylist probably of the twentieth century, imparted this respect for the work in hand and for care and precision without preciosity in language to many other writers of the time, including the two analysed here (Calvino was an influential reader and commissioning editor with Einaudi as well as a practising novelist and essayist). There is the attentiveness of the observer who, however, has given up illusions of mastery: you observe in order to observe, not predicting or betting on the outcome, aware that the outcome of observation might be less, not more, light. It seems that the act of observing is more important than the object or the outcome, and this may have an ethical dimension to it. This is an attentiveness to small details, whose overall significance, if any, is not contained by any overarching discourse, as though by the close observation of detail the observer might hope to break free of ideology or, if the achievement of that hope is known to be impossible, to signal at least the hope. With the alleged disappearance of 'grand narratives' in postmodernity, echoed in Celati's remarks quoted above, comes not so much the apocalyptic sense of discourse (or culture) being smashed to fragments as a boundless fluidity traversed, by these writers at least, with rather un-postmodern impulses of desire.

9.4 Epilogue: a weekend in April

A week after the narrow victory of Romani Prodi's centre-left Union at the polls had put an end to the longest-serving post-war government, led by Silvio Berlusconi at the head of his House of Freedoms coalition, two readers settled down to peruse the weekend cultural supplements dated 22 and 23 April 2006, backed up with the 'Cultura' sections of Italy's two bestselling current affairs magazines, *L'espresso* and *Panorama*, which had appeared the previous Thursday. This is what they found:

(1) ***tuttoLibritempolibero*** (***ttl***), 22 April 2006: Saturday supplement of *La Stampa*. It used to be called *Tuttolibri*, but the marriage of books with lifestyle ('free time') has long been consummated. In fact, book reviews or book-related articles occupy the first half of the supplement. *La Stampa* is published in Turin; the city, Piedmont and neighbouring Liguria are well represented in its cultural coverage. This number opens with the inauguration the same day of Turin as 'World Capital of the Book', a UNESCO-sponsored event which lasts a year before the baton passes to Bogotà in April 2007. Turin has been chosen, one might surmise, because it already hosts a very successful annual book fair (Salone del Libro). You have to go to another publication to discover that Turin will share this honour with Rome. The year of the book will begin with 'Book-Stock', a thirty-hour 'rave party' at the Palalsozaki.

There follow:

- a notice about BUR's 'futuro passato' series, an eclectic selection of titles comprising politics, recent history, memoirs, literary classics and the ever-popular 'pillole', small-format books selling at €5;
- an extract from a book about western Liguria illustrated by a photograph of Calvino when young and panoramic shots from the 1980s of San Remo

(where Calvino grew up) and Noli; there is a back-up piece about how 'magical' the region used to be;

- a review by Alessandro Defilippi of Don DeLillo, *Body Art*, which is on sale with copies of *La Stampa* ('€5,90 plus the price of the paper', with a free phone number to ring, 8 a.m. to 8 p.m. on weekdays).

Fiction reviews come next. From Italy: Cesare De Marchi's new novel *La furia del mondo* (Feltrinelli): the novel is set in eighteenth-century Germany and Rome and the review is illustrated by a Rubens engraving of Jonah being thrown into the sea. Andrea Cortellessa reviews Luca Rastello's *Piove all'insù* (Bollati Boringhieri). Cortellessa, a prolific reviewer, begins by observing: 'To produce "the" novel of the Seventies is the great unspoken ambition of Italian writers. And you can see why. What "produces" masterpieces are historical traumas, wars, big wars and small wars, "objective" and inner wars. The years of "peace" which followed this last conflict [1970s terrorism] (never declared and so never really ended) – the Eighties of Appearance, the Nineties of Falsification, even the Noughties of Confusion – have already had their narrators. But the most recent shared wound is still to be worked through, still awaits its interpreter' (p. 4). Another critic has suggested Nievo as a model for Rastello's novel; Cortellessa suggests Fenoglio. Decades are labelled, lineages established, the wait for the novel of the seventies suggests a wish for fiction on the model of the Great American Novel (a rare event in recent Italian fiction). Sergio Pent reviews Giancarlo Marinelli, *Ti lascio il meglio di me* (Bompiani), a crime writer reviewing a crime novel, not very enthusiastically.

Reviews of fiction from abroad make no mention of the quality of the translation: the translators, though credited in the book details, are silenced in the reviews. A small army of low-paid people undertake this work, which is a mainstay of the Italian publishing business.

Other items with a literary connection include pieces on how a plan was hatched to rescue Benedetto Croce when the Germans occupied Sorrento in 1943, a selection of books on / of Jewish literature, electronic books on demand, and personalities like Iris Murdoch and Arthur Schopenhauer, before the supplement moves on to gardening, cooking, DVDs, art exhibitions and travel, with more on Turinese cultural highlights on the back page.

(2) ***Alias***, 22 April 2006: Saturday supplement of *Il manifesto*. The left-wing daily was founded, originally as a monthly, twenty-five years earlier (the first issue came out on 28 April 1971). Several other papers draw attention to this anniversary and the forthcoming autobiography by one of the founders,

Valentino Parlato, but not this issue of *Alias*. Instead it devotes its front page, followed by pp. 2–6, to the 8th Far East Film Festival, taking place in Udine until 29 April. Richly illustrated in colour, all the photographs are of seductive women singing, dancing, succumbing. Page 2 has a column on an iconic photograph of Samuel Beckett, and there is a feature dedicated to Mario Iacomini, 'founder in 1996 of the Tagliacozzo Film Festival' and owner of the 'Cantina del Brigante', which is described as an 'experimental and theoretical stage of healthy food and taste as well as a research space for the cultural avant-garde'; there is a fetching photograph of Iacomini (pp. 8–9).

After more short pieces on film, bands, new releases, tours and classical recordings, and an interesting article by Giovanni Vacca on the tradition of 'industrial song' from nineteenth-century Britain to Ewan MacColl, we come to the *la talpa libri* section, six pages of book reviews followed by theatre and art. The books selected for review are demanding: recent books on/of American poetry reviewed by the academic Massimo Bacigalupo; editions of the baroque poet Marino, under the headline 'Who is still afraid of the Baroque?'; a volume on Mantegna; and an edition of Italian medieval poetry (*Poesie dello Stilnovo*) published by Rizzoli, praised for the quality of its commentary, 'which will appeal both to specialists and users from the schools' (p. 22) – an audience which might well be that of *la talpa libri*.

(3) ***Almanacco dei Libri***, 22 April 2006: supplement of *La Repubblica*. The issue leads with Simonetta Fiori interviewing Silvia Ballestra, who has just published her new novel, *La seconda Dora* (Rizzoli), 'a Fascist Jew, forced to sacrifice her own identity in order to save her skin', as the rather clumsy *Repubblica* headline puts it. The centrepiece is a short story by Björn Larsson, with a background story on the author and his books and a drawing by Tullio Pericoli, an accomplished artist specializing in literary themes and figures, dated 1982, and reproduced on the cover of this book.

The rest of the supplement is devoted to reviews, some of them very short, as well as the bestseller lists and recommendations from individual booksellers (who change from week to week) which are a regular feature of the literary/cultural supplements.

(4) ***Domenica***, 23 April 2006: Sunday supplement of *Il Sole 24 Ore*. This is the heavyweight of the weekend supplements, containing well-written reviews of high quality covering a very wide range of disciplines in the arts, literature, humanities, social science, economics, philosophy and so on.

This issue includes the opening pages from a translation of Andrea Levy's novel *Small Island*, an extract from Marc Fumaroli's preface to his edition of

Jean-Baptiste Seroux D'Agincourt's *Histoire de l'art*, which will set its purchasers back a cool €700, and a review by the activist film critic Goffredo Fofi of Paul Theroux's *Dark Star Safari* (in Italian translation). The veteran novelist Raffaele La Capria has just published a well-received short novel, *L'amorosa inchiesta* (Mondadori), which is reviewed here as elsewhere. Other pages of *Domenica* include two articles on Gödel, various contributions inspired by the exhibition *Tempo Moderno: Da Van Gogh a Warhol* which has recently opened in Genoa to celebrate the centenary of the trade union organization CGIL, a theatre initiative in a poor district in Naples, and a tribute to Alida Valli, the star who has just died at the age of 85.

(5) ***Cultura***, 23 April 2006: supplement of the Milan-based *Corriere della Sera*; this section merges seamlessly into TV programmes and sport. The issue includes some serious academic reviewing: Dante Isella on a new edition of Fenoglio's *Ventitre giorni della città di Alba* (Einaudi), Cesare Segre on a book on Dante, Mario Andrea Rigoni on a book on Leopardi, as well as more standard fiction reviews. The novelist Giorgio Montefoschi defends his right to criticize Italo Calvino (very mildly) against fellow novelist Pietro Citati, while Alida Valli here gets two full pages with photographs: 'Farewell to the most beautiful gaze in cinema' (pp. 36–7).

(6) ***L'espresso***, 20 April 2006: the 'Cultura' section is on pp. 126–57, between 'Reportage' and 'Economia'.

The cultural journalism of *L'espresso* highlights its freshness, fashionableness and 'must-know' quality. Fabio Gambaro reports 'from Paris' on the buzzy ideas of Michel Onfray under the heading 'Corpo, sesso e felicità' ('Body, sex and happiness'); Andrea Visconti reports from New York on 'Scandaloso Philip Roth', on his new novel *Everyman* (which the journalist has read, the headline makes clear, 'in anteprima' – pre-publication); and there is an interview with Björk, or rather her husband, on a whaling boat, it seems. These pages run through art, architecture, TV, CD, opera and books, including in the books section an enthusiastic review by Marco Belpoliti of a newly published collection of stories by Gianni Celati, *Vite di pascolanti* (Nottetempo).

All of these book reviews are very short, as are most of the other pieces except for the three or four lead articles. Perhaps this is to do with the fact that the magazines, to a greater extent than the newspaper supplements, are designed to be flicked through, expecting an attention span of not more than thirty seconds per page, and liberally interspersed with full-page advertisements which are made to catch the eye. This week's advertisements, from which one might gauge something about the readers, or at least the readers' aspirations, are: Pal Zileri (menswear) (128); Luck in Luck (menswear) (131); UPS Express (134); zerorh+ (sunglasses, modelled by Giancarlo Fisichella) (139); Sony sat-nav (140); Baileys Original (linked to holiday cruises) (142); *Romance & Cigarettes* (film by John Turturro) (145); Grandi Navi Veloci (ferries/cruises) (146); Docksteps (shoes for men, also linked to boats) (148); Terme dell'Emilia Romagna (healthy vacations) (150); Nokia Nseries ('Aggiorna il tuo blog con una fotocamera ad alta definizione': 'Update your blog with a high-definition camera' – is it a phone as well?) (152); Harmont & Blaine (menswear, modelled/signed by Fabio Cannavaro) (154); Ministero per le Pari Opportunità (campaign against female genital mutilation) (156); London Guide on sale next week with *L'espresso* ('Scoprire l'anima di una grande città è una questione di stile': 'Discovering the soul of a great city is a question of style') (158–61).

(7) ***Panorama***, 20 April 2006: the 'Cultura' section is on pp. 228–50.

In general, *Panorama* is more downmarket, more conservative, conventional and reassuring than *L'espresso*, a little less secular. Its readers are not only assumed to be anxious about keeping up with the new (whistle-stop tours of must-see exhibitions are despatched in a couple of columns, one of them with the title 'E l'andar per mostre m'è dolce in questa Pasqua': 'And going to shows is sweet to me this Easter'; attentive readers who discern an echo of the last line of Leopardi's 'L'infinito' will appreciate how deep into the linguistic and cultural memory of Italy that celebrated line has reached); they are also assumed to be anxious about losing the familiar. The 'irresistible new book by the humorist Flavio Oreglio' is flagged up as the second feature under the heading 'Quante "cazzate" sparano i filosofi' (roughly translatable as 'What a load of old cobblers from the philosophers'), with ample extracts from the irresistible new book illustrating the thesis. More intriguingly, an opinion piece signed by Lorenzo Arruga talks about how bold and esoteric (classical) music was absorbed by the Italian public in the twentieth century, making it 'ours', but arguing that now things are different. In the twentieth century 'we' had to start from 'our' own nation and learn from outside. But now 'the universe has arrived in our house, we are invaded by images, languages, experiences and thoughts, and it's almost as though we don't even have our own beliefs and our own country' (p. 264). This is the first sign we have found in this tiny sample of weeklies of the fear of immigration, particularly from outside the European Union, which has become prevalent in Italian society at large, finding its way on to the cultural pages of a major national publication.

We do not draw any conclusions from so limited and arbitrary a sample, except perhaps to urge the much more systematic study, in the case of Italy, of the contemporary embedding of literature in the variable multitude of representational practices as a whole. Literary journalism, like cultural journalism more widely, has its own rules, which are determined by the modern need for constant renewal and variety within a framework which is reassuringly familiar. From this perspective, the cultural pages of the twenty-first century printed media, profoundly different in content and tone though they are, would not be unrecognizable to their eighteenth- or nineteenth-century ancestors. Indeed, in one respect today's literary-cultural palette bears more resemblance to its earlier than to its more recent forerunners. There is a striking lack of consensus about what literature – however that term might be defined – is *for*. More pertinently, there is a striking lack of interest in the question. In retrospect, it becomes apparent that for a very large part of the chronological period covered by this book, roughly between the 1790s and the 1960s, literature had firmly assumed a central role in the education, the acculturation, the mental and spiritual formation of an increasingly rapidly expanding cohort of habitual readers. Its history was tied up with that of the standardization of the Italian language over many decades, with the formation of a national consciousness, and at the same time with the cultivation of many different ways of thinking about subjectivity, often playing on the tension between the shifting claims of public and private spheres. Its history was inexorably connected to the triumph of the medium of print on a mass, near-universal, scale in Italy. That period, as what is now discernible as a distinct historical moment, has ended. That does not mean that literature has disappeared, nor its readers. Its semiofficial role as a kind of secular religion almost certainly has. Its readers, by all the evidence, are indestructible.

References

This list contains only those books and articles which are specifically referred to with the author-date system in the text. For more general titles and further reading, please see 'Further reading' below.

Alfieri, V. (1951): *Vita scritta da esso*, 2 vols, ed. Fassò, L. [*Opere di Vittorio Alfieri da Asti*, vols 1–2], Casa d'Alfieri, Asti.

Alfieri, V. (1978): *Parere sulle tragedie e altre prose critiche*, ed. Pagliai, M. [*Opere di Vittorio Alfieri da Asti*, vol. 35], Casa d'Alfieri, Asti.

Bacchelli, R. (1919): 'G. Scalvini, un caso letterario', *La Ronda* I(3), 61–5.

Banti, A. M. (2004): *Il Risorgimento italiano*, GLF Editori Laterza, Rome.

Baretti, G. (1932): *La Frusta letteraria di Aristarco Scannabue*, 2 vols, ed. Piccioni, L., Laterza, Bari.

Barlow, H. C. (1866): *The Sixth Centenary Festivals of Dante Alighieri in Florence and at Ravenna*, By a Representative [i.e. H. C. Barlow], Williams and Norgate, London.

Beccaria, C. (1958): *Opere*, 2 vols, ed. Romagnoli, S., Sansoni, Florence.

Bellina, A. L. and Caruso, C. (1998): 'Oltre il Barocco: la fondazione dell'Arcadia. Zeno e Metastasio: la riforma del melodramma'. In: Malato, E. (ed.), *Storia della letteratura italiana*, vol. VI, Salerno, Rome, pp. 239–312.

Bellorini, E. (ed.) (1943): *Discussioni e polemiche sul romanticismo*, 2 vols, Laterza, Bari.

Bellucci, N. (1996): *Giacomo Leopardi e i suoi contemporanei*, Ponte alle Grazie, Florence.

Benjamin, W. (1973): *Illuminations*, Fontana, London.

Berchet, G. (1972): *Opere*, ed. Turchi, M., Fulvio Rossi, Naples.

Berengo, M. (1980): *Intellettuali e librai nella Milano della Restaurazione*, Einaudi, Turin.

Branca, V. (ed.) (1953–65): *Il Conciliatore: foglio scientifico-letterario*, 3 vols, F. Le Monnier, Florence.

Brand, C. P. and Pertile, L. (eds) (1999): *The Cambridge History of Italian Literature*, 2nd edn, Cambridge University Press, Cambridge.

Burney, C. (1971): *Memoirs of the Life and Writings of the Abate Metastasio, Including Translations of His Principal Letters* [1796], 3 vols, Da Capo Press, New York.

Caesar, M. (1999): 'Contemporary Italy (since 1956)'. In: Brand and Pertile 1999: 561–606.

Il Caffè (1993): *'Il Caffè' 1764–1766*, eds Francioni, G. and Romagnoli, S., Bollati Boringhieri, Turin.

Calvino, I. (1978): *Il sentiero dei nidi di ragno: Con una prefazione dell'autore*, Einaudi, Turin.

Calvino, I. (1985a): *Palomar*, Einaudi, Turin.

Calvino, I. (1985b): *Mr Palomar*, tr. Weaver, W., Secker and Warburg, London.

Cannistraro, P. V. (1975): *La fabbrica del consenso: fascismo e mass media*, Laterza, Rome and Bari.

Capponi, G. (1882–90): *Lettere di G. Capponi e di altri a lui*, ed. Carraresi, A., 6 vols, Le Monnier, Florence.

Celati, G. (1975): *Finzioni occidentali*, Einaudi, Turin.

Cerruti, M. and Mattioda, E. (1998): 'La letteratura nel neoclassicismo: Vincenzo Monti'. In: Malato, E. (ed.), *Storia della letteratura italiana*, vol. VII, Salerno, Rome, pp. 289–378.

Corti, M. (1978): 'Neorealismo'. In: Corti, M., *Il viaggio testuale*, Einaudi, Turin, pp. 25–98.

Croce, B. (1974): *La letteratura della nuova Italia: Saggi critici VI*, Laterza, Bari.

Cucchi, M. and Giovanardi, S. (eds) (1996): *Poeti italiani del secondo Novecento 1945–1995*, intro. Giovanardi, S., Mondadori, Milan.

De Ceccatty, R. (2006): 'Venise, Napoléon et la Pisana', *Le Monde des livres*, 7 July.

Del Giudice, D. (1985): *Atlante occidentale*, Einaudi, Turin.

Dombroski, R. (1999): 'The rise and fall of Fascism (1910–45)'. In: Brand and Pertile 1999: 493–530.

Dooley, B. (2002): 'The public sphere and the organization of knowledge'. In: Marino 2002: 209–28.

Duggan, C. (1994, rev. 2002): *A Concise History of Italy*, Cambridge University Press, Cambridge.

Eco, U. (1990): *The Limits of Interpretation*, Indiana University Press, Bloomington and Indianapolis.

Eco, U. (1994): *Apocalypse Postponed*, ed. Lumley, R., Indiana University Press, Bloomington and Indianapolis, and BFI Publishing, London.

Falaschi, G. (1976): *La resistenza armata nella narrativa italiana*, Einaudi, Turin.

Felici, L. (1999): 'La poesia del Settecento'. In: Borsellino, N. and Pedullà, W. (eds), *Storia generale della letteratura italiana*, vol. VII, Federico Motta Editore, Milan, pp. 116–244.

Fenoglio, B. (1976): *I ventitre giorni della città di Alba*, Mondadori, Milan.

Fido, F. (1999): 'The first half of the Settecento'. In: Brand and Pertile 1999: 343–62.

Fogazzaro, A. (1983): *Scritti di teoria e critica letteraria*, ed. Landoni, E., Edizioni di teoria e storia letteraria, Milan.

Forgacs, D. (1990): *Italian Culture in the Industrial Era 1880–1980: Cultural Industries, Politics and the Public*, Manchester University Press, Manchester and New York.

Forgacs, D. and Lumley, R. (eds) (1996): *Italian Cultural Studies: An Introduction*, Oxford University Press, Oxford.

Foster, K. and Grigson, J. (trs and eds) (1964): *Alessandro Manzoni* The Column of Infamy *Prefaced by Cesare Beccaria's* Of Crimes and Punishments, intro. D'Entrèves, A. P., Oxford University Press, London.

Giocondi, M. (1978): *Lettori in camicia nera: Narrativa di successo nell'Italia fascista*, G. D'Anna, Messina and Florence.

Giorgetti Vichi, A. M. (ed.) (1977): *Gli Arcadi dal 1690 al 1800: Onomasticon*, Arcadia, Accademia Letteraria Italiana, Rome.

Goldoni, C. (1969): *Opere*, ed. Folena, G. with Mangini, N., Mursia, Milan.

Gordon, R. S. C. (2005): *An Introduction to Twentieth-Century Italian Literature: A Difficult Modernity*, Duckworth, London.

Gozzano, G. (1981): *The Man I Pretend To Be: The Colloquies and Selected Poems of Guido Gozzano*, tr. and ed. Palma, M., intro. Montale, E., Princeton University Press, Princeton, NJ.

Gozzano, G. (1983): *Opere*, ed. Baldissone, G., UTET, Turin.

Gozzano, G. (1987): *The Colloquies and Selected Letters*, tr. Nichols, J. G., Carcanet, Manchester.

Graziosi, E. (1992): 'Arcadia femminile: presenze e modelli', *Filologia e critica* 17(3), 321–58.

Gronda, G. (ed.) (1978): *Poesia italiana del Settecento*, Garzanti, Milan.

Gussalli, A. (ed.) (1857): *Opere di Pietro Giordani*, vol. 11, Borroni e Scotti, Milan.

Hallamore Caesar, A. (2000): 'The novel, 1945–1965'. In: Panizza, L. and Wood, S. (eds), *A History of Women's Writing in Italy*, Cambridge University Press, Cambridge, pp. 205–17.

Hanlon, G. (2000): *Early Modern Italy, 1550–1800*, Macmillan, Basingstoke.

Hobsbawm, E. J. (1995): 'Art of darkness', *Independent Weekend*, 21 October.

Hulten, P. (ed.) (1986): *Futurismo e futurismi*, Bompiani, Milan.

Jacobson Schutte, A. (2002): 'Religion, spirituality, and the post-Tridentine Church'. In: Marino 2002: 125–42.

Kimbell, D. (1999): 'Opera'. In: Brand and Pertile 1999: 363–70.

Lejeune, P. (1975): *Le Pacte autobiographique*, Editions du Seuil, Paris.

Leopardi, G. (1984): *Canti*, ed. De Robertis, D., 2 vols, Il Polifilo, Milan.

Leopardi, G. (1991): *Zibaldone di pensieri*, ed. Pacella, G., 3 vols, Garzanti, Milan.

Leopardi, G. (1998a): *Epistolario*, 2 vols, eds Brioschi, F. and Landi, P., Bollati Boringhieri, Turin.

Leopardi, G. (1998b): *The Letters of Giacomo Leopardi 1817–1837*, sel. and tr. Shaw, P., Northern Universities Press, Leeds.

Lumley, R. (1998): 'Some thoughts on the mass/popular culture question', *Italianist* 8, 130–4.

Luperini, R. (1981): *Il Novecento: Apparati ideologici, ceto intellettuale, sistemi formali nella letteratura italiana contemporanea*, 2 vols, Loescher, Turin.

Luperini, R. and Cataldi, P. (1999): *La scrittura e l'interpretazione: Storia e antologia della letteratura italiana nel quadro della civiltà europea*, 6 parts, Palumbo, Palermo.
Macchia, G. (1981). *Pirandello o la stanza della tortura*. Mondadori, Milan.
Manzoni, A. (1981): *Scritti di teoria letteraria*, ed. Sozzi Casanova, A., Rizzoli, Milan.
Manzoni, A. (1984): *On the Historical Novel*, tr. and intro. Bermann, S., University of Nebraska Press, Lincoln, NE, and London.
Manzoni, A. (1986): *Tutte le lettere*, ed. Arieti, C., 3 vols, Adelphi, Milan.
Manzoni, A. (1997): *The Betrothed, and History of the Column of Infamy*, eds Forgacs, D. and Reynolds, M., J. M. Dent, London.
Manzoni, A. (2000): *Del romanzo storico e, in genere, de' componimenti misti di storia e d'invenzione*, intro. Portinari, F., eds De Laude, S. and Danelon, F., Centro Nazionale Studi Manzoniani, Milan.
Marino, J. A. (ed.) (2002): *Early Modern Italy 1550–1796*, Oxford University Press, Oxford.
Metastasio, P. (1947–54): *Tutte le opere*, 5 vols, ed. Brunelli, B., Mondadori, Milan.
Montale, E. (1976): *Sulla poesia*, ed. Zampa, G., Mondadori, Milan.
Montale, E. (1996a): *Tutte le poesie*, ed. Zampa, G., 7th edn, Mondadori, Milan.
Montale, E. (1996b): *Il secondo mestiere: Prose 1920–1979*, ed. Zampa, G., 2 vols, Mondadori, Milan.
Montale, E. (1998): *Collected Poems 1920–1954*, tr. Galassi, J., Farrar, Straus and Giroux, New York.
Montani, G. (1827): '*Versi* del conte Giacomo Leopardi', *Antologia* 28(83–4), 273–5.
Moretti, F. (2005): *Graphs, Maps, Trees: Abstract Models for a Literary History*, Verso, London and New York.
Muratori, L. A. (1971–2): *Della perfetta poesia italiana*, ed. Ruschioni, A., 2 vols, Marzorati, Milan.
Natali, G. (1929): *Storia letteraria d'Italia: Il Settecento*, 2 vols, Vallardi, Milan.
Nievo, I. (1999): *Le confessioni d'un italiano*, ed. Casini, S., 2 vols, Ugo Guanda Editore, Parma.
Ory, P. (2004): *L'Histoire culturelle*, Presses Universitaires de France, Paris.
Palazzolo, M. I. (1985): *I salotti di cultura nell'Italia dell'800: Scene e modelli*, Franco Angeli, Milan.
Papa, E. R. (1974): *Fascismo e cultura*, Marsilio, Venice.
Parzanese, P. P. (1856–7): *Poesie edite ed inedite*, 3 vols in 1, Stamperia dell'Iride, Naples.
Passerini, L. (1987): *Fascism in Popular Memory: The Cultural Experience of the Turin Working Class*, Cambridge University Press, Cambridge.
Pavese, C. (1972): *Il carcere: La casa in collina*, Mondadori, Milan.
Pertile, L. (1986): 'Fascism and literature'. In: Forgacs, D. (ed.), *Rethinking Italian Fascism: Capitalism, Populism and Culture*, Lawrence and Wishart, London, pp. 162–84.

Petroni, G. (1948): 'Il mondo è una prigione', *Botteghe oscure* I, 3–89.

Pirandello, L. (1936): *Maschere nude*, Mondadori, Milan.

Pirandello, L. (1973): *Tutti i romanzi*, ed. Costanzo, M., 2 vols, Mondadori, Milan.

Quondam, A. (1982): 'L'Accademia'. In: Asor Rosa, A. (ed.), *Letteratura italiana*, vol. 1, *Il letterato e le istituzioni*, Einaudi, Turin, pp. 823–98.

Ragone, G. (1983): 'La letteratura e il consumo: un profilo dei generi e dei modelli nell'editoria italiana (1845–1925)'. In: Asor Rosa, A. (ed.), *Letteratura italiana*, vol. 2, *Produzione e consumo*, Einaudi, Turin, pp. 687–772.

Rao, A. M. (2002): 'Enlightenment and reform'. In: Marino 2002: 229–52.

Reeve, C. (1999): 'The progress of romance, through times, countries and manners'. In: Kelly, G. (ed.), *Bluestocking Feminism: Writings of the Bluestocking Circle 1783–1785*, Pickering and Chatto, London, pp. 163–275.

Ricuperati, G. (1976): 'Giornali e società nell'Italia dell' "Ancien Régime"'. In: Castronovo, V. and Tranfaglia, N. (eds), *Storia della stampa italiana*, 2 vols, vol. I, Laterza, Rome and Bari, pp. 71–372.

Saba, U. (1988): *Tutte le poesie*, ed. Stara, A., intro. Lavagetto, M., Mondadori, Milan.

Saba, U. (2004): *Poetry and Prose*, sel. and tr. with notes Moleta, V., Aeolian Press, Bridgetown, Western Australia.

Sanvitale, F. (ed.) (1995): *Le scrittrici dell'Ottocento: Da Eleonora De Fonseca Pimentel a Matiilde Serao*, Istituto poligrafico e Zecca dello Stato, Rome.

Smith, L. R. (ed. and tr.) (1981): *The New Italian Poetry, 1945 to the Present: A Bilingual Anthology*, University of California Press, Berkeley, Los Angeles and London.

Sorba, C. (2002): 'Il Risorgimento in musica: l'opera lirica nei teatri del 1848'. In: Banti, A. M. and Bizzocchi, R. (eds), *Immagini della nazione nell'Italia del Risorgimento*, Carocci, Rome, pp. 133–56.

Stendhal (1959): *Rome, Naples and Florence*, tr. Coe, R. N., J. Calder, London.

Svevo, I. (1966): *Epistolario*, intro. Maier, B., Dall'Oglio, Milan.

Svevo, I. (1972): *Romanzi*, ed. Maier, B., Dall'Oglio, Milan.

Symcox, G. (2002): 'The political world of the absolutist state in the seventeenth and eighteenth centuries'. In: Marino 2002: 104–22.

Tani, S. (1986): 'La giovane narrativa italiana: 1981–1986', *Il Ponte* 92, 120–48.

Timpanaro, S. (1969): *Classicismo e illuminismo nell'Ottocento italiano*, 2nd edn, Nistri-Lischi, Pisa.

Tommaseo, N. (1827): Review of *I promessi sposi*, *Antologia* 28(82), 101–19.

Tommaseo, N. (1841–2): *Canti popolari toscani corsi illirici greci*, 4 vols, Girolamo Tasso, Venice.

Verga, G. (1987): *Vita dei campi*, ed. Riccardi, C., Le Monnier, Florence.

Virdia, F. (1967): *Silone*, La Nuova Italia, Florence.

Further reading

This short bibliography is limited to books which take a broad view of their subject and often themselves supply extensive additional bibliographies. In a few cases, because of its wider interest, a title appears here which has already been listed in the references above. The list concentrates on works published in English, except in the first section, which reflects the substantial output of high-quality manuals of literary history from Italy during the past two decades.

General

Asor Rosa, A. (ed.) (1982–96): *Letteratura italiana*, 10 vols, Einaudi, Turin.

Bethemont, J. and Pelletier, J. (1983): *Italy: A Geographical Introduction*, Longman, London.

Bondanella, P. and Bondanella, J. C. (eds) (1979): *The Macmillan Dictionary of Italian Literature*, Macmillan, London.

Borsellino, N. and Pedullà, W. (eds) (1999): *Storia generale della letteratura italiana*, 12 vols, F. Motta, Milan.

Brand, C. P. and Pertile, L. (eds) (1999): *The Cambridge History of Italian Literature*, 2nd edn, Cambridge University Press, Cambridge.

Brioschi, F. and Di Girolamo, C. (1993–6): *Manuale di letteratura italiana*, 4 vols, Bollati Boringhieri, Turin.

Cecchi, E. and Sapegno, N. (eds) (1987–8, 2003): *Storia della letteratura italiana*, 9 vols [twentieth-century vols rev. 2003], Garzanti, Milan.

Ceserani, R. and De Federicis, L. (eds) (1991–3): *Il materiale e l'immaginario*, 5 vols, Loescher, Turin.

Dionisotti, C. (1967): *Geografia e storia della letteratura italiana*, Einaudi, Turin.

Duggan, C. (1994, rev. 2002): *A Concise History of Italy*, Cambridge University Press, Cambridge.

Farrell, J. and Puppa, P. (eds) (2006): *A History of Italian Theatre*, Cambridge University Press, Cambridge.

Ferroni, G. (1991): *Storia della letteratura italiana*, 4 vols, Einaudi, Turin.

Hainsworth, P. and Robey, D. (eds) (2002): *The Oxford Companion to Italian Literature*, Oxford University Press, Oxford.

Lepschy, A. L. and Lepschy, G. (1988): *The Italian Language Today*, Routledge, London.

Luperini, R. and Cataldi, P. (1999): *La scrittura e l'interpretazione: Storia della letteratura italiana nel quadro della civiltà e della letteratura dell'Occidente*, 4 vols, Palumbo, Palermo.
Maiden, M. (1995): *A Linguistic History of Italian*, Longman, London.
Malato, E. (ed.) (1995–): *Storia della letteratura italiana*, 10 vols, Salerno, Rome.
Migliorini, B. (1984): *The Italian Language*, abridged, recast and rev. T. Gwynfor Griffiths, Faber, London.
Panizza, L. and Wood, S. (eds) (2000): *A History of Women's Writing in Italy*, Cambridge University Press, Cambridge.
Russell, R. (ed.) (1994): *Italian Women Writers: A Bio-Bibliographical Sourcebook*, Greenwood Press, Westport, CT.

From the eighteenth century to the present

Baranski, Z. G. and Lumley, R. (eds) (1990): *Culture and Conflict in Postwar Italy: Essays on Mass and Popular Culture*, Macmillan, Basingstoke.
Baranski, Z. G. and Pertile, L. (eds) (1993): *The New Italian Novel*, Edinburgh University Press, Edinburgh.
Baranski, Z. G. and West, R. (eds) (2001): *Modern Italian Culture*, Cambridge University Press, Cambridge.
Biasin, G.-P. (1985): *Italian Literary Icons*, Princeton University Press, Princeton, NJ.
Bigazzi, R. (1969): *I colori del vero*, Nistri-Lischi, Pisa.
Bondanella, P. and Ciccarelli, A. (eds) (2003): *The Cambridge Companion to the Italian Novel*, Cambridge University Press, Cambridge.
Bono, P. and Kemp, S. (eds) (1993): *The Lonely Mirror: Italian Perspectives on Feminist Theory*, Routledge, London.
Burns, J. (2001): *Fragments of 'impegno': Interpretations of Commitment in Contemporary Italian Narrative 1980–2000*, Northern Universities Press, Leeds.
Caesar, M. and Hainsworth, P. (eds) (1984): *Writers and Society in Contemporary Italy*, Berg, Leamington Spa.
Cannon, J. (1989): *Postmodern Italian Fiction*, Associated University Presses, London and Toronto.
Carpanetto, D. and Ricuperati, G. (1987): *Italy in the Age of Reason, 1685–1789*, Longman, London and New York.
Clark, M. (1996): *Modern Italy 1871–1995*, Longman, London.
Debenedetti, G. (1976): *Il romanzo del Novecento*, Garzanti, Milan.
De Mauro, T. (1976): *Storia linguistica dell'Italia unita*, Laterza, Rome and Bari.
Forgacs, D. (1990): *Italian Culture in the Industrial Era 1880–1980: Cultural Industries, Politics and the Public*, Manchester University Press, Manchester and New York.
Forgacs, D. and Lumley, R. (eds) (1996): *Italian Cultural Studies: An Introduction*, Oxford University Press, Oxford.
Ginsborg, P. (1990): *A History of Contemporary Italy: Society and Politics 1943–1988*, Penguin, Harmondsworth.

Ginsborg, P. (2001): *Italy and Its Discontents: Family, Civil Society, State 1980–2001*, Allen Lane, London.
Gordon, R. S. C. (2005): *An Introduction to Twentieth-Century Italian Literature: A Difficult Modernity*, Duckworth, London.
Hainsworth, P. and Tandello, E. (eds) (1995): *Italian Poetry since 1956*, supplement 1 to *Italianist* 15.
Hearder, H. (1983): *Italy in the Age of the Risorgimento 1790–1870*, Longman, London.
Lucente, G. (1986): *Beautiful Fables: Self-Consciousness in Italian Narrative from Manzoni to Calvino*, Johns Hopkins University Press, Baltimore.
Mack Smith, D. (1988): *The Making of Italy 1796–1866*, Macmillan, London.
Moliterno, G. (ed.) (2000): *Encyclopedia of Contemporary Italian Culture*, Routledge, London.
Ragone, G. (1999): *Storia dell'editoria in Italia dall'Unità al post-moderno*, Einaudi, Turin.
Raimondi, E. (1997): *Romanticismo italiano e romanticismo europeo*, Mondadori, Milan.
Springer, C. (1987): *The Marble Wilderness: Ruins and Representation in Italian Romanticism 1775–1850*, Cambridge University Press, Cambridge.
Tranfaglia, A. and Vittoria, A. (2000): *Storia degli editori italiani: Dall'Unità alla fine degli anni sessanta*, Laterza, Rome and Bari.
Venturi, F. (1972): *Italy and the Enlightenment: Studies in a Cosmopolitan Century*, Longman, London.
Wood, M. (2005): *Italian Cinema*, Berg, Oxford.
Woolf, S. (1979): *A History of Italy 1700–1860: The Social Constraints of Political Change*, Methuen, London.

Index